D1568210

THE JEWISH HOLY DAYS

THE JEWISH HOLY DAYS

THEIR SPIRITUAL SIGNIFICANCE

MOSHE BRAUN

JASON ARONSON INC.
Northvale, New Jersey
London

Excerpts from *The Handbook of Kabbalah and Astrology*, by Shlomo Pasmanter, copyright © 1985, published by Friedman Press, are used by permission of the author.

This book was set in 10 pt. Palatino by Alpha Graphics of Pittsfield, N.H.

Library of Congress Cataloging-in-Publication Data

Braun, Moshe.
    The Jewish holy days: their spiritual significance / by Moshe Braun.
       p. cm.
    Section 3, "The Light of Chanukah," originally published:
Brooklyn, N.Y. : Z. Berman Books, 1979.
    Includes index.
    Contents: The Days of Awe — The joy of Sukkos — The Light of
Chanukah — The celebration of Purim — The freedom of Pesach —The
revelation of Shavuos.
     ISBN 1-56821-553-3 (alk. paper)
  1. Fasts and feasts—Judaism. 2. Judaism—Customs and practices.
3. Hasidism. I. Title.
  BM690.B76 1996
  296.4'3—dc20   95-40428

Manufactured in the United States of America. Jason Aronson Inc. offers books and cassettes. For information and catalog write to Jason Aronson Inc., 230 Livingston Street, Northvale, New Jersey 07647.

לזכר נשמת

מוה"ר ישראל בן הגאון וצדיק תמים
מוה"ר חיים ברוין ז"ל
מעיר באניהאד שם אמו אסתר שינדל

מרת מלכה בת איש החסד
מוה"ר משה אשר זילבער ז"ל
מעיר סאבאסלא שם אמה גיטל

מוה"ר משה מרדכי בן התמים
מוה"ר שמואל זאב הי"ד
מעיר סאלאש שם אמו יוטא

מרת מלכה בת הרה"ח
מוה"ר יצחק אייזיק הי"ד
מעיר סעמיהאלי שם אמה לאה

Contents

Foreword

Rabbi Aryeh Kaplan (zt"l)

ike everything in Judaism, the Jewish holidays have an infinite dimension of depth. Every rule, every law, every custom has deep inner significance. There is no such thing as "mere custom." It is taught that, "If [the Jews] are not prophets, they are the sons of prophets" (*Pesachim* 66a). Therefore, even Jewish customs can be said to be based on Divine inspiration, and can therefore be found to contain layer upon layer of meaning.

Many books have been written on the inner meaning of the laws and customs surrounding the holidays. Many of these are based upon the Kabbalah, and without a great deal of interpretation are inaccessible even to the average talmudic scholar. There is, however, one book that explores the holidays in depth and in a manner that is accessible even to the average thinking Jew. This is the *Sfas Emes* by the great Rabbi Yehudah Aryeh Leib Alter (1847–1905),

the second leader of the famed chasidic dynasty of Gur. His analysis is a combination of depth and clarity that has made the author's works famous among all Judaic scholars.

Unfortunately, until now, this vast treasury has been inaccessible to readers who are not fluent in talmudic Hebrew. My good friend Moshe Braun has therefore done an immeasurable service to the English-reading Jewish community by providing this book on the Jewish Holy Days based on the *Sfas Emes*. Not only will it give people an opportunity to learn about the holidays in depth, but it will introduce them to the profound depth of thought that is the hallmark of the *Sfas Emes*.

Of course, in its entirety, the *Sfas Emes* covers many topics. This book is therefore only a taste of the profound insight that is available. It is hoped that this will only be the first of many works based on this most important Jewish classic.

Preface

For the Jewish people, there are the ordinary days of the year, and the holidays. Literally, they are holy days, bringing with them divine gifts of holiness, and a pause to reflect upon our heritage and traditions. The holidays contain, by commandment, custom, and tradition, the foundations of our faith.

The Talmud views the human body as having 248 vital parts, for each of which there is a positive commandment in the Torah; and 365 sinews, for each of the negative, forbidden commandments. These add up to the 613 commandments. The 365 days of the year are reflected in the 365 sinews, veins, and arteries of the human body. Through the flow of blood, and communication of the nervous system, they maintain the body's functions. But there are also vital organs, without which a person's life would be in grave danger. Each of those is reflected in one of the holidays.

The Sabbath is the queen mother of all the holidays. Its holiness began with the creation, as a day in which all creatures return to their Creator. On that day, they renew their life and negate themselves to God. They bathe in the primordial light, and delight in the Creator's presence.

Just as the soul is the vitality for the body, Sabbath is the soul of the six workdays, and adds a spark of holiness to each of them. And one can collect these bits of holiness from each of the six days and bring them back to the Sabbath. That collection forms the energy for the coming week. And the cycle is repeated.

The Sabbath, undoubtedly, can teach us critical lessons. We learn that only six days are for work, but on Sabbath we work for no one. We are free men, slaves to no one, nor anyone's laws, rather, servants of the one and only God. As a result, the laws guiding us are not necessarily the natural laws that dominate the six workdays, they are, rather, the divine laws. And our salvation lies in having no attachments to the mundane, material world, but to escape to God's refuge and bask in his light.

Thus, each of the holidays is some aspect of the Sabbath. During Passover we relive its aspect of freedom, declaring that although slaves to Pharaoh, we were set free by God. We learned our lesson, as we quickly threw off his yoke. On Shavuos, the holiday of Pentecost, we rejoice with the divine law we received from Mount Sinai. We are bound to divine laws of a higher authority and not intimidated by the forces of nature. Then on Sukkos we escape from our mundane attachments, build a hut, and remain in God's refuge. And on Rosh Hashanah we declare the sovereignty of God as our king and master of the world.

Purim and Chanukah, too, commemorate miracle tales of heroics and freedom, as we were saved from terrible oppression and free to serve God once more.

What we learn from all the holidays, added together, equals one Sabbath.

It is clear then that every holiday, and its celebration, is really another aspect of the Sabbath. They are the vital organs of one's spiritual body without which a Jew would be in grave danger and barely alive. But when a Jew observes the Sabbath, and the holidays, he can enjoy spiritual health and divine closeness.

There is yet a deeper way to understand the Sabbath and the holidays. Our experience merely skims the surface of the multidimensional world in which we live. Very few of us have a clear grasp of the space-time continuum, and far fewer would fathom the meaning of additional dimensions. Generally, though, the spiritual worlds are understood as reflections of the apparent world. That which happens in the heavens, also, in some form, happens on the earth. And that which we do on earth directly influences the nature and configuration of spiritual reality. Thus, in Sabbath we imitate the essence of spiritual reality. It is the day of the soul, unity, peace, and tranquillity. It is as spiritual as it can possibly be within the limitations of a material world. We do no work of consequence and hallow the spiritual aspect of nature by not altering it in any permanent way. We do not plow, plant, or reap. We do not shear, spin, or weave. We do not produce fire, cook, or take the life of a living being. We thus live the day in a hallowed and spiritual state.

We can compare this to a microbiologist studying cells. He describes, in details as small as molecules and atoms, that which we observe on a far larger scale. He can either start from the large scale and explain the microscopic—or start with the microscopic and end with the observation. They are, after all, two sides of the same coin. Similarly, when we observe the Sabbath, we mimic and reflect the spiritual reality of the heavens. Or, one who has knowledge of the "heavens" can tell you that what you are doing on Sabbath is similar to what he had observed in heaven.

This is also true of the holidays. What became manifest in Jewish history is a dimension of the spiritual. When Moses led the Israelites out of Egypt, it was a dimension of the freedom inherent in the heavenly realm, which, by a wrinkle in time or cosmic wormhole, was manifest in the material world for that moment. And each year, celebrating that freedom, we open the channels for that dimension of heaven, again, to be manifest on earth. This is true of all the holidays. They are glimpses, tiny rays breaking through cracks in the laws of nature, shining into our lives. They transform us, and we, by reflection, transform it. The very fabric of the multidimensional universe is transformed because of our deeds, and again, reflectively influencing us. It is a lifelong reflective process as two mirrors facing each other, infinitely influencing each other's image.

How can we ever hope to experience the holidays in their fullness? Only by learning and delving into their essence in all their dimensions. And we can do this by turning to those teachers who devoted their lives to raising the spiritual consciousness of their followers. From among them I have chosen the chasidic masters, who, in my opinion, have revealed, illuminated, and clarified the deep secrets and symbolism of the Torah. They base their teachings on the Kabbalah, which contains the innermost secrets of

our relationship with God, the Creation, and the meaning of Torah verses. Their teachings simplify the Kabbalah by using comparisons, analogies, and parables. In that way, even an unschooled person can understand it.

Chasidic teachings touch not only your mind but also your emotions. Therefore, they relate to one's personal life and existential struggles.

I have based my writing on the teachings of a preeminent chasidic master, the famous Rabbi Yehudah Aryeh Leib Alter, the second leader of the chasidic dynasty of Gur. He was born to the first Gerer Rebbe, Rabbi Mordechai Alter, who was the only son of the Chidushei Ha'rim, in Warsaw, on the eve of Rosh Chodesh Iyar, in 1847. Orphaned as a young boy, he was educated by his grandfather, who was one of the greatest Torah sages of that time. Even at that young age, he learned Torah with great diligence, eighteen hours a day. To visiting scholars, his grandfather would say, "Look at my grandson how he studies Torah!" When the grandfather passed away, the chasidim wanted to appoint him as the next Gerer Rebbe. Being merely nineteen years old, he refused, and instead went as a pupil to the Rebbe of Aleksander. Four years later the Rebbe of Aleksander passed away and again the chasidim urged him to take on the yoke of leadership. This time he accepted. He molded Gur as a center of Chasidus, attracting tens of thousands·of followers from all over Europe. His commentaries on the Talmud made him renowned as a great Torah scholar as well as a brilliant leader. For more than thirty years he counseled his followers to live with fervent devotion to the Torah, both in study and deed. In 1905, at the age of fifty-seven, a few days before he passed away, he had written the last of his written words, "Lips of truth, Sfas Emes, stand firm forever" (Proverbs 12:19). Because they were the last words of his earthly sojourn, his sons chose them as a lasting tribute and named all his writings, Sfas Emes.

The Sfas Emes on the Torah, which is the basis for this book, has a uniquely deep and exciting approach to interpreting its verses and topics. Besides their depth, they encompass a wide spectrum of quotations, analogies and comparisons from the Talmud, Midrash and Zohar. His teachings are constantly bursting with new ideas in every sentence, phrase, and word. He is like a brook, endlessly bubbling forth new ideas, that tastes differently each time you drink from it.

It was some fifteen years ago that students who were intellectually gifted came on Shabbos to study Torah with me, seeking the profound guidance from the portion of the week. I had tried a variety of commentaries till I discovered the Sfas Emes. The Sfas

Emes, too, was challenging. There were too many new ideas to explain in each paragraph and we never got to finish a complete thought. I decided then to focus on central ideas and clarify them by explanation and parables. After a time we discovered themes and patterns. We compared and contrasted, until the approach of the Sfas Emes was slowly discovered. This book represents what we had understood of his commentary—our learning, our struggle to comprehend and explain. No doubt, it is not the only interpretation. And most certainly there will be differing opinions on what the Sfas Emes actually meant. As the Gerer Rebbe himself said: The Israelites stood at the foot of Mount Sinai. When they understood that they were merely at the foot of the mountain, without understanding, then they were lifted up to the heavens and received the Torah from God Himself. The Torah, therefore, is meant for learning. Although I cannot hope to understand all its teachings, God in His mercy has allowed me to understand some small portion. This is the part I would like to share with you. These are not, however, the very words he spoke, but rather, an approximation.

From this book, I pray you will learn to appreciate chasidic teachings and catch a glimpse of the Kabbalah. Also, you will acquire a taste of the deeper significance of the holidays, giving you vitality throughout the year.

I pray that these teachings will sustain you year round.

Moshe Braun

Acknowledgments

 would like to thank Rabbi Aryeh Kaplan of blessed memory for his encouragement to write this series of books on the holidays. His great scholarship, humility, and prodigious writing are a beacon of light for all of us. Even more, I am grateful to my family, whose humor and love has given me the patience to continue to the end. To my dear wife, Leah, who can think and write far better than I, and my dear children: Zevy, Pessie and Chevele; Shaindy, Sruly, Surala, Shmuel Zevy, and Gitty; Mutty, Gitty, Yisroel Rueven, and Chayala; Chavy, Daniel, and Yisroel; Chaya Yitty, and Yosef Yitzchok. May they all be blessed with clear todays and bright tomorrows, and live to see the Redemption soon in our days.

I

THE DAYS OF AWE

Introduction

From the first shofar blast on the first day of *Elul* to the last shofar blast at the end of Yom Kippur, the Jewish people remain in awe. With fear and trembling they stand before their Creator, Who judges every living thing: "Who will live, and who will die?!" The sound of the shofar calls out, "Awake! Dreamers, awaken from your slumber!" It warns of danger ahead if they continue on their crooked path. It alerts them to battle; the enemy has broken through the city walls and has taken up residence inside our home. Who is so arrogant as not to heed its call?

What can convey the feeling better than this sublime prayer on the New Year:

> You remember the deeds done in the universe, and you recall all the creatures fashioned since earliest times. Before You all hidden things are revealed and the multitude of mysteries since the beginning of Creation, for there is no forgetfulness before Your throne of Glory and nothing is hidden from before Your eyes. You remember everything ever done, and not a single creature is hidden from You. Everything is revealed and known before You, God our Lord who keeps watch and sees to the end of all generations. . . .
>
> The remembrance of all created beings comes before You, man's deeds and mission, the accomplishments of his activities, his thoughts and schemes, and the motive behind his deeds.

God judges man's every deed, action, and motive. Will we not take note? Will we not tremble?

The awesomeness of these days is powerfully pictured in another prayer, one of the most stirring of the holiday, the "*Unesaneh Tokef*":

> Let us now relate the power of this day's holiness, for it is awesome and frightening. . . . It is true that You alone are the one Who judges, proves, knows, and bears witness; Who writes and seals, counts and calculates; Who remembers all that was forgotten. You will open the Book of Remembrance—it will read itself, and everyone's signature is in it. And a great shofar will be sounded, and a still, thin sound will be heard. Angels will hasten, a trembling and terror will seize them. . . . All mankind will pass before You like members of the flock. Like a shepherd pasturing his flock, making sheep pass under his staff, so shall You cause to pass, count, calculate, and consider the soul of all the living. . . .
>
> On Rosh Hashanah will be inscribed and on Yom Kippur will be sealed how many will pass from the earth and how many will be created; who will live and who will die; who will die at his predestined time, and who before his time; who by water, and who by fire; who by sword, and who by beast; who by famine, and who by thirst; who by storm, and who by plague; who by strangulation, and who by stoning. Who will rest and who will wander. . . .
>
> He is likened to a broken shard, withering grass, a fading flower, a passing shade, a dissipating cloud, a blowing wind, flying dust, and a fleeting dream.

Not only are the common people awed by the judgment of God, but even the great and righteous rabbis of generations past were awed by His judgment, as we have been taught by our sages:

> When Rabbi Yochanan ben Zakai took ill, he was visited by his students. Upon seeing them, he started to cry. His students said, "Our rabbi, the light of Israel, the central pillar, the great hammer, why are you crying?" He answered them, "If I would be taken before a king of flesh and blood,

3

who is here today and tomorrow in the grave, and even if he became angry, it is not an everlasting anger; and if he imprisons me, it is also not forever; even if he kills me, it is not an eternal death. And I could even calm him with words or bribe him with money—still I would be crying. Surely now, that they are taking me before the King of Kings, the Holy One blessed be His Name, who lives eternally, for ever and ever, and if He becomes angry at me, it is forever; and if He imprisons me, it is forever; and if He kills me, it is also forever; and neither could I calm Him with words nor bribe Him with money. And more so, I have before me two paths, one to *Gehenom* and one to the Garden of Eden, and I do not yet know which path I will be led—should I not cry?"

Yet the Days of Awe have a twofold message. As severe and exacting is the judgment of God, that is how powerful and imminent is His call to repentance and His readiness to accept those who return with all their hearts.

But how is the stray sheep ever to find its way back to its master? How is a rebellious son ever to return to the palace, to his father's embrace?

The Baal Shem Tov, the first leader of the chasidic movement in the eighteenth century, illustrated this return to God with a story about a king who normally stayed in the palace. While the king was in the palace, it was hard to contact him or communicate with him. But when he left the palace to travel to other cities and was met on the road and in the field, there, anyone could approach him and even speak to him. Thus, all year, God is in His "palace." But during the Days of Awe, the days of judgment, when God is "in the field" examining His troops, then anyone can approach Him and speak to Him.

It is not enough, though, just to know that God is in the fields, approachable and waiting for every creature to return. We must ponder the deeper meaning of these days, so that our awe can motivate us to reach a level of intimacy with God unattainable the year-round.

From Part I of this book I pray you will learn to acquire a taste of the deeper significance of the Awesome Days while learning to abandon falsehood and illusion, and start a life of truth and authenticity.

By fully appreciating the Days of Awe, you will be granted true and lasting repentance. You will be born anew as you return to the root and cause of all vitality.

1

The Month of Elul

"Ani l'dodi, v'dodi li"
I BELONG TO MY BELOVED, AND MY BELOVED
BELONGS TO ME.

The month of *Elul*, which begins the Days of Awe, is traditionally set aside for repentance. Our sages have said that the word *Elul* is an acrostic for four words found in the Song of Songs of Solomon the King, which expresses the great love between the Jewish people and God: *"Ani l'dodi, v'dodi li*—I belong to my beloved and my beloved belongs to me" (Song of Songs 6:3). Therefore, during the month of *Elul* we recognize our closeness and belonging to Him as well as His closeness to us.

Ani L'dodi, V'dodi Li

The Jewish people are living witnesses that God created the world. They ceaselessly proclaim His sovereignty with such intensity that other witnesses are not needed. They are so insistent in their witnessing that other nations copy them. These other nations too begin to proclaim, in a smaller measure, that God is the creator of the universe.

That God is the refuge for all His creatures is recognized through the activities of the Jewish people. While the storm of confusion and challenges to God's rule rages all around, the Jewish people stand their ground and prevail. Now, however, near the year's end, we examine what we have accomplished and find ourselves lacking. We realize that we too had better get ourselves into God's refuge.

At year's end, the Jewish people are like a man who was helping others find their way to shelter during a blinding snowstorm. Suddenly there were gusts of wind, and he himself was in danger of being buried alive. He quickly abandoned his attempt to rescue the others and rushed into the shelter for his own safety. In *Elul*, the last month before the New Year, we dash off to God's refuge, as it is written, "I belong to my beloved, and my beloved belongs to me" exclusively.

Let us therefore run to the refuge of God and save ourselves during these forty Awesome Days.

Although the Jewish people are aware of their closeness to God, they occasionally feel estranged and distanced from Him. But just at that time God draws closer to them, and they feel His closeness. They are neither prepared for the sudden intimacy nor have the vessels to receive it. Thus the closeness, as easily as it came, can also be lost.

This is like a millionaire who proposed marriage to a woman in a distant land and brought along many gifts. His advisors were optimistic, but had some doubts about whether his proposal would be accepted. A few weeks later, when they heard that she had ordered a mansion built for the two of them, they were confident that their marriage plans were serious.

The "marriage plans" of God and the Jewish people, of Passover and Shavuos, were very tentative and temporary. We were not ready to keep Him as our God. Soon after the Exodus, we worshiped a Golden Calf and proclaimed it as our liberator from Egypt. We then had to spend the entire month of *Elul* repenting for our sin. Our repentance prepared a dwelling place for God's closeness. The words "and my beloved belongs to me" mean that His love is felt constantly through our preparation. Will we experience God's closeness this year, or will we not? That is the judgment of Rosh Hashanah and Yom Kippur.

Now that *Elul* has arrived, and with it God's closeness, let us not waste any time, but immediately prepare vessels for Him so that His closeness may be permanent.

It is written, "I have formed this people for myself and they shall proclaim my praises" (Isaiah 43:21). There is no greater need of the Jewish people than to say the praises of God. This is their essence and mission in the world. When they proclaim God's praises, they are in effect saying, "I belong to my beloved . . . ." My essence is not mine, but belongs to God, my beloved. Likewise, God answers us, saying, "If you realize why you exist, I too will show you openly what I realize; that the entire creation has meaning and purpose only if the Jewish people live to tell about it."

This is like a king who sent one of his trusted servants to administer a distant city. When the servant arrived in that city, he set up a minipalace, proclaimed laws, established courts, and persuaded the citizens to be loyal to the king.

When the king heard of these actions, he dispatched a caravan of luxurious gifts to honor and bring comfort and joy to his servant. "Let everyone know that the luxuries of my palace are at the disposal of he who establishes my kingdom. After all, to what use is my palace if not for my kingdom. Hence, my palace belongs to my servant."

During *Elul*, the Jewish people finally return to the task of proclaiming the kingdom of God and say, "I belong to my beloved. . . ." Then God, too, makes known that all of the creation is empty and meaningless without the Jewish people: ". . . and my beloved belongs to me."

Let us therefore not hesitate to return to our mission and heartily proclaim God as the master of the universe.

It is written, ". . . and Mount Sinai was full of smoke . . . as the smoke of a furnace . . . and the whole mountain trembled . . . and the sound of the horn was gaining in strength . . ." (Exodus 19:18–19).

Several events prepared the Israelites for the revelation at Mount Sinai. They had been humbled through slavery, had witnessed the Ten Plagues; had experienced a miraculous Exodus; had walked through the parted Red Sea; had defeated their enemies while all the time being protected by the clouds of glory; had eaten the manna, bread from heaven; and had drunk water from a miraculous well. Each one of these miracles elevated them and prepared them to stand at Mount Sinai to receive the Ten Commandments. They were ready to revitalize the entire world, as it is written, "And you shall be my special treasure among all the nations . . ." (Exodus 19:5), meaning that all the nations will be uplifted through Israel's chosenness to God.

The preparation was to no avail. The nations were not ready to be uplifted by the Jewish people, and that vacuum caused the Israelites to sink to the level of idol worship. They made the Golden Calf, thus losing all of their spiritual gains.

After this tragic downfall, Moses stood on Mount Sinai for forty days and forty nights begging God to elevate the Jewish people once more. Those forty days correspond to the forty Days of Awe that start on the first day of *Elul* and end on Yom Kippur. Moses succeeded, and God issued the "second tablets of stone" on which were carved the Ten Commandments. Those tablets were very different from the first set. The second ones were given privately and quietly, without noise or fanfare, and belong exclusively to the Jewish people.

This is like a king whose son was getting married. On the wedding day, the king readied gifts for the bride and groom and all the guests. Some of the guests became arrogant and bragged how deserving they were of the presents. And the prince too, hearing the bragging of the guests, spoke disrespectfully. Surprised by the outbursts, the king declared, "I will not give my gifts publicly as planned. I will give my son his gift in private."

During the Days of Awe we can relate to God on a private and intimate level. We are in the king's palace then and are about to receive precious gifts. Let us not waste this opportunity, but prepare for it through our good deeds.

It is written, "I belong to my beloved, and my beloved belongs to me." Our sages of the Talmud have taught: The world was created for the use of those who serve God (*Shabbos* 30b). This teaching refers to the Jewish people especially; if they stray or fall short of serving God, they are discordant with God's intentions. Therefore, during the Days of Awe, when we repent and remember our duty, our soul calls out, "I belong to my beloved . . . ."

Still, this is not always so. Although our duty is clear, we can slip off the path because of our desires and curiosity of mind.

We can compare this to a fruit tree that grew apples each year. During the long, cold winter months, it would wonder about other fruit: "Ah, if only there could be other fruit on this tree. How beautiful those oranges, lemons, or pears would be! Why do I grow only apples, year after year?" Yet, when spring again arrived, the sun warmed the air, and its buds bloomed into apple blossoms, the tree had second thoughts. "Perhaps it is best this way," it thought. It put its fantasies aside and spent its time producing delicious apples.

When we harness our mind to fulfill our duty and purpose, it is truly noble. And if we do so without thinking and wavering, it is better still. As it is written, "Man and beast will be helped by God" (Psalms 36:7). The Talmud comments: They are connivingly wise as men, but assume the posture of animals. They are capable of using their minds for the service of God, but they do even better and serve God with their essence, as a beast under her yoke (*Chullin* 5b).

Therefore, as the New Year approaches, the anniversary of the creation, each creature can revert to its essence. Each one of us can stop our conniving and straying thoughts and let our true purpose shine through. Then our being will cry out, "I belong to my beloved . . ." and God will answer, ". . . and my beloved belongs to Me."

There is a divine portion in each and every Jewish soul. This portion can neither be corrupted nor defiled. It forever remains in its purity and holiness.

Unfortunately, because of our errors, that purity becomes obscured. It becomes concealed with the impurity of our ways; yet, it is there in all its strength. When the Days of Awe arrive, each of us repents and returns to God and reconnects to the center of purity, which remains, although it is obscured by our deeds.

Therefore, the astrological symbol for the month of *Elul* is Virgo the virgin. She says to her beloved, "Behold I am pure and undefiled." Similarly, we too say to God, "I belong to my beloved."

In response to this declaration, God grants the Jewish people special gifts. As it is written, "God said, I will make a covenant before all your people, and I will do miracles that have never been brought into existence in all the world, among any nation" (Exodus 34:10). How does God make this covenant? God relates to us with His Thirteen Virtues of Kindness. No other nation experiences these virtues in their pure form as we do.

This is like a king who was forced to wage war and defend his kingdom. He needed to leave the palace to lead his troops and summoned his most trusted servant. He placed his signet ring in his servant's hand and said, "Here is my seal. Guard it with your life; no matter what the enemy destroys, the ring must stay intact so I can re-establish my kingdom when I return."

The servant made a small cut in his leg and hid the ring there. Later the enemy overran the city and took many captives. The servant was dragged from place to place, unkempt, thin and weak, and clothed in rags. The palace and the king were faint memories in his tortured mind.

After many months of war, the king successfully routed the enemy. The servant heard that the king was about to retake the prison and set the loyal citizens free. He immediately forgot his pain and suffering and instead remembered the king's seal. As the king approached his cell, the servant was removing the ring from its secret hiding place. He was suddenly overtaken with emotion. He realized then that his relationship with the king was as strong as ever. The king, too, was overjoyed to see his loyal servant and showered him with gifts.

In *Elul* the King is on His way to free everyone from the prison of sin. Let us remember our eternal purity and return to God Who waits for us always.

Each of us is born into the world with a personal purpose and goal. To reach it we must find the path, a path clearly defined in the Torah. Whoever strays from the prescribed Torah path also strays from his personal purpose and goal.

There was a king who gave his servant a huge sum of money with which to buy carpets for the palace. The servant traveled to a distant country and examined many carpets in order to choose the most suitable one. He also chose a few for himself. As the days passed and he saw more and more materials, he put more aside for himself. Soon he had a nice selection and started selling them at a profit. Business was good, and he forgot about his mission.

One day a messenger arrived with a letter from the king to remind him of the pattern for the guest room. He trembled and cried as he read the king's words. "What have I done?" he moaned. "I have forgotten my real mission for the king's sake and instead only thought of my own desires!" He quickly quit his business and spent all his time from then on in the king's service.

Similarly, in the Days of Awe, we receive the letter from the King and are reminded: "I belong to my beloved. . . ." We are here for the service of God only. Let us abandon our erring ways and return to the path of God.

———————

It is written, "I belong to my beloved, and my beloved belongs to me." Yet in another verse the order is reversed, "My beloved is mine, and I belong to him" (Song of Songs 2:16).

When the Jewish people are vessels for the Divine presence, they can experience God's desire to be with them always. Similarly, on special occasions we feel this desire to be with God. Sometimes it is brought about by our own work, and at other times it starts in the spiritual spheres and descends to us.

The Days of Awe have both these qualities. We desire to repent and return to God and the path of righteousness. And God too desires us, just as He did even after the worship of the Golden Calf. Therefore, it is the best time of the year to return to God, with the desire coming both from us and from God. "I belong to my beloved," and "my beloved is mine."

When such great events are happening, let us not stand on the sidelines. Let us connect to the desire of our people and of God who desires us.

———————

When the Jewish people made the Golden Calf, Moses prayed for forty days and forty nights. Finally, God declared His forgiveness, with Thirteen Virtues of Loving-kindness, as it is written, "And God passed by before Moses and proclaimed, God, God, Omnipotent, merciful and kind, slow to anger, with tremendous resources of love and truth. He remembers deeds of love for thousands of generations, forgiving sin, rebellion and error" (Exodus 34:6–7).

These Thirteen Virtues are the life-giving vitality that creates the world and keeps it in existence always. All creatures that have the capacity are filled by them, but those who stray from the path of life abandon the gifts of God.

There are no better vessels for these virtues than the Jewish people. And therefore, even before the world was created, the plan for the Jewish people was already in place. Symbolically, then, the Jewish people always precede the creation.

Rosh Hashanah, the New Year, is the anniversary of the creation: the emanation of the Thirteen Virtues. Therefore, before they arrive in this world, the Jewish people precede creation with their repentance and good deeds. And thus they show that they are indeed the ones who receive the fullness of the creation.

This is also symbolized by the first and second tablets that God gave to the Jewish people. The first were carved and written by God; the second were also written by God, but were carved by Moses. The first tablets symbolized that, even before the Jewish people do, God is already doing for them. They are chosen by Him, even before they do good deeds. The second tablets symbolized that if you want to receive, you must first have vessels.

Had we received the first tablets only, we would have thought that one must be perfect in order to receive the gifts of God. But with the second, we realized that even after one sins, but returns to God, one too can prepare vessels for God's gifts.

This is like a king's daughter who was of the age to get married. The king finally found a suitable prince in the adjoining kingdom, had him brought to the palace, clothed him in royal finery, and schooled him in etiquette and courtly conduct. After months of education the king was satisfied, a huge royal wedding was prepared, and the young couple was wed.

During the first week of marriage the young prince mistreated the princess. The king was furious and summoned his daughter home. The young prince realized his mistake and appeared before the king to beg his forgiveness. The king listened patiently, and said, "Before you were wed I schooled you, but, it seems, to no avail! Now go and school yourself. Come back in one month and show me that you are ready to take my daughter to your home and treat her with respect and dignity!"

We have all strayed and erred in our conduct. Let us therefore mend our ways, make vessels, and carve tablets for God's divine message that He seeks to etch into our hearts. As it is written, "I belong to my beloved, and my beloved belongs to me."

WE ARE HIS OWN, HIS PEOPLE

"Know that God is the Lord, He has made us (*v'lo anachnu amo*), we are His own, His people, the flock that he shepherds" (Psalms 100:3) .

The Hebrew word for "and to Him" is written *v'lo*, with the last letter an *aleph* meaning "and not"; we are not His people. However, it is read as if it was written with a *vov*, *v'lo*, "and to Him." If we combine the written form of *v'lo* with the vocalized form of *v'lo*, we get the word *Elul*, alluding to the month of repentance.

———————

God is the master of the world. Whoever humbles himself and accepts this fact becomes a vessel for His divine presence. But a person who behaves arrogantly and thinks that he is his own master leaves no room for the truth. Similarly, when the Jewish people acknowledge that they cannot exist without God, then they are His nation. If *v'lo*, we are not, which is the truth, then *v'lo*, we are His people. Similarly, if *v'lo*, we are not, we do not give primary importance to our physical needs as if they were the focus to our life, but rather, *v'lo*, and to Him, our focus is only to God, then we are His people. When we humble ourselves and subordinate all our needs to the service of God, then we are vessels for God's divine presence.

This is like a king who sent his servant to administer a city. The servant set up a minipalace, with all the trappings of a king. The servant soon started to feel as if he were a mini-king and raised his head with arrogance. When a messenger came to deliver new ordinances from the king, he treated him with disdain.

Hearing of the servant's petulance, the king decided to pay him a visit. When the king appeared, the servant immediately realized the foolishness of his ways and promised to serve the king with proper humility. During the long year, we too stray onto mistaken paths of arrogance. When the Days of Awe draw near, however, and we sense the approach of the King, we immediately humble ourselves and assume the proper posture before the Master of the World.

It is written, "*v'lo*—and to Him we are His people and the flock that He shepherds." "*v'lo*—if we are not, then to Him we are a people." This means that if we humble ourselves before God, we are His people. And considering ourselves as His people causes us to humble ourselves properly. But to reach this awareness one must possess understanding. As it is written, ". . . man and beast alike will be helped by God" (Psalms 36:7). Our sages add, "They are wise as men but humble themselves as animals."

Only through wisdom does one realize one's predicament. When we are aware that we are His people, and not our own masters, we can be the flock of the shepherd. This same idea is expressed in the verse "I was a dolt without knowledge, I was a mere beast in thy sight, O God" (Psalms 73:22). I stand before the Creator as if I know nothing and can do nothing. The verse ". . . and you are my sheep, the flock that I shepherd, you are people . . ." (Ezekiel 34:31) also expresses this idea. When you humble yourself as sheep before God, then you are truly men.

This is like a king who would buy his candelabras from one silversmith. The king favored his intricate hand carving, which was unsurpassed. The smith became an arrogant fellow and considered himself royalty. "After all," he thought, "is it not my work that adorns the castle and lights the way for the king." He shunned his "lowly" neighbors and became more and more conceited.

One day the smith was summoned to the palace and ushered into rooms filled with decorative silver pieces from every part of the world. His eyes widened as he examined the variety of craftsmanship and designs. After hours of viewing thousands of pieces, the smith realized that his was a very small silver shop producing one piece in several months. He felt ridiculous comparing himself to royalty, to immense wealth. He realized that he was a good smith, but not much more than that.

As we start the Days of Awe in the month of *Elul*, let us dwell on the great and helping God and our comparative insignificance and helplessness. Let us be wise and be truly humbled before our Maker Who shepherds us as His flock.

AT A DESIRABLE MOMENT

It is written, " As for me, may my prayer come to You, O Lord, at a desirable moment; O God, in Your abundant faithfulness, answer me with Your sure deliverance" (Psalms 69:14). The Talmud comments that "At a favorable moment" means the Days of Awe, the month of *Elul* (*Rosh Hashanah* 18a).

God is *ein sof*, without limit and infinite. His loving-kindness, flowing to the world without interruption, is also infinite. How can the finite creatures receive anything from the infinite God? This itself is God's kindness—that He limits and channels His kindness through thirteen vessels called the Thirteen Virtues of Loving-kindness. Within those confines the creatures are able to receive.

We who receive must also prepare vessels. How? By guarding the energy that God gives us daily and not allowing it to go to waste. The better vessels we prepare, the less waste there is, and the better we can contain the gifts of God. There are times during the year when God's kindness can be received with ease. These are the holidays, which act as vessels themselves. And this is even more true during the Days of Awe, when we repent and return to God; those days are the strongest vessels of them all.

Let us therefore participate in the repentance of these days and be proper vessels for God's gifts that flow without limit.

Before the creation of the universe there was no time as we know it. There was only the pure unaffected will of God to create the world. All was then at the epitome of spiritual purity. With the creation there appeared a reality on a lower level. Still, even the creation can connect to that level of timelessness during special times of the year. This is especially true during the Days of Awe before the New Year, the anniversary of the world's creation. "May my prayer come to You, O Lord, at a desirable moment."

On the level of timeless desire, God is constantly giving; there is no time during which He is not giving. This is not true of the recipients, however. Those who are arrogant are only interested in the material portion of the gifts. In contrast, the humble ones, the righteous servants of God, wish to be connected to the very will from whence the gifts emanate. They would rather have that infinite and timeless will than its limited manifestation. On a higher level this is the meaning of the verse "As for me, may my prayer come to You, O Lord, at a desirable moment. . . ." My prayer, yearning, and desire are only for the favorable moment; I want to be connected to Your desire, which is infinite.

Each one of us can humble himself in this favorable moment of the Days of Awe and be connected to the infinite will of God.

Each catastrophe visited upon the Jewish people contains a small measure of punishment for the sin of the Golden Calf worshiped by the Israelites in the desert. As it is written, "And in the day that I visit I will visit their sin upon them" (*Sanhedrin* 102a; Exodus 33:34).

That grave sin created a negative energy that continues to sap the strength of our faith for all generations to come. Still, it was followed by repentance of great sincerity. This, during the forty days that Moses spent atop Mount Sinai, ending with God's granting the second set of tablets. These forty days left a positive energy for all generations to come. It is a "desirable moment"—our desire to return, and God's desire to accept us.

This is like a king whose most trustworthy servant rebelled against him. The king ordered him banished from the palace. The servant felt remorseful and pleaded and begged to be readmitted. After many days of ceaseless begging, he was finally allowed to enter the throne room. Upon entering, he broke down and cried about his grave sin and how much he desired to serve the king. The king pardoned him, and the servant resumed his former position.

Each year, on the anniversary of the rebellion, the king called his servant and said, "Do you remember the time that you rebelled, how you begged and cried, how you desired to serve me?" Although the king remembered the rebellion well, he remembered the servant's repentance even more.

Let us treasure this precious opportunity to awaken our yearning at this "desirable moment" and to earnestly return to God.

Even before God gave the first tablets to the Jewish people, they proclaimed, "All that God has spoken we will do and we will listen" (Exodus 24:7). They accepted the Torah wholeheartedly, as *tzaddikim*, unblemished righteous servants of God. But then they sinned and worshiped the Golden Calf. Moses broke the tablets of stone, the divinely forged Ten Commandments. The Jews were no longer unblemished, but were sinful and distanced from God. Soon they begged, clamored, and cried to be reaccepted. Their yearning was so strong that it produced the second tablets of stone.

The second tablets were therefore granted to the *baalei teshuvah*, repentants who yearn for God. And this great yearning took place during the forty days that Moses stayed on Mount Sinai. These are the forty days from the first of *Elul* until Yom Kippur and are set aside for great yearning and repentance.

We can compare this to a king who gave his loyal servant a signet ring with the royal seal. This made him arrogant, and he spoke to the king disrespectfully. The king removed the ring and banished the servant from the palace. The servant realized his error and begged and beseeched the king to forgive him. After many days and nights, the king finally allowed him to return, saying, "You will no longer wear my signet ring, but one with your own name on it." Each time the servant saw the ring, he remembered his yearning to be readmitted to the palace. The first ring was no longer important to him and was soon forgotten.

The second tablets are a symbol of yearning and repentance; therefore they are remembered. The first ones were slowly forgotten.

Let us return with the energy of the second tablets and yearn to return to God with all our hearts.

In comparison with the kingdom of God, we are as a speck of dust in the endless ocean. Rosh Hashanah, the New Year, is the anniversary of the creation of the world, God's kingdom, and as it draws near, we feel more and more our triviality and unimportance. We realize that our arrogance is ludicrous and that we do not even have anything to be humble about. Thus we resolve that there is nothing better for us to do than serve God in truth. That is our desirable moment.

———————————

It is written, "God is near to all those who call Him, to those who call to Him in truth" (Psalms 145:18).

During the month of *Elul* the Israelites prayed for forgiveness, and the heavenly gates of prayer opened. It is therefore a month in which we can pray without difficulty. And those who pray "in truth" open the gates for "all who call to Him."

2

Rosh Hashanah

SHOFAR

And in the seventh month, on the first day of the month, you should have a holy convocation; you should do no servile work: it is a day of (*t'ruah*) blowing the trumpet for you. (Numbers 29:1)

e are commanded in the Torah to hear the sounding of the shofar on Rosh Hashanah. Three soundings must be heard, and each of these is called a *t'ruah*, as it is written, ". . . a day of *t'ruah* for you." And each and every *t'ruah* must have a *t'kiah* (uninterrupted sound) before it and after it. That makes a total of nine soundings. We are not certain what a *t'ruah* is. It may be one of the three following sounds: either a *shevorim*, a sound broken into three; a *t'ruah*, a sound broken into nine tiny ones; or a combination of *shevorim* and a *t'ruah*. Therefore, with the *t'kiah* before and after each of the above, we have a total of thirty soundings in all.

It is written, ". . . The voice is the voice of Jacob . . ." (*Genesis* 27:22). Although the voice belongs to Jacob and the hands belong to Esau, still Jacob can also have hands, as when he does *mitzvos*, the commandments of God. But his real connection is to the voice within the action, within the creation, the divine essence in the universe. Therefore, although Jacob can misuse his hands, as when the Israelites worshiped the Golden Calf, the Jewish people will not misuse their "voice." It is protected from defilement and ruin.

The Midrash compares this to a king who gave his servant two crystals to guard. He carelessly broke one of them. The king summoned the servant and said, "You have already broken one. Now be mindful not to break the second." Similarly, after the Israelites worshiped the Golden Calf, God said to them, You have already bungled your promise of ". . . we will do . . .", now be mindful and don't ruin your promise of ". . . and we will listen."

As much as the descendants of Jacob can ruin their actions and deeds, they cannot touch their voice, the voice within the creation. And so God counsels them: be very careful with the voice; it is still whole and unbroken. And by guarding the voice of Jacob you can again reconnect yourself to your original promise of "we shall do."

We can compare this to a prince who received two gifts from his father: a horse and a whistle. One day while riding in the fields he spotted a stream and dismounted to drink. After the prince quenched his thirst and admired the landscape, the horse strayed out of sight. The prince looked up and saw his horse walking off. He quickly grabbed his whistle and blew several shrill blasts. Soon his horse came galloping and stood beside him.

Similarly, another year has just passed and we stand before God as empty vessels. We have long abandoned our good deeds, the "we will do." It is time for renewal; the New Year has arrived. We therefore grab the shofar and blow several blasts. We pray, ". . . and He has commanded us to hear the voice of the shofar" (*Prayer Book*, Rosh Hashanah). We must be very attentive to the voice of Jacob, as it is written, "Bless the Lord, you, His angels, that excel in strength, that do His commandments, listening to the voice of His word" (Psalms 103:21). We again become connected to His commandments by listening to the "voice."

Let us therefore be very attentive to the sound of the shofar. In it we hear our own promise to do and listen, we hear Jacob's voice proclaiming God's kingdom, and ultimately we hear the "voice" of our creator as He created the world. And just as when God created the world there was no difference between word and deed, as it is written, "And God said let there be light, and there was light" (Genesis 1:3), we too can do and listen.

———

The shofar proclaims God's kingdom, and there are two aspects of this proclamation. One is that God is the absolute ruler of the universe and tends to one and all with uncompromising judgment. The other is that therefore we are pitifully empty and broken creatures who constantly need God's loving-kindness to survive.

We can compare this to a king's servant who rebelled against him. He left the palace and traveled from kingdom to kingdom to find a place where he could live in comfort. After many months of searching, he returned weary and embarrassed. Begging and pleading, he was finally allowed to appear before the king. He bowed and said, "O great and mighty king, your rule extends to many lands. Your riches are unsurpassed, and your palace is replete with a thousand pleasures. Your army is mighty." "Stop that!" interrupted the king. "My greatness I'm sure you have not forgotten. But what about you? How do you feel now about yourself?" "And I," continued the former rebel, "I am your humble servant who has nothing in this world, except to serve your royal highness!"

Similarly, the broken sounds of the shofar remind us of our true condition as creatures. We are therefore told, "When the Jewish people blow the shofar, the Creator rises from the throne of judgement and sits on the throne of loving-kindness" (*Midrash Rabbah, Vayikrah* 20:2). If we listen carefully and reassess our condition, then we are worthy of loving-kindness.

———

In the beginning when God created the heaven and the earth, He called to the creation to appear. On the sixth day he called to the dust of the earth and man came forth: "And He breathed into him a breath of life" (Genesis 2:7).

God calls to every creature in the universe, and each one responds to His call. Only man responds in the "image of God." This calling and responding form the relationship that God has with the universe.

In man it reaches its highest level. Adam had the opportunity to nurture this relationship to its limit. Unfortunately, he failed and ate from the Tree of Knowledge (Genesis 3:17). Finally, Abraham came and answered God's call with loving-kindness. His son Isaac answered it with stern judgment. The third of our forefathers, Jacob, found the sublime balance, which was the ultimate and most beautiful one. With Jacob, man's response to God was on the highest level. Jacob is therefore equated with responding, as in "the voice is the voice of Jacob." Thus, whenever Jacob or his children are in trouble they call out to God, as in, ". . . and the Israelites called out to God" (Exodus 14:10).

This is like a king who had a beloved son and responded to his every wish. The prince grew up and unfortunately befriended a band of thieves and soon left the palace. He traveled with them from town to town and took part in their exploits.

One day the king went to visit his subjects and passed through the town where his son happened to be. As the royal coach passed, the king caught a glimpse of the thieves' leader beating the prince. "Father, father, save me, please!" the prince shrieked. The king stopped his coach and ordered the prince be taken inside. He said, "When you called out to me like that, then I knew that I am your father and you are still my son."

The sound of the shofar is our own response to God's call. It is the voice of Jacob, the ultimate relationship with God. And when we respond properly, we can be sure that God's call to us, as His creatures, is in its fullest strength. The world is in order again; it is beautiful and sublime.

———

God is one.

God willed a perfect world to come into existence, and in His will it did not lack perfection. But the creation itself, once it materialized, was not perfect. Although God has neither beginning nor end, the creation has a beginning and an end and therefore is not perfect.

The creation constantly moves toward its end. Material things slowly crumble; living things wither and die. Their cells deteriorate and must constantly be renewed. New cells are born; the old ones are discarded. Human beings, too, are always in need of renewal in order to stay alive.

There is a realm, however, where renewal is not even necessary. This is the realm of God's pure will, the utterly hidden aspect of existence. There, everything is perfect and without fault. In such a place every brokenness becomes whole and full of life.

We can compare this to a prince whom the king sent to a distant land. The prince needed to stay away from home several years until his objectives were accomplished. After three years, the prince experienced great problems. He had huge expenses, but was totally out of funds. He wrote to his father asking for help. His father sent him money, but the prince still faced additional hardships. By the time he had completed his father's mission, the prince was penniless, desperate, and near physical collapse. The king heard of his son's imminent arrival and waited for him with every possible comfort. The prince too fantasized about the pleasures he would soon request. The palace doors opened, and servants carried the prince to his chambers. When the prince saw the elaborate preparation for his welcome, he scampered onto his bed, sank quietly into his pillow, a smile spreading over his face. He no longer needed anything.

Holidays are a time of renewal. But on Rosh Hashanah we want to be in the place where renewal is not even necessary. This is the "hidden" realm of existence, the pure will of God where everything is perfect. There, even brokenness gets straightened out.

Therefore when we blow the shofar, we start with a *t'kiah* (prolonged blast). *T'kiah* also means to rivet, to connect with force. We want to connect our lives to the hidden realm, the world beyond renewal. Then we continue with the sounds of *shevorim* and *t'ruah*, the broken sounds. Once we are in the world of perfection, even our brokenness, faults, and erring ways are transformed and become alive again. Not only are they renewed but they are as if they had never been broken.

Let us therefore reach out to the world beyond renewal where perfection and bliss abound.

When God created the world, He did so with judgment. Everything existed in stern precision and exactness. The world, however, could not possibly exist that way. Therefore God combined judgment with loving-kindness so that the world could survive.

Rosh Hashanah, our New Year, is like the creation. As we recite in our prayers, "This is the day, the beginning of your deeds, a reminder of the very first day . . ." (*Prayer Book*, Rosh Hashanah). Rosh Hashanah, too, starts with judgment; God is ready to judge the entire human race, but surely they would not survive with stern exactness. Therefore we blow the shofar. It is a prayer that we may be worthy that God will use His virtue of loving-kindness, and we will survive.

The Jewish people particularly need God's loving-kindness, although collectively they may have an abundance of good deeds. And even if as a people they would be judged with sternness and exactitude the Jews would be vindicated. Nevertheless, they humble themselves and plead for their lives. And God replies, "Yes, my children, I will deal with you, and with all of humanity with loving-kindness."

This is like a king who prepared a royal feast for his servants. After much partying and drinking, the guests took to ridiculing the king and his policies. When the king overheard their *chutzpah*, he ordered all of them out of the palace immediately. The palace guards quickly expelled every last one of the guests. The prince, who was among the guests during the turmoil, was expelled too.

The servants were extremely embarrassed, but the prince thought that his father's wrath was directed only at him. He took courage and went to his father, bowed, and begged forgiveness.

"No, my son," said the king, "not you, not you! You are my beloved child. You don't need my mercy. But you just made me remember how much I love you . . . and all my servants; they too may return."

The Mishnah states that the shofar of Rosh Hashanah may be of a straight horn (*Mishnah, Rosh Hashanah* 3:3). This means that the Jewish people can come before God even straight, with stern judgment. They need not plead for mercy. However, because of their righteousness they use a bent shofar. They bend and humble themselves for the sake and welfare of the rest of the world.

"Three times a year all your males should appear before God, the God of Israel" (Deuteronomy 16:16). The Talmud comments, "Just as you come to see Him, He too comes to see you."

During the three holidays the Jewish people work for the revelation of God's kingdom. Therefore, God too moves closer and reveals His kingdom to them.

This is an act of love that emanates from the heart of the Jewish people. And the response from God is to love them and to choose them even more. On Rosh Hashanah, however, this love is concealed, and instead of anything concrete, we only have God's voice. We hear it and respond with awe.

We can compare this to a prince who had left the palace on a secret mission to establish his father's kingdom. The king came personally and thanked each province that swore allegiance to him. Once on his travels, men who were unaware of his identity and mission mistook the prince for a common criminal and imprisoned him. The prince was terribly frightened, until the day his father's voice was heard within the prison's hallways. He waited with awe and trembling. Still, he knew that as soon as his father saw him, he would shower him with love.

The three holidays are times of God's open display of love. Not so on Rosh Hashanah. The whole world stands in judgment, and God's love seems to have been suspended indefinitely. Then, just as suddenly, the sound of the shofar is heard, announcing the arrival of the king, the Lord of Israel. Although we stand in awe, still we are relieved. We are sure of His love for us always.

God gives the world life, vitality, and renewal. Without these qualities, the world would deteriorate and die. This cycle of decline and renewal is symbolized by the phases of the moon. The moon fills progressively with more light until mid-month when it is full. Then the light from it diminishes daily until it fades entirely and disappears from view. Then, just as suddenly, it reappears, and the cycle is repeated again.

Similarly, as the Jewish people reveal God's kingdom, they make light in the world. When they succeed, the light increases; when they fail, the light decreases and sometimes is altogether absent.

This cycle is dramatically represented in the life of Abraham. He realized God's existence at an early age and proclaimed it to his idolatrous people. His work gained in intensity, until light was shining from one corner of the earth to the other. Then God ordered him to sacrifice his son Isaac. That event was the eclipse, the absence of light. But just as suddenly, a voice from heaven stopped him, and he discovered a lamb. He was set straight and continued to spread light throughout the world.

The Jewish people, too, went through a similar cycle. Jacob established the twelve tribes to educate and reveal God's kingdom. His "moon" was full, until his descendants were oppressed by Egyptian slavery. Then life was dark, and they nearly abandoned their goal. With the force of great miracles, they finally were released from slavery. And God called to them, "This month shall be the head month for you" (Exodus 12:2). Their "moon" again started to have some light, as they marched forth from Egypt with strength and vigor.

Is the world completely lost during the cycle of darkness? The answer comes on Rosh Hashanah. Although the moon is dark on Rosh Hashanah, the shrill sound of the shofar pierces the air and announces, "God is King!" How can this be? Because as long as there is a Jewish people, God's kingdom is inevitably revealed. And although to all appearances it looks as if it is the end, it is only the beginning.

The Midrash says, "Balak the Moavite king asked Balaam the sorcerer to curse the Jewish people. Balaam answered, '. . . the Lord their God is with them, and the trumpeting of the king is in them. [acclaimed among them as king]' (Numbers 23:21). 'The Lord God is with them, so what can I do? They are protected in the merit of Moshe.'

"'Then curse the next generation,' said Balak.

"'That I can't do either,' said Balaam, 'because of the merit of Joshua. He, too, has God with him; he blows the shofar and the walls of Jericho came tumbling down'" (*Numbers Rabbah* 23).

The relationship between Moses and God was direct, and God spoke to him face to face. Moses also received food directly from heaven: the manna and the brook. This relationship is as direct as the Written Law, which is manifest and clear. In contrast, God's relationship with Joshua was indirect. The manna stopped when the people entered *Eretz Yisrael*, and the sound of the shofar was used at the battle of Jericho.

A direct and manifest relationship is visible to all, although it is only its exterior part. A voice, in contrast, is indirect and concealed, but comes from the deepest depths of one's being. It is the life force itself and breaks through all barriers, even impenetrable walls such as the ones at Jericho.

Thus, although the Written Torah Law of Moses is powerful because it is direct, the Oral Torah Law of Joshua, is, in its own way, even more powerful because it comes from the very essence of our being.

This is like a prince who rebelled against his father and joined a band of thieves. One day the army arrested the entire band, including the prince, and threw them in jail. The following day they were all brought before the king and awaited his judgment. Suddenly the king heard a familiar voice pleading, "Father, please forgive me. I have been very bad, but I am truly sorry, father!" The king was overcome with emotion, stood up from his throne, and examined the thieves with a stern look. "Which one are you, my son? Come to me at once! Please."

Similarly, on Rosh Hashanah we come to God with our "oral" Torah Law. We present our very essence and plead with Him with the sound of the shofar. And He, ignoring all appearances, which seem like walls that separate us, breaks through them all and brings us close to Him.

It is written, ". . . man thus became a living creature" (Genesis 2:7). The Targum translates this as "and man became a talking being." The essence of man is speech: his ability to communicate with a system of complex symbols. He needs to be focused in order to fulfill his true nature. If he is not focused, then some parts of him will go in one direction while his essence goes in another direction. His feet may walk aimlessly about; his arms may seize objects and strike out to maim and kill. As it is written, "The voice is the voice of Jacob, but the hands are the hands of Esau" (Genesis 27:22). Jacob represents the man who is in touch with his essence, whereas Esau is an errant and straying person whose hands strike out and cause harm.

During the past year we have allowed parts of us to go astray. But on Rosh Hashanah, the Day of Remembrance, we remember our essence. We pray to God, ". . . hear the voice of the shofar," to listen intently to the voice within us, our unique ability and superiority over the other creatures.

The universe is vast and awesome. In comparison, we seem as insignificant specks of dust. We look about and marvel, "What are we doing here?" But then we remember. We remember our soul, our very essence, which is from the spiritual realm. And we realize that we are creatures of God, Master of the universe, with a special mission to proclaim His kingdom. And if we don't forget our duty, then God is our God. But if we abrogate our mission, go astray, and think that we have created ourselves, then we are very mistaken.

The Jewish people, as a whole, does not forget. They remember why they exist and proclaim, "Hear O Israel God, our God, God is one" (Deuteronomy 6:4). And then God also remembers and says, "They are, after all, my creatures and I must provide for them abundantly."

The Jewish people remember, also, because they have been made sensitive to listening. They were trained on Mount Sinai to hear the sound of their essence, when they heard the sound of the shofar and the Ten Commandments. Their collective ears are sensitive to even the faintest reminder, and therefore they proclaim, "Hear O Israel. . . ." And likewise in heaven, God contemplates His creation and thinks, "As long as there are human beings who proclaim my kingdom I can love my world and treat it with mercy."

Rosh Hashanah is the Day of Remembrance; we blow the shofar and proclaim, "Please God, be king over the entire world." And because the Jewish people proclaim Him as master, the rest of the world has a king too. And just as the Jewish people

listen and remember, God listens and remembers us also.

It is written, "You are my servant, Israel, through whom I shall win glory" (Isaiah 49:3).

The relationship between God and the Jewish people is like that between a father and his child; it is full of love and compassion. But the Jewish people are humble and consider themselves undeserving of such intimacy. Instead, they consider themselves as servants and God as their master.

This is like a king whose son was one of the royal guards. One day, when the guards rebelled, soldiers quickly surrounded them to protect the king. The king called out, "All who are loyal to the king come forth!" Some of the guards, including the prince, moved forward and bowed at the king's feet. "My son," the king remarked, "surely I didn't mean you." "Still," answered the prince, "I too am your loyal servant."

On Rosh Hashanah the children of God blow the shofar proclaiming God as their master and king. And because of their humility, God has even more compassion for them and treats them with lovingkindness.

It is written, "Man and beast alike are helped by God" (Psalms 36:7). The Talmud comments, "They are cunning as men, but consider themselves mere animals" (*Chullin* 5b).

Man enjoys a special relationship and intimacy with God that is unavailable to other animals. He was created in a special way, as it is written, ". . . and He breathed into him the breath of life" (Genesis 2:7). It is this Godly breath that makes him equally close to heaven as he is to the earth. It is his closeness with the spiritual, however, that is the source of his wisdom. Because God is All-Knowing, the closer we are to Him, the more wisdom we possess. Still, man, as every other animal, is usually preoccupied with his physical survival and forgets his lofty origins. He forgets his soul and spiritual nature. He forgets his royal household, that he is the "son of the king."

Then on Rosh Hashanah, he hears the blast of the shofar proclaiming God as king and master of all creatures. He suddenly remembers who he is and his spiritual origins. This remembrance enlightens and infuses him with wisdom, as it is written, "Praised is the nation who has the wisdom of the shofar blast" (Psalms 89:17). It is the sound of the shofar that brings wisdom to those who hear it. And the verse ends with the words, "God, they will walk in Your light." Whoever acknowledges his own lofty origins, his soul, and his wisdom will be bathed in God's light and loving-kindness.

Therefore, whoever considers himself an animal, a created being, will enjoy the intimacy of God and receive wisdom.

The world was created on Rosh Hashanah, and of its completion, it is written, "And it was evening and it was morning, the sixth day" (Genesis 1:31). Our sages comment: "Why is it called *the* sixth day, as if it was very special? The sixth day is very special; on the sixth day of *Sivan* the Ten Commandments were given on Mount Sinai. And God said to the Israelites on that sixth day, 'If you accept my Torah on this sixth day, I will give life to my world, and if not I will destroy it.' Thus, the final seal of approval for the creation was at Mount Sinai, when the Jewish people accepted the Torah" (*Genesis Rabbah*).

Why is the creation so intricately bound with the Torah? Because the Torah is the blueprint, formula, and trade secret of the creation. Therefore, on Rosh Hashanah when we hear the blast of the shofar, we remember that God is our king, the creator of the universe by means of the Torah. Thus, our prayer to be inscribed in the Book of Life actually means the Torah, as it is written, "It [the Torah] is a tree of life for those who hold on to it" (Proverbs 3:18).

We can compare this to a king who sent his young wife on a goodwill tour to a distant country. Wherever she went, she was greeted with great pomp and celebration. She was so overwhelmed that she momentarily forgot her mission. Days passed; she moved from party to party, from one testimonial to another. Suddenly, at one affair, as the band started to play, the queen stood up in surprise as she heard the melody of her wedding march. She was overcome with emotion as she remembered her wedding day and was ashamed how quickly she had forgotten her husband's bidding.

When we hear the sound of the shofar, we remember the piercing shofar blast of Mount Sinai and how God had chosen us to be His own. We are overjoyed in our chosenness, but remorseful for our shortcomings.

There are three types of sounds we blow with the shofar: a *t'kiah*, a steady blast; a *shevorim*, a broken note; and a *t'ruah*, a shattered quavering note. They symbolize our prayers on Rosh Hashanah.

During the year when we pray, we approach our creator directly, as we do in the *Amidah*, the silent prayer, which originally consisted of eighteen separate prayers. We stand before God in awe, fear, and trembling, and we bow and sing His praises. Then we cry, plead, and beg, as creatures, for our life and sustenance. We then exit from our encounter with praise and honor to God.

On Rosh Hashanah we pray with the shofar. The steady blast of the shofar, *t'kiah*, signifies our direct approach to God. We need not travel, but are immediately before Him. We thus realize that we are His creatures, impotent, broken, and shattered. These are the sounds of the *shevorim* and the *t'ruah*. They are expressed, not in words, but in sounds that bellow forth from our inner being and essence as creatures. Once we have made this intimate encounter, we exit and praise God with another steady blast. There are a total of three short notes and nine shattered notes, corresponding to the twelve prayers of the *Amidah* dealing with life and sustenance.

Let us open our heart on Rosh Hashanah to experience the true brokenness of our being and our exile as a people. Then God will answer with the steady blast of the shofar, signaling our total redemption.

There will come a day when all the crooked will be straightened, all the valleys will be raised, and all the mountains will be lowered; God will reign supreme, and all will know that He is one. The World to Come will be ushered in with an infinite, piercing, steady sound of the shofar.

We have already heard this shofar sound, collectively, on Mount Sinai. There too it was revealed that God is our father and we are His children; He is our king and we obey Him as servants.

On Rosh Hashanah, the sound of the shofar evokes in us the shofar sounds from the past and the future. Then we straighten our crookedness, humble our arrogance, and assume the role of a child, a prince in God's kingdom.

Abraham was commanded to take his son Isaac and sacrifice him on a mountaintop. Abraham walked for three days, and "On the third day, Abraham saw the place from afar" (Genesis 22:4).

This is like a king whose son was away at sea. When they were a great distance from home, the sailors decided to become pirates, to loot and plunder. The king got word of this, dispatched his navy, and soon brought the mutineers under control. In the confusion, the prince was tied in chains with the rest of the crew. The prince's eyes were fixed on the port where his father was waiting with thousands of soldiers. Soon he saw his father, and although in distress, still he was hopeful. "Soon the nightmare will end," he thought, "and I will be safe at home."

On Rosh Hashanah we are seized with the rest of the world for judgment. We fear for our lives and are filled with anxiety. Then we hear the trumpets from the king's palace, and although fearful, we know that we are almost home.

THE SOUND OF THE SHOFAR

It is written, "The voice is the voice of Jacob" (Genesis 27:22). Jacob's voice is his own, pure and undefiled in prayer and study. His voice is flawless and unerring. Yet, Jacob too sometimes goes astray, and his voice becomes tainted with other sounds, with impurity and ungodliness. Later, he realizes his mistake and tries to correct his ways. Then he abandons all the crooked, broken sounds and is left merely with the pure and melodious sound of his own.

We hear the blast of the shofar and say, "He has commanded us to hear the voice of the shofar." The sound of the shofar is at first smooth and pure as the real voice of Jacob, but then it is broken into bits with the sound of the *shevorim* and further crushed with the *t'ruah*. The brokenness of Jacob is not permanent, however, and a final clear blast is sounded to signal the complete restoration of Jacob's voice.

This same cycle is repeated in the life of the Jewish people. At their origins, standing at Mount Sinai, they are straight and pure. Later, in the periods of exile, they go astray, with idol worship and assimilation. Finally, when the *Mashiach* (Messiah) appears, they again hear the piercing blast of the shofar and return to their pure and straight nature once more.

We can compare this to a magician who performed rope tricks before a large audience. He held a rope in his hand that seemed to be whole as he tugged at it. Then he folded, twisted, and manipulated the rope to appear as if it were two ropes. Suddenly he pulled hard on both ends, and "presto!" the rope was whole again.

The Jewish people are compared to a rope, as it is written, "Jacob was the (*chevel*) lot of His heritage" (Deuteronomy 32:9). *Chevel* means rope, and although they may appear crooked, twisted, and erring, the Jewish people are collectively actually straight, whole, and genuine.

It is written, "Praised is the nation that understands the quavering sound of the shofar" (Psalms 89:16).

The quavering sound of the shofar is the utter brokenness and impotence of all creatures before God the Creator. This is the truth of our being: we exist only by the grace of God's purely unaffected will and mercy every instant. Thus, whoever understands his own brokenness also understands God's will in its purest form. As it is written, ". . . and the trumpet blast of the king is in him" (Numbers 23:21). The will of God is to do whatever He deems good for His creatures. This is the divine judgment: precise, exact, and unerring. It is understood by those who understand the *t'ruah*, their own brokenness as creatures. Still, we pray for mercy and loving-kindness on Rosh Hashanah. What more can we ask for?

We can compare this to a patient who was diagnosed as having a large brain tumor and chose a reputed surgeon to remove it. The surgeon informed the patient of all the details, consequences, and prognosis. Finally the day of surgery arrived. Although he believed the doctor would be precise, exact, and unerring, still the patient had tears in his eyes. "Please," he pleaded, "I understand the operation fully. Just, I beg you, each time you cut, think of me and my life. Think of how I will feel it." Thus, although he was confident the operation would be done with pure judgment, still he begged for loving-kindness. We want God to take our life into account the way we experience the judgment. We want the good that God does to be also the good that we experience.

This idea is beautifully taught in the Talmud: "When the Jewish people blow the shofar on Rosh Hashanah, God rises from his throne of judgement and sits down on a throne of mercy" (*Rosh Hashanah* 18a).

On Rosh Hashanah we pray in the purest form for spiritual guidance and understanding. We want to choose a life based on the needs of our spiritual well-being. We no longer want to go astray with lust and desire for the impermanent.

Normally, during the entire year, we pray for our physical needs. Then we pray with our physical being: our throat, tongue, teeth, and lips. But on Rosh Hashanah we use only our breath, our spiritual essence, and blow into the shofar. The shofar sound is our Rosh Hashanah prayer to God: "May this year be one in which we seek the path of spiritual benefit, and not purely physical lusts."

It is written, "They call and God listens" (Psalms 34:18). The Midrash asks, "What is inherent in their call that guarantees the attention of God?"

The Jewish people are forever humbled before God with prayers and supplications. They recognize God as the Creator and assume the role of creatures. And since the Creator is always good to His creatures, He listens and answers their call. The gift of heartfelt prayer we have inherited from our forefather Isaac. He blessed his son Jacob and said, "The voice is the voice of Jacob." The voice belongs to him always in all generations to come. And when Jacob prays as a creature before his Creator, he needs no mercy. It is decreed by divine judgment that every creature shall receive sustenance. Thus, Jacob received his voice, and his sustenance, as an inheritance from his father Isaac, who represents the virtue of strict judgment.

This is like a kingdom in which all legal matters were judged by the king with the help of a panel of judges. On occasion, the king overruled the judges, saying, "I know the law, but this case, because it is pitiful, is an exception." Once, the prince himself presented a legal matter before the judges. His father ruled in his favor, and the judges added, "In this case we rule that whoever is like the prince, so loyal and faithful, deserves what his father grants him."

On Rosh Hashanah, as soon as we make our voice heard through the sound of the shofar, God had already listened.

The Midrash comments: Whoever heard the voice of Jacob came to love him more and more each time (*Genesis Rabbah* 27). Jacob's voice comes from his essence and is pure, sweet, and lovable. But it is merely his voice. Esau, in contrast, has words. Words are formed with the throat, tongue, teeth, and lips. While Jacob's voice is always the same, the words of Esau change according to circumstances. Therefore, Isaac's love for his son Esau also depended upon circumstances, as it is written, "And Isaac loved Esau because he brought food to his mouth, while Rebecca loved Jacob" (Genesis 25:28). Her love for Jacob, as his voice, was unconditional.

The voice of the Jewish people too is beloved by God. It is the voice of Jacob, essentially unchanging and eternally pure and sweet, as it is written, "My dove, that hides in holes in the cliffs or in the secret places on the high ledges, let me see your face, let me hear your voice; for your voice is pleasant, your face is lovely" (Song of Songs 2:14). On Rosh Hashanah when the judgment of the Jewish people is still secret and the outcome obscure, they let their voice be heard. The sweet unchanging voice of Jacob, represented by the shofar, is heard. And God Who hears it immediately loves them more and decrees life for the coming year.

God created the world with Ten Commands. The first of them is the word *Bereishis*, "in the beginning," that the universe should have a beginning. And this beginning is the Torah, which is the essence of all. It is the plan and wisdom of every created thing. And whose wisdom is the Torah? It is the wisdom of the Creator Himself. Whoever is connected to the Torah has life; without this connection, he withers and dies. As it is written, "Wisdom preserves the life of him that has it" (Ecclesiastes 7:12). And in contrast it is written, "They die, even without wisdom" (Job 5:21). Those who are connected to wisdom have life, whereas those who are without it wither and die.

On Rosh Hashanah we hold dearly the piercing sound of the shofar, the sound of Mount Sinai, the sound of the Torah itself. Then we are revitalized as in the beginning and are immediately transcribed to life.

Shortly after the Israelites left Egypt, the nation of Amalek attacked them at Rephidim. Moses instructed Joshua to fight Amalek, and while he fought, Moses held his hands high and the Israelites prevailed. But when he let his hands down, Amalek prevailed (Exodus 17:8–13).

The Mishnah asks: were the hands of Moses responsible for the fate of the battle? The reason is thus: when Moses lifted his hands and the Israelites' attention was turned to their Father in Heaven, they prevailed. But when his hands were lowered, they only thought of the conduct of the war, and so they were defeated (*Mishnah Rosh Hashanah* 3:8).

The voice of Jacob, his tongue, is physically raised above the hands of Esau. He can always overpower the hands of Esau if his tongue is active in prayer and Torah study. Esau, on the other hand, tries to keep the spirit of the Jewish people enslaved.

Jacob needs only to rise above his physical enslavement: Egypt and Amalek. Then his voice is heard clearly above the sounds of battle, and he attains complete freedom. This is alluded to in the talmudic teaching, "It was on Rosh Hashanah that Joseph was freed from prison." Joseph was connected to the voice of his father Jacob, and, with this connection interpreted the dream of Pharaoh and was released from prison.

On Rosh Hashanah, with the sound of the shofar, we all leave our prisons and are victorious over the enslaving power of Esau.

It is written, "All of them you have made with wisdom" (Psalms 104:24). Everything in the world contains the wisdom of God. And this is true even of the dimensions of space and time, so that every dimension of the universe is worthy of close examination. As we are taught by our sages, "Who is wise? He who learns from every being" (*Ethics of Our Fathers*).

The Baal Shem Tov amplified this truth in this way: Every encounter we have with the world, no matter how trivial it may seem, nevertheless can be instructive. And when the dimension of time of Rosh Hashanah arrives and we are filled with fright and anxiety about God's judgment, we can learn from that too. We learn that God is the master of the universe, and we are totally helpless without Him. And by accepting the role of creatures, we are humbled and in need of God's loving-kindness. Judgment is transformed to mercy.

The Baal Shem Tov compares this to a king whose servant was in a foreign country on a crucial mission. A short while later the king sent an emissary to call the servant back to the palace. When he heard of the emissary's arrival, the servant hurriedly cleaned his house, borrowed and gathered the best of everything, and prepared a feast. His guest was received with great honor and ate a sumptuous meal. The following day, he toured the city with him, followed by dinners and feasts in the finest banquet halls. Finally, at week's end the servant returned to the king. "Why have you tarried so long?" the king asked. "I was too busy honoring your special emissary," answered the servant. "You fool," the king scolded, "you should have come at once! Is it not I who has sent for you?"

On Rosh Hashanah we are frightened because of God's judgment of the world. But judgment is merely God's emissary. Should we spend time with the emissary or attend to the king? We should immediately run and appear before Him and pray for our lives. Therefore, although we pray for the details of our needs in our daily prayers, and receive them with judgment, on Rosh Hashanah we merely sound the shofar to declare God as King and Judge, and as humble servants we beg for life.

It is written, "Blessed are the people who know the sound of the *t'ruah*" (Psalms 89:16). A *t'kiah* is a whole sound, but a *t'ruah* is broken and fragmented and represents stern judgment.

This is like a king who was angered by his son's behavior and was about to punish him. The prince's mentor begged, "Please, Your Majesty, don't punish all at once, but each time you want to be kind to him, give him a little less."

Loving-kindness flows in a steady and uninterrupted stream, like the sound of the *t'kiah*. Stern judg-

ment, if it were to come all at once, would be unbearable. It is therefore broken into smaller pieces, like the *shevorim* and the *t'ruah*. But as small pieces, they are no longer judgment, but bits of kindness instead.

When God created the world, each thing was complete and wholesome. Then these things deteriorated and were no longer pure; man, animals, the vegetation had to return to the very earth itself. But one day, and it is sure to come, everything will return to its original state of perfection. We yearn to see this soon in our days, to see *Olam Habah*, the World to Come.

The world, flawless from the beginning is as the *tzaddik*, the righteous one who stands without blemish before God. The corrupt world, waiting for redemption, is as the *baal teshuvah*, the repentant who waits for God's mercy to return him to his flawless beginning.

We experience renewal twelve times a year, once each month with the sighting of the new moon. Each of the eleven months represents one of the eleven tribes, the *baalei teshuvah*, who yearn for and receive renewal. The twelfth new moon, or Rosh Hashanah, symbolizes Joseph, the *tzaddik*, the flawless one who never strayed and is as he was in the beginning.

The world begins because God remembers us, and we pray on each of the New Moons, "May you please remember us on this day of the new moon." But on Rosh Hashanah, the day itself is a day of remembrance; it is the day of the *tzaddik*, who is flawless as when he was created. It is the utmost beginning; it cannot even be experienced and is therefore in concealment, *ba'keseh*.

Let us therefore connect ourselves to the energy of Joseph, the righteous one, on this Day of Remembrance. And we too will merit being immersed in the flawless beginning and will always be remembered.

The truest definition of our being is that we are nothing but powerless and completely impotent without God. This is profound understanding and the greatest wisdom. Therefore the Hebrew word for wisdom is *chochmah*, made of two short words—*koach* and *mah*—the absence, the negation of strength at the root of all things, and that is God.

Who possesses this wisdom? Those who are cunning as humans, but consider themselves mere animals. As we recite in our morning prayers, "For what more is man than the animal: nothing!" Those who can negate themselves completely before God are therefore connected to God's wisdom, which is "nothing"; it is not a thing, not a created thing, but God Himself, wisdom and knowledge in its purest form. This is represented by the pure sound of the shofar—no words, no confusion, but rather a primal scream, an animal's gut bellowing, crying out to God. As it is written, "She opened her mouth with wisdom . . ." (Proverbs 31:26), she merely opened her mouth, she calls out as a creature before her maker. That is true wisdom.

Let us allow the sound of the shofar to pierce through our rationalizations. We then connect with the *ayin*, "nothing," the source of all wisdom.

On Rosh Hashanah all the world is judged. We take full note of the seriousness of the day and approach with awe, fear, and trembling. In the spiritual sphere, all this is superficial. Concealed within are loving-kindness and compassion. Is it not the anniversary of the creation of the world? And God would have created it with stern judgment, but had to combine loving-kindness so that it can survive. Therefore, it is the anniversary of the fact that the world cannot survive without kindness, which is what we pray and hope for. "Please, God, You know that the world cannot survive without kindness, so why apply the rule of law and strict judgment to us? You know that we will not survive. So just begin with kindness and we will live."

In the laws pertaining to the fiftieth year of the *Yoval*, the Jubilee year, the shofar is mentioned twice, as it is written, "Then you should send abroad the sounding trumpet of the shofar on the tenth day of the seventh month, in the day of atonement you should send abroad the shofar throughout the land. And you should proclaim liberty throughout all of the land and the inhabitants thereof . . ." (Leviticus 25:9–10). But in the laws about Rosh Hashanah the shofar is mentioned only once: "And in the seventh month, on the first day of the month you should have a holy gathering; you should do no servile work: it is a day of blowing the shofar for you" (Numbers 29:1).

The sages of the Talmud deduce from these verses that whenever we are commanded to sound the shofar the sounding should be identical (*Rosh Hashanah* 33b); since the word shofar is mentioned three times, there ought to be three series of sounds.

What do we learn from the comparison of Rosh Hashanah to the Jubilee? That on each Rosh Hashanah we too can hear the shofar blast of the Jubilee that sends all slaves free. We need no longer be

enslaved by the illusions of habit and impermanent circumstances. We can attain freedom from attachments and deceptive rationalizations. This is symbolized with the three sets of sounds—*t'kiah, t'ruah, t'kiah*—three times three. They represent our three forefathers, Abraham, Isaac, and Jacob, who were all connected to the plane above the natural world, the World of Freedom. There, one is free from the three strongest attachments of the physical world—idol worship, incest, and murder—which are caused by the three appetites of jealousy, lust, and seeking honor.

How do we attain freedom? By purging and emptying our being of all attachments and illusions. By being like the shofar, a hollow vessel with open ends. Can the shofar possibly be a *vessel* with both ends open? Yet it is the ultimate vessel for carrying the voice of God, for passing through it without attachments. Our lives are like that too. We too are but hollow vessels with open ends. Whatever we have is merely the will of God, and not really ours.

The sound of the shofar alludes to this idea as well. It comes from the trachea, the windpipe, and is pure and simple, without words. The esophagus, or food pipe, in contrast, is involved with the digestion of foodstuffs and has more attachments to the physical world.

When we hear the triplicate sound of the shofar, let us immediately assume our freedom and enjoy the world beyond enslavement.

This world would not exist were it judged sternly and with exactness. It must have the mercy, compassion, and loving-kindness of God. And we are worthy of compassion only when we realize that we are beings, flawed, imperfect, and dependent on our Creator. That is true wisdom.

The document in which this wisdom is stored is the Torah, which is open and accessible to one and all. The mercy that we desperately need on Rosh Hashanah comes to us through the Torah. The Torah is therefore called *Rachmono*, the merciful one, because by the means of its wisdom, God has mercy on His creatures and we survive.

This is like a servant of the king who was sent on a secret mission. One night as he led his horse near a cliff, he slipped and tumbled down the side of the mountain. He lay in pain and agony, unable to move. Finally he managed to open a flask of whiskey, and emptying it with desperate gulps, he fell into a drunken stupor. Passing soldiers heard his moans and, not knowing his identity, brought him before the king. The servant, who was actually the prince in disguise, mumbled drunkenly while the king contemplated his fate. All at once, the prince found the royal seal in his pocket, took it out, and played with it. Then he fell and prostrated himself before the king with the seal still in his hand. The king, astonished, called out, "Aha! Now I see who he is. Take him to my chambers and fetch the royal physician."

On Rosh Hashanah let us hold tightly the Torah, which is the seal of the King, and remember its teachings. Then God will remember us too with compassion.

———————

It is written, "The Lord is gone up with the sound of the *t'ruah*, God with the sound of the shofar" (Psalms 47:6).

Abraham's ethical teaching was to be compassionate in all circumstances. Yet, this man of great compassion was asked to take his son Isaac and sacrifice him on a mountaintop. He had to obey God with exactness and stern judgment. It was a great ordeal for Abraham. Then, God called to him, he stopped his attempt to kill Isaac, and sacrificed a ram instead. As a reward for his great devotion, God promised Abraham to bless his descendants and protect them always.

From that moment on, whenever there ought to be stern judgment, there is compassion instead. And we say, "The Lord [*Elohim*, symbolic of judgment] is gone up with the sound of *t'ruah*." When there ought to have been *Elohim*, judgment, as with a sinner who repents, now it is gone up, it is uplifted and transformed to mercy and compassion. The verse continues, ". . . God, [symbolic of mercy, when dealing with the righteous] goes straight up with the sound of the shofar"—the *t'kiah*, which is flawless.

May God remember the covenant He forged with our forefather Abraham and transform and uplift us unconditionally.

———————

All may be servants of God, yet one is a *tzaddik* who has never sinned, and the other is a *baal teshuvah*, a repentant.

The *tzaddik* follows the prescribed path and is witness to God's kingdom. He is symbolized by the three major holidays, when "Three times a year all your males shall appear before God your Lord in the place where He chooses" (Deuteronomy 16:16).

The *baal teshuvah*, although he sinned, is on a higher level than the *tzaddik*, as the Talmud assures us, "The place where the *baal teshuvah* stands, even the completely righteous cannot stand" (*Berakhos*

34b). Why? Sins are attachments to the realm of space and time. And they bring their own punishment—being unable to rise above the physical realm to the spiritual realm. Thus, when the *baal teshuvah* returns to God, he is returned to the state of singularity before the creation, before time or space, when only God prevailed. Sin exists only in space and time; thus in God there is no sin. And therefore the *baal teshuvah*, who is transported to the throne of God, the realm of preexistence, is immediately cleansed, completely and totally.

Rosh Hashanah too is from the realm of beginnings, of preexistence, prior to space and time. And thus, when we hear the sound of the shofar, we quickly come before God Who will transform us as if we were unblemished from time immemorial.

IN THE CONCEALMENT

"Blow the shofar at the moon's renewal, at (*ba'keseh*) the time appointed for our festival" (Psalms 81:4). The word *ba'keseh* also means concealed. All the other holidays are celebrated when the moon is visible. Only one is celebrated when the moon is concealed. This holiday is Rosh Hashanah, which is celebrated on the first of the month of *Tishrei*, when the moon is still not visible.

———————

It is written, "And God saw that the light was good" (Genesis 1:4). The original light was extraordinary, and one could "see with it from one end of the universe to the other." Therefore God concealed its quality and hid it for the *tzaddikim*, the righteous, for use at a future time (*Genesis Rabbah* 1).

The special quality in the light is called "good" and is revealed during the holidays. Therefore, each holiday is called *yom tov*, literally a good day, because each possesses some of the good light. On Rosh Hashanah, this good light is concealed because it is so solemn a day, and it is set aside for judgment. Still the light is there in great abundance, but, *ba'keseh*, in concealment.

———————

It is written, "And your people are all righteous" (Isaiah 60:21). And a great reward is in store for them: "A harvest of light is sown for the righteous" (Psalms 97:11).

There is a hidden light inside each Jew that has the nature of the Throne of Honor, the highest of spiritual realms. Therefore, the Jews are called the children of God because their soul is an offshoot of God's spirituality. It is the highest privilege and honor to be called the children of God, and the jealousy of the other nations is intense. God, therefore, must hide this light from the other nations. Still, that does not change the fact that the Jews possess God's light.

This is like a king who sent his son on a secret mission. It was so secret that only the king and his son knew the details. The king gave his signet ring to his son and said, "I never remove this from my finger nor give it to anyone. But this is an exception." The prince carefully guarded the ring and hid it beneath his clothing. He never even looked at it for fear of discovery.

One day he was captured by a band of robbers and taken to a mountain hideaway. The king was informed of his son's plight and dispatched soldiers who nabbed the band. In the confusion, for fear of losing the ring while being searched and questioned, the prince swallowed it. Finally he was brought before his father. The king dismissed everyone from the room to welcome his son. "I knew that we were close," said the prince, "but I did not experience fully this closeness until I guarded it as a secret."

On Rosh Hashanah when the moon is concealed, the Jewish nation is in judgment together with the rest of the world, and our closeness to God is concealed too. It is then that we feel the power of that closeness as we hide it from the jealousy of the world.

Although Rosh Hashanah is a day of judgment, fear, and awe, it is a festival nevertheless.

We can compare this to a prince who was invited to feast at the palace of a neighboring monarch. An entourage of guards and noblemen accompanied him. The party was lavish, and the guests regaled with unrestrained merriment. The prince and his men, while drunk, exchanged some loud banter and vulgarities. When his father got word of this behavior, he summoned the scoundrels to appear before him at once. Still not fully sober, they stood trembling before the king. The king said, "You are all banished from the palace for a month. Instead you will work in the fields with the other prisoners."

The king thought sadly, "I had to punish my son too so he can learn to behave, but I can hardly wait for his return." The prince was pining, "I wish the month was over and I could be with my father again."

Similarly, we acknowledge our judgment and are awed by the precision and strictness of the judge. Still we cannot wait for the judgment to be over and to rejoin God in His palace as His children. And although we are judged on Rosh Hashanah, soon we will be in the refuge of God, in the *sukkah*, and rejoice with Him.

INSCRIBE US TO LIFE

Every being in the world is judged on Rosh Hashanah. The sages of the Talmud have taught: "Three books are opened on Rosh Hashanah, the righteous are immediately inscribed and sealed for a good life. The wicked are immediately inscribed and sealed for death. And the ones who are neither too good nor too bad are left suspended; if they repent till Yom Kippur, they are inscribed to life, and if not, they are inscribed to death" (*Rosh Hashanah* 16b). Therefore, our prayers on Rosh Hashanah are replete with the words "Please inscribe us to life."

No doubt, each one of us wants life and does not want to die. Still, when God inscribes us, it is to a more lasting life than the physical one. It is a permanent and everlasting inscription. It is the life at the center of our life—the soul—which is the kernel of divine spirituality in each one of us. But if it is eternal, then why does it need renewal? Why must we pray and beg for God's mercy?

A prince was sent on a secret mission by his father, who entrusted him with his signet ring. The prince sailed and was at sea for many months. A hurricane came and tore the ship apart, leaving the survivors clinging to driftwood. After days afloat and near death, the prince was finally washed ashore on a remote island. Marooned there for months, he struggled to survive. But this attempt too ended in disaster, and he was captured by pirates. Years passed before he was able to resume his original plans. By then his only identity was the signet ring, but alas, it was completely tarnished and impossible to recognize. The prince realized his hopelessness and cried about his plight. His father appeared in a dream and said, "My son, do not be afraid. The inscription on your ring is still as clear as the day I gave it to you. Just scrub, scrape, and clean it off and everyone will realize that you are my son."

When we pray, "Please, God, inscribe us," we mean to say, "Please, God, your inscription in us, our soul, is all tarnished and hardly visible. Please renew, rejuvenate your inscription, our 'life' our vitality in us."

On Rosh Hashanah we repeat many times the prayers, "Please remember us to life. Please inscribe us to life." We are certainly concerned and anxious about being judged on Rosh Hashana. We are afraid. It is surely a day of fear and trembling. However, the fear itself should be lifted to a higher spiritual level. It should not be negative, a fear of losing our health, or even our life, but rather a concern and worry about not being separated from life, the Tree of Life, the Torah, the blueprint of our very life. For the Torah is truly the Book of Life, guiding us to the pure and true life always.

This is like a prince whose father gave him the sacred book of princely conduct. The prince was then sent on a dangerous voyage and was beset by menacing storms. One storm was so severe that everyone, including the prince, abandoned ship and jumped into the lifeboats. The prince was frightened as the waves washed over his head. He clutched the sacred book close to his bosom to protect it from harm. "I better guard this if I ever hope to live like a prince again," he said.

We too are more concerned about our separation from the Torah, our sacred book of life, than even about death itself.

It is written, "And God formed the dust of the earth, and formed a man, and breathed into his nostrils the breath of life. Thus man became a living creature" (Genesis 2:7–8). This alludes to the three books of judgment that are opened on Rosh Hashanah. In one, the wicked are inscribed for death. This is the "dust of the earth," those who cannot rise above their physical natures, sin constantly, and end in dust. In another book, the righteous are inscribed to life. This is "the breath of life," those who infuse their bodies with the vitality of their souls. The third book is for those who are neither righteous nor wicked. This is reflected in the phrase "man became a living creature"; they are living, but merely as creatures. They strive for the life of the soul, but still cling to their creaturely lusts.

Thus the *tzaddik*, the righteous one, is called alive, because he receives his life from his soul. His focus is spiritual, and his body is merely a vessel through which he attains his ultimate goal. Even when he dies, the *tzaddik* is called alive because that which was his true life is still alive—his immortal soul. In contrast, the wicked shun the light of their soul and indulge merely in physical lusts. They are called dead even while living, because they do not allow their true life to shine through.

As the years pass, we may go astray and forget our true life, our immortal souls, and occupy ourselves purely with physical needs. We may harness our soul to attain our physical goals, instead of harnessing our body to attain our spiritual goals. The light of the

Torah, our Book of Life, dims in us. We are in danger of being declared dead. We need to change.

Rosh Hashanah is the time for renewal and we beg for life: "Please God, restore our life, our soul, to its original strength, and allow us to live in its light."

It is written: "You alone are God; You made the heaven, the highest heaven with all its host, the earth and all that is on it, the seas and all that is in them. You preserve (*mechayeh*) all of them, and the host of heaven worships you" (Nehemiah 9:6).

The universe is physical and behaves according to natural laws. But these are not the laws that give it life. The life of the universe is God, as the word *mechayeh* implies: You, God, give it life. But it is a life hidden and veiled by the regular, predictable, and expected behavior of the material world. God is hidden behind nature; the miraculous world is concealed. And for the average person, the natural world is all he will ever experience. The *tzaddikim*, the righteous ones, are more fortunate, as they attain a glimpse of the miraculous world from time to time. And when they do, they really know where the life and vitality of the universe come from.

The miraculous world was also revealed to the Israelites when they left Egypt and stood at Mount Sinai. God spoke to them and said, "I am God your Lord who brought you out of Egypt" (Exodus 20:2). Do not think that you left Egypt by some natural accident. No, you didn't. I, God, am the one who was behind all that.

On Rosh Hashanah, we too beg God to grant us a glimpse of the true "life," the life behind the veil of nature, the spiritual life.

Every living thing received its nature from God when it was created. Man has both a physical and a spiritual nature. His body ages, withers, dies, and returns to dust. His soul, in contrast, is immortal; it lives on to bask in the light of the spiritual world forever.

On Rosh Hashanah, we yearn for the eternal life, the life of the soul. And the more we serve as a vessel to receive the spiritual essence, the more we have it the entire year. Therefore we beg, "Please, God, inscribe us to life," inscribe in us the true life, our soul, in a most permanent way.

We recite in our Rosh Hashanah prayers, "Please remember us to life, O King who desires life, and inscribe us in the book of life, for Your sake, the Living God."

Although we ask for life, we do not ask for our sake, but for Yours. If we get life, You, God, will be honored. As it is written, "I have formed this people for my sake; they will say my praises" (Isaiah 43:21). If You let us live, we will say Your praises; You will have a people who will proclaim Your kingdom throughout the world. But if we perish, then who would be left to say Your praises?

There are thousands upon thousands of types of living creatures, and millions of each type. Still, the crowning glory of the entire creation, from the tiniest virus to the largest blue whale, is man. Man is the creature who has the power to bend the entire creation either to the positive or the negative side. On a practical level, observe the environment, the well-being of the entire ecosystem. If man acts with his capacity of understanding, compassion, and ability to organize, he brings life to all creatures including himself. On the other hand, he can act with lust, disregarding and harming the very earth that sustains him. The fate of the world, even the most physical, is in his hands.

Therefore, on Rosh Hashanah, we plead, please God, restore in us the life of the crown of the creation. Help us rise to the occasion, and give us the strength to lead the world toward the good: both the physical well-being of the creatures and the spiritual elevation of mankind.

Before God created the world He reigned in His Majesty. Nothing else existed: not matter, not time, not space. Where was there room for the creation? God, so to speak, contracted His being, and in that infinitesimal place matter was created. Therefore, on some level, where there is matter, there is not the fullness of God's vitality and life-giving forces. The universe expanded and the more it did, the farther and farther it moved from the divine vitality, and consequently, the closer it came to the realm of death. Then man was created, and God breathed into Him a breath of life. He breathed into him that which the universe needs. It needs to be in touch with the life-giving breath of God.

Man is therefore at the center of the entire universe; between God, on the one hand, and "dead" matter, on the other hand. It is in his power to tilt the creation from one side to the other if he so chooses. He can bring God's life-giving spirit back into the world of nature, a nature that is constantly running away from it. Therefore, we beg, God, inscribe us to

life, that we ourselves be connected to divine vitality and revitalize the world with its life-giving powers.

A human being's body has many parts, organs, and members. It has vital organs without which man cannot survive, such as the brain and the heart, the lungs and the liver. But it also has other organs that are not vital to our survival, such as our limbs, teeth, and appendix. Without doubt the organ that is the most vital is the brain, our head. And, therefore, wherever our head is, our body is sure to follow. The focus of our thoughts, whether physical or spiritual, whether merciful or wicked, determines the activities of the rest of our body.

Our body contains 248 organs and 365 tendons, corresponding to the 248 positive commandments, or mitzvos, in the Torah, and the 365 negative commandments. Thus our head can lead our body to become alive with mitzvos, good deeds, or it can ruin the body to become defiled with misdeeds. We can draw the life-giving force from God into our body by means of our head. When we focus our thoughts, yearnings, wishes, daydreams, lusts, and passions to attain spiritual vitality and strength, then our actions will follow. And the divine life will flow into us, and we will "live."

That is the life that we beg for on Rosh Hashanah. "Please God, let us have the thoughts and focus necessary for the real life with You. No other life is really worth as much."

The physical world can pursue lust and material gratification, and it runs away from the spiritual world. While the spiritual world is full with the life-giving power of God, the physical world runs toward death. However, God will never again let the physical world reach the point of no return, as happened in the days of Noah when a flood nearly wiped out all living things. God promised then, "I will never again kill every living creature, as I have just done. While the earth lasts, seed time and harvest, cold and heat, summer and winter, day and night, shall never cease" (Genesis 8:21–22).

Similarly, God promised the Jewish people that they will bring His life-giving forces to the world and its inhabitants. But how much good can the Jewish people do? Nothing limits them but their will. If they choose to work hard, they can uplift the world to great heights. And if they lack initiative, they let the world flounder. Still, the responsibility will not be given to another people.

And so we beg, "Please, God, give us the strength to bring life into a dead world again."

It is written, "Seek God when He is found" (Isaiah 55:6). The Talmud comments, "When is God found? In the days from Rosh Hashanah till Yom Kippur" (*Rosh Hashanah* 18a).

Does this mean that God is not found at other times? No. God can always be found. He has placed into each one of us, has inscribed on our hearts the awesome message of "I am God your Lord who brought you out of Egypt" (Exodus 20:2). Then why don't we constantly hear this message? It is because our sins separate our mind from the purity contained in that message. As the sages taught, "One should always imagine that the holy one is dwelling inside his body." Always, even after a person has sinned, the holiness is there inside in its original purity. Then why did he sin? Because his corruption separated his physical being from his spiritual being. Thus, life is always inside us, but we are not always connected with it.

We can reconnect with the divine energy inside us by repentance, by returning to God with all our heart and soul. As it is written, "Return O Israel *and* to God your Lord, for you have stumbled in your evil courses" (Hosea 14:2). How far is "*and* (till) God your Lord"? It is until the words "I am God your Lord . . ." of the Ten Commandments, the words that God inscribed into us.

On Rosh Hashanah, when the whole world is judged and renewed, we can reconnect to the pure life that is inscribed in each one of us, and pray fervently, "Please God, reinscribe that life in us again."

God created the universe, something, from nothing: in *yesh mei'ayin*. But do not think that the "nothing" is our common usage of the word. It only seems to us that it was nothing, because that is all we can say about God: nothing. During the period of nothing, there was no matter, but there was the One and Only God. Therefore the *yesh*, the something, needs to negate itself to the nothing. Whatever we have or do must be focused on nothing. We should not start with matter, but should give it direction by looking at the nothing from whence it came.

Compared to the *ayin*, nothing, which is life itself, the *yesh*, the material world, is death. Thus, if we negate the material world, our physical life, and our possessions to the *ayin*, the realm of God, then we give them all life. And so we beg God in our prayers,

"Please, God, inscribe us to life. Help us uplift our physical world to the realm of nothing, the place and origin of the universe, which is Your holy place, where You are the one and only."

PASS BEFORE HIM LIKE FLOCKS OF SHEEP

The second mishnah in the tractate of *Rosh Hashanah* reads:

> The world is judged at four periods in the year: on Passover for grain; on the Festival of Weeks, Shavuos, for the fruits of trees; on the New Year, all the inhabitants of the world pass before Him, like flocks of sheep, as is written, He Who fashions the hearts of them all, Who understands all their doings; and on the Festival of Tabernacles, Sukkos, they are judged for water.

The Talmud comments: The judgment of God on Rosh Hashanah is done in one glance, in one instant (*Rosh Hashanah* 18a). How does this happen?

It is written, "So God formed out of the ground all the wild animals and the birds of the heaven. He brought them to the man to see what he would call them, and whatever the man called each living creature, that was his name. Thus the man gave names to the cattle, to the birds of heaven, and to every wild animal" (Genesis 2:19–20).

Man is the crown of creation. He was created with intelligence that can plan and render the fate of all the other creatures. On a physical level, he can help all living things, plants, and animals to survive by deliberate caring. Or, he can cause the demise and extinction of whole populations of living things by his hurtful behavior—by polluting, removing environments, and slaughtering. At its absolute worst, this extinction was attempted by the Germans during the Second World War, as they planned and executed the annihilation of the Jewish people.

God placed the entire world in the hands of man, and said, "Go find a place for each and every creature. Determine how each fits into the plan, and help them survive." And thus "man called names" for each of the creatures by assigning its place. He sensed where each one belonged in the total scheme. But how did he know? By negating himself to the Ten Commands with which God created the world. Those Ten Commands define the nature and purpose of each creature in the universe. Thus, by being in tune with the Ten Commands, man "knew" the animals' real names and how to care for them. Therefore, when God judges His creatures, He needs only to look into the hearts of mankind to know the condition of them all. Because all the creatures are in the heart of man.

When God looks into the hearts of each of us on this day, is He going to see our selfish desires? Or will he see the Ten Commands, His Will, in us? Now is the time to decide.

It is written, "In the light of the king's countenance is life" (Proverbs 16:15).

A king was judging the case of the men who plotted to kill his son. On the same day a group of survivors of a recent shipwreck arrived to beg the king for help. He ignored the pitiful souls and continued with the case. The shipwrecked sailors waited outside the king's chambers forlornly. After many hours, they were ushered in to the king. The king was still brooding about the previous case and did not look at the delegation. Finally, he looked up, and said, "Yes! What can I do for you?" The sailors were thrilled with the king's attention and sensed that they would be helped.

Similarly, it is written, "And God saw all that He had done and it was very good" (Genesis 2:30). When God looks, when He cares for and is attentive to the creatures, they then have life. If He turns away from them, they wither and die, as it is written: "All of them look expectantly to you to give them their food at the proper time. What you give them they gather up; when You open Your hand they eat their fill. When You hide Your face, and they are restless and troubled; when You take away their breath, they fail and return to dust from which they came. But when You breathe into them they recover; You give new life to the earth" (Psalms 104:27–30).

Thus when God "looks" at us, when He looks us over on Rosh Hashanah, from that glance we have life.

It is written, "As the rose among the thorns, so is my love among the daughters" (Song of Songs 2:2).

The nations of the world are as thorns. Although the thorns protect the roses from being plucked, still, which of them is more beautiful: the thorns or the roses? The roses are the Jewish people who are the witnesses for God's kingdom, and they all are judged.

The nations of the world do not want to be judged. They do not have much to be proud of and have to be forced to stand in judgment. But the Jewish people come willingly, with their good deeds and merits,

and are judged among them. And they do not have the same fear as the nations, because deep in their hearts they know that they are good. As it is written, "Show me your face, let me hear your voice; for your voice is pleasant and your face is beautiful" (Song of Songs 2:15).

It is written, "Remember the days of old, think of the generations of long ago (*shnos dor v'dor*)" (Deuteronomy 32:7). *Shnos*, each year, has its particular problems, crises, dilemmas, and perplexities. And to help humans solve those problems, God gives them understanding that is suited precisely for that year. And with that understanding they are able to solve their problems and rise above their limitations. Thus when we are judged on Rosh Hashanah we pray to God, "Just as the shepherd, when he counts his sheep, glances at them to appraise their needs, so You too, dear God, understand our hearts, and know just what sort of understanding we need for our problems. Please grant us that understanding for this year."

The Judgment of Rosh Hashanah

On Rosh Hashanah each and every being is judged, as we recite in our prayers:

> On Rosh Hashanah it is written and on Yom Kippur it is sealed: How many will pass from the earth and how many will be created; who will live and who will die. Who will die a timely death, and who an untimely death; who in water, and who in fire; who by the sword, and who by wild beast; who by famine, and who by thirst; who by storm, and who by the plague; who by strangulation, and who by stoning. Who will rest, and who will wander; who will live in tranquility, and who will be harried; who will live in peace, and who will suffer; who will be poor, and who will be rich; who will be degraded, and who will be exalted.

Although Rosh Hashanah is a day of judgment, it is also a holiday of joy and pleasure. But how can anyone who is being judged, who is hanging between life and death, celebrate? The answer is that God's judgment emanates from a chamber in the spiritual world called *heichel z'chus*, the chamber of merit. It is the place for the defense of the Jewish people collectively. In that chamber they are always proven innocent and merit acquittal. The end result of each judgment and sentence is to cleanse the defendant of all sin and move him on to the next level of spirituality.

This process is alluded to in our prayers, which repeat three times the word *b'chein*, which is numerically equal to 72 and is thus also equal to the word *chesed*, "kindness," which equals 72. Add *b'chein* three times, and it totals 216, which is the equivalent to *gevurah*, judgment. This alludes to the teaching that kindness adds up to judgment, and judgment adds up to kindness.

This is like a king who gathered his family and said, "A year has passed since I asked you to help with my work. Now I will judge all of you and decide who deserves to be rewarded and who deserves to be punished." Each member of the family was frightened about the results of the judgment. Still they were all confident that their father loved them and would continue to need them.

Thus, although we are judged, we know it is done with kindness, to give us life, and therefore we celebrate.

KINGSHIP, REMEMBRANCE, AND SHOFAR

In the additional Musaf prayers of Rosh Hashanah, we recite ten sets of verses. One set is named *Malchiyos*, concerning the kingship of God; the second, *Zichronos*, concerning the remembrance of God, and the third, *Shofros*, concerning the shofar blasts. The Talmud asks: Why do we include these verses in our holiday prayers? We recite *Malchiyos* to help us accept God's kingdom; we recite *Zichronos*, in order that our remembrance shall ascend to God, and with what means? With the shofar.

It is written, ". . . and the trumpet blast of the king is in him . . . [acclaimed among them as king]" (Numbers 23:21). The heart of the Jew yearns to be the servant of God. He wants to negate his desires and be true to his faith and trust. But the evil in the world weakens him and prevents him from reaching his goal. In contrast, the nations of the world, even the most devoted and loyal servants of kings, would rather be without the yoke of the king upon their shoulders. They would rather be "free."

A king left the country and entrusted the palace to his son and advisors. The advisors did their best to maintain the king's rule. They constantly worried what might happen if the king returned and found something amiss. The prince, on the other hand, thought about his father, how he missed him, and how happy he would be to find everything in order when he returns.

One day, the gardener fell ill and left no one to tend the garden. The prince asked for volunteers, but no one came forward. Each of the servants wanted the other one to do the work. The prince thought, "It is our garden, and it will go to waste." Finally, the prince gathered a few able-bodied men and tended the garden until the gardener returned.

The trumpet blast of the king, the word of God, is in the heart of each Jew. He feels responsible for the spiritual well-being of the world as if it was his own. He wants to serve God's purpose in the creation and does, unless stopped by evil.

Therefore, it is fitting for the Jewish people to welcome the kingship of God on the day when God is proclaimed king by all living beings. The honor belongs to them more than to any other nation.

How is it possible to establish the kingdom of God in the world? Only by learning about God. And the best source of knowledge of God is the Torah. Those who are taught by the Torah or connected to the Torah know that God is the master of the world. And what about now when Torah knowledge is so weak among the nations of the world? In such circumstances we have to pray that the world will become more receptive to the kingdom of God. We need it, and God, so to speak, needs it too.

Our sages of the Talmud have taught: If one prays for a friend, and is also in need of that very thing, he gets helped first. The question is: if he needs help, why is he praying for a friend? Would he not be better off praying for himself first? It is possible that the lesson of the Talmud deals with the specific case, in which a person feels responsible for the condition of his fellow man, as in the case of Abraham. When Avimelech the king took Abraham's wife, Sarah, to the palace, he and all his servants were punished. After Avimelech returned Sarah and apologized, Abraham prayed for Avimelech's recovery. All the women in the palace gave birth. And soon after, Sarah too was pregnant and gave birth to Isaac.

Abraham felt responsible for the afflictions of Avimelech and therefore prayed for him first. And because Abraham needed the very same thing, a child, he was answered first.

It is the same way with the kingdom of God. We wonder why God is not recognized as the king of the universe by the entire human race. It must be that we are at fault. We are not doing enough to witness, educate, and disseminate the truth. And because we take the blame and we need God to be recognized as king, we are answered first. And God proclaims His kingship over us, the Jewish nation, first, before anyone else.

Thus we pray:

Please, God, Reign over the entire universe in Your glory; be exalted over all the world in Your splendor, reveal Yourself in the majestic grandeur of your strength over all the dwellers of Your inhabited world. Let every thing that has been made know that You are its Maker, let every thing that has been molded know that You are its Molder, and let every thing with a life's breath in its nostrils proclaim, "God, the Lord of Israel, is King and His kingdom rules over everything." (*Prayer Book*, Rosh Hashanah)

We pray for God's kingdom to be revealed over all the world, and therefore it is revealed to us first.

It is written, "Is Ephraim my most precious son or delightful child, that whenever (*midei dabri bo*) I speak of him, I remember him more and more? And so my heart yearns for him; I am filled with tenderness toward him" (Jeremiah 31:20). The sages comment that *midei dabri bo* should be read as *dai diburi bo*—it is enough that My Word is in him.

God gave the voice to the Jewish people as a gift from the days of Jacob: ". . . the voice is the voice of Jacob." Thus when the Jewish people call out to God, He hears His own voice echoing from them. Then He is filled with tenderness toward Himself, so to speak. This very voice is the sound of the shofar. When we sound the shofar, God hears the voice of Jacob, remembers the deeds of our ancestors, and reveals His kingdom.

This is like a prince who was kidnapped by a band of thieves. The king and his men searched for him throughout the kingdom to no avail. Finally one day the king heard a child's voice calling from the forest. "That is him," thought the king, "his voice is exactly like mine."

When the Jewish people call to God with their voice, the voice of the shofar, God recognizes it immediately, responds with tenderness, and comes with the fullness of His power to be king over them.

We beg God to remember us on Rosh Hashanah. But what kind of remembrance is this? Is its purpose to remember everyone and judge them? Who would want that kind of remembrance? That might be dangerous; one could get sentenced to die! Perhaps it would be better if God forgot us and not judged us at all! This begging for remembrance itself is the merit of the Jewish people. They know how crucial it is to be remembered by God. It is the only way that

anyone can attain enlightenment, life, and the kingship of God. And although it is laden with danger, the danger of being judged, still they yearn and pray for it. And God rewards them with great tenderness, mercy, and blessings for a good and healthy year.

Two events in history established God's kingdom in the world. One was the creation, and with it every creature became a servant of God. The second was the Exodus, when God established an exclusive relationship with the Jewish people. They were no longer on the level of servants, but rather became children of God.

All human beings, the nations of the world, have a share in the event of the creation. They can all realize that God is the Creator and can respect Him and be in awe of Him. They can even "fear God" and serve Him with great devotion. But only the Jewish people have a share in the Exodus. It was then that God separated them; they smeared the blood of the Passover sacrifice on their doorposts and the lintel, making a permanent division between them and the nations of the world.

The creation, which no human being witnessed, is believed with faith and trust. It is something that is described by God to Adam and passed on to all generations. But the Exodus was seen by the Jewish people with their own eyes; they witnessed that God is the unchallenged ruler and master of the world and that all events, large and small, emanate from Him.

A prince lived in the palace with the king's advisors. Each day the advisors and the king met to discuss the administration of the kingdom. The prince was not invited to those discussions and complained to the king. "If you love me, why not allow me to attend?" the prince asked. All the king said was that "some day you will understand." One day, an advisor asked the prince how the king was feeling, whether he slept soundly, and what they ate for breakfast. Suddenly the prince realized that although he cannot attend official discussions, he is the king's son and is closer to his father than anyone at court.

The month of *Nissan*, the anniversary of the Exodus, is a special time for the Jewish people. The anniversary of a Jewish king's reign is always celebrated in *Nissan*. The month of *Tishrei*, in which Rosh Hashanah falls, on the other hand, is special for the entire human race, for all the nations of the world.

Although the message of *Tishrei* is for all the nations, it still has a special significance for the Jewish people. By realizing that God created the world, we also realize that He can parcel out any part of it to the Jewish people. He can take a piece of land from the nations and give it to His people, as the land of *Eretz Yisrael*. And therefore we proclaim God's kingship on Rosh Hashanah, not only for the entire world but also for the Jewish nation.

What is the proper awe for the kingdom of God? One must be prepared to sacrifice one's very self for God's sake rather than commit the three carnal sins: idol worship, incest, and murder. One who accepts God as King is then free of idol worship. One who surrenders emotional responses to God then repairs the sin of incest. And when we blow the shofar we remember that God blew the breath of life into the first human being, that he was created in the image of God, and we thereby refrain from murder.

These three correspond to the verse, "And you shall love God your Lord with all your heart"—no part of your heart should be committed to an idol; "with all your soul"—no part of your feelings should be aroused for incest; "and with all your resources"—if we realize that all our possessions are a direct gift from God, then we would not covet and kill others for what they have nor for what we lack.

When all of our actions are pure and are cleansed of evil, we can truly proclaim God as our king and be witness to His kingdom.

There were Ten Commands with which God created the world, followed by the Ten Plagues in Egypt, and then by the Ten Commandments on Mount Sinai. After the creation the universe, collectively, was a witness that God is the Creator. With the Ten Plagues, the Jewish people were particularly chosen and separated to be the witnesses for God's kingdom. When the chosen ones were released from exile, they stood face to face with the king, in absolute clarity and certainty, and proclaimed His kingdom forever.

We find these three phases in the cycle of exile and redemption. First we are with God, then we are exiled and suffer, and then we are redeemed as we again come back to God.

This cycle of exile and redemption is similar to another cycle. God clearly controlled the creation. Later, people forgot about God, His kingdom became concealed, and the laws of nature were thought to dominate. Finally, when the Messiah will appear, the world will be renewed to its original perfection.

This cycle is repeated in our own lives. Before we are born, our soul is pure and knows that God is king. After birth, we are in the exile of physical confusion

and are no longer sure of God's Kingship/Sovereignty. Later, when we die, we are liberated and return to the pure state once again. This cycle is repeated many times: we are born pure, we sin, we then return to God and are made pure again.

This basic threefold cycle is symbolized by the three types of shofar blasts: *t'kiah*, *t'ruah*, and again *t'kiah*. *T'kiah* is the first phase of the cycle; it is an uninterrupted sound that reflects our direct uninterrupted relationship with God. *T'ruah*, a quavering sound, is the second phase; it symbolizes the sound of our whimpering and crying because of the exile. And finally, the third and final phase, another *t'kiah*, is the uninterrupted sound, symbolizing our return to the presence of God again.

Thus, *Malchiyos*, the kingship of God, is the first phase when God's kingdom is clearly manifest and we are basking in His presence. *Zichronos*, remembrance, the second phase, represents our suffering in the exile, a world where God's kingdom is in concealment and where we call out to God to remember us. And finally, we return, with the third phase of *Shofros*, the blowing of the shofar, proclaiming the kingdom of God that is back in all its strength.

The three types of prayers of Rosh Hashanah are symbolized by our forefathers, Abraham, Isaac, and Jacob. Abraham symbolizes the kingship of God, the one who traveled and proclaimed God as king of the universe wherever he went. As stated in Maimonides, Abraham gathered crowds at every stop in his travels to teach his newly discovered revelation about the one and only God. Isaac, who was bound and nearly sacrificed on a hilltop, represents the exile and our prayers for redemption, "Please God, remember us." And Jacob, who created a miniature nation with the birth of the twelve tribes, symbolizes completion; God is king and His people is Israel.

Abraham is symbolized by the *t'kiah*, the uninterrupted sound of the shofar, as he continued to declare God as king without interruption. Isaac is symbolized by the *t'ruah*, the quavering sound, as he calls out to God, although bound and helpless and totally resigned to his fate. And Jacob is represented by the last *t'kiah*, when all returns to its perfect and proper order.

The Midrash teaches us another lesson from the story of Abraham. Abraham pleaded with God, "You commanded me to take my son and sacrifice him. I did not protest. I was silent and did your bidding. In the merit of that deed I want something in return for my descendants. When they call out to you, when they make impossible demands on you, when there is no way out of their predicament and they cry for help, don't answer that You cannot help them. God, please remain silent. Help them anyway although there is no way. Be there with them although You can't."

The sages of the Talmud have taught, "Every commandment that the Jewish people originally received with joy, they still perform with joy" (*Shabbos* 130a). Rosh Hashanah is the head of the year, and wherever the head is, the body is sure to follow. Therefore, we must accept upon ourselves the kingship of God with great joy, so that it will remain with us throughout the year.

From everything that we have, we offer the first part to God. This *mitzvah* teaches us concretely that just as we received from God we return to God. The Jewish people themselves are the chosen first of all the nations and therefore must be the first ones to give themselves back to God by accepting upon themselves the kingdom of God.

It is written, "The Torah was commanded to us by Moses; it is an inheritance to the congregation of Jacob. Then a king arose among Yeshurun . . ." (Deuteronomy 33:3–4).

The Torah teaches us the true nature of the world. From it we realize that God is the creator and king. Similarly, Abraham investigated and discovered the nature of the world and started to believe in one God. Thus it is only through the education and understanding of the Jewish people that God's kingdom is revealed to the nations. On Rosh Hashanah, when we feel the power of His kingdom in the awesome Day of Judgment, it is compelling for us to crown God as the king, so that His kingdom prevail over all the nations.

It is written, "The kindly one with a good eye will be blessed" (Proverbs 22:9). A person who shares and is generous will receive abundance so that he can share even more. And it is this attitude of the Jewish people that makes them want to include the nations in everything they receive. As much as they yearn for God's kingdom, they pray that God will reign over the whole world, all the nations without exception.

Abraham exemplified this teaching with his loving-kindness to one and all without exception. And because he shared his kindness with everyone, God increased it and elevated him spiritually. While naturally the kinder and more tender hand is weaker than the hand of strict judgment, in the case of Abraham the kinder hand overpowered the strong hand, as symbolized in the binding of Isaac. Abraham with his loving-kindness overpowered the strict judgment of Isaac. With love he had the strength to do the most unnatural act—a father having to sacrifice his son. And this gave the strength for his descendants later to be fiercely brave in the most extreme circumstances. It was their love that gave them strength far beyond their physical capacity.

Thus on Rosh Hashanah, when the whole world is being judged, we have the opportunity to share all our gifts with the entire human race. And when we do, we will reap even more of God's blessings, without measure or limit.

King David's son Absalom rebelled against his own father. King David was forced to leave the palace and Jerusalem in disgrace. Finally, after much intrigue, the war ended with a surprise attack by King David, which left Absalom's troops in shambles and Absalom himself dead. Now the tribes came to reinstate David as king. He sent a message to the elders of Judah, "Why should it be you who are last to return David to the throne?"

It is the same with the kingship of God on Rosh Hashanah. The Jewish people want to be the first ones to proclaim God as king. And although the nations of the world gather, clap their hands, and declare that God is king, still the Israelites preceded them at the Red Sea as soon as they were free men.

This tradition started even earlier with Abraham, who was the first to proclaim publicly that God is king. And his descendants have the merit to continue and do the same.

The yearning of the Jewish people is that God reveal His kingdom to them, and then all the world will realize that He is the creator. This is similar to *Eretz Yisrael*, where it is written, "A land that God looks after and on which His eyes rest from the beginning of the year to the end of the year" (Deuteronomy 11:12). Because He looks after the land of *Eretz Yisrael*, He also tends to the other countries too. Thus whatever the other countries receive is in the merit of *Eretz Yisrael*.

The Jewish people are thus the conduit for the blessings that emanate from God to the entire world.

When Jacob ran away from his brother's wrath, he stopped to rest. He slept and dreamed of a ladder reaching from the ground to the heaven. He saw angels going up and down the ladder. When he awoke, he realized that he had had an awesome experience.

The Midrash comments that Jacob was asked to ascend the rungs of the ladder but refused.

Jacob's ladder is the world and the laws of nature that belong to the four kingdoms and the seventy nations. Jacob did not want to repair the world in the realm of nature, but instead, wanted it repaired miraculously, with the power of the infinite. Abraham also wanted such a world in which all would work with loving-kindness. He realized that the world cannot exist if governed merely by strict judgment; it must have kindness, the infinite, and miraculous as well. Then when Isaac was bound as a sacrifice, both Isaac and his father, Abraham, defied the laws of nature. Isaac was therefore given the virtue of strict judgment as his own. Even the laws of nature that sometimes seem opposed to the Godly life were given to the servants of God: ". . . you have not (*chosachto*) spared your son Isaac." The Hebrew can also be read as *choshachto*, "to darken." Your son, Isaac, did not fall under the control of the dark forces, of strict judgment, but on the contrary, he took control of them. This is the blessing that God gave to Abraham: ". . . and your offspring shall inherit the gates of their enemies" (Genesis 24:60). What are these gates that the enemy has? They are the gates of power and strength. Within the confines of the laws of nature, the strong and more numerous win. Even those gates will be in the hands of the Jewish people.

Thus on Rosh Hashanah we take hold of judgment and control it, transform it into kindness; the natural consequences, once transformed miraculously, become kindness. Instead of death to the sinner, now there is life. We ascend the ladder, but still come out ahead of the laws of nature and the nations of the world. How? Miraculously.

THE ABSENCE OF *HALLEL* ON ROSH HASHANAH

The Midrash teaches: The angels ask God, "Why don't the Jewish people say *Hallel*, [the prescribed psalms recited on joyous occasions and anniversaries] on Rosh Hashanah?" And God replies, "What?

The king sits in judgment with the book of life and the book of death open; who can then sing praises of the Lord?" (*Rosh Hashanah* 32b).

There are two worlds: the physical world ruled by the laws of nature and the spiritual world, which is infinite and miraculous. The wicked are only connected to the physical world, which withers and dies. Therefore, they themselves are called dead; their world is finite and must perish. But the *tzaddikim*, the righteous who are in touch with the spiritual, infinite, and miraculous world, even though they die, are alive. They are just as alive as the world with which they were connected.

According to the laws of nature, whatever was alive is alive unless something kills it. A man dies, and we ask, "What was the cause of death?" We know that death must be caused; otherwise the man would still be alive. Death is natural and expected. We only say *Hallel* for unexpected events, such as miracles, unusual victories, or joyous anniversaries. But life given to us on Rosh Hashanah is with strict judgment. And since we were alive yesterday, it is not surprising that we are alive today.

Then why do we beg for life on Rosh Hashanah? We do not beg to have life; that we have. We beg to receive the real, infinite, everlasting life that comes from a direct connection to God. We do not want to have; we want to receive.

The Zohar admonishes people not to bark like dogs and beg for food and sustenance! Why then do we pray at all for life and sustenance? We do not pray to have life; that we already have with judgment. We pray to receive life.

The angels would want to recite the joyous prayers of *Hallel* and rejoice in the kingship of God. They know that the Jewish people will be pardoned in the end and that God will be proclaimed king of the universe. But the Jewish people are on a higher level than the angels and see that it is not right to say *Hallel* then. They repent and reach a higher level than even the angels. As our sages have taught, "In the place where repentants stand, even the wholly righteous cannot stand" (*Berakhos* 34b). And from that vantage point they see that it is more important to respond with humility. And while the judgment is being decided, *Hallel* should not be recited.

Similarly, the Israelites were pursued by the Egyptians into the Red Sea. The Israelites walked through the dry river bed while the Egyptians were drowning. Then too the angels wanted to say *Hallel*. But the Israelites understood that it is proper humility not to speak at all while judgment is meted out. When the ordeal was over, then the Israelites sang a song of praise about their miraculous rescue.

Let us therefore be joyous to the utmost in our hearts that we have merited to live and see God crowned as king of the universe. At the same time we must be very discreet about our joy and respectfully stand in awe of the judgment that is taking place.

We have learned that from each *mitzvah*, each commandment that we perform, an angel is created. Whether we do the *mitzvah* with thinking, with speaking, or with activity, in each case an angel is created. There *is* a difference, however, between performing the commandment with thought or action. If we actively perform a *mitzvah*, then whatever went into it is all there is. For example, if a beggar comes to our door and we offer him a slice of bread, that is the extent of our charity. If we add a few kind and encouraging words, they too are part of the *mitzvah*. We may invite him in to eat, give him a change of clothing, allow him to rest, and help him get a job; there is no limit to how great the *mitzvah* can become. But when we think about doing a *mitzvah*, it is infinite. It has not yet been limited by action; it is still in the world of the possible.

Therefore, on Rosh Hashanah when the Jewish people realize that it is the anniversary of the world's creation and the kingship of God, they want to rejoice. But how could they celebrate, with the Books of Life and Death open before the Eternal Judge? Thus, rejoicing stays in their thoughts and is infinite. The angels that are created from these thoughts want to concretize their beings by saying *Hallel* in the hearts of the Jewish people. But it is far beyond the possible universe, and they too fall silent. And that silence is the greatest praise of God, because He is so great as to be beyond words.

The world, although replete with natural laws that we have only begun to understand, is called the world of darkness. Breakdown, weakness, and death lurk and follow its every move. It inescapably moves toward disintegration. Whatever is composed of parts breaks down and dies, whether rocks, plants, animals, or man. The place of the true, everlasting life is the spiritual, the miraculous, and infinite world. And the only source of it is God.

On Rosh Hashanah the world is renewed, and the angels want to say *Hallel*. But they are reminded that the Books of Life and Death are open, and they fall silent. Of what are they reminded? They realize that, although the world is renewed, the Book of Death is still open. It is open for every created thing. And because this world will come to an end, we cannot be overjoyed about it. It is not perfect enough for *Hallel* to be said. But what we can do is beg God to grant us the true life from the infinite world. And for that life we will say *Hallel*, in a future era, when the infinite will be revealed: ". . . then our mouths will fill with laughter and our tongues with glad song" (Psalms 126:2).

RENEWAL OF THE WORLD

Rosh Hashanah is the anniversary of the creation of the world. And on this day the whole creation celebrates its being by renewing itself. Thus the entire creation is renewed, including man, who is the crown of the creation. This is especially true of the Jewish people, who were chosen from among all of mankind to proclaim the kingdom of God.

It is written, "God, when He made man, made him straightforward, but man invents endless subtleties of his own" (Ecclesiastes 7:28).

There is a straight path, and whoever walks on it reaches his goal. It is focused, deliberate, and direct. One does not lose one's way on it, but continues on until the mission is accomplished. This is the path of the Torah, wherein is told the origin of the universe and what man can do to live a worthwhile, meaningful life with everlasting benefits.

Although such a path exists, man, who is naturally curious, is not satisfied to follow it. He would rather figure it out by himself. He wants to know why he exists, what he should do, and why he should do it. Even when he discovers the just life, his doubts persist, and he continues to wonder about other choices. He is constantly full of calculations of all sorts and gets tangled in mazes and endless labyrinths. Finally, Rosh Hashanah arrives. The straight path is renewed and laid bare for the entire creation. Every creature has the opportunity to straighten out his life—to leave the convoluted, meandering, and tangled paths that go nowhere and to follow the one path that leads to the goal. God is calling to us, "Get up now, out of the dust, and start walking this wonderfully clear path that leads to your destination." Will we listen?

It is written, "It is a land which God your Lord tends from the (*mi'reishis*) beginning of the year to the end of the year" (Deuteronomy 11:12). The sages of the Talmud comment: the word *rei'shis* can also be read as *reish'is*, meaning poor, to teach us that a year that is poor at its beginning will be prosperous at the end (*Rosh Hashanah* 16b).

How does the world ever get renewed on Rosh Hashanah? Is not everything getting old, deteriorating, falling apart, and dying? From where would one get life? The answer is that all creatures get life from the Creator, the originator and giver of life. Whoever wants it must get it from the source. But how can you ask for life if you already have life? The only way then to get new life from God is by thinking, speaking, and acting as if we have no life without Him. "Please, God, I have no life without You. I am nothing without You, but dust, ashes, a blob of cells. Please God, give me life." That is the prayer of one who negates his being in the presence of the Creator. And when one does, then one is worthy of life and receives it; it is renewed.

This is true also for the entire Jewish nation, as it is written, "Who, O God, is like you, who pardons iniquity and overlooks transgression for the (*l'sh'eiris*) remnants of His heritage?" (Micah 7:18). The Talmud comments: Is this as the delicious tail end of an animal, which has a thorn stuck in it and cannot be eaten? No, it is better. God overlooks transgressions for the remnant, but that does not mean that there will be only a remnant left from the entire Jewish nation. The remnant means that God will forgive the one who stands before Him as a remnant, *shirayim*, as leftovers, just as the dust of the earth. But isn't the verse about a sinner who of course feels like leftovers? Why would such a person be arrogant? (*Rosh Hashanah* 7b).

True, a sinner would not be arrogant. On the contrary, he feels dejected. He feels so guilty that he expects never to be close to God again. Therefore, he must be told: Do not think you are dust and leftovers forsaken by God. No. Because you are *sh'eiris*, leftovers, God has compassion for you and brings you close. The word *sh'eiris* changes to *reishis*. From dust it becomes a new beginning, connecting the remnant to the source of life. As long as the sinner does not give up and continues to believe that he still has a connection with the Torah, he can still renew his life and live.

This is our task on Rosh Hashanah, the day of renewal: to reaffirm our faith in God, the Torah, and the unity of the Jewish people. Then we too will be worthy to receive the life that God readily gives to all those who stand in total humility before him.

As the year progresses and we repeatedly engage in materialistic pursuits, the encrustation around our soul becomes thicker and thicker. It reaches a point when hardly any life-giving energy can reach us.

This is like a prince who built a tree-house in his father's orchard. He failed to care for the tree and allowed vines and thorn bushes to grow around it. Soon the entire tree was covered by brambles, and it was impossible to approach it. Fortunately, the royal gardener inspected the orchard once a year and repaired all damages. With his professional tools he cleared the vines, and the tree was free to breathe and grow again.

On Rosh Hashanah, God releases every one of His creatures from prison and renews his life. On this day we have the rare opportunity to cut away all obstacles, become free men, and renew our life from its source.

It is written: "Remember (*y'mos olam*) days long gone by. Ponder the years of each generation. He set up the borders of nations to parallel the number of Israel's descendants. But His own nation remained God's portion; Jacob was the lot of His heritage" (Deuteronomy 32:7–8).

The years of each generation are connected to the *y'mos olam*, the beginning of the world. Just as in the days long gone by the creation just came forth from the source, from the Cause of all causes, the spring and root of life, so too creation occurs each year; the world is renewed on Rosh Hashanah.

As we stand in judgment, we must remember that we stand also at the very beginning of time. We watch as the universe is being created anew. We can almost sense the power of the Giver of Life as He causes creatures to appear one after the other. We quickly throw away the old, worn-out habit-formed life and stand ready to receive the new life from the Source.

Our sages have taught in the *Ethics of Our Fathers* (6:1):

The world was created with Ten Commands. What does this come to teach us? Indeed, could it not have been created with one command? This was to exact punishment from the wicked who destroy the world that was created with ten commands, and to bestow goodly reward upon the righteous who sustain the world that was created by ten commands.

How could the world have been created with one command? And which one would it have been? It would have been the first one, "In the beginning...," which includes all the others. The first command means, Let the universe begin! Let everything be the way it is supposed to be. The entire universe down to the last detail was in the will of God before the creation. Then every creature was in perfection. In that perfect state everything was all together. At the creation, as they spread apart, they become less and less perfect. It would have been more perfect had it remained one command. It became less perfect with each additional command.

Each of the commands corresponds to each of the ten days between Rosh Hashanah and Yom Kippur. The first command corresponds to Rosh Hashanah, the first day of the year. Thus, Rosh Hashanah contains the whole year in potential. The year unfolds from Rosh Hashanah, which is like the seed, like *Bereishis*, the first command.

This is the hope and prayer of the Jewish people—that the world should return to the perfect state of the one command when everything existed in potential and perfection. It is symbolized by the shofar blast, which was used in the Israelites' sojourn in the desert to gather together the people, as it is written, "Make two trumpets of beaten silver and use them for summoning the community and for breaking camp" (Numbers 10:2). The trumpet sound unifies; it restores the world to its original state. And then the world is renewed and has new life.

The world was created, *yesh*, something, from *ayin*, nothing: from the nothing came something. This means that God caused the world to become. This is the underlying truth about all of creation; behind the something there is always nothing. Take the human body, for example. The body is built of tiny cells barely visible to the human eye. The control center of the cell is in the nucleus, which contains tiny components known as genes made up of intertwined DNA and RNA molecules. And finally, those molecules are made up of atoms, which are made up of a nucleus of protons and neutrons. The atom itself is mostly plain, ordinary, empty space, or void.

The work of the Jewish people, and of each and every righteous person, is to return the *yesh*, some-

thing, to the *ayin*, the cause, source, and origin: to God the creator of the universe.

Thus, Rosh Hashanah, being the beginning of the year, has a good chance to reconnect to the cause. It is nearly there, as the year has just started, and it can be the renewal of the world.

Adam was created on the sixth day and then Eve, and together they enjoyed the Garden of Eden. They were commanded not to eat from the Tree of Knowledge, sinned by doing so, were expelled from the Garden, and then repented. All this happened on the sixth day. Still, the Torah describes the sixth day, "And God saw all that He had done, and it was very good. And it was evening and it was morning, the sixth day" (Genesis 1:31). Why is it considered a good day, although Adam sinned? Because although Adam and Eve sinned, they repented, yearned, and prayed for the world to be as perfect as before. Thus, starting with the first human beings and continuing throughout the generations, the righteous yearn to restore the world to its original state.

Rosh Hashanah, the beginning of a new year, is also such an attempt. By repentance, prayer, and acts of charity we hope to renew the world.

Everything ultimately is returned to God, as it is written:

Remember your creator in the days of your youth, before the time of trouble comes and the years draw near when you will say, "I see no purpose in them." Remember him before the sun and the light give place to darkness, before the moon and the sun grow dim, and the clouds return with the rain—when the guardians of the house tremble, and the strong men stoop, when the women grinding the meal cease work because they are few, and those who look through the windows look no longer, when the street doors are shut, when the noise of the mill is low, when the chirping of the sparrow grows faint, and the song birds fall silent; when men are afraid of a steep place and the street is full of terrors, when the blossom whitens on the almond tree, and the locust's pouch is swollen and caper buds have no more zest. For man goes to his everlasting home, and the mourners go about the streets. Remember Him before the silver cord is snapped, and the golden bowl is broken, before the pitcher is shattered at the spring, and the wheel broken at the well, before the dust returns to the earth as it began and the spirit returns to God who gave it. Emptiness,

emptiness, says Koheles, all is emptiness. (Ecclesiastes 12:1–8)

Thus, when we return everything to God, even our very life, then we are face-to-face with Him and are immediately renewed.

Repentance on Rosh Hashanah

Rosh Hashanah, in addition to being the first day of the new year, is also the first day of the Ten Days of Repentance that end with Yom Kippur. It is especially important to repent on the first day of the year and to make a good and fresh start.

———

Our sages have taught:

> Ten things were created on the Sabbath eve at twilight. They are: The mouth of the earth; the mouth of the well; the mouth of the donkey; the rainbow—Noah's sign that there would be no future floods; the manna; the staff; the shamir worm; the script; the inscription; and the Tablets. Some say also destructive spirits, Moshe's grave, and the ram of our forefather Abraham. And some say also tongs, which are made with tongs. (*Ethics of Our Fathers* 5:8)

Adam and Eve were created on the sixth day. On the same day, they sinned by eating from the Tree of Knowledge, were banished from the Garden of Eden, and repented. After that, ten things were created at twilight, evening came, and it was the Sabbath.

This teaches us that, even after sin, God keeps on creating the world. If we repent, then He reveals to us those special parts of creation that no one had ever seen. This is especially so if we repent on Rosh Hoshanah, which is the head of the year and gives the rest of the year direction and focus. If the head of the year begins with repentance, we can be certain that the rest of the year will unfold with repentance. And although banished from the Garden of Eden, God will grant us other aspects of the creation that are nearly as sublime as those primordial days.

———

It is written, "I will heal their backsliding, I will love them freely: for mine anger is turned away from them" (Hosea 14:5).

There are two distinct aspects of the love that God has for the Jewish people. When they live according to Torah teachings, then of course God loves them. After all, they are following His teachings and accomplishing His plan. But even when they backslide, when they sin and stumble off the path, even then God loves them.

The soul of each Jew is, so to speak, a child of God; it is of a spiritual essence that is very different from the material world. And therefore the Jewish people are called the children of God; they embody God-like characteristics. And God loves the soul of the Jewish people always, without conditions or reservations. They are always pure and undefiled, spiritual and holy. In a minuscule way they are so much like Him, as it is written, ". . . God's share is His own people" (Deuteronomy 32:8).

Therefore, even when they stumble off the path, they are still beloved. As our sages have taught: Any love that depends on a specific cause, when that cause is gone, the love is gone; but if it does not depend on a specific cause, it will never cease (*Ethics of Our Fathers* 5:19).

So too this aspect of God's love for the Jewish people is not dependent on anything—neither good deeds nor righteousness. God just loves us always. As it is written, "Many waters cannot quench (*ha'ahavah*) the love, no flood can sweep it away" (Song of Songs 8:7). *Ha* signifies the special one. Which love cannot be quenched? The special love, the love that does not depend on the good deeds of the Jewish people.

A king took his young son to the market, which was packed with customers. The prince let go of the king's hand for an instant and was suddenly separated from his father. Turning this way and that and not seeing his father's face, the prince cried and wailed. He rubbed his eyes as he cried and imagined himself all alone and lost forever from his father. His father turned, looked down, and saw his son. He bent down and took hold of him and said, "Here I am, son; don't cry, I haven't gone anywhere. I was here the whole time next to you. You are not lost. Come, let's go home."

No matter how far and miserably we have strayed, we are still next to God, and as close to Him as ever. Our distance from Him is like an illusion, and if we but turn, in one instant, we will see that we are standing next to Him.

3

Aseres Y'mei Teshuvah— *The Ten Days of Repentance*

THE SIGNIFICANCE OF THE TEN DAYS

he Ten Days of Repentance start with Rosh Hashanah, the New Year, and end with Yom Kippur, the Day of Atonement. It is traditional to increase the usual amount of prayers, charity, and repentance during these ten days. In many parts of the world, additional prayers, *slichos*, are said before the daily morning prayers.

Every Jewish man and woman returns to God with complete repentance before the New Year arrives. Still, what more beautiful way is there to start the New Year than with repentance. In addition, Rosh Hashanah, being the first day of a new year, is a day of judgment for all mankind. Three books are opened in the heavenly court. The righteous are inscribed and immediately sealed to life. The wicked are inscribed and sealed immediately to death. And those who are in between are given until after Yom Kippur to repent. If they do, then they are inscribed in the Book of Life, and if not, they are inscribed in the Book of Death.

Who would be so arrogant as to think that he is without fault and worthy of life? All are humbled before God and assume that they have much to improve and are in between the wicked and righteous. They repent with all their hearts and souls for their sins. As it is written, "Inquire of God while He is found; call upon Him when He is close at hand. Let the wicked abandon their ways and evil men their thought: let them return to God, who will have

pity on them, return to our God, for He will freely forgive" (Isaiah 55:6–7). The Talmud comments that the phrase "when He is found" refers to the ten days between Rosh Hashanah and Yom Kippur, when God makes Himself accessible.

The chasidic masters taught: Some people in a village needed help and wanted to approach the king and plead for mercy. The king, however, was far away in his palace, and the villagers had no way to reach him. One day they heard that the king was traveling, and the entourage would pass directly through their village. They were thrilled and prepared for his coming. The day came, and the villagers went into the fields to greet their king as he passed through. How happy they were when the king stopped his coach and chatted with them casually and attentively. They were able to propose any request, and the king listened to every word.

Similarly, during the Ten Days of Repentance the King is in the fields waiting for those who yearn to see Him, to approach Him with prayer, repentance, and good deeds. Won't you come to see Him now?

Normally the week has seven days—six work days and the Sabbath. So why are there ten days of repentance?

When God created the world, the first three days were in the highest form of perfection. The days that followed were already a mixture of perfection and imperfection. Then when the creation was finished, God took the perfection of the first three days, named

37

y'mei kedem, days of long past, and hid them. Thus we say, "O God turn us back to yourself, and we will come back; renew our days as in times long past" (Lamentations 5:21). We want to return to those days of perfection when there was no evil and no sin. And God in His mercy gives us the *y'mei kedem*, adding them to the seven days. And so we have seven plus three equals ten. Therefore, if we return now, we have the added spiritual strength of the three primordial days of perfection. And with their spiritual power we can visualize how our soul looks without the slightest blemish or fault. Then we cry out to God, "Yes, that is where I want to be! Please, God, help me get there!" And God in His mercy breaks through the crust around our soul and frees it to soar.

It is written, "You open Your hand and give what they desire to every living creature" (Psalms 145:16). Yet, on Rosh Hashanah we pray, "Everyone believes that Your hand is open." God's hand is already open during the Days of Repentance for all those who want to return. But during the year we have to pray for that hand to open.

This is like a king who was about to marry a princess, when she was suddenly abducted by a band of robbers. They took her to a remote island and locked her in a thick-walled dungeon. It was nearly impossible to get in. The king discovered the hideaway and arrived with his troops. When he saw the impregnable prison, he called the princess by name. She answered in great excitement. They called to each other several more times. Suddenly the king seized a thick log and ran toward the door. The door cracked like a dry twig from the power of the blow. The king rescued the princess and brought her back to the palace to be married.

Similarly, God always wants to be close to the Jewish nation, but our sins cause a thick crust to form around us that separates us from Him. However, when the Ten Days of Repentance arrive, the love of God is manifest in the strongest way and breaks through all the walls and doors. Nothing is in the way now.

Let us soften our hearts and leave them open for God's advance. Then we will see how in one second our life can be turned from the prison of our sins to the splendor of the palace.

When man sins he defiles that which is holy in him. How deep is the level of defilement depends on the sin and the number of times it is repeated. And sin-

ning can go on and on until it reaches a point when defilement can go no further. Yet, there is a portion of the Jewish soul, a kernel of holiness that cannot be defiled. This is the portion that God tends to during the Days of Repentance. Whoever wants to change his life, to turn his life toward the Torah and God's advice, the Days of Repentance are the easiest time of all. Now all of us can connect to that part of ourselves that is pure as it always was.

Why are there many days of repentance instead of one day? Because there are many levels of repentance, and we can go higher and higher, as the sages have taught. Repentance is great, as it can reach until God's Throne of Honor. That is the highest level attainable.

The person is made up of the body, for action; the spirit, for speech; and the soul, for the intellect. And when man repents he must repair each of those, from the lowest, physical level, to the highest, spiritual level, which reaches to the Throne of God.

There are many levels of repentance for another reason. Some people repent because they fear the pain of punishment; others repent because they yearn to be close to God again. They know how sweet it is to be close to Him. These two levels are based on the virtues of Abraham and Isaac, the love and the fear of God. The third level of repentance is found in the person who recognizes the truth of his actions, how wicked he is in contrast to the kindness of the Creator. This is based on the virtue of Jacob, who strived for truth, as we recite in our prayers, "Give truth to Jacob."

Thus in each of the three parts of us—in the physical, verbal, and mental, in the material body, spirit, and soul—we can repent, correct, and repair our life with fear, love, and truth. By repenting in all the combinations of these elements, we fill up the ten days until we reach the highest level, at the Throne of Honor.

The Ten Days correspond to the Ten Commands with which the world was created. And just as each command created another facet of the universe, so too the repentant creates another part of his life on each of the ten Days of Repentance.

Our sages have taught: Why was the world created with Ten Commands, when surely one would have been enough? It was in order to reward the *tzaddikim*, the righteous, who keep the world that was created with Ten Commands, and to punish the wicked who destroy the world. As high as the righteous are, the repentant is even higher. Because the righteous only keep the ten "old" commands, while the repentant renews the commands. Because one who was wicked and destroyed the world, now that he repents, rebuilds the world that he destroyed.

Thus, on the New Year when the world is renewed, the repentant has the best opportunity to repair and rebuild the world that he destroyed. Should we not also take part in its rebuilding?

It is written: "Wash yourselves and be clean. Put away the evil of your deeds, away out of my sight, Cease to do evil and learn to do right, pursue justice and champion the oppressed; give the orphan his rights, plead the widow's cause. 'Come now let us reason together,' said God. 'If your sins be as scarlet, they may become white as snow; though they are dyed crimson, they may yet be like wool'" (Isaiah 1:16–18).

The prophet's ten exhortations symbolize the Ten Days of Repentance. Then after we repent, each day in a different manner, we reach the tenth day, Yom Kippur, the Day of Atonement, when God transforms our blood-red deeds to be white as snow. The question is: How can blood-red sins become white as snow? That is just not normal! And that itself is the answer. Repentance is not of the normal, natural, and orderly world. It is from a realm higher than and preceding nature. Therefore, even the red garment becomes white as snow, as no natural law interferes with a repentant from reaching up to the Throne of God.

Repentance

We are commanded in the Torah to repent. Maimonides explained this to mean that, for there to be a complete repentance, the sinner must have such remorse that even God could affirm that he will never sin again. He must forever, finally, and unconditionally leave his sinful ways and obligate himself to do the will of God from that moment on. And although a sinner may have done his evil often and over a long period of time, even to the end of his days, and only then at the end realizes the truth and repents, he too is an authentic *baal teshuvah*, who is entitled to all praise that the prophets have uttered.

There is no good time or bad time to repent. God's hand is always open to accept he who repents, and He wants that more than anything else, more than punishment or the death of the wicked. But there *is*

a best time to repent—the ten days between Rosh Hashanah and Yom Kippur, when God is especially attentive to His creation and helps all those who want to be near Him, with infinite wisdom, strength, and loving-kindness.

The world was created in six days, and after each of them it is written, "And God saw that it was good." What was good? The "good" was the light that God created and hid for the righteous for a future time. Where did God hide this light? He hid it in each item of creation. Only the *tzaddikim* were spiritually sensitive enough to discern this light. And therefore, when a *tzaddik* relates to the world, he relates not merely to its physical characteristics but also to the hidden light, which is really God's vitality in all things.

Unfortunately, we are not all *tzaddikim*, the righteous without sin, and we stray from the path of God. Our eyes are no longer able to sense the light of God in the creation. Instead we see but the darkness of the material world. And we live in the darkness thinking that it is light. How can we ever get out? By turning to God and by begging Him to let us see the light again. As it is written, "Remember the days of old, consider the years of many generations: ask your father and he will show you; the elders, and they will tell you" (Deuteronomy 32:7). The days of old are the days of creation when God hid the light in each created thing. And how do you get to see it? By asking your father, your elders, the previous generations, our ancestors—Abraham, Isaac, and Jacob. When you are ready to return to God, they will help you find the way. They will instruct you in ways to see the light again.

Let us not miss this opportunity. In these ten days we can repair our being to live with the light of God once more.

It is written, "And the living creatures ran and returned, as the appearance of a flash of lightning" (Ezekiel 1:14).

When God created the world with the Ten Commands, it was expanding without limit.

This is like a man who had walked in the snow for many hours and was thoroughly chilled. He went into his house and sat down near the fire. The heat was awesome, but he hardly felt it. Slowly he thawed. Then he started to feel the heat, and finally he had to move away from the fire. Slowly he cooled, until he started to feel the chill again. He returned again to sit near the fire. And this was repeated many times.

The creation cannot be too near the fire of God's presence, lest it turn into nothing again. It therefore moves away and back, away and back, in a motion repeated thousands of times, like a flash of lightning. But it must always return to its roots, to the warmth of the fire, lest it cool and die altogether. But in our case, sins prevent us from returning to the root. And thus in these ten days we cry out to God, "Please remove the impediments from our path and let us return to You."

The Midrash teaches: When God created the world, He looked into the Torah. The Torah was the plan, the inner reality, the vitality of the creation. And just as there is a speck of holiness in each material thing, so is there a soul inside man's body. And it is written, "The lamp of God is man's soul" (Proverbs 20:27). And it is also written, "A *mitzvah* is the lamp, and Torah is the light" (Proverbs 6:23). Just as the Torah is the wisdom and light of the entire creation, so too it is the wisdom and light of man. Why then is man's life not full of light? It is because of his sins that extinguish the light.

Our sages have taught, "A sin can extinguish a *mitzvah*, but it cannot extinguish the Torah" (*Sotah* 21:1). A *mitzvah*, a commandment, is the lamp, and sin can block light from reaching it. Torah, however, is the light itself, and nothing can extinguish it. Thus with the light of the Torah, everything was created, and everything that was damaged can also be fixed.

We must therefore rededicate ourselves to the Torah; then we will return to God with a complete *teshuvah*.

It is written, "I reveal the end from the beginning, from ancient times I reveal what is to be; I say, 'My (*ah'tzosi tokum*) purpose shall take effect, I will accomplish what I please" (Isaiah 46:10).

Ah'tzosi tokum also means, My purpose shall be made to stand. The purpose of the entire creation is that everything shall stand; it should not fall nor get destroyed. If it is about to fall because it is damaged, then it should be fixed so that it does not fall. That is the power of the Torah—to lift things from their lowest state of mere material to the loftiest heights imbued with spirit. From the greatest distance from God to the closest point near the root of all vitality.

Let us therefore reestablish our link with the Torah, and return to God with all our hearts.

It is written, "Is not my word as a fire? said God; and like a hammer that breaks rock in pieces?" (Jeremiah 23:29).

Sometimes people sin, stray from the Torah, and live a different sort of life. Each time they sin, they form a crust around their hearts. They repeat their mistake again and again until their sinful path becomes as hard as rock, and worse, it becomes the rock itself. Others may try to break through that rock, but cannot do so. But there is one thing that can break through even the hardest of rocks, and that is the Torah. There is no rock too hard for the Torah. As soon as the Torah touches it, it shatters into fragments.

A prince was sent away to school, befriended by a group of ruffians, and became estranged from the king. The king sent pedagogue after pedagogue to reform him, but to no avail. Finally, as a last resort, he removed a map of the palace from the prince's room, on which the prince used to plan his days of fun. The king sent it to the prince by messenger. When the prince received it, his heart just melted as he remembered all the good times he had playing within the palace walls. He said goodbye to his friends and returned to his father.

Similarly, when we are attracted by the physical nature of the world, hardly a thing can call us back. But if we allow the Torah to enter our hearts and sense the path of the King's palace neatly laid out before us, the spiritual delights planned for us, then our heart melts, the stone around it breaks, and we return to the King's palace with great love.

It is written, "By deeds of terror answer us with victory, O God of our deliverance, in whom men trust from the ends of the earth and far-off seas" (Psalms 65:6). The Midrash comments: The gates of prayer in heaven are like a *mikvah*, the ritual bath; they are sometimes open and other times closed. The gates of repentance, on the other hand, are always open like the sea (*Midrash Rabbah, Eicha* 3).

Just as there are gates of prayer and repentance in heaven, so too there are gates in a man's heart. When we are in need or in distress, we do not always turn to God. Whether we do so depends on our spiritual state. If we are sinful, our heart is blocked from reaching out to God. And, therefore, prayer is like a *mikvah* that is not always open. But repentance is the act of negating one's being to God, and that can be done any time with nothing in the way. Because as soon as we are humbled and allow God to be our king, then we already stand before Him. When we start to return, we have already returned.

———————————

It is written, "Rend your hearts, and not your garments; turn back to God your Lord; for He is gracious and compassionate" (Joel 2:13).

Punishment is meted out by the great Judge, and we must plead for mercy with great fervor. But that is not the complete *teshuvah*, repentance, although it affects the garments, the outside layer of a person's life. The change that God wants from us is to change our hearts—to rid our sinning, crooked hearts, and make them clean and pure again.

It is even too easy to make changes on the outside, like tearing our garments and putting on new ones, as some people do when they repent. They literally change their appearance, wear different clothing, change their hair style, and so on. The more difficult and lasting change is on the inside, in the deepest depths of our heart. That is the change that God desires, and we should be prepared to do it.

———————————

It is written, "Return you backsliding children, and I will heal your backsliding" (Jeremiah 3:23).

There are two distinct types of relationships with God. We can worship Him as servants or can do His will as children. The relationship of servants to their master is characterized by awe and fear; there is great respect and a wish to follow the master's commands to the minutest detail. In contrast, a child's behavior with his father is characterized by love and the special feelings that accompany familiarity.

We express this sentiment in our morning prayers, "Bring us back, our Father, to Your Torah, and bring us near, our King, to Your service." The words "Our Father" reflect our relationship to God as His children; the words "our King" reflect our relationship as servants. If we return to God because of fear for our lives, then our relationship is as servants. And just as a king pardons his servants when they beg forgiveness, God forgives too. But if we return because of our love for Him and the Torah, then our relationship is as children, and God is like a father who not only forgives his child but also draws him near with greater warmth and love than before.

As our sages have taught, "If one repents because of fear, then the sins which he did intentionally are transformed as if he did them unintentionally. But if one repents because of love of God, then his sins are considered as if he did good deeds" (*Yoma* 86b).

A prince joined a group of his father's servants in mutiny. The king overpowered the mutineers and had them bound and thrown into the dungeon. Several days later, without food or drink, they were brought before the king in irons. The king looked at them sternly in silence. He studied each of their faces for some time. Finally, they broke down, cried and wailed about their evil deeds, and begged the king for his pardon. The king called out, "Silence! You are all pardoned. But I warn you, the slightest deviation and you will be in irons forever!" He then turned to his son and had him turned loose and brought to his throne. He hugged him and said, "My son, my son! Now, after your backsliding, I know how much I love you and how dear you are to me." Just like the backsliding becomes part of the love that the father feels for his son, so our sins become part of our closeness to God.

———————————

It is written, "O God turn us back to Yourself, and we will come back . . ." (Lamentations 5:21).

When we repent and return to God, at first it is from fear. We cannot have true love of God in our hearts, because our sins prevent us from feeling close to Him. In that stage we need help from God to accomplish our repentance. Once we have decided to leave our sinful ways, and start performing the commandments of the Torah, then slowly the love of God takes hold in our heart until we repent with love as well.

This is exemplified in the lives of Noah and Abraham, who were both righteous men. Noah is described as, ". . . with God, Noah walked" (Genesis 6:9). On the other hand, Abraham is told, "Walk before Me, and be perfect" (Genesis 17:1). Noah needed God's support to help him walk, but Abraham was able to walk on his own. Noah's motivation was external; he feared only God's wrath. Abraham's motivation was internal; he had the fire of the love of God burning in him, which kept him on course.

Similarly, it is written, "Turn from evil and do good. . ." (Psalms 37:15). The phrase "turn from evil" means repentance as we abandon evil because of our fear of punishment. "And do good" is the next stage when we draw near to God because of love.

Let us therefore quickly abandon our errant ways; God is nearby to help. And we will surely continue repenting until our entire life will be renewed with new vitality and love of God.

———————————

It is written, "I will heal their backsliding, I will love them freely . . ." (Hosea 14:5). Rashi interprets the words to mean, Of my own bounty I will love them. I will give them love out of my own generosity.

We are commanded to love God: "You shall love God your Lord with all your heart" (Deuteronomy 6:5). The philosophers have asked: How is it possible to command anyone to love? Love is a feeling of closeness and intimacy; how could one be commanded to feel it? The answer is that one cannot. The commandment is that we should yearn to love God, to wish and hope that we could love Him. Then God too plants the love into our hearts as a gift. God gives His love to us as a bounty, a gift.

On a deeper level, the love for God is always in the hearts of the Jewish people, just as God's love for His people is ever present. Yet, the sins of the individual do not let him feel the love for God and also separate him from God's love. However, as soon as the sinful behavior is removed, the heart of the Jew feels the love for God, and God's love is also able to reach him.

Let us reach out for this love in the most opportune time of the year and live with God's love always.

———

Our sages have taught: If one says "I will sin but repent, sin and repent," he will not be granted the privilege to repent completely. Why not? Because he is using repentance as a vehicle with which to sin. He is, in effect, saying, God, please overlook my sin, because I will repent, and overlook it each time, because I will repent again (*Yoma* 85b).

The opposite is also true. One who repents because he fears punishment, then is afraid that the desire to do evil will induce him to sin again and so repents even more and with more remorse and fervor, will not be given the opportunity to sin again. Because he is using sin as a vehicle for his repentance, sin will never have control of him again.

Let us therefore return to God who receives us with great kindness and generosity.

———

It is written, "He found him in a desert land, in a waste, and howling void" (Deuteronomy 32:10).

The question is: if it is a land, then it is not a desert; if it is a desert, then is it not a land? The answer is that those who understand that the land is really a barren waste, without God, they will inherit the land too. But those who think that it is a land will have merely the desert.

There is the physical world, and directly below the surface lies the spiritual world. Compared to the spiritual world, the physical world is a mere desert. It is empty and desolate and does not bear fruit. The

spiritual world, on the other hand, is full of life, is fertile, and grows all life-giving food. We should always strive to connect with the spiritual in each thing. Then, we relate to its essence, instead of the dead material portion. Thus we have the land instead of merely the desert.

———

It is written, ". . . and call heaven and earth to witness (*V'o'eedo bom*) against them" (Deuteronomy 32:28). The word *bom* also means with them; with the Jewish people I will have witnesses for the heavens and the earth. The Jewish people are the witnesses that God created the universe, and everything that is discovered about it is a song of praise to God.

When scientists make great discoveries in any of the areas of inquiry, the one who makes the discovery is praised. The Nobel Prize is awarded to the one who contributed to the most outstanding discovery in a field of science. Praise is heaped upon the instrument that was able to measure or test a theory. But we Jews, after each discovery, testify about the Creator and praise Him. When the Jewish people sin and stop witnessing for the Creator, the heavens and the earth no longer say the praises of God. The only ones who are praised are the star-gazers. But when they repent, as we all do during these Ten Days, they resume their role as witnesses.

———

It is written, "Then my anger shall be kindled against them in that day, and I will hide my face from them, and they shall be devoured, and many evils and troubles shall befall them; so that they will say in that day, 'Are not these evils come upon us, because our God is not (*b'kirbi*) among us?'" (Deuteronomy 31:17).

We believe that in every Jew there is a soul, a speck of spirituality from heaven. God is literally *b'kirbi*, in me. His holiness, His presence sustains us always. If we sin, however, there is a separation between us and God. We no longer feel Him among us; in fact, we feel as if He is not among us.

Let us therefore reestablish the connection we have with Him and believe and feel His presence among us always.

SEEK GOD WHILE HE MAY BE FOUND

It is written, "Seek God while He may be found; call upon Him while He is near" (Isaiah 55:6).

Repentance is accepted by God any time of the year, but especially in the days from Rosh Hashanah to Yom Kippur. Those are the days when God is found and is near. And it is in those days that every Jew must encourage himself and feel the urgency of the moment. Now is the time—do not wait or hesitate.

———————

It is written, "Am I a God near at hand, says God, and not a God from afar off?" (Jeremiah 23:23).

The truth is that God is very far removed from us; His thoughts and His ways are not human, and He is the opposite of anything that exists. But at the same time, He is so near that nothing can be as near. How can this be? God made the whole universe from nothing. Whatever exists is still connected to the nothing that it came from. God is right next to each item and helping it to exist. If not, it would just disappear and cease to exist. Thus as different and as far removed as God is from the creation, He is also right there near it.

During the year, rather than His closeness, we might feel God's distance from us. It is during the Ten Days of Repentance that God makes the hearts of the Jewish people sensitive to His closeness. And that is the ideal time to draw close to Him, with repentance, prayer, and acts of charity.

———————

The world is composed of the material and the spiritual inner portion. It is natural for us, human beings, to relate to the physical aspect of the world; after all, we are physical beings. How then do we learn to relate to the spiritual aspect of the world? From the Torah. The Torah is the master plan of the whole universe and the path for reaching the inner reality. Therefore, by being connected to the Torah we can connect to the spiritual world.

Unfortunately, sins are a barrier between man and the Torah, and consequently between man and the inner reality. The only solution is to repent, to break down the barriers, and to become close to God again. And there is no better time to do so than the Ten Days of Repentance, when God avails Himself to all who want to be close to Him.

———————

It is written, "The utterances of God are pure" (Psalms 12:7). The Midrash comments:

> The utterances of God are pure, but the utterances of human beings are not pure. Why? A king arrives in a city and is greeted warmly by his subjects. He is moved and declares, "My dear subjects, very soon

I will start building the stadiums that I have promised; soon, I will send architects to bring water to your city." Everyone applauds and cheers. That night he goes to sleep and dies. Where are his utterances? Where are his promises? But God is the king, the source of life, Who lives forever, and His utterances and promises come to pass. (*Leviticus Rabbah* 21)

The world was created with Ten Commands. Yet, it could have been created with one. For our sages have taught, the words "In the beginning" are the first command, and in it all the ten are included.

If the universe would have been created with one command, there would have been no free will. The creation would have been clearly and undeniably the work of God. Therefore, it started with the command, "In the beginning," followed by a separate command for each particular item, such as ". . . let there be light." God's word was hidden within nature. And therefore, it was no longer clear whether it is God or whether it is nature. Thus we have free choice.

In the story of creation the name of God is *E-LO-HIM*, meaning the master of all the energies. What energies? The dual energies that we experience in the universe. We experience the singular energy of God, of the words "In the beginning," and we experience the energy of the laws of nature. Therefore, the name of God, *yud heh vov heh*, is not mentioned in the story of creation. That name signifies the creative force in the form of singularity.

What does the sinner do wrong? Instead of responding to the singular clear message of God, instead of seeing God in every particle of creation and responding accordingly, he responds to the plurality, to the laws of nature, and the physical aspects of the world. He goes astray and sins.

What happens when he repents? He abandons the world of plurality, of the many, and returns to the world of the One. He leaves the realm of the Ten Commands and enters the realm of the single command, "In the beginning." Thus the repentant goes back to the very beginning of creation, before free will, before the possibility of sin.

This same lesson is taught in two places in the Torah. One place is the Ten Commandments, "I am God your Lord," which mentions both names of God, *yud* and *heh* and *vov* and *heh*, and also *E-LO-HIM*. This means that one can experience the singular within the plural: one can find God within the natural world. This lesson is also taught by the verse, "Hear O Israel, God our Lord, God is one." Here too both names of God are used, and the verse concludes that God is one. Although you may experience plurality, because you find God in the many aspects of the world, still, you must know that God is one: a singularity unchanging and unchangeable.

This aspect of God is close to us during the Ten Days of Repentance. We should seize the moment and return to God with all our hearts.

"Seek God. . . ." refers to the Torah, as it is written, "It is hidden from the eyes of all creatures, and from the birds of the heaven it is closed" (Job 23:21). The Torah was hidden from mankind for 2,000 years and was finally revealed. And it is only through the Torah that man can find God again. Therefore, during the Ten Days of Repentance, God makes the Torah accessible to all. Whoever is wise returns to receive instruction from the Torah, and with it finds his way back to the path of life. As it is written, "For they are life to him who finds them" (Proverbs 4:22).

The Hebrew word for seek is *b'himotzo*, which literally means, in where he is found. This instructs us that a person should not excuse himself and think, "Those other people are having an easy time serving God and repenting, because their lives are so different than mine. If my circumstances were different, I might also do the same. But look at my situation! It is nearly impossible for me to do the right thing. And certainly it is hardly possible for me to change!"

Therefore the prophet declares: "Seek God . . . in the very circumstance of life that you are found. Where you are, right there, you have the opportunity to do the right thing, to overcome the oppression of your life and return to God with all your heart. There is no other life, but the life that you have. And when you are ready to find Him in the very life where you are found, where you find yourself, then you will find Him directly and immediately."

DELIBERATE SINS BECOME MERIT

The sages of the Talmud have taught:

> Reish Lakish said, *Teshuvah* is great, because the deliberate sins are transformed as if they were done unintentionally. As it is written, "Return O Israel till God your Lord, for you have stumbled in your evil courses" (Hosea 14:2). "Evil" refers to willful sins, and still it is called "stumbled," which means unintentionally. But didn't Reish Lakish once teach that *teshuvah* is great because the deliberate sins are transformed into merit? As it is written, ". . . and when a wicked man gives up his wickedness and does what is just and right, he shall live" (Ezekiel 33:20). When he gives up his wickedness, it is as if

he has done justice and mercy. Our sages explain, when a sinner repents because of fear, his deliberate sins become as if done without intention. But if he repents with love, his sins become merit. (*Talmud Yoma* 86b)

If we repent with love, then our sins become merit. But if our repentance is caused by fear, the willful sins become as if they were done unintentionally. The question is what difference did the motivation make, as long as the result was repentance and return to God. There should be no difference!

The truth is that without love of God it is impossible to return to God. Fear only drives one away from sin, but does not bring one to God. How then does a sinner, who has not the slightest feeling of love for God, ever return to God? It is because he thinks, "I am frightened of my sins. I don't want to die, or lose my fortune. I don't want my children to die because of my sins. But I have no idea how to get close to God again. I wish I knew, but I don't. What shall I do now?" And because he yearns to be close to God, God gives him a spark of love as a gift. As it is written, "I will heal their backsliding, I will love them freely . . ." (Hosea 14:5). And with the spark of love in his heart he returns and repents, and lives a Torah life. But he whose heart is awake with great love of God and yearning to be close to Him again, he can fix all his sins even if done intentionally, and they become merit.

We wonder, from where does the love come into the heart of the sinner?

It is written, "Many waters cannot quench love, no flood can sweep it away" (Song of Songs 8:7). The love that the Jewish nation collectively has for God was given to them as a gift at the time of the Exodus. God took us to Himself as His people, the seed of the great man of faith, Abraham, who united the world to believe in one God. That love is engraved so powerfully in the Jewish heart that no nation can weaken it and no oppression can remove it. This Jewish consciousness is never extinguished, even if the person assimilates or even converts to another religion. It is always there in the deepest depth of the heart, and when there is an opportunity, it becomes manifest.

Let us then meditate on this unquenchable love in our heart. And when we dwell on it, we will realize that just as we love God always, God loves us also.

It is written, "He forgives (*nosei*) iniquity" (Exodus 34:7). The word *nosei* means lifts up. Our sages disagree about what God does with our sins when we repent. One opinion is that on the scale of judgment the sins are lifted up, forcing the side with the merits to outweigh the sins. The other opinion is that the side with the merits is pushed down, thus outweighing the sins.

These two opinions speak of two different circumstances. Sometimes we are suddenly overcome with fear when we realize the terrible effects of our sins. We are sickened by the depravity of our deeds and wish they would never have happened. Then the power of the sins becomes weaker and lighter, and their side of the scale is lifted. The merits then outweigh them. At other times we are overcome with yearning for holiness by being close to God. We are sorry that we sinned, that the evil influence of sin prevents us from being immersed in Torah and *mitzvos*. It is our appreciation of Torah and *mitzvos* that propels us toward repentance. Hence, the good deeds we have done become magnified and weigh down the side of merit. They outweigh the sins.

We have the opportunity to tip the scale now during the Ten Days of Repentance. Only a fool would be inactive.

HE WHO OPENS THE GATE

There are many spiritual gates, and some are open and some are closed. But the gates of repentance, whenever anyone knocks on them, they are opened.

Who are those who constantly knock on the gates in repentance? They are our forefathers—Abraham, Isaac, and Jacob—who have etched into the hearts of the Jewish people a desire to return.

A prince rebelled and stayed in the mountains with a band of thieves. The king sent his most trusted servants to find him. They disguised themselves as nomads and roamed the mountains. At night they kindled a fire to keep warm, played their harp, and sang songs about palaces and kings. Soon, the thieves befriended these interesting men and stayed in their company. Each night they sat around the fire and joined in singing the songs of longing. Many days passed, and finally the prince thought, "I too am longing for my father. I can't remain here any longer. It is time to run away."

Similarly, our ancestors planted into our hearts the longing to be in the King's palace. Thus we knock on the gates and enter.

In the beginning when God created the heaven and the earth everything was (*tohu va'vohu*) desolate and bare, and darkness on the face of the deep. Then God said, "Let there be light," and there was light.

Before anything new was created, there had to be total desolation and nothingness because the creation was something from nothing. And if there is already something, then a new creation cannot come from it. Therefore, if the repentant wants a new life, he must first totally negate his old life. He must consider himself nonexistent in God's presence. He must think that he has no life at all without Him. When his self is totally annihilated before Him, he can then receive a new life.

The word *teshuvah* has the same Hebrew letters as *tohu va'vohu*, "desolate and bare," as well as the letter *shin*, signifying *choshech*, "darkness." This teaches that a repentant is one who has thoroughly humbled himself and thinks that he is in darkness without God. Then God can re-create him and make him a completely new creature, a new man.

It is written, "Blessed is the man who hears me, watching daily at my gates, waiting at the posts of my doors" (Proverbs 10:34).

There are doors within doors. The first door can be opened by knocking. The second is not opened by knocking, but responds to the knocking on the first door. The more one knocks on the front door, the more the second door opens. The first door is our response to the call of God to return, "Return you backsliding children." The second door is God's response to our efforts. When we knock in repentance, God opens the second door.

A king was in his private chamber, a place that not even his most loyal servants entered. One stormy night, there was a loud banging on the outside gate. It was the knocking of the prince who was outdoors and had been caught in the hailstorm. He banged to be let in, but in his desperation he woke the king. The king, who had already retired, heard the terrible noise and decided to investigate. He opened the door to his chambers and went to open the gate. By then, servants had opened the gate, and the prince was already inside. When the king saw his son, he said, "My boy, look how wet you are. Come quickly into my chambers and get dry and warm."

4

Sabbath of Repentance— Shabbos Teshuvah

THE SABBATH AND REPENTANCE

ne of the days of the Ten Days of Repentance is the Sabbath. Being the holiest day of the week and one that falls on the holiest of the yearly holidays, this Sabbath is also the best day for repentance and return.

On each day of the creation it is written, ". . . and God saw that it was good."

When God contemplated the creation and saw that it was good, His satisfaction gave the creation the energy to exist. And from the totality of the satisfaction and charm of all the created things is formed the seventh day, the Sabbath. As it is written, "Thus heaven and earth were completed with all their mighty throng. On the sixth day God completed all the work He had been doing, and on the seventh day He ceased from all His work. God blessed the seventh day and made it holy, because on that day he ceased from all the work He had set Himself to do" (Genesis 2:1–3).

Thus, the Sabbath is a day of complete and total satisfaction and charm in the eyes of God. And therefore when we repent on the Sabbath and resume being the man with whom God was satisfied at the creation, we add to the holiness of the Sabbath. Similarly, the holiness of the Sabbath that we feel comes from the energy of God's satisfaction with us.

Now that it is the Sabbath of Repentance, let us not pass by this great opportunity to give God satisfaction from His creation.

There are six work days and the Sabbath. However, it is not as if Sabbath is a separate entity apart from the other six days. On the contrary, all the holiness that is hidden in the six days is revealed and concentrated in the Sabbath. The holiness of the Sabbath lifts up the work and striving of the entire week. It focuses spiritual energy, which brings everything back to its roots.

Similarly, it is written, "One thing I ask God, that I shall seek: that I dwell in the house of God all the days of my life; to behold the sweetness of God and contemplate in His sanctuary" (Psalms 27:4). If you seek one thing and one thing only, then you will find that one thing in everything you do and every day of your life. Thus, if it is holiness and holiness only that you are looking for, then you will certainly find it. And that one thing is the Sabbath, which is all the holiness contained in the six work days.

Sabbath, then, is just like repentance, because it collects all the spiritual energy and reflects it back to its roots. And just like *Shabbos* makes us look for holiness in our six work days, so too repentance makes us look at our actions to see if they lead to God.

Let us therefore use the Sabbath to gather all of our stray energies and focus them toward the one primary goal, the source of all life: God.

In the beginning when God created the world, He said, "Let there be light, and there was light." The light of creation was special; one could see from one end of the universe to the other with it. To prevent the wicked from enjoying it, He hid it for a future time. However, He did not hide it until after the Sabbath was done. Thus, during the first Sabbath the primordial and spectacular light still shone because, although the Sabbath is part of the physical world, its holiness is so powerful that it can be a vessel for things purely spiritual.

Similarly, our sages have taught: The Sabbath is a reflection and of a similar nature of the World to Come. But how can that be? Is not the Sabbath a day of rest in this physical world while the World to Come is of a totally different nature? The answer is that God created the Sabbath to be a vessel to contain the spirituality of the six days of the week.

Thus, during the six work days, we may not see the light of God and see only the physical world. Our concern is about the welfare of our possessions, our body, our children. And out of fear for our life and limb we return to God. But on the Sabbath, we can see from one end of the universe to the other with the supernal light. Then we yearn for a higher level of spirituality and return to God with love.

The difference between the six weekdays and the Sabbath is work. Work, however, is not guaranteed. You can either find work or not. The Sabbath is different. What we earn during the six days with work we receive as a gift on the Sabbath. And that gift is guaranteed with God's promise: ". . . between Me and the Jewish people it is a sign forever" (Exodus 31:17). Thus, although our sins stand in the way of our repentance during the six work days, they do not affect us on the Sabbath. Whoever wants to can repent with ease on the Sabbath. And when he does, he will immediately be granted the gift of forgiveness.

A similar thing happens with the soul. During the week, we have to labor to keep our soul free of the pollution of sin and evil. But on the Sabbath we receive an extra portion of spirituality, the *neshama yeseirah*, the extra soul, which is untouchable by sin. It stays clean regardless. It is a gift from God in honor of the Sabbath and does not depend on our deeds.

Let us be wise and avail ourselves of this wonderful opportunity to repent on the Sabbath day—a day untouchable by sin—and with a soul unsoiled by wickedness.

The Sabbath evening prayer says that the Sabbath is celebrated "in memory of the work of creation." What kind of work of creation did God do on the Sabbath? None. Then how does it help us remember the work of creation?

Each thing that was created has a physical part. It also has a spiritual part—the Sabbath. Sabbath is the inner reality inside each created thing. And although

we can destroy the physical reality of the creation, we cannot affect the inner reality, the Sabbath. Thus on the Sabbath day we can gather all of the untouched inner reality of the entire week and lift it up to its roots. This is just like repentance. When we repent we also take our deeds and lift them to God. As the Baal Shem Tov once explained, When a person sinned with lust and wants to repent, how should he start? He must ask himself from where the emotion of lust comes. It has its roots, of course, in the spiritual realm, and finally in God Himself. God loves all His creatures unconditionally, and therefore there is love in the hearts of mankind. When this love is misused, then it is lust. How could we use this wonderful virtue, which emanates from God, against the will of God? We must not abuse it, but return it to its roots, to God Himself. And then we receive love from God again, all new. We must use it to serve Him and proclaim His kingdom. So, too, must a repentant gather all the inner reality of all his actions and return them to God.

When we repent on the Sabbath, we can go directly to the highest levels of spirituality and be cleansed of sin in one instant.

It is written: "The Israelites shall keep the Sabbath, they shall keep it in every generation as a covenant forever. It is a sign forever between me and the Israelites, for in six days the Lord made the heavens and the earth, but on the seventh day he ceased work and (*vayinafash*) refreshed himself" (Exodus 31:16–17).

The word *vayinafash* means, it became spirited; a new spirit filled it. During the Sabbath everything returns to its roots, the source of life and all vitality—God—and thus becomes filled with a new spirit. But to receive this new spirit we must nullify our very existence before God Who is the source of life. So too, a repentant, if he wants to be filled with a new life, must first rid himself of the old one by nullifying and humbling himself totally.

The word *Shabbos* means to rest, as when one works and then needs rest. However, it also means to cease to be, as when we constantly cease to be and nullify our life before the source of life and thus receive new life. And what does a repentant need more if not a new life? Therefore, the Sabbath is the most favorable time to repent and get new life directly from the source.

There are the weekdays and the Sabbath. Because the weekdays are a time for activity and physical accomplishment our daily prayers deal with our activities and we beg for success. The Sabbath is a day of rest, and all we ask for is to be reunited with the root of life: God.

This is similar to repentance. There is the act of turning and of repentance. In the act of turning we decide to start a new life and wish to be connected to the root of life. Then there are many details to the repentance itself, such as remorse, abandoning the wicked ways, and a commitment for the future.

Thus, on the Sabbath, in one instant we can be at the root of all and face to face with God.

There are forty-nine gates of impurity, and we can escape from them one at a time. Then begin the forty-nine gates of purity and holiness. After working through the forty-nine gates of purity we stand before the fiftieth gate. It is locked and does not open as a result of anything that we can do. It only opens as a gift from God.

The identical thing happened when the Israelites left the land of Egypt. They were oppressed and enslaved within the forty-nine gates of impurity. When they were released from the impurities, they were catapulted through the forty-nine gates of purity in a single instant. Then, in the midst of the Red Sea, they entered the fiftieth gate, and the lowliest of them prophesied with the power of the greatest prophet. God opened the fiftieth gate for them, and they entered.

This is similar to the six workdays and the Sabbath. During the six workdays we work very hard to elevate ourselves and the world around us to a higher spiritual plane. But the Sabbath day is given to us as a gift from God.

Thus the Sabbath is similar to the Exodus. Both have a gate that opens after our hard labor. Therefore, our sages have taught, "If only the Israelites would have kept the first Sabbath after the Exodus, then no nation could have enslaved them again" (*Shabbos* 118a). If they would only have appreciated the spiritual significance of that first Sabbath, they would have stayed in the realm of freedom, the fiftieth gate, and would never have been enslaved again. But they did not and therefore missed the opportunity. Each year, however, the first Sabbath of the year follows Rosh Hashanah. This is the Sabbath between Rosh Hashanah and Yom Kippur, *Shabbos Teshuvah*. And, again, if the Jewish people observe that Sabbath, then no nation can oppress them. And furthermore, the Sabbath is the best vessel for repentance since it is the fiftieth gate, opened by God, as a gift.

It is written, "Return to Me, and I will return to you" (Malachi 3:7). There are two movements. One is the yearning and movement of the Jewish people toward God. The other is the movement of God toward the Jewish people. Where do they meet? At the Throne of Honor.

A king's son rebelled and refused to return to the palace no matter how many times he was asked to nor whom the king sent for him. Finally, the king mounted his horse and said, "I am going to meet him myself." When the prince heard that his father was approaching, he quickly started out also toward him. They met on the road, embraced, and cried.

Similarly, just as we move toward God, He moves toward us. And we meet between the heaven and the earth, between the physical and spiritual worlds. We meet at the Throne of Honor, the source of all the Jewish souls.

The Throne of Honor is the vessel for the divine presence created by the Jewish people. How do they create this vessel? By completely negating their being and humbling themselves as the dust of the earth to the awesome reality of God. When they do that, they return their every morsel of energy back to its source. They lift up all their deeds to the heavens. And God too descends from His lofty place, so to speak, and meets them at that point, the edge of the physical world, the ethereal realm, the heaven, the Throne of Honor.

The six weekdays and the Sabbath can also be compared to these two movements. During the six weekdays we work in the physical world to lift it to the heavens, and on the Sabbath God comes toward us with the heavens. And therefore it is very easy to return to God during this first Sabbath of the year, the Sabbath of Repentance. And we must do our utmost to observe this first Sabbath, as our sages have taught: If only the Israelites would have kept the first Sabbath, then no nation in the world could have oppressed them. The first also refers literally to the first Sabbath of each year; the way we keep the first one will determine how the rest will be kept.

Let us therefore quickly return to God on this first Sabbath and be happy to know that God is returning to us too.

Our sages have taught, "Whoever observes the Sabbath has all his sins forgiven" (*Shabbos* 118a). A sin is an act against God's commandments, and impurity settles upon the person for two reasons. First, the rebellious act against God's will produces impurity.

Second, the act itself is obviously impure if God forbade it. The state of impurity separates man and God. Sabbath, on the other hand, is just the opposite. It is written, ". . . between Me and the Israelites it is a sign forever . . ." (Exodus 31:17). The words "between Me and the Israelites" testify that the Sabbath is an intimate relationship between God and the Jewish people. Therefore, when we keep the Sabbath there is no longer any separation between us and God; it has been removed.

If observing the Sabbath forgives a man's sins, how careful must we be to observe this first Sabbath of the year, to repent, and to return to God.

In the Sabbath Eve *Kiddush* service we recite, "And Your holy Sabbath, with love and desire did You give us as a heritage."

The Sabbath day that was given to the Jewish people has two qualities. The first is love, reflecting a unique relationship that God has with the Jewish people for no reason. They have a kinship and connection that are prior to and above any deeds. The other level is longing and desire; God granted us the Sabbath because He desires to benefit us.

Similarly, there are two levels for those who observe the Torah. There are the *tzaddikim*, the righteous, and the *baalei teshuvah*, the repentants. The righteous have a relationship with God of love, and they observe the Torah for no particular reason. The repentants, on the other hand, have a longing and a desire to observe the Torah; they have a reason for doing it.

Since the Sabbath has both qualities of love and desire, it is therefore very easy to repent on that day. And one who does will find the love and desire of God helping him reach his goal.

It is written, "Moses answered, 'Do not be afraid. God has come only to test you, so that the (*yiraso al p'neichem*) fear of Him may remain with you and keep you from sin." (Exodus 20:20). When God appeared on Mount Sinai in His awesome majesty, the only possible reaction was humility. Who could entertain a thought of self-worth, strength, or wisdom before the terrible strength and ultimate wisdom of God? The Jewish people were wiped out both physically and spiritually. It was nearly the All of the All and would have left all of them dead. Although they survived, they experienced such deep shame, the deepest humility of their insignificance before the Creator. *Yiraso al p'neichem* literally means His fear on your faces—the shame that you bear deep in your consciousness that prevents you from doing evil.

Thus, the fear and shame in the presence of God are never erased, no matter what you do. They are always with you. Similarly, they are always present on the Sabbath, as our sages have taught. The Hebrew letters in the word *Shabbos* can also spell *boshes*, meaning shame. When a Jew comes into the presence of the Sabbath day, he immediately feels the awesome presence of the Creator, and he is utterly ashamed and humbled.

Therefore, it is very easy for one to repent on the Sabbath day, as it is a day of great fear, awe, and shame in the presence of God.

It is written, "I reveal the end from the beginning; from ancient times I reveal what is to be; I say, My purpose shall take effect, I will accomplish all that I please" (Isaiah 46:10).

Our life is full of unanswered questions, both about us and the world around us. To what purpose are these things happening? The answers are not readily available and sometimes never come. But there will come a time in the future when all the questions will be answered, all the mysteries solved, and everything will lead to a logical and decisive conclusion. That will be when the *Mashiach* comes and all of God's plans will be bared and revealed. Then, from the end we will understand the beginning, the purpose God had in all events since the beginning of time. We will see that everything that happened served a purpose for the good of mankind and for all the individuals involved.

As it is written, "I will give all peoples once again pure lips, that they may invoke God by name and serve him with one consent" (Zephaniah 3:9). In the end everyone will have pure lips to call the name of God. Simply, God is saying, Everyone will repent in the end because that is My desire and purpose. I want everyone to be forgiven; I want everyone to be righteous.

Therefore, since the Sabbath is like the future time, it contains the vision of the end that answers the beginning. It has the answers to the aimless wanderers who are far from home and getting nowhere. Then, on the Sabbath, they will be home, and their questions will be answered: "I wandered for reasons clear to me now, and I'm finally home," they will say. On the Sabbath it is very easy to repent, to come back from the lost places, and to find one's way.

At the future time there will be a total Sabbath, without any confusion, and all will be repaired. All the sinners will have returned, and all wrongs will be righted.

It is written: "Wisdom has built her house, she has hewn her seven pillars; she has killed a beast and spiced her wine, and she spread her table. She has sent out her maidens to proclaim from the highest part of the town, 'Come in, you simpletons.' She says also to the fool, 'Come dine with me and taste the wine I have spiced,'" (Proverbs 9:1–5).

The world was created in seven days. Those seven days are the pillars of the world. They are the laws of nature, the way it has been since the beginning, and the way it will be for a long time to come. This regular path is the one for the *tzaddik*, the righteous who stays on the right path from the beginning until the end. And therefore it is written, "And the righteous one is the foundation of the world" (Proverbs 10:24). He helps the world continue on its regular course.

The *baal teshuvah*, on the other hand, has erred, has strayed, and is lost. But then he did find his way. We wonder how did he ever stumble on the regular path. Should not it be impossible for someone to repent? Yes, it is. Except there is yet another path, a new, irregular one that existed even before the creation. It is the path of *teshuvah*, which cannot be found among the laws of nature nor among the regular tried-and-true paths. Nevertheless it exists, above and beyond the world of nature. It is a path that no sin could make crooked, no problem could upset. It is untouchable by evil and totally out of this world.

The Sabbath is exactly like that path. It is of the world beyond the natural, a world unaffected by the corruption of the regular, the everyday. And because Sabbath and repentance have the same nature, each invigorates the other. Thus, the Sabbath is the most welcome day for repentance.

Our sages have taught: If the Jewish people had kept the first Sabbath, then no nation on earth could have oppressed them.

Man was placed in the Garden of Eden and commanded not to eat from the Tree of Knowledge. Yet, Adam and Eve sinned, ate, were banished, the sun set, and it was the Sabbath. Therefore, just as the first sin came to the world before Sabbath, we can repair everything that was damaged by observing the Sabbath. The Sabbath has to be remembered always, and it is impossible to remember it unless we observe it properly. Therefore, we must observe this first Sabbath of the year in absolute holiness and purity and remember it every instant. Then God will protect us and save us from all oppression and from all evil forces.

On the Sabbath, the Jewish people witness that God created the heavens and the earth. Anyone can do this except the sinner. A sinner is not an acceptable witness. This is a big problem for the wicked because the purpose of every Jew is to be a witness that God is the master of the universe. As it is written, "You are my witnesses, says God, and I am God" (Isaiah 43:10). Thus, a sinner cannot be a real Jew.

Yet, there is a solution to a sinner's problem. If he stands up and is ready to bear witness for God, to show his commitment, then he is already forgiven. As it is written, "Happy is the man who follows these precepts, happy the mortal who holds them fast, who keeps the Sabbath (*meichalelo*) undefiled, who refrains from all wrongdoing" (Isaiah 56:2). And our sages have taught, the word *meichalelo* can be read *mochel lo*, meaning, he is forgiven. Therefore, if someone keeps the Sabbath holy, he is forgiven.

A king's servant rebelled and joined a group of disloyal soldiers in the hills. After some months, the entire city population rebelled. The servant had a change of heart. He thought of the king and the kingdom, and said, "These men want to destroy this beautiful kingdom of ours. I will not permit it!" He quickly mounted his horse and, galloping from town to town, exhorted the mobs to stop their madness. The villages quieted down, and the servant returned to the mountains.

When the king heard of his servant's exploits, he sent him an urgent message, "Come to the palace at once, my loyal servant!" As the servant entered the royal chamber, the king announced, "All is forgiven! Don your royal robes and resume your service for the king!"

The same is true of a sinner who braves opposition and keeps the Sabbath day holy in all its details. God forgives him too because he made a commitment to be God's witness.

Therefore, those who keep the first Sabbath of the year can repent easily and return to God.

The mission of the Jewish people is to proclaim the kingdom of God. When a sinner goes astray and does not observe the Torah, he forgets God. The righteous, on the other hand, always remember God and think of Him constantly.

It is easy to forget God during the six work days. After all, we work, we accomplish, and we take the credit. We forget that God is the one who gives us the strength to do everything. As it is written:

Take care not to forget God your Lord and do not fail to keep His commandments, laws, and statutes which I give you this day. When you have plenty to eat and live in houses which you built, when your herds and flocks increase, and your silver and gold and all your possessions increase too, do not become proud and forget God your Lord who brought you out of Egypt, out of the land of slavery. . . . Nor must you say to yourselves, "My own strength and energy have gained me this wealth," but remember God the Lord; it is He that gives you strength to become prosperous . . . (Deuteronomy 8:12–18).

All that is true of the six workdays. But when the Sabbath comes and the Jewish people bear witness that God created the heavens and earth, they remember, as it is written, "Remember the Sabbath to keep it holy." It is a day to remember, to set our minds straight after six days of going astray. And by remembering God on the Sabbath we will remember Him during the six workdays too. And therefore, the Sabbath is the ideal day for repentance; even a sinner who has forgotten God remembers Him on that day.

It is written, "Our God shall come, and not keep silence: a fire shall devour before him, and it shall be (*nisaroh*) very tempestuous round about him" (Psalms 50:3).

Our sages have taught: "In the World to Come the righteous will each have a canopy and enjoy the Divine glory. And if one were to attempt to intrude upon another, they will get burned" (*Bava Basra* 78a). Even the righteous, although they enjoy the Divine glory, would like to be closer to God than they have merited. The yearning causes them pain, although it stems from the love of God.

When the wicked repent because they fear the fires of *Gehenom*, of Hell, they run from pain to the refuge of God. But the righteous run to the refuge of God from yearning for the Divine glory. And if he is unable to come close to God because of any sin, he cries out to God to overcome the obstacle.

Similarly, of Cain who killed his brother Abel, it is written: ". . . but Cain and his gift He did not receive. Cain was very angry and his face fell. Then God said to Cain, 'Why are you so angry and cast down? If you do well (*s'eis*) you are accepted; if not, sin is a demon crouching at the door. It shall be

eager for you, and you will be mastered by it'" (Genesis 4:7). If you do well and *s'eis*, lift up your soul to soar toward God, overcoming obstacles along the way, then you will do well. If not, then the door will be clamped shut before you because your sins will prevent you from escaping the fires of *Gehenom*.

The Sabbath is also an indicator of how close you are to God. When the Sabbath, which is a reflection of the World to Come, arrives and we are connected to it, then we are prepared for the World to Come too. But if we are not prepared, then it must be our sins separating us from the Sabbath, and we must repent immediately. We do so with yearning and love for the closeness of God.

Let us therefore be inspired by the Sabbath to yearn for the purest holiness and return to God with love.

It is written, "Give ear to what I say, O heavens, earth, listen to my words." And later, "He made him ride on the heights of the earth and fed him on the harvest of the fields" (Deuteronomy 32:2,13).

Man is made both of the heaven and the earth. He has a lofty soul that rides on the heights of the heaven, as well as a lowly body of the earth. It is the rare person in which one can find the synthesis of these two opposites. Moses was one of those rare individuals who was called a "man of God." He was part man and part God, our sages say. He was able to lift up even his physical body to the level of the heaven, although he was of the earth. If he would have entered *Eretz Yisrael*, he would have taught the Jewish people how to transform their involvement with the earth, their farming into spiritual activities.

The Sabbath is a day when both the soul and the body are uplifted. Both reach for a higher level of spirituality, the World to Come. Then, the entire universe, the earth and the heaven, the physical and the spiritual will be restored to its original state of perfection as it was before the sin of Adam and Eve.

What better time then is there to repent than the Sabbath day? Let us therefore reach up, even with our lowly bodies, and touch the heavens, returning to God with all our hearts.

RETURN O ISRAEL

The Haftorah reading for the Sabbath during the Ten Days of Repentance is Hosea 14: 1–10.

Return O Israel (*ahd*) to God your Lord; for you have stumbled in your evil courses. Come with your words ready, come back to God; say to Him, "Take away all iniquity. Accept our plea: so we will render as bullocks the words of our lips. Assyria shall not save us, nor will we seek horses to ride; what we have made with our own hands we will never again call gods; for in You the fatherless find a father's love."

I will heal their backsliding; I will love them freely; for my anger is turned away from him. I will be as dew to Israel that he may flower like a lily, strike root like the poplar and put out fresh shoots, that he may be as fair as the olive and fragrant as Lebanon. They that dwell under his shadow shall return; they shall revive as the corn and grow as a the vine: the scent thereof shall be as the wine of Lebanon. Ephraim shall say, What have I to do any more with idols? I have heard him and observed him: I am the pine tree that shelters you, to me you owe your fruit. Let the wise consider these things and let him who considers take note; for God's ways are straight and the righteous walk in them, while sinners stumble.

It is written, ". . . for you have stumbled in your evil courses." Any evil that a Jew does is only a stumbling. His essence, his soul, a spark of divine holiness, is pure and untouchable by impurities.

Sins are merely superficial, marring the physical aspects of the person. When we repent, the inner essence and purity are revealed. And this revelation is accomplished in one instant.

A prince went off to befriend some peasants who were his age. He played with them in the mud and got badly soiled. When he returned he was quickly ushered into the royal bath, his soiled clothing was removed, and he was scrubbed from head to toe. In a few minutes the prince emerged, looking better than ever. Admiring his image in the mirror, he said, "I don't understand. I was just as full of mud as the peasant boys, yet after I am washed I am a handsome prince. But when the peasant boy is washed, he is still nothing but a peasant!" The king laughed and said, "You are a prince, clean or dirty. Even if you get dirty, all it needs is some cleaning. But the other boy is a peasant, and no matter that he is washed, he remains a peasant."

It is written, "Return O Israel (*ahd*) to God your Lord. . . ." Our sages have taught that *ahd* also means witness; God is a witness that this repentant will never again return to his evil ways.

There is the conscious and the unconscious. A person can be thinking about repentance. But even before he thinks about it, it may already be present in his mind in some form, perhaps in the form of a pathway in his brain or the beginning of pathways that later will form thoughts of repentance. God knows those thoughts, although they are not yet formed. And He helps make those fragments into complete thoughts of repentance.

We must allow God to find thoughts of repentance in our hearts, and no matter what form they may have He should help them grow into full-fledged desires and yearning to return to God.

It is written, "Return O Israel (*ahd*, till) to God your Lord. . . ."

As strongly as you exert yourself to reach God through repentance, so will be God's closeness. If you push yourself and get all the way up there next to God, then He too will be there right next to you.

It is written, "Return O Israel (*ahd*) to God your Lord. . . ." It is not enough to repent. One has to continue on and on until he reaches God Himself with his repentance.

And where will he reach God? Right below the Throne of Honor, the source of all life and souls of mankind. And even if he is already as pure in deeds as a unblemished righteous man, he does not have to stop there. He can continue until he gets to the Throne of God.

It is written, "Return O Israel (*ahd*) to God your Lord. . . ."

The Rambam, Rabbi Moses ben Maimon, comments: One should repent to the degree that God Himself could be a witness that the repentant will never return to the path of evil. Is this not too severe? Who could possibly repent to that degree? The answer is that the Rambam is not speaking about where repentance starts, but rather where it ends— the scope and extent of repentance. Repentance starts with the tiniest fragment of a thought—*ahd*—till, the very extreme, when even God could be witness about it. And what is this extreme? It is when the repentant gives up his free will rather than sin. His prayer is, "Please God, I know that you have given me free will to do what I choose. But look where that has led me. I am sick of where I am. I want to be close to you always. So, please, You could have my free will back, if You want it, and as for me, I will serve you without my will for the rest of my life."

Repentance with such devotion, with disregard for personal gain, is the highest form, which will heal all of the Jewish nation when the *Mashiach* comes. And it is this selfsame repentance that is meant in the teachings of our sages, "The place where the repentants stand even the wholly righteous cannot stand." Why? Because the sinner has been on all the crooked paths, and he returns them all to God, and says, "No, thank You!" He no longer wants the free will to roam the multitude of paths. And his new path is a place that a wholly righteous person has never been.

Let us therefore completely escape from under the influence of sin, corruption, and the multitude of paths, and follow God all the way to the Throne of Honor.

———

It is written, "Return O Israel (*ahd*) to God your Lord. . . ."

When a person sins, he thinks he is the master of his life and he can do what he pleases. In effect, he is not allowing God to be the king everywhere. Thus when he repents, he again reestablishes God's kingdom, and returns, *ahd*, till the very presense of God.

This is like a prince who grew rebellious and locked himself in his room. No amount of pleading by his tutor or the wise men made him open the door. Finally the king himself came, but he too was refused entry. "This room is my kingdom," the prince yelled from behind the locked door. "You have no jurisdiction here!" After a day, the prince relented and opened the door for his father. "Come in, Father, I decided to give the room back to you."

———

It is written, "Come with your words ready, come back to God; say to Him, 'Take away all iniquity. Accept our plea: so we will render as bullocks the words of our lips.'"

When God finished creating the world and saw everything that He had made, He said, ". . . and behold it is (*tov meod*) very good." *Tov*, "good," refers to the righteous, and, *tov meod*, "very good," refers to the repentants.

God saw that some people are going to do good, and others will do evil, but in the end everyone will repent, repair all the damage, and the world will again have the perfection of the Garden of Eden. And this is the plea of a repentant, "Please God, help us arrive at that end, the end of time, when all will be restored to its original condition."

A king gave a beautiful painting to the experts to have it restored. They took apart the frame, tacked the painting to a board, and worked on it. When the

king entered the room, he was shocked by the sight. Small mixtures of paint were lying all over the room; tacks, hammers, pliers, and many other tools lay nearby. The painting no longer looked like the masterpiece he had given the experts to fix. The experts sensed the king's dismay and said, "Your majesty, do not worry about appearances. When we finish, everything that appears out of place now will be completely restored. The painting will look like the masterpiece that you love."

Whose energy helps the repentant? The return of Adam after he sinned gives energy for all the generations of mankind to repent too. How do we know this? Since his sin caused death to the entire mankind, then the good, his repentance, surely brought repentance to all of mankind.

———

It is written, "Return O Israel (*ahd*) to God your Lord. . . ."

Why have the sages chosen a verse from the prophets to teach us about repentance, rather than a verse from the Torah? The Torah also discusses repentance:

> When these things will happen to you, the blessing and the curse of which I have offered you the choice, if you and your sons take them to heart there in all the countries that God your Lord has banished you (*veshavtah*), you will turn back to Him and obey Him heart and soul in all that I command you this day, then God your Lord will show you compassion and restore your fortunes. He will gather again from all the countries to which He has scattered you. Even though He were to banish you to the four corners of the earth, God your Lord will gather you from there, from there He will fetch you home. (Deuteronomy 30:1–5)

The verses in the Torah are an oath that sinners will return to God. The prophet, on the other hand, is urging the Jewish people to repent, teaching us the great importance of repentance.

Thus, we can be sure that the Jewish people will repent. And there are two movements: One is God's movement toward us, which is like an oath that we will all repent in the end. The other is the movement of the Jewish people toward God, as in the words of the prophet, "Return O Israel. . . ."

Just as God chose the Jewish people, they chose Him too, as it is written, ". . . you have chosen God this day. . . ." And just as God's choosing of us is eternal, as it is written, "I, God, do not change. . . ." So our choosing of God is also guaranteed by God, as it is written, ". . . and you shall return. . . ."

The reason that the Jewish people can return to God is because God loves them for no reason. As our sages have taught, God desires to bring merit to the Jewish people. He therefore gave them an abundance of Torah and *mitzvos*. Why did God desire the merit of the Jewish people if they had not yet done anything? It is because God's love for the Jewish people precedes deeds, precedes the material world, and precedes consciousness. Thus, although we have gone far astray and have not observed the commandments, still, we can return to the desire of God, which precedes the Torah.

It is written, "Return O Israel (*ahd*) to God your Lord. . . ."

Our forefather Isaac had two sons, Jacob and Esau. Jacob's name was given to him when he was born and was grasping the heel of his older brother. That is the material level of Jacob. It is the very bottom, the heel. He can deal even with the lowest levels. Later, he struggled with an angel and prevailed. He then received the name *Yisrael*, Israel. That is his highest level. When the Jewish people sin, their level of Jacob, being close to the earth and the material world, gets affected by it. But in his spiritual level as Israel, it is as if he stumbled or made an unintentional mistake that does not affect his essence. Thus, "A Jew even if he sins, is still a Jew," is on the level of Israel. But on the level of Jacob, he could lose his heel as it gets stuck in the mud.

Therefore, "Return O Israel." Israel can always return to the Throne of Honor, because he is not disabled by sin.

It is written, "Return O Israel (*ahd*) to God your Lord. . . ."

The Torah spoke to all of Israel, to their collective soul, and said, "I am God your Lord who has taken you from Egypt."

The ultimate condition of the Jewish people is that God's name is called upon them as their own; He is their God, and they are His people. Their sins, however, are a barrier between them and their Creator. Therefore, the Ten Days of Repentance correspond to the Ten Commandments; if you return to God, you are catapulted to Mount Sinai and stand before God, while He proclaims, "I am your God."

And these are the words of the prophet, "Come with your words ready, come back to God." Which words? The Ten Commandments. When you hear them you know that you have reached your goal; you have arrived at the beginning again.

COME WITH YOUR WORDS READY

It is written, "Come with your words ready, come back to God" (Hosea 14:3).

Repentance comes because of a dialogue, or it is the dialogue itself. What is this dialogue? God gives the Jewish people the Ten Commandments, and they answer, "We will do and we will listen." Without this dialogue there is nothing going on between God and the Jewish people.

If we are not doing the commandments and instead do evil, then we sleep away the time while God waits for us to awake, as it is written: "I sleep but my heart is awake. Listen! My beloved is knocking: Open to me, my sister, my dearest, my dove, my perfect one . . ." (Song of Songs 5:2). I am sleeping from the commandments; I am not doing them, however, my heart is full of the conversation that God had with me on Mount Sinai; I can never forget it. Yet our sins fill our hearts with confusion and noise, and we are unable to hear the call of God. How then is our heart woken up? By breaking the crust of our heart with humility and lowering ourselves as the dust of the earth. Then we can hear the words of God again.

When we blow the quavering note of the shofar on Rosh Hashanah, it is meant to break our heart and enable us to hear. And when we do, we stand before God's throne and continue the dialogue with Him. "Come with your words ready, come back to God."

It is written, "Come with your words ready, come back to God."

The prophet Isaiah said, ". . . and as the rain and snow come down from heaven and do not return until they have watered the earth, making it blossom and bear fruit, and give seed for sowing and bread to eat, so shall the word that comes from my mouth prevail; it shall not return to me fruitless without accomplishing my purpose or succeed in the task I gave it" (Isaiah 55:10–11).

Each human being has within him the seeds of purpose, which he must bring to fruition during his lifetime. The purpose of the Jewish people is a special one: to reveal the kingdom of God. Each one is seeded with God's words, which must grow and blossom. But if they go astray and lose their way, those words lie dormant—nothing happens with them. Finally when they repent, they resume their mission and can still complete it. They come before God with His words and say, "I have returned to report that I made Your words grow and bear fruit in the world."

Unfortunately one who sins cannot return to the Creator empty-handed: ". . . it shall not return to me fruitless without accomplishing my purpose" (Isaiah 54:11). But as soon as he repents, he can resume to cause the words of God to grow into fruitful activity and come before Him.

Let us then quickly take the words of God and place them in enriched and fertile soil. Then we will again be on course and continue our purpose and accomplish it.

It is written, "Come with your words ready, come back to God."

The words of God are man's soul that was placed in him, as we say in our prayers, "The soul which you have placed in me is pure. You have created it, You have formed it, You have breathed it into me. And You watch it in me, and You will take it from me and return it to me in time to Come." Our sages have taught us that the physical body is like a scroll and the soul are the letters. The body is what the message of God is written on, to accomplish the purpose of God.

When a person sins, he blocks the soul from being the message, and the body stumbles along a false path. Still, we can repent and remove all obstacles from our soul and can resume striving toward our goal.

If we are wise, we would abandon our errors quickly and focus all our energy to fulfill our purpose.

It is written, "Come with your words ready, come back to God."

The Jewish people are vessels to contain the words of God; they have the ears and heart for that purpose. They humble themselves so they can listen to God's words. That is because they are slaves to no one, and their ears and heart are their own, and can turn them to listen. A slave cannot really listen to the words, as it is written: "Mere words will not keep a slave in order; he may understand, but he will not respond" (Proverbs 29:19).

Now that it is the time of repentance let us free our hearts from enslavement, and hear again the words of God that call us to return to Him.

5

Yom Kippur—
Day of Atonement

he Days of Awe start with the first of *Elul* and end with Yom Kippur. Likewise, the Ten Days of Repentance start with Rosh Hashanah and end with Yom Kippur, the final day of forgiveness and atonement for all the Jewish people. As it is written:

All this shall be an eternal law for you. Each year on the tenth day of the seventh month you must fast and do no work. This is true of both the native born and the proselyte who comes to join you. This is because on this day you shall have all your sins atoned, so that you will be cleansed. Before God you will be cleansed of your sins. It is a Sabbath of Sabbaths to you, and a day upon which you must fast. This is a law for all time. (Leviticus 16:29–31)

God spoke to Moses saying:

Only (*ach*) on the tenth of this seventh month shall be a day of Atonement for you. It is a sacred holiday when you must fast and bring a fire offering to God. Do not do any work on this day; it is a day of atonement, when you gain atonement before God your Lord. If anyone does not fast on this day, he shall be cut off [spiritually] from his people. Similarly, if one does any work on this day, I will destroy him [spiritually] from among the people.

Do not do any work on this day. This is an eternal law for all generations, no matter where you live. It is a Sabbath of Sabbaths to you, and a day when you must fast. You must keep this holiday from the ninth of the month until the next night. (Leviticus 23:26–31)

Yom Kippur is certainly, in many aspects, considered the holiest day of the year. It is the one and only time that the *Kohen Gadol*, the High Priest, enters the Holy of Holies in the *Beis Hamikdash*, the Holy Temple in Jerusalem. In this room was found the Ark of the Covenant containing the Ten Commandments on two stone tablets.

The elaborate rituals of Yom Kippur, with the *Kohen Gadol* immersing himself in a *mikvah*, changing his clothing, washing his hands and feet, confessing on the heads of the sacrifices, sprinkling the blood, and sending the goat are all a result of the love and kindness that God has for the Jewish people. Not one day nor two does God wait for the wicked to repent, but many days. From Rosh Hashanah when the doors open wide until the end of Yom Kippur, with the *Ne'ilah* prayer when the doors close, God waits patiently for each and every one of us to repent. And do not think that only those who are obvious sinners need to return to God. The commandment for repentance is an invitation and obligation to every single Jew to examine his life and correct his errors and improve his habits. Even the righteous have this obligation, and we are never excused from it to the day we die. The more righteous a person is, the more he repents for his shortcomings. We know of countless sages and righteous men and women whose life was pure in every way who would spend the entire Yom Kippur crying for their shortcomings and praying to live long enough to improve. From the start of the *Kol Nidrei* service to the shofar blast after the *Ne'ilah* prayers, we must ceaselessly pray to God to forgive our shortcomings and to give us the strength to improve all aspects of our life. May this Yom Kippur be the one when we leave our faults behind and start our life again as a babe newly born.

THE SIGNIFICANCE OF YOM KIPPUR

It is written, "And no man shall be in the Communion Tent from the time [Aaron] enters the sanctuary to make atonement until he leaves" (Leviticus 16:17). Our sages have taught that "no man" means that when the *Kohen Gadol* enters the Holy of Holies, he is no longer a man, but an angel. He is elevated because of the holiness of Yom Kippur.

Yom Kippur is a reflection of the World to Come, when perfection will return to the world with a new heaven and earth. And God gives us the opportunity, just as on every Sabbath, to taste the coming world. We can soar and be as angels, pure and enlightened.

Where does all this spiritual energy come from? It comes from the devotion and fervor of the Jewish people, clamoring to return to their Creator. After forty days of using every means to show their intent—fasting, charity, prayer, repentance, and acts of loving-kindness—the Jewish people create a cosmic storm. And in answer to that storm, there descends from heaven a most sublime spirituality that transforms the very essence of men's natures.

A similar event occurred with the Israelites in the desert. They received the Ten Commandments at Mount Sinai, turned to idol worship, and then built the Tabernacle. On the eighth day, after the priests prepared the sacrifices, it is written: "Moses and Aaron came out of the Communion Tent, and when they came out, they blessed the people. God's glory was then revealed to all the people.

"Fire came forth from before God and consumed the burnt offering and the choice parts on the altar. When the people saw this, they raised their voices in praise, and threw themselves on their faces" (Leviticus 9:23–24).

Again, where did this spiritual energy come from? There, too, it came as a response to the repentance of the Israelites. They were so utterly remorseful about their sin of the Golden Calf that they wasted not a moment to beg God for mercy. And the response from the realms of the infinite was a consuming fire. It showed them that, although their actions are physical and limited, the response from the spiritual realm will be infinite.

Our sages tell us that the heavenly response for Yom Kippur is so strong that the day is not even part of the natural year. It is totally removed from physical time, the year of 365 days. And during the 365 natural days, the Satan has dominion and influence, except on Yom Kippur, a day apart from nature. As it is written, "... and in Your book are written all my destined days when (*v'lo echod bohem*) as yet there was none of them" (Psalms 139:16). The words *v'lo echod bohem* are said to mean: *v'lo*, and to Him; *echod*

bohem, that one single day from among all the others belongs to God Himself. That is Yom Kippur, which belongs entirely to God and no one else.

On this day, when the gates of repentance are wide open, when we have no physical obstacle in our path of repentance, when the Satan is inactive, we have a great opportunity to return to God completely and wholeheartedly.

Our sages tell us that when Aaron donned the robes for the service in the Communion Tent, he did not do so for his own honor. Rather, he did so to lend respectability to the service and to respect God. That was on the physical level. On a spiritual level, Aaron's garments, the garments of his soul, became holy. Because of his service, his soul was lifted to such heights that his body too was elevated. And for that reason when the *Kohen Gadol* finished the service and left the Holy of Holies on Yom Kippur, his appearance was heavenly, was not altogether human. As we recite in our Yom Kippur prayers:

And so, how majestic was the *Kohen Gadol* as he left the Holy of Holies in peace. Like the heavenly canopy stretched out over those who dwell above was the appearance of the *Kohen*. Like lightning bolts emanating from the radiance of the Celestial creatures. Like the fringes attached to the four corners. Like the image of the rainbow above the clouds. Like the majesty in which the Creator clothed the creatures. Like a rose that is placed in midst a precious garden. Like a crown that is placed on a king's forehead. Like the graciousness granted in a bridegrooms face. Like the purity that was placed on the turban pure. Like the one who sat in concealment to plead before the king. Like the morning star on the eastern border was the appearance of the *Kohen*.

Yom Kippur is our opportunity to escape the mundane and ordinary pathways of returning and repentance. We can be transformed to angels if our desire is strong enough.

When God formed man from the earth it is written, "... (*vayitzer*) and God formed man dust from the earth ..." (Genesis 2:7). The word *vayitzer* is written with a double letter *yud*, and our sages interpret that to mean that man was formed with two desires: a desire to do good and a desire to do evil. These opposing desires in the same person are present because man is physical and imperfect. Had he been perfect he would only have one singular desire—to do good—just as the angels who have one desire and a singular mission to accomplish. When Yom Kippur comes, the *yetzer hara*, the desire to do evil, is gone. Satan and the evil forces have no jurisdiction during that one day, as it is written, ". . . and in Your book are written all my (*yomim yutzaru*) destined days when (*v'lo echod bohem*) as yet there was none of them" (Psalms 139:16). In this verse, *yutzaru* is written with one *vov*, meaning a single formation, a single desire. On Yom Kippur all of Israel has one desire—to resume their task and proclaim God's kingdom. But how could man, made of a physical body and a spiritual soul, have one single desire? Is he not made of two opposites? Yes, but on Yom Kippur the physical becomes spiritual too. Just as the angels, with one heart, do not eat nor drink, so too, all of Israel does not eat or drink.

Therefore on this holiest of days let us make one heart out of its fragments. Then we will no longer desire anything except repentance.

It is written, "I am dark and beautiful, daughters of Jerusalem . . ." (Song of Songs 1:5). Our sages say: I am dark the year-round and beautiful on Yom Kippur. The year-round my physical self opposes spirituality, but on Yom Kippur, all of me has but one singular purpose. Even my body is uplifted and together with my soul soars to new heights.

Therefore, although the Holy of Holies is not a place for a human being, the *Kohen Gadol* can enter it on Yom Kippur. His body is transformed to something more than human. As it is written, "(*ach*) . . . but on the tenth day. . . ." The word *ach* means merely, meaning that on Yom Kippur you are to be only, merely, and exclusively one, the singular purest thing. And if you are, you too will enter the Holy of Holies to the place of your soul, the Throne of Honor near God.

It is written, "God is my light and my salvation." The righteous are written and sealed in the Book of Life on Rosh Hashanah, and on Yom Kippur they already see the light. But the mediocre people, those who are neither good enough nor very evil, need lots of help until Yom Kippur to be written in the Book of Life. As it is written, "Your righteousness is like mighty mountains—Your judgment is like the vast deep waters. Man and beast will be saved by God" (Psalms 36:7). The words "your righteousness" mean the

righteous who can be as sure of their fate as the mighty mountains that stand firmly. The words "your judgment" speak of the wicked who are judged to the very depths. But the mediocre ones, who have both human and beastly parts and repent by Yom Kippur, will be saved by God.

Who is that arrogant to think of himself as a complete *tzaddik* without sin or blemish? Let us then not consider ourselves more than the mediocre ones and quickly repent and be saved by God.

It is written: "Also unto You God belongs mercy: for You render to every man according to his work" (Psalms 63:13). Our sages ask: if you render according to a man's deeds, you use strict judgment. Then that is not mercy. If you use mercy, then you do not use strict judgment. The answer is: first there is strict judgment on Rosh Hashanah followed by mercy on Yom Kippur.

This is similar to what our sages have taught about the creation. At first God desired to create the universe with the virtue of strict judgment. Because he foresaw that the world would not stand with strictness alone, He therefore combined it with loving-kindness.

On Rosh Hashanah, God examines each and every human being with strict judgment. The whole human race becomes extremely frightened and returns to God. But how can a human being hope to return to the extent of the exactness demanded by strict judgment? Therefore, God lends His loving-kindness to help man repent fully and accomplish his desire.

Now that it is Yom Kippur and our quest for repentance is supported with the abundant loving-kindness of God, let us not hesitate for a moment. We should not be frightened but should quickly seize the opportunity and run to the refuge of God, Who waits with open arms for all who call to Him with truthfulness.

It is written, "The Lord's arm is not so short that He cannot save, nor His ear too dull to hear; it is your iniquities that raise a barrier between you and your God; because of your sins He has hidden His face so that He does not hear you" (Isaiah 50:2).

In the physical world, everything is made of matter. Although everything is basically the same, there is great diversity. On the surface the differences are outstanding. A zebra is very different in appearance from an apple tree, a chair from an octopus. But if we probe deeper we notice that the pronounced differences are only superficial. Beneath the surface all things are made of cells and those of molecules. All molecules are made of atoms. Finally, everything in the universe is made of subatomic particles, which are all the same. We can therefore say that the entire universe is made of the same exact material. Everything is more similar than different; the difference lies more on the surface than at the level of inner truth.

This is true also on the spiritual level. Although each human being may be different from the other, they are more the same than different. Although each Jew may be different from the other, they all share a common soul. And although we are as different from God as heaven and earth, we share something with Him; our soul was created in the "the image of God." It is a reflection of His spirituality. Thus we have something in common with God and with each and every Jew.

When we sin, all this changes. Our sins emphasize our physical nature, the superficial part of us, which sets us apart from others. This causes us to feel separated from and to dislike others. We create a barrier between us and our fellow Jew, between us and God.

Therefore, on Yom Kippur, the Day of Atonement, our sins are removed, the barriers are broken, and we unite again with God. But how can we unite with God, if we have not united with all of Israel? If we are still stuck on our differences with others, how can we be God-like? Therefore our sages have taught, "Wrongs between people, even Yom Kippur does not remove unless we have asked forgiveness" (*Yoma* 85b).

Furthermore, Rabbi Akiva has taught that "You shall love your fellow as your self" is a (*klal godol*) great rule in the Torah (*Shabbos* 8a). The word *klal* also means community. The Torah is similar to the love we should have for our fellow. Although the Torah is written with individual words, which all seem to be different, on a deeper level they are of an identical material. The entire Torah is composed of the names of God, and they are one and the same; they are all one community, one family. We and our fellows too are one community, one family. If we emphasize our differences, however, we tear the fabric to pieces and create barriers between family members.

When we unite with the rest of Israel, we are also able to unite with God. Then the Torah becomes whole, and the names of God shine into every creature. As it is written, "The Torah was commanded to us by Moses: it is an inheritance of the congregation of Jacob" (Deuteronomy 33:4). When Jacob con-

gregates, and becomes one community with love, then the Torah is their inheritance. It enriches and unites them even more.

It is written, "Go to it then, eat your food and enjoy it, and drink your wine with a cheerful heart; for already God has accepted what you have done" (Ecclesiastes 9:7).

Why do the Jewish people want to be forgiven and pray and beg for forgiveness? It is so they can resume their special mission with a pure, unblemished heart. As it is written, "There is forgiveness with You, so that You should be feared" (Psalms 130:3). The reason we ask forgiveness is that You should be feared; we want to help others fear You.

What is the sign, then, that our begging forgiveness was for God's sake and not to escape the fires of Hell? It depends on what we do after we are forgiven. If after Yom Kippur we resume our mission to proclaim God's kingdom with great joy, then we repented for God's sake. As the prophet said, "Go eat, and drink"—learn Torah and perform the commandments with a cheerful heart, because if you do, it is proof that God accepted your prayers for repentance.

We can understand this concept on a deeper level as well. Although in the physical world we move from the past to the present to the future, on God's level, there is no sequence to time, no future or past, but one Divine present. Thus the service that you will perform later, after Yom Kippur, with happiness, God takes into account as you beg forgiveness. God has accepted what you have done. Why? Because you went later to "eat and drink," to the Torah and commandments with joy.

On this Yom Kippur may God accept our prayers for a pure heart and soul. May God see our later joy when we start fresh, as we do the commandments as if for the first time.

It is written, "For God gives to a man that is good in His sight (*chochmah*) wisdom, and (*daas*) knowledge, and joy . . ." (Ecclesiastes 2:26).

The word *chochmah* represents Rosh Hashanah, when we sound the shofar horn, which our sages called *chochmah*, wisdom, and not work. What type of wisdom does the shofar give us? It reminds us of the omnipotence of God and of our nothingness compared to Him. It makes us humble, which is true *chochmah*, or *koach mah*—an absence of strength, an absence of activity, total humility before God. After all, what is true wisdom if not the negation of our wisdom? As expressed in the verse "The beginning of wisdom is the fear of God . . ." (Psalms 111:10), true wisdom starts with fear and humility before God and also ends with humility and fear of God.

Yom Kippur, on the other hand, removes the barriers to God's forgiveness, and we climb the ladder out of the forty-nine gates of defilement to the realm of understanding. Each level of evil that we leave behind brings us to a higher gate of knowledge until with our complete repentance we reach the fiftieth gate of knowledge.

A prince rebelled and ran away from the palace. The king sent loyal advisors to entice him to return, but to no avail. He answered, "I refuse to listen to my father. I will do what I decide is best for me." Finally, after months in the forest, his heart softened, and he decided that his father is the king and that he will behave as a son. But how would he find his way back to the palace? He waited. Finally, the king sent a messenger that all is forgiven. The prince followed him out of the forest and back to the palace and soon stood before the throne of his father.

Similarly, even after we are humbled on Rosh Hashanah we cannot find our way back to God. But with the forgiveness of Yom Kippur, we climb out of wrongdoing, gain understanding, and finally stand before God on the fiftieth level of understanding. As King David said, "He sent from above, He took me, He drew me out of many waters" (Psalms 18:17).

Let us quickly escape the mistaken life of sin and wickedness, with true humility run the path of wisdom, and reach the highest gates of understanding.

Each Sabbath is a reflection of the World to Come, and Yom Kippur is the Sabbath of Sabbaths. During the Sabbath the extra spirituality, *neshama yeseirah*, that descends enjoys the bodily pleasures that we have in honor of the Sabbath. Similarly, on Yom Kippur our soul elevates our body to the level of the World to Come. Our body is then able to perceive spiritual pleasures. Just as there is no eating, drinking, or physical pleasures in the World to Come, they are absent on Yom Kippur too. Although normally we can only imagine spiritual pleasure, on Yom Kippur we can actually perceive it.

Let us therefore leave our lusts and passions, our pleasures and physical yearnings for this one singular day of the year to soar as the angels who have but one heart and desire for the will of God. Then we will abandon all evil and stand before the Throne of God with truth and humility. Then we will be at the root of all holiness, of time and space, of spirit and soul, as the *Kohen Gadol* who enters the Holy of Holies on the holiest day of the year.

THE CLEANSING OF YOM KIPPUR

Yom Kippur is a day of atonement and cleansing. All who are dirty with sin, no matter what the sin was, can be cleansed on this holy day, with confession and repentance. Three times during the Yom Kippur Temple service, the *Kohen Gadol* performed confession on the heads of the sacrifices. The first and second confessions were for his own sins and for the sins of the House of Aaron. And the *Kohen Gadol* would say the following: I beg of You, God, I have erred, been iniquitous, and willfully sinned before You, I and my household. I beg of You—with Your Name, God, forgive now the errors, iniquities, and sins that I have erred, been iniquitous, and willfully sinned before You, I and my household. As it is written in the Torah of Moshe, Your servant, from Your honored words: This is because on this day you shall have all your sins atoned, so that you will be cleansed. Before God you will be cleansed of your sins.

The third confession, for the sins of the nation of Israel, was performed on the head of a goat. And the *Kohen Gadol* would say the following: I beg of You, God, they have erred, been iniquitous, and willfully sinned before You, Your people Israel. I beg of You with Your Name, God, forgive now the errors, iniquities, and willful sins that they have erred, been iniquitous, and willfully sinned before You, Your people Israel. As it is written in the Torah of Moshe, Your servant, from Your honored words: This is because on this day you shall have all your sins atoned, so that you will be cleansed. Before God you will be cleansed of your sins.

The *Kohen Gadol* mentioned God's name three times in each confession and once more when he chose the goat for the sacrifice, for a total of ten times; each time he mentioned God's name, all the *kohanim* (priests) and the people who were standing in the courtyard would kneel and prostrate themselves, and fall upon their faces and say, "Blessed is the Name of his glorious kingdom for ever and ever."

Similarly, we repeat the confession prayer ten times to remember the Temple service.

Thus, the entire day of Yom Kippur was taken up with the act of cleansing the Jewish people of their sins. As the prophet said, "Then I will sprinkle clean water upon you, and you shall be clean: from all your filthiness, and from all your idols, will I cleanse you" (Ezekiel 36:25).

It is written, "Then I will sprinkle clean water upon you, and you shall be clean: from all your filthiness, and from all your idols, will I cleanse you" (Ezekiel 36:25). The clean water is the Torah, as it is written, "Come, you who are thirsty, come to the water . . ." (Isaiah 55:1). Whoever connects himself to the Torah will be cleansed by its life-giving waters.

There are two words in the Jewish tradition signifying closeness to God: *kedushah* and *taharah*, holiness and purity. What is the difference between them? *Kedushah* is the level of closeness to God before we sin. It is the very level of our soul before we are born; of our teacher Moses, whose prophetic vision was flawless as the clearest glass; of the Jewish people as they stood by the foot of Mount Sinai and received the Ten Commandments; of the Written Law, which is precise, clear, and unambiguous; and of *Shabbos*, the holy day in which the good is clear and at hand.

Taharah, purity or being cleansed, on the other hand, is found after we have sinned and are trying to return to God. We then must constantly purify our actions, strive to do the good, and separate the good from the evil in our life. This is the condition of the soul after we are born; of the Jewish people after they worshiped the Golden Calf; of the other prophets who see through an obscured glass; of the Oral Law, which needs careful study until the purity of its logic is revealed; of the six weekdays with their activities of good and evil; and of our constant vigilance to do the right thing.

This is like a prince who grew up in the palace. There were rules for every activity—for dressing, eating, playing, studying, greeting royalty, and relating to his parents, the king and queen. All was carefully taught as royal etiquette. It was all clear and concise with hardly a deviation.

When the prince was older, he was sent to a distant country. Suddenly everything changed. He was now in the company of men who had their own agendas, some of which contradicted the king's plans. He heard opinions contrary to those of his father. He observed behavior unacceptable in the palace. The prince no longer had the pure mind with which he was nurtured. He had to think carefully before he ventured an opinion or gave an order. He had to choose constantly between good and evil, between loyalty and treachery.

We too, before we are born, are in the king's palace. There everything is clear, like the written law, "the rules of the palace." But after we are born into the world with its mixture of good and evil, the rules

are not as clear. In this place we must work hard to separate the good from the evil. We are no longer on the level of *kedushah*, but, it is hoped, we are on the level of *taharah*.

Let us therefore connect ourselves to the Torah, whose waters will bring us the cleansing we await on this holiest of days.

It is written, "This is because on this day you shall have all your (*chatoseichem*) sins atoned, so that you will be cleansed. Before God you will be cleansed of your sins" (Leviticus 16:30). The word *chatos* signifies a sin done unintentionally. Why, on Yom Kippur, are all sins classified as a *chatos*? Because the congregation of Israel, as a collective entity, repents, even if merely out of fear. And the intentional sins of one who repents from fear are transformed into unintentional sins, which are mild enough for the powerful cleansing power of Yom Kippur to erase. Thus in our prayers we proclaim, ". . . for the sin befell the entire nation unintentionally."

We must at least be included in the category of unintentional sinners. Then we too will merit the cleansing of God on Yom Kippur.

It is written, "Blessed is he whose transgression is forgiven, whose sin is covered" (Psalms 32:1).

There is a spiritual balance in the universe; there is good and there is evil. And where is the root of the evil? The Zohar tells us (*Portion of Emor* 240) that all evil comes from the depth of the sea, which is the place of refuse of the *sefirah* of *malchus*, "kingdom." Consequently, when we repent we send the sin back to the deepest part of the sea, as was done in the Yom Kippur service when all the sins of the Jewish people were placed on the head of a goat that was sent away to the desert.

The kingdom of God is all pervasive—there is nowhere where He is not found. How then is there evil? The balance for God's kingdom is the evil, the *sitra achra*, the other side, the negative kingdom. Its source is the bottom of the sea, as it is written, ". . . and cast into the depths of the sea all their sins" (Micah 7:19). When ugly evil raises its head, then sin is not covered up. On the contrary, sin is displayed, and the kingdom of God is eclipsed. Finally, when we repent, we gather the evil, the spiritual energy of our evil deeds, and throw it back into the depths of the sea.

We have the opportunity to reclaim the world for

God's kingdom and to banish its opposite, the negative kingdom, back into the depths of the sea. It requires but one act: repentance. And that would cleanse us of all sin and the world of evil.

Our sages have taught:

> Rabbi Akivah said, Praised are you of the Jewish nation, before whom do you cleanse yourselves and who cleanses you in return? Your Father in heaven, as it is written, "Then I will sprinkle clean water upon you, and you shall be clean: from all your filthiness, and from all your idols will I cleanse you" (Ezekiel 36:25). And also, "The (mikvei) hope of the Jewish people is God" (Jeremiah 17:3). Just as a mikvah cleanses those who are defiled, so too God cleanses the Jewish people" (Yoma 85b).

When God created the world, He separated the upper waters from the lower waters. As it is written:

> God said, "Let there be a sky spread in the middle of the water, and it shall divide between water and water." God thus made the sky spread, and it separated the water below the sky from the water above the sky. It remained that way. God named the sky "Heaven." It was evening and it was morning, a second day. God said, "The waters under the heaven shall be gathered to one place and dry land shall be seen." It happened. God named the dry land "Earth," and the (mikvah) gatherings of water, He named "Seas." God saw that it was good. (Genesis 1:6–10)

The upper waters are heavenly; they symbolize the perfection of God's Divine Providence; the lower waters, the mikvah, are of the earth and symbolize the confusion of good and evil. The upper waters are flowing in great abundance without interruption; the lower waters sustain only when the good has been separated from the evil.

The word mikvah means a gathering of water. When it is gathered and controlled then it is beneficial for people. If it overflows without boundaries it can be harmful. Similarly, the spiritual blessings that are of the earth are helpful when they are gathered together—when the good is separated from the evil. If you have separated good from the evil in your life, purified yourself until you remain an empty vessel to receive the blessings of God, then you may get those blessings. If you have not purified yourself, you do not receive these blessings.

Therefore, on Yom Kippur when God showers all those who return to Him with an abundance of love, He does so with the upper waters, directly from the source, that flow without interruption.

A prince was in a foreign country far from home. Whenever he needed something he would send a message to his father and would receive it by special messenger. Once, when the messenger arrived the prince had already left to go to a different country. Another time, a storm delayed the messenger, and the prince did not receive what he needed. Finally, after months of travel he arrived home. He entered the gates and stood before his father. His father welcomed him warmly and asked, "My son, you have traveled far. Is there anything that you need?" The prince looked at his father lovingly and said, "No, Father. Now that I am home, I don't need anything!"

On Yom Kippur, God takes the baalei teshuvah, the repentants, and connects them to the root of blessing, the upper heavenly infinite waters. In that realm there is no lack, nor sin, defect, or deficiency. There is only the abundant providence of the Almighty. We have finally arrived at the King's palace, and with one stroke, we are cleansed.

Isaac wanted to bless his son Esau. Rebecca, the mother of both Esau and Jacob, wanted Jacob to be blessed but not Esau. Jacob protested, saying, "But my brother Esau is hairy . . . I am (cholok) smooth skinned. Suppose my father touches me. He will realize that I am an imposter!" (Genesis 27:11).

The Midrash comments: The word cholok also means portion, as in, "But God's (chelek) portion was His own people, Jacob was His allotted heritage" (Deuteronomy 32:9). The word cholok also means smooth, without dirt. While all year they are dirty with sin, come Yom Kippur and God cleanses them smooth (Genesis Rabbah 27).

The Jewish people are God's portion; they are a reflection of God's image and spirituality. Their souls are pure and unblemished by sin. Their sins are like dirt and can be washed off. As it is written, "I am dark and beautiful, daughters of Jerusalem, like the tents of Kedar, or the tent curtains of Solomon" (Song of Songs 1:5). The tents of Kedar can be washed and made very clean, so clean that they are worthy to be the tents of the king himself.

A prince played with the gypsy boys in the mud until he was unrecognizable. The boys were still covered with mud from head to toe, when the king passed and yelled, "How dare you do this to yourselves!" A servant was summoned and quickly washed them all. The king watched sternly as, one after the other, the boys' faces appeared. Finally, he saw the face of his own son. The king called excitedly, "Ah, so here you are. Go and change to a new outfit and come sit near me in the throne room!"

On Rosh Hashanah God judges the whole dirty and encrusted human race. He judges them all sternly, with the strictness of truth, and there is doubt whether anyone will be found innocent. His own (chelek) portion, the Jewish people, repent and cleanse themselves with fasting, prayer, and charity. When the Ten Days of Repentance pass and Yom Kippur is over, God surveys His world and sees that His people are really pure and (cholok) smooth, without dirt. His judgment is then announced with great kindness. "I declare; those who are clean can now enter my palace!"

Therefore, after Yom Kippur we go directly into the Sukkah, God's tent, the tent of Solomon, made from the dirty linen washed pure and cleansed of all blemish.

Moses and Aaron

The establishment of Yom Kippur as a day of forgiveness for all generations was brought about by Moses and his brother Aaron. As it is written:

When God finished speaking to Moses on Mount Sinai, He gave him two tablets of Testimony. They were stone tablets, written with God's finger. Meanwhile, the people began to realize that Moses was taking a long time to come down from the mountain. They gathered around Aaron and said to him, "make us an oracle to lead us. We have no idea what happened to Moshe, the man who brought us out of Egypt."

Aaron collected gold and had someone cast it and formed it into a golden calf. Aaron also built an altar and announced, "Tomorrow there will be a festival to God." The next morning they continued to celebrate. God then told Moses to get off the mountain because the people have made an idol and worshiped it. He was ready to destroy them. Moses pleaded with God. Finally after much pleading, God refrained from doing the evil that He planned for His people.

Moses then turned, descended the mountain, and saw what the people had done. Moses threw the tablets from his hands in anger and shattered them at the foot of the mountain. He ground the Golden Calf into dust, scattered it on the water, and gave the people to drink it. He reprimanded Aaron also. (Exodus 32:19–25)

That day was the seventeenth day in the month of Tamuz.

A month and a half later, on the first day of the month of Elul, Moses went back up the mountain and pleaded with God. He stayed up in the mountain forty days and forty nights and did not eat or drink. Finally at the end of forty days, God forgave the Israelites and gave a new set of stone tablets to Moshe. That was on the tenth day of the month of Tishrei, which is now named Yom Kippur.

———

When Moses ascended Mount Sinai on the first day of Elul, all the people fasted, and on the last day of his stay, the fortieth one, they fasted night and day. God forgave them and established the day as a Yom Kippur, a Day of Atonement for all generations.

Aaron, although he meant to restrain them, participated with the Israelites in the sin of the Golden Calf by collecting gold and making announcements to the people. Surely he was also the organizer of their repentance. Therefore, the Temple service of Yom Kippur was given to Aaron and the other high priests.

When the people repented, they regained what they had lost. They had lost half of their promise, "Whatever God will say we will do and we will listen." They lost the words, "we will do," because they did not do the right thing. Now, with the fast, they did the "right thing" even before God commanded them. They actually performed the Yom Kippur service even before God commanded them to do so. And why is this? It is because the love between the God and the Jewish nation is etched into each of their hearts, as the Ten Commandments are etched on stone. On Yom Kippur, they received a new set of stone tablets and also the etching of God's love in their hearts—His words, softly spoken, saying, "Open for me, my sister, my love," which stand as a dam blocking the raging waters of the nations roaring disapproval about our steadfast worship of one God.

———

Aaron repented for his own participation in making the Golden Calf and, by example, he helped all the people to repent too. But it was Moses whose spirit permeated Yom Kippur. Moses was the one who brought down the second set of tablets from Mount Sinai on Yom Kippur. How was he able to accomplish such a difficult feat? After he broke the first tablets, he uplifted the people, united them, and encouraged them to return to God with all their hearts. He pleaded, cajoled, and stirred them to a complete repentance. He participated by repenting with them, again and again, and he begged God for mercy.

Moses is called a man of God, and with his great

humility, he wished to lift all the people to his level. As it is written, "I have said, You are gods; and all of you are children of the most high" (Psalms 82:6). And although the people could not remain on the level that Moses had hoped for, his efforts bore fruit. For when he descended with the second tablets, lo and behold, the whole of Israel was on the level of angels who had neither food nor drink, but communed with God.

Thus, the spiritual energy of Yom Kippur was given to the Jewish people as a gift from our teacher Moses. And because it is a gift, it belongs to the congregation as a whole and to no individual.

Thus, our sages have taught in the Mishnah:

Raban Simon ben Gamliel said, There were no happier days for Israel than the fifteenth of Av and Yom Kippur, the Day of Atonement, for on them the daughters of Jerusalem used to go out dressed in white garments which were borrowed in order not to shame the one who had none. All the garments required immersion in a *mikvah*. And the daughters of Jerusalem used to go forth to dance in the vineyards. And what did they say? "Young man, lift up your eyes and see what you will choose for yourself; don't set your eyes on beauty, but fix your eyes on family. For charm is deceitful and beauty is vain, but a woman who fears God she shall be praised; and it says further, Give to her the fruit of her hands and let her deeds praise her in the gates. And it says moreover, Come out, daughters of Zion, come out and welcome King Solomon, wearing the crown with which his mother had crowned him, on his wedding day, on his day of joy. On his wedding day, is the day of the giving of the Torah Law; and on his day of joy is the rebuilding of the Holy Temple. May it be rebuilt speedily in our days! Amen!" (*Mishnah Taanis* 4:8)

The beautiful ones symbolize the righteous. Those who say, "Don't look at the beauty but the family," are the simple people whose merit is due not to themselves but to their ancestors. There are even those who wanted to repent, but just were not able to complete their desire. All of them come together as one nation, as Moses had intended, in a dance of joy, and they come to God with love.

ADDING ON TO YOM KIPPUR

Our sages said, "It is written, And you shall fast on the ninth of the month" (Leviticus 23:27). Does that mean that one ought to start fasting on the ninth? It says, therefore, "in the evening." But does evening mean from the time it gets dark? No, because it says the words, "on the ninth." How are these two words reconciled? We must start fasting before dark while

it is still the ninth day. This teaches us that one must add some of the weekday to the holy day. Yet we add not only in the beginning but also at the end. We add from the weekday to the holy day, as it is written, "from evening to evening." This includes both the evening before and the evening after (*Yoma* 81b).

It is written, ". . . and you shall fast. On the ninth day . . . in the evening. . . ." Our sages comment: Do we fast on the ninth day? Is not the fast of Yom Kippur on the tenth day? The answer is, obviously, that whoever eats on the ninth day is as if he is fasting on the tenth day. Similarly, we also learn from those words that we should add on to the holiday both before and after.

Yom Kippur is a day deeply loved by the Jewish people. It is the day of atonement for all their sins and for cleansing of their souls. How they all long for that day; how grateful they are that they have it. When Yom Kippur arrives their hearts are so full of joy they can hardly contain it. Yet they cannot express it in merriment and celebration. They are angels and do not eat or drink on Yom Kippur. They express their joy in two ways: by celebrating on the ninth day, the day before Yom Kippur with food and drink, and by taking a few minutes of the weekday and adding to Yom Kippur, before and after the holiday.

This is like villagers who were imprisoned by a tyrant and later freed by their king. The king invited them to a great celebration at the palace. The villagers gathered from all over, and as they met on the road they began to eat, drink, and make merry. The palace gates opened, and the villagers entered with a rush of joy.

Similarly, the Jewish people cannot wait for Yom Kippur and start to celebrate the day before. But as the holiday approaches, they excitedly start observing it, even before it officially begins.

Why would the Jewish people be interested in adding on to Yom Kippur? Because Yom Kippur is a *mikvah*, waters that purify. The *mikvah* of Yom Kippur is God Himself Who purifies the Jewish people when they humble themselves to the very earth. Who would not want to experience more of that purification? We certainly do and therefore add on to the length of the day, before and after.

The day before the seventeenth day of *Tamuz*, the Satan worked hard to mislead the Jewish people, and he did. He showed them an image of Moses lying on a bed lifeless. This led them to make the Golden Calf. Moses broke the tablets, as the Satan had planned, so that the Jewish people did not receive them. Finally Moses ascended the mountain. On the day before the tenth of *Tishrei*, when Moses was scheduled to come down with the second tablets, the people were cautious. They knew that the Satan would try again to mislead them. They repented and prayed and shook the gates of heaven pleading for forgiveness. But neither did the Satan rest. He clamored and worked to mislead them. Finally, Moses brought down the tablets, and it was Yom Kippur.

The merit for the second tablets, and the merit for the cleansing of Yom Kippur, is what the Jewish people did the day before, on the ninth of the month. And therefore, Yom Kippur eve, the ninth of *Tishrei*, is a great and joyous holiday, just as Yom Kippur is a Day of Atonement.

May we be worthy to receive the ninth and tenth day with joy, and be thankful for the wonderful gift of forgiveness that God has given us.

6

Laws and Customs of Elul, *Rosh Hashanah, and* Yom Kippur

LAWS OF *ELUL*

1. The forty days from the first day of *Elul* to the end of Yom Kippur, the Day of Atonement, are days of acceptance for those who return to God.

2. Starting with the second day of *Elul* until the eve of Rosh Hashanah, the shofar is sounded. The reason is to stir up the "sleeping," those who are not awake with Torah and commandments.

3. On the eve of Rosh Hashanah we do not sound the shofar, to distinguish between the voluntary shofar sounds and the mandatory shofar sounds.

4. Many have a custom to fast ten days for repentance. Since we do not fast on the two days of Rosh Hashanah, the Sabbath following, and the day before Yom Kippur, those four days are fasted before Rosh Hashanah; the first day of *slichos*, the eve of Rosh Hashanah, and two other days in between, usually a Monday and Thursday.

5. Many fast on the eve of Rosh Hashanah until the afternoon.

6. It is customary to bathe and cut one's hair in honor of the New Year. And although it is a Day of Judgment, the Jewish people are different from the other nations and are confident in a positive outcome.

7. It is also a custom on the eve of the New Year to recite the absolution of vows (see Chapter 7).

8. From the New Year until after Yom Kippur the word *l'eilah* in the *Kaddish* is repeated: *l'eilah, l'eilah.*

9. During this period, there are several changes in the *Shemonah Esrei* prayer. Instead of *hakeil hakodosh*, we say *hamelech hakodosh*; instead of *ohev tzedakah*

u'mishpat, we say *hamelech hamishpat*; and we add short prayers in the beginning and the end of the *Shemonah Esrei* prayer (refer to the daily Prayer Book).

LAWS OF ROSH HASHANAH

1. On the first evening of Rosh Hashanah, the New Year, after the evening prayers, it is customary to greet one another with this phrase, "You should be inscribed and sealed for a good year!"

2. During the feast of the night, it is customary to eat foods that symbolize good qualities about the year to come. For example, bread and apples are dipped in honey and a prayer is said, "May it be Your will that this year shall be renewed and be good and sweet." The head of a sheep or fish is eaten, and a prayer is said, "May we be the head and not the tail!" Some sweetened carrots are eaten, and a prayer is said, "May it be Your will that our merits multiply." There are a variety of customs for the foods and the prayers that are said.

3. The sounds of the shofar are as follows: the *t'ruah* is the blowing of nine short sounds; the *shevorim* are three blasts, each the length of three short *t'ruah* sounds; and the *t'kiah* is one simple sound. When a *t'kiah, shevorim - t'ruah, t'kiah* are sounded, the *t'kiah* should be as long as the *shevorim - t'ruah*. When a *t'kiah, t'ruah, t'kiah* are sounded, then the *t'kiah* should be as long as the *t'ruah*.

4. It is also customary to sound the *shevorim - t'ruah* with one breath before the *Musaf* prayers, and with two breaths during the *Musaf* prayers.

66

5. Before the sounding of the shofar, the *baal tokeiah* recites two blessings: Blessed are You, God, our Lord, King of the universe, Who has sanctified us with His commandments and commanded us to hear the sound of the shofar. Blessed are You God, our Lord, King of the universe, Who has kept us alive, sustained us, and brought us to this season. The congregation answers, Amen, and refrains from speaking until the very end of all the shofar blasts.

6. In Sephardic communities the shofar is sounded even during the silent prayers. In Ashkenazic communities the shofar is only sounded during the prayers of the *chazzan*, who leads the prayers.

7. The shofar is sounded after the prayer of "Kingship," "Remembrance," and, "Shofar Blasts." After each of these prayers, *t'kiah, shevorim - t'ruah, t'kiah; t'kiah, shevorim, t'kiah*; and *t'kiah, t'ruah, t'kiah* are blown.

8. The sum total of all the shofar sounds is 100.

9. One who has fulfilled his obligation with the shofar and needs to blow it for others may also say the blessings. But if the others are women, he should do it before the shofar blowing in the synagogue.

10. It is customary to occupy oneself with prayer and study during the day of Rosh Hashanah. Some permit themselves to nap after the conclusion of the prayers of the morning.

11. In the afternoon of the first day, it is customary to go to a stream outside the city and where fish abound, and recite the prayer of *Tashlich* as set out in the prayer books.

12. On the second night of Rosh Hashanah, authorities differ whether the *shehechiyanu* blessing is recited. Therefore, one should place a new fruit on the table so that the *shehechiyanu* applies to the fruit also.

Laws of the Ten Days of Repentance

1. The Ten Days of Repentance are obviously for repentance, and each person needs to examine his deeds with care and to repent for each and every wrong. It is customary to increase the amount of prayers, Torah study, and charity during these days. But even more so, the wrongs between people, such as lying, stealing, slander, and the like, must be carefully mended before Yom Kippur, the Day of Atonement.

2. The Sabbath within these ten days is called *Shabbos Teshuvah*, the Sabbath of Repentance.

Laws of Yom Kippur Eve

1. On the eve of the Day of Atonement, it is customary to take a male chicken for a male and a hen for a female, and both a male and female chicken for a pregnant woman, and say the *kaporos* prayers while turning the fowl around one's head. The prayer, "This is in exchange of me," does not mean that the fowl atones for one's sins. Rather, it means that whatever is done to the fowl should really be done to the sinner. And with remorse and correction of his conduct, his repentance will be accepted by God.

2. It is mandatory to feast on the eve of Yom Kippur, the ninth of *Tishrei*, and it is accounted to him as if he fasted both the ninth and the tenth days of *Tishrei*.

3. One should reconcile any misunderstandings that one may have with fellow men, either verbal wrongs, hurting another's feelings, or damage of property, before the Day of Atonement. The person whose forgiveness is sought should forgive with all his heart, should not seek vengeance, nor should he bear a grudge.

4. It is highly commendable to immerse in a *mikvah* on the eve of Yom Kippur, being careful that nothing intervenes between any part of one's body and the water.

5. It is also customary to light a candle in memory of departed relatives.

6. At the afternoon service, after the silent prayers, the *vidui*, confession, is said. Even sins that he had not committed since the past Yom Kippur, nevertheless he should confess them again.

7. In late afternoon, the final meal is eaten. One should conduct this meal as a holiday meal by dipping the bread into honey and eating light foods. The meal must be concluded before nightfall, thus adding from the weekday to the day of Yom Kippur.

8. It is customary to bless the children before entering the synagogue and to pray that God grant them a healthful year, and they not be punished for their parent's transgressions.

9. It is customary to wear a white robe, a *kittel*, both because it is the garment of the dead and because it is pure and white as the angels that we resemble on Yom Kippur. The *tallis* is also worn for the evening prayers.

Laws of Yom Kippur

1. Before *Kol Nidrei*, the Torah scroll is removed from the Ark and walked around the reader's platform. When kissing it or honoring it in another fashion, we beg forgiveness for being lax with the commandments of the Torah.

2. In the *Shma*, the prayer "Blessed is the Name of His glorious kingdom for all eternity," which is normally said in a whisper, should be said in a loud voice on Yom Kippur.

LAWS CONCERNING THE FAST

1. On the Day of Atonement, eating, drinking, bathing, anointing, wearing leather footwear, and cohabitation are forbidden. It is also forbidden to do all forms of work that are prohibited on the Sabbath. All is likewise forbidden before twilight on the eve of Yom Kippur and after the appearance of the stars at the conclusion of Yom Kippur.

2. The priests for the service or the ill may wash their hands in the usual manner.

3. Footwear made of material other than leather is permitted.

4. Pregnant and suckling women fast until the conclusion of the fast.

5. If a person is dangerously ill, even if the doctors say that he can survive without food and fasting will not worsen his condition, but the ill person says that he must eat, then he may be given food. In any event, a rabbinical authority should be consulted before anyone partakes of food on Yom Kippur.

6. The Ne'ilah prayer, at the conclusion of Yom Kippur, is recited when the sun reaches the tops of the trees, shortly before sunset.

7. At the conclusion of Ne'ilah, the congregation recites "Hear O Israel . . ." once, "Blessed is the Name of His glorious kingdom for all eternity" three times, and "God is the Lord" seven times. These prayers are followed by the Kaddish, with a shofar blast, to announce the conclusion of the fast and the Day of Atonement.

8. After the evening prayers, the Havdalah service is recited. The blessing for the fire, "He creates the light of the fire . . ." should be recited only on a fire that was not used for work the entire day of Yom Kippur.

9. At the conclusion of the Day of Atonement we are happy that God has accepted our repentance and eat and drink with rejoicing. We immediately busy ourselves with the commandment of building a Sukkah.

Thus concluded, we pray that our repentance and good deeds will tip the scale of judgment and we will be inscribed and sealed for a year of life, health and happiness. We move confidently to the next mitzvah, the commandment of sukkah, God's refuge.

7
Prayers and Blessings

Rosh Hashanah

Annulment of Vows

 n the eve of Rosh Hashanah one should annul one's vows. Three men sit as a court of law while the petitioner says the following:

Listen, please, my masters, expert judges—every vow or oath or prohibition, or restriction that I have adopted by use of the term konam, *or the word* cherem; *that I vowed or swore whether awake or in a dream; or that I swore by the means of the holy names that are not erased; or by means of the name* yod *and* heh *and* vov *and* heh, *blessed be He; or any form of nazirism that I accepted on myself, except the nazirism of Samson, or any prohibition, even a prohibition to deprive enjoyment from myself, that I imposed upon myself or upon others by means of any expression of prohibition, whether by specifying the term prohibition, or by use of the terms* konam, *or* cherem, *or any commitment, even to perform a* mitzvah—*that I accepted on myself, whether the acceptance was in terms of a vow, a voluntary gift, an oath, nazirism, or by means of any sort of expression, or whether it was made final through a handshake; any form of vow or voluntary gift, or any custom that constitutes a good deed to which I have accustomed myself, or any utterance that escaped my mouth, or that I vowed in my heart to perform, any of the various optional good deeds, or good practices, or any good thing that I have performed three times, without specifying that the practice does not have the force of a vow; whether the thing that I did related to me or to others, both regarding vows that are known to me and those that I have already forgotten—regarding all of them I regret retroactively and ask and request of your eminences an annulment of them. I am fearful that I will stumble and become entrapped, Heaven forbid, in the sin of vows, oaths, nazirism, cherems, prohibitions, konams, and agreements.*

I do not regret, Heaven forbid, the performance of the good deeds I have done; rather, I regret only having accepted them upon myself with an expression of a vow, or oath or nazirism, or prohibition or cherem, *or* konam, *or agreement or acceptance, of the heart, and I regret not having said, "Behold I do this without a vow, oath, nazirism,* cherem, *prohibition,* konam, *or acceptance of the heart."*

Therefore I request annulment for them all. I regret all the aforementioned, whether they were matters relating to money, or whether they are matters relating to the body, or whether they were matters relating to the soul. Regarding them all I regret using the terminology of vow, oath, nazirism, prohibition, cherem, konam *and acceptance of the heart.*

Now behold, according to the law, one who regrets and seeks annulment must specify the vow, but please be informed, my masters, that it is impossible to specify them all because they are many. Nor do I seek annulment of those vows that cannot be annulled; therefore may you consider as if I had specified them.

The judges then repeat three times:

May everything be permitted unto you, may everything be forgiven you, may everything be allowed to you. There do not exist any vow, oath, nazirism, cherem, *prohibition,* konam, *ostracism, excommunication, or curse. But there does exist pardon, forgiveness, and atonement, And just as the earthly court permits them, so may they be permitted in the Heavenly Court.*

The petitioner then makes the following declaration:

Behold I present the following declaration before you and cancel from this time onward all vows and all oaths, nazirisms, prohibitions, konams, cherems, agreements, and acceptances of the heart that I will accept upon myself, whether while I am awake or in a dream, except for vows to fast that I undertake during the Minchah *service. In case I forget the conditions of this declaration and I make a vow from this day onward, from this moment I retroac-*

tively regret them and declare them that they are all totally null and void, without effect and without validity, and they shall not take effect at all. Regarding them all, I regret them from this time and forever.

Eruv Tavshilin

When Rosh Hashanah falls on Thursday and Friday, an *eruv tavshilin* is made. Two foods are held and the blessing is said:

> *Blessed are You, God, our Lord, King of the universe, Who has sanctified us in His commandments and commanded us concerning the* mitzvah *of eruv.*
>
> *Through this* eruv *may we be permitted to bake, to cook, insulate, kindle flame, prepare, and do anything necessary on the festival for the sake of the Sabbath, for ourselves and for all Jews who live in this city.*

Kindling Lights

On each night of Rosh Hashanah two blessings are recited. When Rosh Hashanah falls on the Sabbath, the woman kindles the lights, covers her eyes, and recites these blessings.

> *Blessed are You, God, our Lord, King of the universe, Who sanctified us with His commandments, and commanded us to kindle the light of [the Sabbath and] the Festival.*
>
> *Blessed are You, God, King of the universe, Who has kept us alive, sustained us, and brought us to this season.*

It is customary to recite this prayer after kindling the lights:

> *May it be Your will God, my God and God of my forefathers, that You will show favor to me (my husband, my sons, my daughters, my father, my mother) and all my relatives; and that You grant us and all of Israel a good life; that you remember us with good and blessed memory, that you consider us with a consideration of salvation and compassion; that You bless us with great blessings; that you make our household complete; that You cause Your presence to dwell among us. Privilege me to raise children and children's children who are wise and understanding, who love God and fear God, people of truth, holy offspring, attached to God, who illuminate the world with Torah and good deeds, and with many works in the service of the Creator. Please hear my supplication at this time, in the merit of Sarah, Rebecca, Rachel, and Leah, our mothers, and cause our light to illuminate that it be not extinguished forever, and let Your Countenance shine so that we are saved. Amen.*

Kiddush Service

When Rosh Hashanah falls on Friday night, one begins the *Kiddush* service here:

> *(Whisper) And it was evening and it was morning;*
> *The sixth day! And heaven and earth were complete; then with the seventh day, God completed His work which He had made, and with the seventh day, He ceased from all His work which He had made. And God blesses the seventh day and made it holy, for with it He had ceased from all His work which He, God, brought into existence in order to continue the work of creation upon it.*
>
> *Welcome my teachers, rabbis, and all others!*
> *Blessed be You, O God, our Lord, King of the universe, Creator of the fruit of the vine.*
>
> *Blessed be You, O God, our Lord, King of the universe, Who has chosen us from among all peoples, exalted us above all tongues and has sanctified us by His commandments. And You have given us, O God, our Lord, in love, (Sabbath for rest) festivals of assembly for rejoicing, feasts of rallying and seasons for delight, (this Sabbath day and) the day of this Day of Remembrances, a day of (remembrance) shofar blowing (in love), a convocation to the Sanctuary, a remembrance of the Exodus from Egypt. For You have chosen us; You have sanctified us from among all peoples, (and the Sabbath) and Your holy festivals of assembly (in love and in favor) in joy and delight You have given us as an inheritance. Blessed be You, God, Who sanctifies (the Sabbath) Israel and the (festive) seasons.*

At the conclusion of the Sabbath, two candles, with flames touching, are held up, and the following blessings are said:

> *Blessed be You, God our Lord, King of the universe, Creator of the flames of fire.*
>
> *Blessed be You, God, our Lord, King of the universe, who has made a distinction between holy and profane, between light and darkness, between Israel and the nations, between the Seventh Day and the six days of work. You have made the holiday, and You have sanctified the Seventh Day above the six working days; You have set apart Your people, Israel, and sanctified them by Your holiness. Blessed be You, O God, Who has made a distinction between holy and holy.*
>
> *Blessed are You, O God, our Lord, King of the universe, Who has kept us alive, and has preserved us, and Who has brought us to this season.*

Omens for the "May It Be Your Will" Prayers

On the night of Rosh Hashanah, we eat special foods and pray for a good year. Each of these special foods has its own prayer.

• Dip apple into honey and say: *Blessed are You God, our Lord, King of the universe, Who has created the fruit of the tree. May it be Your will, God, our God and the God of our forefathers, that You renew for us a good and sweet year.*

- Carrots: *May it be Your will, God, our God and the God of our forefathers, that our merits increase.*
- Leek or cabbage: *May it be Your will, God, our God and the God of our forefathers, that our enemies be decimated.*
- Beets: *May it be Your will, God, our God and the God of our forefathers, that our adversaries be removed.*
- Dates: *May it be Your will, God, our God and the God of our forefathers, that our enemies be consumed.*
- Gourd: *May it be Your will, God, our God and the God of our forefathers, that our decrees be torn, and may our merit be proclaimed before You.*
- Pomegranate: *May it be Your will, God, our God and the God of our forefathers, that our merits increase as the seeds of the pomegranate.*
- Fish: *May it be Your will, God, our God and the God of our forefathers, that we be fruitful and multiply as the fish.*
- Head of a sheep or fish: *May it be Your will, God, our God and the God of our forefathers, that we be as the head and not the tail.*

Prayers before Blowing the Shofar

The *tokea*, the one who blows the shofar, recites Psalm 47 before blowing the shofars.

For the conductor, by the sons of Korach, a song. All you nations join hands—sound the shofar to God with a cry of joy. For God is supreme, awesome, a great King over all the earth. He shall lead nations under us and kingdoms beneath our feet. He will choose our heritage for us, the pride of Jacob, that He loves, Selah. God has ascended with a blast; God with the sound of the shofar. Make music for God, make music, make music for our King, enlightened one. God reigns over the peoples, God sits upon His holy throne. The nobles of the peoples gathered, the nation of the God of Abraham—for the protectors of the earth belong to God, and He is raised above them all.

This prayer is said for the *tokea*, the one who blows the shofar:

May it be Your will, God, the God of heaven and the God of earth; the God of Abraham, the God of Isaac, the God of Jacob; the great, the mighty, and awesome God, that You send me all the pure angels, the ministers who are trustworthy in their mission, and who desire to vindicate Your people, Israel. The great angel who is appointed to draw forth Israel's merit at the time when Your people Israel sound the shofar; the great angel who is appointed to make heard the merits of Israel to alarm the Satan when they are blown; the great angels who are appointed over the shofar blast, who raise our shofar blasts before the Throne of Your Glory; the angel appointed over the t'ruah; and the angel appointed over the t'kiah-shevorim-t'ruah-t'kiah. May they all be ready for their mission, to raise our shofar blasts before the heavenly curtain and before the Throne of Your Glory. May You be filled with mercy

upon Your people, and may You contemplate the ashes of Isaac, our forefather, that are heaped upon the altar. May You deal with Your children with the attribute of mercy and may You overstep for them the line of the law. Remember for their sake the akeidah *of Isaac for his offspring, for You are God, the faithful King, Who remembers the covenant. Blessed are You, Who remembers the covenant.*

May it be Your will, God, our God and the God of our forefathers, that Your mercy suppress Your anger from upon us and Your mercy overwhelm Your attributes. May You have mercy on Your children, and through their shofar blasts, may You change for their sake from the attribute of judgment to the attribute of mercy and remember for them the merit of the three Patriarchs. May they be engraved upon the Throne according to the order of their birth: Abraham above, Isaac opposite him, and Jacob in between, and may no error or sin intervene. May you enter for their sake beyond the boundary and find favor for me before You and have mercy on me. Amen.

The *tokea* and then the congregation repeat this prayer:

From the straits I have called upon God; God responded by giving me expansiveness.

You have heard my voice; do not shut Your ear from my prayer for my relief when I cry out.

Your very first utterance is truth, and Your righteous Judgment is eternal.

Be Your servants guarantor for good; let not willful sinners exploit me.

I rejoice over Your word, like one who finds abundant spoils.

Teach me good reasoning and knowledge, for I believe in Your commandments.

Please accept with favor the offerings of my mouth, God, and teach me Your judgments.

May it be Your will, God, our God and the God of our forefathers, God of judgment, that in the merit of these holy names, that are derived from the initials of the following verses—God, please bring near the salvation of those who long for You. Turn about those that fear You, bring them forth from their confinement. Redeem the storm tossed, open the eyes of the blind, they long for Your right hand. Draw up the oppressed, gather the scattered, support, O God our falling—that now be a propitious time before You. May You tear up in Your great mercy all the curtains that have separated between You and Your people Israel until this very day. Remove from before You all the accusers and prosecutors of Your people Israel. Seal the mouth of Satan that he may not accuse us, for our eyes are turned toward You. I will exalt You, my God the King, God of judgment, He who hearkens to the sound of the shofar blasts of His people mercifully.

God has ascended with a blast, God with the sound of the shofar.

Blessed are You, God, our Lord, King of the universe,

Who has sanctified us in His commandments and has commanded us to hear the sound of the shofar.

Blessed are You, God, our Lord, King of the universe, Who has kept us alive, sustained us, and brought us to this season.

T'kiah Shevorim—T'ruah T'kiah
T'kiah Shevorim—T'ruah T'kiah
T'kiah Shevorim—T'ruah T'kiah

May it be Your will that from the T'kiah Shevorim— T'ruah T'kiah *blasts that we sound, You fashion a crown of them, that it may ascend and sit upon the head of the God of Hosts, and may He do with us a sign for the good. And may You be filled with mercy upon us. Blessed are You, Master of Mercies.*

T'kiah Shevorim T'kiah
T'kiah Shevorim T'kiah
T'kiah Shevorim T'kiah

May it be Your will that from the T'kiah Shevorim T'kiah *blasts that we sound, You fashion a crown of them, that it may ascend and sit upon the head of the God of Hosts, and may He do with us a sign for the good. And may You be filled with mercy upon us. Blessed are You, Master of Mercies.*

T'kiah T'ruah T'kiah
T'kiah T'ruah T'kiah
T'kiah T'ruah T'kiah

May it be Your will that from the T'kiah T'ruah T'kiah *blasts that we sound, You fashion a crown of them, that it may ascend and sit upon the head of the God of Hosts, and may He do with us a sign for the good. And may You be filled with mercy upon us. Blessed are You, Master of Mercies.*

Praiseworthy is the people who knows the shofar blast; o God, in the light of Your countenance will they walk. In Your Name they will rejoice all day long, and through Your righteousness they will be exalted.
For You are the splendor of their power, and through Your will shall our pride be exalted.

Tashlich

On the first afternoon of Rosh Hashanah, it is customary to recite the *Tashlich* prayer near a stream that contains fish.

Who, O God, is like You, Who pardons iniquity and overlooks transgression for the remnant of His heritage? You do not let Your anger rage forever, but delight in love that will not change. Once more You will show us tender affection, You will suppress our iniquities, and cast our sins into the depth of the sea. Grant truth to Jacob,

kindness to Abraham, as You swore to our forefathers from ancient times (Micah 7:18–20).

From the straits I called to God, God answered me with expansiveness. God is with me, I have no fear—how can man affect me? God is with me, through my helpers; therefore I can face my foes. It is better to take refuge in God than to rely on nobles (Psalms 118:5).

Yom Kippur

Kindling the Lights

The woman lights the candles, covers her eyes, and recites these blessings.

Blessed are You, God, our Lord, King of the universe, Who sanctified us with His commandments, and commanded us to kindle the light of [the Sabbath and] Yom Kippur.

Blessed are You, God, King of the universe, Who has kept us alive, sustained us, and brought us to this season.

It is customary to recite this prayer after kindling the lights:

May it be Your will, God, my God and God of my forefathers, that You will show favor to me [my husband, my sons, my daughters, my father, my mother] and all my relatives; and that You grant us and all of Israel a good life; that you remember us with good and blessed memory, that you consider us with a consideration of salvation and compassion; that You bless us with great blessings; that you make our household complete; that You cause Your presence to dwell among us. Privilege me to raise children and children's children who are wise and understanding, who love God and fear God, people of truth, holy offspring, attached to God, who illuminate the world with Torah and good deeds, and with many works in the service of the Creator. Please hear my supplication at this time, in the merit of Sarah, Rebecca, Rachel, and Leah, our mothers, and cause our light to illuminate that it be not extinguished forever, and let Your countenance shine so that we are saved. Amen.

Blessing of the Children

It is customary to bless the children before going to the synagogue.
For a boy:

May God make you like Ephraim and Manashe. May God bless you and keep you. May God illuminate His countenance for you and be gracious to you. May God turn His countenance to you and give you peace.

For a girl:

May God make you like Sarah, Rebeccah, Rachel, and Leah. May God bless you and keep you. May God illuminate His countenance for you and be gracious to you.

May God turn His countenance to you and give you peace.

For a boy and girl:

May it be the will of our Father in heaven, that He instill in your heart His love and reverence. May the fear of God be upon your face all your days, in order that you not sin. May your craving be for the Torah and the commandments. May your eyes gaze toward truth; may your mouth speak wisdom; may your heart meditate with awe; may your hands engage in the commandments; may your feet run to do the will of your Father in Heaven. May He grant you righteous sons and daughters who engage in the Torah and the commandments all their days. May the source of their prosperity be blessed. May He arrange your livelihood for you in a permissible way, with contentment and with relief, from beneath His generous hand, and not through the gifts of flesh and blood; a livelihood that will free you to serve God. And may you be inscribed and sealed for a good, long life, among all the righteous of Israel. Amen.

Kol Nidrei

The *Kol Nidrei* prayer is the declaration to nullify all types of oaths and vows.

With the approval of the Omnipresent, and with the approval of the congregation; in the convocation of the court above, and in the convocation in the court below, we sanction prayer with the transgressors.

[Kol Nidrei] All vows, prohibitions, oaths, consecrations, konam *vows, or equivalent terms, that we may vow, swear, consecrate, or prohibit upon ourselves, from the last Yom Kippur till this Yom Kippur, and from this Yom Kippur to the next Yom Kippur, may it come upon us with good—regarding them all we regret them henceforth. They will be permitted, abandoned, canceled, null and void, without power and without standing. Our vows shall not be valid vows; our prohibitions shall not be valid prohibitions; and our oaths shall not be valid oaths.*

This verse is then repeated three times:

May it be forgiven for the entire congregation of the Children of Israel and for the stranger who dwells among them, for the sin befell the entire nation through carelessness.

Please forgive the iniquity of this people according to the greatness of Your kindness, and as You have forgiven this people since Egypt and to this point. And there it was said:

And God said, "I have forgiven according to your words."

The leader then recites the following blessing and the congregation repeats it and finishes the last word before the leader:

Blessed are You, God our Lord, King of the universe, Who has kept us alive, sustained us, and brought us to this season.

Yom Kippur Temple Service

The order of the Temple service for Yom Kippur is clearly elucidated in the Torah in Leviticus 16:1–34; in the *Mishnah Yoma,* chapters 1–8; in the Talmud *Yoma* consisting of 88 *dafim,* or 173 pages; and in Maimonides' *Laws of the Yom Kippur Service,* in the section on the Service of the Sacrifices.

The order of the Yom Kippur service is as follows:

At about midnight, the *kohanim* choose who should do the separation of the ashes. The woodpile on the altar is put in order, and the altar is cleared until the time comes to sacrifice the Daily Sacrifice. Then a linen cloth is spread between the *Kohen Gadol* and the people. He removes his weekday garments, immerses in the *mikvah,* dons the gold garments, and washes his hands and feet, as prescribed. He cuts the neck of the Daily Sacrifice and allows someone else to finish it. He receives the blood in a vessel and throws it on the altar. Then he enters the sanctuary, burns the incense of the morning, and prepares the lights of the Menorah. He then burns the parts of the Daily Sacrifice and the [*havitin*] and pours the wine and oil as prescribed. After doing so, he sacrifices the ox and the seven goats of *Musaf,* the additional holiday sacrifices.

Then he washes his hands and feet, removes his gold vestments, immerses himself in a *mikvah,* dons the white garments, and washes his hands and feet. He approaches his ox, which is standing between the sanctuary and the altar, its head toward the south while the *Kohen* is standing on the east and facing west. He places both his hands on its head and says the following prayer:

I beg You God, I have erred, been iniquitous, and willfully sinned before You, I and my household. I beg You, with Your Name, God, forgive please the errors, iniquities, and willful sins that I have erred, been iniquitous, and willfully sinned before You, I and my household. As it is written in the Torah of Moshe, Your servant, from Your glorious expression: For on this day He shall atone for you to cleanse you; from all your sins before God.

Then he draws lots for the two goats, ties a red ribbon on the head of the one sent away, and places it near the gateway facing its destination. Then he approaches his second bull, places both his hands on its head, and says the following prayer:

I beg of You God, I have erred, been iniquitous, and willfully sinned before You, I and the children of Aaron, Your Holy people, I beg You, with Your Name, God, forgive please the errors, iniquities, and willful sins that I have erred, been iniquitous, and willfully sinned before You, I and the children of Aaron, Your Holy people. As it is written in the Torah of Moshe, Your servant, from Your glorious expression: For on this day He shall atone for you to cleanse you; from all your sins before God.

Then he cuts the neck of the bull, receives the blood in a vessel, and gives it to [the *kohen gadol*] so that it should not congeal. It is placed on the fourth row outward from the Temple. The priest then takes the light shovel, clears away fire from the top of the Altar near the western side, as it is written, "from on the Altar, before God," and descends and places [the vessel] on the row that was in the courtyard. They bring out the spoon and a vessel full of incense, which is thinner than thin. He scoops with his cupped hand handfuls, which are not leveled and not overflowing but are well filled, each according to the size of his hand, and places them in the ladle. To carry a sacrificial item with the left hand is forbidden, so the priest should carry the spoon of incense in his right hand. However, because the shovel is so hot and heavy, he would not be able to carry it in his left hand to the Ark. Therefore, he takes the spoon in his left hand and the shovel in his right hand. He goes through the Temple until he reaches the Holy of Holies. He finds the curtain held back [by a clasp on the north side and the inner curtain held back on the south side, so as to make room for entering without exposing the view of the Holy of Holies]. He enters the Holy of Holies and approaches the Ark, where he places the shovel between the staves of the Ark, [two poles used to carry the Ark. During the Second Temple period he would place it on the Foundation Stone—according to tradition, it is the spot from which the world started to form]. He grasps the spoon with his fingertips or with his teeth, pours the incense using his thumb, and fills his cupped hand with it as it was before. Then he piles the incense onto the remote part of the hot coals on the shovel, so that the incense should burn closer to the Ark and away from his face and not burn him. He waits until the whole room is full of smoke and then leaves. He walks backward little by little, facing the Holies with his back to the Temple until he exits the curtain. And there he prays a short prayer, so as not to frighten the people, lest they think he had died inside the Temple. And he prays thus:

May it be Your will, God, and the God of our forefathers, that if the year must be hot, let it be rainy. Let not a leader be absent from Judah, and neither should Your people depend on one another, nor the prayers of the wayfarers enter Your presence.

During the burning of the incense in the Holy of Holies, all the people move away from the Temple proper, but not from between the Temple and the Altar. Moving away from there is required daily—when the incense is being burned and when the blood is sprinkled.

Then the *Kohen Gadol* takes the blood from the one who is stirring it, takes it into the Holy of Holies, and sprinkles it eight times between the staves of the Ark. He then exits the Holy of Holies and places the blood on a golden shelf on one of the walls. Then he exits the Temple, cuts the throat of the goat, receives the blood in a vessel, and returns to the Holy of Holies. Again, he sprinkles the blood eight times between the staves of the Ark. He exits and places the vessel on another golden shelf. Then he takes the blood of the bull from the shelf and sprinkles toward the curtain in the direction of the Ark eight times. He then puts down the blood of the bull and again takes the blood of the goat and sprinkles it toward the curtain eight times. Then he pours the blood of the bull into the blood of the goat and pours that mixture into the first vessel so that they mix very well. And he stands inward from the Golden Altar, between the Altar and the Menorah, and sprinkles the mixed blood on the corners of the Golden Altar. And he circulates and sprinkles it on the outside of the corners, starting with the northeastern corner, to the northwestern, to the southwestern, and to the southeastern corner. On all the corners he puts the blood in an upward motion, except the last one, which is directly before him. On that corner he sprinkles the blood in a downward motion, in order that his clothing not get soiled. And then he moves the coals and ashes on the Golden Altar this way and that until the gold can be seen. Then he sprinkles the mixed blood on the cleaned-off part of the Altar seven times, on the southern side where he had finished putting the blood on the corner. He exits and spills the leftover blood on the western foundation of the outer Altar. Then he approaches the goat that would be sent away [to the Azazel], and places his two hands on its head, and says:

I beg of You God, they have erred, been iniquitous, and willfully sinned before You, Your people the family of Israel. I beg You, with Your Name, God, forgive please the errors, iniquities, and willful sins by which Your people the Family of Israel have erred, been iniquitous, and willfully sinned before You. As it is written in the Torah of Moshe, Your servant, from Your glorious expression: For on this day He shall atone for you to cleanse you; from all your sins before God.

Then he sends the goat to an isolated land. He removes the innards of the bull and goat from which he had already taken blood and puts them in a vessel. The rest of the animals he sends to the place of ashes to be burned. He exits to the women's courtyard and reads from the Torah, after the goat has already reached the isolated land.

Then the *Kohen Gadol* washes his hands and feet, removes his white clothing, and immerses in the *mikvah*. He then dons the golden vestments, washes his hands and feet, and does the service of the goat on the outside, which is part of the *Musaf* sacrifices. He then sacrifices his sheep and that of the people, as it is written, "And he shall exit and do his sheep and that of the people." He then burns the innards of the bull and goat. Then the *Kohen Gadol* does the daily afternoon sacrifice.

He then washes his hands and feet, removes the golden garments, immerses in a *mikvah*, dons his white garments, washes his hands and feet, returns to the Holy of Holies, and removes from there the spoon and the shovel.

He then washes his hands and feet, removes the white clothing, immerses in the *mikvah*, dons the golden vestments, washes his hands and feet, burns the incense of the afternoon, and prepares the lights, as every day.

He then washes his hands and feet, removes the golden robes, dresses in his own garments, and exits to his own home. All of the people accompany him to his home. And he would then make a celebration, for he came forth in peace and unharmed from the sanctuary.

May we too be worthy to see the rebuilding of the Holy Temple and the resumption of the Temple service, soon in our days. Amen.

The service of Yom Kippur is over, and we reaffirm our faith in the Creator:

Hear O Israel, God is our God, God is one. [once]
Blessed is the Name of His glorious kingdom for all eternity. [three times]
God is the Lord. [seven times]

NEXT YEAR IN JERUSALEM!

II

THE JOY OF SUKKOS

Introduction

A Psalm for the thanks offering:

Make a joyful noise to God all the lands! Serve God with gladness! Come into His presence with singing! Know that God is the Lord. It is He that made us, and we are His; we are His people, the sheep of His pasture. Enter His gates with thanksgiving and His court with praise! Give thanks to Him, bless His name! For God is good; His steadfast love endures for ever, and His faithfulness to all generations. (Psalms 100:1–5)

ur holidays are a time of joy and gladness. Joy in being with our family, friends, and our people. Joy in reaping the fruits of our labor in the land of Israel and joy in our well-being. Joy in the uplifting of our hearts that sends our spirit soaring to new heights. The one holiday that emphasizes this joy to the utmost is Sukkos. As it is written, "Rejoice in your holiday, and you should be only happy" (Deuteronomy 16:14). No doubt this joyous holiday should leave its mark on us for the rest of the year. It teaches us that there is joy in the world and that it can be found.

This teaching is true despite all appearances to the contrary. Whoever opens his eyes sees a world with suffering, death, and misery in great abundance. Not only is there much apparent suffering but even our joys are impermanent. Joys come and go, and we cannot seem to get a good hold on them. They slip through our fingers as sand, with but few grains remaining. People grope in darkness seeking joy of the body and of the spirit, only to find illusion.

Rabbi Nachman of Bratslav, a giant among chasidic masters, once said, "The world to come, the perfect world, we at least believe in. But, this material world, the one here and now, how can anyone believe in it? The only thing to do is to run to the refuge of God."

True joy is the product of harmony. When every facet of our life is in harmony and rooted in God, then we are able to make contact with the world of essence, the divine, infinite, and lasting reality. This rootedness we find in the commandment of *sukkah*.

In the earlier third of the twentieth century, Sukkos was a nearly invisible holiday in America. Walking on the American streets then, even in Jewish neighborhoods, there was little visible sign of the holiday. If at all, it was only at the synagogue or temple where one found a *sukkah* in which to eat holiday meals.

To some American Jews, Sukkos was apparently too brazen a sign of Jewishness. How embarrassing it might have been to have neighbors watch the construction of a temporary hut in a twentieth-century city! What for? Even today there are embarrassed Jews who do not enjoy the depth and meaning of the Torah way of life. Yet, Sukkos is no longer invisible. American Jews are filled with a new courage and pride in their heritage and traditions. The Torah too is brighter for them as they watch the world at large slipping into an abysmal darkness, a darkness of aimless groping and insecurity. The Torah way is increasingly popular.

One can now walk through Jewish neighborhoods in many parts of the world and see the *sukkah* and see grown-ups and children walking to the synagogues with the *esrog* and *lulav*. It is beautiful to take part in one's traditions, to rejoice with family and friends, to feel pride in one's people. With pride must come a deeper understanding of the true essence of the holiday of Sukkos. What strengths do we gather from the *sukkah* and the four plant species? We must learn how the holiday elevates each one of us by its absolute escape from the world of illusion and running to the refuge of God.

The chasidic masters have taught: Each time one does a *mitzvah* it should be done as if for the very first time. We should not say, "Oh, Sukkos? That's what we did last year!" The *sukkah* of this year should be totally new and elevated compared to last year's.

How can we accomplish this? By learning and relearning the significance of this joyful holiday. I pray you will acquire a taste of the deeper significance of Sukkos while learning to abandon falsehood and illusion to find peace in God's refuge.

By participating fully in Sukkos, you will be granted true and lasting joy. You will find the roots of your soul as you bask in God's protection. You will unite as one with your people and live with their collective strength.

8

Time of Our Rejoicing

You shall keep the feast of booths seven days, when you make your ingathering from your threshing floor and your wine presses; you shall rejoice in your holiday, you and your son and your daughter, your manservant and maidservant, the Levite, the sojourner, the fatherless, and the widow who are within your towns. For seven days you shall keep the feast to God your Lord at the place which God will choose; because God your Lord will bless you in all your produce and in all the work of your hands, so that you will be altogether joyful. (Deuteronomy 16:13–15)

here is great awe and fear during Rosh Hashanah and Yom Kippur, followed by a great rejoicing during Sukkos.

A king prepared a feast for the royal family and servants. The banquet was ready and the king entered the hall. Everyone was filled with great awe and fear, and they stood motionless. After the formal greetings, the guests sat down to eat. Those who were intimately friendly with the king relaxed and talked with him. They talked and joked and enjoyed his company. The ones who were but mere servants remained respectfully quiet during the entire meal. When we are filled with awe and fear on Yom Kippur, it seems as if we are strangers to God and afraid of Him. When we rejoice on Sukkos, however, it becomes clear that our awe and fear of God stem from our closeness to Him.

Similarly, Abraham named his son Isaac, which means laughter. Why Isaac? Is he not the one with the virtue of stern judgment; why call him laughter? Because his awareness of the stern judgment of God brought him great joy. It made him laugh.

When Abraham was about to offer his son Isaac

to God, he was stopped by a voice from heaven. Instead, he found a ram tangled by its horn in the thicket. This ram's horn is used on Rosh Hashanah to make the sound of awe and fear, but it is really laughter. The laughter of Rosh Hashanah is concealed until the holiday of Sukkos. Then it all becomes perfectly clear. We do not fear for our lives. God has long ago forgiven—but we are awed by God's greatness, which we admire with awe and laughter.

Each Rosh Hashanah, the Creation receives new vitality and resilience. On a deeper level, the world is constantly being created and renewed. This constant "creation" is revealed at special times during the year.

When the world is re-created, there is Divine choosing and great joy. The ideal path, ideal teachings, and teachers are chosen anew. On Rosh Hashanah the Jewish people, who are concealed among all the nations of the world, are judged. Finally, they are chosen anew, set aside, and placed into the *sukkah*. The world is clearly re-created, and this brings great rejoicing.

"God's honor will be forever and God will be happy with His work" (Psalms 104:31).

True happiness is present when God's name is completely revealed in the world. Such revelations will not occur until the nature of the world changes from deception and illusion. Revelation is "light," for it is written, "The light is planted for the righteous."

It is planted and concealed in the earth at present, but "for the straight of heart, there is joy" (Psalms 97:11). To be straight without illusion or deception belongs to some future time.

A repentant, however, can transport himself into the World to Come. He transforms time into the infinite by restoring his past and revitalizing his future. He catches a glimpse of the straight path leading directly to the Throne of Honor, the Divine essence. In that place there is true happiness.

Therefore, after the repentance of Yom Kippur, we are transported to an island of the World to Come where we find true happiness and great rejoicing. This is the *sukkah*.

The *sukkah* reminds us of the Holy Temple. In the days of old, all the Jews would leave their homes and journey to its courtyard. So too, all Jews leave their homes and go to the *sukkah*.

Whenever we are reminded of the Holy Temple, we cannot help but be happy. As it is written, "I was happy when I was told, 'Let us go to the house of God'" (Psalms 122:1). People would say to King David, "When is this old fellow going to die so that we can start building the Holy Temple" (*Makkos* 10a). David knew that the Temple would be built only after his death. Still he was happy to hear people yearning for its construction. Moreover, David continues, "Jerusalem, built as a city which is bound firmly together." The hearts of all of Israel are bound together in this city of Jerusalem. Similarly, in the *sukkah* every Jew can find his place. Therefore, as soon as one hears that one is going to the *sukkah*, a living symbol of the Holy Temple, one immediately rejoices and is glad of heart.

The Torah has three references for joy during the holiday of Sukkos.

1. "And you should rejoice in your holiday" (Deuteronomy 16:14).
2. "...and you should be only joyous" (Deuteronomy 16:14).
3. "...and you should rejoice before God your Lord seven days" (Leviticus 23:40).

Why is Sukkos especially propitious for joy?

Joy grows from harmony. On a small scale, when each member cell of an organ supports the life of the other cells, then there is joy. When all the organs give life and vitality to each other, there is joy for the whole being. However, if health, vitality, and life are lacking, there is instead want, yearning, and pain.

Harmony is disrupted by having want, and instead of joy, there is sadness.

This is also true on a larger scale for mankind as a whole. Mankind's pivotal role in creation is to reveal the true nature of the universe, which is that God is the Master and nature is Divine.

The Divine nature of the world is in exile until man redeems it. How does he redeem it? By dealing with it in a Divine manner. Each item that is thus redeemed becomes part of the redeemed universe, part of the harmony and joy of being.

God wants all the nations of the world to be part of this harmony and joy. As it is written, "God wants for the sake of His righteousness" (Isaiah 42:21). He wants all the nations to share in the righteousness, but they refuse to do so.

The task of the Jewish nation is to transform the world so that all of mankind participates in its harmony and joy. In order to fulfill this task, the Jewish people needed to be prepared in stages. First they needed to be separated from all erroneous paths. This was accomplished with the Exodus from Egypt, which severed them from idol worship and the "abominations of Egypt." When they received the Torah on Mount Sinai, they were further separated from the erroneous paths of the other nations. Therefore, the holidays that commemorate these events, Passover and Shavuos, lack the fullness of harmony and joy. Not only are the other nations not included but, on the contrary, they are excluded. However, with Sukkos finally comes a taste of true joy. The Jewish people make offerings for all the seventy nations and bring harmony to all of mankind.

Similarly, the Jewish nation shares three names with their ancestor Jacob: Jacob, Yisrael, and Yeshurun. Jacob is he who runs away from his brother Esau and chooses instead the Godly way. This name corresponds to Passover, for the humble nation runs away from the arrogant one. Yisrael contains the two Hebrew words, *Li Rosh*, meaning I have a head. The head is wisdom—the wisdom of the Torah; therefore, this name represents Shavuos. Finally, Yeshurun means not merely straight, but "making straight," referring to the work of the Jewish nation. They make all of mankind and the entire creation straight. This last name corresponds to Sukkos. Thus, harmony is at its peak during Sukkos, and it is accompanied with great joy.

Let us also participate in the work of redeeming the world, bringing with it joy to all of mankind.

"Go eat your bread with enjoyment, and drink your wine with a merry heart for God has already approved what you do" (Ecclesiastes 9:7).

The Jewish people are connected to the Divine roots of the world. When they sin, there is separation, and it seems as if the world is in chaos. When they repent, however, their connection to the Divine roots becomes clear again, and all is restored to its proper place.

The root of all souls is God's Throne of Honor, *Kisei Hakavod*. Therefore, our sages have taught, "Repentance is so great that it reaches to the Throne of Honor" (*Yoma* 8a). Similarly, the image of Jacob's face, the sum of all Jewish souls, is carved into God's Throne.

By repenting on Yom Kippur, each of our souls finds its original place in God's Throne. Everything is back in order and restored. As it is written, ". . . for God has already approved . . ." Everything is approved retroactively as if it were in its original order. This brings the great joy of Sukkos. Sukkos is when we rejoice for the restoration of all that appeared out of place. The great joy comes from realizing that it was really in order all of the time.

"As the apple tree among the trees of the forest . . . for in his shade I have yearned to be . . ." (Song of Songs 2:3).

The apple tree gives little shade, and very few turn to it as a refuge from the sun. Similarly, the path of Divine illumination is difficult and was rejected by the arrogant nations; nevertheless, the Jewish nation yearned to be in His shade and ignored the hardships. They walked with Moses into the desert, from slavery to God's refuge, and they yearned to remain there forever.

The joy of being in God's refuge gave birth to a great yearning to remain there. This is the commandment of the Sukkah, a refuge for those who seek God. Joy is there in abundance for anyone seeking the Divine shade.

The ideal place for man on earth was the Garden of Eden. This was the most harmonious spot and state of being for him. Unfortunately, man was expelled from this ideal state and set into "exile" to "work the earth." Still on special occasions, places, and spiritual levels, a glimpse of the Garden of Eden is revealed. One such place is the *sukkah*; therefore, it is a source of joy and boundless rejoicing.

Our souls come from the Divine realm. The light of our souls shines through the dark and obscure nature of this world and leads us to the right path. Thus, we are illumined and enlightened by the power of our soul. If we err and sin, however, the world becomes more obscure, and the light of our soul no longer illumines us. This is corrected by *teshuvah*—repenting and returning to God. Our soul is restored to its former strength and shines through the darkness of the apparent world. It gives light for our life and for choosing the correct path of God.

Each one of us has two energies that are neither touched nor harmed by even the most vile acts. One is a kernel of absolute holiness in us that is forever undefiled. This energy is called *tzaddik*, the righteous one. The other is an energy in each of us that seeks home, the Throne of Honor, God's refuge. This energy is called *baal teshuvah*, the repentant one.

When we return to God on Yom Kippur, both of these energies shine within us, through us, and for us. We feel their strength on Sukkos when we run to the refuge of God. Our happiness and joy know no bounds; we are whole and alive once more.

9

The Sukkah

THAT YOUR GENERATION MAY KNOW

You shall dwell in booths (*sukkos*) for seven days; all that are native in Israel shall dwell in booths, that your generations may know that I made the people of Israel dwell in booths when I brought them out of the land of Egypt; I am God your Lord. (Leviticus 23:42–43)

ust as when a man meets a woman, chooses her to be his wife, and then takes her to his house, which is symbolized by the *chupah* (canopy), so too God chose the Jewish people in the Egyptian Exodus and then took them to His house, the *sukkah*. This act can be compared to the behavior of a shepherd in the time of rain. He quickly gathers his belongings and runs to the shed. What does he take? His personal belongings. The rest he leaves outside. The same is true of God and His relationship to the nations of the world. He chooses a portion who are closest to Him and brings them into His refuge.

Is it not strange that God chose only a portion of mankind to teach them the path, the law, and the wisdom? Would not it be more perfect and complete if He would have chosen all of mankind?

The truth is that the Jewish people among the nations are like the soul inside the body. The soul is the pure vitality and spiritual essence present in each person through which man can be illuminated completely. So too the Jewish people have been chosen for the task of illuminating and bringing wisdom to the world. Therefore, as we sit in the *sukkah*, we should be glad that we have been chosen for God's refuge. At the same time, we must exercise humility and not misuse our choseness. We must serve as the soul and vitality for the world with our teachings of justice and mercy.

The *mitzvah* of *sukkah* brings illumination and blessing to the home. This light surrounds the home while the illumination of the *mezuzah* protects the inner light from harm.

"And they camped in *sukkos*" (Exodus 12:37).

We can compare this to a king who was looking for a wife. After meeting many women, he chose one whom he felt would be the most loyal. He realized then that his other woman friends would be jealous. So he quickly took his chosen one, clothed her in royal garments, took her to the palace, and married her. Now she was protected from the jealousy of the others. The *sukkah* is the "palace" of God. Here He surrounds us with His protective tent and saves the Jewish nation, his bride, from the jealous glares of the nations of the world.

"And they camped in *sukkos*" (Exodus 12:37).

We can compare this to a king who had many sons. One son, however, was outstanding in his commitment to his father. The king realized this and chose to groom him for a more responsible position. When the other brothers heard of this decision, they reacted with jealousy and annoyed the favorite brother. To avoid this taunting, the king called his favorite son and conferred with him in his private study. There the king and his son were all alone: there he was protected from the annoyance of the brothers. Thus, in the *sukkah*, we too can experience a privileged privacy with God.

In the Sabbath prayer, we say, "He spreads a tabernacle of peace." The Hebrew word for "spreads" is *haporeis*. *Poreis* also means to break off a piece, a fragment. The Jewish people are the chosen fragment of the world. They are responsible for teaching the path of God.

"But why did God choose a fragment rather than the whole?," the nations ask.

The answer is that God dwells within the brokenness. By breaking one's ego, one becomes a vessel for God's indwelling. A vessel unbroken is not a vessel for God. Therefore, the broken one is ready for absolute completeness and infinite wholeness, and the unbroken one is actually the incomplete one. *Haporeis* means when broken off; *sukkah* can be a tabernacle, a protected area of peace; and *shalom* is completeness and infinite calm.

The completeness of anything lies in its vital part. However, the vital part is only part of the whole. Still it is this vitality that lends value to the rest. We can compare this to food that is ingested by the body. There is vitality in the food, although it is a small portion that makes it worthwhile to eat.

This is the position of the Jewish people among the nations of the world. It is through the Jewish nation that the other nations come to share in God and His teachings. When we sit in the Sukkah, we realize our responsibility of serving as the vitality of the world. We come before God as broken vessels and are filled by God's essence.

When we prepare ourselves, we then have vessels for God's goodness, illumination, and light. There are, however, two types of light. One is inside; it glows and fills us. The other is outside; it surrounds us. One is our inner space, our mind and psyche, and one is our surrounding space, our life in the world. Likewise, our home too is filled with God's light. The protection for the inner light of our home is the *mezuzah*. For the outside light, it is the *sukkah*. When we are in the *sukkah*, we are generating the protection of the Divine light that surrounds our life outside our home.

God's goodness is constantly flowing to the world. If there is a vessel to receive it, then it becomes full.

And how do we prepare ourselves to be vessels for God's goodness? We do so by opening our hearts to the fact of our creatureliness, our apparent lack of any substantial possession. We do this by verbally acknowledging that we are empty vessels before our Creator. That is prayer.

There are two types of prayer. One is prayer that we offer when we are really and actually in need. We are empty, and our need is apparent. The other type is prayer that is offered when we are full, and our need is not obvious. Each of these two types has an advantage and a disadvantage. When we are desperately in need, we naturally think of ourselves as broken vessels that require the help of God's abundant goodness. But our thinking is not pure because we are desperate. What else can we do but beg? When we are full, however, then our stance is pure. If we then stand before our Creator as a broken vessel, it is not out of need. Yet we still have a struggle. Can we acknowledge that all our fullness is from God?

These are the two types of prayer cited in the Psalms. One is "a prayer of the poor man" (Psalms 102:1); the other is "a prayer of Moses" (Psalms 90:1). To pray at a time when we are "the poor man" is certainly proper. After all, to whom should we address our problems if not the Creator of the world? Yet it requires no great effort nor taking of a stance. The difficulty arises when we are not in need because then our prayer is really a stance; it is "a prayer of Moses."

We can compare this to the child who was away from home and soon found himself penniless, lonely, and desperate. He wrote a letter telling his father how much he missed him and needed him, and asked, "Please send some money." When the father received the letter, he realized that this is not a stance. His son had not yet realized how much he needs a father. It was only because of his desperate situation that he had turned to his father. Later, the boy got a job and became prosperous. Again he wrote to his father how much he missed and needed him close by. The father then realized that his son had finally learned a truth about their relationship that he had not known until that time.

Sukkos is the time of our joy and gladness. It is the time of the year when we gather what we have sown, grown, and reaped from the spiritual harvest of the entire year. We then pray "a prayer of Moses," the rich man's prayer. It is especially at this time that we must prepare our hearts as vessels for this goodness. We pray that what we receive should not go to waste, but rather should bring vitality to the whole of mankind.

It is written "Blow the shofar for the New Moon, in the hidden time, on the day of our holiday" (Psalms 81:4). This refers to Rosh Hashanah (*Rosh Hashanah* 86) when the moon is still hidden.

On the New Year all of mankind is judged. Then what is hidden? The Jewish people are hidden and concealed within the judgment of the world. Two weeks later when the moon is full, the vital role that the Jewish nation has in the world becomes clear.

We can compare this to a teacher who is giving a test to his class. During the test, the few who are devoted to their studies are hidden within the rest of the class. But as soon as the tests are marked, it becomes very clear whom this test has selected. When this revelation happens, the selected ones need protection from their jealous classmates.

This is the *sukkah*.

What was hidden on Rosh Hashanah is revealed during Sukkos. When we enter the refuge of the *sukkah*, the results of the judgments of Rosh Hashanah become clear to us and to all mankind.

It is written, "I remember the kindness of your youth, your love as a bride, how you followed me to the desert, the unseeded land" (Jeremiah 2:2).

It is the virtue of the Jewish people that since the Exodus, they are ready to discard all their worldly possessions and follow the path of God. How do they come by this virtue?

The connection between God and the Jewish people is not coincidental, but one of essence. Their soul is essentially fused with God. When an individual Jew subordinates himself to the Jewish nation, he can then taste this connection. He will then taste how important God is to him.

We can compare this to the leaves on a tree. When a leaf "acknowledges" its leafness and its essential nature as part of the tree, then it can even taste its connection to the roots. It is part of the whole tree. However, when a person is arrogant and feels like an independent entity, he cuts himself off from his roots, which is God Himself. He shows his arrogance by acting outside God's will, the Torah path. Then he becomes desensitized from experiencing his roots.

It is during Yom Kippur that we cleanse ourselves of our arrogance and redefine our being as an integral part of the people who walk the path of God. We are then ready to part with our earthly belongings and walk with God in the desert. This is the *mitzvah* of *sukkah*. When we move into the *sukkah*, we are

uniting with our people. As we learned, "All of Israel could suffice with one *sukkah*" (*Sukkah* 276); then we are ready to relinquish our possessions, our home and house, and be a part of the larger house, the "house of Israel."

There is a Divine order and Providence, *Hashgocho Protis*, for each and every creature in the world. The amount that each one of us is to receive and is receiving does not change. It is preordained.

God's giving has two phases. The first phase is in the spiritual realm. The second phase is manifest in our physical life. In the first phase, the giving is infinite. When it reaches the second phase, it is already within a vessel and no longer possesses the quality of the infinite.

At least so it seems!

The truth is that the limitations we experience are an illusion. Our habits and attitudes about the world are vessels and borders. Our body ends here; the object starts there. We experience the world physically in terms of borders and limitations; therefore, we conclude that it actually has limits. The experience of our bodies, however, is not the complete picture. Just beyond the illusion, the universe is without limit. The amount of Providence we receive comes from God. It has no limit. Yet, the infinite Providence needs an infinite vessel, and we, who are of flesh and blood, are limited. How then do we receive infinite blessing from God? When we realize that our limitation (i.e., our ego) does not cause us to receive the blessing. It is, rather, a direct gift from God. When one acknowledges that, one removes the concealment of appearances and meets the true nature of the world.

It is written, "Blessed is the man who trusts in God, and God will be trustworthy to him" (Jeremiah 17:7). To trust means to acknowledge that whatever you receive is God's will, and that what you receive is good enough for you and could not be better. You trust His judgment in providing for you. Then what you receive is Godly, infinite, and limitless.

The opposite attitude is to think that what we receive is an entity outside God. This is "idol worship." It is cut off from the roots and is dead matter. Idol worship is a dead end; it is disconnected and dislocated from the Divine nature of the world. A person who takes a stance of arrogance by disconnecting himself from God is a *rasha*, an evildoer. A *rasha* is considered as if dead; he has broken away from the life and vitality in the universe. Thus, when we enter the *sukkah*, we envelop ourselves in God's refuge. We trust in His protection and encounter the infinity of Divine Providence.

The responsibility of the Jewish people is to reveal the Divine nature of the world, to remove the concealment, and to demonstrate clearly and manifestly that God is the Master of the universe.

One can do this work in three spheres: time, space, and spirit. Each of these needs restoration and uplifting. When the various elements of a sphere are in proper order, then the Divine nature of that sphere is manifest. Sukkos is the effort to bring the nature of space out of concealment and to demonstrate clearly that "the world is full of His honor." The walls and roof of the *sukkah* envelop "holy" space. We enter a dimension of infinity that universal space represents.

Isn't this a contradiction? How can the infinity of space become manifest within the apparent limitation of the *sukkah* walls? This is precisely the beauty of the commandment. The path of God, the *mitzvah*, breaks through the limitation and encounters the infinite that is close at hand and beyond the illusion. When we enter the *sukkah*, we can free ourselves from all spatial limitations as we enter Divine space.

The universe has Divine order and unity; however, the unity and order are hidden from us by its material nature. The apparent nature of the world is one of limitation, fragmentation, and confusion. It gives us a false and mistaken impression; therefore, it leads us to untrue conclusions. The Jewish people are in the world to reveal God's mastery and break through the concealment. Thus, they are in constant battle with the confusion created by the illusory nature of the world. When they win, they restore and reveal its unity and Divine essence.

During the battle, the Jewish people are designated by the name Yaakov (Jacob), meaning "footstep"; a battle is won by a systematic step-by-step approach. This approach is represented by Jacob's ladder. When the battle is won, the Jews acquire the name Yisroel (Israel) which means "to do battle with Divine forces" and to succeed. In this approach the Jewish people skip and have a direct encounter with the true nature of the universe. They skip the steps on the ladder and affect the revelation of God's presence in the world.

These two approaches are also represented by the *lulav* on the one hand and the *sukkah* on the other hand. The *mitzvah* of *lulav* consists of four plants: the palm, myrtle, willow, and citron. Each one in turn represents a different level of mankind in their encounter with God. Some are on a lower level and some on a higher level. There are those with knowledge and deed (citron), those with only knowledge (palm), those with only deeds (myrtle), and those with neither knowledge nor deeds (the lowly willow). Levels are illusions manifest in the world of material things. The *lulav* is therefore Yaakov, the footsteps going up the ladder one level at a time.

In the Divine nature of the world, there are no levels at all. This is the *sukkah*; we skip to God's refuge and meet Him directly as Yisrael. The battle is already won. There is no need for strategy and systematic warfare.

Therefore, Yom Kippur, a day of battle against concealment, falsehood, and confusion, gives us the *mitzvah* of the *lulav*, a gradual step-by-step climbing. Finally, we enter the *sukkah*, which is the truth of our condition; there really is no confusion or falsehood.

We can compare this to a king who led his loyal and faithful servant blindfolded into the dense forest. He then sent soldiers to feign an attack on the servant. The servant battled valiantly. The soldiers convincingly played the role of a battling and retreating army. They battled fiercely, but they finally withdrew. The servant had vanquished the king's enemies! "Now it is clear once more that the king rules this forest," he thought. Suddenly, the king came out of hiding. The servant soon realized that the king had only been hiding, and the entire battle was nothing but illusion. The king was present all of the time, and his sovereignty was never in question. When we step into the *sukkah*, we realize the Divine nature of the world. We realize that we are in a direct encounter with God. We know that, although we battled, it was only to come to the ultimate truth; no battle was necessary after all.

There are two opposing forces in the world. There is Divine Presence and unity on the one hand, and there is concealment and confusion on the other hand. The nation that represents the former is the Jewish people; those that represent the latter force are the Amalekites.

With two opposing forces, when one is strong, the other weakens. As one becomes stronger and approaches the midpoint, the opposition reaches its apex. Then the stronger force begins its decline into weakness.

When the Jewish people left Egypt, a revelation was about to take place that would have ended all concealment. It occurred when the opposition was strongest and Amalek appeared for an attack. This was the appropriate time for the protection of the clouds that God provided for them. Likewise, when we are victorious after Yom Kippur, the opposition is the strongest, and we need the protection of the *sukkah*. Thus, as we enter the *sukkah*, we remember that this time we are making a total commitment to reveal the Divine presence in the universe. It is also the time that we are likely to experience the most opposition. We must take refuge within God's protection, the *sukkah*, to withstand this opposition.

God is the master of the world; however, His indwelling and presence are not manifest. They are concealed by the appearance and illusory nature of reality. It is through the work of the Jewish people that the concealment recedes and the revelation of God's mastery is revealed.

This indwelling is called *Shechinah*, the Divine presence that pervades every part of the universe. In the *sukkah* it is represented by inviting in the seven patriarchs—Abraham, Isaac, Jacob, Joseph, Moses, Aaron, and David—each one of whom was instrumental in the revealing of God's presence in the world.

When there is concealment, there is also great yearning. Every particle in the universe yearns to be realized for what it really is and not according to appearances, illusions, and the concealment of vessels. This is the meaning of the verse, "In His shadow I have yearned to be . . . and I have stayed" (Song of Songs 2:3). Shadow is the period of hiddenness. Moreover, there is yearning. This yearning is as strong as the degree of hiddenness.

During Rosh Hashanah, the hiddenness is very strong. As it is written, "Blow the shofar during the new moon in the hiddenness of our holiday . . ." (Psalms 81:4). The Jewish people are yearning for the revelation of God's sovereignty, and they call out, "O King, reign over the world in glory!" This is the time of shadow and yearning. However, on Sukkos the *Shechinah* is revealed: "I have stayed in it."

Our experience of Sukkos depends on our yearning for the *Shechinah*. As we enter the *sukkah*, we invite the patriarchs who strived for the ultimate revelation. We realize that we must participate to make God's indwelling manifest, and if we do, we can rejoice with gladdened hearts.

The Jewish people have the responsibility of declaring God's kingdom. They must use their time and energy to realize that responsibility. There are many distractions, and therefore, they must banish the distractions that work against their primary responsibility. They must focus their activities on fulfilling their mission in the world. The Jewish people accomplish this task by separating from the other nations. We are then free from involvement that misdirects our energy. Our energy is then focused to enable us to accomplish our goal.

The Holy Temple in Jerusalem served this very purpose. It represented a private space for our people that made focused effort possible. The *sukkah* too is such a space. Therefore, during the holiday of Sukkos, sacrifices are offered for all the nations. When we are able to carry out our mission, then all the nations benefit. As the Talmud says, "If the nations would know how much they benefit from the Holy Temple, they would decorate it with gold" (*Numbers Rabbah* 1).

When we sit in the *sukkah*, we should realize how much benefit we could be to the world. We must prepare and consecrate our energies for this mission. Then the private space of the *sukkah* becomes charged with Divine Light that shines out in all directions.

CLOUDS OF GLORY

". . . because I have made the children of Israel dwell in *sukkos* . . ." (Leviticus 23:43).

"There is a disagreement among the sages. One says these were real booths. The other says they were clouds of glory that came in the merit of Aaron (*Sukkah* 11b).

The clouds came in the merit of Aaron, the chief of the priests.

What was Aaron's work? He made peace between man and man. When two people quarreled, he went to one and said, "Your brother is very sorry for what he did, but he is too embarrassed to apologize. Please forgive him." Then he would go and tell the other one the very same thing. Thus, Aaron prevented the fabric of the Jewish nation from being torn to pieces. Similarly, the clouds of glory protected them from all harm, as a tent of fabric protects those inside.

Aaron brought peace in two basic types of quarrels. One was between people who quarreled because of a misunderstanding. Aaron helped them see their mistakes and regain their friendship. The other type of quarrel was between people who had actually wronged each other. These people, too, Aaron drew near. He embraced them and showered them with love. In turn, they were very embarrassed and repented with all their hearts and souls.

The clouds too in Aaron's merit protected those who were worthy and those who really were not worthy. Likewise, a *sukkah* protects all. It stands as a protection of love over all Israel, and it urges those who are far to be far no longer.

"In *sukkos* you shall live for seven days . . ." (Leviticus 23:42). The Torah is saying, "Go out of your permanent dwelling and go to live in a temporary one."

The world functions according to sets of laws of which we are aware through daily observation. The laws of nature are "dependable." If the sun rose today, it is "sure" to rise tomorrow. It is our "permanent" dwelling. It is that aspect of the universe that we experience as a constant. In contrast, there is also the unexpected, dynamic, and miraculous. This is the divine aspect of the world with which we have contact from time to time. It is its "temporary" aspect. We can hardly expect to relate constantly to the miraculous. After all, our senses tell us that this world is what it appears to be, nothing more and nothing less.

The Torah, therefore, commands us, "Go out from your permanent dwelling," and do not regard the world as permanent. It tells us to move into the "temporary" and to experience the Divine and the miraculous. "In order that you should know that I have made the Jewish people live in Sukkos when I liberated them from Egypt" (Leviticus 23:43).

How will we know from sitting in our *sukkah* what God did many generations ago? The answer is that we were liberated from the ordinary laws of nature at the Exodus; therefore, we can again experience that liberation. God promised the Jewish people that they will never fall into the "enslavement" of the world of nature again. They were given "wings" with which to rise above the ordinary world and go to Sukkos, the dwelling of the Divine. As it is written, "And I will lift you on the wings of eagles and bring you to Me" (Exodus 19:4).

After the cleansing of Rosh Hashanah and Yom Kippur, we are ready to be on the level of the miraculous and the divine.

When a farmer reaps his crop, the stalks argue with the kernels. The stalks say, "It is because of us that all the planting was done!" The argument continues until the time the farmer threshes his crop. The straw and chaff are allowed to be blown by the wind while the kernels are gathered together and stored (*Genesis Rabbah* 39).

In the same way Abraham stood among the people of the world. The people thought that they would have the responsibility to declare God's kingdom. Then God spoke to Abraham and said, "Go forth from your land . . . to the land I will show you" (Genesis 12:11). It is then clear who was chosen for that awesome responsibility.

We can compare this to a beachcomber who was sifting sand on the beach to find a treasure. As the sand fell through the sifter, he kept saying, "No, this is not what I was looking for." But soon the sand emptied from the sifter and there appeared a diamond. He called out, "Yes, this is it! This is why I let all that sand fall through the sifter, just to find this diamond!" (*Genesis Rabbah* 39).

Likewise, the nations of the world lived together with the Jewish nation in Egypt. The nations thought, "Surely ours is the responsibility of God's work in the world." As soon as the Exodus took place, the Jewish nation followed God into the desert. It then became clear which was the grain and which was the chaff.

Similarly, every being in the world is judged on Rosh Hashanah and Yom Kippur. There is suspense, as they are all judged equally. Then the judgment is over. The Jewish people go into their *sukkah*, the tent of faith. Suddenly, it is clear who is innocent and who is guilty. Therefore, Sukkos is called the Holiday of Ingathering. Just as the ingathering from the field makes clear which is the grain and which is the chaff, so too does the *sukkah*.

The *sukkah*, therefore, is firmly linked to Abraham and Aaron. As we read, "I remember the kindness of your youth" (Jeremiah 2:2). This is Abraham who initiated the youth of the Jewish nation. "The love of your gatherings" is Aaron whose energy came from the congregation of the Jewish people. Abraham took himself aside to one side of the river and set up his tent. Aaron distinguished himself by working for the unity of all the people. Thus, it is clear which is the chaff and which is the grain.

When we sit in the *sukkah*, we know that all the judgments, pains, and hardships we endured were experienced to establish clearly our innocence and our willingness to walk with God even in the desert.

"And they moved from Raamses and came to *sukkos*" (Numbers 37:6).

What type of *sukkos* were they? Real *sukkos* or protective clouds? Still, the very fact that they reached the *sukkos* was in the merit of Aaron. How so?

God sent Moses to effect a complete redemption; however, because of their great suffering, the Jewish people had no patience to listen to him. Therefore, Moses took along Aaron, who was a pillar of kindness, and he gave them the strength to be redeemed. As it is written, ". . . that I made them live in sukkos . . . when I brought them forth from Egypt" (Leviticus 23:43b). The *sukkah* is supported by the pillar of kindness. Thus, whoever wants the blessing of kindness should connect himself to the *mitzvah* of *sukkah*.

God is the ultimate perfection. When this perfection manifests itself in our own flesh and blood, then we can say that God's kingdom is being revealed. This is the *Shechinah*: unity and peace.

There is another aspect of God's being that forever remains concealed. This is the essence of God that is unknown and inconceivable. The unknowable is the fact that God is king; the revelation is His kingdom. God as king is heaven; God's kingdom is earth.

The two brothers, Moses and Aaron, related to these two aspects of God. Moses related to God the King and Aaron to God's kingdom. Moses climbed Mount Sinai and carried down a teaching for the children of Israel. He linked the Jewish nation with the unknowable and hidden, and he brought the word of heaven to the earth. On the other hand, Aaron unified the Jewish nation by making peace. He made God's kingdom manifest on the earth.

In essence, what was Aaron's work? He made people—who are separated from each other, from the Jewish nation, and from God—come together. He made them realize that at the root level everyone is connected to the other and all divisiveness is an illusion. It is only on the level of husks, the very outside of things, that there is any division. At the root, there is only unity.

Thus, Aaron's work was to make manifest the connection and unity of all and the all-encompassing nature of God. Therefore, everything is subordinated to His protection. These were the "clouds of protection" in the merit of Aaron. This is also the "tent of protection," the house of God, the *sukkah*. To bring everything in the world under God's wings and shadow.

When "rust" accumulates on us, we have difficulty seeing the connectedness of our roots. Consequently, after Rosh Hashanah and Yom Kippur when we remove the dross and rust, it becomes clear that we were never actually separated. We immediately enter into the *sukkah*. There, we again experience our unity and oneness with each other and with God.

Moses and Aaron each related to a different aspect of God. The life of our teacher Moses was one of struggle. When he was born, he was cast into the water. He struggled at Pharaoh's palace and in the workfields among his brethren. He struggled to flee Egypt, and he had no rest at the well where he met his future wife. He struggled with Pharaoh until Pharaoh released the Jewish people; but neither did Pharaoh nor the Jewish nation give him any rest. He struggled with the angels to receive the Torah; then again he struggled with his own people when they made the Golden Calf. He struggled with the Amalekites for it is written, "When Moses lifted his hand, the Israelites were victorious; when he lowered his hand, the Amalekites were victorious" (*Rosh Hashanah* 25a). The path of Moses was victory, *netzach*, and this required struggling. The disadvantage of this path was and still is that one cannot always be victorious. There can be situations when a battle is lost.

The path of Aaron was different. His approach was to create situations in which battle and struggle were not even necessary. Therefore, Aaron is the peacemaker, and he makes offerings in the Holy Tabernacle, the *Mishkan*, which expiate the sins of the people. He prevents plagues and pestilence from attacking the community. He even removes accidental murders from among the Jewish nation, and he minimizes evil thoughts from their minds. His way is honor, *hod*, and the one who emulates him does not struggle for honor. One receives honor by virtue of his deeds.

In the kabbalistic scheme of Divine attributes, or *sfiros*, these two paths of victory, *netzach*, and honor, *hod*, reach a balance in foundation, *yesod*. The active and passive paths of victory and honor of Moses and Aaron are the foundation of the Jewish nation. Therefore, the clouds of glory are in the merit of Aaron. There is no struggle, but there is the de facto peace and honor. Likewise, it is the honor that one gains when one sits in the *sukkah*.

Sukkah is the foundation of peace.

It is written, "'Peace, peace to the one who is far, and one who is near.' said God" (Isaiah 57:19).

One who is near is the *tzaddik*, the righteous one who has never sinned. Although this world is incomplete and full of strife, the *tzaddik* can still reach some measure of completeness and peace.

One who is far is the *baal teshuvah* who is returning to God after going astray. He brings completion and peace from the highest place, for he is considered higher even than the *tzaddik*.

The *tzaddik* is represented by Moses who dwelled with God in the mountain for forty days; the *baal teshuvah* is represented by Aaron who was involved in the making of the Golden Calf. Therefore, Sukkos, which comes after the days of repentance, is in the merit of Aaron. When we have turned again to God as our refuge and sit in the *sukkah*, we receive peace from the highest place.

The kindness of God spreads without limit and pervades the minutest particle of the universe. It is this kindness that is the essence of each and every item in existence. The kindness of God is infinite and indestructible. The vessels, the husk, the illusory appearance of things are only limitations, and they ultimately must perish.

The permanence of things is God's loving-kindness in them. The stronger we are connected with this love, which ignores the apparent separateness of the husk, the more we are vessels to receive the unity and oneness that characterizes the *sukkah*. The *sukkah*, the protection in and by the loving-kindness of God, unifies all souls in Divine infinity.

The activity that thickens the finiteness of the creaturely world is sin. Therefore, it is also that which produces a gap between creature and creature, and between creature and God. Thus, after Rosh Hashanah and Yom Kippur, when the cleansing is complete and purity returns to the soul, the world is open again to the infinite love of God. Then one can walk directly into the *sukkah*, the elling of Divine infinity.

Separation is only an illusion. By treading the path of the Torah, we lessen the illusion, and the true nature of the world becomes apparent. Returning to God is the act of connecting to the essence and ignoring illusion. After Yom Kippur we are pure and have thinned out the illusions of our separateness. We are more in touch with the truth about this world, and we sit in the refuge of God, the protection of the *sukkah*.

REMEMBERING THE KINDNESS OF YOUR YOUTH

The word of God came to me, saying, "Go, and proclaim in the hearing of Jerusalem," thus says God. I remember the kindness of your youth, your love as a bride (of your gatherings), how you followed me in the wilderness, in a land not sown. (Jeremiah 2:2)

God's loving-kindness fills the world. All the liberation and illumination one needs emanate from Him every instant. However, this kindness needs to be contained in a vessel. It needs to enter the world of flesh and blood, and it does so when we do deeds rewarded by God's kindness. It makes us deserving because our physical deeds bring the kindness into the material world.

There are times, however, when the infinite kindness of God miraculously enters our lives without vessels. Such kindness has no place in this world and is lost. What can we do to keep this miraculous kindness? We must quickly flesh it out with deeds. Then it can remain with us forever.

This was precisely our predicament when we left Egypt. We were liberated undeservingly and miraculously. Therefore, we needed to bridge the infinite kindness to this world through our deeds. As the prophet says, "I remember the kindness of your youth . . . when you followed me into the desert . . ." (Jeremiah 2:2). This infinite kindness became permanent in the form of clouds of glory that surrounded the Jewish nation. Flesh-and-blood deeds bring the kindness of God into physical vessels, which protect it from disappearing.

When kindness has vessels, it can even stand up to the scrutiny of judgment. It is protected. Therefore, after Rosh Hashanah and Yom Kippur, the Days of Judgment, it is clear that we deserve God's kindness. We have prepared vessels for it through our good deeds, and it has the protection of the *sukkah*.

"I *remember* the kindness of your youth. . . ." After an event happens, it is no longer in the world. It is finished, yet it can be remembered. Memory is a vessel for events that otherwise would no longer be in the world. God's kindness during the Exodus would have ceased to be if we would not have made vessels for it. Therefore, it can be remembered, for memory is its vessel and protects it from utter extinction.

The *sukkah*, too, is the materialization of our good deeds and a "remembering" of God's kindness. The strength of our *sukkah* experience is directly related to how much we deserve God's loving kindness. May we all be worthy of it.

In each and every thing in the universe, there is a speck of Divine vitality, its essence and soul. If this essence would be manifest, there would be no doubt that God is the Master of the world. But it is concealed, and so is God's sovereignty. It is concealed in the material world of illusion and masks of falsehood. Nevertheless, it is in man's power to reveal the Divine roots and essence of the world. He can do this by Godly deeds. By acting according to the Torah teachings, he uncovers the Divine nature of the world. Then the concealment is but a garment for

God's presence, and the Holy Name of God then rests upon the individual.

When the whole Jewish nation helps reveal God's kingdom, He is then called "the God of Israel." The Jews are then but a garment for God's presence, and they are powerfully tied to His essence and vitality. This connection protects them and is their "tent of peace." (In Hebrew, the word for tent, *ohel*, has the same letters as God's name, *Eloha*.)

Peace is the manifestation of God's kingdom in the world. War comes from divisiveness, contradictions and opposition, quarrels and differences. These qualities are born from the material sphere of illusion. The true essence of the world lies in its unity in God. God is one, and He brings peace.

The *sukkah*, too, is the garment that the Jewish nation "wear" after their hard labor throughout Rosh Hashanah and Yom Kippur. They worked strenuously to reveal God's name in the world. They have connected strongly to the Divine roots and now have peace. When we sit in the *sukkah*, we all realize how rooted we are in the Master of the World; we are one and, therefore, we have peace.

"And they journeyed from Raamses and camped in *sukkos*" (Numbers 37:6).

In Raamses they were slaves. Their only master was Pharaoh, a being of flesh and blood; their only credo was limitation. However, in the *sukkos* the opposite was true. Their master was now God, the creator of heaven and earth; their credo was liberation.

But how is it possible to change so quickly from a slave mentality to a constant Divine consciousness of free choice? In natural circumstances it is hardly possible. But this transformation was a miracle. The infinite or Divine aspect of the universe came into contact with the nation of Israel, making the transformation possible. Nevertheless, miraculous events are only temporary. We can no longer come to the liberated place of "Sukkos" without a great deal of hard work. Therefore, each year Sukkos is preceded by Rosh Hashanah and Yom Kippur, the Days of Awe that are the Jewish people's preparation to move out of bondage and the worship of the material world to freedom and worship of our Creator. Thus, the energy of Sukkos remains in our flesh-and-blood life.

"In *sukkos* you should live for seven days . . ." (Leviticus 23:42). The gateway of the infinite world is open to man. He enters the divine order of the universe, and all limitations vanish. Thus, this liberation from slavery brings great joy and renewal.

When an individual is a slave, he slowly loses his will. Each "free" area of his life is slowly enslaved by the master. Soon there is no area in which he exercises desire or will. However, in the *sukkah*, which is the house of God and the gate to freedom, there is a renewal of desire and yearning. The heart and mind are alive again and full of joy.

There is an inner order and an outer order. The latter is the world of appearance and material reality. This is the world we encounter with our senses; it is the world of illusion.

A more complete picture of the world is that "God's honor fills the universe" (Isaiah 6:3). Its true nature is Divine and infinite. Our experience with it, however, is finite and limited. Why? Because the world presents itself as finite, and we react accordingly.

In order to encounter the infinite that is the world, we must prepare ourselves. We must be proper vessels to relate to it. If we are not prepared, we are likely to miss such contact even if we happen to find it by chance.

We can compare this to a newborn baby. The babe has fingers, but they are yet too weak to grasp anything but the lightest objects. If he should happen to grasp something a bit heavy, he will very likely lose it. He lacks the vessels to contain it.

When the Jewish nation left Egypt, they had not yet formed the proper vessel to encounter God. Yet they did encounter Him when they crossed the Red Sea. During the crossing of the Red Sea, "even a maid saw more than the prophet Ezekiel" (*Mechiltah, Beshalach* 2). They had no firm grasp on this encounter, and they almost lost it.

Why is it so easy to lose spiritual gains? Because there is a spiritual balancing in the world. When illumination and enlightenment increase, so do the energies of concealment, confusion, and ignorance. There is an internal dynamic in the universe. On the one hand, life; on the other, death. On the one hand, growth; on the other, desolation—a desert.

This is symbolized by the Jewish nation leaving Egypt and journeying through the desert. The desert is not only empty of growth, but it is also full of such harmful animals as snakes and scorpions. When the vessels are being formed, one needs protection. Therefore, God hid the newly born nation inside the "protective clouds." These would protect them from both spiritual and physical opposition.

When vessels are being formed, there is a struggle. One must expend great energy to retain the encounter with the Divine. To contain within them the revelations of the Exodus and the Red Sea, the newly formed nation had a most difficult struggle. Moreover, on the physical level, they had to struggle with the Amalekites.

When a person struggles, his energy is not focused on his ultimate goal. He wastes the energy just to retain his position. If the struggle is won, then he can again refocus all his energy toward that final goal. Thus, before the Jews are in the *sukkah*, they are struggling. This is the great effort of Rosh Hashanah and Yom Kippur. Finally, when the struggle is over, they can walk directly to an encounter with God. This is the *sukkah*.

If one is willing to move away from comforts and smugness, go to the desert, seek God, and prepare vessels, then one can enter the House of God, the *sukkah*, and receive His protection. Therefore, when God will judge the world, at *Mashiach*'s (the anointed redeemer of the Jewish People) coming, the *sukkah* will be used. "And this will be the sin of the nations, that they will refuse to celebrate the holiday of Sukkos" (Zechariah 14:10). The nations will not leave their smugness and risk an encounter with God.

When we leave our house to walk into the *sukkah*, let us be prepared to risk—to struggle until our vessels are developed enough to receive the Divine nature of the universe and to live in the protection of God's house.

"So that your generations should know that I have made the Jewish people live in *sukkos* when I took them from Egypt" (Leviticus 23:43). There are two opinions concerning the word *sukkos*. One says the *sukkos* were clouds of glory, and one says they were actual *sukkos* (*Sukkah* 11b).

The clouds that protected the Jewish people in the desert were a clear indication of God's presence. They made it clear to the generation of the Exodus that God dwelled among them. When it is clear to us with unbending faith, then it is also reflected in the material world. When our faith weakens and we are confused by the illusions of our senses, the Divine presence also slips into obscurity and concealment. The protective clouds disappear, and only the frail, little *sukkah* is left. Still, God's spirit is ever present with us, and it is not removed one iota. Only the appearances have changed.

A prince started out on a journey. The king sent faithful guards to protect him from all harm, and they traveled at his side. One day the prince had an argument with them. The guards became enraged and refused to travel at the prince's side. Still, they did not dare disobey the king's wishes and so hid in the for-

est to continue to protect the prince until he reached his destination. The prince was sad when the guards left him. Still, when he noticed his horse and saddle with the king's seal, he remembered his father's promise to bring him home safely. He was consoled. He did not know how his father was doing it, but he trusted that his protection is constantly with him.

So, too, when we enter the *sukkah*, the tent of "faith," we remember the promise of our Father in Heaven to protect us always. He is always with us with His Divine presence and the "clouds of glory." Furthermore, when we look at the walls with pure faith, we know that they are not the "temporary" walls of illusion, but they are the permanent walls from the world of truth. They are not the finite walls of material, but the infinite ones of spirit.

"When God created the universe it was full of light with which one could see from one end of the world to the other" (*Genesis Rabbah* 1). The true nature of the world is Divine, and it has a quality of unity and oneness. The vessels, however, are material, fragmented, and opaque. We see only that which is in front of us: borders, limitations, and superficiality. Our senses encounter the vessels, and that is as far as we see.

When we recognize the impermanence of the material world, then the supernal light is able to shine through its opaqueness. We are then in touch with its divine nature. Our attitude toward the world as impermanent brings us closer to the permanent. Therefore, to the degree to which we connect ourselves to the impermanence and frailty of our physical *sukkah*, there will be the revelation of the heavenly *sukkah* of "clouds." The more we are aware of the illusory nature of the world, the stronger is our connection to the permanent and Divine nature of the world.

This also happened to Abraham. Because he left the illusory world of his father's idol worship, he was told by God to go to "the land I will show you" (Genesis 12:11). When we turn our backs on ignorance, we are able to see the promised land. Our eyes become vessels for the Divine Light that shines from one corner of the universe to the other. We are told by the Kabbalists that the word *sukkah* means to see, or *soche*. As we turn our backs on the illusion of permanence, which our homes represent, and run to the *sukkah*, our eyes open. We can then "see" our life and that of the universe from one end to the other.

When God liberated the Jewish people from Egypt, He wished to elevate them spiritually. He devised a path for them that is above the natural world in order that they should be connected to the miraculous and Divine aspect of the universe. As it is written, "And God did not lead them through the land (*derech eretz*) . . ." (Exodus 13:17). *Derech eretz* also means the way of the land, the natural, material, and illusory world.

The Zohar relates that had they been worthy the Jewish people would still have the Holy Temple. They sinned; therefore, they lost that level of holiness. But through repentance, we can return to that abandoned path. After Yom Kippur, the day we return to God with all our hearts, we are given a glimpse of the Holy Temple. Though we seem to be here within our physical boundaries and limitations, we are there in the Holy Temple. Those who have returned to God become vessels to "taste" the miraculous world. This is the *sukkah*.

When the *Mashiach* comes, God will remove the protective covering that shields us from the sun, and He will ask everyone to come into the *sukkah*. Those who have become accustomed to the comfort of the material world will not be able to tolerate the brilliant spiritual light. Only those who yearn for high levels of spirituality will be prepared to receive that unique illumination. Thus, in the *sukkah* it becomes clear that our return has been a complete one. We can then bask in the sunshine of Divine light and revelation.

The Jewish people are vessels to receive the Divine light and to relate to the miraculous aspect of the world. In Egypt they were enslaved and saturated with the illusory, transitory, and superficial nature of the world. In Egypt their universe became dense and opaque, limited, fragmented, and ordinary. Then God shone His light onto them, and they tasted the sweetness of the infinite world. They gathered their few belongings and set out to follow the Master of the Universe into the desert.

As Divine vessels, the Jewish people did not find their place in Egypt. Their place in the world was only with God and the miraculous. Therefore, after the Jews left Egypt, they went to live in *sukkos*, which were God's "place." Likewise, each year after Yom Kippur, we cleanse ourselves from the opaqueness of our relationship with this world. Then we go directly to the *sukkah*, God's "place," our place. There we find our home and our true nature.

The *sukkah* reminds us of the "clouds of protection" that surrounded the Jewish people. What was their merit? The Jewish people ran to God for their refuge. They put themselves completely in God's hands, and God received them completely.

Why were they able to do this? Because the slavery of Egypt was unbearably painful. At the first opportunity, they ran to God's refuge lest they fall back into the clutches of their oppressors.

This happens also on a spiritual level. We all are capable of choosing, and God grants us the freedom. There are times, however, when our choices are so painful that we would rather not have any choice. All we want is not to tread on the mistaken path. Then we ask God, ". . . and lead us in a straight path . . ." (Psalms 27:11). You lead us, God. We do not want to choose!

We can compare this to a man who was overweight and could not adhere to his diet. Finally, he developed complications and had a severe heart attack. The doctors were barely able to save his life. They warned him that, if he continued to eat excessively, he would die. He hovered between life and death for several weeks. Finally, he was out of danger, and he spoke to his doctor, "Please do something so that I will never have this condition. I don't ever want to feel this kind of pain and fear of death again." He chose not to have a choice rather than to face the consequences of a poor decision.

During Rosh Hashanah and Yom Kippur, we realize that our behavior is leading us to ignorance and death. We turn our hearts from the mistaken paths and proceed toward God's refuge. This is done out of fear of the pain that awaits us if we remain in our present condition. When Rosh Hashana and Yom Kippur have passed, we sense the purity of our hearts. We realize the great loving-kindness that God has granted us. He has taken us under His protection, changed our hearts, and drawn us near to Him. We forget about our pain and fear, and we run to His refuge with great love. This is the *sukkah*.

A father and a child strolled together among the rose bushes. After a time the child was not careful and walked into the thorns. The child cried bitterly while his father scolded him to be more careful. A little while later, the child again stumbled into the thorn bushes and burst into tears. This time he held up his hands to his father to lift and carry him lest he stumble and hurt himself again.

His father reached down and lifted his child. The boy snuggled into the warm embrace of his father. He felt the safety and comfort of his father's closeness. Suddenly, he forgot about the thorns lurking below among the rose bushes. His only thought was about how much his father loved him and how wonderful that felt.

When we are in the *sukkah*, we realize how secure

it is to be in God's refuge. Our minds is filled with the love God has for us; our fear of our painful mistakes recedes to the background. We are home.

Sukkos following Yom Kippur

And God said to Moses,

> On the tenth day of this seventh month is the day of atonement; it shall be for you a time of holy convocation, and you shall afflict yourselves and present an offering by fire to God. And you shall do no work on this day, for it is a day of atonement, to make atonement for you before God your Lord. For whoever is not afflicted on this day shall be cut off from his people. And whoever does any work on this day, that person I will destroy from among his people. You shall do no work: it is a statute forever throughout your generations in all your dwellings. It shall be to you a sabbath of solemn rest, and you shall afflict yourselves on the ninth day of the month beginning at evening, from evening to evening shall you keep your sabbath.
> And God said to Moses,
> Say to the people of Israel, On the fifteenth day of this seventh month and for seven days is the feast of booths to God. (Leviticus 23:26–35)

God promised, ". . . not one will be cast away" (Samuel 14:14). Not one Jewish soul will be cast away from returning to God. Rather, each one will have the opportunity to cast off his evil ways and to return to the refuge of God. Not only does God allow you to return but He also opens His "hand" wide and helps in every way. "Open up for me in your hearts a tiny opening, the size of a needle's eye, and I will widen it as the gates of a palace" (*Song of Songs Rabbah* 5:3).

We are glad that God allows us to return, yet it does not seem "just" to extend such help and kindness to sinners. "Where is justice?," the evildoers ask.

The answer is that justice decrees that everyone receives what he deserves. There are many who have purity, holiness, and goodness, yet are unable to make those qualities real because of overpowering circumstances. God in His great mercy smooths the difficulties, and the purity, holiness, and goodness are transformed into reality. Then justice says, "This person truly deserved kindness. Look how beautifully he did."

We can compare this to a king who had summoned his subjects to the palace for a great feast. It was a three-day journey to the palace. On the second day, there was a severe rainstorm. The waters loosened huge stones from the mountainside and uprooted trees. The floodwaters formed the stones, trees, and mud into a thick wall that blocked the path

to the palace. When the king's servants reached the wall, they became confused and discouraged. The wall was impregnable; it hardly seemed possible to cross over it. Many of them turned back dejectedly and went home. But others refused to surrender. They began to pull bits and pieces from the wall with their bare hands. Hearing of their loyalty, the king quickly sent soldiers with equipment and dismantled the wall. The servants arrived at the palace and thanked the king for his kindness. Their hearts were filled with joy and gladness as they sat down for the great feast. When the others who had turned back heard of this, they complained, "Why did you help them come to the palace?" they grumbled. "They didn't deserve it more than we! It isn't just!" The king answered, "When I took away the obstacles, I didn't do it for them! I only wanted to see who was really on the way to the palace and who was really on his way home!"

Those who arrived at the palace were on their way to the palace.

The *sukkah* is the dwelling place of God, for it is written, ". . . and I will dwell with the humble . . ." (Isaiah 57:15). Those who humbled themselves during the Days of Atonement are treated with justice. God removes the obstacles, and it becomes clear where they were heading.

"Everyone that is proud in heart is an abomination to the Lord" (Proverbs 16:5).

God is the Master of the world, and no one has an independent power outside Him. Yet there are some people who are arrogant enough to claim power in this world. They claim that there is a place in this world that is empty of God's power. What are these arrogant people doing? They are creating a place empty of God, which is impossible to do, and it is therefore nonexistent. It is these, the arrogant ones, who have no true place in this world.

When an arrogant person returns to God, he relinquishes his claim to the place from which he had banished God. Thereby, he regains a place to exist in this world. Moreover, God gives this place to him with infinite loving-kindness.

A servant of the king rebelled and fled to the mountains. There he attracted a band of outlaws and established his headquarters. The king's servants were no longer safe in the mountains where the rebels roamed. The king, however, did not relinquish his control of the region and dispatched troops to reassert his dominion. After a time the rebels were overtaken and banished. Somewhat later, some of the rebels regretted their deeds and humbled themselves before the king. The king realized their sincerity, pardoned them, and granted them a place within his palace. While in the mountains, they had been confined and had no right to rule. Now, in the palace, they had royal power and influence.

Sukkah is the infinite space for the arrogant ones who have humbled themselves on Yom Kippur. The *sukkah* is the palace of God, and we enter it with great humility so that it can be filled entirely with God's presence.

"God wanted to create the world with judgment but saw that the world could not exist. He therefore combined it with loving-kindness" (*Genesis Rabbah* 1:1).

To receive sustenance with judgment, one must be perfect; however, this world cannot be perfect because it is created. Each created thing is in need of its creator, and it is lacking and imperfect. It therefore must have loving-kindness and mercy in order to exist.

At times we are arrogant and insist that we are perfect enough to exist even in stern judgment. Obviously we are mistaken and in danger of being cut off from life because no creature is perfect and deserving according to the infinite judgment of God. If we accept even God's stern judgment, we are then totally humbled and realize our true plight as His creatures. Then we are worthy of receiving God's mercy and live through the power of His kindness. Not only by virtue of mercy are we worthy but we are also worthy according to the concepts of strict judgment.

A king had issued laws for the administration of his kingdom. There was one servant who thought the king's judgment mistaken and his laws unfair. He argued against the law in public, and this action came to the attention of the king. The king sent a stern message that the servant cease from his rebellious activity, but that servant persisted. The king summoned him to judgment and said, "Because you do not accept the laws governing my kingdom, you have forfeited your rights to stay here. You will be banished at once!"

The servant was banished and after a time felt remorse. He sent the king a letter that he wished to see him. The king accepted. During the audience, the servant said, "I realize now that your laws are just, and I am willing to accept even the law dealing with rebels like me!" When the king heard the sincere humbled words of his servant, he said, "The law for a truly humbled person like you is to receive the kindness of his master. Therefore, not only can you return to the kingdom, but you will live in my palace and be my advisor."

When we accept the stern judgment of Yom Kippur, we are worthy of kindness. We enter the *sukkah*, God's palace, the Divine refuge, and we enjoy the peace and loving-kindness that surround us.

When the world was created, "God said, 'Let there be light,' and there was light" (Genesis 1:3). Likewise, with each and every item of existence, God said, "Let there be . . ." and there was. These pronouncements are the will of God becoming manifest as material reality. The word of God is that which keeps each item of the creation continually existing without cessation. "With the word of God the heaven was made; and with the breath of His mouth, all its hosts" (Psalms 33:6).

The words of God, however, are hidden within the material world. They are concealed to the senses and to our usual relationship with material things. Only through faith in the Master who constantly "breathes" Life into His world do His words become manifest. Our faith in God we express verbally, and this is prayer. Then our word reaches within and uncovers God's word in the material world.

When we arrogantly claim mastery to manipulate the world, we divorce ourselves from the word of God. With an arrogant attitude we also lack faith and we speak empty prayers. When we humble ourselves, we can again relate to the primeval words of creation and "recite" our faith.

Therefore, our humility caused by the Yom Kippur fast brings us to faith and prayer. We pray all day long, ceaselessly bringing our word in contact with the word of God.

Deeper still, the word of God is in each one of us. Did not God say, "Let us make man in our image" (Genesis 1:26)? This "word" is concealed within our material body and sense experiences. But in suffering and pain, we become humbled, and the word of God within us shines forth. The luminescence within us comes in contact with the light within the Creation, and suddenly we are praying. We are redeemed from the exile of concealment.

The pain of our Yom Kippur fast redeems us and brings us to the word of God. This is the *sukkah*. The *sukkah* is a space containing the word of God, and we are enveloped within it. We have arrived.

Sukkos is the time to gather the grain from the field and pile it in storage. First the unwanted portion is removed and cast away. This is the chaff. Then the grain is separated, the best part is taken as food, and the rest is used for animal feed.

This sifting takes place on Rosh Hashanah and Yom Kippur, as we learn, "Three books are opened on Rosh Hashanah; the purely righteous are written and sealed for a good life, the purely evil ones are written and sealed for death; and those in between are pending till Yom Kippur; if they return they receive life" (*Rosh Hashanah* 16b).

After sifting, the grain is taken home. We enter the *sukkah* with resolve and purity. It is a clear sign where we stand in our commitment to God.

———————

The Jewish people left Egypt and shortly afterward stood at Mount Sinai. There they received the highest revelation and teaching of all time. Shortly thereafter, they demanded to have an idol to guide them. Aaron assisted them by collecting gold jewelry and melting it to form a Golden Calf. Aaron repented after his participation in making the Golden Calf even though he had noble intentions. Later, Aaron was chosen to work in the Holy Tabernacle, the *Mishkan*, and he was the only person allowed to enter the Holy of Holies once a year.

What makes Aaron worthy of having such a close encounter with God?

We can compare this to a servant of the king who rebelled against him. His disobedience took place before the entire royal court. The king banished him into exile. Some time later the servant humbled himself and realized his great error, but he was too embarrassed to go directly into the palace because of his infamy. So one night he hid in back of the palace and tapped on the window of the throne room. The king turned and saw his former servant. He opened the window and listened to him beg forgiveness and express a complete humbling before the royal presence. The king told him to dig a secret passageway near the back wall leading into the king's private chamber. This was done, and the former rebel met intimately with the king. The king said, "You can't come in through the front gates because of the opposition. I must therefore take you in through a different path, but then we can even be alone and have a closer encounter."

The righteous walk through the front door of the palace and have an encounter with God. The repentants, *baalei teshuvah*, must dig their way into the palace in secret and unused paths. This path leads to the Holy of Holies, an intimate encounter with God. This was Aaron's entrance into the Holy of Holies on Yom Kippur. Even if Moses was on the highest level, still it was Aaron who came through the secret passageway and was able to come into that most holiest of places.

After the repentance of Yom Kippur, the Jewish people too are ready to come into God's palace and have an intimate encounter with him. This is the *sukkah*. The *sukkah* may be rickety and not palatial in appearance. It may even look like the back of the palace, but it is precisely where one can be close to God. Let us enter with humility and joy in order to be worthy of such closeness.

———————

God is the Master of the world. Yet this mastery is not manifest, but concealed within the creation. The natural world of causes and effects may appear as a world without a master. It is therefore called the world of untruth and illusion.

When the truth is manifest, so is the kingdom of God. Then it becomes clear that the world is His creation, and He is the root of all power. Each and every item of Creation, from the highest to the very lowest, is dependent on God. This faith is represented by God's Throne of Honor. When we realize the truth of the Creation, it is as if we saw the very throne of God manifest on this earth.

The Throne of Honor represents also the highest and deepest ideas concerning the Creator. It is a place in spiritual awareness that few people can reach. Yet one who returns, a *baal teshuvah*, reaches the Throne of Honor (*Yoma* 17b). Why is this so?

Once again we can compare this to a king whose servant was rebellious. When the king would talk about his dominion and how he ruled over all the citizens, the servant would chuckle. He would insist that the king could not possibly rule over everyone.

One day the servant ran away from the palace. In the city he removed his royal garments and became a thief. His acts of thievery became bolder and more daring. Soon he committed his first murder and continued to terrorize the citizens.

The king dispatched a large group of soldiers to capture him. They caught him and brought him to the palace. The king sent everyone out of the room, and said to him, "You see now how I rule over even the lowliest . . . like you!"

When the sinner turns to God, he realizes that even a lowly creature like himself is ruled by God. This conviction is like seeing the Throne of Honor. It also raises the *baal teshuvah* to the Throne of Honor. The *baal teshuvah* ironically becomes the link to God's presence, a link from the highest to the lowest; therefore, the *baal teshuvah* is catapulted from the lowest to the highest.

He who reaches out to touch God's "throne" also

brings it down to earth. He who proclaims anew that God's power prevails to the lowest makes manifest God's kingdom on earth. Thus, after the repentance of Yom Kippur, the name of God becomes manifest. This is the *sukkah*. *Sukkah* is God's "throne," which we have reached by repentance. When we, as *baal teshuvah*, enter the *sukkah*, we proclaim God's kingdom from the highest to the lowest.

"As an apple tree among the trees of the forest, so is my beloved . . . to sit in its shadow was my yearning and I did stay" (Song of Songs 2:3). The Midrash comments, "The apple tree has very little shade and people avoid sitting under it. But the Jewish people persisted and sat under its shade" (*Song of Songs Rabbah* 2:3).

The kingdom of God, which brings tranquility and peace, is concealed in this world. One must have faith to believe that it is there and be consoled by its strength.

We can compare this to a king who was exiled from his own land and then traveled around the country. Some of his faithful servants went with him and served him as always. People criticized the "foolish" servants for following a king who no longer had any power. The servants answered, "Perhaps it seems to you that the king is powerless. But wait! You will see that he still rules this land!" Some time later, the king returned to the capital with a powerful army, recaptured the palace, and ruled the land once more.

Similarly, when God's kingdom is concealed, the chosenness of the Jewish people is also concealed. Therefore, on Rosh Hashanah when judgment is meted out to every human being, the Jewish people are concealed. They are concealed within the judgment of the whole world, and it is called "in the hiddenness" (Psalms 81:4). After Yom Kippur, however, the righteousness of the Jewish people becomes clear, and they are vindicated. The King too returns to His palace. Again, it is manifest that He is the ruler, and one can find protection in His "shade." This is the shade of the *sukkah*.

When we sit in the *sukkah*, we have to realize how fortunate we are for being able to see its shade while the nations of the world cannot.

Man cannot live without God, even for an instant. When he realizes this, a great yearning awakens in his heart. He yearns to have a meaningful encoun-ter with God and to possess illumination, wisdom, and holiness. He realizes that without this he is but a broken vessel, empty and constantly in need of fulfillment.

Often, however, man is content with the fulfillment of his physical needs, and he has no concern with spiritual enlightenment. Certain aspects of his life become obstacles to reaching out for God. But should those obstacles be removed, he would realize how much he needs God and how much he wants Him. This is done by creating a deficiency in his life to make him feel his creatureliness and brokenness.

Therefore, on Yom Kippur by denying our physical needs, we are humbled before our Creator. When we feel the emptiness of our lives, we yearn for the fullness of a life with God. This yearning is a pain that prepares us to receive blessings and goodness.

We can compare this to a servant who rebelled against the king and left the palace. He went to live on a beautiful nearby mountain. The king sent his soldiers to fill up the wells of the servant with sand. The servant was thirsty and went to draw some water. Instead he pulled up only sand. He was upset and yearned for his good life in the palace. After suffering for some time, he decided to return. He was brought to the king in chains. The king said to him, "Why didn't you draw your water from elsewhere?!" The servant answered, "When I had no water, I suffered. I thought of the delicious spring water in the royal garden. This made me realize that my place and home are really here with you in the palace."

Our deficiency is in three dimensions: space, time, and life. The yearning for a spiritual space is the holy land of Israel; spiritual time is the World to Come; and spiritual life is the Torah, the path of life.

These three dimensions are represented by the *sukkah*. The *sukkah* is holy space; it contains peace and is therefore "a time for peace" (Ecclesiastes 3:8) that is from the World to Come. It is also a vessel for life since we enter it after being granted life on Yom Kippur.

When our yearning is awakened on Yom Kippur by the pain of denial, we are ready to enter the *sukkah*. In the *sukkah* we arrive at the fulfillment of our deepest needs and desires.

The essence of each creature is rooted in Divine existence. When this fact is revealed by our deeds, then God's indwelling occurs. God's kingdom is at hand. When it is concealed, there is exile. The divine and holy sparks that reside in every particle of creation are as if wasted. There is an emptiness, a gap, and yearning for fulfillment. He whose deeds reveal the holy sparks also consequently prepares himself as a vessel to receive God's kingdom.

The era in which God's kingdom will be totally revealed is called *Olam Habah*, the World to Come. Those who have prepared "garments" in their lifetime will be allowed to experience the World to Come.

Still, not only the righteous do good deeds. What happens to the garments and vessels created by evildoers? This energy is transferred to the righteous who are committed to the revelation of God's kingdom and the redemption of those holy sparks. As it is written, "And I have separated you from the nations . . ." (Leviticus 20:36). This means that God has separated you to reveal His name; however, from where does your energy come? "From the nations. . . ." You receive the energy from the occasional good deeds of the nations. This is the reason for the offerings during Sukkos for all the nations of the world. The "turning" of Yom Kippur puts us in a position to gather the holy sparks from the nations.

This was also the hiddenness of Rosh Hashanah. The kingdom of God was in a state of hiddenness, and now it is being revealed. All, who pray, shout out, "The King!" This is followed by Yom Kippur when we prepare vessels for this kingdom.

The Zohar tells us that a *baal teshuvah* who returns to God restores all his "tattered garments," and they become vessels for Divine revelation. Therefore, the *sukkah* is a vessel restored, for it is created from the sins of the penitent.

A servant rebelled against the king and abandoned the palace. He gathered rebels, made a flag, and proceeded to march on the palace. On the way he suddenly felt remorse and changed his mind. He returned to the palace to beg forgiveness. He took the flag and had it sewn into a suit to appear before the king. When the king saw his humility, he pardoned him and accepted him back into his retinue. Similarly, the former sins of the *baal teshuvah* become his garments with which to appear before the king.

It is written, "Praised is he whose sins have been uplifted and whose transgressions are covered" (Psalms 32:1). Covered means wearing a garment. A garment was made out of his transgressions. Likewise, the roof covering of a *sukkah* must be made of the undesirable portion of the grapevine and grain. This teaches us that our *sukkah* is created from our undesirable actions, the sins and transgressions for which we have repented on Yom Kippur.

When we sit in the *sukkah*, we can become connected to its highly charged energies. Our sins were brought about by arrogance, evil yearning, jealousy, stubbornness, rebellion, anger, cynicism, lying, and cheating. Now that we have returned to God, all those energies and strong emotions are transformed and channeled into the holiness of the *sukkah*, the service of God, and into the revelation of His Kingdom.

"And you should rejoice during your holiday, and you will be only joyful" (Deuteronomy 16:14).

What is not joy? We all know the answer. When we are in need, there is no joy. When our yearnings are unfulfilled, our desires unaccomplished, then too we have no joy. Joy is when our essence and soul are where they should be. This is when our present self and who we want to be are united as one.

The truth about our present self is that we are creatures created by the Master of the World. In the ultimate sense, we have no power independent of the Master. Therefore, when we desire independent power, we forfeit our creatureliness. On the other hand, when we desire our creatureliness, then we are wholesome. That wholesomeness brings joy.

There are varying degrees of realizing our creatureliness. On a simple level, we come to realize our physical limitations and frailties. We see plainly that our bodies are prone to illness and breakdown and that our life is balanced on a delicate thread. We know that despite our "great" accomplishments, we are but a small step away from death and oblivion. We are grateful to the Master of the World for keeping us alive and sustaining us in our everyday struggles.

There are times, however, when our contemplation takes us to the farthest corners of the universe. Our minds ignore all boundaries and dare to realize the greatness and awesomeness of God's existence. We realize that the furthest expanse of space down to the tiniest particle in the atom is filled with God's glory. We comprehend that He has made, is making, and will make everything that there ever will be. Then our soul is filled with awe, and our total insignificance fills us with sheer terror. We shrink from our arrogant haughtiness to our true size before God's awesome power. There is nothing we can do; we have no independent power; we are totally in the hands of God. Then the idea of our creatureliness resounds in us with devastating clarity, and our hearts are full of joy.

On Rosh Hashanah and Yom Kippur, the Days of Awe, we realize our insignificance as we stand in judgment before God. Our powerlessness becomes clear to us, and we acknowledge our sheer and utter creatureliness. Then we enter the *sukkah*, God's refuge, in great joy, and we rejoice with our Creator, the Master of the World.

"Jacob gathered himself and his children, and this saved him from the intrigues of his brother Esau" (*Genesis Rabbah* 32:8). Similarly, the *sukkah* is a refuge from the intrigues of our prosecutors of Rosh Hashanah and Yom Kippur (*P'siktah* 28b). Therefore, it is called "the holiday of gathering" (Exodus 34:22). Even the *lulav*, the tallest of the four plant species around which the others are gathered, is symbolic of Joseph, "the righteous one." In Joseph's dream he saw, "And behold we were gathering sheaves in the field, and mine stood up and all of you gathered around . . ." (Genesis 37:7). So too is the *tzaddik*, the righteous one, who leads those around him in the proper direction toward God's refuge.

We read in the Sabbath evening prayer, "He spreads over us a *sukkah* of peace." The *sukkah* is God's refuge. It brings us back to fulfillment, wholesomeness, harmony, and peace, all of which are found in God. God is the fountainhead of all the good that exists in the world. He also placed in each of us a drop from that holy fountain. Though only a mere drop, it is still infinite as the fountain itself. This holy drop that is inside each of us never becomes dirty or soiled. No matter what we do, it remains in its infinite purity.

What happens when man errs or sins? He blocks the holiness of his soul from purifying all his parts.

We can compare this to a king who had a garden. The gardener, his servant, rebelled and blocked the waters from reaching the outermost plants. Then he became more angry, and he blocked the waters closer to the fountainhead. Soon the waters stopped flowing altogether. Slowly the plants and trees withered, and hardly any life was left in them. The king passed the garden and saw the woeful sight. He thought, "If I start from the outer edges, I might be too late to save the entire garden." Instead, he went directly to the fountainhead, cleared the debris, and the water flowed freely again. It filled the channels and canals, and it fed the garden. Soon the withering plants began to regain their strength and to bloom again.

Similarly, when we go astray and do sinful acts, we block the life-giving waters from our spiritual wellsprings. The outer edges of our being dry up and wither. If we continue on the path of falsehood, we block the waters at our very roots, and we totally wither away.

Then God sees our sorrowful state and helps us experience an encounter with Him. The intensity of this closeness breaks through all barriers and clears all the debris strewn in the path of the "spring of life." We are then alive once more. We have returned to God and to His refuge. This occurs in the days of Rosh Hashana and Yom Kippur. As it is written, "Peace to those who are far, and those who are near" (Isaiah 57:19). Thus, peace is experienced when the soul revitalizes our physical being.

The arrogant evildoers do not allow their debris to be cleared, and they remain cut off from their source of life. As it is written, "And the evildoers are as the tumultuous sea" (Isaiah 57:20). They cannot experience tranquility and peace.

Therefore, after God opens our wellsprings on Yom Kippur, we are reconnected to our roots and source of life. We go directly into the "*sukkah* of peace." When we sit in the *sukkah*, we can open our hearts to the spring of life that bubbles forth from us. We can revitalize every cell in our body, every utterance of our speech, and every concept and image of our thoughts. In the *sukkah*, we can experience harmony and peace coming from the infinite roots of our Creator.

"When I sit in darkness, God is a light for me" (Micah 7:8). "Happy is a nation who knows the sound of the trumpet, *t'ruah* [*t'ruah* also means brokenness, bitter crying], God, they go with the light of your countenance" (Psalms 89:16).

What is the experience of light and darkness for us? We experience light when our eyes respond to a source emitting light energy. We experience darkness when no energy is being emitted or when we do not have functioning organs for receiving the light. Our eyes are receptors for certain wavelengths of light energy, but they are not proper receptors for ultraviolet and infrared light. However, we can assist our eyes by using instruments that are sensitive to those extremes of light. Even if no other light is available and it is apparently dark, the instrument "sees" everything; and it is "light."

God fills the universe with light, but we are only creatures of flesh and blood and can receive only a limited amount of this light. For the portion of light for which we have no receptors, it might as well be dark. We simply have no way of experiencing it. It is dark for us, but in truth the light is at its greatest intensity. Therefore, "when I sit in darkness," one knows that, "God is a light for me." His intense light must be there since the individual does not have proper receptors to experience it.

It can then be said that the light is hidden in the darkness. We see an instance of this in Abraham whose virtue was loving-kindness. His virtue was hidden inside his son, Isaac, who had the virtue of stern judgment, seemingly the opposite of his father. Isaac subsequently gave birth to Jacob who had the virtue of mercy and judgment. The light of Abraham, which is finally revealed in Jacob's life, was always hidden in Isaac.

The loving-kindness of Sukkos is hidden in the Days of Awe of Rosh Hashana and Yom Kippur. Thus, it is written, "From distress I have called God, and He answered me in a large place" (Psalms 118:3). Although the Days of Awe seem full of judgment and tightness, when Sukkos arrives, we see the expanse that was concealed in them. Likewise, "Peace to those who are far, and to those who are near" (Isaiah 57:19). At first it seems that God is far, but then one realizes that this perception is actually caused by His closeness.

When we enter the *sukkah*, we experience the loving-kindness of God, which is too intense for our receptors. We gain strength for the whole year when the darkness seems so real to us. We then know that the darkness has hidden the most intense light of God.

"God wanted to create the world with stern judgment, but He saw that it would not stand. He, therefore, fortified it with loving-kindness" (*Genesis Rabbah* 1).

Whenever something is being created, the door of kindness opens anew. This happens when one turns to God in repentance and becomes as a totally new creature: the doors of kindness open wide.

Abraham crossed the river to be on the side of God while the others stayed behind with their idol worship. He then circumcised himself. This was a promise that not only he but also his children would stay with God, for it is written, "And he sat by the door of the tent . . ." (Genesis 18:1). This verse means that by turning entirely to God Abraham opened up the "door" of kindness, which became his seal and lifework.

When Aaron returned to God after the incident with the Golden Calf, he received the virtue of loving-kindness in great measure. He was now connected to that door, and he could open it for others. Thus, he became an angel of love and peace among his people. When we turn to God after Yom Kippur, we are ready to enter the door of the tent, the *sukkah*, a new house built with the virtue of loving-kindness.

The world is created once more, and each one has a new chance to obtain life.

In descending order, there are three spheres of creation: creating, forming, and doing. Corresponding to these spheres are the soul, spirit, and life of man that vitalize him. When man sins, he disrupts the order in the celestial and spiritual spheres. When man wants to restore the three spheres, he returns to God. He first returns in the sphere of doing, which are his actions; he straightens them to correspond with holiness. Then he corrects the sphere of forming, which is his speech. Finally, he needs to restore the sphere of creation. This sphere has the closest connection to the Creator, and it is the most difficult to reach. It can only be obtained by Divine mercy, for it is written, "Return to me, and I will return to you" (Zechariah 1:3). Therefore, when one returns to God with all his heart, then one is created anew. Moreover, the individual, who has just been created, is still connected to the energy of the Creator and is fitting to be in His refuge.

God's refuge is the *sukkah*. When we enter, we go as newly created beings who still taste the energy of the creative moment. We are able to open our eyes anew in order to see the glory of God and to praise His name.

"God has made man upright, yet they sought out many calculations" (Ecclesiastes 7:29).

When a person follows the Torah, he is directed toward God and has a singularity of purpose. Otherwise, he has a multiplicity of desires and flounders in aimlessness. These are the "many calculations" of the one who is astray and disconnected from Torah holiness. When we return to God on Yom Kippur, we again affirm our singularity of purpose and are made straight again. We know exactly where we are going, and we go directly to God's refuge.

The repentance that is valued most stems from joy rather than fear. During the Days of Awe, Rosh Hashanah and Yom Kippur, we are afraid for our very lives. The King, Master of the World, judges each and every human being. Who will live? Who will die? Being in doubt about our merit and worthiness, we fear God's judgment and return to Him immediately. God promises every penitent forgiveness.

Sukkos follows the Days of Awe. It is a holiday of

great rejoicing and happiness. We are no longer in fear for our lives, but we are confident that God has forgiven us with kindness and mercy. Our repentance is even deeper and more meaningful.

We can compare this to a servant of the king who rebelled and left the palace. During his absence, he committed crimes against the king and royal family. One day he read a decree, "All rebels are commanded to surrender within the next ten days or suffer great punishment." The servant knew that this decree would bring him death. He willfully but begrudgingly made his way to the palace. He surrendered to the king and begged forgiveness. The king was merciful to him and let him live, "You needn't worry. You are totally pardoned and are a free man. Do what you please!" Now the servant's heart truly softened, and he desired to remain with the merciful king. "Please let me stay," begged the servant. The king considered his request and said, "Now I know that you are my faithful servant once again. You are returning now without fear or worry."

We enter the *sukkah*, God's house, with joy and gladness. We would rather stay there than anywhere else in the world. This is the highest form of repentance.

There are two stages of repentance. The first is to abandon the ways of evil. The second is to focus our actions and walk the path of God. During the Days of Awe, our objective is to abandon our evil ways. On Sukkos we continue by entering the house of God and following the path of righteousness.

"It is the abomination of God those who are arrogantly proud" (Proverbs 16:9).

God's power fills the universe, and there is no place where His power is absent. When someone claims to have independent power, he denies God's omnipotence. The virtue that is true to fact is humility.

It is true that we are powerless, even lifeless, without God. The humble person therefore relinquishes his own space and leaves room for God. True humility means to stand in awe before God as a powerless creature. This humility is reached in the Days of Awe, Rosh Hashanah and Yom Kippur, when we stand before God in judgment. After these days, we enter the space relinquished to God: the *sukkah*. The *sukkah* is a space for people who take up no space.

When we sit in the *sukkah*, let us take up so little room that we leave much room for guests and especially for God. We are therefore taught: "All of Israel has room in one *sukkah*" (*Sukkah* 27b). Any why not? Not one of them takes up any room, but each one opens up a place for the indwelling of God and the creation of His refuge.

REFUGE OF FAITH

"Come and see, when a man sits in this dwelling, a tent of faith, the Divine Presence, *Shechinah*, spreads her wings over him from above, and Abraham and the other five righteous ones come to dwell with him" (Zohar, Leviticus 103).

"Whoever has a share in the holy nation sits in the tent of faith and greets the guests, to be full of joy in this world and the world to come" (Zohar).

"To be under the shelter of wisdom is as good as to be under the shelter of silver (*kesef*)" (Ecclesiastes 7:12).

The highest level, wisdom, is housed in one's head, and the lowest level, instinct, is manifest as the feet. One can be led by wisdom or plainly by one's feet—instinct without thought. The feet are constantly yearning to be enlightened by wisdom. In man it is his wisdom that guides the bodily organs and protects them from harm. The feet move the body from place to place and also out of harm's way.

Likewise, in the spiritual sphere, there are two refuges. There is one refuge that is born from God's wisdom. There is another one that is born from man's yearning to be with God. Man yearns to have wisdom in every part of his body, including his feet. Even his feet, so much removed from wisdom and understanding, should move toward God by yearning alone.

The feet do not "know" what they are doing, yet they follow the head by faith, almost as if by instinct. This is the *sukkah*, a protection of God emanating from His wisdom. It attracts even those on the "foot" level who are yearning and following by pure faith. Therefore, it is called "the shadow, the refuge of faith," for even those who are in it by faith find their home there.

"Many waters cannot quench love" (Song of Songs 8:7).

The love between God and the Jewish people is unquenchable and is constantly present. Still, when they sin, the love is then concealed. It is uncovered again with repentance during the Days of Awe.

The *sukkah* is the revelation of the love between God and the Jewish people. It is the refuge where each heart can find a home and protection. Even those who have sinned and returned are now included, for it is written, "Love covers all sins" (Proverbs 10:12).

A king had married a princess. One day she became disenchanted with him and left the palace. After some time she wanted to return, but was afraid of the king's anger. She heard a rumor that unless she returned she would be punished severely. She started back, but was interrupted by a raging storm. She braved the winds and fought on, saying, "What does it matter? Either way I will die!" Finally, she stood at the palace door. The king was at the window watching to see if she was coming. She looked up and saw him. Her heart opened to him, and she was filled with her previous love. The king also remembered that he had loved her all along, and he forgave her, saying, "The distance between us has brought us closer than ever."

When we sit in the *sukkah* with love of God, it is then a refuge, a protection and cover, that hides our former sinful ways.

"And God said, 'Let there be light,' and there was light" (Genesis 1:3). What happened to this original light? It was hidden for the righteous (*Genesis Rabbah* 1:3).

When God formed and created man, he was barely above the other animals. His distinction lay in his being created in God's image. Man himself can create. He is aware of his own being and that of the universe and of God. This is surely a Godly trait. It gives him the ability to create language and communicate his awareness. "And man was a living being" (Genesis 2:7)—he had the ability of speech. This is the hallmark of man's being.

Man is the pivotal point between the infinity of God's existence and the finiteness of the created world. Man touches both spheres. On the one hand, he is a creature, and on the other hand he is a creator. He can see no more than an ordinary animal, yet he can see God in the world and "call in the name of God" (Genesis 4:26).

Which light shines infinitely from one end of the world to the other? It is the name of God, a revelation that the infinite power of God is there in all its glory. When could man see with this light? The answer is when he is in God's image. Therefore, the light had to be concealed because man was not worthy and had refused to call in the name of God.

Abraham came and the creation was renewed. It is written, "And He called them man when they were created *behibera'am*)" (Genesis 5:2). One can read it not as *behibera'am* but as *beAbraham*, which means "with Abraham." The world was created anew with Abraham. How? Abraham assumed the pivotal role that man was to occupy within the structure of creation, the role of creating and re-creating the universe. He therefore saw with the supernal light from one end of the world to the other. "He called in the name of God"—he showed people how God's glory is revealed in each and every item of the creation.

"God separated between the light and the darkness" (Genesis 1:4). He "separated"—some light will be unseen and will have the illusion of darkness. Likewise, when we call in the name of God, we separate ourselves as did Abraham. He too crossed the river in order to separate from the idol worshipers and to proclaim God's glory.

The *sukkah* is the resting place of God's name; it is a microcosm of the world. Although it is limited in space and time, it embodies the infinite quality of both. Moreover, in it we are "man" again, and we assume our role as those who proclaim God's kingdom. When we sit in the *sukkah*, we experience the ultimate refuge of God—here God is God, and man is man. It is therefore the root of all blessing for the year-round.

God watches over us constantly without interruption, yet this watchfulness is concealed. Only in times of unusual closeness is this attention revealed. One such time was during the travels of the Jewish nation in the desert from Egypt to the Promised Land, for God's care was clear to one and all.

The *sukkah* too is the tent and refuge of faith. We enter it with complete faith as our forefathers did in journeying through the desert. We leave our home and walk into a temporary dwelling to stay with God in complete faith and trust. Thus, we are surrounded by the clouds of glory in a refuge of God's watchfulness that is with us constantly.

Who is free, and who is a slave? One can depend on a free man because he has power. A slave, however, is not dependable and does not own anything. Everything belongs to his master, including his offspring.

Why is this so? Because a slave has relinquished his power to someone else, and he has cut his own actions from their roots. He is disconnected and dead. On the other hand, a free man brings forth his actions from his being. Whatever he does is still attached to his essence, for they are all part of him.

On a deeper level, we are all dependent on the infinite power of God. If we cut ourselves off from the source, our finiteness becomes quickly manifest, and we wither and die. When we are servants of God, we are free. When we cut ourselves off from Him, we becomes slaves.

How is this manifest on a practical level? Those who are arrogant are cut off from their Divine roots and are slaves. When the Jewish people attempt to break away from God, they become slaves unto slaves. They become enslaved to the arrogant nations of the world. They soon realize that they have exchanged their true freedom for a state of enslavement to the nations.

Aaron constantly worked to unite the Jewish people with God. When he was successful, the Jewish nation was free from foreign domination. Therefore, it was in the merit of Aaron that the clouds of glory surrounded and protected the Jews in the desert.

We can compare this to an accident in which a person's hand was severed at the wrist. It was now detached from its roots and would soon wither and die. Doctors frantically worked to reattach the hand sinew by sinew. Blood flowed again through the microscopic blood vessels. The hand was now "protected"; it was receiving life from the roots.

This was the work of Aaron. When we sit in the *sukkah* and the clouds of glory surround us, we experience our connection to God and our true freedom.

LEAVE YOUR PERMANENT DWELLING

"In booths you shall dwell for seven days." (Leviticus 23:42).

"The Torah has stated, leave your permanent dwelling place and dwell in the impermanent dwelling" (*Sukkah* 2a).

"The rabbis have stated: All the seven days one makes the *sukkah* the permanent dwelling place and his home as if temporary. How? If he has beautiful vessels, he brings them to the *sukkah* and beautiful spreads too; he eats, drinks and lounges in the *sukkah*.

"The rabbis have stated: 'You shall dwell . . .' (Leviticus 23:42), as you dwell all year in your home" (*Sukkah* 28a).

". . . and I will place walking ones among those who are standing" (Zechariah 3:7).

The angels are called standing beings. They experience God on such a high level that they stand in union with God. They are awed by His infinite majesty and stand absolutely still.

We can compare this to a person who journeys to reach his destination. While en route, he must keep moving, but when he arrives, he stops and is still. There is nowhere else to go.

This is true of angels who are on a high spiritual plane. Man, however, is different. He must constantly move about, climb to higher levels, and travel to accomplish his mission on earth. He climbs from level to level, consolidates his position, and then moves upward again. He gains experience, finds synthesis, and advances again. Man's way is to move, stop, and proceed until the end of his days.

When man has found God, no matter on what level that may be, he is then standing still. It is a very safe and secure position. But how will the kingdom of God become known? Man must move and proclaim God's name in the world. This is a risk, and it is not easy to take it. Man must have faith that he will not lose his present levels of attainment by moving again.

A king loved a princess and wanted to marry her. "If you want to marry me," said the king, "then you must go forth and proclaim me as the king." The princess was very upset. "How can I be sure that you will still want me when I return?," asked the princess. "Trust me," said the king, "and we'll be married when you return."

Abraham was climbing from level to level; he consolidated his position and then stood in awe of the Creator. Then God spoke to him and said, "Go forth from your country and your father's house to the land which I show you" (Genesis 12:11). Go and proclaim my kingdom to the world. This move required great faith, and Abraham went forth according to God's commandment.

How do we obtain this great faith? By standing in absolute awe before our Creator, realizing that we have neither existence nor power without Him. The Yom Kippur prayer reads that we are as "a shadow of a bird passing over the field, a withering flower, crumbling clay." We experience this feeling during the Days of Awe of Rosh Hashanah and Yom Kippur.

On Rosh Hashanah every cell in our body is judged. Our whole being is stilled under the scrutiny of the judgment of our Master. Everything is one; the universe, including our very being, is one. Thus the prayer "Hear O' Israel, God our Lord, God is One" symbolizes Rosh Hashanah. When we say "One," we are unable to move. Where is there to go? There is only one place and time. There are no differences or plurality—only "One." We are one with the One. There is nothing else! Therefore, we proclaim God as king on Rosh Hashanah, for His Kingdom is infinite and all encompassing.

On Yom Kippur, our souls are at their peak of yearning, and we are elevated to the level of angels. The angels sing, "Praised is the name of the honor of his kingdom for ever and ever" (*Yoma* 35b). Whoever recites the song means to say, "We are not independent; all we can say is that God's kingdom is for ever and ever." Therefore, we too recite this prayer on Yom Kippur. Like the angels, we also stand in awe of the great mercy and kindness showered on us by our Creator on Yom Kippur. Again we stand very still.

What have we gained at the end of the Days of Awe? Our sins are forgiven; we are as a newborn child. Our spiritual strength has been renewed. We are strong in our faith and yearn to follow the path of God. We are now ready to journey forth. "Go forth from your country. . . ." "Get out of your permanent dwelling and go into the temporary one" (*Sukkah* 2a). We go forth to proclaim God's name in the world, for it is written, "And you should love God with all your heart, all your soul, all possessions" (Deuteronomy 6:5). "You should make God beloved . . ." (*Yoma* 86a). This is the essence of the *sukkah*—our love for God, and God's love for us.

Walking out of the house on the way to the *sukkah*, we take a step with complete faith. There are no doubts in our minds; there is only the absolute and complete trust in God. For no matter where we go, He is with us in all His strength and glory.

———————

"For I am your passing guest, a sojourner, like all my fathers" (Psalms 39:13).

The existence of man on earth is on two levels. On the one hand, the essence of his being is infinite. On the other hand, he is a creature of flesh and blood who perishes in time and is no more. Nevertheless, that which perishes seems most real. The material world, composed of myriads of atoms and molecules, is destined to disintegrate. It is the only world we can know, but it eventually turns into a form that is unfamiliar and unrecognizable.

A clear example of this change is the death and decomposition of animals and human beings. When a human dies and decomposes, he is no longer recognizable. He becomes molecules of various elements that become part of the earth. If anyone would examine that bit of earth, he would hardly recognize the remains as human. Therefore, the reality of the world is more of an illusion than true to fact.

The other level of human existence, the Divine kernel, our soul, is eternal and infinite. It is the combination of both of these factors, the corporal and the spiritual, which is the total man. Thus, when we are in touch with our total being, we realize that we are a passing guest on the earth. Therefore, Abraham was told, "Go forth from your country . . ." (Genesis 12:11). It is a lesson he had to learn immediately. This earth is not as it appears. We are here but for a short time, and we must soon move from our place. The place we occupy is impermanent, and we must soon relinquish it. "Go forth" is the truth about our very being.

At times we go astray and lose ourselves in the world of illusion. We sink into a mistaken notion of the world and stagnate in the realm of dying and decomposing entities. Yet our eternal soul yearns for the permanent, and we seek and return to God. We leave our errors behind as a man who flees from fire. "Go forth" is our connection to our forefathers who totally understood the two levels of existence—to flee from the world of illusion and take refuge in God's permanent house.

We leave our illusory permanent house and go into the *sukkah*. "Go forth. . . ." We can hear God's command, and we follow enthusiastically.

———————

There is a controversy in the Talmud as to whether a *sukkah* should be an impermanent building or a permanent one (*Sukkah* 21b). Both of these opinions are correct, for the *sukkah*, which seems only impermanent, actually represents the true permanent nature of the world.

A king sent his servant on a special and crucial mission to another country. The nature of his mission did not allow the servant to set up a permanent residence. Rather, as he traveled across the land, he set up temporary resting places and then proceeded again. The king kept track of the servant's journeys, and he would come to visit him late at night. Other servants of the king thought themselves to be more fortunate to have permanent headquarters. They felt sorry for their friend who had to roam the countryside without a permanent home. They were mistaken. It was that servant who was the closest to the king and the royal secrets of the kingdom. His work was to safeguard the permanence of the kingdom throughout the land.

This parallels our leaving of our homes and our entering into our *sukkah*. We pitch a temporary tent to proclaim God's name. It is therefore the most permanent dwelling anyone can have, for it assures the revelation of God's kingdom on this earth.

———————

The Talmud concludes that the *sukkah* need not be a permanent dwelling (*Sukkah* 21b). The *sukkah* is the shadow and refuge of God. In it we have an encounter with God on the level of the World to Come. Such an encounter with God is not for the masses, but for the *tzaddikim*, the righteous, who walk constantly with God. Everyone else is yearning and striving to be with God, yet does not attain it. This yearning, however, is valued by God as the whole of the World to Come.

Therefore, the *sukkah*, which can hold all of the Jewish people, is impermanent. Let us leave our permanent way of being with God. Then we can yearn for a level of total closeness, the World to Come. Although we cannot maintain this way permanently, at least we can experience it temporarily.

10

The Four Plant Species

And you shall take on the first day the fruit of a beautiful tree, branches of palm trees, and boughs of leafy trees, and willows of the brook, and you shall rejoice before God your Lord seven days. (Leviticus 23:40)

ukkos is the time when God draws nearer to the Jewish people with great love. Similarly, we draw closer to Him. We experience the abundant shower of blessing and love that comes to us from heaven, and we are inspired to move toward God.

Sukkos is the last of the holidays of the year. Each one of them adds a dimension to the revelation of God's kingdom. This is the ultimate knowledge. Sukkos brings this knowledge to completion and helps us maintain it for the entire year. Therefore, it is written, "So that your generations should know that I have placed the Jewish people in *sukkos* . . ." (Leviticus 23:43). Sukkos is the holiday of knowing, and it is a blessing bestowed on us by God. We prepare to receive God's blessing to the depths of our heart. Moreover, it also is written, ". . . take unto yourselves . . ." (Leviticus 23:40)—take the blessings until you are full.

The Midrash compares this to a king who invited some of his servants to his private dining room. They never before had this privilege and were reluctant to eat. The king said, "Would I invite you if I didn't want you to eat?" Similarly, God is saying to us, "Take! When I am giving in abundance, take unto yourselves."

The beautiful fruit is the *esrog*, a citron, which symbolizes the heart. We should fill our hearts with the knowledge of God in order that it should remain with us for the entire year.

This is actually possible for us after Yom Kippur. We have purified our hearts and prepared them for

God's blessing. Now we are ready to be united with all of Israel; it is this union that makes our purified hearts better vessels to receive God's blessing.

This union is symbolized by the four plant species. The lowest is the willow of the stream, for it has neither taste nor smell. It symbolizes Jews who have neither good deeds nor Torah. However, even they, because they join together with the rest of the nation, receive the blessing from God.

The world has two aspects. One is the reality of our senses. This is the material or "real" world. The other is the Divine aspect of the world, which we have no vessels to perceive.

The Torah teaches us a path, a way of life, that is true to the actual nature of the world. God's kingdom, honor, and glory are contained within the illusion of material reality: they are the "holy sparks" trapped in exile. *Mitzvos*, the Torah way of action, reveal the Divine aspect of the world, and they release these holy sparks.

This release occurs on two levels. Some *mitzvos* raise the holy sparks of the inner nature of things. Others reveal divinity even in ordinary physical nature.

We can compare this to a patient who was critically ill, and doctors had already given up all hope of his recovery. Finally, a great healer was found at the far corner of the earth, and he agreed to treat the patient. His method of treatment was to have the patient regain his interest in life, health, and strength. The healer spoke softly but firmly; his encouraging words sunk deeply into the patient's heart. Slowly, the patient moved from his despair and became encouraged. His resolve improved and he wanted to live; however, there was no improvement in his illness. When asked about the patient's condition, the healer said, "It will take some time until you will see an improvement in his body. But once the inside is working properly, the outside is sure to follow."

We can compare this to a servant who was invited to the palace by the king. The king was in a very charitable mood and said, "Ask and it will be granted to you!" The servant was truly humble and was thinking, "How fortunate I am to be in the king's palace." The presents were not meaningful to him.

Sukkah, too, is a *mitzvah* that affects the inner wisdom of our hearts, for it is written, "In *sukkos* I have made the Jewish nation dwell . . . so that your generations should know . . ." (Leviticus 23:43). The *mitzvah* of *sukkah* restores a pure "knowledge" deep in our hearts. Yet, Sukkos is a time when all of Israel gathers together in joy and happiness during the harvest. This ingathering was a group offering during the Temple period. When all of Israel is together, they have an energy and power to break through all obstacles and barriers.

Therefore, we gather in the *sukkah* and tie the four kinds of plants together. Every part of our body, every type of Jew from the lowest to the highest, restores the outside material world while God's wisdom sinks inside into the deepest part of us.

The *sukkah* is God's refuge and garden. It is the Garden of Eden and the World to Come. Nevertheless, the Jewish people are not satisfied with that, for they want to hold this holiness in their own hands. This is the *mitzvah* of the four plant species.

We can compare this to a servant who was on his way to the palace. Meanwhile, the king chose him as his advisor. The news traveled quickly, and the enemies of the king banded together and began to chase the servant. He ran for his life. Finally, he entered the gates of the palace and stopped to catch his breath in the king's garden. The king entered and offered delicious fruits to him. "If I can have anything," said the servant, "honor me in letting me hold your hand."

After Yom Kippur, the Jewish people emerge humble, pure, and holy. The arrogant people chase them, and they run to God's refuge, the *sukkah*. They are safe there and quite happy, yet they want more. They desire to hold onto the refuge itself and rejoice with God, their Creator. These are the four plant species that we hold dearly in our hands.

There is wisdom and good deeds—Torah and *mitzvos*. In plants there is flavor and fragrance. The *esrog* has both, and it symbolizes those who have both Torah and good deeds. Some people only have wisdom, and this is the *lulav*; others only have good deeds, which is the *hadas*. Still others have neither, and this is the willow, *aravah*.

The great yearning to follow God can only be evoked by the joining together of each and every one of us. Why? Because if only a select few belong with God, then it is "logical" for God to choose us. He chooses only those who are worthy. Yearning is beyond reason, and so is our chosenness. God chooses even those who are "not worthy." Therefore, in order to gain entry into God's refuge, we must humble ourselves totally and join even those whom we considered as the lowliest of our nation. In truth they are held in the same regard as the "more worthy" among us.

Thus, on *Shabbos* we need not take the *lulav*, the myrtle branches, including the other three species, because it is a day when all of Israel comes together. "The secret of *Shabbos* is," says the Zohar, "that all gather together in the secret of the one." All souls find their place together with all the others, and there is unity and peace.

The four kinds of plants represent the parts of the body. The myrtle leaves, or *hadas*, is the eyes; the willow leaves, or *aravah*, is the mouth; the citron, or *esrog*, is the heart; the date palm leaves, or *lulav*, is the spine. When we hold these four, we consecrate the energy of our entire body and direct it to God. Nevertheless, it is a very difficult feat to accomplish, but we have help. We have the help of the *mitzvah* itself.

Each *mitzvah* is a promise that the deed is possible. When God commands, "Honor thy father and mother," or "Thou shalt not steal," it is a Divine promise that these *mitzvos* will be in the realm of the possible. Although there will be obstacles posed by circumstance, in the end we will be able to perform them. Thus, the four plants of the *mitzvah* of *lulav* are a promise that one can focus one's entire bodily energy toward God, no matter what powerful forces act against it in this world.

Sukkos is a time of joy, for it is written, ". . . and you should rejoice in your holiday" (Deuteronomy 16:14). True joy is when the soul is at home, strongly rooted and feeding from the wellsprings of life. A person can experience this only if he humbles and subordinates himself totally to the rest of Israel, for the soul of the entire nation is surely connected to the wellsprings of Divine holiness. On his own level, each individual is fed from the foundation of life and wisdom, for it is written, "and you should take unto you" (Leviticus 23:40). Each one of you should take the holiness that suits your particular soul.

The Jewish people humble themselves and do not even take what is offered. They go to God Himself even if they have not vessels for it. As it is written, "The king had brought me to his private chambers, I will be glad and rejoice with you" (Song of Songs 1:4). Although the king has offered me the innermost chambers, the deepest levels of spirituality, still I will be happy only with Him. When we hold the *lulav, esrog, hadas,* and *aravah* together, we join all of Israel to seek only God; may it be our will always.

What is prayer? When we pray, we make manifest our faith and yearning. When we have nothing—neither wisdom nor deeds—we pray and yearn for God's help. Since there is prayer in the world, it is a witness that there is also God's help in the world!

The willow leaf has neither flavor nor fragrance, neither wisdom nor deeds. What then does it have—who needs it? It has the shape of a mouth; it is prayer. One who has nothing is praying all the time. As King David said, "And I am prayer . . ." (Psalms 109:4). He constantly thought of himself as lacking and unworthy; therefore, he prayed all the time. The psalms that he authored are a witness that God's help is in the world. If there is a book full of prayer and yearning, then there is also one full of God's assurance and help.

This was Isaac's blessing to Jacob: ". . . the voice is the voice of Jacob . . ." (Genesis 27:22). The redemption of Jacob, of the Jewish people, will come by the voice and by their prayer. Therefore, the redeemer, *Mashiach* (may he soon come) is born from David's descendants. Where else would help come from if not from one who prayed constantly?

The willow leaf, which we thought is lowly and empty, is really the one that ushers in the Age of Peace. Let us therefore hold tightly those who seem empty, for it will be their prayers that will bring the redemption to us and our children.

Sukkos is the time of the harvest. All summer long, grain was growing in the field. Now it is cut, gathered, threshed, and piled in the storage place. It is the time when a farmer could assess his crop. During the summer, when the grain stood in the stalks, he might have had an illusion about the size of his crop. How-

ever, now he is able to break through the illusion. He sees clearly how much of the crop is chaff or rubbish and how much is precious food.

Similarly, after the powerful cleansing of Yom Kippur, each of us can take stock of our state of affairs. It is harvest time, a time to take an honest look at how we fared during the year. Consequently, each of us takes hold of the four *mitzvos* of *lulav*. As it is written, ". . . and you should take unto yourselves . . ." (Leviticus 23:40), which also means, and you should take yourself. Each one of us should take hold of ourselves and take a long, hard look where we are and where we are going.

Sukkos is the time of harvest when the grain is gathered into our household. We take the four types of plants from the field into the *sukkah*, God's refuge, and we rejoice there with God.

A field symbolizes that which is forlorn and forsaken and open to everyone's selfish hands and feet. A field is open to stealing and trampling. As it is written, ". . . because in the field, he had found her; and the girl was screaming, but there was no one to help her" (Deuteronomy 22:27).

When we are out in the open field, when we have no direction, we can be blown away by the wind. As it is written, "Not so are the evildoers. They are as the chaff that is blown away by the wind" (Psalms 1:4). Those who are not yet in God's refuge are easily blown by the wind and go to waste.

When we hold the four types of plants, we rejoice that we, no matter how lowly, are privileged to be in the *sukkah*. We have found our way to the refuge of God, and we are sheltered from dangerous winds.

The four types of plants are a prayer for water, the scarcity or abundance of which is judged during Sukkos. Water comes from the highest place as rain, and from the deepest place as brooks and wells. It is the entire Jewish nation that can open the well in order that the water can flow without interruption. This deed can only be accomplished if all of us, from the lowest to the highest, gather in holy unity. Therefore, holding the plants together is already a prayer for water; for when we are together, the shower of blessings come. As it is written, "Spring up, O well!—Sing to it!—the well which princes dug, which the nobles of the people delved, with the scepter and with their staves . . ." (Numbers 21:18). These represent the four types of Jews: the "princes" are our three forefathers who are symbolized by the myrtle branch, which has leaves of three covering its stem. The "nobles," who "gave of themselves," are the willow leaves that have but the yearning of their hearts to offer. The "scepter," the lawgiver, is the *lulav* or palm leaves that have flavor or wisdom. Finally, the "stave" is the *esrog* or citron, for the stave is something on which one can lean and depend. It is the heart of man, of a man with wisdom and good deeds. Thus, when we are joined together, we open the wellspring of blessing, and the blessing of water flows abundantly.

The revelation of God's kingdom in the world is God's name. Those who walk on the path of the Torah are writing God's name in the world. Likewise, those who break God's laws erase His name.

Each of the plants—the *esrog*, *lulav*, *hadas*, and *aravah*—represents one of the four letters of God's name. By uniting with the four kinds of people, we also accomplish the writing of God's name. This causes panic in the arrogant nations of the world. They claim to have power independent of God and shudder at the thought that God's name will be revealed in the world. Therefore, the Jewish people who take hold of the four species of plants are hidden inside the *sukkah*. It protects them from the nations' opposition, for it is God's refuge.

There are two levels in man: his wisdom that resides in his mind and his actions that reside in his body. It is incomplete and senseless to consider man as only one of these two components. If a man has wisdom but is totally paralyzed and unable to communicate, then what sort of man is he? If man is only a body that lacks even the slightest rudiments of human wisdom, then too how can we speak of him as man? Therefore, to fulfill God's intention in the Creation, which is to serve God as human beings, we need both wisdom and physical activity.

These two levels are represented by the *tefillin*, or phylacteries, one of which is tied on the head and the other that is bound on the upper part of the left arm. The *tefillin* that is worn on the head directs our wisdom toward God; the *tefillin* on the arm directs our physical activity.

The holiday of Sukkos also has these two components. The *sukkah*, God's refuge, is God's name, His Wisdom, which flows to us in abundance and loving-kindness. How do we receive His Wisdom? We must prepare vessels, and the vessel for wisdom is activity. Therefore, when we restore our activity

during Yom Kippur by returning to God, we then possess vessels for God's loving-kindness of Sukkos.

Likewise, there are two components within our spiritual life. There is "the voice of Jacob" and the "hands of Esau" (Genesis 27:22). The "voice of Jacob" is the Torah and our yearning and prayers to live a Torah-directed life. We have the power to convert the "hands of Esau" into vessels for the "voice of Jacob." We can make physical activity a manifestation and revelation of the kingdom of God.

Similarly, this is the battle that occurs on Yom Kippur. The hands of Esau try to prosecute the Jewish nation before the heavenly court. They present evidence that they have won this battle. "Look, the Jewish people are full of evil deeds," they say. However, despite the overwhelming accusations and evidence, we return to God with all our heart and soul. We are not intimidated by our detractors, but we vigorously plead to God. Finally, at the close of Yom Kippur, each one stands acquitted by the One and Only Judge of the Universe, who says, "I forgive; I make pure." The hands of Esau are vanquished; the voice of Jacob is victorious. Now the Jewish nation has vessels to receive God's wisdom. The hands of Esau become infused with the voice of Jacob.

The victory of Yom Kippur is symbolized by the *lulav*, a sword, and the other plant species are also likened to other implements of war. The plants are a prayer for rain, that is, God's infinite Providence. Our prayers, the voice of Jacob, were victorious against the hands of Esau.

When we enter the *sukkah* with the four species, we rejoice with God in our victory to prepare vessels for the gift of wisdom. We stand completed with mind and body, and we turn to God's refuge in order to "stay in His house all the days of our life" (Psalms 29:4). Then the *sukkah* becomes the protective tent of peace over us—peace, a sign to the end of striving. May we be worthy to experience such completion. Amen.

There are three realms: space, time, and life. The holiness of space was concentrated in the holy land of Israel, in the holy city of Jerusalem, in the Holy Temple. The holiness of time is concentrated in our holy days of *Shabbos* and the holidays. The holiness of life is concentrated in the soul that God placed into each one of us.

The most powerful portion of holiness is at its beginning. Therefore, the first day of the holiday is most propitious for the performance of the *mitzvah* of *lulav*. When the holiness of time is at its greatest strength, the *lulav*, representing our deeds, connects us to the root of blessing. The blessings of Sukkos shower upon us in abundance and without limit.

In the Holy Temple, however, the holiness of space accompanies the holiness of time. Therefore, the *mitzvah* of *lulav* is performed there on each of the seven days of Sukkos. When the Temple was destroyed, this custom ended, and the *mitzvah* of *lulav* was performed only the first day.

Rabbi Yochanan ben (the son of) Zakai rectified this law and proclaimed that the *lulav* should be taken all the seven days, even in the absence of the Temple. Although the Temple is absent in the physical realm of space, it is still present in the realm of life. The soul of the Jewish people always yearns for the Holy Temple. As it is written, "Our rejoicing was transformed to a mourning" (Lamentations 5:15). This means that what was previously accomplished by rejoicing is now equally done by mourning. The mourning, the emptiness of our hearts, sustains the spiritual being of the Holy Temple among us. Therefore, we perform the *mitzvah* of *lulav* during the seven days of Sukkos.

The three realms of time, space, and life are alluded to in the recitation of the *Hallel* (Psalms 113–118), the special prayer for the holidays. "Servants of God, praise the name of God. May the name of God be praised for ever and ever"—this is the realm of time. "From the east where the sun rises till where it sets, God's name is praised." This is the realm of space. "God is most high upon all the nations . . ." This is the realm of life.

As we hold the four plant species close to our hearts in the *sukkah*, let us remember the Holy Temple. The *sukkah* is the Temple of God where God's name is holy and powerful. Our heart is a "Holy Temple," where we yearn for the revelation of God's kingdom. May we see this in our lifetime in the holy city of Jerusalem before the eyes of all mankind.

God's Providence showers all creatures with infinite goodness. Each one, however, prepares different vessels to receive that goodness. Some only prepare vessels for the material parts of God's gifts. Some work harder and receive vitality on a spiritual level. Finally, those who are very fortunate receive the essence of the Providence, the kernel or the soul and vitality of the goodness itself.

We can compare this to a king who invited his favorite servants to a party. After the royal feast, the king expressed how pleased he was with each one of them and that they each deserved to be rewarded. They could ask him for whatever they wished, except the crown and kingdom. The servants were overjoyed. Each one went off in a corner to decide on his once-in-a lifetime choice. Eventually, they were all ready. One asked for the royal chef with limitless foodstuffs. The other asked for the royal coach, horses, and driver. The third asked for the royal baths. The last one said, "I ask for only a small favor. I want to marry the princess." The king smiled and said, "You have made the wisest of all choices. Whoever has the princess also has everything in the royal palace."

A similar incident happened when Solomon first became king. In a dream, God permitted him to "ask and it will be granted." Does he want riches, power, or long life? Solomon asked for wisdom. "And God said, 'You have asked well.'" For whoever has wisdom has also everything else.

Likewise, the Jewish people ask for the essence, the kernel or the soul of God's goodness. This is Divine wisdom, God's name, the Torah, and the soul in each one of us. It is the princess herself.

We can compare this to a king who loved his daughter very much, and he finally found a suitable husband for her. When the day of the wedding arrived, he said to the young man, "It is very hard for me to part with my daughter, yet I have promised her to you. Please do me a favor and build a small guest house next to your palace. Then whenever I yearn to see her, I will stop by and stay in the guest house."

When you take the princess, you must be ready to welcome the king himself. King Solomon, who asked for wisdom, built the Holy Temple, the "small guest house," to receive God's Divine presence. The Jewish people who ask for the essence of Providence cleanse their hearts until they are fit dwelling places for God Himself. This is symbolized by the *esrog*, which represents the heart, and the *lulav* or leaves of the date palm, the Hebrew letters of which also spell *lo lev*—"he has a heart." We take the heart of wisdom, the princess, into the Sukkah, the small guest house, in order to receive and to rejoice with God.

There are *tzaddikim*, those who walk on the path of God constantly without any interruption, and there are *baalei teshuvah*, those who have stumbled but have finally returned to God. The *tzaddik* has chosen the straight and holy path, yet he is not without difficulties and setbacks. Each level he reaches is a new challenge to his righteousness, commitments, and convictions. Still he struggles and persists. He meets each challenge as it comes and battles through difficulties. For example, suppose he chooses the holy path of kindness. Each time he is about to do a deed of kindness, he is confronted by the circumstances of the moment. Perhaps his kindness is unacceptable within his society, such as being kind to a drunk or a vagabond on the street. Is someone making fun of the *tzaddik*, or is the opposition only in his mind? The *tzaddik* has a battle in either case. On the other hand, he can do acts of kindness when it is very acceptable, such as lending sugar to a neighbor or aiding his best friend who is ill. In that case, he has no challenge. Therefore, the difficulties arise for the *tzaddik* only if his chosen path is challenged.

The *baal teshuvah*, the penitent, is different. In the past he has been confronted by every type of obstacle to the path of God. He had not dealt properly with the challenges and confrontations. On the contrary, he traveled the road of opposition while floating along with the current. Thus, he took each obstacle and made it part of himself. They were internalized. When idols challenged his faith, he chose idols. When lust challenged his purity, he chose lust. When inertia challenged his good deeds, he chose the path of not doing.

Therefore, when the sinner returns to God, he brings with him all the challenges of his past. Thereby he is elevated to a level even higher than the *tzaddik*. He comes face to face with God in an instant.

"The *tzaddik* will blossom forth as a date tree" (Psalms 92:13). It takes a long time for the date tree to mature its fruit, and so it is with the *tzaddik*, but of the *baal teshuvah*, it is written, "And he will blossom forth as the rose" (Hosea 14:6). The rose opens its blossoms quickly, and so does the penitent.

Therefore, on Sukkos we take hold of the date palm and shake it vigorously. The trembling and shaking are the activity of a penitent attempting to reenter the palace of the king. The *baal teshuvah* is reaching the level of *tzaddik*. The rose is becoming a date blossom.

When we hold the *lulav*, a date palm, in the *sukkah*, God's refuge, let us bring to God all our straying desires and actions. Let us consecrate them to the revelation of God's kingdom.

The night before the Jewish people left Egypt, they were commanded to "take branches from the *azov* bush" (Exodus 12:22). The Talmud compares that "taking" to the verse "And you should take on the first day the fruit of a beautiful tree, a bunch of date palm, myrtle branches, and willow branches" (Exodus 23:40).

As slaves in Egypt, we were as low as the *azov* bush. God then lifted us to great heights. Moreover,

God desired that every generation of Jews reach those heights by repentance and good deeds. This is the *lulav* that symbolizes our returning, our thrashing, and vigorous efforts to be with God.

During the Exodus, the redemption was accomplished with pure loving-kindness. Later we became deserving through our persistent efforts. At first we were received with kindness alone; later we were received with stern judgment. Therefore, the kindness of Sukkos comes after the days of judgment of Rosh Hashanah and the forgiveness of Yom Kippur.

There are two kinds of tying. As it is written, "I will betroth, or tie, you to myself forever. I will betroth, or tie, you to myself with righteousness, judgment, kindness and mercy" (Hosea 2:19). We are at first tied to God and brought close to him with great humility. Although we have nothing and are undeserving, still God redeems us. This is the *azov* of the Exodus. Finally, we are tied to God with judgment, repentance, and good deeds. This finally is the *lulav* and the other plant species.

God says, "Return to Me and I will return to you" (Zechariah 1:3).

When a person indulges in sin, he loses the power of his spiritual essence. When he repents and returns to God, God returns the power of his spiritual essence to him. As it is written, "Take for yourselves on the first day. . . ." On Sukkos each one of us can accept the spiritual essences in their full strength. This brings completeness and true joy to us. As it is written, "Take . . . and rejoice before God seven days" (Leviticus 23:40).

Each one of the four species represents one of the four spiritual essences. When they are "tied" together, there is true joy. On *Shabbos* day, when the realm of spiritual essences is "united in the secret of the one" (Zohar, *Tazriah*) and all is one without divisiveness, there is no need for the *lulav*. The union is accomplished through the holiness of time, the *Shabbos*.

The willow leaf, or *aravah*, is shaped like a mouth, which symbolizes both prayer and Torah study. The Jewish people are always connected to these, as it is written, "The voice is that of Jacob" (Genesis 27:22). This "voice" is the inner portion and kernel of holiness. The outer portion, the husk that protects it, is the "fear" of God. He who is awed by the Creator focuses all his energies for an encounter with Him.

We can compare this to a treasure house. The one

who possesses the keys to the roomful of treasure also possesses the treasure. However, unless he has the keys to the outer doors, he is likely to lose the treasure to intruders. The outer doors are the fear of God (*Shabbos* 31b).

The Holy Temple in Jerusalem was the ultimate place of prayer in the world, for wherever a Jew is, he directs his prayers toward Jerusalem. As it is written, "From Zion shall go forth the law and the word of God from Jerusalem" (Isaiah 2:3). It is the treasure house, yet it also is the outer gate where one can reach the highest level of fear of God. Jerusalem, or *Yerushalayim*, can be divided into two Hebrew words—*yoreh sholem*, "complete fear." In Jerusalem a person can reach the ultimate level of fear of God. He now has the inner and outer keys.

Therefore, we take the *aravah*, the willow, and shake it with the *lulav*. The four species tremble and pray together. "God, the inner doors are open for us always, and so, too, is the depths of our soul. Please open the outer doors for us!" As it is written, "Open up for me the gates of righteousness, let me come in them to praise God" (Psalms 18:19).

――――――――――

The *aravah* has neither flavor nor fragrance, and it symbolizes the individuals who have neither Torah wisdom nor good deeds. It is also symbolic of those generations that have nothing at all, but who can only pray for God's help. As it is written, "He turned to the prayer of the destitute, and he did not reject their prayers" (Psalms 102:18).

Not one of the four species stands by itself. Each plant represents a different type of person, and they stand only by joining together. They give each other life and strength. As they give life "horizontally," to each other, they also give life "vertically," to the following generations. Thus, each generation gives strength to the next one, even to those who have nothing to offer.

Yet we have strong ties to the previous generation through our beliefs and customs. Traditionally, we always possess Torah, wisdom, and good deeds even

if they are not our life goals and priorities. But we pray, "Please God, may we be worthy to have our habits as our way of life." Therefore, the *aravah* is called a "custom of the prophets." We yearn that our customs of habit should become an essential part of us.

We shake the four species, which includes the *aravah*, as a prayer. Even if we are empty of wisdom and good deeds, even if we are on the lowest level of habits, it ties us to those who have had more. It is a link between the generations.

――――――――――

The myrtle leaves have no flavor, but a good fragrance. This is symbolic of those who have no Torah wisdom yet possess good deeds. The triple leaves on each row of the branch symbolize our forefathers, Abraham, Isaac, and Jacob. Although they did not yet possess the Torah, they still did many good deeds.

What is the nature of this good fragrance? A fragrance can be detected far from its source. A fragrance also lingers after the source is gone.

This can be compared to a prince who rebelled against his father and ran away from the palace. He changed into common clothing and walked in the slums among the poorer citizens. He was not recognized by anyone because of his altered appearance. However, when he passed a blind beggar, the beggar called out to him, "Stop there! You who come from the king's palace! I cannot ever forget that fragrance! Who are you, pray tell me?"

Our forefathers blessed us that we should never lose the fragrance of the palace. This sweet odor comes from our past, and it also comes from our future. Every Jewish soul will experience the perfection of the World to Come. This future is this residual odor.

When we hold the *hadasim*, or myrtle branches, we pray that their lovely fragrance should never leave us. Our good deeds should always be with us. They should not merely be an odor, but should be rooted in Torah wisdom, which constantly generates and gives forth the good fragrance forever.

11

Sukkos Nights

SIMCHAS BEIS HASHOEVAH—REJOICING BY DRAWING THE WATER

The water libation, how was it done? A golden flagon holding three logs was filled from the pool of Shiloah. When they arrived at the Water Gate, they sounded a prolonged blast (*t'kiah*), a quavering note (*t'ruah*), and a prolonged blast (*t'kiah*). He went up the ramp and turned to his left where there were two silver bowls. . . . And they each had a hole like a narrow spout, one wide and the other narrow, so that both were emptied out together, the one to the west was for water, and that to the east was for wine.

With one log they could do the libations all the eight days. (*Sukkah* 48a)

The sages have said, "Whoever has not seen the rejoicing at the Libation Water Well has never seen rejoicing in his life."

At the close of the first holiday of the festival of Tabernacles (Sukkos), they went down to the Court of Women where they made an important rearrangement. The golden candlesticks were there with four golden bowls at their tops and four ladders to each one, and four youths from young *kohanim* with pitchers of oil holding a hundred and twenty logs in their hands, which they used to pour into every bowl.

For the worn-out drawers and girdles of the *kohanim*, they made wicks; and with them lit up, and there was no courtyard in Jerusalem that was not lit up with the light at the Libation Well Water ceremony.

Pious men and men of good deeds used to dance before them with burning torches in their hands and sang before them songs and praises. And the Levites on harps, and on lyres, and with cymbals, and with trumpets, and with other instruments of music without number upon the fifteen steps leading down from the court of the Israelites to the Women's Court, corresponding to the fifteen songs of Ascent in the Psalms; upon them the Levites used to stand with musical instruments and sing hymns. (*Sukkah* 51a)

Rabbi Joshua the son of Chananya said:
"When we rejoiced at the Libation of the Water-Well, we did not sleep at all." (*Sukkah* 53a)

hat was the great rejoicing when the water was drawn from the well? It was because they drew with it the holy spirit (*Sukkah* 50b).

Joy is when a being is in harmony with itself and is totally connected to its roots. Joy is the result of vitality and life; sadness comes from illness and death.

The holy spirit in man is the spirit of God, as it is written, "And He breathed into his nostrils a spirit of life . . ." (Genesis 2:7). When man was created, God defined his being by breathing into him. Man's body is of this world, yet he has God's breath within him. He stands, therefore, between the heaven and the earth. He has the delicate task of combining these two spheres in order to be man. If he succeeds, he is then connected to his roots and is filled with vitality. If not, he is in danger of losing his life as a human being.

There are two kinds of joy. One is the genuine joy that grows from within the individual. When a person is in harmony, every part of his being is at home with the others; then he is filled with joy. The other is artificial joy that grows from without. As it is written, "And now take a musician and let him play for me, and the holy spirit will descend upon me" (2 Kings 3:15). This joy is empty, and the state of being empty is like a vessel. The vessel has the potential to be filled. Because the holy spirit produces joy, one who is joyous is prepared to receive the holy spirit.

Therefore, those who rejoiced at the water drawing could not sleep at all. How can one sleep when one is constantly rising to new heights of life, vitality, and total being?

Let us also rejoice, so the holy spirit may rest upon us.

"You should rejoice in your holiday and be only joyous" (Deuteronomy 16:14). The word "only" alludes to times when we could be other than joyous. Although you may have reason not to be joyous, still one should be "only joyous." Even in the dark and dismal days of exile, when there seems to be nothing to rejoice about, one should be "only joyous"! And so especially on this night, the most joyous of all nights of the holiday.

". . . and He breathed into his nostrils the breath of life, and man became a living being" (Genesis 2:7). The Targum interprets this as, "and man became a talking being."

God's breath in man makes him what he is. Man can breathe out Godly breath by speaking truth and words of Torah. The more he breaths out Godliness, the more the breath of God becomes part of him.

When a child is old enough to speak, the father teaches him to say, "The Torah was commanded to us by Moses; it is an inheritance to the children of Jacob" (Deuteronomy 33:4). When a child starts to speak, he is defining himself as a human being. The breath of God is forming within his body. Immediately, we put the stamp of God onto his breath by teaching him to say words of Torah.

This Godly breath is also the source of prophecy. Even those who never reach a level of biblical prophecy can still obtain some prophetic level. As the Talmud relates, "The Jewish people, even if they are not prophets, still they are the children of prophets" (*Pesachim* 66a). On some level each one of us who breathes out Godly breath is a prophet.

A person who breathes Godly breath is in touch with his essence. He is filled with true life and vitality, which is the greatest joy. Let us rejoice on these nights when we can touch our true wellspring from the waters of life. Let God's breath enter us and breathe out songs of praise to His holy Name.

"And the spirit of God hovered over the water" (Genesis 1:2).

The entire Creation is subordinated to God, and God's spirit hovers over it. Who would not be happy with this situation? Only one who is arrogant and credits himself with independent power. He is not happy to serve God and to follow His prescriptions. This arrogant one falls into the clutches of like-minded people, and they enslave him. As it is written, "Because you did not serve God with joy and gladness . . . you will now serve your enemies" (Deuteronomy 28:47).

When we remind ourselves that we are servants of the Creator, it should bring us the greatest happiness. Moreover, when we rejoice by being "covered by the water," then God's spirit hovers over us. These are the "waters" of life that are drawn on the nights of Sukkos. On the holy night, we have the opportunity to become humble servants of God, to rejoice in our choice, and to be revitalized by the infinite spirit.

There are three realms: time, space, and life. In each of these three, there is Divine joy. In the realm of time, there is the holiday of Sukkos, for it is written, "And you should rejoice in your holiday" (Deuteronomy 16:14). This is additionally called "the time of our happiness" in the *Amidah* prayers.

There is joy in the realm of space, the Holy Temple. As it is written, ". . . the joy of all the land" (Psalms 48:3). The joy of all locations on earth is concentrated within the Holy Temple.

Finally, in the realm of life, there is the Jewish nation. As it is written, ". . . the heart of those who seek God should be joyous" (Psalms 105:3). Are there people who seek God as do the Jewish people? Therefore, they can be the source of joy for all mankind.

When the joy of the three realms merge, it is the greatest rejoicing in the world. This occurred during the holiday of Sukkos when all of Israel celebrated in the Holy Temple. Thus, we connect ourselves to the joy of time, space, and life as it was in the Holy Temple. At that point we experience true joy.

On Yom Kippur the Jewish people are purified. It becomes manifest that they are the ones chosen by God to declare His kingdom. Likewise, it is clear that they have chosen God as their ruler. This is the greatest of joys; for it is written, "God will rejoice in His creation" (Psalms 104:31) and "Israel will rejoice in his Maker" (Psalms 149:2).

When the Creator and the created become manifest, a song of joy rises to heaven. As it is written, "This nation I have formed for myself; they shall proclaim My praise" (Isaiah 43:21). When the forming of My people is clear, then My praise rises from the earth.

Yet, the angels too praise the Creator. Then whose songs of praise are sweeter?

We can compare this to a kind and just king whose servants rebelled and forced him to leave the palace. He disguised himself in rags and wandered in the city. He wandered among the poor and working classes, asking for food and lodging. To many he revealed his identity and asked for their help. He was pleased to hear their promises of loyalty. After many months, the king was certain that most of the citizens were loyal to him. The masses organized, and soon the king's cause captured the hearts of the entire province. The king sent word that he was ready to march on the palace. They amassed and approached the palace walls.

At that point, the king's ousted generals emerged from hiding and greeted the king, "Praised be the name of our kind and just king for ever and ever." They discussed strategy and organized the people for the assault. The citizens felt belittled. "Now that the generals are here," they thought, "we are not so important anymore!" The king sensed their doubt and said, "If not for you, would my kingdom ever have become manifest?"

There is no sweeter praise than the Jewish nation singing of God, the Creator of heaven and earth. There is no greater joy than these nights of Sukkos when this becomes clear before all of mankind.

"At the celebration of drawing water in the Holy Temple, Hillel would say, 'If I am here, all is here.'" (*Sukkah* 53a).

The Jewish people are the vessels for the revelation of God's kingdom. When they were in Jerusalem, it was a thriving city, and the Temple stood before all mankind. When they were exiled, the Temple, together with Jerusalem, was destroyed. The kingdom of God was concealed, and the light of the world was extinguished.

On the nights of Sukkos, our crucial role in the revelation of God's kingdom becomes very clear to us. This is surely the greatest joy. As it is written in the evening prayers, "May our eyes see, and our hearts rejoice, and our spirits be gladdened in Your help when it will be told Zion; behold your king reigns."

They brought a pitcher of water and poured it onto the altar. As if God is saying to them, "Pour the water before me so that your yearly rain be blessed" (*Taanis* 2a).

Water is the essence of blessing both in the physical and spiritual sense. Every living thing is primarily water. Water helps things grow, thrive, and flourish. However, rain can fall and go completely to waste. There must be vessels for the raindrops in order for rain to be purposeful.

To have purpose, all the parts of the vessel must be concentrated in one place. If the parts are scattered and wandering aimlessly, then they cannot receive the Divine blessing. Sukkos is the time for ingathering. Yom Kippur has helped us cast off unwanted parts and consolidate our vessels. We concentrate our beings individually and as a people. Therefore, we become proper to receive God's blessings. On the other hand, the evildoers are fragmented and dispersed. They are not appropriate vessels to receive the blessing from heaven.

When it rains, it rains on the righteous and evildoers alike. Therefore, on Sukkos there were offerings for all the seventy nations. Thus, all the nations benefit from the "rain" that falls on the Jewish people.

On Yom Kippur we separate and purify ourselves as the angels in heaven. We cleanse our hearts and secret places. We prepare our innermost parts to be vessels for holiness and Divine blessing. God takes us into His private quarters and "hides" us. He pours Divine vitality into us, away from the glares of the jealous and arrogant nations of the world. As it is written, "Hide them in the *sukkah*, from the quarrels of tongues" (Psalms 31:21). Let us therefore open our hearts to the Divine blessing and rejoice in the refuge of God.

"For God had not yet made it rain, and man was not yet there to work the land" (Genesis 2:5).

When there are vessels to receive the Divine blessing, the rain comes. Rain brings food and sustenance to all living things. It is a true gift that is given undeservedly with infinite kindness.

When one realizes the benefits of rain, one does not take it for granted. One thinks, "I have it today, but tomorrow my benefactor may not give any more." Only man, who recognizes his Creator, can really appreciate the gifts of God. The Jewish people desire "rain" for one reason. They want to serve God without distractions. They fully recognize the gift. Therefore, it is also God's will that rain should fall only through the desire and longing of the Jewish people.

There are two ways that rain descends. It is written, "He gives rain on the face of the land, and sends water on the outside streets" (Job 5:10). In the land of Israel, the vessel for all blessing that God "gives" is rain. It is as if we are given this gift directly from the hand of God. God "sends" the rain to other lands because they are at a distance from Him. They do not receive rain directly from His hand.

Similarly, when the Holy Temple will stand in Jerusalem, "God will open for you His storagehouse and give rain for your land in the proper season" (Deuteronomy 28:12). However, there is destruction and exile, and the channel of gifts has now become an indirect one. Nevertheless, the Divine gifts keep flowing with great kindness, for where there is sustenance, there is also great joy. This is the rejoicing of Sukkos. The gifts come in abundance. Thus, we go to draw the holy waters from the wellsprings of help.

———

"And God separated between the water under the heavens and the waters upon the heavens" (Genesis 1:7).

There are the upper waters and the lower waters. The lower waters complained to God, "We, too, want to be close to You. Why are we unlucky to be so far away?" (*Genesis Rabbah* 1:7). God answered, "There will come a time when you too will be close, when water will be poured on the altar during the holiday of Sukkos to celebrate the drawing of the water" (*Tikunei Zohar* 5).

Man is composed of flesh and blood from the earth and a soul from heaven. He is capable of revealing the Divine nature of his being. To help him in this process, he received the Torah, teachings that guide his life. If he lives according to the Torah, the Divine nature of his flesh and blood also will become revealed. This brings peace between the earth and heaven.

On Yom Kippur the Jewish people become pure as the angels of heaven. This takes them directly into the *sukkah*, which is the tent of peace. We celebrate the coming together of the earth and the heaven. Likewise, we can also rectify the gap between the lower and upper waters. We can reveal that there are no lower waters at all. The truth is that all waters are Divine and belong near to God "on the altar."

Let us, who feel downtrodden, abandoned, frustrated, vanquished, and weak, take strength from our joyous holiday. It is within our power to raise "lower waters" and the earth itself to the heights of heaven. Let us then rejoice and celebrate and receive the refreshing waters of life and vitality for us, our children, all of Israel, and all the nations of the world.

12

Hoshanah Rabbah—
Begging for Help

What is the ritual of the willow branches? There was a place below Jerusalem called Motsa. They went down there and collected young willow branches, and they came and set them upright along the sides of the altar with their tops bent over the top of the altar. They then sounded a prolonged blast (of the shofar or *t'kiah*) and a quavering note, *t'ruah*), and a prolonged blast (*t'kiah*). Each day they walked in procession once around the altar and recited, "We beg you, God, please help! We beg you, God, please help us succeed!" (Psalms 118:25). . . . But on that day they walked in procession around the Altar seven times. (*Sukkah* 45a)

nd he will kiss me from the kisses of his mouth . . . for your love is better than wine" (Song of Songs 1:2).

One can hold one's child's hand with love, stroke his hair, or hug him. These are all signs of love. The mouth, however, is the essence of man. Our mouth, our speech, distinguishes us from animals. Our mouth is the "voice of Jacob." When we kiss with the mouth, the essence of one touches the essence of the other.

The connection of God to the Jewish people is not dependent on the coincidences of deeds. It is one of essence. The spiritual kernel, our soul, is connected to the most infinite spiritual level, which is God.

Wine is a liquid that contains color and flavor, the fermented juice of grapes. Water, however, contains nothing but the liquid essence. It is this water for which we pray on Hoshanah Rabbah, "Please, God, help!" Therefore, we want the purest *aravah*, the willow branches that grow near water. This love is better than wine.

The willow leaves have neither taste nor fragrance, and they represent those of us who have neither Torah wisdom nor good deeds. We plead to God, not because of our good deeds but because of the essential connection we have with Him, "the kisses of His mouth."

Deeper still . . .

Neshikah, the Hebrew word for kiss, comes from the root *hashoko*. *Hashoko* is a law regarding two pools of water that are next to each other. One is in accordance with all the laws of *mikvah*, or ritual bath, which contains natural or rain water. The other pool contains water that was poured in by vessels. However, if a tubular opening is dug between the two pools and the water from one "touches" the water from the other, both pools can be used as a *mikvah*. When the waters touch each other, it is called *hashakah*, a kissing of the essences.

We may have neither Torah wisdom nor good deeds, but God's essence is touching us. We are infused with holiness and purity. On Hoshanah Rabbah we plead not with the merit of our deeds for what do our deeds amount to? We plead, "God, we are Your children. No matter what we do, we remain Your children. Please help us. Let us see Your kisses, Your ever closeness to us!"

On Hoshanah Rabbah we pray with the *aravah*, the willow branches. The *aravah* has nothing; it can only yearn and pray for help. The leaves are smooth and long; it is constantly praying. *Aravah* also means sweet. The "voice of Jacob" is sweet to be heard. One who humbles himself has charm and finds favor in the eyes of his benefactor. *Aravah* also means to mix together. We are essentially mixed and united with God. Let us then humbly plead to God in a sweet voice from the depths of our hearts, for His help is surely coming.

———————————

"Man and beast alike will be helped by God" (Psalms 36:7). It is written in the Talmud, "This verse refers to people who have the wisdom of man but consider themselves no higher than beasts" (*Chullin* 5b).

How can man be arrogant? He realizes that as smart as he is, there is always someone smarter. Obviously he thinks man is the smartest in the entire world. But this too is false. As we say in our daily morning prayers, "What are we, what is our life, our kindness, our help? What can we say before You, God? Are not all the heroes like nothing before You, and the famous as if they never were; and the wise man like ones without understanding." Therefore, no one can boast of his wisdom as he stands before God. Moreover, the person who can imagine himself as standing before God is a vessel for the help of God. Thus, on Hoshanah Rabbah we stand empty, as beasts before their master, without power or wisdom, waiting and yearning for the help of God to come.

———————————

"He has turned to the prayer of the destitute, and He did not reject their prayer" (Psalms 102:18).

The lowly, desolate, poor, and empty person can only pray. He has nothing to claim as merit before his Master. God too ignores all prayers in order to listen to the prayer of the poor and lowly. It is therefore written, "He did not reject their prayer" (Psalms 102:18). The prayers of all the others, filled with wisdom and good deeds, are accepted only together with the poor man's prayer.

We can compare this to a kingdom that was hit by a fierce storm. The winds wrought havoc and devastation upon rich and poor alike. Trees were uprooted, houses destroyed, and fortunes lost. Those afflicted came before the king to plead for help. First, of course, the rich were allowed in to plead their case. They cried to him about their mansions, their orchards, their purebred horses that were all lost in the storm. Their pleas fell on deaf ears. Soon the poor people were ushered in to the king. They stood before the king in their rags. They had nothing to ask. The storm took nothing from them; they had nothing worth taking. They looked up at the king and cried and cried. For the first time, the king felt the devastation of the storm. Now he was ready to help all those who were afflicted by it.

The willow leaf is like a mouth. It pleads before God. As it is written, "As a line of scarlet are your lips, and your speech (*midboreich*) is beautiful" (Song of Songs 4:3). *Midboreich* means "your desert." When you come to God as a "desert," empty and desolate, then your lips are beautiful.

On Hoshanah Rabbah we can lift up all the prayers of mankind to be accepted before God. Let us stand as the poor beggar before the King. Then the Divine kindness will flow abundantly to a world so much in need of His help.

———————————

The willow leaf is smooth; it does not have any raised parts. It is a pure and empty vessel to receive the blessing of God. It has nothing and can only pray. As King David said of himself, "And I am prayer" (Psalms 109:4). I can only pray. I have nothing to bring as merit before God.

To pray with the *aravah* on Hoshanah Rabbah is called a "custom from the days of the prophets" (*Sukkah* 44a).

We can compare this to a mother who loves her baby very much. She hugs, holds, nurses, plays, and sleeps with the baby. When her baby cries, she already knows what she wants. Her friends say to her, "Are you a prophet to know what your baby wants?" She answers, "We understand each other." When two people are very close, each knows the other one's heart.

Similarly, the connection that God has with the Jewish people is heart to heart, for it is one of essence. The Jewish people are all prophets, and they start customs that grow out of their relationship with God.

The arrogant nations of the world ignore our chosenness when it is based on our deeds. It is logical and natural that "as you sow, shall you reap." However, they are ready to annihilate us over our chosenness when it is beyond deeds. They know we have a special relationship with God before we even do a single good deed. They oppose the *aravah*, the willow that is without flavor or fragrance, for it is special in the eyes of God. For this opposition alone, we need great help. God should protect us from their jealousy.

In our present exile, the opposition of the arrogant nations embarrasses us. God's kingdom is concealed, and we are downtrodden. How dare we say we are chosen? But there will come a day when this will change, for it is written, "I will find you in the marketplace; I will kiss you; still they will not shame me" (Song of Songs 8:1). "I will kiss you" symbolizes the relationship of essence before and beyond any deed. The Jewish people will not be ashamed of that. It will be clear to the world as God's Kingdom.

On Hoshanah Rabbah we come to God as prophets who understand each other's heart. We all need the redemption—for our sake and for Your sake.

The four species each represent a component of the Torah. The *lulav* has only flavor; that is Torah wisdom. The myrtle has only fragrance; that is *mitzvah*, or deeds; the *esrog* with flavor and fragrance are *mishpatim*, laws with logical reason; and the *aravah* with neither taste nor fragrance are the *chukim*, laws without reason.

Likewise, there are four components in impurity. There are the four exiles of Babylon, Persia, Media, and the present one, Edom. Moreover, there are the four most severe transgressions: idol worship, incest, murder, and hatred without cause. The present exile corresponds to the hatred, which comes without flavor or fragrance.

Why are we in exile? The answer is because we do not have faith in God's love for us. He loves us even if we are empty of flavor and fragrance.

Why do we hate? Because the other person has neither flavor nor fragrance. This reflects our lack of belief in God's love for us; therefore, we are in exile.

Hoshanah Rabbah is the time when we can rekindle our faith in God's love for the Jewish people. We hold the *aravah* tightly with great love, even if it has neither flavor nor fragrance. We pray to God, "We are all empty vessels ready to receive Your Divine Providence. We stand together with all the people regardless of their emptiness. This is the way You love us, God. Now please redeem us, your lowly ones, from exile."

The one thing the willow leaf could do is yearn for help. It has nothing, but hopes to receive help from God. Likewise, Hoshanah Rabbah is the last day of Sukkos, which symbolizes King David. In the *Amidah* prayer, we say, "The sprouting of Your servant, David, You should bring forth speedily in our days." We pray and yearn with the *aravah* for the Redemption that should come in our days.

During all of Sukkos, we keep the four species together, those that have Torah wisdom and good deeds with even those who have neither one. We are then in the *sukkah*, the house of God, and we are able to unite. After Sukkos, however, we are influenced by our exile. This exile originated with the destruction of the Second Temple in Jerusalem. It happened

because of hatred. This hatred still haunts us today, and it does not allow us to hold the four species together. We therefore hold the *aravah*, which is now separated from the *lulav*.

What then can we do to escape the curse of the exile? We must humble ourselves to the very earth. We must realize our emptiness and insignificance. We are only willow leaves with neither flavor nor fragrance. Therefore, on Hoshanah Rabbah we take the *aravah* separately and lower it to the ground. Not only do we lower it but we also strike it on the ground again and again. The sound of that beating is a prayer. "Please, God, even if we are only as the *aravah*, so bare and lowly, listen to our prayer. Even if we cannot unite with the rest of Israel because of the exile, help us! See our humility! We know we are truly empty. Redeem us quickly for Your sake."

"I was poor and He helped me" (Psalms 116:6). It is because we realize our poverty that God helps us. As it is written, "Not because you are more numerous than the other nations, . . . you are but the minutest of all nations" (Deuteronomy 7:7). Because you humble yourselves more than the other nations, therefore you are a vessel to receive God's Providence.

The Jewish people realize that they are undeserving when they receive gifts from God. They don't say, "See, we deserve it!" On the contrary, the more often they receive, the more humbly they think, "God keeps giving to us, but surely we don't deserve a thing!" Even when He helped me, still I was poor. The Jewish people never thought they deserved it. God gives to His people only because of His Divine kindness.

There are some, however, who use their humility as a source of arrogance. It is used as a social ladder in order to climb higher than others. This is why serrated willow leaves are not to be used. The humility must be smooth, for one must subordinate one's self to those who are better and higher.

On Hoshanah Rabbah we humble ourselves in order to become vessels to receive *hoshanah*, the help from God. The lower we are, the more likely is our redemption that we hope and pray will soon come in our days.

The Jewish people were blessed with the virtue of poverty and humility, which stems from their essential relationship with God. They stand before Him and realize their utter insignificance. As it is written, "Man and beast alike will be helped by God" (Psalms

36:7). They consider themselves no more than the beast; therefore, they are helped. On the simplest level, How can anyone be arrogant? Is he not an animal like other animals? What is there to be arrogant about?

It is this virtue of humility that makes the Jewish people vessels for all of God's gifts. As it is written, ". . . may water flow forth from his pails (*dolyov*)" (Numbers 24:7). *Dolyov* also means the poor ones. The water of life, the Torah, will flow from those who are poor. They are proper vessels to receive the gift of wisdom. Therefore, we take the lowly willow leaves that grow near the water. The water is flowing—God's gifts come in abundance. Those who lower themselves properly are the correct vessels to receive it. This is Hoshanah Rabbah, the great help on this last day of Sukkos. We resign ourselves to the wonderful Jewish virtue of humility and prepare for the redemption.

The *aravah* has neither wisdom nor good deeds. Then in what way is it connected to God? With faith. The leaves are smooth and flowing. Our hearts yearn and flow; they follow God even into the desert. As it is written, "Draw me to follow you and I will run . . ." (Song of Songs 1:4). We follow God even on the level of an animal being drawn by its master.

We can compare this to a king who had one son and many servants. They all lived in the palace enjoying the benefits of royalty. Then tragedies befell the kingdom. There was famine, which was followed by war and pestilence. Little by little, the servants abandoned the king. Soon there was hardly a loyal servant left except the king's son. He was asked, "Why do you stay with the king after all these tragic events? "Why do I stay with the king?" he answered. "The king is my father!"

A son inherits from his father on two levels. On one level he receives wisdom. On the lower level, the son is the "footstep, or knee, of his father" (*Eruvin* 70b). The son follows his father and walks in his footsteps. This is beyond understanding, sense, or logic. It is faith alone.

Parents teach their children with elaborate explanations. Yet, there are some things for which they neither give rhyme nor reason. The children experience neither flavor nor fragrance, yet they follow the customs of their parents.

This is the level of *aravah*, the lowly willow: it is the level of pure faith. Therefore, the *aravah*, which we hold on Hoshanah Rabbah, is but "a custom from the days of the prophets" (*Sukkah* 44a). Customs and faith go hand in hand.

As it is written, "If you do not know the beautiful one among the women, go therefore to the heels of the sheep . . ." (Song of Songs 1:8). If you are not positive who among the nations belong to God, go and see who are those following the heels. Who walk in God's path with pure faith when all have abandoned Him because of difficulties? The Jewish people, the ones who have pure faith.

Likewise, the inception of our people was the Exodus. Before we had flavor or fragrance, we already followed God with pure faith. These are our roots and foundation. Similarly, our redemption will come through faith. When we are lowly as the willow, when we have neither flavor nor fragrance but the yearning in our heart, then the redemption will come.

The *aravah* is shaped like a mouth. The mouth is the power of the Jewish people, for it is written, ". . . the voice of Jacob" (Genesis 27:22). We hold the *aravah* and pray to God for His help.

The mouth has two lips. Why two? One represents talking, the other quiet. One is the open lip; the other is the closed lip. We likewise use two branches of *aravah*. One represents the "open lips," Moses our teacher. The other is the "closed lips" of Aaron, as it is written, "And Aaron was quiet" (Leviticus 10:3). Moses was the most humble individual on the face of the earth; however, he is not the one who brings peace and love among men. He is the teacher who imparts the teachings and the law of God. It is the one who is quiet, receptive, and accepting who can bring true peace. Aaron is called "he who loved peace and pursued peace" (*Avos* 1:12).

Similarly, to speak evil, argue, and cause dissension and hatred is the worst of sins. It rends asunder and destroys. Therefore, one who is quiet at such times upholds the entire world. His power is great and infinite.

Ultimately, one is dependent on the other. To the degree that a person is able to hold his lips together, that is how well he can open them. The quiet one then can speak the words of law. For it is written, "As the kiss of lips, so is he who answers properly" (Proverbs 24:26). One whose lips are "kissed" together in quiet is worthy to answer properly.

The *aravah* that is tied to the *lulav* with the other species is the open lips. It is connected with those who have Torah wisdom, and it participates with them. The *aravah* of Hoshanah Rabbah is the quiet one who has nothing to say, but yearns for the help of God and the complete redemption.

When we lower the willow branches to the ground, let us do so in complete silence. Let us break this exile of hatred, evil talk, argument, and quarreling. Then we are worthy to have our lips opened and to sing a song of praise of our redemption.

―――――――――

The willow, without flavor or fragrance, symbolizes the Jewish people. They know truly that only God possesses power and all the gifts one may need. They know also that they are not chosen due to any merit, but their chosenness comes from an essential relationship with God. As it is written, "And I have planted you as a noble vine; all are true seed" (Jeremiah 2:21). As a seed is related to the tree, so is the Jewish people related to God.

Deeper still . . .

Beings of flesh and blood can do things unrelated to their characters. They can lie, cheat, fool, and pretend; however, when they have a child, that is the moment of truth. One's essence becomes manifest, and that is truth. Thus, when a tree gives forth seeds, that is truth; from that seed will grow the same type of tree as the original one.

The truth is that we are powerless without God. Therefore, the Hebrew letters of *aravah* have the same numerical value as *zera*, "seed." We know the truth about our existence; the truth manifests itself. It is a seed.

The Seer of Lublin once said, "If one feels no connection with God, it is because he realizes that he is an empty vessel, possessing neither Torah wisdom, nor good deeds, and is nothing and nobody. This is the truth . . . and he therefore is in fact connected to God, who is the God of truth."

On this day of Hoshanah Rabbah, let us realize the truth and be seeds of truth before God. This will make us pure and empty vessels to receive the redemption.

―――――――――

The *aravah* grows by the water, as it is written, "willow branches of the stream (*nachal*)" (Leviticus 23:40). The Hebrew letters for *nachal* are an acrostic, *nafsheinu chicsoh lashem*—"our souls yearn for God" (Psalms 33:20). The yearning of our hearts opens the source of water, the "waters of help."

We are like the willow, empty and desolate, thirsting for water, yet unfulfilled by all the waters in the world. Our thirst remains unquenched until we drink the purest of all waters, the waters of Torah.

Similarly, this was Jacob's blessing to Joseph's children: "Let them multiply as the fish in midst of the land" (Genesis 28:16). Fish, who live in the water, still jump up toward the raindrops and are constantly thirsty for a new drop of water. So too the children of Israel should never be satisfied with any water until they obtain the purest water. Let them be like the parched, tired, dry land; for no matter how much water it is given to drink, it is not satisfied until the purest water comes.

On Hoshanah Rabbah we can reevaluate the type of water that we have been drinking. To make our souls thirsty and empty for the purest water, let "our souls yearn for God" alone. We dare not be satisfied with any substitutes. Then we are vessels, for "He is our helper and our protector" (Psalms 33:20, end of verse).

―――――――――

"For in the field he did find the girl, she screamed but there was no one to help her" (Deuteronomy 22:27). The Talmud comments, "If one does hear her pleas for help, he may take the attacker's life" (*Sanhedrin* 73a).

Our opposition, the evil in the world, is attacking us. We scream and plead for God's help. Why then does He not take the life of the attacker? Why does He not erase evil from our midst? The answer is "in the field," the field of aimless and desolate emptiness. We have exposed ourselves to evil.

Dare we complain?

On Yom Kippur, however, we have become pure and focus our life and soul toward God. Now we could scream out for the help of God, and He would answer us. Especially today, on Hoshanah Rabbah, when we are as the lowly willow, as empty vessels that are ready to receive the help of God.

Let us then cry out with our hearts and souls, "Please, God, once and for all, remove the evil from among us! Redeem us totally and finally for the sake of Your holy name."

13

The Additional Holiday

SHEMINI ATZERES—THE EIGHTH DAY

On the eighth day you shall have a solemn assembly: you shall do no laborious work, but you shall offer a burnt offering, an offering by fire, a pleasant odor to God. . . . (Numbers 29:35)

he Divine nature of the world is hidden within natural laws. Everything appears to operate according to laws that are totally divorced from spirituality. This is all an illusion. During Sukkos the Jewish people have a strong experience of the spiritual nature of the world. This experience is incongruous to the illusion of the natural world, and it must remain protected inside the *sukkah*.

The eighth day, Shemini Atzeres, is different. It is beyond the seven natural days, and it is beyond nature. It is actually the World to Come; the Divine nature is clear and manifest without the slightest concealment.

The Divine nature of the world is also revealed through the Torah. The Torah is the word of God. It reveals to each person the nature of the world and where his place is within it. Therefore, the celebration of Torah is most fitting on Shemini Atzeres.

Similarly, during the seven days of Sukkos, we make offerings for all the seventy nations. However, on the eighth day, only one offering is made. This offering is only for the Jewish nation. On this day the relationship between God and the Jewish people is clear. The Divine reality needs no protection; consequently, we do not sit in the *sukkah*. This could be the meaning of the talmudic conclusion: "We do sit in the *sukkah*" (*Sukkah* 47a). Thus, on the eighth day, it is as if we are sitting in the *sukkah*. The protection comes of itself.

"On the eighth day, you shall have a solemn assembly" (Numbers 29:35). The Talmud compares this to a king who made a celebration for his trusted servants. There were seven days of royal feasts, banquets, and lavish entertainment. When it was over, the servants were preparing to leave. The king said to them, "It is very hard for me to part with you. Please prepare a small homemade dinner without any embellishments. Let us sit down as small-town friends and enjoy each other's company" (*Sukkah* 55b).

The Divine gifts constantly flow to the world in great abundance. Often the creatures have not even the vessels to receive what God gives them. Out of His great mercy God concentrates His gifts into channels small enough for mankind to receive. This is the situation for all the nations of the world. However, the Jewish people are intimately bound to God, and they have a permanent, albeit constricted, channel to receive God's gifts. This channel is the "small homemade dinner" of Shemini Atzeres. It the eighth day with prayers for "rain" to sustain the world throughout the year.

What do the Jewish people do? They take the constrictedness of the material world and broaden it into infinity. They do this by following the Torah formulas for the revelation of the Divine nature of the world. They become vessels to experience the fullness of God's gifts to them.

When we pray for Divine "rain" on Shemini Atzeres, let us prepare the appropriate vessels for it. Then infinite blessing will come into our lives.

"The eighth day you shall have a day of solemn assembly" (Numbers 29:34). On the eighth day, a person can reach the level of assembly or gathering that is so small and insignificant that the only life he receives is directly from God.

The Baal Shem Tov said, "We can compare this to a man who has come in from the cold winter air to warm himself by the blazing fireplace. He is shivering with cold and comes directly in front of the fire. Soon his clothes and skin thaw and start to warm. Then he becomes warmer and warmer until he is too hot to stand close by the flames. He moves back where there is less heat. Soon his body cools, and again he draws near the fire. This too is our relationship with God. When one is too close, he can burn; when one is too far, he becomes too cold. As it is written, 'And the celestial creatures run forth and back'" (Ezekiel 1:14).

When we realize what insignificant specks we are compared to the infinite consuming fire, the warmth enters us. The Jewish people have this virtue; whenever they receive a blessing from God, they gather and humble themselves totally. Thereby, they receive His blessings in greater measure.

During the holiday of Sukkos, we receive an abundance of gifts and humble ourselves totally. As a result we receive the holiday of Shemini Atzeres, which is Divine beyond any limitations. Therefore, let us become like gathered dots, for no part of which is whole or fulfilled. Therefore, the blessings will come to us in great abundance.

We move from our homes into the *sukkah*, God's refuge. On the eighth day, we return to our homes with the gifts that we received in the *sukkah*. What gifts did we receive? On a simple level, each of us received renewed strength, vitality, and faith. On a more complex level, the gift was the very fact of our staying in the house of God and our refusal not to leave it for seven days. This is the greatest gift of all; we have drawn close to God.

The Zohar relates, "There are two types of penitents. One feels badly about the evil he had done, and he returns to God out of remorse. While this certainly is repentance, it still lacks completeness. The complete and most genuine return is when one finally focuses all his energies to seek God."

We can compare this to a king who married the princess, a girl whom he had known since his youth. They were happily married for several years. One day she did something terrible, and he banished her from the palace. After some time she felt very bad about

what she did, but she felt even worse about being separated from the king whom she loved very much.

There are those who are sorry that they acted against their Creator. That can start them toward a deep repentance; however, even deeper are those who yearn to be close to God again. But their misdeeds stand in the way.

On Sukkos we rejoice that God had forgiven our sins. We are now cleansed of the troublesome deeds of our past. On Shemini Atzeres the rejoicing is deeper. Now we fully experience that God has removed all obstacles from our path to Him again.

There are three crowns: the crown of kingdom, the crown of Torah, and the crown of priesthood. Each corresponds to one of the three holidays. "Kingdom" is the Passover Exodus when we became a nation and God became our king. "Torah" is the Divine encounter at Mount Sinai when we received the Ten Commandments. This is the holiday of Shavuos. Finally, "priesthood" represents the clouds of glory that came in the merit of Aaron, the *kohen*. This is the holiday of Sukkos.

Why is there another holiday of Shemini Atzeres? As we have learned, "The crown of a good name is higher than all of them" (*Avos* 4:17). The three holidays are Divine gifts, but Shemini Atzeres is a result of what we had accomplished by our own deeds. The "good name" is a result of all our efforts.

Similarly, we had three forefathers: Abraham, Isaac, and Jacob. This can be compared to a stool with three legs. Out of the three forefathers grows a fourth leg on the stool; this is David. David's descendent will be the *Mashiach*, who will redeem and end all exiles forever. He will usher in an era of true peace and tranquility called the Age of the *Mashiach*.

The last day of Sukkos symbolizes the end of days, King David and the advent of the *Mashiach*. Shemini Atzeres follows directly from that concept. It will usher in the era of peace—the good name for the whole Jewish nation.

"When King Solomon finished building the Holy Temple in Jerusalem, he made a celebration for seven days. On the eighth day, he sent everyone home" (1 Kings 8:66). This is also the eighth day of Sukkos, Shemini Atzeres.

We can compare this to a king who prepared a banquet for all his servants. He erected large tents to accommodate the guests, and he also used the huge gardens. When the celebration was over, the guest started to leave, and the king turned toward the palace. Everyone took their leave except the royal family and the king's inner circle. They accompanied the king even to his chambers.

Similarly, during Sukkos, all the world celebrates with the Creator. All the seventy nations receive gifts of Divine blessing. Then it is time to go home ". . . on the eighth day he sent everyone home." The nations take their leave; they had no other interest except to acquire something and to run. But the king's family accompany him to his chambers. When they receive their bounty from him, they realize how insignificant they are without him and how much they want to be with him. This parallels God's presence that is above and beyond the material world. It is beyond the seven days of creation; it is already eight.

Let us then appreciate the value of our gifts and not abandon the King. Preferably, let us remain with Him and be led into His inner chambers.

———

The Kingdom of Heaven is now concealed in this world. Therefore, the close relationship between the Creator and His people is also concealed. Thus, it is the task of the Jewish people to make it manifest. During each holiday, some basic aspect of this special relationship becomes revealed. Because Shemini Atzeres is the last of the year's holidays, it is also the "final" revelation. This day gives us the energy to reveal God's kingdom all year.

The year starts with great concealment. The loving-kindness of God is hidden, and all the world is placed in judgment. It seems as if the world will be destroyed for surely no one is worthy. As it is written, "Blow the shofar (the horn) on the new moon in the hiddenness of our holiday" (Psalms 81:41). This hiddenness forces the Jewish people to work very hard. They do the work for which they are best suited, and they then work constantly for twenty-one days. Finally, it is the eighth day, Shemini Atzeres, and God's name is clearly manifest in the world.

Shemini Atzeres is the Divine nature, the World to Come. It can only be miraculously manifest in this world as a holy day, for it is not a regular day. Therefore, it is connected to the name of God, which also means, I will be. It is not yet to be, but it will be. The name is spelled aleph, heh, yud, heh, and it has the numerical value of twenty-one. These are the twenty-one days that the Jewish nation toils to reveal God's kingdom, the World to Come—that which will be.

Similarly, it is written, "You should rejoice in your holiday, and you should be only happy" (Deuteronomy 16:14). The Hebrew word for only is ach, which is spelled aleph, chof; it also has the numerical

equivalent of twenty-one. When you work twenty-one days, from the hiddenness of Rosh Hashanah until the total revelation of Shemini Atzeres, then you are worthy of "only" happiness in its simplest purity.

Therefore, Sukkos is called the time of ingathering and of strength. All the energies of the year are gathered to be revitalized and focused in the service of the holy work. When this is done, one is exposed to great dangers and is in need of protection. Thus, God takes us into the sukkah.

Similarly, on Shabbos we gather the energies of the entire week and consecrate them for the Divine purpose in the Creation. Then too we do need protection. Shabbos is given a tent of peace that is spread over us, for we recite in the Sabbath prayers, ". . . He who spreads His tent of peace over us and all of Israel and Jerusalem."

We can compare this to a shepherd who allowed his sheep to graze in the pasture. While the sheep ate, he lay under a tree playing his flute. Now it was time to gather and lead them home. He needed to be alert, and he watched his flock carefully lest a danger should befall them. Once the sheep reached their destination, the shepherd could again relax.

Throughout the entire twenty-one days, we work on the ingathering of all our energies. On the twenty-first day, we have arrived at a dimension of time that is out of time—"I will be"—but it is not yet to be; it is the World to Come.

Many of the greatest tzaddikim yearned to taste the World to Come. What would that infinite joy taste like? How peaceful is Divine peace? Yet here is a day that is the World to Come in which we can "taste" the Divine presence. Those who taste it are lifted to ecstatic heights outside the natural dimensions of time and space. They sing and dance in joy while expressing the pure sense of peace within their souls.

———

The holiday of Sukkos is finished, yet the Jewish people add another day of celebration. This is Shemini Atzeres.

We can compare this to a villager, a subject of a king, who was invited to the palace. The man came and politely took part in royal meals and enjoyed the palatial pleasures. When his stay ended, he thanked the king graciously and took his leave.

The next day a friend of this villager came to him for dinner. When the family sat at the meal, the guest noticed some curious new customs. He said, "I have never before noticed that you use table napkins or silver, and now you do. Why so?" The host answered, "I have just been to the palace. Now I want the palace to come to me."

Similarly, after the six weekdays, we enter into the holiness of *Shabbos*. When we leave *Shabbos*, we take some of it along into the following week by adding several minutes onto the *Shabbos*. Likewise, on Shemini Atzeres we take the palace, the holiness of the *sukkah*, into our realm for the year-round.

Each of the holidays has a special commandment associated with it. Passover has *matzos*; Shavuos has the two loaf offerings; Sukkos has the *sukkah*. But Shemini Atzeres has nothing but the concept that "you should be only happy" (Deuteronomy 16:15). This day we can move out of the material realm totally. Then we need absolutely nothing except the joy of our encounter with the Divine presence.

The *sukkah* is the refuge that God opens for those who repent and return to Him.

The world was created with the Hebrew letter *heh*, ה (soft h), the softest and easiest sound to make in the alphabet. It is nothing more than a breath—and the world was there. Examining the shape of the letter, we notice a large opening on the bottom and a small one on top. This symbolizes that if a person wants to abandon his special mission and topple out of the bottom, he has an abundance of room. However, he can still return, although with much greater difficulty, through the small opening at the top.

Similarly, a halachically, or technically, valid *sukkah* needs "two complete walls and the third even one cubit wide" (*Sukkah* 6b). This is the same shape as the *heh*, ה; therefore, it is the refuge of the penitent.

Likewise, it is written in a Yom Kippur prayer, ". . . His hand is open to accept those who return." The Hebrew word for hand is *yad*, which is composed of two Hebrew letters, *yud*, י, and *dalet*, ד. Both letters together form the letter *heh*, ה, the symbol for the penitent.

However, there are two dimensions of "opening" for the penitent. One is the opening that emanates from the Divine sphere, the door that God opens for us with great mercy and kindness. The other is the door that we open through yearning and prayer. The door that God opens for us is always open, and its opening is infinite. Whether the door that is opened with yearning and prayer is indeed open depends on our sincerity and resoluteness. The Divine door is like the sea; it is always open. Our door is like a *mikvah*, a ritual bath, which is sometimes open and sometimes closed (*Lamentations Rabbah* 3:34). There are special conditions that validate a *mikvah*. If the conditions are not met, the *mikvah* is not "open." Similarly, if our hearts are not prepared properly for God, then our door is not open.

The door that God opens on Sukkos is open for all of mankind. Each of the nations may enter if it so desires. On the eighth day, the door of yearning and prayer is opened. This door is miraculously unlocked on this day for the Jewish nation. They gather together to pour out their hearts before God, and they beg for "rain," that Divine gifts should come to them. Thus, when the infinite doors are open to us on Shemini Atzeres, even our finite doors are transformed miraculously, and they become infinite. Nothing is in our way. The path is clear. Let us return to our Creator without reservation.

The holiday of Sukkos is the season of ingathering, when the Jewish people gather for blessing and peace. They receive a special blessing that their gathering should bring peace. Therefore, their gathering also ends with peace. As it is written, "On the eighth day you should have a solemn assembly" (Numbers 29:33). On the other hand, the arrogant evildoers gather to do evil. Evil is separation, fragmentation, and destruction. It leads to the opposite of peace.

This is clearly illustrated in the time of war. As it is written, "When you near a city to make war with her, you should call out to her and make peace" (Deuteronomy 20:10). The way of righteousness unites, binds, and builds. Evil destroys, for it is written, "Peace, peace, but there is no peace" (Jeremiah 6:14). When evildoers gather and ask for peace, it ends with disunity and destruction.

On the day of Shemini Atzeres let us gather our energies totally and finally. Let us hold them together for the entire year as a source of blessing and peace to us and those whom we touch.

"In the beginning when God created the heavens and earth, the earth was desolate and bare . . ." (Genesis 1:1).

There was nothing but God before the Creation. When the material world was created, it started to spread and spread. Then God said, "Enough!," and it stopped spreading. This "enough" (*dai*, in Hebrew) is one of the names of God, *Sha-dai*. For it is written, "He who said, 'Enough!' to His world" (*Genesis Rabbah* 1:1).

To where was the world spreading? On a simple level, it was spreading deeper and deeper into materialism. At first the Divine nature of Creation was crystal clear because the world was very close to its Divine roots. Then, as it spread it moved deeper into the world of illusion.

The mission of the Jewish nation is to reiterate the original command of "Enough!"—to reestablish the Divine nature of the world and to reveal its true roots. This is done on Sukkos on an elementary level. It is the time of ingathering, the holding together, lest materialism should spread. This becomes more true on the eighth day, a day of solemn assembly. It has the special blessing of holding together as Atzeres signifies. We truly can reveal the Divine roots of the world on this day through the Torah, which is the ultimate revelation of Divine roots in the world. Thus, the eighth day is connected with the Torah, and we rejoice for them both.

"Six days you should eat *matzos*, and the seventh is a day of solemn assembly" (Deuteronomy 16:8).

When the Jewish nation left Egypt, they were not completely free. The Egyptian army chased after them to the Red Sea. Finally and miraculously, they were saved on the seventh day. For six days there was still *matzos*, which also means *mitzo*, "quarrel and conflict." On the seventh day, they were finally assembled in freedom.

Similarly, during the Sukkos holiday, although they are protected, the Jewish nation is still in battle. The battle started with the judgment of Rosh Hashanah, the New Year. They are judged together with the entire world. The question or battle is: "Who will be vindicated?" On Yom Kippur, the battle is still raging. The Jewish people clamor for the acceptance of their purification. Finally, on Sukkos they enter God's refuge, yet there is still room for the other nations. Therefore, offerings are made for the seventy nations of the world. On Shemini Atzeres, all is quiet. The battle is won. We are totally assembled in peace.

". . . You should celebrate the holiday for seven days. The first day is a rest day, and the eighth day shall be a solemn rest" (Leviticus 23:39).

If the holiday is for seven days, how does the eighth day become mentioned?

The seven days of Sukkos represent the material world. The material world is made up of fragments, and we assign numbers to these fragments. However, the number eight represents the Divine nature of the world. It is not an ordinary number, but a singularity; therefore, the eighth day unifies all the seven days that passed before.

The arrogant nations of the world each have the ambition to rule the world. Their actions are divisive and fragmenting. Therefore, on Sukkos, offerings are made for them all. Their connection is with the fragmented numbers of the "seven" days. On the other hand, the eighth day is one of unity, oneness, and true peace. This day is reserved for the Jewish people who yearn and pray, hope and do, and make the world a place where ". . . nation shall not lift sword against nation, neither will they know war any more" (Isaiah 2:4).

". . . and Moses declared to the people of Israel the feast days of God" (Leviticus 23:39).

Each of the holidays brings a special blessing to the Jewish nation. These blessings come in the merit of our forefathers, Abraham, Isaac, and Jacob. The blessings could come, but how are they received? This was accomplished by Moses. He connected the holidays to the heart and soul of the Jewish people.

We can compare this to a father who gave his son an expensive gift. The son did not appreciate the gift because he was ignorant of its value. A friend of the boy came and showed great interest, surprise, and amazement when he saw the gift. He admired and praised its worth. Slowly, the son also started to comprehend a sense of the gift's worth.

Moses was totally saturated with Torah energy. The Torah that he taught instructs us how to receive those teachings. Therefore, Moses' declaration of the holidays opened the Jewish people's hearts to receive God's bountiful gifts. This was and is the uniqueness of Shemini Atzeres; it opens all hearts to receive the blessings of the other holidays.

"On the eighth day you shall have a solemn assembly" (Numbers 29:34). When people unite for the sake of God, the unity remains even after the project is completed. Sukkos is the time for ingathering. Still, when it is over, the unity remains through the eighth day. This brings the unity of Sukkos into the calendar year, and it never leaves us.

Prayers for Rain

From what time should they begin to mention the Power of Rain?

Rabbi Eliezer says, "From the first day of the festival of Tabernacles (Sukkos)." Rabbi Joshua says, "From the last day of the Festival of Tabernacles." Said Rabbi Joshua to him, "Since rain during the holiday is but a sign of a curse, why should one make mention of it?" Rabbi Eliezer replied to him, "I did not really say to pray for but merely to mention, Who causes the wind to blow and the rain to fall in its proper season?" He answered him, "If so, one should mention it at all times." (*Taanis* 2a)

The opinion of Rabbi Joshua is accepted.

The world was created on Rosh Hoshanah, for we recite in our prayers, "This is the day You have started to make the world." It was formed and shaped according to laws that continue without interruption. Man also is part of this creation, and it is for him to look after God's work. Therefore, before man there was no rain "because God did not yet bring rain on the earth as there was no man to work the soil" (Genesis 2:5). When man was created, he looked around and realized that the earth needed rain. He yearned and prayed. The rain came.

When you are positive that something will happen, you neither yearn nor pray for it. Why pray when you need but wait and it will be there? Yet, when there is doubt, then there is also yearning and prayer. Rain is a phenomenon that we can never be positive of its coming. Therefore, when man looked at the parched earth, he prayed for rain. Thus, in order to pray, we must step out of the familiar in our hearts and evaluate our needs. We need rain, the blessings of God, the holy Torah. Let us yearn and pray.

The three holidays—Passover, Shavuos, and Sukkos—correspond to the three blessings we all need: children, life, and sustenance. Passover is for our children, for we retell the story of our Exodus. Shavuos is the day when the Torah was given; the Torah is our life. Finally Sukkos is the time when we beg for "rain," sustenance from our Creator.

The season of sustenance is a time of joy. In turn, the Creator is joyous in providing for His creatures. Similarly we too should provide sustenance to others. This brings even more blessing from the storehouse of God. This storehouse is opened both physically and spiritually. Our hearts receive a new gift of Torah light that gives us life. Let us, therefore, pray for rain on this day of "only" happiness—the day of the most generous Divine giving.

"And from Midbar [they came] to Matana" (Numbers 21:18)—names of places. Another meaning is, "and from the 'desert' they came to 'having a present.'" When one empties himself as the desert,

then one is ready to receive God's gift. In the desert one gift was a brook of fresh water that followed the Jewish people constantly. Likewise, if we are as a desert, we also receive water.

During each of the three holidays, the well becomes manifest. On Passover and Shavuos, this well is incompletely manifest. It becomes more manifest on Sukkos. It becomes a reality on the eighth day. This is alluded to in the story of Isaac and the wells:

> But when Isaac's servants dug in the valley and found there a well of spring water, the herdsmen of Gerar quarreled with Isaac's herdsmen, saying, "The water is ours." So he called the name of the well, Esek, because they contended with him. Then they dug another well, and they quarreled over that also, so he called its name Sitnah. And he moved from there and dug another well, and over that they did not quarrel; so he called its name Rehovos, saying, "For now the Lord has made room for us, and we shall be fruitful in the land" (Genesis 26:19–22).

The gift of Passover was not yet complete because the Egyptians were in pursuit. The gift of Shavuos, the acceptance of the Torah at Mount Sinai, was also incomplete for the arrogant nations of the world thought it was unfair that the Jews were chosen. At last, the gift of Sukkos became complete, when "fruitfulness" descended and filled us. This concept especially recurs on the eighth day, for it is a microcosm of the previous seven days.

To do acts of kindness is the ultimate desire and pure will of God. There is great rejoicing in the world when God is giving and the creatures receive. And the highest joy is reached on Shemini Atzeres when we pray for rain. Therefore, let us rejoice on this day of days with the Creator of the world "who opens His hand and feeds all living creatures" (Psalms 145:16).

> When they came to Marah, they could not drink the water of Marah because it was bitter . . . and God showed him a tree, and he threw it into the water, and the water became sweet. . . . Then they came to Elim, where there were twelve springs of water and seventy palm trees; and they encamped by the water. (Exodus 15:23–27)

God's gifts of water flow through the twelve springs, the twelve tribes. By way of many channels, the seventy nations of the world receive sustenance too. The work of the Jewish nation is to sweeten the water and to see that it not flow into wasteful places. When we pray for rain, let us purify our hearts and have the proper vessels for the gifts that God gives us in abundance.

In Israel the water or rainy season starts after Sukkos. The summer begins with Passover. During the rainy season, the farmer does not work. He prays and watches the rain vitalize his fields. His primary work occurs during the summer; it is in that season that he does everything.

Similarly, on a spiritual level, most of the worship in the Holy Temple took place during the summer months during the three major holidays. The rainy season contains in potential that which becomes manifest later in the summer. Moreover, now that we have completed all our work, it is time for God to start doing His. Thus, we pray for rain. Let the rain come down from the heaven, for we are prepared.

"Pour before me water during your feast day in order that the rain for the year will be blessed" (*Taanis* 2a).

"When God created the heavens, He separated the upper waters and the lower waters. The lower waters cried constantly that they want to be near God. In turn, God promised to have them poured on the altar and to offer salt with the sacrifices" (*Tikunei Zohar* 5).

The separation of the lower waters and their distance from God are but an illusion. Actually, all water is equally close to the Creator. It needs only clarification to make it manifest. Still we find no preparation of the water. On the contrary, it is poured on the altar in its natural state. This shows that water, no matter if it is higher or lower, is close to God.

However, wine requires much toil before it can be offered on the altar. Grapes must be cut, pressed, strained, and cleaned. In contrast, water is pure and acceptable as is; therefore, God allows the true nature of the lower waters to be manifest during Sukkos. This happens during the ceremony of pouring the water on the altar.

When we pray for rain during the eighth day, we are yearning for Divine Providence. It is our yearning, together with the yearning of the lower waters, that reveals the Divine nature of things.

"The strength of rain is mentioned . . ." is found in the second part of the *Amidah* prayer. The Talmud comments, "Why the word 'strength'? Because it falls with strength" (*Taanis* 2a).

Each and every creature in the world receives sustenance from God. All this emanates from God's infinite loving-kindness that excludes no one. Yet there are those who receive even according to strict judgment.

We can compare this to a benevolent king. Every day of the week, the king's subject would come to see and to beseech him for royal favors. The kind king was favorably inclined to their requests. However, one day a week most of the favor seekers did not come. This was on Tuesday when the king sat in judgment. On this day, only those who were certain to survive the king's stern decisions dared to come to him. Everyone, that is, but the king's son. The prince ignored the days of the week completely, saying, "To me, the king is always kind. After all, even the strictest father is kind to his own children. I can come to him even on the day of judgment."

God's sustenance comes to the Jewish people even when they are judged. As it is written, "He turns the rock into a pool of water, the flint into a spring of water" (Psalms 114:8). Even the rock, the hard strictness of judgment, is turned into flowing kindness. It is also written, "You open Your hand and satisfy the desire of every living thing" (Psalms 134:16). "Hand" always refers to the left hand, which symbolizes strict judgment. Nevertheless, for those who deserve, even the left hand is open and satisfies their desires.

On the eighth day, Shemini Atzeres, it had finally become clear who deserves sustenance. Thus, let us stand before God as His children and receive fully from His open hand.

14

Great Rejoicing

n the eighth day, Shemini Atzeres, it is customary to make a celebration with the Torah. Outside *Eretz Yisrael*, Israel, it is celebrated on the ninth day, the last day of the holiday, commonly called Simchas Torah.

The chasidic masters have celebrated it so that it corresponds to the celebration in Israel. They celebrate both on Shemini Atzeres and the next day of Simchas Torah.

REJOICING WITH THE TORAH—SIMCHAS TORAH

There are two levels of happiness with the Torah. One is the happiness that comes from learning something new, which is related to the clarity of understanding. The other is being happy with the mere fact of receiving the word of God.

This can be compared to a king who sought the best possible mate for his son. After many years of searching, he finally found the most suitable girl in all the world. The prince trusted his father's efforts and married the girl. Each day he was with her, he discovered a new virtue that she possessed. This made him immensely happy. Yet, his happiness was even deeper than that. Each time he saw a good trait in her, it reaffirmed his trust in his father and the quality of his choice.

Similarly, it is written, "The Torah was commanded to us by Moses; it is an inheritance (*morasha*) to the congregations of Jacob" (Deuteronomy 33:4). Do not merely read *morasha* to mean an inheritance, but read it as *meorasa*, which means married to. When a person learns Torah, he must be on the level of "marriage" with God's word. He should know the Torah like a wife; he should rejoice in every revealed and hidden meaning and interpretation. Yet the deeper level is *morasha*, an inheritance. The Jewish people accept the Torah as the gift that is an inheritance from God.

This level of inheritance is not attained by everyone. A person must humble himself so that his particular share in the Torah comes by being part of all of Israel. The taste of the gift and the inheritance that the Jewish nation received bring the deepest happiness. On Shemini Atzeres the doors are open for *atzeres*, "assembly." Therefore, let us assemble and reconnect ourselves to the Jewish nation and receive the Torah as a gift and inheritance.

Rejoicing with the Torah occurs at the beginning of the year. The joy, singing, and dancing open our hearts and make us yearn for a life filled with Torah. Even before the Torah enters our head, it enters our feet, the lowest level. Our feet walk with regularity and consistent habit; the daily routine of our lives must first be saturated with Torah. This happens when we rejoice and dance. When the lower levels are filled with Torah, the rest of the body follows; as it is written, "I have thought about my ways, but my feet bring me back to Your Torah" (Psalms 119:59).

"And you shall love God your Lord with all your heart, all your spirit, and all your possessions. And these words, which I command you today, shall be on your heart; and you shall study them ..." (Deuteronomy 6:5).

These verses symbolize the fall holidays: "with all your heart" symbolizes Rosh Hashanah, the Day of Judgment when we consecrate our entire heart to God; "with all your spirit" represents Yom Kippur, which is a day when our spirit is withheld sustenance; and "with all your possessions" is Sukkos when we gather our produce from the fields and abandon our homes to sit in a temporary dwelling.

If one participates in those three holidays, then one is worthy of "and these words which I command you today shall be on your heart." After Sukkos one is ready to place the words of Torah deeply into one's heart. This is symbolized by the word *atzeres*, which means assembly. During the sacred assembly we pull together tightly and safely in a vessel; we hold the Torah in the innermost part of our hearts. This brings great joy, and we are able to rejoice with the Torah.

The Kabbalists divide the year into two spheres. The winter months are the potential, whereas the summer months are for revelation of the potential through activity. Passover and Shavuos in the summer months correspond to Sukkos and Shemini Atzeres in the winter months.

The holiday of Shavuos commemorates the day we received the Ten Commandments, and it is called Atzeres, "solemn assembly." Moreover, the eighth day of Sukkos, Shemini, is also called Atzeres, and we celebrate and rejoice with the Torah. The fruit that started growing on Shavuos has finally ripened. It is time for the harvest, and there is gladness and joy in our hearts.

The Torah contains the entire story of the Holy Temple, the offerings, the pouring of water on the altar, and other holiday traditions. We no longer have many of these traditions because the Holy Temple was destroyed. Therefore, our celebration during the Sukkos holiday turns into a celebration with the Torah, which contains the fullness of the holiday.

"In the shadow of His refuge, I yearned to be; and His fruit was sweet to my palate" (Song of Songs 2:3). "His refuge" means the days of Sukkos; "His fruit is sweet" is the eighth day when we rejoice with the Torah.

The Torah is the blueprint of the world, for it is written, "In the beginning when God created . . ." (Genesis 1:1). God created the world by looking into the Torah, which is called the beginning, the root of the world. On the Eighth Day of Solemn Assembly, we pull all our energies to gather and connect them at their roots. Thus, we are simultaneously connected to the Torah, the roots of the creation.

How do we reach this level? Arrogance is the dispersion of the ego and its attachment to the outside world. Humility is the opposite. We pull our attach-

ments together into ourselves until they form one tiny speck that insignificantly disappears. This is the same as *atzeres*, "assembly," a concentration of our energies and humbling ourselves before God.

"The Torah was commanded to us by Moses; it is an inheritance to the congregation of Jacob" (Deuteronomy 33:4).

Each of us has a share in the Torah; our roots are connected to the roots of the Torah. It is through our ties with the Torah that we are able to unite as a people. Because of the Torah, we are able to be a "congregation of Jacob."

Let us therefore unite our souls with the Torah and thereby with our people. This brings the greatest joy and celebration.

From the mouth of babes, You have founded strength to put to rest the enemy and the avenger. Who is man that You should remember him, and son of man that You should look after him? And You have made him but less than the Divine, and You have crowned him with honor and—You have let him rule over Your handiwork, all You have placed under his feet. (Psalms 8:3–7)

These verses refer to the fall holidays. "Who is man that You should remember him?" refers to the Day of Judgment, which is Rosh Hashanah. Man's very existence is in doubt; therefore, they are the "Who?" It is not yet clear who they are nor what will happen to them. "You made him but less than the Divine" refers to Yom Kippur when all of Israel purify themselves and are likened to angels. "You have crowned him with honor" refers to Sukkos when God surrounded the Jewish nation with clouds of honor. "You have made him rule over Your handiwork" refers to the eighth day where it is written, ". . . a day of solemn assembly it should be for you"; it is in your hands and your power.

The Midrash relates how God was about to give the Torah to the Jewish nation and the angels complained, "Who is man that You should remember him?" (Numbers 29:35). Yet with effort man can be "but less than the Divine"; he can pull himself to great spiritual heights.

Furthermore, before giving the Torah to the Jewish nation, it was first presented to the other nations of the world. The descendants of Esau refused it because of the commandment against killing. The children of Ishmael refused it because of the prohibition against robbery. Ishmael was the son of Abraham who symbolized kindness, the right hand. Esau was the son of Isaac who symbolized stern judgment, the left hand. Today, Ishmael attempts to usurp the chosenness of the Jewish people by outdoing their right hand by doing acts of kindness. In addition, Esau tries to usurp the chosenness of the Jewish people by outdoing their left hand through acts of stern judgment.

However, the Torah is more powerful than these opposing hands. As it is written, "The strength of His deeds He has related to His people . . ." (Psalms 111:6). This means that through the Torah we regain the strength originally intended for us. This strength is expressed by being witnesses to the Creation and God's sovereignty. When we are connected to the roots of our being, the Torah, then we regain the use of both our hands. This happens on the eighth day, Shemini Atzeres, the day of solemn assembly when we gather our energies that have gone astray. Therefore, ". . . a solemn assembly it should be for you"— we regain the energies. These energies are returned to the Jewish people again through the power of the Torah.

The Torah is the inheritance of the children of Jacob, whose energies are in his voice, for it is written, "The voice is that of Jacob, but the hands are those of Esau" (Genesis 27:22). The voice of Jacob is poised in balance with the hands of Esau, and on the eighth day the balance tips completely. The energies become focused and clear. The arrogant nations are excluded totally, and the Jewish people are able to do their work unhampered. Let us rejoice on this holy day and celebrate the victory of the voice over the hands, the Torah over arrogance.

Every day is the same as the previous day; nothing changes. There is constancy, continuum, and the irreversible laws of nature; nothing is new.

If the above statement is true, then *teshuvah*, the return to God, is impossible. If only the old well-trodden paths exist, what can one do to deviate from one's old well-trodden but mistaken path? Nothing.

Yet there is *teshuvah* in the world, for it is written, "Let the evildoer abandon his path, and the sinner his thoughts and return to God who will treat him with mercy, and the Lord, for He is all forgiving" (Isaiah 55:7). This is only possible because there is renewal in the world. The world is constantly being created and re-created, pulsating into existence every infinitesimal instant. It appears the same, but is always different.

If a person connects himself to the sameness, he

sinks in quicksand; there is no change for him. However, if he is connected to renewal, then a new path opens for him, and suddenly he discovers himself at the side of God.

The world of renewal is basically concealed except on special occasions during the year. It is revealed during the New Moon and the holidays, at which times we can experience it with more ease. By the time the last holiday, Shemini Atzeres, occurs, the revelation of the world of renewal is at its peak. Let us come to the eighth day with yearning; this is the day in which rejoicing is always being renewed.

It is written, "Blessed is he who trusts in God, and God will be trustworthy to him" (Jeremiah 17:7).

Each item of creation appears as material reality. Yet, its true Divine essence is concealed. We can compare this to a kernel of wheat that is inside its husk. The true nature of wheat is hidden from view while the outside appearance is incomplete and misleading.

We can relate either to the illusion or to the true nature of things. If we relate to the illusion and ignore the Divine essence, then we create an idol, a power independent of God. Because there is no power independent of God, illusion has no life nor existence at all. In contrast, if we relate to the true nature of the world, the Divine, we give it existence and life, and we receive life in return.

Torah is life. It is written, "And you who are connected to God are alive . . ." (Deuteronomy 4:4). Therefore, whoever is connected to the Torah actually is connecting himself to the life within it.

On the eighth day, our trust in God, which started growing on Rosh Hashanah, reaches maturity. Similarly, our connection with the Torah is at its peak. Let us rejoice in God, with life and the Torah for the light and length of our days.

"A man came to Hillel and said, 'Teach me the Torah while I stand on one foot.' Hillel replied, 'Do not do unto others what you do not want done to you. This is the whole Torah; the rest is an explanation'" (*Shabbos* 31a).

The entire Torah is summarized in the commandment, "Love your neighbor as your own self" (Leviticus 19:18). The whole Torah is a prescription that produces one singularity from all the many parts. Therefore, the commandments are an explanation; each one makes clearer how the singularity is to be accomplished.

Similarly, the eighth day is a day to accomplish singularity, as it is written, ". . . a day of solemn assembly it should be for you" (Numbers 29:35). When we assemble all our energies, we are moving in the direction of Torah. Let us rejoice with the Torah and our good fortune of uniting with our people.

On the eighth day, we pray for "rain" and we celebrate with the Torah. The rain falls and helps things grow. The growth is not pure; there are the fruits as well as the husk that covers them. The fruit sustains life, but it too contains impurities, contents that cannot be absorbed by the body. This is the natural way of receiving gifts from heaven.

The food we received in the desert, the *manna*, was different. Every molecule of that food was absorbed by the body. There were neither impurities in the food nor impurities in the vessels that absorbed it. The *manna* had no husk. It was not limited by a surrounding impurity; therefore, it was infinite. Similarly, the sustenance we receive from the Torah is pure and infinite.

We must prepare vessels to receive its great energy, and we can do so on the eighth day, Shemini Atzeres. Atzeres, the day of assembly, is the time when we focus and consecrate our desires into a singular goal and purpose. Our unity with the rest of Israel forms an impregnable fortress of a pure vessel to receive the Divine and infinite portion of the Torah. Thus, on this day, our every cell absorbs the inner blessing of the Torah. Let us rejoice and be glad.

"Let us rejoice and be glad with the Torah because it is our strength and light" (Prayer Book, holiday prayer).

The Torah is a clear and infinite light. As from a lamp, the light comes from a flame that is attached to a wick. It is written, "The *mitzvah* is a lamp and Torah is the light" (Proverbs 6:23). In order to have Torah, one must make a vessel for it by performing the commandments. If not, the flame is left hanging in the air, and it is soon extinguished.

As a nation, we understand this when Moses asked us whether or not we would accept the Torah. We answered, ". . . we will do and we will listen" (Exodus 19:8). We realized that the only way we can have the light of the Torah is if we first do. Then we have the lamp, the wick, and the oil in which the Torah is contained.

The Jewish New Year, which starts in the month of *Tishrei*, is especially full of *mitzvos*; therefore, this time is especially receptive to the light of the Torah. The saturation of deeds starts with the *mitzvah* of shofar, blowing the horn on Rosh Hashanah. This "*mitzvah* saturation" continues with Yom Kippur and with Sukkos, with its *sukkah, esrog, lulav, hadasim,* and *aravos*. It finally culminates in Shemini Atzeres, the eighth day. The eighth day is the completion of the lamp in which the light of the Torah will be contained.

Let us rejoice, for we now have the lamp and the infinite light for the path of life.

Just as the Jewish nation rejoices with the Torah, the Torah also rejoices with them. It is written, "In the beginning when God created the heaven and earth . . ." (Genesis 1:1). The first word in the verse means "with the beginning"; God created the universe with the plan and intention of its beginning, its roots, and the Divine nature of all things. Moreover, the Divine nature of all beings is represented by the Jewish people.

Therefore, the Jewish nation rejoices, for the true intention of the universe becomes revealed. This revelation is the fact that the Torah is the Divine plan and intention of the Creation. Furthermore, the Torah rejoices that the Jewish nation reveals itself as the people of the Divine nature. This becomes clear after Rosh Hashanah, Yom Kippur, and Sukkos. Thus, on the eighth day, the two meet and celebrate together.

"If one learns from his friend one chapter, even one law, even one letter, he is to treat him with honor" (*Avos* 6:3). Surely, this applies to the Torah itself, which teaches us constantly to serve God faithfully. We can honor the Torah by constantly studying it day and night, for it is written, "If you seek her, it will elevate you" (Proverbs 4:8). One should seek Torah as a poor person who gleans the fallen stalks of wheat after the reaping is done.

The Torah is infinite. Each verse, word, and letter contains limitless teachings and is connected to celestial worlds. We are able to grasp only fringes of the fallen stalks. If we humble ourselves to lift up the stalks, then we are uplifted in return. God gives us the infinite teaching as a gift.

Similarly, when the Jewish nation was about to accept the Torah, they went to stand "at the foot of the mountain" (Exodus 19:17). They understood that they only have vessels for the "fringes" of the Torah. This humility made them vessels for its infinite nature. Likewise, we should bend down to look for

Torah teachings in each and every thing we encounter. This too reveals the Divine nature of the universe and the Torah that is found within each item of the Creation.

Deeper still . . .

The Torah is really a singularity. It is Divine, neither fragmented nor made up of parts, and it is "the name of God." It is written, "God wanted to benefit His righteous, that the Torah be magnified and strong" (Isaiah 42:21). The Talmud comments, "He wanted to make the Jewish people worthy; therefore, He gave them Torah and *mitzvos*" (*Makkos* 23b). This means that God conjugated and combined His Holy name in many different ways so His people could learn and live it through the form of deeds.

Let us humble ourselves and rejoice with the name of God that is in each letter of the Torah. This infinite teaching shows us the light in every step of our life. Let us open our eyes and hearts to the Torah that is contained in each and every item of creation. It will lift us to the sphere of Divine and infinite enlightenment, and we will experience true joy and gladness forever and ever.

"This is the Blessing"—*Zos Habrachah*

On the last day, Simchas Torah, it is customary to read the last portion in the Torah, *Zos Habrachah*, "This is the blessing." It is read with a special tune, followed by the reading of the very first portion of the Torah, *Bereishis*, "In the beginning. . . ."

"God has come from Mount Sinai and was shining forth from Seir . . ." (Deuteronomy 33:1). God took the Torah to all the nations of the world to see if they would accept it. They did not; however, the Jewish nation did accept it finally. The Zohar says that the nations' refusal generated a more powerful light than we were to have received. How so?

The Torah can be understood on many levels. If it were given to the angels, it would have been understood on a far less physical level. If it would have been given to the descendants of Esau and Ishmael, it would have been understood on a much more physical level. Therefore, when the nations refused the Torah, we received their levels of understanding too. This is why the Torah starts with the story of Creation. In this manner, we can understand the Torah even on the level of nature and physical events.

"From His right hand came the fire of Law" (Deuteronomy 33:1).

The Torah is like a fire that would consume those who come near it. It is higher than human understanding, and it is only by the mercy of God that we can learn it. Thus, Moses wandered onto the mountain of God "and behold the bush is burning, but it is not consumed" (Exodus 3:2). Therefore, even those who are not consumed by the fire and fervor can still benefit from the Torah by being part of the burning bush, the Jewish nation.

"The Torah was commanded to us by Moses; it is an inheritance to the congregation of Jacob" (Deuteronomy 33:4).

The Jewish nation at Mount Sinai asked Moses to speak to them saying, ". . . let not the Lord speak to us lest we die" (Exodus 20:19). They knew that if God spoke directly to them, the revelation would not last forever. There are no vessels in the universe to contain the intensity of the Mount Sinai revelation. The reason the congregation of Jacob has the Torah as inheritance is because "the Torah was commanded to us by Moses." For his level, they had vessels.

"And this is the blessing that Moses blessed . . ." (Deuteronomy 33:1).

"If one is leading the blessings with the congregation and makes a mistake, another person should continue from where the first one had stopped" (*Deuteronomy Rabbah*). Moses too started where Jacob had stopped. Why does the Midrash use this explanation?

The Jewish people are a vessel ready to receive God's blessing. Even if there are evildoers among them, there is always somebody who is able to restore the vessel. The true blessing is that, when one ceases, there is another one who is able to continue. Where Jacob's blessings end is where the blessings of Moses begin.

"He also loves the nations, all the holy ones in your hands, and they pressed themselves to Your feet and are led by Your word" (Deuteronomy 33:3).

There are four levels of being: the inanimate, the growing plant, the animal, and man. In order to reach any level in its full maturity, one must restore the lower levels to their Divine essence. If the plant is to mature, the inanimate in it must be pure. Similarly, the animal is incomplete if the vegetation it ingests is not the finest and purest. Man too must first connect all the lower levels to their proper roots if he is to be complete. Therefore, the Jewish people bring offerings for all the seventy nations in order that they will be able to come to their level. Thus, in order for Jewish people to be "led by Your word," they first must press themselves to the feet of God, to humble themselves, and to lift up all the lower levels that constitute the sum of their nature.

"And they have pressed themselves to Your feet" (Deuteronomy 33:3). The Jews were miraculously saved from the slavery of Egypt, and God was ready to present them with the Torah. However, their spirits were too inflated, and their arrogance was increasing. They were not appropriate vessels to receive it. Therefore, God took them through the desert for seven weeks. Finally, they regained their humility and were ready for the Torah.

Similarly, after Rosh Hashanah and Yom Kippur, we are redeemed from the slavery of our evil desires. Again there is the inclination to arrogance; therefore, we are asked to leave our comfortable homes and to enter the *sukkah*. We regain our humility, and after seven days, we are able to rejoice with the Torah. Thus, the degree that one humbles himself to the "feet of God" is the degree that one receives the Torah. The Zohar says, "If one be as the doorstep, constantly trodden, then the *Shechinah*, the Divine Presence, lifts him up to great heights" (Zohar, Deuteronomy 33).

"And God came from Sinai, and shone forth from Seir, came forth from Paran, and with Him multitudes of angels" (Deuteronomy 33:2).

There are four levels of learning. One is the literal translation (*pshat*); two is the explanation (*remez*); three is the exegesis (*derush*); and four is the hidden meaning (*sod*). The first three are constantly threatened by evil. *Sinai* also means hatred, for the arrogant nations hated the Jews after they received the Torah. *Seir* are the descendants of Esau and *Paran* are the children of Ishmael, two nations that constantly threaten the Torah. Only one level is not threatened. That is the secret and hidden. No one can touch that for it is the Divine realm—the "multitude of angels."

Similarly, the three holidays—Passover, Shavuos, and Sukkos—each correspond to one of the forefathers: Abraham, Isaac, and Jacob. Each of those had been threatened, but Shemini Atzeres

represents King David, the one who will bring the complete redemption. That day is free from evil entirely.

"All the holy ones are in Your hand; they press themselves to Your feet and they follow Your word" (Deuteronomy 33:3).

The Jewish people are the witnesses that God is the Master of the world. It is written, "... 'You are my witnesses,' says the Lord" (Isaiah 43:12). How can the Jews be witnesses if they are as close to God as children are to their father? The truth is that the Jewish people do not say witness. They are special, chosen, uplifted, and living on a high standard of social morality. Still they humble themselves as the lowest of people. Why? Because they know clearly that God is the ultimate Master and no other power exists beside Him. When people see the humility of the Jewish people, they realize that the world has a master. When people see that the Jews are pressed to the feet of God, the nations realize that the Jews follow His word. Thus, the nations also become witness to God.

"And among the Jewish nation, there was a king" (Deuteronomy 33:5). King means the Torah, and it also means Moses. How are these two interpretations reconciled?

Just as Moses gave us the Torah, the Torah gave us Moses. Therefore, each time people gather to study Torah, the teaching energy of Moses is evident.

Furthermore, the Torah is composed of the names of God, His garments are the twenty-two letters of the Hebrew alphabet. These are as the garments of a king. When he "wears" them, they are different than when he has them hanging in the closet. Similarly, we must be connected to the garments of God, the Torah, as if He is wearing them. Our connection should be to God Himself rather than to the garments. The connection should be to the King; thereby, we have the Torah and Moses, our teacher.

"And this is the blessing with which Moses blessed the Jewish people" (Deuteronomy 33:1).

We recite a blessing before and after reading the Torah scroll. We can compare this to the blessing we make before and after we eat. Before eating we thank God that He is providing sustenance for our starving body. After eating we thank Him for the vitality and energy that our body is absorbing and digesting from the food.

Similarly, there are two holidays in which we celebrate the giving of the Torah. On Shavuos we rejoice over the very fact of receiving the Torah. On Shemini Atzeres, the eighth day, we rejoice in absorbing the Torah. Just as the rain falls and fertilizes the seeds, enabling them to grow and bloom, so too the Torah makes our hearts fertile and vitalized.

This growth in one's heart bears fruit. This fruit is the "Torah" that one originates creatively. Therefore, we say in the prayer before the Torah reading, "And everlasting life He has planted in us. . . ." This energy to create and originate interpretation, the Oral Law, was given to the Jewish people by Moses. He planted it inside us. Therefore, it is written in the blessing after the Torah reading, "And this is the blessing that Moses blessed. . . ." This blessing, which symbolizes the absorption of the Torah and the blossoming of the Torah deep in our bones, is the Oral Torah that each one of us innovates. This blessing was given to us by Moses.

May we be worthy of the Divine "rain," so that the words of Torah seep into our bones and shine forth from us in greater strength.

The blessing after the Torah reading is, ". . . that He gave us a teaching of truth." Should not the words have been "that He gave us a true teaching . . ."?

The answer is that the Torah is the document that reveals the Divine truth. This world is one of illusion, falsehood, and lies. The Torah breaks through this sham and deceit and openly declares the Divine truth to mankind. This is because the Torah is the Divine nature of every existing thing. Therefore, if there is any truth, it is the Torah that is the foundation of that truth.

Similarly, the true humanity of man is revealed when he is connected to the Torah. Therefore, the words "The Torah was commanded to us by Moses— *Torah Tzivah Lonu Moshe.*" The first Hebrew letter of each word spells *tzelem,* "image." Man does not possess his true image unless he possesses the Torah, for the Torah helps reveal the fullness of his image.

"The Torah was commanded to us by Moses; it is an inheritance to the children of Jacob" (Deuteronomy 33:4).

The Torah is Divine and the true nature of all things. However, it is concealed and requires revelation by the Master of the world. Yet, in rare instances one is pure enough to relate to its concealed nature. This was possible for our forefathers, Abraham, Isaac, and Jacob, who lived a Torah life long before the Mount Sinai revelation.

We inherited a sensitivity to the Divine from our ancestors, for we recite in the morning prayer, "He planted in us an everlasting life." The everlasting life, the Torah, is planted deep within us as an inheritance. This is the Oral Law, the Torah that grows out of one's own life and being. The Written Law is the key that opens up the hearts of the Jewish people to find the treasure within each Jew. Thus, the revelation at Mount Sinai presented the Jewish people with keys for their inner inheritance. "The Torah was commanded to us by Moses"; thereby, it revealed to them the inheritance within their hearts.

"And all of the firm hand that Moses had done before the eyes of the Jewish nation" (Deuteronomy 34:12). "In the beginning when God created the heaven and earth . . ." (Genesis 1:1).

The purpose of the creation is to reveal its Divine nature. This inner nature has been revealed from time to time, but this revelation especially occurred to the Jewish nation during their sojourn in the desert. These were the "miracles" that Moses showed to them, for it showed them the inner essence, the roots, and the beginning of all existence.

This brings the teaching of the Torah full circle. What is the teaching? That the true nature of the world is miraculous as Moses clearly showed the Jewish nation. This is the "beginning" spoken of at the outset of the teaching.

May we be worthy to experience the world in its true form through the light of the Torah.

"And this is the blessing which Moses blessed . . ." (Deuteronomy 33:4). "In the beginning when God created the heavens and the earth . . ." (Genesis 1:1).

Why does the creation of the world start with a *beis,* the second letter of the Hebrew alphabet? Why not the *aleph,* the first letter? Because *aleph* is used to spell *arur,* "cursed"; and the Creation (Torah) is a blessing. Moreover, *beis* can spell *brocha,* "blessing"; God looked at the world and blessed it, saying, "I do hope it will last!" (*Genesis Rabbah* 1:1).

The Torah that was presented at Mount Sinai, the Ten Commandments, starts with an *aleph*—*Anochi,* "I am. . . ." There is no fear of *arur,* curse, because the Torah is the root of blessing. It transforms even the curse into a blessing. This is also the path of the righteous, for it starts with thorns and ends with a smooth road.

Likewise, the "curses" mentioned in the Torah are actually blessings when we are connected to the Torah. The Divine nature of all evil is the greatest kindness. Whoever is a vessel, receptive to the inner nature of the universe, receives the curses as a blessing even on a material level.

"And this is the blessing. . . ." The Torah starts with blessing, although concealed in one letter, and ends with the full expression of blessing. Those who are worthy and prepare themselves to be vessels for the blessing experience its fullness in the end.

"The Torah was commanded to us by Moses . . ." (Deuteronomy 33:4).

The souls of the Jewish people are the lamps on which the flame of the Torah can rest. It is written, "The commandment is a lamp and the Torah is the light" (Proverbs 6:23). Furthermore, "The lamp of God is a man's soul" (Proverbs 20:27). The more we prepare ourselves to be vessels to the flame, the more the Torah is part of us.

Some generations have better vessels than others to receive the light of the Torah, and others have pitifully poor vessels. In their case the Torah is in exile, for it is written, "With him I am (*Anochi*) in trouble" (Psalms 91:15). When the Jewish people are in trouble, then the "I am" (*Anochi*) of the first of the Ten Commandments is also in trouble.

Therefore, let us lift ourselves to be appropriate lamps for the Torah flame.

". . . all the signs and wonders . . . and the strong hand . . . that Moses had done before the eyes of all the Jewish nation" (Deuteronomy 34:12). "In the beginning when God created the heaven and earth . . ." (Genesis 1:1).

The world was created with the Torah, which is its concealed essence. Yet the "world was desolate and bare," (Genesis 1:1) until the Jewish people revealed that which was hidden. Therefore, through the intervention of Moses, the true nature of the universe was revealed. Because of "the miracles . . . before the eyes of the Jewish nation," it became clear that, "In the beginning when God created. . . ."

"And this is the blessing. . . ."

Each one of our forefathers—Abraham, Isaac, and Jacob—blessed the Jewish nation. Where the blessing of one ended, there the next one started. Each of their blessings corresponds to one of the three holidays of Passover, Shavuos, and Sukkos. The blessing of Moses corresponds to the eighth day, Shemini Atzeres, which is a holiday unto itself. The blessing of the Torah rests on Shemini Atzeres; therefore, we read the portion of, "This is the blessing that Moses blessed. . . ." It brings blessing for the entire year to be saturated with Torah light.

"And all the firm hand . . . which Moses did before the eyes of all the Jewish nation" (Deuteronomy 34:12). "In the beginning . . ." (Genesis 1:1).

Moses performed all his miracles with the energy of the "beginning," which is the Torah, the root of the entire universe. Likewise, every item of Creation can be restored to its proper place with Torah energy. If the world can be created with the Torah, surely it can be "fixed" with it.

Let us suffuse ourselves with Torah energy and fix ourselves and everything with which we come in contact.

How is the end of the Torah connected to the beginning? The story of Creation was concealed, hidden, and not understood. Finally, when Moses revealed the Torah, the Creation was revealed with it. Therefore, let each one of us delve deeper into the Torah, and the world will shed its concealment.

"And this is the blessing that Moses blessed the Jewish people . . ." (Deuteronomy 33:1).

God blessed the Jewish nation with the Torah, the Divine essence of the universe. The Jewish people are the vessels to receive the blessing. When these three come together completely, there is great rejoicing in the world; and all is whole and at peace.

"And this is . . ." (*v'zos*).

The eighth day of Sukkos is connected to the eighth day of Chanukah, which is called *zos* Chanukah. Both days are the culmination of their respective holidays. They are on the level of eight, the world of the miraculous. In that miraculous world we realize that *zos*—this is it. There is a time and basic essence in the world, and it is the Divine.

15

Laws, Customs, and Prayers of Sukkos

PRAYERS UPON ENTERING THE *SUKKAH*— INVITING THE HOLY GUESTS

 pon entering the *sukkah* for the first time, one should receive the "holy guests" and invite them with great joy and pleasant voice. One says:

Come in, holy heavenly guests; come in, holy heavenly fathers, to sit in the heavenly refuge of faith. Come in, Abraham, the merciful one, and with him Isaac, who was brought to the binding; and with him Jacob, the completed one; and with him Moses the faithful shepherd, and with him Aaron, the holy kohen-priest; and with him Joseph, the righteous one; and with him David, the king—the Messiah. "In the sukkos, you will sit." So please sit, dear holy guests; sit, please; sit, faithful guest, please sit.

After sitting down, it is customary to say:

I am prepared and ready to perform the mitzvah *of* sukkah, *as commanded by my Creator, blessed be His name, "In Sukkos you should dwell for seven days, and all that are native in Israel shall dwell in Sukkos. So that your generations should know that I made the Jewish people dwell in Sukkos when I took them from Egypt" (Leviticus 23:42). Sit, please, sit, my heavenly guest. Sit, please, sit, my holy guests. Sit, please, sit, my faithful guest. Please sit in the refuge of God, blessed be His name. Praiseworthy is our share, and praiseworthy is the share of all the Jewish people. As it is written, "For his nation is God's share, and Jacob is His continued inheritance" (Deuteronomy 32:9).*

The Kabbalists have authored the following prayers:

For the sake of the unification of the Blessed Holy One and His Divine Presence, with awesome reverence and love, to unify the name Yud Heh *and* Vov Heh, *in perfect union, in the name of all of Israel through that which is concealed and hidden, in the name of all of Israel.*

May it be Your will, God, my Lord, God of our fathers, that Your Divine Presence shall rest among us, and spread over us Your tent of peace, for the sake of the unifying of the Holy One, Blessed be His name, and the Divine Presence with awesome reverence and love. To unify the Yud Heh *with* Vov Heh *in a complete union, in the name of all of Israel. And please surround us from the splendor of Your holy and pure honor. This is spread over our head as an eagle protects her nest. And from there should emanate an emanation of life to Your servant (insert name). And in the merit that I left my dwelling to be outside, and do run after Your commandments. May it be considered as if I moved far away. Clean me thoroughly from my sins and transgressions. And from the heavenly guest, the faithful guest, my ears should hear many blessings. And make me worthy to dwell and to have protection in the refuge of Your wings when I leave the world; and be protected from the stream and rain when You will rain coals of fire on the wicked. And may this* mitzvah *of* sukkah, *which I am performing, be considered as if I kept it with all the details and exactness and conditions, and all the commandments that are bound to it. And You should produce a good seal for us, and make us worthy to live a long life on the earth, the holy land, with Your service and awe. Blessed be God forever, Amen and Amen.*

It is fitting that one who enters to eat in the *sukkah* say this:

Master of all the universe! May it be Your will, that the mitzvah *of dwelling in the* sukkah *be considered by You, as if I had kept it with all the details, and exactness, and the 613 commandments bound to it; and as if I meditated on all the meditations of the men of Great Assembly.*

On the second evening and day say:

Come in, Isaac, who was brought to the binding; and with him Abraham, the merciful one; and with him Jacob, the completed one; and with him Moses, the faithful shepherd; and with him Aaron, the holy kohen; *and with him Joseph, the righteous one; and with him, David, the king—the Messiah.*

The First Chol Hamoed

On the third night and day, say:

Come in, Jacob, the completed one; and with him, Abraham, the merciful one; and with him, Isaac, who was brought to the binding; and with him, Moses, the faithful shepherd; and with him, Aaron, the holy kohen; *and with him, Joseph, the righteous one; and with him, David, the king—the Messiah.*

The Second Chol Hamoed

On the fourth night and day, say:

Come in, Moses, the faithful shepherd; and with him Abraham, the merciful one; and with him, Isaac, who was brought to the binding; and with him, Jacob, the completed one; and with him, Aaron, the holy kohen; *and with him, Joseph, the righteous one; and with him, David, the king—the Messiah.*

The Third Chol Hamoed

On the fifth night and day, say:

Come in, Aaron, the holy kohen; *and with him, Abraham, the merciful one; and with him, Isaac, who was brought to the binding; and with him, Jacob, the completed one; and with him, Moses, the faithful shepherd; and with him, Joseph, the righteous one; and with him, David, the king—the Messiah.*

The Fourth Chol Hamoed

On the sixth night and day, say:

Come in, Joseph, the righteous one; and with him, Abraham, the merciful one; and with him, Isaac, who was brought to the binding; and with him, Jacob, the completed one; and with him, Moses, the faithful shepherd; and with him, Aaron, the holy kohen; *and with him, David, the king—the Messiah.*

Hoshanah Rabbah

On the seventh night and day, say:

Come in, David, the king—the Messiah; and with him, Abraham, the merciful one; and with him, Isaac, who was brought to the binding; and with him, Jacob, the completed one; and with him, Moses, the faithful shepherd; and with

him, Aaron, the holy kohen; *and with him, Joseph, the righteous.*

A PRAYER UPON LEAVING THE *SUKKAH*

On Shemini Atzeres, the eighth day, when one is ready to leave the *sukkah* for the last time, one should say:

May it be Your will, O God, our Lord, the God of our fathers, just as I have performed and dwelt in this Sukkah, *I should be worthy in the next year to dwell in the* Sukkah *made from the skin of the Leviathan.*

Master of the world, may it be Your will that the angels who are assigned to the mitzvah *of sukkah and the* mitzvah *of the four species—lulav, esrog, hadas, and aravah—that are performed on the Sukkos holiday, should accompany us when we leave the* sukkah *and should enter our homes with us to life and peace. They should constantly watch over us in Divine watchfulness from Your Holy Dwelling place, to save us from all sins and transgression and from all ill happenings, and all bad times which quickly come to pass. Pour out on us a spirit from on high and renew our understanding to serve You with truth, with awe, and with love. Let us diligently study Your Torah, to learn and to teach. The merit of the four species and the* mitzvah *of sukkah should uphold us, that Your patience be long, until we return to You with full repentance. We should be worthy of both tables, without pain and worry, my household, all my children and descendants and myself. We should all be quiet, peaceful, and at ease, full of sap and vigor, and true servants of God in truth as You want us with Your Good Desire, included among all of Israel.*

May it be the will of God to accept the utterances of my mouth and the thoughts of my heart; God is my rock and my redeemer.

LAWS OF TYING THE *LULAV*

1. It is a *mitzvah* to tie the *lulav* and the myrtle and willow branches with a full knot. Two knots, one on top of the other, should be made. They can be tied with any material.

2. Anything that is tied on to beautify the *lulav* does not invalidate it.

3. If a person had not tied it before sunset at the start of the holiday, he can tie it with a bow.

4. Hold the *lulav* with the spine facing you. Then place the three myrtle branches on the right side a bit higher than the two willow branches on the left.

5. The three species above are all tied together in order that one may lift them at once when saying the benediction.

6. It is also customary to tie two more knots on the upper part of the *lulav* in order to beautify it.

PRAYER WHEN TYING THE *LULAV*

This prayer is said when one ties the *lulav* with the myrtle and willow branches:

May it be the will of God, my Lord, and the God of my fathers, that through the tying of the lulav, *they should also be tied together with the Divine virtues of Greatness, Strength, Beauty, Victory, Majesty; for everything in heaven and earth, to You, God, is the kingdom. Through the three myrtle branches that represent Abraham, Isaac, and Jacob; and through the two willow branches representing Moses and Aaron; and the* lulav *and* esrog *representing Joseph and David; should accomplish the joining the four letters of Your great and holy name. Through the three myrtle branches will be joined the* Yud *of Your great name; and through the two branches of the willow will be joined the full* Heh *of Your great name; and through the* lulav *will be joined the full* Vov *of Your great name; and through the* esrog *will be joined the full* Heh *at the end of Your great name. And from Your holy name should emanate to Your servant (insert name) Your true and good life, which is the numerical values of* hadas, *and the numerical value of* lulav, *including all the letters. And please, God, give my children the blessing of "wholesome, wise, and righteous," which equals the numerical value of* aravah *(including the word). And give me a good and wholesome heart to understand the Torah, which is the numerical value of* esrog *(including the word). And may I be worthy to soon tie them together in the holy Temple, speedily in our days, Amen.*

LAWS OF TAKING HOLD OF THE *LULAV*

1. While standing, take hold of the *lulav* in the right hand and the *esrog* in the left.

2. First hold the *esrog* with the stem on top, for it is the part that is cut from the tree. Then lift the *lulav* and say the blessings. On the first day, there are two blessings; on the other days there is only one blessing.

3. Then hold the *esrog* in the reversed position so that the stem is on the bottom, and then shake it.

4. It is the kabbalistic custom from the Holy Ari, Rabbi Yitchok Luria, to say the blessings and to shake the *lulav* in the *sukkah*.

5. Hold the *lulav* and *esrog* together, touching one another, with the spine of the *lulav* facing the individual.

6. Move the *lulav* and *esrog* away from the body, while facing east, in the following directions: south, north, east, up, down, west; move them toward each direction three times. (Other customs are to shake it in these directions: east, south, west, north, up, and down; east, north, west, south, up, and down; east, north, south, west, up, and down; and east, south, north, up, down, and west.)

7. Do not eat before fulfilling the *mitzvah* of the *lulav*. Do not smell the fragrance of the myrtle leaves or the *esrog*.

8. On *Shabbos* one does not perform the *mitzvah* of *lulav*. Therefore, it may not be carried even in the house. The *esrog*, however, may be carried in the house on *Shabbos* and may be smelled.

A BEAUTIFUL PRAYER TO SAY BEFORE TAKING HOLD OF THE *LULAV*

May it be the will of God, my Lord, and the God of my fathers, that the fruit of the beautiful tree, the palm leaves, the myrtle branches, and the willow leaves, which symbolize the letters of Your singular name, should be brought together one with the other, and they should be as one in my hand, and to know that Your name is being called upon me, and others should fear to come near me, and when I shake them, an emanation be directed to me from the Divine wisdom to the canopy dwelling place, the foundation of our house of God. The mitzvah *of the four species should be considered before You as if I had performed it with all its particulars and roots and the 613* mitzvos *that are bound to her. Because my intention is to unify the name* Yud Heh *and* Vov Heh *in perfect union in the name of all of Israel, Amen. Blessed is God forever, Amen and Amen.*

BLESSINGS FOR THE *LULAV*

Take the *lulav* and *esrog* and say:

> *Blessed are You, O God, our Lord, King of the universe, who has sanctified us with His commandments and instructed us to take hold of the* lulav.

On the first day only:

> *Blessed are You, O God, our Lord, King of the universe, who has kept us alive and has preserved us, and who has brought us to this season.*

KIDDUSH SERVICE

On the first, second, and last two nights after inviting the holy guests, one should recite the *Kiddush*. If these nights follow on a Friday, one should add in a whisper:

And it was evening and it was morning, the sixth day! And heaven and earth were complete; then with the seventh day, God completed His work which He had made, and with the seventh day, He ceased from all His work which He had made. And God blessed the seventh day and made it holy, for with it He had ceased from all His work which He, God, brought into existence in order to continue the work of creation upon it.

One should then continue reciting the *Kiddush*, saying:

Welcome my teachers, rabbis, and all others!

Blessed be You, O God, our Lord, King of the universe, Creator of the fruit of the vine.

Blessed be You, O God, our Lord, King of the universe, Who has chosen us from among all peoples, exalted us above all tongues and has sanctified us by His commandments. And You have given us, O God, our Lord, in love, (Sabbath for rest) festivals of assembly for rejoicing, feasts of rallying and seasons for delight, (this Sabbath day and) the day of this Festival of Tabernacles, the season of our rejoicing (in love), a convocation to the Sanctuary, a remembrance of the Exodus from Egypt. For You have chosen us; You have sanctified us from among all peoples, (and the Sabbath) and Your holy festivals of assembly (in love and in favor) in joy and delight You have given us as an inheritance. Blessed be You, God, Who sanctifies (the Sabbath) Israel and the (festive) seasons.

At the conclusion of the Sabbath, add the following:

Blessed be You, God our Lord, King of the universe, Creator of the flames of fire. Blessed be You, God, our Lord, King of the universe, who has made a distinction between holy and profane, between light and darkness, between Israel and the nations, between the Seventh Day and the six days of work. You have made the holiday, and You have sanctified the Seventh Day above the six working days; You have set apart Your people, Israel, and sanctified them by Your holiness. Blessed be You, O God, Who has made a distinction between holy and holy.

On the first night of Sukkos this blessing is said before "That You let us live . . ."; on the second night, it is said after it.

Blessed are You, O God, our Lord, Who made us holy with His commandments and instructed us to dwell in the Sukkah.

Blessed are You, O God, our Lord, King of the universe, Who has kept us alive, and has preserved us, and Who has brought us to this season.

Laws of Dwelling in the *Sukkah*

1. During the seven days of Sukkos, one should make the *sukkah* one's main residence for eating, sleeping, walking, drinking. All one's needs should be met in the *sukkah*.

2. One should not use the *sukkah* to do menial work such as washing pots and pans.

3. If one eat even an egg-sized piece of bread as a meal, it must be eaten in the *sukkah*.

4. Fruit, wine, liquids, meat, and cheese can be eaten outside the *sukkah*.

5. If a person refrains even from drinking water outside the *sukkah*, he is praiseworthy.

6. One must sleep in the *sukkah*. However, presently, there are legitimate reasons for not sleeping in the *sukkah*, especially if one is married.

7. The first night one is obligated to eat bread in the *sukkah*. If it is raining, one recites the *Kiddush* and completes eating one *kezayis* (olive-sized) piece of bread. One can finish the rest of the meal in the house.

8. Each time a person sits to eat a meal, he is obligated to recite the blessing, "Blessed are You God, our Lord, who has sanctified us in His commandments and instructed us to sit in the *sukkah*."

9. Women, children younger than the "age of obligation," and the sick are not required to sit in the *sukkah*.

10. A *sukkah* must have at least two completed walls and the third wall must be even one *tefach*. (A *tefach* equals approximately 3¾ inches.) However, it is best if it has four complete walls.

11. The roof can be made from any material that grows and is now cut off from its source.

12. The *sukkah* must be at least seven *tefachim* wide and long and at least ten *tefachim* high.

13. It is customary to cover the walls of the *sukkah* with beautiful tapestries and to hang nuts, wine, honey, flowers, and other decorations from the roofing (*sechach*) and sides.

Selecting Choice Species for the *Mitzvah* of the Four Species

The following rules will be an assistance in selecting "beautiful" species. If the particular species is not perfect, it may still be valid to be used for the *mitzvah*. However, in that case, one needs to consult the Code of Jewish Law or a rabbinical authority.

One need not buy the four species in order to have the *mitzvah*. One can use those that belong to someone else. Nevertheless, if one can afford it, one should try to obtain them without any blemish.

Selecting a Choice *Esrog*

The *esrog* should be a "beautiful" fruit, and it should have these naturally beautiful characteristics:

1. It should have no parts missing or punctured.

2. The *pitum* (pestlelike protuberance on the upper portion of the *esrog*) and the *shoshantah* (flowerlike growth) should be whole.

3. It should be clean, without any spots, especially on the uppermost part.

4. The *esrog* should be fresh in appearance and to the touch.

5. It should not be round. It should be wider near

the bottom portion, gradually narrowing toward the upper portion.

6. It should be a matured fruit.

7. An additional aspect of beauty for the *esrog* is symmetry.

8. The skin of the *esrog* naturally has bumplike elevations.

9. The *ukotz* (peduncle, stem, the part cut from the tree) is naturally recessed in the flesh of the *esrog*.

10. The minimum size of an *esrog* is the measure of one egg, preferably a large egg.

Selecting a Choice *Hadas*

1. The leaves of the *hadas* should surround the stem as follows: each row of leaves should have three leaves emerging on the same level (not one above nor below the others.) It should appear as a linked chain surrounding the stem uprightly.

2. The *hadas* should not have more berries than leaves. This includes even the green ones, but especially the red or black ones.

3. The *hadas* should be fresh and green, especially the uppermost leaves.

4. It is best if the top of the branch is whole.

5. It is best if all the leaves of the *hadas* are whole, especially the uppermost ones.

6. If there are small branches between the leaves, they should be removed, but not on a *Yom Tov*.

7. The *hadasim* should be longer than 11½ inches.

Selecting a Choice *Aravah*

1. The *aravah* should have long, smooth-edged leaves that are on a red stem.

2. It is best to obtain those that grow near the water.

3. The top of the twig should be whole.

4. It is best if the leaves are firm and healthy looking and they are all present.

5. The *aravah* should be at least 11½ inches long.

III

THE LIGHT OF
CHANUKAH

Introduction

"And the earth was desolate and bare, and darkness upon the surface of the deep . . ." (Genesis 1:2). The Midrash comments, "Darkness, these are the Greeks who darkened the eyes of the Jewish nation with their evil decrees" (*Genesis Rabbah* 2).

The darkness that the Midrash refers to is that which existed before the creation of light; there was not one single ray of light anywhere, and darkness was total and absolute. Very few of us have ever experienced such total darkness. Even when we are in a dark windowless room, there usually is some light, even just a few rays, filtering in from some tiny crack. But "darkness on the face of the deep" is like blindness—sheer, utter, and total. Why couldn't the Midrash choose a less extreme example such as night or the darkness of a cave? How terrible the Greek exile must have been if our rabbis found no better analogy than the darkness of creation, which is the most extreme.

As a child I would listen to my teacher telling the story of Chanukah. He would emphasize the oppression, whippings, killings, and torture. I would sigh with each new decree and wince with every new tyranny.

Years later I discovered that the real story was slightly different. I was quite disillusioned to hear that, physically, the Jews lacked nothing under Greek rule. Quite the contrary. The Greeks introduced them to their culture of social and political "wisdom," built stadiums and sports arenas for them, and generally wished them no harm. The Jews dressed, spoke, and lived as Greeks and enjoyed life. They were well off.

The truth is, however, that they were indeed in exile—an exile of the worst kind. If the darkness is not total, one can still contrast it with the rays of light that filter in. But if the darkness is total, there is nothing else, and a person is unable to ascertain that he is indeed in the dark. When the Jews aren't aware of their exile, that is the worst exile!

Looking around today, I see that, for the most part, we are left alone by our host countries, thank God. Our hosts say to us, "Come to us; we'll show you the good life!" We have no lack of material wealth and comforts; indeed, we have them in abundance. We too are well off!

But woe is to us! We too have entered a darkness so complete that after a time we no longer know that it is dark. Where are we, after all, spiritually? How much time do we spend on our spiritual needs? How is our Torah study, our relationship to God and to man? What do we feel on *Shabbos* or other holidays? What is our praying like? What do we want, and where are we heading?

In truth we cannot deny that we are now locked within a sheer and dismal exile so dark, so blinding that we are insensitive to our predicament.

Yet a miracle did happen. God beamed His light directly into the abysmal darkness of the exile. Suddenly the Jews realized the severity of their condition and also, miraculously, the way out of the exile. They tasted its bitterness and realized what they lacked. A moment before, their eyes were blinded by the darkness; suddenly they were filled with Divine light! Can you imagine what the Chanukah lights meant to them then?

In our present exile, how very much we need that Chanukah light, how greatly our souls are yearning for it, how our hearts are hungry for it! If only we could learn about Chanukah and taste its wondrous light. Even that, however, is beyond our reach. The books that reveal the deepest Chanukah secrets are only accessible to scholars who have had adequate preparation. Yet there must be a highly readable book for the general public, which can imbue one with the flavor of this miraculous holiday.

The chasidic masters have taught that each *mitzvah* should transform the one who does it. From reading this section on Chanukah, I pray you will learn to appreciate chasidic teachings and catch a glimpse of Kabbalah. Even more, you will taste the sweetness of Chanukah when you learn what to see in it. You will open your heart and allow God's light to penetrate. Then you may suddenly realize the darkness of our exile and yearn for God's permanent light.

Chanukah will fill you with blessing and light. It will give you encouragement and spirituality, hope and yearning. You will be transformed and uplifted. You will always have a key to release yourself from prison and personal exile. You will rediscover your faith in God and love for your fellow man. The light of Chanukah will light your way within the darkness, and you will be redeemed.

16

The Essence of Chanukah

What is Chanukah? The rabbis taught: The twenty-fifth day of *Kislev* is Chanukah. There are eight days on which we are not allowed to eulogize or fast. When the Greeks entered the Temple, they defiled all the oil that was there. When the kingdom of the House of Hasmoneans grew in strength and vanquished them, they searched thoroughly but found only one small jar of oil with the seal of the High Priest (*Kohen Gadol*), and it contained enough to light for one day. A miracle happened and they lit from it for eight days (*Shabbos* 21b).

When the Jewish People are enslaved, they cannot do God's bidding and be His servants. They yearn to be free from oppression so that they can carry out God's special mission in this world. The Jews named the holiday Chanukah, from the word *chanu*, "they rested," to emphasize the cause of their rejoicing. Their happiness was due to their freedom from enslavement and wars. Now they were free to accomplish their Divine task again.

What is Chanukah? Chanukah is a holiday that comes from such a high place that we constantly need to ask, "What is it?" When we think we are satisfied that we know what it is, we must still ask about it because we can never fathom its depth and understand all its meaning. Chanukah comes from that spring of infinity where God is revealing Himself within the natural world. Therefore, even if we seem to know Chanukah clearly, the next instant it is renewed by fresh waters from the spring, becoming something new to us again (*Shabbos* 21b).

The beauty of Chanukah is that we will never tire of asking, "What is Chanukah?"

The holidays of Sukkos and Chanukah share several common characteristics: (1) Both last eight days; (2) Sukkos commemorates the clouds of glory that surrounded the Jews in their wanderings, which God gave them in the merit of Aaron, the high priest, and the battles of Chanukah were fought by the Hasmoneans, a priestly family (*kohanim*); (3) Both have laws pertaining to beautifying the *mitzvah*, for example, to take a beautiful *esrog* on Sukkos and to kindle more beautiful lights on Chanukah.

Therefore, in a mysterious sense, Chanukah is the mirror image of the holiday of Sukkos. And like a mirror, rays of light bounce off the person to the mirror and back again to the person's eyes, and the same with these two holidays. Rays are bouncing back and forth between these two holidays, through the interim months, so that one is a reflection of the other. The quality of your Sukkos will most likely be reflected in the quality of your Chanukah. And the spirit with which you celebrate Chanukah will be reflected back to Sukkos.

"Like a woman who is pregnant, when she nears the time of her delivery, and is in pain and cries out in her pangs, so have we been in Your sight, O God" (Isaiah 27:18).

Childbirth is a beautiful miracle. Why then is the woman crying out? Because of her pains she momentarily forgets what it all is leading to.

The same is true of our exiles. We cry in pain from the pressures of oppression only because we do not see the nearing redemption. When God redeems us, it is like childbirth. A child is born flawless, but at the same time it needs much training to accomplish its mission in life.

When we are redeemed we are as the newborn child, pure and innocent, yet we need lots of training. Therefore we named the holiday of our redemption Chanukah, from the word *chinuch*, "training." When we stand near the Chanukah lights, we are renewed as the newborn, and we need only start our training in the service of God.

The earlier generations had a better relationship with God than later ones. The earlier ones only needed the three main holidays—Passover, Shavuos, and Sukkos. Later, however, the generations were further removed from spirituality and they needed more holy days during the year to help them survive. For this reason the three main holidays are called *regalim*, which can be read as *raglayim*, "feet." During the year the Jews had three feet, a good and steady support. Later, this was not enough, and Purim was added. Later still, Chanukah was officially declared a holiday, when the Jews realized that they simply could not survive an entire year without the additional boost from another holiday.

On each of the three holidays, the Jewish People would go to the Holy Temple in Jerusalem to celebrate. When they arrived they took part in prayer, learning, and celebration. They became spiritually uplifted and were thus suffused with spirit until the next holiday. All this, however, was preceded by much preparation and cleansing to become holy. If a person was not prepared, he would gain nothing from his holiday.

Chanukah is a more accessible holiday than the other ones. No preparation is necessary—it comes to you as you are. The light reaches out to you, though when it does your heart must be open to receive it. Allow it to shine into you, and you will experience an uplifting none of the other three holidays could provide. You soar to the place of infinite light and have a glimpse of the complete redemption.

Pain and joy come from two different sources. Pain comes from the shell and husk of things. The inside, the essence, the spiritual part of anything knows much joy. It is aware that God does everything and is equally happy with it all. The spiritual essence gladly does a *mitzvah*, but the body may not like it.

Doing a *mitzvah* with only your body is a risk. The *mitzvah* may have the same fate as the material body. It could wither and die. If, on the other hand, you do a *mitzvah* with all your soul, it will last forever, being connected to eternity by means of your spirit whose roots are God.

The Jews built a holy tabernacle during their desert wanderings. It was finished precisely on the 25th day of *Kislev*. They brought gifts of gold and silver from which the tabernacle could be built with a joy and happiness that reached beyond the limitations of the material world. This tabernacle would surely last forever. Later, when the Holy Temple was built, the tabernacle was hidden. Yet the joy of the original tabernacle has lasted. It has raised the twenty-fifth day of *Kislev* to the realm of the infinite. This was the reason why the Jews rededicated the Holy Temple in the Greek exile on that very date, which was already transformed through great joy.

As we stand near the Chanukah lamp, we must receive its light with great joy. If we do, we will not only enjoy its light the entire year but also for many years to come.

The three main holidays—Passover, Sukkos, and Shavuos—are in the merit of Abraham, Isaac, and Jacob. There shall be twelve other holidays in the merit of the twelve tribes when *Mashiach* comes.

The miracle of Chanukah was the last miraculous redemption before our final redemption. Its name Chanukah (*chinuch*, "training") says, "Allow this holiday to train you for the twelve new holidays you are about to receive."

In our personal lives we should allow Chanukah to train us to yearn in anticipation for great gifts from God.

There is a difference between oil and water as they pass through a wick. After all the water passes through, there is a last drop that stays in the wick. Oil is burned away by the flame to the very last drop. This tells us that the Jewish people belong to God to the last drop. No matter what conniving and subterfuge the nations may use in order to trick us, it will not work. The oil will continue to adhere to the wick to the very end.

The three major holidays are called *regalim*, which also means feet. The spiritual year cannot stand without these three feet. But even the three feet were only enough to support the previous generations who were strong in fear of God. Later the sages saw that their generation would never survive spiritually with only the three holidays. They sensed that a miracle was about to be caused that would be celebrated as a holiday. This was eventually the holiday that came to light up the darkness.

Although the three major holidays are more important because they are written in the Torah, the minor holidays of Chanukah and Purim are better in one respect. We can fulfill our obligations fully and totally during Purim and Chanukah, but not on the major holidays. There are services during those three major holidays that require the presence of the Holy Temple, which we unfortunately do not have. When the Temple will be rebuilt, speedily in our days and the service will be restored, then all the holidays will be at their highest level once more.

The Greeks wanted to uproot the power of the Jewish people. And what is the source of their power? They have the power of renewal. And whenever something is being renewed, the Jewish people are connected to it, as is the case with the new moon. When the moon becomes new, the Jews celebrate. The Greeks were determined to stop these celebrations.

Finally the Jews were victorious. They not only were able to celebrate the beginning of the month, but even began celebrating the end of the month. This is the holiday of Chanukah, which is at the end of the month.

Many nations have oppressed the Jewish people. Each one subjected them to endless pain and oppression. During their years of oppression they were in contact with a nation of evil actions and deeds. They lived among them, observed them, and constantly interacted with them. Did not all this contact have an influence on the Jewish people? Yes, and some were influenced in a harmful way. But those who were God-fearing used the evil behavior that they observed for the worship of God. How? They observed arrogance, violence, fierce oppression, and the unfettered use of force. In turn they thought, "Ah, that is how strong and persistent we have to be when we observe the Torah way of life." When the oppression ended, the Jews emerged spiritually stronger than before.

In order to make fire you need three things: material, kindling temperature, and oxygen. When the material reaches the kindling temperature, oxygen combines with it and it burns. From where does fire get its energy? From the used energy of the material and the oxygen. The fire gives light. But what is light itself? Light in its purity comes from God.

When man makes light, in order to have it he consumes something . But when God gives light, nothing is lost. It is just there. Similarly, in the service of God, we have to involve and use up something in order to ascend to higher levels of spirituality. But when we do, God shines His light to us, a light which causes no loss.

It is written, Start a boy on the right road, and even in old age he will not leave it (Proverbs 22:6).

The Jewish people accepted some commandments with great excitement and rejoicing. Those commandments remained forever with a special connection and meaning to them. One of these commandments was the building of the holy Tabernacle in the desert, after the Exodus. That was in the early days of the Jewish nation. Therefore, when the Temple was defiled by the Greeks and later rededicated, the Jewish people again felt that resurgence of joy. In their "old age" they felt the joy of their youth.

The nations of the world have many times attempted to destroy the Jewish people physically. They enslaved, oppressed, and finally killed some of them. Still worse, some attempted to destroy the Jewish people spiritually. Such was the case with the Greeks and much later, in our lifetime, with the Russians. These nations attempt to erase from the minds and hearts of the Jewish people the Torah and *mitzvos*, our Jewish heritage and teachings. Their scheming, in the end, ends with failure, because God will never allow the Jewish nation to disappear. So when the Greeks attempted to Hellenize the Jews, to cut them off from the wellsprings of the Torah and the Jewish way of life, they were defeated. The nation of God threw off the Greek yoke from upon their necks, and they returned to their way of life with more commitment than ever.

———

The Greeks would not have harmed the Jews if they had agreed to assimilate and live as Greeks. All they asked was that the Jews abandon the study of the Torah and its *mitzvos*. Some Jews stubbornly refused to do so. They did not want to live without God's guidance. Therefore, when God helped them vanquish their enemies it was "His" fight. As we say in the Chanukah prayer, "And You fought their fight." You, God, fought, because the Jews' fight was identical to Your fight. They were fighting only for God's sake and the Torah.

———

The heavens are truly wondrous! There are the movements of the planets, constellations, and stars. There exist the nebulae and interstellar dust, galaxies, radio stars, black holes, and endless space. Yet, as mind boggling as it all is, the study of the heavens does not lead everyone to the same conclusion.

We can compare this to a king who sent an emissary to his faithful servant. When the guest arrived, the servant was so impressed with him that he forgot to ask him why he had come. Instead, he delighted in entertaining his guest with everything at his disposal. He prepared elaborate meals and invited important neighbors to meet the King's emissary. As the hours passed the king was gradually forgotten.

The universe is a messenger of God's greatness. But the Greeks got no further than being impressed by its greatness. And therefore the numerical equivalent for Greek, or *yavan*, equals *galgal*, meaning the celestial sphere. They get stuck there, and they went no further. On the other hand, the Jewish people raise their eyes and declare, "The heavens declare the glory of God, and the expanse of the sky tell of His handiwork" (Psalms 19:2). In their case there is another word, *elokecho*, "your God," also with the numerical equivalent of *galgal*. Because when the Jews look at the heavens they remember that it is only an emissary of God that comes to inform them of its Creator.

———

Every time a nation subjugates the Jewish people, it leads them to idol worship. This happens for two reasons. One is that their spirits are so broken and they are tired of the pain. The pain and misery are so unbearable that they worship idols to appease the enemy. They think they will be spared. The second reason is that they are misled, copy the culture of their host nation, and assimilate.

And so when the redemption comes, it is as if an idol worshiper becomes a Jew. He gives up the beliefs of his father and mother and worships the one and only God. As it is written, "Because my father and mother has left me, but God will gather me up" (Psalms 27:10). It was as if he were born anew. A newly born child who needs to be taught from the very beginning. As it is written, "Start a boy on the right road . . ." (Proverbs 22:6).

When we start to teach, it is called *chinuch*. So the holiday commemorating the redemption of the Jewish people from the idol-worshiping Greeks is called Chanukah, because we start to teach anew. A newborn nation of Israel is again starting to learn about worshiping the one and only God.

———

When the Jewish people study the Torah and live according to the commandments, they do not need miracles. God helps them while they live a natural and ordinary life. When do they need miracles? When they have strayed from the path of the Torah and fall into the hands of their enemies and dangerous circumstances.

During the Greek period of oppression many Jews assimilated and became alienated from the Torah. They could not be saved with ordinary help. They certainly needed a miracle.

———

When a miracle occurs, everyone who witnesses it becomes inspired to serve God. It is because of this new devotion that God grants miracles again. Although the miracle of Chanukah happened long ago, still, if we are inspired by it, God will again grant us miracles. . . . in the form of the final redemption.

———

It is written, "I never called my neighbor by an unflattering surname given him by myself or others" (*Taanis* 28a). The word for surname is *chanicho*. We can use this word to understand the story of Chanukah. How did the Greeks have the power to stop the Jews from studying the Torah? By ordering them to translate the Torah into Greek, it gave them a "share" in it. As it is written, May God extend Japheth's bounds, let him dwell in the tents of Shem" (Genesis 9:26). The Greek descendants of Japheth will dwell in Shem's houses of study. Their language will be used in studying the Torah of Shem's descendants, the Jewish people.

The language is merely a surname to the essence of the Torah. Therefore, when the Jews became free of Greek domination, they became free of their *chanicho* also. That is why the holiday is called Chanukah.

"You fought their battles," we say in the prayer for Chanukah. When the Jewish people are determined, and do battle, then You, God, take it over as Your battle.

We can compare this to a prince who was playing with his friend. Suddenly the other boy made an insulting remark about the king. The prince was shocked and yelled at the boy. The king overheard this and went to see what the commotion was all about. When he saw the anger of his son, he too raised his voice to reprimand the boy.

The Jewish people battled the Greeks not for their own honor and comfort, but for the honor of God. And therefore it was God's battle too, and He intervened to help them.

The word *Chanukah* means they rested on the twenty-fifth day of *Kislev*. The Jews rested from the battles that they fought against the Greek oppressors. But why choose a name that tells of war, battles, and the day of victory? It is because the Jewish people fought their battles for the sake of God and the Torah, and not for their own safety. This elevated the battles to a spiritual level and established the name of the holiday.

The Jewish people struggled with the persecution and terrible decrees of the Greeks. They fought prolonged and difficult wars against all odds. Finally, after many battles they were victorious, retook Jerusalem and the Holy Temple, and resumed the worship and sacrifices. All this ended on the twenty-fifth day of *Kislev*, and the holiday is therefore called Chanukah, meaning they rested on the twenty-fifth.

There is a very difficult question about the name Chanukah. When they stopped fighting on the twenty-fifth day, there simply was a cessation of all hostilities. Perhaps the major battles were over, but how could they possibly have rested? Rest has the quality of calm, peace, and tranquility. They certainly could not have attained that quality so suddenly. That quality is something to strive for.

We can compare this to a prince who was captured by a band of thieves and forced to live in the hills. He tried his best to maintain royal standards in the way he spoke and acted. He flatly refused to curse and swear, neither did he rob and kill. He stubbornly awaited the day when his father would find him and return him to the palace. One day while his captors argued over the loot, he surprised his guard and escaped. The thieves gave chase and nearly caught him several times, but the prince outran them through brush and thorns, lakes and swamps. Finally he entered the palace gates where he collapsed into the waiting arms of his father. He cried momentarily, but was soon fast asleep. He was home.

The Jewish people, the ones who are faithful to the Torah, never felt comfortable with the Greek culture. They stubbornly fought the Greeks tooth and nail on every decree. They felt like prisoners in their own land and could not wait to be free. They awaited the redemption of God so they could study the Torah freely and live as Jews. Their minds and hearts were full of a calm resolve and determination never to submit to the enemy. Finally when the redemption came, nothing more was needed. Their hearts were at complete rest, quiet, and peace. They were home.

Sometimes we wonder, "When will we have the peace and tranquility that we need in order to worship God with all our hearts and souls? How could we possibly live a life devoted to the Torah with all the interruptions, troubles, oppression, and harassment? When will we live free of all evil?" To answer this question, God causes a miracle to happen. The Jewish people are suddenly redeemed and accomplish the impossible. And they suddenly realize that nothing is really impossible. Circumstances are not to be considered. We must persist even against all odds.

The lesson to us is obvious. Often we are in a situation that is a good excuse for inaction and laziness. We cry about our circumstances and declare that as soon as things improve we will fulfill our obligations. But the miracle of Chanukah teaches us to disregard our circumstances. Just as in those days the Jews ignored their harsh treatment and oppression and observed the Torah, we can do the same. And by going beyond the limit, a miracle, an "impossible" event, is caused to happen. May we be worthy to see it in our lifetime.

There are two ways of doing something that are very different. One is to act without thinking, out of habit. The other is to act with thinking and wisdom. The first is very physical; the other is cerebral. The physical part of the action, just as the body that does it, ages and gets old. The part done with thinking, just as wisdom itself, does not age.

The same is true in a person's own lifetime. His physical being, his body, keeps aging, while his intellect stays fresh. So that when you start to do your actions with thought, choice, and intellect, you bring youth to the place where aging dominated.

The Jewish people in their exile fall into the ways of habit. Their study and rituals become stale and grow old. This was also true during the Greek exile. Then came the miracle of Chanukah. It shone the light of intellect into the place of habit, youth and vitality into the place of aging. There was renewal—in the Temple and in all of Israel.

"God has called your name a green olive tree . . ." (Jeremiah 12:16).

"Why are the Jewish People likened to an olive tree? With olives, the more you beat them the more oil they give. So too with the Jewish People; the more they are oppressed by the nations of the world, the more good deeds they do. Just as olive oil does not mix with any other liquid, the Jewish People don't mix with other nations. Just as olive oil rises on top of other liquids, so too, the Jewish People, in the end, will be on top" (*Exodus Rabbah* 28).

This Midrash provides a very good description of the Greek exile. The Greeks oppressed the Jews and beat them, but the Jews are like the olives who give out oil when beaten. The Jews had a resurgence of the Oral Law at that time. The Greeks attempted to force the Jews to assimilate, but they are like oil and they did not assimilate. The Greeks attempted to humiliate them, but they are like oil and rose to the top.

Each one of us can take courage from this Midrash. God has blessed us with great strengths. We have no excuses for most of our shortcomings. Then when we kindle the oil in the Chanukah lamp, we allow the miracle of olive oil to enter our hearts. We acquire three strengths from the olive and remain loyal to the Torah.

17

Impure Oil

The Greeks defiled all the oil in the Holy Temple, and only one small jug of pure oil was found. (*Shabbos* 21b)

s it possible that the Greeks overlooked any oil? Hardly. Then where was this small jug? It seems that the jug was hidden miraculously, and it took up no space.

This is how the soul exists inside us. It is spiritual and infinite, but takes up no space at all. Yet, if we want its power we must seek it with all our yearning and desire. When we discover our soul, it shines with such brilliance that it lights up everyone around us.

Any creature with a little sense knows that God is the Master of the world. The wiser you are, the clearer this is to you. Therefore, the essence of wisdom is to humble yourself before God, King of the universe. And even if our wisdom should tell us the opposite, even if we are slightly arrogant and think that with our wisdom and skills we do not need God, still we have complete faith that it is not we who have power but only God.

Our faith protects our wisdom. Our faith is like a lamp, and our wisdom is the oil. The Greeks ruined our faith. They screamed, "We are the masters!," and they were able to reach in and defile the oil, our wisdom.

The Chanukah miracle put everything back in order again. The light shines into our hearts, reassuring our faith and protecting our wisdom.

Wisdom is usually found in written form. Writing is made up of small letters and some small symbols.

The position of a small mark such as a comma or a period can make a big difference.

The Greeks screamed, "We are the masters of the world!" They lied. They were not! Then how could they say it? They only changed a small mark in punctuation—replacing the question mark with an exclamation point—and suddenly they are now the masters.

To counter this error God gave us the miracle of Chanukah: a small bit of oil, humble but pure. And into our bodies He placed a soul, a tiny Divine mark, inside us. When we kindle the Chanukah lights, the beam shines from one tiny mark, the tiny flame, into our souls, which is the other tiny mark, and a brilliant light streams forth.

One of the differences between the Written Law and the Oral Law is that we are not permitted to add on to the Written Law, but we may add on to the Oral Law. The lighting of the Chanukah lamp is a *mitzvah* from the sages and is part of the Oral Law, and we can therefore add on to it. Thus, there is a rule that at a minimum one lamp should be kindled per household. A more adorned way, however, is to kindle a lamp for each family member, and an even better way is to kindle different numbers of lamps each night.

The heroes in the period of the Greek exile had great reverence for the Torah. Those who honor the Torah, and God's word is important to them, are as the Oral Law and therefore cause an increasing number of lights to be turned on.

The sages in the time of the Greek exile suffered great pain from the edict to produce a Greek translation of the entire Torah and to present it to the king. They understood this intrusion into their literature to be an imminent danger. They feared that once the Greeks were able to study the Torah, they too would be masters over its contents. After much discussion, however, they decided to allow the project to commence, basing their decision on verses in the Torah. This halachic decision is still binding, although the Greeks have no power over us today as they did then. But why? Why is it still permissible to translate the Torah into Greek? It is because the Greeks are no longer a nation of any consequence and therefore no longer have any power over us. They cannot possibly gain power over the contents of the Torah now.

"... the evil Greeks ruled over the Jewish People and attempted to efface the Torah from their memory ..." (*Prayer Book, Al Hanisim*).

Historically, we know that the Greeks were oppressing the Jews long years before the Chanukah miracle. Why did God wait until the last minute. What if it had been too late?

The answer is that, as long as a nation does not threaten the survival of the Jewish Nation or the Torah, it is allowed to continue its subjugation of the Jews. But as soon as it threatens Jewish survival, God destroys it.

What if the Jews are in exile but do not have any merit of their own to redeem them? How do they escape from their exile? God leaves the oppressors alone until they nearly threaten Jewish existence, and then He destroys them.

We too must have faith. When we see that everything is going wrong, we ought to say, "At this point God will intervene!" Similarly, the Jews were about to give up looking for oil, and just then the small jug was found.

18

Miracle with a Small Jug

Then they found a small jug of oil sealed with the High Priest's seal and they used it to light the Chanukah lights for eight days. (*Shabbos* 21b)

Why did the miracle happen with a small jug of oil rather than with no oil at all? After all, God did not need any material thing with which to make the miracle. This is the pre-eminence of the miracle of Chanukah—that, instead of avoiding nature, God used nature itself to bring a miracle into the world.

This miracle showed God's great love for the Jewish People. How? Because a miracle is God's business, whereas the commandment to light the Menorah was the business of the Jewish people. God could have made the Menorah light up miraculously without oil. Instead, out of His love for the Jewish Nation, He thrust the miracle into the small jug of oil. Now His people could accomplish their responsibilities on their own.

We too, when we pour the tiny amounts of oil into the Chanukah lamp, should remember how much God "goes out of His way" to help us do His commandments.

The Greeks defiled all the oil in the Holy Temple. Still, miraculously one jug of oil stayed pure and was not destroyed by the Greek soldiers. This teaches us a great lesson. If we see a group of people who have become corrupt, then we should search for the one who is still good and decent. If we find ourselves drifting away from the path of God, we should not be dismayed, because surely there is still purity left in us somewhere.

Only recently we have witnessed this truth. When the Germans imprisoned the European Jews in their concentration camps, they proceeded to torture, vilify, debase, and dehumanize them incessantly. Some succumbed. But there were a significant group of others, my father of blessed memory included, who kept their faith, dignity, and humanity under the most extreme conditions. As much as the Germans wanted to defile them, the Jews stayed strong and fierce as leopards to do the will of God.

19

Miraculous Glow

The Greeks oppressed the Jewish People and made decrees against the Torah. The Jews fought the Greeks and were victorious. Then they found a small jug of oil from which they lit the Menorah. The small bit of oil miraculously burned for eight days. That was the miracle of Chanukah. (*Shabbos* 21b)

od created the world in six days and rested on the seventh. Everything that exists in the universe, including rest, was created within those seven days. The number seven therefore symbolizes the corporeal universe, which is dominated by space and time. The number eight, however, is beyond the limitations of that universe and is touching the infinite. It is outside the world we live in and has no connection to it.

There are periods in the history of the world, within space and time, in which the Jewish people are terribly oppressed and God intervenes to redeem them. He takes the Jews out of their misery by granting them more space and more time in which to fulfill their vital task as messengers of God. He removes them from the exile.

The redemption of Chanukah was even stronger. God not only lessened their exile but also gave them strength to endure it. The Jews were still under Greek rule, yet God granted them a glimpse of the ultimate redemption. This glimpse was from the infinite world beyond space and time, the world after the number seven. A light shone from the world of eight into the world of seven. Every Jew had a taste of eternity, and his soul was renewed.

The light of this miracle still shines into our hearts from the eight days and eight lights of Chanukah. It heartens our spirit to know that even within the dark exile, the space and time we now experience, there

shines an infinite light without bounds or limitations. The number eight lights our way.

The Greeks oppressed the Jewish nation by immersing them in the everyday. They were eager to interest the Jews in materialistic pursuits so that they would ignore the spiritual world entirely. They were overawed by natural phenomena, laws of nature, and orderliness in the universe. They emphasized the ordinariness in the world and mocked the miraculous. They ridiculed the Divine election of the Jews, arguing that every nation is entitled to chosenness.

Orderliness leads to ordinariness; ordinariness leads to forgetfulness. This was a true exile for the Jews who always remember. They remember that God is the Master of the world, no matter how much apparent evidence they see to the contrary. They do not forget.

The Greeks thrust the material world in the Jews' faces, saying, "Look, do you see any god here? Look again, do you see any god there? Why should you choose a special god? Do as we do. All our gods are ordinary people. And all people are the same. There's nothing special or outstanding in the world!"

Forgetfulness occurs when you turn away. The Jewish People are stiff-necked (Exodus 32:9) and do not turn easily. They refuse to forget. Neither does God ever forget them. He broke the orderliness and ordinariness of the world for them. Ordinarily the strong defeat the weak, the many vanquish the few, the evildoers beat the righteous. God made the opposite happen: the weak defeated the strong, the few vanquished the many, the righteous beat the wicked, and the Jews were victorious. This was a great miracle. Yet, it was not enough to counter the

Greek exile. "What about the ordinary, the plain, the everyday? Where are You, God, in all of that?" the Jews asked.

To counter this oppression, God revealed specialness in the ordinary. A small jug of oil burned for eight complete days. How wondrous, how special! Even the ordinary is special. God is in the everyday! This new and special light shone through the thick darkness of the Greek exile and whispered to each Jew, "You needn't turn away and forget. I never forget you; I am with you always!"

"Therefore hear this, you who are afflicted, and drunken but not with wine" (Joshua 51:21).

There are times when the Jewish nation is afflicted with terrible troubles. Their oppression is then so severe that they are not able to fulfill their true desire, which is to proclaim God's kingdom. They may get so tired, depressed, and forlorn from their enslavement that they are about to despair. Just then God redeems them.

During the dark and dismal Greek exile the Jews were about to fall into despair. But God, in His great mercy, intervened and saved them. Yet this was not enough. They were still *drunk* from the exile and very depressed.

We can liken this to a drunk who was lying unconscious on the street. A kind person found him and compassionately carried him home. He bathed, dressed, and fed him. The drunk explained that he started drinking when he lost his job and had been drinking ever since. He hardly ever had food to eat or a place to sleep. He did not want to live anymore. The kind benefactor was at a loss to help him. He knew how to bring him out of his drunken state, but he could not raise him from despair.

Similarly, while the Jews were physically redeemed by their victory, their spirit was still broken. To lift their spirit, God showed them His love. He shone the soft miraculous lights into their hearts and whispered to them, "Do not despair, my children, for I am with you even in the exile. Even while your light is darkened, let my light shine for you."

As we look into the tiny soft lights of the Chanukah lamp, we should allow ourselves to be uplifted from our exile, dejectedness, and despair. Our hearts should fill with joy.

There were many Greeks and only very few Jews who would fight against them. The Jews could easily have said, "We are so few. How dare we fight the enormous Greek armies?" But their hunger for freedom was so powerful that they ignored the risks and fought them anyway.

Later, they found a small jug of oil with which to light the Menorah. They could have said, "There is so little oil. Let's wait till we have more. It's no use to light with it. How can we expect it to burn for more than a few hours?" But their yearning to do God's bidding was so strong that they disregarded the futility of their efforts and lit the Menorah anyway.

The miracle of Chanukah should shine into each Jewish heart the power of the so-called inadequate. "My brain, heart, guts, strength are too small to serve this demanding God," we hear people say. Yet God doesn't ask of us what He Himself has not placed in us. In each of us is the kernel of spirituality, our soul. The soul is flowing from the fountain of infinite wisdom and power. To the extent that you truly yearn for these qualities, to that degree you can tap the source within you. And if you truly yearn, you will see the miracle of Chanukah repeated in your own life; the small and the inadequate will be victorious.

The material world withers and dies. Renewal and eternal life are found only in God. To the degree that creatures can connect themselves with the spiritual fountain, God, so will be their power of renewal. Even if a creature succeeds in making that connection, his body must wither and die, but his spirit is renewed and lives on. In man, his outer portion, his body, dies, while his inner part, his soul, lives on.

Man connects himself to God by means of the Torah, which is God's teaching to His people. Even the Torah, however, has an inner and outer portion. The inner portion is the spiritual and hidden fountain that flows directly from God. Whoever drinks from this water is immediately renewed and finds life. There is also the outer portion, which is as the husk is to the kernel. It is the outer shell excluding any spiritual connection. The outer part of the Torah can be viewed as wisdom and the object of scholarly scrutiny.

The Greeks quibbled with the Jews over this very point. They said that there is much wisdom in the world and the Torah is but one example of such wisdom. The Jews argued that the Torah is God's teaching and is superior to any earthly knowledge. The Greeks wished to add the knowledge of the Torah to their collection of wisdom. They wanted to place the Torah alongside all the other books they had acquired from other nations and asked that a Greek translation be made. And one was made. But the Jews knew that the Torah is not just another book of wisdom. It is the path to life, renewal, and God. Yet they found themselves in an exile in which the oppressors screamed at them, "Your knowledge is no more special than any of the others!"

We can compare this to an art collection that is housed inside a splendid building. A tourist, hearing so much about the paintings, decides to go visit the museum. When he arrives, he meets another visitor outside. The visitor points to the great beauty of the building's facade, architecture, and design. When the tourist wants to enter, the visitor insists that there is nothing at all beautiful inside. All the beauty, he argues, is on the outside. He argues for so long that the tourist actually begins to doubt his own judgment.

Similarly, while the Jews were in exile among the Greeks, the Greeks attempted to make them forget the inner part of the Torah, the source of life.

But God did not forsake His people; He opened the doors of redemption. He broke through the shell of material darkness and death. He forced the inner spirituality to surface and illuminate the night of the exile. He showed them that, although a small jar of oil must burn up and die out, the inner part of it can become renewed and can burn indefinitely.

This can also be applied to our own personal exiles. We will forever remain in exile if we are only linked to the outer shell of things. Instead, we must tie ourselves to the inner spirituality that is forever being renewed.

Chanukah connects us with spirit, life and renewal. May it always be so!

"Many waters cannot quench love, neither can the floods drown it . . ." (Song of Songs 8:7).

Aaron, the brother of Moses, was the greatest peacemaker in the world (*Ethics of Our Fathers* 1:12). He constantly sought people who were quarreling and made peace between them.

When Aaron met one of the quarrelers, he would say, "I just met your partner and he is very sorry for what happened and wants to be friends. Only he's too embarrassed to speak to you personally." When he met the other one, he would tell him the same thing. Naturally, when the two would meet they would embrace with true forgiveness and love (*Avos de'Rabbi Noson* 12:3).

What did Aaron really do? He saw that people have love that is exposed and easily lost. Aaron took this love and locked it back into their hearts securely and eternally. Many waters cannot quench love . . .

There is love between God and the Jewish people. This love is locked within the kernel of spirituality that God placed in each Jewish heart. The love is locked with such power that absolutely nothing can disturb it. It is there always and eternally. ". . . neither can the floods drown it. . . ."

The Greeks oppressed the Jews by denying their chosenness. "Why should God choose you instead of us?" the Greeks argued. They virtually refuted the love between God and the Jewish People. The Greeks, of course, worked in vain. "Many waters cannot quench love. . . ."

God revealed His eternal love and redeemed the Jews miraculously. And where was the sign of God's love? They searched and found a small jar of oil *sealed* with the seal of the High Priest (*Kohen Gadol*). No one could touch or spoil this small jar. The oil is the love locked into a jar, the Jewish heart sealed by the High Priest, Aaron. ". . . neither can the floods drown it. . . ."

When we look at the lights of Chanukah, let us allow them to shine into that part of us that has never yet been defiled, where our love for God and God's love for us have never been stronger. This is the part locked in by the peacemaker Himself, the part that whispers to us, "Many waters cannot quench love, neither can the floods drown it."

"From Zion shall come forth Torah, and the word of God from Jerusalem" (Isaiah 2:3).

The Holy Temple was the light of the Jewish People and of the whole world. Jews came there to pray, rejoice, thank, and cry to God for forgiveness. They also came to ask, debate, learn, and clarify. Torah and the word of God constantly streamed forth from the Holy Temple.

The Greeks transformed the Temple into a house of idol worship, Greek propaganda, and oppression. No longer did light stream from the Temple, the word of God was silenced.

Then God forcefully intervened, and the Greeks were expelled from the Temple. The lamp was lit again, and the rays streamed outward to light the darkness outside.

The human being is a temple of God's holiness. In our personal exile, too, we must rid our temple of all idols and foreign gods so that the light shines out of us again.

"Give thanks to God, for He is good, because His mercy endures forever. Let Israel now say that His mercy endures forever. Let the house of Aaron say that His mercy endures forever. Let them now that fear God say that His mercy endures forever" (*Psalms* 118:1–4).

When all is as it should be, and the Jewish nation lives in peace, we are aware of God's mercy. When we are in exile, we begin to doubt the power of His mercy. But when God redeems us, we realize that His mercy is forever and that He was with us even in the exile.

There are four exiles: Babylon, Medea, Greece, and Edom. Each one corresponds to one of the verses above. Greece is the third exile in which redemption was brought about by a priestly family, the *kohanim*, the descendants of Aaron. And we say, ". . . His mercy endures forever."

Let us, as we suffer from our own exiles, look at the Chanukah lamp and remember the house of Aaron, who were just about to give up hope but fought on and, in the end, said, "His mercy endures forever." This reaffirmation of faith will bring the last, final redemption from our present exile. Then we can sing, "Let them now that fear God say that His mercy endures forever."

God is the total and absolute Master of the universe. His power is in every particle of the universe, at all times. It is, however, concealed within the natural world; it is passed over and unnoticed. One can live one's whole life and never once notice God's power nor His rule over the world.

The mission of the Jewish People is to declare God as the Master despite His concealment. Yet when the Jews are in exile, they themselves are concealed. They are therefore unable to affirm God's absolute power.

During the Greek exile the Jews were in that exact predicament. They were later miraculously redeemed and resumed their chosen task, revealing God's power. And they prayed, "Please, God, please don't hide Your control and reign ever again. May Your kingdom be always revealed." God heard their prayers and rewarded them with the miracle of the Chanukah lights. The lights were usually hidden inside the Holy Temple on the Menorah, and hardly a soul ever heard mention of them. After the miracle, however, the lights were the most popular topic of conversation. The lights were hidden no longer; they were revealed fully.

We, who suffer exile after exile in our daily lives, must look well into the Chanukah lights. The Chanukah lights will then shine into our eyes. Our eyes will open to see the revelation of God's kingdom in our own lives and the lives of our people.

The lamps of the Menorah were lit each day in the Holy Temple, with enough oil to burn through each

of the nights, even the long winter nights. But in the morning, even after the other lamps went out, one still kept burning. This was the westernmost lamp that burned miraculously. The flame that shone on it was not natural. It was not of this world; it was eternal. Therefore, it is there even today and forever.

This is symbolized by our own menorah. It is the light of the westernmost lamp. It is eternal even in the absence of the Holy Temple.

Light has a visible and an invisible spectrum. We have vessels to perceive the visible light: our eyes. But we cannot perceive the portion of light on the extremes of the spectrum; we cannot see ultraviolet or infrared light. Yet, we know that if we could perceive those rays we would be able to see so much more, as some animals are able to do. Lately, technicians have made devices that can detect those "invisible" light rays. And how much more of the world is made visible through them. It is even possible to see in total darkness.

On a spiritual level, too, there is light and the hidden light. The plain light is for those who walk in the path of God. But then there are some who risk their lives to keep the light of the Torah shining throughout the darkness. They merit the hidden light. And with it one can see from one end of the world to the other.

This miraculous everlasting light is the light of Chanukah.

We believe with unshakable faith that each and every event that happens to the Jewish people is ordained by God. Therefore, even the miserable suffering of the exile is a Divine plan for the improvement and betterment of the Jewish people. Perhaps at the present, very few of us recognize this fact, but there will come a day when we and all of mankind will plainly see that the unfolding of history was actually guided all along by the Hand of God.

This too was true of the Greek exile. While they tortured, enslaved, and oppressed the Jews, many thought that their actions were just a lot of bad luck. But then after the spectacular victory and redemption it was plain that God's Hand was at work again.

The world works in balance. When the good increases, so too does the evil. And likewise, when the evil increases, there is a corresponding increase in the good.

Therefore, because the Greeks wanted to make the Jewish people forget the Torah, they remembered it so much more. So, after the victory the Jewish people were stronger than ever in their resolve never to allow the Torah to be forgotten.

"*Vayehi erev vayehi boker*—And it was evening and it was morning . . ." (Genesis 1:5).

The word *erev* also means confusion and mixture. The evening, *erev*, comes with darkness and impurities. Man needs to remove the impurities, to simplify the confusion, and to make light from the darkness. When he accomplishes this, then comes morning.

"And God saw the light that it was good. And He separated between the light and the darkness. He called light day, and the darkness night" (Genesis 1:4–5). The light, these are the deeds of the righteous; the darkness, these are the deeds of the evildoers. So then how do we know which ones God favors? "'And God saw the light and it was good.' It is obvious that God favors the deeds of the righteous" (*Genesis Rabbah* 1:1).

Likewise, in the Greek exile the misdeeds of the evildoers brought great confusion among the Jewish people. But those Jews who were committed to the tradition of "light" fought to rid themselves of impurities. They moved the nation out of the gloom of the Greek night into the morning of Godly light, and it was morning.

Why do the Jewish people need miracles? Can't God take care of them in an ordinary and natural way?

This can be compared to a king who had a son whom he sent on a special mission. The prince was in danger from the first moment. Highwaymen were after his treasures, and traitors were after his head. Each time he was in trouble, however, the royal guards appeared and saved his life. When the boy returned he asked, "Father, why did you have to send me to such a dangerous part of the country where you had to come and save my life so many times? You could have sent me on a much safer way, and I could have fended for myself!" The king answered, "You know how precious and dear you are to me. I wanted you to realize how much I always take care of you, and without me you couldn't survive!"

The same is true with the Jewish nation. In natural circumstances the Jews would long ago have disappeared. They are constantly bothered, oppressed, maligned, and murdered. They are the children of the King, and everyone is jealous of them. How then do they survive? Only through divine intervention—miracles. Their survival is miraculous, and God leads them through stormy paths of history in order to save them with miracles. He wants them to realize that without miracles they couldn't possibly exist.

A clear bright day is full of light. The night is a mixture of darkness and the light of the stars. Similarly, when the Jewish people are free to live by the Torah in the land of Israel, then it is light. If they are dominated by other nations and in exile, then they are in darkness. But even in the darkness they manage to search for and find the light. And when they do, they are rewarded with even a brighter light than the daytime.

"There was a river flowing from Eden to water the garden, and when it left the garden it branched into four streams" (Genesis 2:10). God will give the nations a cup of poison from the place where judgment emanates. The four streams are the four kingdoms (*Genesis Rabbah* 16:7).

The nations of the world immediately separate and go on their own way. And because they are forever separating, they separate from God also. This act will bring judgment upon them. The Jewish people, on the other hand, are always seeking their roots in the ultimate singularity, in God. Even when they fall into the hands of the nations, they preserve their integrity by staying connected to their source.

This was also the power of the twelve tribes, the sons of Yaakov. Although they were twelve, still they were united as one, and called themselves *Bnei Yisrael*, the children of Israel. And when their father died, they promised, "Hear O Israel, God, our God, God is one." "Just as in your heart there is only one, so too, in our hearts there is only one."

Therefore in the end of days, each will return to his original nature. The nations will separate as they really are, and that is their judgment. And the Jewish people will be united in their homeland under one leader to worship the one and only God forever.

There are three major holidays in the Torah: Pesach, Shavuos, and Sukkos. These are the holidays of the Written Law, and each of them shines a light into the Jewish soul. Then a reflected light shines back and creates a new holiday. These are the holidays of the Oral Law. Shavuos, which commemorates the granting of the Ten Commandments at Mount Sinai, created the holiday of Purim with its rededication to

Torah study. Sukkos, which was celebrated by elaborate sacrifices in the Temple, created the holiday of Chanukah with its rededication to the worship of the Temple. And Passover has also created a holiday of redemption, a redemption still to happen, as it is written, "I will show miracles as in the days when you left Egypt" (Micah 7:15).

———————

Chanukah is the first holiday in the winter season, and is needed to train us in receiving the other holidays that follow.

The sages during the Greek exile must have sensed something special about the holiday of Sukkos, which preceded the Chanukah miracle. They sacrificed many animals for the sake of the nations of the world. They must have felt that their service had a strong effect on the nations. In addition, they must have also had the sign of the moon. It is traditionally believed that on the last night of Sukkos, on Hoshanah Rabbah, one can foretell the future with the shadows of the moon. Using this intuition they sensed that the end of oppression and the redemption were close at hand.

———————

The Jewish people must have taken the sanctity of the Holy Temple too lightly. And so the Greeks were able to overpower them and breach the walls. However, when they later repented and fought the Greeks, expelled them, and rebuilt the Temple walls, they established ritual bowing. This corrected their levity in respecting the Holy Temple.

We can compare this to the king's servant who rebelled and escaped from the palace. One night he sneaked back and wrote graffiti on the palace walls. When the king heard of this, he was very upset. Later the servant relented and begged to be taken back. "I not only will erase all those words," pleaded the servant, "I will cover each stone with gold and adorn it with the king's royal crest." "You have learned your lesson," replied the king. "You may enter."

———————

The Jewish people sometimes relate to God as children, and at other times they relate as servants. As it is written, "You are children of God . . ." (Deuteronomy 14:1), and otherwise, "We are but servants, and in our servitude have not forgotten our God" (Ezra 9:9). When all is well, then we relate as children to God, and God in turn relates to us as a

father. But when we stray from the Torah way and end up in the clutches of exile, then we are merely servants and God is our master.

During the Greek oppression many Jews assimilated and became Hellenists. Many strayed off the path and pursued the culture of a foreign nation. We were then on a lower level as are servants. Still, a sizable group of faithful fought and vanquished the enemy. Suddenly God caused a miracle to happen, and the little jug of oil burned for eight days. The Temple service was renewed, and the Jewish way of life flourished once again. Our relationship returned to that of the children of God as it was meant to be.

Yet the miracle happened when we were only servants. Therefore, it gives us strength in today's exile. We reassure ourselves, "Even if we are not the best generation and we are spiritually weak in so many ways, still God is with us and may even cause miracles to happen with us."

———————

God is infinite, and even the entire universe is too limited to contain Him. Yet despite His magnitude, we believe that His Divine Presence fills each and every particle, even the most lowly. This is the preeminence of God's greatness. Similarly, the mark of any mortal's eminence is that, no matter how important that mortal is, he is still simple enough to mix with the lowly.

There were two brothers, Moses and Aaron, who brought gifts to the Jewish people. Moses, our teacher, brought us the tablets from Mount Sinai. Aaron, the High Priest (*Kohen Gadol*), served in the Holy Temple. The tablets were stone, but the words on them were God's Divine Presence. How could the infinite rest on such tiny letters? Yet this is God's greatness. It is incomprehensible how God can do this, but He does it. The Holy Temple was only a house, but God was always present within it. This too brings out the greatness and humility of God. Similarly, it points to the humility of Moses and Aaron who brought God's gifts to us. Moses was "the most humble of all persons on the face of the earth" (Numbers 12:3), whereas Aaron respected even the lowliest creature and tried to bring him peace and love.

The tiny letters containing God's presence (the Torah) last forever. The Menorah with its tiny lights, representing the Holy Temple, also lasts forever. Why? Because God's spirit was thrust into the lowliest places, and therefore it survives even in the lowest of generations and exiles.

The miracle of Chanukah was that the Almighty God descended and made the tiny flames stream with light. This is in the merit of Aaron; and we place the lamp directly opposite the *mezuzah*, which symbolizes the Torah scroll, which is in the merit of Moses.

We too, high and mighty as we are, must humble ourselves and prepare a dwelling place for God inside our hearts. And when the Chanukah lights shine there, they sparkle always and forever. The infinite meets the lowly. The spirit meets flesh and blood. We too should follow the example of God, Moses, and Aaron, mingling with the lowliest and affirming God's love for each and every Jew.

20

Placing the Lamp

The Chanukah lamp should be placed outside the front door opposite the *mezuzah*, so that if one is facing the entrance, the *mezuzah* is on the right and the Chanukah lamp on the left. (*Shabbos* 22b)

an experiences God's presence in two distinct ways, openly or concealed. The truth is that, even in things and places where God seems to be absent, His vital holiness is there in full measure. Man's task is to relate to the Godliness that is within the concealment and to ignore its hiddenness completely.

Every *mitzvah* brings honor to God's name and is thus a manifest holiness. To experience God in a *mitzvah* is expected and commonplace, just as one expects to find strength in one's right hand. But to find power in one's left hand is a sign of even greater strength, because strength was found where there is usually weakness.

Similarly, the light of Chanukah shone within the darkness of suppression. Through the efforts of the Jewish people who ignored the darkness of concealment, the light became manifest and shone with greater strength than the light of any other *mitzvah*.

Therefore, while a *mezuzah* is placed on the right side where we expect to find the strength of God's presence, the Chanukah lights are set on the left side—a sign of even greater strength, of God's presence within the concealment.

If you want to receive blessing and holiness, you must open the door of your heart. You will then be filled with yearning and heightened expectancy, which is good. Opening the heart, however, raises the possibility of danger. The heart is then open to aimless yearnings and mistaken paths, because it is also a time of multiple possibilities and choices. There is the possibility of confusion and, therefore, *conceal-ment*. Your only hope is to reach for the light that is shining inside the concealment.

Chanukah is a time when doors are open for new revelations, and, likewise, new choices. We want the lights on the *left*, to light our way in the concealment.

The Torah is a treasure-house of deeds, *mitzvos*. This treasure is locked inside our hearts in the form of potential deeds. Fear of God gives direction to our deeds and is therefore the key to the treasure-house.

While the treasure is still in our hearts, it is an inner light, our private domain. When it becomes manifest as deeds, it is then the public domain. The light travels from one domain to the other through the doors of our hearts. These doors need protection, but some public elements come and defile the pure light in our private domain.

In the miracle of Chanukah we were able to protect our domain from intrusion by the enemy; we protected the Holy Temple. We show this by placing the lights at the doors of our houses.

"There is long life in her right hand, and in her left hand riches and honor" (Proverbs 3:16). If you, fortunately, have chosen the *right* path, God grants you life. But even if you have stumbled along on the left path, God may still save you miraculously if you yearn and struggle to find your way. Certainly, this doesn't equate the right with the left, but it does show the strength of God's grace.

In the historic period of Chanukah, all the oil of the Temple became impure. The impurity of the nations crept into the Jewish culture through assimilation. Still, some pure oil was found; there were a pure family and pure followers. The Jews were miraculously saved from the wrong path. Even on the *left* (side of the door) the miraculous lights shine brightly.

In order for anything to be redeemed, it must have at least some part remaining in its original pure form. God has guaranteed the Jewish People that they will always have a redeemable portion.

During the Greek oppression, the Jewish People needed redemption. On the physical level, this was symbolized by the small jar of oil found in the Temple. On the spiritual level, it was the kernel of undefiled holiness that is forever within each Jew.

Therefore, long before the destruction of the Temple, God prepared a redeemable portion. He brought about a miracle that transformed the Menorah into an everlasting form. These are the Chanukah lights, which will last until the advent of the *Mashiach*, and they will be followed by the Menorah in the next Temple.

As we learn in the Midrash, "Open for me an opening the size of a needle's eye, and I will open for you the doorway to a palace" (*Song of Songs Rabbah* 3). This means that the tiny but pure light enables the door to the next Holy Temple to open, speedily in our days.

Our life is finite; we live a short time, at most ninety to a hundred years. On the other hand, the World to Come is everlasting and infinite. Compared to that infinity, our lifetime is a fleeting moment, a spark that flickers for an instant and then is no more.

What activities should we then pursue? Activities that make our short physical existence possible, or rather should we be busy ensuring that we live forever in the World to Come? It is logical that we should pursue the latter. We could even say that if a person pursues his physical life, his lusts, ambitions, and appetites, then he is making a big mistake because he is neglecting his eternity, his everlasting life.

So then what are we to do with this world? How should we deal with our everyday affairs?

There are two approaches. One approach is to push aside the everyday affairs of this world and to focus only on actions that guarantee us everlasting life. We find this approach taken by earnestly religious people, pious servants of God, whose every waking moment is in the interest of doing good deeds and following the *mitzvos* of the Torah.

But there is another way, which is equally valid. And that is to look for the everlasting in all our physical actions. To find the holy in the mundane, to look for the light within the darkness. The one who chooses this path does not despise work, does not disregard his dwelling, does not hate his food, does not shun his wife. On the contrary, he deals with all of them as opportunities to serve God. And he finds a path that leads to everlasting life through them.

This is the symbol of the Chanukah lamp that brings light within the darkness. It is on the left, so that even if we are partaking in the "left," in short-lived activities that are minor compared to eternity, still there is light within it. It is our task to find it.

It is written, "Long life in her right hand, in her left hand riches and honor" (Proverbs 3:16).

Torah leads us to life, as it is written, "I offer you the choice of life and death, blessing and curse. Choose life" (Deuteronomy 30:19). And life means the long everlasting life in the World to Come. All this is in her right hand, the better and more important of the two choices, while riches and honor are placed in the second and less important hand. In the lifestyle of one who follows the guidance of the Torah, the pursuits of the material world should occupy a secondary, minor position compared to the pursuit of the spiritual values and goals.

When we place the Chanukah lamp on the left, we want its light to illuminate the secondary, material portion of our life. We want God's light to shine into everything we do and to show us the path of life even in the darkness.

The original custom was to light the Chanukah lamp at the door outside the house. Nowadays most people light it on the inside by the window. Why?

There were times when our homes were pure, were full of the fear of God, and Torah was our guide. The threat of assimilation came from the outside as strange influences spread through our communities. We then put the menorah on the outside as a protection against the evil influences. But today the forces of evil have already penetrated our homes. Our doors have been weakened with the attacks of foreign beliefs and culture. So today we place the menorah inside to shine its good influence on us and to purify our hearts from all evil and misguided paths.

The *mezuzah* is on the right side of the door, and the Chanukah lamp on the left" (*Shabbos* 22b).

The *mezuzah* is a small scroll containing one chapter of the Torah. It represents the Torah, with its clear, steady light guiding us throughout our life. On the other hand, the Chanukah lamp is a lesser light, but gives us light in the darkness.

We can compare this to a prince who ran away from the palace and was lost in the woods nearby. When night came, he was in total darkness and could not see where he was going at all. Fortunately, large torches were lit on the palace grounds each night. The light filtered through the forest, and the prince was able to find his way home. Once inside the palace gates, the prince enjoyed the steady light that streamed without pause. He thought, "It is far better to be here in the light than to find my way through the darkness."

Although we are very impressed with the light of the Chanukah lamp, and that God gives us light even in the darkness of the exile, still we would rather have the steady light, the light of the Torah. Therefore we place the Chanukah lamp in a secondary position on the left side of the door.

The Holy Temple had thirteen doors. In defiance, the Greeks tore thirteen breaches in the wall around the Temple. Thus, they aimed to defile the private domain of the Jewish People, where the purest manifestation of God could be found in its original form. But God miraculously saved us from them. Not only did our domain remain pure but it even shone into the public domain, which was dominated by impurity (the Greeks). This light broke down the Greek walls, the obstructions and separations between God and the Jewish People.

They wanted to leave us open to defilement, to break our walls and set up their walls—but instead, purity burst forth from within us, broke their walls, and brought us even closer to God.

The Talmud says that the Menorah is witness that God's presence is with the Jewish people. How so? Because surely God does not need the light of the Menorah; its presence shows us that God's light is with us all the time.

There is an even deeper reason. The Menorah was on the opposite side of a curtain from the ark that contained the Torah. God gave His very presence with the Torah, which obviously never leaves us. And the Torah too is always present as witnessed by the light of the Menorah, shining constantly adjacent to the Torah.

The *mezuzah* is also a witness that God's holiness dwells among us. The first reason is because it is a small Torah scroll. Second, the doorpost itself was a witness in Egypt when we were chosen as a people. We were commanded to smear blood on it the night before the Exodus. It is witness that we are slaves to no one but Him and He in turn is our God.

The Greeks wanted to suppress and enslave us. They attempted to sever the special relationship that God has with us. Their efforts, however, were futile. We will be slaves to no one; we remained, as always, God's People.

These are our two witnesses, the light of the Menorah shining near the *mezuzah*. The Torah scroll, the doorpost, and the lights all publicize God's presence with us.

Chanukah was the time when we threw off the yoke of strangers and rededicated ourselves to the kingdom of heaven. This was accomplished through our great yearning and desire to hear the word of God, to listen to our Torah.

If your ear is not yearning to hear God's word, your hearing must be faulty. If you are not tuned in to the real master, you will have a stranger as master. Therefore, the servant who refuses to go free has his ear trained on the doorpost that witnessed in Egypt our servitude to God.

As we read in Proverbs 18:43, "Rewarded is the one who listens to me, to frequent my doors each day." The *mezuzah* represents listening; it contains the *Shma* (listen), and the Chanukah lamp is the rededication to the kingdom of heaven.

This is why Chanukah is the only holiday with varying degrees of performing the *mitzvah* of lighting the lamp beautifully. Yearning has no limit. The more the door of a person's ears and heart is open, the more God opens the doors for him to holiness and understanding.

"The *mezuzah* is on the right, Chanukah lights on the left, and the man with a *tallis* and *tzitzis* in the middle" (*Esther Rabbah* 1).

There are three dimensions: space, time, and spirit.

The manifestation of God's holiness must encompass all three. Space is represented by the *mezuzah*, which brings holiness into the space of a household. Time: The Chanukah lights are within the holy period of the year in which we celebrate. Spirit: *Tzitzis* and *tallis* represent the special soul of the Jewish People.

The Zohar says that just as Jacob loved Joseph more because he was born in his old age, and he made him a coat of many colors, so too the Jewish People came long after the creation (although they were the primary intention of God's creation), and received a special soul over which the other nations jealously fight constantly. This special soul is physically experienced as the *tallis* with the *tzitzis* (Zohar, Genesis 605).

This is what the Greeks were fighting for, to rob us of our special dimension. Therefore, we publicize our specialness by lighting the lamp near the door.

A door needs protection. When it opens, anything can enter and anything can exit. So it is with new revelations that enter your heart. First the heart needs protection that you should receive them. Then it needs protection that you should not lose them.

The *mezuzah* on the right enables the holiness to enter the house. The Chanukah lights protect the holiness from being lost.

Doors allow both friend and foe to enter and need to be closely guarded. We therefore place the Chanukah lamp next to the door opposite the *mezuzah*.

Similarly there are twelve doors for the channels of God's providence. These are also the twelve borders of the land of Israel for the twelve tribes detailed in the Torah (Numbers 34:2). Each of those borders also has to be watched, because they are doors.

The essence of the twelve tribes is summed up in two of them—Joseph and Judah—because they are the sum total of promises that God made with the Jewish people. Joseph did not succumb to the temptations of the wife of Potifar and therefore represents the foundation, that no child will be lost from the Jewish nation and all children born will belong to God. He represents the physical survival of the Jewish people. Judah, on the other hand, whose mother said at his birth, ". . . now I will thank God . . ." (Genesis 29:35), represents the special relationship that God has with the Jewish people; they can pray to God for all their needs and will be guided throughout their life by His Torah. Judah represents the spiritual survival of the Jewish people. The victorious battles of Chanukah ensured Jewish survival on both counts. Therefore we thank God on the level of Judah and we praise God on the level of Joseph.

Habit, the routine performance of *mitzvos*, is two-sided. On the one hand, it is good to do *mitzvos* constantly without interruption. On the other hand, one may no longer be motivated by the original commandment of the *mitzvah* but by one's earlier performance. Habit leads to forgetfulness, and one may lose the true connection.

The Greeks attempted to make the Jews forget the *mitzvos* on both levels. First, they attempted to stop them from performing the *mitzvos* altogether, thereby causing forgetfulness. Second, even if the Jews continued to do *mitzvos*, the Greeks wanted them to be performed out of habit, without their true depth.

This was the battle of Jacob with the angel of Esau. The angel of Esau touched Jacob's leg (*regel*, which also means habit). The right leg represents the *mitzvos* themselves. The left is the connection to the roots of the *mitzvos*.

The *mezuzah* is on the right, showing that we have overcome Esau on that front. The *mitzvos* are constantly with us, as is the *mezuzah* constantly on our doorpost.

The Chanukah lights are on the left, showing that we overcame even in the battle of habit.

This is also the meaning of the talmudic rule: "One can light the Chanukah lights until all feet (*regel*, also habit) end from the street," i.e., late at night when no one is walking on the streets (*Shabbos* 21b).

A door needs protection. When it is open, anything can enter.

The Greeks endangered the Jewish People by breaking their doors, physically and spiritually. Physically, this refers to the doors of the Holy Temple. Spiritually, they decreed that Jews may not observe *Shabbos*, the New Moon, or circumcision. All three are doorways. *Shabbos* is a doorway of blessing for the whole week, the New Moon is a doorway of blessing for the month, and circumcision is the doorway through which more Jews are brought into the world.

Surely, the Greek domination of the Holy Place was brought about by the lack of proper respect for the Temple. And therefore, when the Jews fought for the honor of God and the Holy Temple, the miracle manifested itself in something that brings honor. These are the lights of the Menorah, which have no practical use. They were there to bear witness to God's presence among the Jewish people.

The doors were secure again.

21

Prayers and Blessings

efore lighting the Chanukah lights, we say three blessings:

Blessed are You, God, our God, King of the Universe, who has commanded us to light the Chanukah lamp.
Blessed are You, God, our God, King of the Universe, who has done miracles for our fathers, in those days, in this time (of the year).
Blessed are You, God our God, King of the Universe, who has made us live, and kept us, and allowed us to arrive to this day.

There are two types of occurrences in this world. One happens within the realm of natural law; the other happens miraculously. We understand natural laws with ease and expect them to recur regularly and always. The sun rises and sets, seeds sprout from the ground, objects thrown in the air fall back to earth, planets move in the sky, bacteria are active under the microscope. We have learned, by constant repetition, that these events happen without fail or interruption. They make sense to us—how could they possibly be otherwise? We call them laws, so they must happen precisely the way we expect them to. We also call them natural, not requiring any special Divine intervention. On the contrary, as long as there is a cause, there will be the awaited effect. No outside force is required to make this happen.

Then one day we stand near the Red Sea while the Egyptians are in pursuit. Our leader, Moses, lifts his staff over the water, and behold, the water splits open (Exodus 14:16–22). We stare in amazement and awe. Never have we seen water split, nor expected it to happen. "This is a miracle!" we call out. "It doesn't just happen! Only God can do it!"

If we think a little deeper, however, we discover something entirely different. Do natural laws just happen? Certainly not. We believe that God created the world, and with His absolute free will He wills the universe to exist every instant. It is impossible to imagine that there is an instant that God should not will it to exist. There would be sheer nothingness then as before the creation. In a Divine sense, God is creating and re-creating every creature at every instant of its existence. Certainly, we expect to see the sun rise tomorrow as we have every other day, but God is the one who is making it rise. It does not just happen, nor does nature make it happen.

Even from our perspective, however, there is another approach. Are the natural laws and occurrences really so simple and expected? They may be simple on the surface, but certainly not if we delve deeper. When you begin to study any natural phenomenon in more detail, you obviously discover new, unexpected, and sometimes startling facts. Whoever is familiar with any one of the natural sciences knows the excitement that accompanies "new" discoveries. Whether in astrophysics, microbiology, quantum mechanics, or biochemistry, new and unexpected findings are constantly being encountered. "Unexpected?" you ask. "How can any natural phenomenon be unexpected?"

On a simple level we answer: natural laws are only simple on the surface; once we delve below the surface they are neither simple nor expected. On a much deeper level, there is not, there was not, and there never will be any phenomenon that happens unless God makes it happen. This includes both the so-called natural and the so-called miraculous. The natural, after all, is just as unexpected as the miraculous once we scratch the surface.

Then what is a miracle? It is when we expect one thing and an entirely different thing happens. We expect the Red Sea to keep flowing, but it is suddenly split before our very eyes. Certainly we believe and know that God is the one who made the water flow, and likewise, He is the one who made it part. Yet, in our amazement, and for lack of a better term, we name it a miracle (from the Latin *mirari*, "to wonder at").

There is, yet, even a greater wonder. This occurs when even what we had expected on the surface suddenly is transformed to the unexpected. We do not expect to see God's intervention in ordinary everyday phenomena. When we do, it is the greatest of wonders. If we could experience just once that God is making the sun rise, that without Him this would not occur, it would be wondrous indeed!

Oil always burns; it is expected to and it is natural for this to happen. If oil refused to burn, we would wonder, "Is this perhaps a miracle?" When a tiny jug of oil burns for eight days instead of one, we see with our own eyes that the expected, natural phenomenon is actually an act of God. Experiencing God's intervention in nature is the greatest miracle of all.

We can liken this to a band of wanderers walking in the darkness. The particular night is so dark that it is absolutely impossible to see anything. They stray off the path and are utterly lost and just about to give up hope. Suddenly, the sun rises! The wanderers freeze in awe and wonder. They cry out, "Look! God has changed the night from darkness to light! Praised be His name!" But what if the sun had not risen? What if, in that dismal and absolute darkness, God had clearly and explicitly revealed to them that He is the One and no one else, who made the night so dark? Would not that be even a greater wonder, that God is making it dark directly, there and all around them?

If the sun rises in the middle of the night, the night is then brilliantly transformed for you. But when God whispers to you that it is He who is making the darkness, how much more brilliant the night becomes for you!

In the miracle of Chanukah, God revealed himself within nature. He showed that the expected is really unexpected, that nature is miraculous, that night is really light, that the everyday is really God. When we realize all this, we praise God saying, ". . . You have made miracles . . . in this time." The miracles appeared within this very time, natural and expected, yet so unexpected and miraculous.

The nations of the world arrogantly claim to be masters of the world. They leave no room for God's kingdom, nor do they allow the Jewish People to proclaim God's sovereignty. They oppress them and lock them in darkness. When God intervenes, however, and redeems them, they realize that in that very exile God is with them. They gain new strength

to continue their special task and declare God's mastery over all.

There are four exiles: Babylon, Medea, Greece, and now Edom. Each one had its particular brand of darkness, and from each one there is a redemption. Each redemption is a revelation that even in that particular darkness God was ever present. Each revelation is therefore a teaching by means of which the Jewish People can endure the next exile.

The same is true with each individual. Each one of us needs to pass through four types of exile and darkness and be redeemed from them. Each darkness we pass through enlightens us in the performance of our special mission.

After we passed through the darkness of Greece, we were granted the redemption of Chanukah. That light was an eternal revelation that God is with us even in the darkness. This is the soft light shining into our hearts, always urging us to do God's bidding. And whenever we see this light we praise God and say, ". . . that You have made miracles . . . in this time [of the year]" (*Prayer Book*, The Blessings of Chanukah). Even in this very time the light of Chanukah lights my way. I know that the dark exile of my own personal life can also be overcome. I need only to hold tightly the drop of pure oil, the holiness, that God has placed in my heart. Then I will overcome my obstacles and impediments and continue to sing God's praise.

God is the source of life for the whole universe. Whoever desires life must find a path that leads to this source. The path we have chosen is the Torah. It teaches us the manner of conduct leading to God. Every moment that we are connected to the Torah, we also have life.

The Greeks strove to separate us from the Torah and likewise from God. Theirs was a path of darkness and death. In the end, however, we were saved and were given back our lives. And so we praise God, ". . . that you have made us live . . ." (*Prayer Book*, The Blessings of Chanukah). You have given life back to us, and we cherish it immensely.

"We are not permitted to make ordinary use of them, but to look at them . . ." (Prayer for Lighting the Chanukah Lamp).

The darkness of the exile and our own lives clouds our vision. We are hardly able to see, but when we experience a miracle, our whole life lights up. We are able to see again.

This is true with the Chanukah lights. Although we should not use them, they help us to look and to see again.

When we light the Chanukah lamp, we say,

"Who has performed miracles for our fathers in those days, in this time [of the year]" (Blessing for the Chanukah Lamp).

Why is it that we recite this blessing only when we kindle the lamp and otherwise do not recite it at all? After all, is not the day itself a time of miracles? So why can't we recite a blessing for the day itself?

There is the natural world in which we live. It is as physical as we are, and we have direct access to it. Miracles, however, are not of this world. They are not natural and have no connection to anything physical. And when a miracle happens, as it did on Chanukah, we need a bridge to help us have a connection to it. That bridge is the act of kindling the Chanukah lamp. If we do not kindle the Chanukah lamp, we have no tangible connection with the miracle at all.

"For Yourself You made a great and holy Name in Your world, and for Your people Israel You worked a great victory . . ." (Prayer for Chanukah).

When the kingdom of God is revealed in this world, then the Jewish people thrive also. And when God's kingdom is concealed, the Jewish people also become covered with darkness. Therefore, when God's name is magnified, after a miracle, and He gets a "new" name, then the Jewish people also get a new "name." The student with the new name must be taught what to do, and therefore the holiday named for the miracle is Chanukah, meaning to teach.

"You delivered the strong into the hands of the weak, the many into the hands of the few, the impure into the hands of the pure, the wicked into the hands of the righteous, and the wanton into the hands of the diligent students of the Torah" (Chanukah prayer).

We know that the nations of the world have "hands" as it is written, ". . . but the hands are the hands of Esau . . ." (Genesis 27:22). Then what kind of hands does the Jewish nation have? Their strength comes from the Torah. Therefore five "hands" are mentioned in this prayer. They symbolize the five books of Moses, the Torah. Also, the world was created with the letter *heh*, which is equivalent to the number five, and it is written h-h, which is five times five. And this power of the hand, *yud* and *dalet*, helps the Jewish people defeat the seventy nations if they need to do so. The letter *dalet* equals 4; 4 times 15 equals 60 plus *yud* (10) equals 70.

The letter *heh*, the fifth letter of the Hebrew alphabet, is mere breath, breath that is used in songs of praise and thanks on the twenty-fifth day of the month of *Kislev*, Chanukah.

There are times when the Jewish People are, unfortunately, in exile. Their oppressors treat them mercilessly, and they exist in sheer darkness. Yet the merciful God shines a heavenly light to them, and they are able to endure. It may not be the most brilliant light, but compared to dismal darkness it shines like day.

The exile of Greece was an especially cruel one. The Greeks denied the chosenness of the Jewish People by claiming to have more wisdom and better teachings. They did not allow the Jews to carry out their responsibilities. They mocked the Torah, the commandments, the Sabbath, and the holidays. They denied the ultimate reason for the existence of the Jewish Nation: to proclaim God's sovereignty. The Jews were totally rejected as a people; there was no longer a *reason* for their existence.

In such a terrible and dark exile, which robbed them of any identity, the Jewish People yearned for God's light. They imagined the great brilliance of such a light even as they longed for God's redemption. They thought, "This will not be just a light. No, this light will be special and more brilliant than ever. It will light up the earth so much that whatever anyone has ever lost will be found again. There will be no hiding place that this light will not penetrate." Despite their yearning, the exile continued. And the Jews cried, "God, we don't need the bright light . . . just give us a sign, even the smallest light, that we are still Your people and have a special reason to be in the world."

The yearning of the Jewish hearts drew down the most brilliant of lights. It was hidden, however, inside the tiny flames of the Menorah. Yet every Jew knew that the Jews had been reestablished as the exclusive messengers of God—teaching wisdom, justice, and mercy.

It was our activity that lit the special light of the Chanukah miracle. And so we praise God saying, ". . . You have commanded us to light the Chanukah lamp." We are the ones who light the lamp as we did during our redemption.

22

Lighting the Lamp

he *mitzvah* of Chanukah is to light one lamp per family. Those who want to beautify the *mitzvah* more light one for each member of the household. And those who beautify *mitzvos* even more light a different number of menorahs each night (*Shabbos* 21b).

Why are varying degrees allowed in the performance of the Chanukah *mitzvah* and not for other *mitzvos*?

There were Jews in ancient Greece who loved to do *mitzvos* and others who did them out of pure obligation. Those who were obligation Jews were not so disturbed by the Greek oppression, but the real *mitzvah* Jews suffered terribly. When the redemption came there was great rejoicing among the *mitzvah* Jews, but sadness among the others.

We must connect ourselves to a love of *mitzvos* by allowing the light to rest among us.

Feet are used basically for two things, to stand and to walk. If a person stands in a place for too long a time his feet fall asleep; they stagnate. You must start to walk to bring a renewal.

When the Jewish nation stays too long in one place, they likewise fall asleep and stagnate. God wants to renew them by moving them from one place to the next. This is the function of exile, to bring life and vitality back to the Jewish People.

The urge to do good is named "a child," whereas the urge to do evil is named "the old man." Why? Because our desire to do good is in constant danger lest it fall into the clutches of evil. It is therefore alert and full of vigor and vitality.

The laws of nature are miracles that happened so many times, stood in one place so long, that they become standing feet. The really miraculous is walking feet. When something can walk out of its plainness, that is miraculous.

As we stand by the Chanukah lights, let us look into our hearts. In how many areas are we standing? Walking? Let the miraculous walking fill our hearts so that we stay renewed always.

The Holy Temple had two periods, one when it was revealed and one when it was hidden. In the first, it was clear that God was among us. In the second, we had to search for Him.

Each one of us is a Temple for the spirit of God. We too must search the depths of our hearts to find God's presence.

During the Greek exile the holiness of the Temple became very hidden. Yet a family of Torah-loyal Jews searched so long that they uncovered it and then felt God's presence in full measure again.

Reb Levy Yitzchok of Berditchev explains: Moses prophesied with the word "this" (*zeh*). It was plain and clear to him. The other prophets used the word "thus" (*koh*). It was blurry and unclear to them. During Chanukah, even the *koh*, the hidden, becomes openly full of light. *Chanu*, they rested; *koh*, even in the hiddenness.

We too should search our hidden places and find God's spirit. Then we will see clearly even in the most dismal places of our hearts.

Space and time can contain God's presence and are then called *moed*, a witness that God dwells among us. When God's Divine Presence descends to be among us, it is called the Written Law. God writes it; He does it. When we draw His presence down to us, this is the Oral Law, that which we have done with our deeds.

Wicks and oils that cannot be used on *Shabbos* can nevertheless be used on Chanukah (*Shabbos* 21a), meaning that even one who cannot get connected to *Shabbos*—perhaps it is too high for him—can still be connected to Chanukah. On that holiday the holiness comes to you. Why? Because the Jews themselves bring it down to the world, and it becomes easily accessible.

How many lamps do we kindle on the eve of Chanukah? Shammai says: The first night eight, then seven, and one fewer each night. Hillel says: The first night one, then two, adding one each night (*Shabbos* 21b).

The lamp has oil and a wick. The oil is consumed to produce the flame. When the flame is bigger, more oil is consumed. The flame represents good and the oil evil. Should one do more and more acts of good or first get rid of the evil?

Shammai holds that first you must rid yourself of all evil and then do good. Hillel holds just the opposite. Increase your good, and the evil will fall away.

As we watch the Chanukah lights burn we look into our hearts to see how much good and evil we find and what we are doing about it. We pray that we shall have the strength either to eliminate the evil or to increase our acts of good.

Man can be the link between God and the world. He has a heavenly soul and an earthly body. If he allows the Divine Presence to enter him, he links heaven and earth. If not, heaven and earth are separated.

How does the Divine Presence enter man? As man craves and yearns for God he becomes a vessel for His holiness and it enters. When the Jewish Nation yearns for God, the entire nation becomes a vessel for His holiness and it enters. Then all the nations of the world make themselves vessels to accommodate the Jewish People with all their needs.

This is how the Menorah is witness that God is among us. Just as the lamp is a vessel to the oil, so too are the Jewish People a vessel.

Each time we prepare ourselves to receive God's presence we are renewed completely. We are connected to the roots and charged with fresh energy.

"We are not permitted to use the lights, but only to look at them" (*Siddur*, Chanukah Prayer).

The light of Chanukah makes you sensitive even to things that you no longer feel. You stop feeling from too much repetition, and the miracle of Chanukah is just the opposite of repetition. It is entirely new.

The light of a lamp is good for searching (*Pesachim* 3b). How does a light search? The flame searches the wick for but another drop of oil to burn. So too God's light, which is in each of us, searches the depths of our hearts to find a place, any place where it can be received.

When you look at the Chanukah lights, allow them to shine into your heart and to spread out to fill you with radiance.

The lamp of God shines into the soul of man, searching out his inmost being (Proverbs 20:27).

That which is hidden can be found only if enough effort is exerted. The Holy Temple is hidden now, but can be found by searching. With what need we search? With the Chanukah lights.

The same applies to the *mitzvos*, the commandments of the Torah. We need to search within our heart of hearts to do the commandments with our entire being with complete vitality. Therefore, A *mitzvah* is the lamp, and Torah is the light (Proverbs 6:23). With the lamp, all hidden things can be found.

In the time of the Holy Temple, the Greeks defiled the Menorah, so that the Jews no longer had a lamp to light. Through searching for the oil, the Menorah itself was revealed. Therefore, we too, although we no longer have the Holy Temple, can have it revealed with our lighting of the Chanukah lights. The lights help us search through the darkness of the exile and find that which is hidden.

We are not the source of our life—God is. We are merely the vessels that contain the life that God grants us. This is very much like the light that resides in the lamp. The lamp is the vessel for the light, but not the source of the light.

As the world turns in its usual everyday habits, people forget who and what they are. It takes the unusual, a miracle, to shake them out of their habitual thinking. Then they realize that they are but vessels, especially if the miracle happens in a vessel, as it did in the Menorah. The Jewish people immediately understood the lesson, that they are vessels to God's light. And by acknowledging this, they can help the whole world understand it too.

Each human being is born so he can add some light to this world. Especially the Jewish people, who know this and have an explicit book of instructions for this very purpose, must constantly take an active role in bringing light to the world. Therefore, as dark as the world becomes, and as much as civilization weakens, so too does the urgency of their task increase. And when the exile becomes very dismal and dark, the Jewish people must shine a light into that darkness.

This was the miracle of the Chanukah lamp—to teach every one of us, with a physical event, that which happened in the spiritual realm. Just as the Menorah lit up the darkness miraculously, so too each human being has the power to light up the darkness far beyond his natural abilities.

———————

God is with the Jewish people regardless of their circumstances. Whether they are worthy or not, many or few, He is with them always. This was revealed through the miracle of the lamp. Although no oil was found at first and then only enough to light for one day, still the lamp burned for eight days. The same is true with us and God's light. Although facts may not merit it, still God is with us always.

———————

Each one of us has a physical body and also a spiritual essence. The physical part of us tends to the darkness and the spirit to light. The body will remain without enlightenment at best, or descend to the abyss of banality at worst. The spirit, on the other hand, will bask in the light of God and enjoy the gift of intellect. How then do these opposite forces come together? The unifying element between the body and the spirit are the *mitzvos*, the good deeds commanded in the Torah. By doing a *mitzvah* the body becomes a vessel to receive the enlightenment of the soul.

Thus it is written, "From distress I have called to God, and He answered me in a wide space" (Psalms 118:5). At first the light of the soul is in a tight place; it is not connected to the body. But then through doing a *mitzvah*, the light of the soul spreads into all the parts of the body. The word for wide space is *merchav*, which has the same numerical value as *ner*, "lamp." When the body is a lamp for the light of the soul, then the two letters of God's name, "YA," expand. They expand by multiplying 10 (*yud*) times the *heh*, which equals 50, which is *nun*, and *yud* is spelled *yud, vov-dalet*, which equals 20-times *heh* (spelled h - h, two *hehs* = ten), which equals 200 (*resh*). Therefore, the expansion of God's name in a tight place, *YAH*, equals and spells the word *ner*, or lamp.

The same is true in the exile. The exile is full of darkness until the light of our good deeds lights it up. And out of the constriction of the exile grows the light of redemption.

———————

The body is a vessel for the light of the soul. But even the soul, as spiritual and as holy as it is, is merely a vessel for the light that emanates from God.

Therefore it is written, "A *mitzvah* is a lamp . . ." (Proverbs 6:23). By doing a *mitzvah* we become a lamp for the light of our soul. However, it is also written, "The lamp of God is man's soul" (Psalms 20:27). Even the soul of man is but a lamp, a vessel for the light of God.

It is written, "The lamp of God shines into the soul of man; it searches out his inmost being" (Proverbs 20:27).

The Hebrew word for searches is *chofeis*, which can also be read as *chofesh*, which means to free. As the light of God shines into us, it raises even the body to spiritual heights. Our body becomes free of attachments. What are these attachments? Lusts and needs that it craves. The body is, to a degree, a slave to those attachments until the light of God sets it free.

———————

It is written, The commandments are the lamp, and the Torah is the light (Proverbs 6:23).

When we do the commandments we create a vessel for the light of God; this is the level of physical activity. The light of God is the Torah, the sacred and divine teachings; this is the level of thinking and intellect. When we praise God for granting us the commandments, this is the level of speaking and communicating. Thus we have all the three components, which together make a complete act—thinking, speaking, and doing. There is another level, which includes all of these, but is even higher. This level is called *mosif ve'holech*—"he adds on and continues to walk." That means that you are constantly using the Torah and *mitzvos*, the commandments, to rise higher and higher.

During the celebration of Chanukah we can connect to all of these levels. And if we do, we will certainly become a lamp, a vessel to receive God's light.

———————

The Hebrew word for lamp is *ner*, the wick is *pesiloh*, and the oil is *shemen*; these words form the acrostic *nefesh*, "soul." To serve God with all your soul you must use your three energies: thought, speech, and action. And when all three are put into the service of God, then the light descends and rests on the lamp, and it burns with a steady flame. But if there is not enough preparation, then the flame flickers and sputters. It does not have a proper resting place.

What is true with each individual is also true with the Jewish nation as a whole. We can be in the best of environments, but may be just unprepared to receive the light. Then, even when we participate in good deeds, the light from them merely flickers and does not really take hold. Similarly, in the time of the Holy Temple, when the Greeks forbade us to learn the Torah and perform the commandments, we were without the steady light. The light flickered and was about to be extinguished altogether. If we had not prepared ourselves properly, the light may have darkened forever. But we struggled and were victorious. Our *nefesh* was again pure, and we in turn received the lamp, wick, and oil with its steady flame. This steady flame is symbolized by the Chanukah lamp and light.

When we want to elevate ourselves in our spiritual life we must do two things. First we must remove ourselves from evil, and only then do good deeds. This is similar to the disagreement between the House of Shammai and the House of Hillel regarding the Chanukah lamp. The House of Shammai says that the first night we should light eight, the second night seven, and so on, always diminishing the amount until on the last night we light only one. The House of Hillel, on the other hand, says that on the first night you light one, the second night two, and so on until on the last night you light eight.

So then, according to Shammai, by minimizing and reducing the power of evil we automatically increase the good. And according to Hillel, we must increase the good in order to rise in our spiritual level. Certainly if we do both we will be heading in the right direction.

Each of us has a body and a soul. The soul is eternal while the body withers away and dies. Still, the body is the "garment" of the soul and has an important assignment.

We can compare this to a king's servant who was carrying material to the palace to be made into royal garments for the king's wedding. On the way he was caught in a storm. He needed to protect the garments from stains and damage. After the storm he was beset by a flood, wild animals, and thieves. He tried his best to preserve the original quality of the material. Finally he reached the palace. The royal tailor spread out the material and examined it. "I can tell that you worked very hard to keep this material pure. Unfortunately, there are a few parts that are soiled. They cannot be used."

Few are those who pass through this world so that each part of their body is pure without sin. But those who do are as a wick that draws oil with a smooth flame. Their body was a proper garment for the soul, so it becomes the royal garments at the final celebration.

One of the differences between the Written Law and the Oral Law is that we are not permitted to add on to the Written Law, but we may add on to the Oral Law. Because the lighting of the Chanukah lamp is a *mitzvah* from the sages and is part of the Oral Law, we can therefore add on to it. The rule is that at a minimum one lamp should be kindled per household. A more adorned way, however, is to kindle a lamp for each family member, and an even better way is to kindle different amounts of menorahs each night. The heroes in the period of the Greek exile had great reverence for the Torah. Those who honor the Torah, and God's word is important to them, are as the Oral Law and therefore cause an increasing number of lights to be turned on.

By ordering the Jews to translate the Torah, the Greeks hoped to take the most precious possession away from them. Their scheme was foiled, and the Jews emerged victorious. The Torah remained untouchable by foreign hands because it is a consuming fire. These are the lights of the Chanukah lamp.

We can compare this to a prince who left the palace to accomplish a secret mission for his father. He was ambushed and taken prisoner by a band of thieves. The leader of the band pestered him to show the secret documents from the palace. "What are they to you?!" the prince insisted. "You needn't know anything about them!" After much harassment the prince finally showed the documents to the thieves. They were puzzled, "What do they say? We can't read them! Come on, read them to us." Fearing for his life the prince read them. "Aha!" said the leader. "Now we know what you're up to!" "And so you do," said the prince, "and what possible use can that be to you? These documents are about helping people live in civilization, while you go around destroying it!"

———————

The *mitzvah* is for him to light one lamp for himself, including his family (*Shabbos* 21b).

What connection does a man's family have to his own *mitzvah*? The answer is: You share a lot of energy with your family. In order to do the *mitzvah* properly, you must bring all of your energies with you.

———————

One who regularly lights the lamp will have children who are scholars, as it is written, The *mitzvah* is a lamp, and the Torah is the light (*Shabbos* 23b).

Material objects will disintegrate, but wisdom will not because it is sublime and does not age. If a person conducts his life with wisdom, neither does he age. A person who lights up his light regularly brings the miraculous light from heaven and renews himself.

———————

The world is a mixture of good and evil. Although we may never reach perfection in our lifetime, we must nevertheless strive toward it.

When Adam and Eve were created and placed in the Garden of Eden, they were in a state of perfection. Good and evil were defined clearly, as it is written, ". . . you may eat from every tree in the garden, but not from the tree of knowledge of good and evil . . ." (Genesis 2:16). After Adam and Eve sinned and ate from the tree, good and evil were in a state of confusion. Later, when the Jewish nation stood at Mount Sinai good and evil became defined clearly again, as it is written, ". . . life and death I have placed before you . . . and you should choose life . . ." (Deuteronomy 30:19). Unfortunately, soon afterward they made the Golden Calf, an idol, and worshiped it. Their spiritual world once more slipped into confusion, and it has been that way ever since. And we can never hope to clear the world of this confusion completely until the final redemption comes. Then all evil will cease, and the entire world will fill with the knowledge of God and the Torah.

This explains the talmudic rule, Till what time in the evening can one light the Chanukah lights? Until the feet end from the marketplace (*Shabbos*, 22b). Literally, it means until late at night when people stop walking around in the street. It also asks allegorically, How long will we be lighting the Chanukah lights? How long will the miracle sustain us? Until the "feet" of the Golden Calf are no longer found among us. And until when is that? Until the very end, the ingathering of all the exiles.

———————

"And the earth was desolate and bare, and darkness was on the face of the deep, and God's spirit hovered over the water" (Genesis 1:2).

Man is made of the earth and is desolate without his soul. When a person does *mitzvos*, he brings God's presence into his body.

We too must allow the light and life of God to come into us . . . then we will live.

———————

"And God said, 'Let there be light.' And there was light" (Genesis 1:3).

The first light was infinite. It only shone for thirty-six hours. These hours symbolize the thirty-six lamps we kindle during Chanukah.

The Greek oppression had brought darkness. But God lit up the darkness with the infinite light, and even in the very long nights of Chanukah the eternal lights did not dim.

———————

"All the nations have surrounded me, but in the name of God I will destroy them. They surround me. Yes, they surround me, but in the name of God I will destroy them. They surrounded me like bees; they are quenched like the fire of thorns: in the name of God I will destroy them" (Psalms 118:8–13).

The Greeks wrecked the Temple and defiled the oil. They did not allow the light to penetrate even from the Holy Temple. This is like a fire of thorns, which burns awkwardly, not with a steady flame. Neither did the Greeks allow the flame of holiness to burn properly.

God finally saved us miraculously and did just the opposite of what the Greeks did. He restored the wrecked Temples, the Jews who were not living Godly lives, who were the thorns that sputtered from the flame; and even they shone with a steady light.

23

Symbol of the Menorah

The Chanukah lamp reminds us of the great miracle when the bit of oil burned for eight days. It is also a reminder of the Menorah in the Holy Temple, which we no longer have today.

The Chanukah lamp is here to console us in the long dismal night of exile. It reminds us of the Menorah in the Holy Temple and of God saying to us, "Although the actual Menorah is gone, I left you an impression of it." This impression is the Chanukah lamp, and it will last until He sends the Messiah to redeem us and build the Holy Temple.

The Chanukah lamp should console each one of us in our personal exile. Although at times we lose some particular holiness, we must not despair, because God is guarding the impression of that holiness in the depths of our heart, and we will some day regain it.

The Menorah in the Holy Temple had six branches, symbolizing the six days of the week. The seven days of creation encompass God's conduct as it relates to the natural world. The Jewish People, however, received a channel from God that is beyond space and time. They therefore were not in need of the light of the Menorah because they had a direct light from God.

This changed with the miracle of Chanukah. Now the light from the sphere above and beyond nature was shining through the seven-branched Menorah. The infinite was being revealed from inside the finite. The seven branches were transformed into eight, the number that represents the world beyond nature. Their light is one that is eternal.

Standing by the Chanukah lamp, we too can experience the transformation of seven to eight. We can, in the glow of the lights, see not only the Menorah of the Holy Temple but also the miraculous one that will be built speedily in our days.

There are two sources of light. One source is from material that is burning, such as the sun or the light of a candle. The other source of light is the independent creation called the Divine light.

The westernmost light on the Menorah burned miraculously without interruption. Its light did not come from burning fuel, but from the Divine light. However, God wanted Aaron to kindle the Menorah each day so that the finite and the infinite should merge and radiate to create an even more penetrating light, a light that would permeate the very actions of man, not merely reflecting off him.

In a similar manner, when we stand by the Chanukah lamp and kindle the lights with open hearts, we are standing in front of the Menorah in the Holy Temple. And as we kindle the tiny wicks, the All Merciful God shines His pure light into our deed. Suddenly we overcome our limitations and our exile. The light passes over the limited oil and wicks and shines forth infinitely.

There is the physical world, and there is its identical twin, the spiritual world. Whatever we do in one prepares us to experience the other. When the Jewish people lit the physical menorah lamp, the spiritual one became lit. Therefore when the earthly one was defiled and extinguished, the light from the spiritual one was not able to reach us.

A miracle was needed to bring back the light of the physical menorah. This came from the spiritual world, where the light always shines.

———————

All the major holidays are connected to the Holy Temple. Prescribed sacrifices and services take place in the Temple during the holidays. In addition there is also the commandment to appear before God, that each male must journey to Jerusalem and rejoice and feast during the holiday. All this required that the Jews should be sovereign over Jerusalem and their land. How is it then that the Jewish people created holidays even during the years of oppression, years when their rights over Jerusalem were taken away and their power crushed?

Their influence over the nations grew out of their worship in the Holy Temple. During the Sukkos holiday they brought sacrifices for the nations of the world that they too should draw near to the worship of the one and only God. Therefore, even under the oppressive hand of the nations they were worthy enough to create holidays.

———————

The nations of the world are constantly bothering the Jewish people about the logic of the Torah and the commandments (*Numbers Rabbah* 19). Of course, some commandments cannot be explained logically. Doing the ones that are least logical requires the most faith. It is only by faith that the Jewish people live and survive as a nation.

Some of the worship in the Holy Temple was understood by the nations. They understood that sacrifices were brought to atone for sins. But they could not find a reason for the lamp in the Temple. "Does God need light?" they asked. It was the least logical worship in the Temple, the one needing the most faith. It was this very lamp that symbolized the devotion that the Jewish people had to the Torah and commandments of God, and it was therefore the most suitable instrument for the miracle that also symbolized God's closeness to the Jewish people.

———————

Even when we are oppressed, God in His great mercy leaves us with some hope of redemption. It was for this reason that, before the second Temple was going to be destroyed, God prepared the way by preserving the Menorah in the form of the Chanukah lamp, so that we do not forget about the Holy Temple and we always keep hoping for its rebuilding.

———————

The westernmost lamp on the Menorah in the Holy Temple was never extinguished. And from that one the *kohen* would light all the five other lamps. This enduring perpetual light symbolizes the Kingdom of God, which never leaves the hearts and souls of the Jewish people. Even if they forget, its mark still remains in the depths of their hearts.

———————

We can learn a great deal from the heroic acts of the faithful during the Greek oppression. They certainly felt miserable about the foreign occupation of Jerusalem. They were indignant about their lack of freedom and the laws promulgated against their culture and religion. They were dismayed and sad to have to fight battles against impossible odds. Still they persisted and emerged victorious. But when they celebrated their victory they did not symbolize it with a sword, only with a menorah, a source of a calm and peaceful light. This symbolized their steady and constant yearning to observe the Torah.

We too, in our exile, are plagued by much trouble. Rather than complain about our physical condition we should yearn to be able to live a spiritual life once more.

———————

The nations of the world subjugate the Jewish people and oppress them. Later God rescues them and elevates them above their oppressors. Thus, in the Greek exile, because the sanctity of the Holy Temple was attacked and defiled, at the redemption the holiness of the Temple shone out more than ever. And since the Greeks attempted to breach the "private" domain of the Jews, God rewarded them by shining a light from their private domain that would light up even the public domain.

———————

The Jewish people in the time of the Greek exile were extremely oppressed and crestfallen. And although the Holy Temple existed then, it still took great effort to perceive the deep spiritual level of the place. And therefore when we pray for the rebuilding of the Holy Temple, we must also pray for much more than the return of the physical building. We must pray that God rebuild and allow us to experience the Holy Temple in all its spiritual levels and aspects.

The *Mishkan*, the tabernacle, was completed on the twenty-fifth day of *Kislev* but was not assembled until the month of *Nissan*. The energy of this preparation was later used to establish the holiday of Chanukah on that very same day.

It is written, when Joseph was intimidating his brothers, "Bring these men indoors, kill a beast and make dinner ready" (Genesis 43:16). In Hebrew, the words *tevach vehochein* contain the letters *cha-nu-kah*. The preparation gives the energy for later deeds. By preparing the dinner the place and time were made ready for the next event.

We can compare this to a prince who loved when his father came to tell him bedtime stories. So he fashioned a comfortable chair fit for a king, brought it up to his room, and placed it next to his bed. The prince said, "Now whenever my father has time, I am ready to receive him."

"A glorious high throne from the beginning is the place of our sanctuary" (Jeremiah 17:12).

"In the beginning, God created heaven and earth" (Genesis 1:1). "Beginning" means the Jewish People, who are the very beginning of creation (*Genesis Rabbah* 1).

The Holy Temple is the "footstool of God" (Lamentations 2:1). It is the place where we can experience God's kingdom in the world. All the world is humbled before His majesty, and no creature dares to deny His sovereignty. He rules not only the heavens but also the earth. And nowhere on earth can we find God's kingdom more clearly manifest than in the Holy Temple. It is a microcosm where God dwells. Symbolically, the Temple is that aspect of creation that humbles itself totally before God, thereby being a place to establish His kingdom. Such a place must exist at the beginning of creation.

The Jews were chosen to proclaim God's kingdom in this world. They are therefore the creatures whose very nature it is to be humbled before God and to prepare the place for God's rule. Thus, they too must have been in existence from the very beginning of creation.

Both the Temple and the Jewish Nation establish God's kingdom in the world. The Greeks aspired to disrupt the Divinely ordained order by oppressing the Jews and defiling the Temple. They were finally defeated. Both the Jewish People and the Temple were liberated, securing God's place in the world once again. The inner deep truth of the universe streamed forth through the Menorah in the Temple, revealing God's sovereignty over the natural world.

The Temple is now in ruins and the Jews are in exile, yet we believe that soon they will both be uplifted and that the final redemption will be accomplished.

When a person kindles the Chanukah lamp, he sees before him the Menorah of the Temple, and it shines into him and realigns his heart with God. The Menorah whispers to him from within the Temple saying, "You and I are dependent partners. Let us do our job together to proclaim God's kingdom." And his heart, which has now been transformed to the heart of the Jewish nation, answers, "Amen. So be it!"

24

To Thank and Praise

The following year they established it as a holiday for praise and thankfulness. (*Shabbos* 21b)

here are two stages in being afflicted with a problem. There is the time of the struggle, and then the time when one is redeemed from it. While struggling, one may not see any benefit from it. But one who has struggled properly and did not succumb has gained not only from the redemption but from the affliction itself.

This is also true when God afflicts the Jewish People with oppressors and then intervenes "miraculously" to redeem them. They think about what happened and realize that they should certainly praise God for the redemption. But also, they finally realize that they have gained even from the problem. For this they offer thanks, or more correctly, acknowledgment that all God had done was good.

There is absolutely no falseness in God. If you want to praise Him it must be on the purest level of truth. But as long as you are still dependent on any earthly care, you cannot really praise God in truth, because compared to truth it is still flattery.

Giving thanks or acknowledgment, however, is different. Even if you are entangled in all sorts of earthly matters and pursuits, you can still thank God fully and honestly for what you have.

This is why King David declares: Praise God you who are servants of God; because only if you are God's servant exclusively can you praise Him.

If a miracle occurs, however, even the praise becomes thankfulness. Certainly one should not praise God's great ability to perform miracles, for there is no difference between creating what is ordinary or what is miraculous. Both are alike in God's ability. Therefore the only thing left to praise is your own good fortune in being redeemed. Could anyone honestly ignore the fact that he doesn't deserve a miraculous redemption? After all, who could deserve it? And as soon as you think that you do not deserve it and how fortunate you are to have it, your ego is entangled in the world. Then the praise is really thankfulness.

The Jewish People belong exclusively to God. Then how is it possible for other nations to have dominion over them? They do it by drawing them away from their loyalty to God. To the degree that the nations succeed in doing so, they are able to oppress them.

What resistance can the Jewish people offer to the oppression of the nations? They must know that their predicament is directed by God and is not due to the power of the oppressor. This itself is a partial redemption, which eventually leads to a complete one.

The truth of this faith was demonstrated powerfully during the Egyptian exile. When God redeemed us, it became unequivocally clear that the exile too was directly from God and did not result from the power of Egypt.

The Talmud states, "Praise God, you who are servants of God . . . but not the servants of Pharaoh" (*Megillah* 14a). It was our miraculous Exodus from Egypt that taught us for always that all exiles are from God.

Therefore, the praise is for the original redemption, while the thanks is for the present exile. For we realize that it is not an exile after all, because we are totally in the possession of God.

There are two levels of happiness. You can either be happy merely because of your good fortune, or your good fortune may make you aware that you are, after all, God's creature, and this realization makes you immensely happy. Certainly, the latter is the deeper happiness.

But how does one connect himself to this deep joy? Obviously, in our hearts where our egos reign supreme, where we are the masters of our own fate, there is no room for this idea. It is only when we humble ourselves and admit our total dependence on God that we accommodate these ideas. Therefore, when we admit our creatureliness, then our ego is not in our way.

This puts thanksgiving before praise. Once you have thanked, you can praise properly.

We can have two distinct experiences of redemption. The first is what we experience in the very instant of redemption. The second occurs after some time has already passed and we have had a chance to think about what happened.

In the first instant of redemption we are still very close to the trouble, and our tears of joy still taste from the saltiness of affliction. Our response of joy comes reflexively, exploding out of our ego, our flesh, and blood. We thank God, we are grateful, we rejoice in our salvation.

Later, after some time has elapsed, we are at a distance and can reflect on the events. We see that what had happened is the unfolding of God's plan. We uncover causes and effects that suddenly fit into a broad pattern leading to our redemption.

The miracle of Chanukah also was experienced in these two ways. Directly after the event the Jews were only capable of giving thanks for the miraculous redemption. Later they were able to praise God. The following year they established it as a holiday of praise and thankfulness to God (*Shabbos* 21b). Why only the following year? Because by then they had the distance to see that the entire score of events was orchestrated by God. The oppression, wars, strife, hostilities, and struggles all added up to the miraculous redemption.

The Jewish People were chosen by God for a special task. Being chosen singles them out for a special relationship with God. The reason for this choice is one of the deepest secrets of the creation. For surely God's choice is not arbitrary or bound to rational considerations. His choice emanates from His essence, and therefore the relationship of the Jewish People to God is one of essence. And to understand the essence of God we need to almost leap higher than our limited understanding, which is impossible.

During our enslavement and oppression by the nations of the world, the unique intimacy between God and the Jewish People is obscured. It is shrouded in shadows and concealment until it is in danger of vanishing even from Jewish consciousness. Then God intervenes. God proves the relationship historically each time He pulls us out of our entanglements and establishes us as His special people.

This is our praise to Him: "Give praise, you who are servants of God" (Psalms 113:1). Praise God for our closeness and connectedness always, without exception.

Thankfulness, on the other hand, is for realizing that God loosens our bonds, clears our obstructions, and unravels our entanglements so that we all realize the essence of our being.

Deeper still . . .

What does it really mean that a creature praises the Creator? We can compare this to a child whose behavior is so exemplary that his very being brings praise to his parents. He need not sing his parents' praises all day long—yet wherever he goes he brings praise to his parents.

So too it is with a craftsman. His works, wherever they are found, are a praise to his craftsmanship.

So too it is with God. Each creature's existence is essentially praise to God's wisdom as a Creator. Therefore, those who are servants of God are praising God by their very being.

Acknowledgment and thankfulness, on the other hand, show not closeness but distance. Surely you do not thank your right hand for putting a gift into your left hand. Neither do we expect thanks from a baby after nursing from its mother. As the distance between the donor and receiver increases, so too does the expectation of thankfulness.

Therefore, the praise that we offer during Chanukah comes from the essential nature of the Jewish People, which is true always and forever. But the thanks comes from the gap that the oppression has caused between God and the Jewish People, which is only temporary. Praise to You, God, from near; thank You, God, from afar.

The spiritual essence of the world is God. Just as man contains this essence in the form of a soul, so too every item of creation has a spirit and Godliness.

When we are fortunate and choose to follow the Divine order and plan, we have a direct connection to the wisdom, immortality, and power of God. We are bound from the essence of our being to the very roots of existence. We are nourished and revitalized from the root of all—the Master of the world.

We can compare this to a farmer who grafts a branch to a tree. If the graft succeeds, the branch starts to be nourished from the root of the tree, and you can taste the flavor of the root even in the branch.

Similarly, we are flesh, and not spirit. But when we are connected to the root of the universe, the spiritual essence, one can taste the flavor of the root in us. When this happens, we become suffused with spirituality and transcend our limitations and creatureliness. There is a ray of light shining from the core of the spiritual foundation to the core of our essence. Our being then is like that of an angel; its very existence is praise to God.

But, unfortunately, we are in exile, the exile caused by our personal daily entanglements and oppression by the nations of the world. The path of light from the root to us is indirect, difficult, and full of obstructions. We are not in a position to readily give praise. Nevertheless, we still feel humbled when God saves us and give thanks for our good fortune.

This is similar to a lamp that was plugged into an electric outlet and lit up a room. Then a thunderstorm passed, and the lamp went out. The owner connected electrical cords of all sorts so that the lamp could reach another outlet. As he was about to connect it to the new outlet, lightning struck. Imagine his surprise when he saw the lamp light up again in its original outlet!

At times God saves us from our difficulty by makeshift wires; at other times by a lightning bolt. The first is the indirect path, and we thank God. But the second path is the miraculous one, which reconnects us right to our very roots. Now we can praise God again.

One of the deepest mysteries of our chosenness is, if God has chosen us outside our will, how do we have free will? Despite this contradiction, we faithfully believe that each human being is free to choose God or otherwise. But each choice does not always require the same amount of effort. Circumstances influence the ease or difficulty of our choices.

When the nations of the world oppress us, it becomes harder and harder to choose God instead of the path of expediency. And although we retain the freedom to choose throughout, the oppression may be so severe that it might appear to us as if we have *no* choice but to submit. And at times we do yield, but with a prayer. We plead to God, "Please, God, redeem us from our exile, even with such force that we'll have no choice, no freedom but to serve You."

At the instant God is redeeming us with power and force, it certainly appears that we have no freedom to choose otherwise. It would be absurd for any person to deny God when he is crossing the Red Sea during the Exodus! But later, upon reflection, we realize that not only do we have freedom of choice now but we even had it during our oppression.

We thank God that we can choose to praise Him— Praise God, you who are servants of God (Psalms 113:1)—that He chose us, but still we are free to choose Him.

When an ignorant person learns a profound lesson , his ignorance strikes him all the more strongly. If he continues learning, each new revelation and depth of understanding will underscore the limitations of his intelligence. He will realize more and more that what he can understand is minuscule compared to the expanse of wisdom in the universe. Therefore, although each new revelation opens doors to him, each only leads to a deeper appreciation of his ignorance. This is certainly painful. On the other hand, each new awareness of ignorance leads to intense yearning for knowledge, for even more brilliant revelations.

The same is true of our exile. Each time God redeems us, a door opens, the bright light shines in, and we gasp, "Oh, how good it can be!" At the same time we suddenly realize what pain we have endured. And even now we are aware that our new "redeemed" condition is imperfect compared to the instant of redemption.

Therefore, each redemption is a preparation for the next exile (our new condition) and awakens a great yearning in our hearts for new doors to be opened.

The yearnings during the first three exiles— Babylon, Medea, and Greece—brought about the redemption in the merit of Abraham, Isaac, and Jacob. Our last redemption was the miracle of Chanukah. Such a great door opened that even the new (and present) condition remained an exile by comparison. Now our yearning is so great for the final door to open that we are able only to pray. Prayer is the weapon of King David, whose descendant will open the final, but everlasting, entrance. Our praise and thanks issue forth from our yearning hearts.

There are times that we thank God and other times that we praise Him. If we encounter a bad situation that later turns out to be good, we thank God. If we immediately see that we are being helped and experience miracles, then we praise God.

The same happened with the Jews during the

Greek oppression and the Hasmonean victory. At first the Jewish people thought that their situation had gone from bad to worse. They were at the edge of despair. Later, they saw great miracles as they defeated a huge and powerful army. Their happiness was twofold. First, they realized that what they had thought was bad was really for the good. They gained a new strength and commitment to the Torah. For this they thanked God. And second, they appreciated the miracles that God performed for them. For this they praised God.

Some people think that the world owes them everything. They are not very likely to be thankful. But the one who feels broken appreciates when he gets a favor. The one who is arrogant is in danger of being misled by the evil urge, because there is no one whom he will accept as a guide or critic. But the one who is broken is protected from the evil urge because he is humble enough to accept guidance.

Therefore, to the extent that you humble yourself, to that same degree you are protected from the evil urge and the more thankful you will be. Thanks and praise go together, and only after you thank are you ready to praise.

"The holiday of Chanukah was established for praise and thankfulness" (*Shabbos* 22b).

We can compare this to a king who had received news of a tragic fire and sent an enormous amount of aid to its victims. The grateful victims came to the palace to thank the king. They were ushered into the opulent royal chamber full of marble, crystal, rubies, and diamonds. Thick rugs cushioned their feet as visual splendor dazzled their eyes. They were overcome with the brilliance of the sight. As they stood before the king, they forgot about their own concerns momentarily. Instead of thanking the king, as they had originally intended, they immediately began to praise him for all his glory.

Thankfulness therefore can be expressed when you still remember who you are, that you were in need but God helped you. Praise occurs when you are so overcome by God's glory that you can only speak of His greatness.

The holiday of Chanukah was established to sing praise and to thank God for the miracles. These songs of praise are the Psalms of King David. This was typi-

cal of the *kohanim*, in the tradition of Aaron, the chief of the *kohanim*, who always pursued the ways of peace. And therefore when the authority over the Jewish people fell into the hands of the priestly family of the Hasmoneans, they were perplexed. They knew that they were the destined leaders, yet they wanted to avoid quarrels over this issue. So they chose the Psalms of King David as songs of praise to show how dear the ruling family of David is to them.

"Though I give him countless rulings in writing, they are treated as invalid" (Hosea 8:12). The Greeks ordered the translation into Greek of the written Torah, and as a result of that the holiness of the Torah diminished among the people. Rather than being a source of spiritual inspiration, the Torah merely became another subject to study in school. Therefore unlike the story of Purim, which is told on a *megillah*, a parchment scroll, the story of Chanukah is related in songs of praise and thanks. It is orally transmitted, by word of mouth, by declaration and song.

We can compare this to a king who regularly sent secret communications with his son. One year a band of notorious criminals hid in the mountains. When the prince rode by, they grabbed him, searched his bags, and took the paper with the secret message from him. They released the prince and used the paper for their nefarious purposes. After this happened several times, the king decided to give his messages orally. The next time the prince passed the criminals, there was nothing they were able to take from him.

The same is true with the Torah. Although it is the holiest of teachings dictated to Moses by God, it is nevertheless a physical document. And being physical, the "hands of Esau," the nations, can tamper with it. But the Oral Law, in one aspect, is even more protected. Being the "voice of Jacob," the hands of Esau cannot touch it.

When the sages established the holidays of Chanukah and Purim, they wanted to accomplish two things. One was to establish the holiday in heaven, that it should have a lasting spiritual validity, and the other was to establish the holiday in the hearts of the Jewish people. Therefore, the purpose of the holiday of Chanukah is to sing songs of praise and prayers of thanks—praise for the light that descends from the heavens above and thanks from the humbled hearts that are ready to receive the spiritual gifts that come with the holiday.

A prince waited by the gates of the palace each day for three months while his father was away on military campaigns. Finally he heard the sounds of the heralds announcing his father's arrival. He could wait no longer and bounded toward his father, jumped up, and embraced him in total ecstasy. Father and son held each other for a long time. Then slowly the prince released his hold and held his father's hand. "My father must be really tired after all the battles," thought the prince. "I must make sure he is not bothered and gets some rest."

At first the prince reacted with love, but that has no vessel and soon disappears. This was followed by fear and awe, which take the feelings of love and place them into a vessel, something real and practical in the physical world. When the prince started to translate his ecstasy into respect for his father's care and well-being, that showed how genuine was his love.

At first when we are redeemed, we are in ecstasy and express great love for God in songs of praise. But is this genuine love? Not necessarily, because we are so overwhelmed by our new freedom. But if we humble ourselves and show fear and awe of God our Creator, we can then say words of thanks. The fear and awe are the vessels for our love and bring them into the realm of the real world.

———

The Jewish People under Greek domination endured many hardships, both physically and spiritually. Miraculously they were saved from them all. For this they thank God. Then they were once again able to serve God with purity and holiness. For this they praise God. But which is more important to them?

We can compare this to someone who fell down a flight of stairs and was injured severely. Both his hands were broken, his teeth knocked out, his legs sprained, and his spine injured. After many months in the hospital he was finally released. He said, "I could tolerate anything but the fact that I couldn't put food into my own mouth! Thank God, I can feed myself now!"

How do we assess what this person's worst hardship was? By listening to his complaints and expressions of gratitude.

The scholars in the time of the Greek exile complained about edicts against celebrating the holidays and performing circumcision; they expressed their gratitude for being able to rekindle the lamp in the Holy Temple. Is there any further doubt about what they considered their exile and redemption?

So too in our time. The lighting of the Chanukah lamp should light the way for our rededication to God's commandments in spite of difficulties and conflicts.

———

We are corporeal beings bound by space and time and the limitations of our material existence. But God has planted in each one of us the kernel of spiritual vitality linking us to the infinite.

There are times when God charges us so strongly with His power that we totally transcend all our limitations. Not only are we then uplifted but the very space and time that we inhabit rise to a higher level. This is what makes a holy-day out of a miraculous redemption. And so we say, "Thank You, God, for helping us; and praise to You that You have chosen us and made us vessels for Your miraculous deeds."

———

Kingdom belongs to the tribe of Judah, yet it was a priestly family of Hasmoneans who defeated the Greeks who were not of that tribe. The Hasmoneans did not feel at all comfortable with their ascension to power: they felt like strangers in their new role. They wanted very much that the celebration in honor of the victory should reflect Judah's rights to royalty. This they did by establishing Chanukah for praise and thanks, which are the hallmarks of King David, the prime symbol of kingdom in the tribe of Judah.

Deeper still . . .

The scholars of that time knew that the days of David's kingdom were over and would not resume until the Messiah would come. They knew that God had just given them a miraculous gift that would continue everlastingly. To preserve King David's kingdom among us, they established the praise and thanks of Chanukah. King David's light shines brightly in our homes and will fulfill our yearnings with the coming of the Messiah.

———

The prophet said, "This nation I have created for me; they will say my praise" (Isaiah 43:21). The Jewish people were chosen for an exclusive mission in the world: to proclaim God's Kingdom. This started with our father Abraham, who taught to all who would listen that the world has a Master. There is a plan, design, scheme, and organization to the world and a Master Author. The task of the Jewish people, too, is to impart this message to the world.

Just as the entire Jewish people bear this responsibility, so too does each individual. But at times we are locked inside constricting predicaments and are unable to fulfill our mission. The Talmud (*Berakhos* 54b) mentions four such troubles that impede our mission: illness, imprisonment, and dangerous crossing of the sea and of the desert. As soon as we are free of our troubles we must immediately return to our task of praising God. And we say, "Thank You God, for granting me, even if undeserving, all the good that You have granted me."

The Jewish people, too, were locked into four exiles: Babylon, Medea, Greece, and now Edom. After being released from each one, they sprang right back to their mission and praised God.

This is symbolized in the four times we bow during the silent prayer (of the 18 blessings). We bow as we say "Blessed are You" and rise as we say "God," bending the knees so we are back in the position of being bound and locked up in prison. This symbolizes the exile. Straightening and then standing erect again symbolizes the redemption. We were already redeemed from three of our exiles and our fourth redemption will occur shortly. Therefore, the praise and thanks of Chanukah, "*Al Hanisim*" (see *Prayer Book*), are said directly after the third, but before the fourth, bowing.

Soon we will be saying the praise for the fourth redemption, and we will never have to be bound and imprisoned again.

The Jewish People were in exile, were oppressed, and were made to suffer pain and humiliation. They were deprived, beaten, and weakened. Nevertheless, they retained their spiritual vigor and vitality by knowing that they were the couriers of the noblest mission and the highest teachings. They consoled themselves that despite their suffering they were still the exclusive teachers of the path of justice and mercy, charity and good deeds, and God's dominion of the world.

The Greek exile was different. The oppressor said to the oppressed, "You claim to have wisdom. Wait until you sample ours! You think you have justice; compare ours. You have teachings, but surely not on our high standards!" This made the suffering absolutely intolerable.

The Midrash (*Mishlei* 30) compares this to the rock badger who chews its cud (which is a sign of a kosher animal), but has no split hooves (a sign of a non-kosher animal). These were the Greeks, who were trying to usurp the chosenness of the

Jewish People with their claims to wisdom and teachings.

Therefore, when the Greeks were defeated, the chosenness of the Jewish People shone once more with even greater brilliance. And what is their cardinal responsibility? To say praise, to proclaim God's kingdom. This is appropriately emphasized in the Chanukah celebration, which is dedicated to praising and thanking God.

The nations of the world express their arrogance by claiming to be masters of their own fate. With their wisdom, skill, and strength they can surmount any problem and difficulty. Their pride leaves no room for God, the Master of the world.

The Jewish People are just the opposite. The most beautiful building within the elegant city of Jerusalem was the Holy Temple. Its magnificence was admired by visitors from the four corners of the earth. Surely this building was the pride and joy of every Jew. It took great wisdom, skill, and strength to build it. Yet in spite of this the Jewish People called the Holy Temple "the footstool of God" (Lamentations 2:1). Even in our greatest achievement we acknowledge God's mastery in the world.

The greatest praise of God is that He alone is Master of the world. When the Jews are in exile, however, they cannot outshout the nations who scream, "We are the masters!" This is the complaint of the Jewish People: "How can we sing the song of Zion on foreign soil?" (Psalms 137:4). The song of Zion, the holy city, the Holy Temple was clearly a symphony to the "footstool of God."

The Greeks defiled the Temple by jeering, "We have wisdom, skill, and power!" They attempted to extinguish the light that proclaimed God's sovereignty over the world.

God miraculously saved us. The light shone once more, and shines Divinely even to this day. Our Chanukah lights glow with the gleam of the Holy Temple. When we see them, we feel at home again. We sing praises near "the footstool of God" and proclaim God's kingdom.

The sages in the time of the Greek exile must have sensed something special about the holiday of Sukkos celebrated in that year of the Chanukah miracle. They sacrificed many animals for the sake of the nations of the world because they must have felt that they had a strong effect on the nations. Furthermore, they possibly had another sign; on the last day on which we pray with the *lulav*, Hoshanah Rabbah, they could foretell the future by observing the shadows. And it must be that during that particular year of the Greek exile, the sages had both these signs so they knew that the end of the oppressor was close at hand.

———

There is the Written Law, the five books of Moses, Prophets, and Kesuvim, and the Oral Law, the Mishnah and Talmud. The Written Law is the Torah that God writes for us. The Oral Law is the Torah that we live.

Other redemptions were brought about by God's direct intervention, by the Written Law. Chanukah, however, was brought about by a great deal of participation on our part. We fought, sacrificed, battled, and were unyielding until the enemy was defeated. This is the Oral Law; we lived the Torah.

To emphasize the predominance of the Oral Law, we praise and thank God orally for helping us bring the Torah back into our lives.

———

The Jewish People have two alternatives in the battle for their freedom. They can fight their enemies in face-to-face combat or at a distance. In face-to-face combat the enemy is very close, and the danger is great. At a distance, even if one is not the mightier, one still may be victorious.

The exiles of Babylon and Medea did not challenge our special mission and chosenness. We were able to risk fighting them at close range. But the Greek exile challenged our very essence as a people. The Greeks said they had wisdom, justice, mercy, and instruction. This is a far more dangerous battle and has to be fought at a distance.

How did we fight this battle? By tenaciously clinging to our position and continuing to proclaim God's kingdom. Our enemies were vanquished because of our distance from them.

A small flame drives away much darkness—from a distance.

Therefore, when we see the flames of the Chanukah lamp we sing the praise of God. We have learned well our strategy for battle.

———

God is constantly opening new doors and new revelations for us. And in order to receive them we need preparation. The more we prepare, the better vessels we become to receive them. But if we are in exile, it is hard to prepare our vessels for new illuminations. Therefore, as a preparation, God redeems us from the exile; then we can receive.

The Chanukah flame is the light that shines through the opened door; the lamp is the vessel of redemption. For the light that God constantly gives, we praise Him. For the vessels, we thank Him.

———

We praise God by saying in the blessing over the Chanukah lights, "He has done miracles for our fathers in those days." Was it necessary for God to perform a miracle so that the Menorah in the Temple could be lit? If all the oil was impure, the Jews certainly were not obligated to do the *mitzvah* of lighting the Menorah.

The miracle, however, served a different purpose. The Jews were very discouraged after enduring all the hardships of the Greek exile. They needed inspiration and reassurance that God was with them. The miracle was heartening for them in those days of trouble.

———

The redemption was received in two distinct ways. Those who withstood the oppression, remaining loyal to God and the Torah, were of course overjoyed. They immediately praised God. But there were others who had succumbed to the Greek culture and ideology. They were at first disillusioned by the Jewish victories. They did not immediately grasp their good fortune and redemption. As time passed, however, and the Jewish People resumed their worship of God in freedom, even these others turned to a Torah-true life. They recognized their error, abandoned the Hellenistic ways, and even thanked God for the miraculous victory.

———

The words of the Ten Commandments were carved into the stone tablets. By accepting the tablets we gained our freedom and independence as a people. But how? Did not the commandments enslave us to our new Master?

We can compare this to someone who was drowning and was pulled from the water unconscious and not breathing. Fortunately, the lifeguard knew the methods of resuscitation. He breathed into the victim's mouth for several hours. During these hours the victim was totally dependent on the lifeguard. He could not possibly survive without him. Finally, however, the lifeguard got him to breathe on his own.

Was the lifeguard enslaving the drowned man? No, he was in fact giving him back his very life, his independence.

When a Jewish heart is where it should be, it is alive and beating with vitality and vigor. When we are connected to what God carved into each one of us, we live and are free. And when we experience this, it is pure joy. And we sing a song of praise to God, "I am Your servant, the son of Your maid, You have opened my chains" (Psalms 116:16). When I am Your servant, my chains open; when my chains open, I am immediately only Your servant.

We are mortal creatures living in the confines of space and time. In our dimension, events unfold one at a time, one after the other. Some things happen before and some after others. We cannot push ourselves back into the past; neither can we project ourselves into the future.

This is all due to our existence within a cause-and-effect universe. In God's dimension of infinite possibility, in contrast, the past, present, and future are all there at once. There are absolutely no confines of space or time. Even if the miracle happened then, it could really be for you *now*, centuries later. And even a miracle that will happen later in the future could be for you now (in its past).

The question is, how do we connect to God's realm of infinity.

This we do by becoming vessels for the miracle. To the degree that you prepare to receive it, that part of the miracle shines into you. The doors in heaven are open; there is no limitation of past and future. You, however, have to open the doors in your heart to this timeless dimension. How? By singing praise to God for *our* miraculous redemption, we tune into the ageless lights that shine into our hearts.

Man is the only creature in the world who is aware of his own existence. Only he knows that there is a universe and a God outside himself, and, most exclusively, that he exists. He is the only one who can establish God's kingdom in the world by humbling himself before the Creator. When he does, all of the creation bows with him. This responsibility was given to Adam in the Garden of Eden.

After Adam, the Jewish People were chosen for this task. They were given the special awareness that enables them to proclaim God's sovereignty. This proclamation sings forth from the souls of the Jewish People and is heard throughout the world.

Evil nations oppress us and hinder our awareness and our "song." When they are defeated, we sing forth again.

God is the Master of the world. Independent of Him there cannot exist any power whatsoever. Those who acknowledge God's power bring honor and sanctity to His name. (But isn't one's existence an instance of power? Yes, it is; however, even that is from God. It is God's vitality and life force that pulsates in every creature.) Those who deny God's power by asserting their independent power are profaning God's name and trampling on His honor. Worse than that, God's vitality, which pulsates in each creature, cries out in anguish from domination by evildoers. In Kabbalah this is called "the exile of the holy sparks."

When the Jewish People are not proclaiming God's kingdom, the nations of the world proclaim their own kingdoms. The nations increase their domination, and more holy sparks go into exile. If the process runs rampant, eventually the Jewish nation itself ends up in exile.

Exile itself, however, is a process making possible the eventual redemption. As the Jewish People are spread to the far ends of the earth, they inadvertently teach their message, "God is the absolute ruler of the universe!" and slowly they free creature after creature from human domination. This is their primary function and task. And finally the work adds up to a total redemption. Then we praise God by saying: "When God is helping me . . . when I attribute all power to God . . . then I will see my enemies fall" (Psalms 118:7). Those who claim to have their own power will perish.

We can experience joy in two distinct ways. One is through the ego; the other is through humility. For example, when two people love each other, each one can be filled with joy. If the joy comes from the ego, one will think, "Look what I can do: see how deserving I am of love." This love is not everlasting. Or one can think, "I am so grateful to love and be loved; I must cherish every moment of it." This love is everlasting since it grows out of humility.

The Jewish People love through humility. Each time God grants them a gift they humble themselves and rejoice in gratitude.

This is the continuous dynamic between the soul and the ego. The soul asserts that all power comes from God, whereas the ego claims independent power. When one dominates, the other is humbled. And so we sing a song of praise, "Praise God, you who are servants of God" (Psalms 113:1). Those of you who are properly humbled before God can have true joy and praise God.

———

As much life as you put into your praise, that is how much you stimulate all living things to say praise, because all of the creation is bound to the fate and destiny of the human race. And it is therefore in the hands of mankind to redeem the creation or to give it a bad future. And when we praise God, we are redeeming the creation together with ourselves.

———

"We affirm in true faith that just as the redemption is God's doing, so too is the exile. And so we praise God: From the east where the sun rises . . . in good times, until it sets . . . bad times, God's name is praised" (Psalms 113:2).

———

"And the snake said . . . the day you eat from it . . . you will be like God . . ." (Genesis 3:5).

The snake wanted to assert a power independent of God. It succeeded in convincing Adam and Eve of such a possibility, and they ate from the fruit.

Before this act, it was very clear to man that all power came only from God. Afterward, confusion set in. There ensued a constant struggle between man's soul and his ego. The latter argues for his own power, while the soul maintains God's supreme power.

The snake was punished. Instead of having an erect posture, denoting ego, it was humbled and made practically to drag its spine on the very earth. God was saying, "No, you have no power of your own. Only I have!"

The spine has eighteen vertebrae (chai = life). If first you humble yourself before God by bending your spine, He imbues you with life. If you do not, there is no room in your life for God. Your ego says that you can stand erect on your own, but you can not. Therefore you have no life.

The life that God fills you with is the vital speck from His own spirituality. That life is absolutely untouchable by any evil in the world. Even the snake never got near it. It is therefore called the good desire, whereas the ego that tasted from the snake's poison is called the evil desire. The task of man is to serve God with both his desires, to bend his spine and humble his ego to God's total sovereignty.

When man arrogantly refuses to humble himself before God he ends up worshiping idols (Sotah 4b). We are told (Sanhedrin 63b) that the Jewish People worshiped idols only to fulfill their desires. Idol and ego worship go hand in hand. Even those who believe that the idol has power only worship it to benefit themselves, to influence events in their favor.

The idol is described (Daniel 2:32) as having "hips made of copper." Its hips are of stiff metal, which prevents it from bowing down to God. It is all ego.

The epitome of all egoistical acts is procreation. To have a child—no, even better, to create a creature in my own image—is there any act more ego-involved than that? Then this is the location for the ultimate battle—to humble oneself even in this act and to acknowledge that all new life comes directly from God.

This is symbolized by the fact that the axis of the spine in bowing is located in the reproductive area (at the hips). Bow even with your hips—your strongest ego area!

The Greeks tried to make us forsake God's power in favor of their power. Their idolatry was ego: "We have wisdom, teachings, and power; we keep our bodies beautiful and intact." They made decrees against circumcision. Why? Because it involved the ultimate ego area, and they could not tolerate its humbling before God. The Greeks refused to allow the Jews to proclaim God's kingdom in the world.

The redemption finally did come, and the Jews breathed "life" again. They had won many battles in wondrous ways, yet they did not choose to sing praises about them. Victory in battle is too much ego—and they had fought the Greeks on that very point. Rather, they chose the unassuming lamp with its (silent) soft light—the small jar of oil all humbled before God, the only Master of the world.

The light of the Chanukah lamp will shine until the coming of the Messiah. His battle will also be ego versus God's sovereignty.

There will be two Messiahs. One will prepare the way for the second. One will be from the tribe of Joseph and the other from David. Both wrestled with the most difficult area of their egos: Joseph, when he was approached by the wife of Potifar (Genesis 39:7–13). and David, when he met Bath Sheba, the wife of Uriah (2 Samuel 11:2–27). Joseph emerged unscathed, but David did not. And so in the final battle Joseph will prepare the way for David.

———

The mission of the Jewish people is to proclaim God's kingdom. If they do their work properly, they light up the world. Whoever hears their message becomes aware of Godliness in the world. His eyes are opened to see that every item of creation shares a common spiritual root. His behavior becomes oriented to the fact of holy sparks within everything.

The nations who allow themselves to be taught and admit to God's sovereignty also allow the Jewish people the space they need for their calling. They know that the Jews are teaching the truth, and they do not meddle in their responsibilities. There is then a coexistence, where the nations deserve their wealth and assets and the Jews teach them the proper attitude toward it.

There are times, however, when the nations are arrogant, denying not only God but also those who are trying to establish His kingdom. Then they do not deserve their prosperity, which only feeds their hunger for more power. This arrogance also extinguishes the light that might have come from the Jews. How? By denying them any room on earth to do their work, they constrict the light until it stays only within the Jewish nation.

This is symbolically represented by the windows of the Holy Temple. They were designed in such a way that the outside frame was much larger and slanted inward to a tiny frame.

The Holy Temple was "the footstool of God," the place that broadcast the kingdom of God to the world. The broadcast did not come by loudspeakers, nor with thunder and lightning. It came by way of a soft glowing light streaming forth from the tiny windows. The light beamed outward, hence the large frame on the outside and the tiny one inside.

Deeper still . . .

The windows say to the nations, "This place that gives light is closed to you. We are the teachers. God has decreed it to be so. You, on the contrary, must make room for our light, lest you sit in darkness with the rest of the world." The Greeks attempted to break open the tiny windows of the Holy Temple. They argued that they had great teachings for the Jewish People, far superior to what the Greeks were learning from the Jews. The Greek teachings, however, were only darkness compared to the light of the Holy Temple, so that by their intrusion they destroyed the space from which the light was flowing. There was darkness. The praise of God was no longer heard, His light no longer seen.

Then the miracle of Chanukah happened. The forces of evil were forced to retreat. The breaches in the Temple walls were mended, and the light was protected once more. It resumed sending forth its soft rays to enlighten all who would listen. The praise of God grew from a whisper to a murmuring to vocalized song: "Thereafter, Your children came to the Holy of Holies of Your House, cleansed Your Temple, purified the site of Your Holiness and kindled lights in the courtyards of Your sanctuary . . ." (*Prayer Book, Al Hanisim*).

"And God said: 'Let there be light' . . . and God separated the light from the darkness" (Genesis 1:4–5).

Every place in the universe is dark until God gives it light. Light is God's gift to His creatures; it is His kindness and goodness that He bestows on every one of His creations. When the light first emanates from God, however, it is so intense that no creature can yet appreciate it. It therefore descends through ten stages and is transformed into a nature that creatures can handle. After descending ten spheres, the light finally reaches our corporeal world, and we have light.

The light we receive is darkness compared to its brilliance when it is first beamed forth from God. What we see, taste, and feel is but the palpable form of God's infinite kindness and goodness. The real thing remains hidden from us.

Nothing is beyond God's infinite power. Even if we, the creatures, have no vessels to hold God's original light, it is not beyond Him to give it to us. He can and He does give us a glimpse of this great light in special places and special occasions.

Although He gives it freely, not every creature receives it in the same intensity. To receive, you must be a vessel; you must be a creature totally and not a master. The more you stand before God as His creature, the greater the capacity of your vessel to receive. The more arrogant and masterly you are, the less you taste and feel.

The greatest praise to God is that He gives freely and that we receive from Him. Therefore, the praise of God is the very fact that we stand before Him as absolute, unconditional, utter creatures. He, on the other hand, is our Master who gives constantly and freely without exceptions.

The place and time that embodied the highest praise of God was the Holy Temple during the Jewish holy days. The Holy Temple, "the footstool of God" (Lamentations 2:1), was absolutely humbled before God. During the holidays, all who were in the courtyard would prostrate themselves before the Master of the world. The most humbling posture, in the most humbled place during a time when God gives a glimpse even of the original light. That is the highest praise to God.

The Greeks attempted to stop the Jewish People from declaring that the world is humbled before God, which is God's praise. Miraculously, they were defeated, and the praise of God resounded once more. And again God allowed His creatures to have a glimpse of the original light that beamed out of the Holy Temple. This was the soft glow from the lights of the Menorah that were lit in the Temple. And they sang a song of praise, "Thank God, for He is good; His mercy endures forever" (Psalms 118:1).

The perfect state of affairs is when God gives and His creatures receive. It is unimaginable that God is not giving. His creatures, however, must make vessels of themselves so that they can receive. If they do not, they ruin perfection not only at their end but also at the source.

We can be compared to a very wealthy man who would spend all his time and money in gift giving. He once announced that he would be in the marketplace at noon to distribute oil. All the people in town assembled at noon and waited for the rich man. He arrived at the appointed hour and wanted to start pouring. He was shocked and disappointed to find that no one had brought any containers in which to take the oil home. The more desperately he wanted to give, the worse he felt. Standing in the midst of the crowd, he felt out of place and helpless.

The same is true of our relationship with God. When we do not prepare ourselves to receive, we do not allow God's giving to be manifest in the world. Then God's Divine Presence is, so to speak, out of place and in exile.

The Greeks defiled our vessels, and we could not receive God's gifts properly. They not only ruined our receiving of light but also meddled with the Divine Presence, the Giver of the light.

When we were miraculously saved from their clutches, the Divine Presence Herself (so to speak) was also saved. The universe swung back to its proper order, which is the greatest praise to the Creator. And we sing a song of praise to Him, ". . . and for Yourself, God, You have made a great and holy name in the world . . . and for the Jewish nation . . ." (*Prayer Book, Al Hanisim*). The redemption of the Jewish nation was great, but far greater was the redemption of God's holy name, His Divine Presence. That redemption is beyond time and infinite and shines to us from the Chanukah lamp.

"And the men did so; and took two milk cows, and tied them to the cart . . . and they placed the ark of God upon the cart . . . and the cows sang on the road . . . as they walked . . ." (1 Samuel 6:10–12).

God is the exclusive Master of the world. He created each and every creature, and He keeps each one alive. Without God's power nothing would exist; all would be annihilated. Anyone who claims to have power independent of God is obviously in error and is a big fool. Whoever submits to such a tyrant is no wiser.

When we are wise, we humble ourselves to God and become vessels for all His infinite gifts. We then receive what is constantly flowing from Him and are sincerely thankful and joyous. We do not consider this a burden as we are laden with gifts. On the contrary, it is our very life and the joy of our days.

This can be compared to a king who had many servants and would constantly give them gifts. Each servant was identified by a special royal uniform. One day a servant wandered out of the palace and met a leader of robbers. He listened to the thief as he told him how they rob from the king's palace. He said, "Why be locked up in the king's palace when you could live freely among us and get the same gifts?" The servant agreed. The leader asked him to disrobe and instead gave him the uniform of the robbers. As time passed, the king ordered more rigorous security, and robbery became virtually impossible. The servant, now a robber, started to wonder. "Why should I be a robber, when I'm getting everything from the king's palace anyway. I might as well stay in the king's palace." He threw off his robber robes, put his royal uniform back on, and went back to the palace.

When the cows carry the holy ark of God, they sing His praise. Whoever makes himself a vessel for God's light and goodness has something to sing about.

The Greeks came to the Jewish nation with a ploy, "Why be slaves to God?" They urged, "Come, learn our ways and enjoy our freedom!" Many Jews were tempted by the reasoning and changed to Hellenistic garments.

Then the miraculous redemption came. The Jewish People took off their defiled garments and put on holy ones. They again received the infinite light from its source. And they sang, "Praise God, you who are servants of God" (Psalms 113:1). You are servants to God; you are now free from all domination and oppression.

Despite that great redemption, we have sunk since then into another exile. Again we carry strange yokes that press down upon us mercilessly. Again we are slaves of slaves, and we are not prepared to receive God's gifts. Yet whenever the anniversary of our redemption comes, we are lifted to a new dimension. In that uplifted place, beyond time, we again experience the proper servitude and humbling before God. We sing out what our soul feels: "Praise God, you who are servants of God" (Psalms 113:1).

We live in a world in which myriads of events are constantly unfolding. They are so many that they boggle our attempts to understand them. Yet, God, the Master of the world, sees them all as sensible and desirable. He is the absolute master, and nothing happens by independent power. No creature can say, "I existed this past instant and in this place by my own independent power."

We can compare this to a child who is watching the preparation of a large feast for the president. Hundreds of waiters, managers, assistants, maids, bartenders, movers, and chefs are bustling to arrange the event. The child might only see a lot of movement and haphazard activity. He may only understand the sense of the simplest components: the tables, chairs, food, and waiters. Yet, he has no comprehension of the smaller details. The head manager, however, has carefully noted where each item is to be placed and how the food is to be prepared, where the flowers are to be placed, and what time the band is to start its music. He did not leave anything up to chance and is in complete control.

At times God allows tyrants to oppress us and finally redeems us with great mercy. Those who are like the child may only appreciate the larger events; there was an exile and now we have a redemption. The wise ones, however, delve into all the complicated details of the exile and redemption and see in them the hand of God's master plan.

One small detail in the miracle of Chanukah is the time of year that it happened. It was during the Jewish month of *Teves*, (corresponding to November-December), when the day is very short and the night is very long. Symbolically, there is a short period of apparent light and a long period of darkness.

God is saying to us, "To you it appears that the darkness is dismal, long, and hopeless. Look carefully and you'll see that in this very darkness there is a light brighter than your day."

Since the light of Chanukah shines in the long dark nights, it is obviously beyond time. It comes from the infinite source of light and glows always and forever. And for this we praise God, "Thank You, God, that You made miracles for our fathers, in those days, in this time (of the year)" (*Prayer Book*, The Blessing of the Chanukah Lights).

The nations of the world claim to be masters of their own fate. They enslave others and force them also to admit to their power.

Man's ego can easily accommodate such ideas.

After all, it is the ego that claims self-mastery and power. Man is the one who does not want God's all-pervading power to apply to his being. The soul, on the other hand, always recognizes who is the Master and is never in doubt.

When a people is oppressed, their souls are yearning and crying out for redemption. Their egos, however, may be quite happy with the state of affairs. Aren't they, after all, in agreement with the claims of the oppressors? Don't they also agree that people have independent power?

When the redemption finally comes, the soul cannot stop singing God's praise: "Oh, how I've yearned; oh, how well I knew that You are my Master!" But the ego is not as ready to appreciate the freedom. It must be humbled to accept the fact that God is the Master and Ruler of the universe.

The mouth is very easily a servant of the ego, by giving orders, bragging, and belittling others. This same mouth must be humbled to acknowledge the sovereignty of God. And when it finally submits, it sings songs of thanks to God for the redemption.

First there must be redemption; then the ego can be made humble before God. Therefore, when we pray, we first speak of our redemption: "Blessed are You, God, who redeems the Jewish people"; and then, "Please, God, open my lips . . . to utter Your praise" (*Prayer Book*, morning silent prayer). The freedom is first experienced by the soul; then when the lips are also humbled, we can start uttering God's praise.

The Jewish People have two kinds of holy days. One is where the time itself is entirely outside the realm of nature. It is holy, spiritual, and infinite. The other is where the time remains within the natural domain, yet within it, miraculously, there is a strand of infinity.

The holidays that are found in the Written Law, the Torah, are beyond time. Chanukah, however, is different. It was a dark and dismal time for the Jewish People. It was also a constricted, confined time because of the Greek oppression.

The Jews fought against oppression. It was their involvement that drew light into the darkness. A beam of eternity shone within the darkness of the exile. This glow will remain forever within that darkness for all those who wish to make contact with it.

During the months of long dark nights, it is dismal outside in the streets, but inside the house the rooms are well lighted. This is natural and expected. But to have light out in the street is highly unusual.

The Jewish People, however, brought the unusual into the usual. They drew eternal time into corporeal time. We therefore place the Chanukah lamp outside, in the street, and sing, ". . . You have done miracles for our fathers, in those days, in this time [of the year]" (*Prayer Book*, The Blessing of the Chanukah Lights). In this very time, corporeal and limited, You have shown us a beam of infinite light to illuminate our darkness.

"And the Lord, God, formed man of the dust of the ground and breathed into his nostrils the breath of life" (Genesis 2:7).

Man's soul comes from God, the fountain of spirituality. The soul is connected to its roots and is constantly aware that God is the Master of all.

Man's body, however, is different. It is composed of elements of the earth, which have a strange and mysterious mode of existence. The existence of these elements is one of the deepest mysteries discussed in Kabbalah. How can anything exist outside God? We know that nothing can exist without God's power and presence. Either God is there, and you have God, or—there is no other possibility. There cannot be any place where God is absent. Then how can the elements exist? Despite this contradiction, both God and the elements exist in the universe. They do so in a mysterious and incomprehensible way. The element is there; yet God is there too. In each element there is the clear and constant knowledge that without God it cannot exist. Yet, and in total contradiction, it also harbors the idea that it is outside God, independent, with a power all its own.

Man is formed of the dust of the ground, of the elements. Therefore he harbors within his ego the thought that he does not need God's power. "I am outside God and the master of my own life!," he says.

A whole nation, too, can assume a posture of pride and arrogance and proclaim itself master of the world. Their haughtiness can also lead them to self-worship, making themselves the idols of their veneration.

"The idol's head is made of gold, his breast and his arms of silver, his belly and his thighs of copper, his legs of iron . . ." (Daniel 2:32–33). Gold, silver, copper, and iron symbolically represent the four elements: fire, water, air, and dust, respectively. Those who are arrogant, claiming their own power, worship their own ego (body), which is composed of the four elements. They worship an idol of their own making and image. When a whole nation does this, they proceed to oppress and enslave others.

The oppression of the Jewish people is a true exile, because they were chosen to proclaim God's sover-eignty. There are four exiles: Babylon, Medea, Greece, and Edom. Each one is represented by one of the elements. Greece was the exile of air. How?

"And God formed man . . . and breathed into his nostrils the breath of life . . ." (Genesis 2:7). Man breathes the breath of life—air. Air is made of the two elements, fire and water. Fire is an element that is constantly rising, whereas water descends to the absolute lowest level it could reach. Fire is rising, yearning, buoyancy, expectancy, and arrogance of the human spirit. Water, on the other hand, is the lowering, receptiveness, dejectedness, dreariness, and submission of the spirit. The "breath of life," therefore, shares the same contradiction as the element from which man was formed. On the one hand, it is arrogant and claims self-mastery; on the other, it humbles itself before God.

Man breathes the breath of life and talks. The Greeks used their speech with great arrogance. They claimed to be the masters of argument, wisdom, and teachings, and they oppressed and enslaved the Jewish People.

The Jews were prevented from breathing life into the world and proclaiming God's kingdom. Instead, they were forced to recite the "wisdom" of Greece, which was nothing but arrogance dressed in fancy garments.

The Greeks were finally vanquished and the Jewish breath of life restored. We are back to vocalizing God's honor in the world. With our buoyant spirits we sing praises to God, and with our humbled spirits we thank God. The element of air is now redeemed. The Jewish People breathe freely again.

Deeper still . . .

There are two distinct parts of speech. One is the voice, as the breath is forced over the vocal cords, and the other is the spoken word, as the sound is articulated. Voice is only breath that has sound. It is still very close to its roots. You can still nearly hear the breath in the voice. Words, however, are much further removed from their roots. They are no longer recognizable as breath and are much more the product of one's own volition and doing. Saying "*my* breath" is not as emphatic as saying "*my* word." Words are therefore more arrogant than voice alone. Words are the ego; voice is the spirit. Voice is the melody: words are the prayer.

We sing songs of praise to God with our spirit. We say prayers of thanks with our humbled ego.

When things are in the proper order, God gives and the creatures receive. To receive, a creature must be a vessel for God's gifts and therefore humbled before His majesty. If he stands arrogantly, he will receive nothing.

There are times, however, when God opens up the doors of heaven and gives to His creatures in great abundance. In such periods, the creatures are more likely to humble themselves rather than miss all His gifts. These are the times of our holy days. The arrogant Greeks who held us in their clutches would not allow us to be humbled before God. They closed our hearts to God's gifts and filled them instead with darkness. Oh, how we cried and yearned for God's gifts pouring forth from the doors, yet passing us by. The Greeks broke *our* doors and put a wall between us and God. We were closed in, the doors of our hearts were closed to receiving, the doors of heaven were open in vain. We cried out: "Open for me the gates of righteousness. . . . I'll come in and praise God" (Psalms 118:19).

The Greeks were finally overthrown. The doors of our hearts, of the Holy Temple, and of heaven were now all in the proper order. Our yearnings were fulfilled: to enter the doors of the Holy Temple, to prostrate ourselves before God, and to receive God's gifts. Now . . . "I will come in and praise God."

The human body is composed of dust and is the ego, whereas the soul is of heavenly stuff and is the spirit of man. The ego is prone to assert its independence, whereas the soul always knows its master. The body, in the end, is totally humbled, returning to the dust, whereas the soul rises to spiritual heights.

There were two trees in the Garden of Eden, the Tree of Knowledge and the Tree of Life. The snake confused man into thinking that by eating from the Tree of Knowledge he would gain complete mastery of the world. This, however, is nothing but the arrogance of the ego and a false and mistaken path. The Tree of Life, on the other hand, was not tampered with and constantly gives pure life to those who connect themselves to it. The root of the Tree of Life is God, and our connection to it is the Torah.

The Greeks desired to confuse us through the Tree of Knowledge. They taught the Jewish People an arrogant form of knowledge that denied God's absolute power. This knowledge, in the end, must lead to complete deterioration and death. The Greeks, indeed, led the Jews on a path of darkness and death.

The Greeks were finally beaten. The Jewish People once again resumed their bond to the Torah, the Tree of Life. Now they praised God, saying: "The dead will not praise God . . . but we will praise Him from now and always . . ." (Psalms 115:17–18).

25

Zos Chanukah:
This Is the Dedication

ach day of Chanukah we read part of the portion of Numbers 7:1–89, which describes the sacrifices of the princes of each tribe when the tabernacle was set up in the desert. On the last day of Chanukah we complete the reading, which ends with the paragraph "This was the dedication of the altar, in the day when it was anointed, by the princes of Israel. . . . The last day therefore is called 'This is the dedication . . . (*Zos Chanukah*).'"

A human being may be strong, rich, wise, and famous. Compared to God, however, none of these attributes has meaning. What are we after all? "Are not all the mighty as non-beings before You, and the famous as if they never existed, and the wise men as if they possess no understanding?" (*Prayer Book*, Morning Prayers). There is no attribute in us that stands up to the test of absolute and infinite power and truth. There is not one quality that we could point to and say, "This is it!" (*zos*).

Yet, God has placed into each one of us a kernel of spirituality that flows from the spring of truth, God Himself. It is to that, our soul, that we can indeed point and say, "This is it!" (*zos*). Each and every significant thing in the universe is *zos*, its own spiritual vitality, the essence of every living creature.

The miracle of Chanukah showed that the natural world is controlled totally by God, that nothing is outside His range of influence. As we kindle the Chanukah lights each of the eight days, we practice this teaching. By the last day we must already know it very well, and therefore call it *Zos Chanukah*—this is it of Chanukah. We have learned the lesson of Chanukah, that in the ordinary world of nature, as in us, there is a portion, *zos*, that is God's spirituality, all true and powerful.

The Jewish People built a tabernacle in the desert during their wandering toward the Holy Land. In this tabernacle there was a Menorah that Aaron kindled every day. The westernmost flame burned miraculously all day long. Why? Couldn't God have had all the lights burning all the time without human involvement? Yes, but He chose rather to teach the Jewish People that through our own involvement we draw God's Divine Presence to rest among the Jewish Nation.

The tabernacle itself was dedicated in this manner. It was the offerings of the princes that brought the tabernacle to completion. Again this showed that the activity of the Jewish People is important and produces everlasting results.

Similarly, the miracle of Chanukah could have occurred without oil. However, God showed the Jews that their activity was needed to bring holiness into the world. They found the oil, and they kindled the lights. This activity is alluded to in the name Chanukah, which means dedication and also training, as in "train (*chinoch*) a child according to his way" (Proverbs 22:6). God trains us in preparation for a higher order of things, the miraculous. As a king who holds his son's hand and trains him to fight in battle, God too lets us do, but holds our hand (so to speak) and trains us for the miraculous order soon to be revealed in the world.

As we stand in front of the softly glowing lights of Chanukah, let us pray, "God, we will do . . . but You, God, please hold our hand. . . ."

Whatever happens during the spiritual year is influenced to a large extent by the major holidays. Therefore, we can safely say that the holiday of Chanukah is closely related to the holiday of Sukkos, which precedes it by sixty-two days. There are several similarities between the two holidays: (1) They both last eight days; (2) the main service, the sacrifices and the Menorah lighting, in both were done by the *kohanim*; (3) in both the merit of Aaron, the chief of the *kohanim*, played a major role—the clouds of honor of Sukkos in the merit of Aaron and the everlasting lighting of the Menorah, also in his merit; (4) in both, the last day encompasses all of the preceding days; in Sukkos it is Shemini Atzeres. *Shemini* means it is made up of all eight, whereas in Chanukah it is *Zos Chanukah, zos* meaning "this" is the entire Chanukah. It also is made up of all the eight days.

When the princes were dedicating the tabernacle, Aaron was sad that he could not have a share in it. "And God said to him, 'Do not despair, Aaron. The work that you do in the tabernacle will last forever'" (*Numbers Rabbah* 7).

The dedication of the princes would not have lasted forever if not for the share of Aaron. His great yearning was transformed into its spiritual equivalent, an existence beyond space and time. It was therefore Aaron who made the dedication last until this very day through the celebration of Chanukah. We celebrate this dedication with the one special commandment of the kindling of the Menorah, of Chanukah.

We must know this for our own lives, that whatever we desire to be everlasting we must do with great yearning. When the doors of our hearts are open, God will shine into us an everlasting and eternal light.

26

An Abbreviated History of the Greek Exile and Redemption

ntiochus Epiphanes, a cunning, evil, unrefined drunkard, was king of Syria and ruled over the Syrian-Mesopotamian region, including the land of Judea (Israel).

Year 175 B.C.E. Yeshua (Jason in Greek), a Greek sympathizer and brother of Hanav the Righteous, bribes Antiochus to grant him the position of high priest (*kohen gadol*). Minalaus, a Hellenist Jew, cheats Jason out of his position by offering Antiochus a bigger bribe; kills opponents. Minalaus can't pay his bribe and is replaced. Antiochus, who is busy quashing revolts, appoints General Adroinach to administer the region. Minalaus bribes Adroinach for the high priesthood and to kill Hanav the Righteous. The masses complain to Antiochus, and Adroinach is executed. Minalaus then bribes officials to execute the Elders of the Jews. Torah-loyal Jews side with Ptolemy (son of Cleopatra), King of Egypt, while the Hellenists stand by Antiochus. Antiochus visits Egypt to bribe officials to support him and later attacks it with his army, capturing Ptolemy. A false rumor spreads that Antiochus died in battle. Jason returns to Jerusalem, slaughters the followers of Minalaus, and flees to Egypt. Jason reports to Antiochus that Jews rebelled against his majesty's appointee (himself) and advises him to break the Jewish kingly and priestly tradition. Antiochus believes Jason and attacks Jerusalem. Hellenists treacherously open the doors of the city and kill all the faithful Jews inside. The Holy Temple is looted. Philip the Terrible is appointed as overseer.

Year 170 B.C.E. Ptolemy, the king of Egypt, plots with Rome to wage war against Antiochus IV the Great, the king of Syria. Antiochus Epiphanes hears of the plot and comes to Egypt in a great rage. Heavy fighting ensues, in which Ptolemy is nearly defeated. Rome, an Egyptian ally, sends an emissary to Antiochus saying that he must stop the fighting or else. Antiochus leaves Egypt shamed and wages war on Israel to avenge his honor. In Jerusalem, he takes 10,000 prisoners, kills many thousands, burns houses, and breaches the wall of the Holy Temple. He declares that the Temple is open for pilfering. Antiochus takes the Golden Altar, Menorah, Holy Table, and other utensils. He builds a huge tower, Akra, to overlook the city. Those who live within it are named *Chakraim* and attack the Temple worshipers from time to time. Antiochus decrees that the Jews may not keep *Shabbos*, circumcise their sons, or make sacrifices in the Temple. He orders the sacrifice of pigs in the Temple and sets up houses for idol worship in all Jewish cities. All offenses are punishable by death.

Year 168 B.C.E. The Greeks halt Jewish worship in the Temple on the twenty-fifth day of *Kislev*. The Greek statue of Jupiter is placed on the Altar. Many Jews abandon the Jewish way for fear of death. On the day of the Greek king's birth, Jews are forced to bring sacrifices to Bacchus and to decorate each door with a wreath in the king's honor. Faithful women who circumcised their sons were murdered together with their infants. Chana and her seven sons die. Hellenizers are showered with gifts, while brides are defiled before marrying their Jewish mates.

Year 167 B.C.E. Apelles the Greek hears that the daughter of Matisyahu, from the priestly family of the Hasmoneans, is about to be married. Matisyahu's son, Yehudah, organizes band of ninety desperate Jews in the Judean wasteland. Apelles comes to

Modyin, sets up an idol, and invites Jews to sacrifice to it. Apelles "honors" Matisyahu by ordering him to carry out the king's will. Refusing, Matisyahu calls out, "I fear *no one*! I do God's will and not that of Antiochus!" A Jew who is a Greek sympathizer comes to the altar to make a sacrifice and is killed by Matisyahu. A battle erupts. Greek soldiers are killed together with Apelles. The altar is destroyed. Matisyahu calls out, "All who are faithful to God come with me!" and escapes to join his son in desert caves. Greeks kill 1,000 Jews in desert caves on a Saturday, on *Shabbos*. Matisyahu convenes the rabbinical court of Hasmoneans to declare that self-defense is permissible even on *Shabbos*. Many Jews join Matisyahu. Matisyahu's followers become brave soldiers and inflict heavy blows on the Hellenists. They destroy the pagan altars.

Year 166 B.C.E. Matisyahu becomes gravely ill. His five sons are at his bedside: Yochanan, Shimeon (advisor), Judah (general), Elazar, and Yonathan. Judah (Yehudah) fights the Hellenists. Apoloni the Greek gathers an army from the surrounding nations. Yehudah springs a surprise attack in which many Greeks, including Apoloni, are killed. General Siron comes to battle against Jews; 800 are dead, among them Siron, after a surprise attack by Yehudah. Philipus sends an urgent message to Ptolemy that is forwarded to Antiochus. Ptolemy and Nikanur come with 20,000 men and 7,000 chariots and camp near Jerusalem. Jews go to Mitzpa to pray. Gurgia, a Greek general, then attacks Jerusalem with 6,000 men. Yehudah, meanwhile makes a surprise attack on the bulk of the Greek army with only 3,000 Jews. He defeats 47,000 men.

Year 164 B.C.E. Lysius comes with 65,000 soldiers. Another surprise attack by Yehudah kills 500 Greeks and the rest flee. Yehudah and his men capture Jerusalem. Hellenists are running to their fort, Akra. Yehudah (Judah Maccabee) and his army enter the Temple and cry over the desecration. They mourn and fast. On the twenty-third day of *MarHeshvan*, they start to clean it. In ten days they clean the Temple, rid all idols from the Temple area, build a new Altar, and mend the walls. They rush to finish by 25 *Kislev*, which will be the third anniversary since the Greeks interrupted Jewish worship in the Temple. On the twenty-fifth day of *Kislev*, they resume the worship of God in the Holy Temple. The Greeks had defiled all the jars of oil. One small jar with the seal of the high priest is found and used in the lamp. The oil burns miraculously for eight days. Jews rejoice over their victory and resume the daily sacrifice, the study of Torah, and the observance of all God's commandments.

27

Laws and Customs of Chanukah—Talmudic Sources

1. Wicks or oils that are not permissible to use for kindling the *Shabbos* lamps still may be used for the Chanukah lamp (*Shabbos* 21b).

2. The *mitzvah* is to have the Chanukah lamp burn from sunset until all feet are gone from the street; no one else is walking (*Shabbos* 21b).

3. Our rabbis have taught that the *mitzvah* of Chanukah is for each person and his family to have one lamp; those who wish to beautify it should kindle a lamp for each one; and those who wish to beautify it even more—the school of Shammai said, the first day eight and each day following one less; the school of Hillel said, the first day one, and each day following one more. What is the reason for their opinions? Shammai counts the remaining days, while Hillel counts the days that passed. Also Shammai compares Chanukah to Sukkos, when each day fewer animals were sacrificed, while Hillel compares it to holiness—one should always ascend and never descend (*Shabbos* 21b).

4. The lamp of Chanukah should be placed by the door. If one lives on an upper level, it should be placed in the window (*Shabbos* 21b).

5. One must have an additional lamp to use for his needs; however, if there is a torch there, nothing more is required (*Shabbos* 22a).

6. What is Chanukah? The rabbis have taught: Beginning on the twenty-fifth day of *Kislev* are the days of Chanukah, eight days in which one is not permitted to eulogize or to fast. When the Greeks entered the Temple, they defiled all the oil. When the kingdom of the Hasmoneans increased in strength and vanquished the Greeks, they searched and found only a small jar of oil with the seal of the High Priest. It had only enough oil to burn for one day, but a miracle happened and they used it to kindle the lamp for eight days. The following year they established it as a holiday for praising and thanksgiving (*Shabbos* 21b).

7. The rule is to place the Chanukah lamp on the left while the *mezuzah* is on the right (*Shabbos* 22a).

8. It is forbidden to count money to the light of the Chanukah lamp (*Shabbos* 22a).

9. "Outside the veil of the testimony (the ark containing the tablets), Aaron should order it (the Menorah)" (Leviticus 24:3). Does he need this light? Impossible! Hadn't the Jews walked for forty years with God's light shining for them?! But it is a witness that the Holy Presence is among the Jewish nation (*Shabbos* 22b).

10. All types of oil are good for the lamp. However, olive oil is the best (*Shabbos* 23a).

11. When a person lights the Chanukah lamp, he should recite blessings; this is true even if he does not light it but only sees it (*Shabbos* 23a).

12. What is the blessing? "You have made us holy with Your commandments and commanded us to kindle the Chanukah lamp." Where has He commanded us (about Chanukah)? In this verse, "Do not stray from the words of the judges neither *right nor left*" (Deuteronomy 17:11) (*Shabbos* 23a).

13. If a person has only enough money to buy oil either for the *Shabbos* or Chanukah lamp, he should kindle the *Shabbos* lamp because it brings peace to his household. However, if the question is whether to spend money on wine for *Kiddush* (sanctifying the *Shabbos* day) or oil for the Chanukah lamp, he should kindle the Chanukah lamp, because it is more important to advertise the miracle (*Shabbos* 23b).

14. One who regularly kindles the lamp will have children who are scholars (*Shabbos* 23b).

15. Where do we mention the "praise" of Chanukah? In the silent prayer, in the prayer of thankfulness (*Shabbos* 24a).

28

The Chanukah Lighting Service

The Chanukah lighting service begins with this prayer:

May it be Your will, God my Lord, God of our fathers, that it should now be a time of acceptance for the observance of this lighting of the Chanukah lamp, as if I fathomed all the awesome secrets that are sealed in it. And my observance should be accepted together with those of Your beloved children who meditate on each and every of Your Holy Names connected with this lighting, and who elevate the unification of Your highest holy attributes, and cause the might of Your Divine Presence to light up the Great Luminaries, and from there an emanation be directed to me, Your servant (insert name) *to receive the Light of Life. For You light my lamp, O God my Lord, You illuminate my darkness (Psalms 18:29).*

Send Your Light and Truth; they will surely lead me to fear and love Your Name, to learn and teach Your holy Torah, the written and the oral, with great diligence, for the honor of Your blessed Name, with the powerful treasure in the Chanukah lamp; make us wise through the light of Your Torah—us, our children, and children's children. May this verse be fulfilled in me: "It shall not depart from your mouth, from the mouth of your children, from the mouth of your children's children, says God, now and forever" (Isaiah 59:21). May my children and my children's children be Torah scholars and devout, beloved in heaven and cherished on earth. Strengthen their hearts in Torah and worship, all according to Your good desire. May I be worthy to see my children and children's children who engage in the Torah and commandments with truth.

Uncover our eyes and allow us to see the wonders of Your holy Torah, and be exact about its truths and secrets. In the merit of Matisyahu the High Priest and his sons, show us wonders, and with Your light may we see light. Purify our hearts to worship You; keep us from evil traits

and aimless thoughts. May our eyes behold Your return to Zion with mercy, when You will rekindle the lamp, and there we will worship You with reverence as in days of old and ancient years.

May the words of my mouth and meditations of my heart be acceptable to You, O God, my Rock and my Redeemer (Psalms 19:15). But as for me, my prayer is to You O God, at an acceptable time in Your great mercy answer me with truth of Your salvation (Psalms 69:14). May pleasantness come to us, O Lord our God, and establish firmly the work of our hands (Psalms 90:17).

The Kabbalists have authored the following prayer:

For the sake of the unification of the Blessed Holy One and His Divine Presence, with awesome reverence and love, to unify the Name Yud Heh and Vov Heh in perfect union, in the name of all of Israel. I come now to perform the lighting of the Chanukah lamp to restore it in its sublime roots.

We recite these prayers before kindling the Chanukah lamp:

Blessed are You, O God our Lord, King of the universe, who has sanctified us with His commandments and instructed us to light the Chanukah lamp.

Blessed are You, O God our Lord, King of the universe, who performed miracles for our fathers in those days, in this time (of the year).

And on the first night we also say:

Blessed are You, O God our Lord, King of the universe, who has kept us alive, and has preserved us, and who has brought us to this season.

We kindle these lamps on account of the miracles and wonders, the victories and battles that You made for our

197

fathers through Your holy priests (kohanim). During all the eight days of Chanukah these lamps are holy and we are not permitted to use them, but only to look upon them, in order to thank You and praise Your great name, for Your miracles, for Your wonders, and for Your salvation.

After the kindling of the lamp the following hymn is sung:

O stronghold, Rock of my salvation, it is very fitting to praise You. You will restore the House of my prayer, and there we will offer a sacrifice of thanksgiving. When You prepare a slaughter, deliverance from the raging foe, then I will complete, with a song of praise, the dedication of the altar.

My soul was filled with troubles; in sorrow he has made my strength fail, they had embittered my life with hardship, during the enslavement of the calf kingdom (Egypt). But with His great hand, He brought forth His chosen, while Pharaoh's hosts and all his offspring sank like a stone into the deep.

To His holy sanctuary He brought me, but even there I found no rest; the oppressor came and exiled me, because I have served alien gods, and I had poured for myself drugged wine. Hardly had I gone away, there came the end of Babylon, Zerubabbel came, and after seventy years, I was saved.

To cut down the stature of the pine (Mordecai) was the aim of the Aggagite (Haman), son of Hamedatha. But this became his own snare, and his arrogance was broken. The head of the Binyaminite (Mordecai) You raised, and the enemy's name You erased, his many sons—his great wealth—You hanged on the gallows.

The Greeks gathered against me, then, in the days of the Hasmoneans; they broke through the walls of my towers and defiled all the oils. And from the remnant in the flasks, a miracle was done for the roses (Jews). Men with insight appointed eight days for song and jubilation.

Bare Your holy arm, and bring close the final salvation. Avenge the blood of Your servants, from the wicked nation. For the salvation is too long in coming for us, and there is no end to the days of evil. Push aside the red one (Esau), into the deepest shadow; raise up for us the seven shepherds.

IV

THE CELEBRATION OF PURIM

Introduction

The rose of Jacob was joyful and glad, when they jointly saw Mordechai robed in royal blue. You have been their eternal salvation, and their hope through the generations. To make known that all who hope in You will not be ashamed; they will not be humiliated, those who take refuge in You. Accursed is Haman who sought to destroy me, blessed be Mordechai the Yehudi. Accursed be Zeresh the wife of my terrorizer, blessed be Esther, who did for my sake. And Charvonah, too, be remembered for good. (*Prayer Book*, prayer after the reading of the *Megillah*)

urim is the celebration of the rescue of the Jewish nation from the clutches of Haman and a reaffirmation of our belief in Divine Providence. We believe that God is directly involved in history, especially with the Jewish people, with whom He has an eternal covenant. And because of His covenant, those who trust in Him will have no regret in the end. Therefore, cursed is Haman, the deputy of Amalek, who through schemes and threats of annihilation attempted to rob us of our faith.

Similarly, in recent history, too, the Germans, as they tortured the Jewish captives, mocked their faith in God. And, therefore, blessed is Mordechai and *tzaddikim*, the righteous of all the generations, who kept the fire of faith burning in the hearts of the Jewish people. They all had the quality of great spiritual strength and uncompromising faith, as it is written, "But Mordechai did not bow, nor did he do him reverence." Mordechai's faith was so strong that he totally ignored Haman and was not intimidated by him in the least.

Hence, our celebration is one of joy in faith. This is clearly seen in the contrast between the two celebrations mentioned in the *Megillah*, one at the beginning and the other at the end. The first celebration mentioned is the drunken, orgiastic revelry of Achashverosh in the company of the elite of Persian society for a period of 180 days or, simply stated, six months! With great splendor, grandeur, pomp, and ostentatious display of the most banal and carnal desires, with music and wine to while away the time, the party went on and on and ended in disgrace.

The second celebration mentioned was when the Jewish people marked Haman's defeat. Their celebration was characterized by jubilation, but with religious and moral content. The theme of their celebration was sharing; gifts of food were exchanged with friends, presents were given to the poor, family reunions were held, and the nation joined in a new commitment to the Written and Oral Law. So fine and genteel were the Jewish celebrations that many non-Jews were attracted to the Jewish religion. Hence, the party ended in honor for the Jewish people, and God's name became known in the world.

Even today, some 2,340 years after the miracle, we celebrate Purim in that same fine spirit. And although we make allowances for an unusual amount of levity and humor, even creating nonsensical "Purim Torah"—jokes with Torah content—and there is an excess of drinking and boundless merriment, still the underlying spirit is the same. It is all done to break through the barriers of the exile—the depression, sadness, and feeling of being abandoned. With the barriers broken, we experience, even if only for a moment, the joy that will be ours in the final redemption of the Jewish people.

As much as we know about Purim, though, its miraculous nature is deliberately hidden. For example, God's name, as it is usually spelled in the Torah, does not appear once in the *Megillah*; the story is told as political intervention, rather than a miracle; Esther's identity as a Jewess was hidden for years; the *Megillah* is part of the written Torah, yet is hidden as if it was merely a letter.

We can compare this to someone who was taking driving lessons. After his teacher showed him what to do, he wrote it down, taped it to the dashboard, and followed the instructions. After mastering driving, he no longer needed the note. Many months later, his son asked him to list the steps for starting a car. He could not remember those steps. It had already become part of his life. He no longer had to think about it.

So too, with the instructions for our spiritual life. There is the Written Law, the Torah, and the portion called the Oral Law. The Written Law is the part that God writes for us; the Oral Law is the part that we live. The *Megillah* has both qualities. It is part of the Written Law, but its essence is the Oral Law, the Torah that we live.

This was personified in the lives of Mordechai and Esther. They were Jews, through and through, to such a degree that writing about it is not even necessary. Everything they did was drawn from the wellsprings of the Torah, their very lives. It did not have to be spelled out; it was obvious. Neither is God's name mentioned; it was obvious to them that God was the author of all historical events. Nor did Esther need to announce her Jewishness; her every action is replete with Torah and Jewishness. The *Megillah* is both a letter, yet part of the Torah; what more is Torah than the actual biographies of Torah people?

The Baal Shem Tov (1700–1760), the founder of the chasidic movement, once said, "If to learn the laws concerning the exchange of a cow for a donkey is considered 'Torah,' then surely, one who actually exchanges a cow for a donkey, how much more it must be considered 'Torah'" (*Al Hatorah*).

When we *live* the Torah, then the Torah is "hidden" in our daily life, but it is Torah nevertheless.

Therefore, on Purim our entire life as Jews is concealed. We go to the synagogue and listen to words of Torah, yet everyone thinks we are listening to a story. We reaffirm our faith in God's divine providence, His intervention in history, yet everyone thinks we are partying. We open our hearts in the truly Jewish way, yet everyone thinks it is a result of too much drink. We even disguise ourselves in masks and costumes to hide our good deeds, as is the Jewish tradition.

The chasidic masters have taught, "Wherever there is hiddenness, there the greatest light is found." And what better place to dig for this great treasure of light than the holiday of Purim, which is masked and concealed, veiled in seven times seven veils.

And what better place to find the deepest meaning of Purim than in the works of the chasidic masters. From reading this part of the book, I pray you will learn to appreciate chasidic teachings and catch a glimpse of Kabbalah. Even more you will grasp the merriment of Purim when you learn what to see in it. You will open your heart and allow God's light to penetrate. Then suddenly you may realize how dull the exile is compared with the exuberance of God's permanent light.

Purim will fill you with merriment and joy; it will give you encouragement and spirituality, hope and yearning. You will be transformed and uplifted. You will always have a key to escape from a personal prison and exile. You will rediscover your faith in God and your fellow man. The happiness of Purim will bolster your hope within the darkness and you will be redeemed.

29

The Portion of Shekalim— Parshas Shekalim

GIVING THE SHEKEL

An entire tractate of Mishnah is devoted to the laws of the half-shekel tax. Every male over the age of twenty had to give the half-shekel tax to the Temple treasury once each year, as commanded in Exodus 30:12–16.

God spoke to Moses saying, When you take the sum of the children of Israel for the purpose of registration, each man shall give a ransom for his soul to God, when you count them; that there be no plague among them, when you count them. As each man passes over to those already counted, he shall give half a shekel by the sacred standard, a shekel is twenty *gerah*, a half-shekel shall be the offering to God. The rich shall not give more, and the poor shall not give less than a half-shekel, when they give an offering to God, to atone for your souls. And you should take the atonement money of the children of Israel, and apply it to for the service of the Tabernacle of the Congregation; that it may be a memorial for the children of Israel before God, to make an atonement for your souls.

The *Beis Din*, the Jewish court, would announce on the first day of *Adar* throughout Israel that every adult male, whether rich or poor, must contribute a half-shekel by the first of *Nissan* to the treasury toward the upkeep of the Temple. From these funds the *korban tamid*, the daily burnt-offering, and the *korban musaf*, the additional offering, were offered from the first of *Nissan* to the following first of *Nissan*.

The first *mishnah* in the tractate of *Shekalim* states: "On the first day of *Adar* they made a proclamation about the half-shekel tax, and about the forbidden admixture."

There are two months in the year that are the most important and primary ones: *Tishrei*, which is our Rosh Hashanah, the New Year, and *Nissan*, which is the month of the Egyptian Exodus and therefore the first *month* of the year. Before the New Year we rid ourselves of old misdeeds by *teshuvah*, returning to God. And therefore the month before Rosh Hashanah is traditionally designated for repentance and charity. The month before *Nissan* is *Adar* and is also suitable for repentance and charity. Therefore, on its first day we give charity and connect ourselves once again to the Holy Temple by giving the half-shekel.

Although we no longer have the Temple, still by listening to the reading, we give the shekel on a spiritual level. This rouses us from our spiritual slumber and helps us give charity on a physical level. In the merit of charity the Third Temple will soon be rebuilt, and then the shekel tax will again be given.

Deep inside every Jewish heart there is a kernel of holiness, the *neshama*, "soul." The *neshama* is otherworldly; it is from heaven and is not material like our body. Nor does it die; it is immortal. It always desires God and spiritual things and has a great capacity to

203

be generous and to share its high levels of spirit. The *neshama* is hidden inside a body of material desires and selfishness. How then does the soul influence the body? When one does a physical act of kindness or charity, although it is only material, the spiritual desire comes forth.

A king was usually kind to his subjects. One day when he was in a very bad mood, a group of poor farmers came to seek his help. The king ignored them as they begged for help. No matter how long they pleaded, the king turned a deaf ear. The court jester noticed this behavior, excused himself, and soon returned with the king's son, a very young prince. The boy ran to his father, climbed on his lap, and whispered into his ear, "Daddy, could I please have some sweets?" The king smiled endearingly at his son and said, "Of course, my son, anything for you!," motioning to one of the pages to give him sweets immediately. As the boy climbed off his father's lap, the king looked around and noticed the farmers. "Now, what is it that you wanted?," he asked with great interest. The farmers were startled out of their gloom and were suddenly excited and filled with merriment.

Similarly in our case, the desire and generosity of our soul lie dormant until we do a physical act of giving. When we give the half-shekel, our hearts open up to sharing and generosity, and we all become filled with joy.

———————————

"On the first day of *Adar* they make a proclamation about the half-shekel tax, and about the forbidden admixture (*kelayim*)" (*Shekalim* 2a).

Each one of us has gifts from God. Some have intelligence, others strength; some have talent, others determination, and so on. We can guard our gifts jealously and not share them with others. If we do that, our gifts are imprisoned in our selfishness. And when our gifts are imprisoned, so are we. But if we share our gifts generously, we release them and ourselves from prison. This causes great happiness and joy.

The Hebrew word for prison is *keleh* and is the root word of *kelayim*, "admixture." When we donate the half-shekel to the Temple, our generosity releases our gifts and everyone else from prison. Therefore, our actions during *Adar* prepare the way for our redemption in the next month of *Nissan* in which is found the ultimate redemption, the holiday of Passover.

———————————

"On the first day of *Adar* they make a proclamation about the half-shekel tax. . . ."

It is written, "A gift opens the door to the giver, and gains access to the great" (Proverbs 18:16).

This verse is about a gift that is promised to be given, but was not yet given. Still, it opens the door, as when one is in a dangerous situation and makes a vow of charity, as is the tradition. The vow releases the person from "prison"—the problem—and sets him free. Therefore the Jewish people make a proclamation, a verbal announcement, a vow that is equal to giving.

A prince was in his father's throne room and was behaving without respect. His bad manners angered the king, who ordered his tutor to lecture the prince about his behavior. The tutor took hold of the prince's arm and was leading him out of the room. The prince felt sad and alone. At that instant he didn't feel like he was his father's son, but rather like a prisoner of his tutor. When he was nearly out the door, the prince turned to his father and with tearful eyes begged, "Please, father, I will not be disrespectful and promise to behave with good manners." The king smiled to his son and motioned for the tutor to release him.

Similarly, when we promise to be charitable, thereby turning to God, we are immediately released from our "prison," our spiritual confinement.

———————————

The Jewish people built the *Mishkan*, the Tabernacle, after their Exodus from Egypt, during the month of *Adar*. They were asked to contribute material and did so with utmost joy. That joy was so great that it was passed from generation to generation. So that each time the Jewish people are asked to give, as in the month of *Adar*, they are filled with great happiness. This creates the additional merriment during this month.

———————————

"Righteousness raises a people to honor" (Proverbs 14:34). The Hebrew word for raises is *teromem*, or *terumah*, "to separate." The act of charity helps separate the Jewish people from the rest of the nations. And because they are uplifted and separated, they are also ready for a complete redemption. And so, in the following month, the Jewish people merit the redemption, when they became a nation at the Exodus from Egypt.

A king sent his son to school together with many nephews of the royal family. Several years later, when they had completed their studies, a graduation ceremony was held in the palace gardens. Each graduate presented the king with a small token of appreciation and then received his diploma. When it was the prince's turn, he presented the king a coin, fashioned by the royal goldsmiths, with the image of the king on it. "Such a gift only you can give, my son! Now come here and stand beside me!" The prince stood next to his father. The other boys suddenly realized that, although they too graduated, the prince was different. He was the king's son.

Similarly, as the nations become more and more civilized, performing acts of justice and mercy and acts of charity, they wonder if perhaps they are all on the same spiritual level. When the Jewish people give their charity, however, their spiritual uniqueness is obvious, they are lifted up, and stand next to God. All realize then, that although they too do acts of kindness, the Jewish people are the children of God.

Each holiday is called a *regel*, literally meaning foot, because each Jewish male was required to go to Jerusalem for the holidays, and most went by foot. Spiritually it means that a person should use even his foot, the limb furthest from spirituality, and go with it up to Jerusalem; one should lift it to the highest level possible.

It is written, "Her feet go downward on the path of death . . ." (Proverbs 5:5). Although the top of things may be out of reach and high up in the clouds, the feet, the lower levels, are more vulnerable, even unto death. As it is written, ". . . and you (the snake) will strike at their heel" (Genesis 3:15). The snake, evil, can strike at and destroy the heel, the lower levels.

What can be used as an antidote for this danger? Charity, as it is written, ". . . and charity is a safeguard against death" (Proverbs 10:2). The act of charity turns over the lowest level, death, and instead gives life. The most appropriate month to give charity is *Adar*, a month that was "turned over" from the sadness of Haman's deadly plot to the rejoicing upon his downfall. The decree of death and sadness comes from the feet, life and rejoicing from the head.

Charity reverses everything; even the feet can be on the highest spiritual level as the feet become the head. Therefore, soon after we give the half-shekel in the month of *Adar*, we can safely walk by foot to Jerusalem in the month of *Nissan* and celebrate the holiday of Passover.

"God knew that Haman will offer shekels as a bribe to King Achashverosh to kill the Jews. Therefore He commanded the Jewish people to give the half-

shekels to counter Haman's bribe. As we have learned, 'On the first day of *Adar* they make a proclamation about the half-shekel tax . . .'" (*Megilla* 15a).

When wheat grows, first the stalks push through the ground, and later the kernels of wheat mature in them. The same is true with every fruit. First the outside shell grows, followed by the fruit itself. A similar thing happened when Rebecca gave birth to her twin sons. First Esau was born and then Jacob. First came the chaff and then the fruit.

Similarly, the Jewish people left Egypt in the month of *Nissan*, the month when grain matures. And as with all births, the last moment is the most dangerous. Similarly, the deepest and darkest moment in exile comes right before the redemption. When the descendants of Jacob are about to be redeemed, Esau's descendants are at their greatest strength. And when Haman threw lots (the *pur*), the month of *Adar* was always chosen; being right before *Nissan*, it was the most dangerous time for the Jews and the easiest time to harm them. The chaff comes before the fruit.

Esau and Jacob are two sides of a coin. Of the descendants of Jacob it is written, "Israel then was holy to God, the *first* fruits of His harvest . . ." (Jeremiah 2:3), and of the children of Esau, it says, ". . . *First* of all the nations was Amalek . . ." (Numbers 24:20). Both Israel and Amalek are *firsts*; Amalek is first to come out of the ground as the chaff, and Israel, the Jewish people, are the first fruit. We can say that the wheat needs the chaff; otherwise how would it grow? Thus the chaff is a vessel for the wheat, as it is written, ". . . and he (the wicked) will prepare clothing, but the righteous will wear them" (Job 27:17).

Our task is to separate the chaff from the fruit. How? We must take the *fruit* immediately before the chaff has a chance to overpower it. Therefore, in *Adar*, the month of the chaff's power, we immediately give charity, our mature fruit. Charity and acts of kindness are what the Jewish people do best. And once they establish the strength of their fruit, the chaff is powerless to harm them.

Much work needs to be done before we have flour for bread. In each step we separate the desired from the undesired; we turn the chaos into order. First the ground is prepared, and the good soil is selected for the seed. The seeds are sorted and planted. When the seed starts to grow, the plant starts to push its way up to the top of the ground. The stalk breaks through the soil and lifts the seeds high above the ground. The wheat kernels grow on top of the stalk, the straw. When fully grown, the wheat is cut and winnowed, the wind blows away the straw, and the chaff is discarded while the wheat is selected and falls to the ground. The wheat is collected and again sorted; it is then milled. The flour is ready for baking. This ends a process of selection after selection.

We too must be very careful how our deeds are done, carefully selecting from the confusion that which is desirable. We have to be selective and choose only the best part of each thought, spoken word, and action because at each step of the way evil is lurking to confuse and confound. This is why Jacob prayed to God and said, "Please save me from the hands of my brother, from the hands of Esau" (Genesis 32:11). He begged to be saved from two types of evil. "The hands of my brother" means even the good deeds that make him seem like a brother. "The hands of Esau" are deeds that are plainly evil and are identified with Esau. We need to be saved both from the good and the evil deeds of Esau.

Therefore, on the first of *Adar*, before the evil ones ever have a chance to promise to do good deeds, we quickly promise to give the half-shekel tax to the Holy Temple. We thereby select the best of charitable deeds and are saved from the hands of Esau.

The first day of the month of *Tishrei* is Rosh Hashanah. It is a day of judgment for the entire world, as we were taught in the Mishnah, "On the New Year all the inhabitants of the world pass before him like flocks of sheep . . ." (*Rosh Hashanah* 2:2). The word *shanah*, "year," also means to repeat. The nations of the world count their year with the sun, which stands still and is repetitious. It seems to have a head, a *rosh*; yet it is only *shanah*, a repeat of the previous one. On the other hand, the Jewish people became a nation in the month of *Nissan*, as it is written, ". . . this month is for you the first of months . . .", "*rosh chodashim.*" The word for month is *chodesh*, which also means new. The Jewish nation counts their year with the moon, which revolves around the earth and is always new. It has a head, *rosh*, and it is *chodashim*, constantly being renewed.

Therefore, *Tishrei*, the New Year for all the nations, is the time of rain. Rain fertilizes and prepares the fields for the growth that follows. Later, in *Nissan*, the grains sprout forth and grow in the fields. This symbolizes the redemption and growth of the Jewish people in the month of *Nissan*.

Similarly, the power of the nations stems from repetition; it is the power of nature and regularity. And its opposite is the power of the Jewish people: renewal, miracles, and the supernatural. The power of the nations gets stronger and stronger after the month of *Tishrei*, when rain falls and the night gets longer and longer. By the month of *Adar* the power of the nations is at its peak. Amalek, the leader of the nations of the world, is about to devour the Jewish people. Haman's schemes are about to become reality. The Jewish people quickly jump ahead and give the half-shekel, their hearts open for the dawn of a new day, the coming of the month of renewal, the month of *Nissan*. They are saved just in time.

First there is the desire and then the deed. Both of these have to be pure and cleansed from all evil. Thus, when the Jewish people were approached by Moses to accept the Torah, to stand at Mount Sinai, and to hear the words of God, they answered, "All that God has spoken we will do and listen" (Exodus 24:8). This means that they promised to keep both their deeds and desires pure. But shortly afterward, they made an idol and worshiped it, and thus their deeds were pure no longer.

In the Midrash we read that a king appointed his servant to watch two crystal vases for him. The servant accidentally broke one of them. The king was very angry and said, "You have broken one, now do be very careful with the other!" (*Exodus Rabbah* 24).

Although the Jewish people did not keep their deeds pure, still their desire to serve God never changed. And therefore when the nations of the world come with their evil deeds, we must jump ahead of them with our good desires. Haman comes with his evil designs and deeds, and we come with the purity of our hearts' desires. We "proclaim," give the half-shekel tax, and all of Israel must *hear*. Our hearing is still good; our desire has not been defiled.

We too, as weak as we are in deeds, should build on our pure desires and thus break the power of evil.

The good is mixed with evil, and every good thing has to be sorted. We sort our deeds too by purifying our intentions. By doing our deeds solely for the sake of God, they are then pure. Therefore, before we even give the shekels, we sort our intentions by announcing that the shekels will soon be collected. We thus focus our thoughts and desires on the good deed we are about to do, and we accomplish it with a pure heart.

Even if a person is not able to accomplish his good desire in deed, at least his good desire forces the evil desires from his heart. Therefore the advice for a person who is enslaved by evil desires and cannot get away from them is to fill his heart with a desire to do good deeds. Once his heart starts beating to the tune of positive desires, he will suddenly feel released from the prison of evil. He will experience a great release of energy and be free to do acts of kindness.

GENEROSITY

Giving the shekel, or any charity, is an act of generosity for which the Jewish nation is well known. As our sages have taught, "There are three signs by which a Jew is recognized; they are merciful, bashful, and generously do deeds of lovingkindness" (*Yevamos* 79a).

It is written, "How beautiful are your sandled feet (*p'omayich*), O Prince's daughter" (Song of Songs 7:1). The Midrash interprets this as "How beautiful is the kindness (*p'omayich*) of the Jewish people, the daughter of Abraham" (*Song of Songs* 7).

The kindness of Abraham was without bounds or limit. He offered his help to one and all, both physically and spiritually: by offering food and lodging, by giving guidance to believe in the one and only God, and by abandoning idol worship. And we too, who are descendants and students of Abraham, should certainly follow his example, to be generous and kind without limit.

A king had an abundance of oil. He announced that whoever needs it should come to the palace gates to receive as much oil as he could carry. How surprised the king was the next morning when hundreds of villagers came for oil! He was even more surprised to see that most of them had brought no vessels to carry the oil home.

It is wonderful to be generous, but one must have containers for the gifts. The *p'omayich*, the generosity, must have sandals to contain the kindness lest it be lost to the wind.

Therefore, when the desire to do kindness is awakened in the month of *Adar*, we must immediately put it into a vessel, a physical act of charity. The vessel is the half-shekel of charity that we give. And each time we give or do a kind deed, our vessel becomes stronger, and more of the good desire is preserved.

Shortly after the Jewish people received the Ten Commandments, they made the Golden Calf and worshiped it. Idol worship is foreign to the Jewish people; it is antithetical to their religion. The antidote to idol worship was God's commandment to give the half-shekel tax. As soon as they desired to be gener-

ous, their hearts softened. This returned them to love God and do His commandments.

A prince ran away from the palace and joined a gang of thieves. The king sent many servants to find him and convince him to come home. All failed, until one of them came to the prince disguised as an old beggar and begged for help. When the prince heard the pitiful words of the "old man," his heart softened, and a surge of emotion filled his entire being. He suddenly remembered his father's generosity to the poor among his subjects. With tears in his eyes and a cracking voice, he said, "I don't want to be here any more; I want to go home to my father."

When the desire of the Jewish people is awakened to be generous, there is no barrier separating them from their Father in heaven. As it is written, "Wear me as a seal upon your heart, as a seal upon your arm; for love is stronger than death, passion cruel as the grave; it blazes up like a blazing fire, fiercer than any flame. Many waters cannot quench love, no flood can sweep it away; if a man were to offer for love the whole wealth of his house, it would be utterly scorned" (Song of Songs 8:6–7).

It is written, "... but for the man himself no partner had yet been found" (Genesis 2:21). When God created the first man, Adam, he did not have a mate. And he looked around and saw that all the other animals have mates, and he yearned for one, too. There was no rain, and nothing grew. As it is written, "... God had sent no rain on the earth..." (Genesis 5:1). And Adam yearned for rain and prayed.

Man was created without perfection so that he would yearn to God for fulfillment. He would not take things for granted, but would feel that he owes God his sustenance and his very life. He would always be looking to God for help, hoping and praying for His assistance.

A king sent his son to a faraway land. Naturally the king made sure that every need was provided for him. The prince left in a comfortable coach, had an abundance of food, and was protected by his father's soldiers. When the prince arrived at his destination, he was surprised to find that his father had forgotten to give him a ring with the royal seal. The prince sent a messenger who soon returned with a ring that bore the seal. In a note the king wrote, "You thought you had everything. You don't. So please don't forget your father."

We realize the truth and know that we owe everything to God, even our very life. And so when we give the half-shekel, we are reminded of our indebtedness and give with great joy.

"He (Raban Gamliel) used to say: Treat His will as if it were your own will, so that He will treat your will as if it were His will. Nullify your will before His will, so that He will nullify the will of others before your will" (*Ethics of our Fathers* 2:4).

A human being has many desires, cravings, and wishes. Some of them run counter to the Torah and its commandments. How can he harness the energy of his desires for the service of God? He can do so by striving to desire only the things that God favors: "Treat His will as if it were your own will." But if you have already strayed too far, then at least you should nullify your will before His will.

We can compare this to the six work days and *Shabbos*. Even during the six work days, it is possible to do everything for God's sake by dedicating everything to God's service. After a week of such devotion, *Shabbos* comes as a crown to all our labor. Despite the spiritual nature of our workdays, they do not diminish the holiness of the *Shabbos*. But if we forget God and the spiritual goals during the work days, and we stray too far, then what effect can *Shabbos* have on us? Then at least we should nullify our will to His will.

We become elevated spiritually and realize that our work is worthless without God. We nullify our desires to God's desire. Similarly, when we give the half-shekel, we open our hearts to God's will and prepare ourselves to be His nation.

It is written, "And you should love God your Lord with all your heart . . ." (Deuteronomy 6:5).

Your heart has many desires and yearnings. You should use every single one of them to love God. A similar lesson was taught with the building of the *Mishkan*, the Tabernacle that the Jewish people built after the exodus. As it is written, "Each of you set aside a contribution to God. Let all who wish, bring a contribution to God: gold, silver, copper; violet, purple, and scarlet yarn; fine linen and goats, perfume for the anointing oil and for the fragrant incense; carnelians and other stones ready for setting in the *ephod* and breast-piece" (Exodus 35:5–8). Each item that is listed is another desire of a man's heart. All of them should be given away to God.

When it comes time to give the half-shekel tax, our hearts open immediately to God. We gather all our desires, consecrate them to God, and are ready to serve Him with great happiness.

The Jewish heart is generous. Still, at times its generosity is in hiding because we live among the nations of the world. We sometimes allow the culture of our hosts to captivate us. We sink to a low level and sad state, and cannot be truly happy. But then the first of *Adar* comes, when every Jew makes vows to contribute generously to God's worship and to pray for the nation's welfare. Then we fill with great happiness, which opens our chains and releases us from the sad oppression. We feel free again, rejoice, and our generosity surfaces. Thus, our true desires are revealed as we give the half-shekel.

We say in our morning prayers, "In His goodness He renews daily, perpetually, the work of creation."

God is generous to all His creatures and sustains them with His goodness. He also planted a kernel of this goodness into the hearts of the Jewish people, so that when they give, there is a kernel of Divine goodness in their giving. It is a gift from God. And therefore they are called *bas nadiv*, "O prince's daughter" (Song of Songs 7:1). The word *nadiv* also means generous. The Jewish people are generous by birth, and they are daughters of generosity; it is part of them, in their very core.

Therefore the commandment is to give a half-shekel to the Temple, or *machatzis*. The word *machatzis* is also found in the verse, ". . . *Bachatzos* . . . in middle of the night I will go out among the Egyptians," (Exodus 11:4), meaning the part of the night that is the "most night." Likewise, when we give the shekel we give it with the *machatzis*, the very essence and core of the shekel, the heart of the giving that is planted within the hearts of the Jewish nation.

It is written, "Then shall the house of Jacob be fire, the house of Joseph flame, and the house of Esau chaff; they shall blaze through it and consume it . . ." (Obadiah 1:18).

When God told Moses that every Jew is required to give a half-shekel coin to the Temple, Moses did not understand what the coin looked like. God then showed Moses a coin of fire identical to the half-shekel (*Exodus Rabbah* 30).

The nature of fire is that even the tiniest spark can ignite a large bundle of straw. If we are ever faced with a massive amount of evil, even if it be as huge as a mountain, we can be sure that a single spark of truth can conquer it. Because evil has no substance, it is not solid; it is only as straw. And as soon as the spark conquers one straw of the bundle, the others soon follow in succession, until the entire bundle is consumed.

The same occurs with the evil Amalekites who gather their forces in the month of *Adar*. They seem so huge and unconquerable. They loom large as mountains and scare the Jewish people to death. But as soon as the Jews kindle their hearts and ignite them with the fire of love and generosity, no evil can intimidate them. The spark of their love burns up the mountains of evil, as a spark that consumes the straw.

It is written, "This month is for you the first of months; you shall make it the first month of the year" (Exodus 12:2). This refers to the month of *Nissan*, the month of the Jewish Exodus. And later in the Torah it is written, "This is the whole offering to be made, *month by month* (chodesh b'chodsho), *throughout the year*" (Numbers 28:15).

This means that during the special month, which is a *chodesh b'chodsho*, "an offering should be made," bought with new coins. The Talmud infers from this that the half-shekel tax should be collected in the month before *Nissan*, or *Adar*, so that new coins will be available during the month of *Nissan*.

The words *chodesh b'chodsho* also mean the "renewal of the renewal." There certainly is renewal in the world, as God helps his creatures gain strength after weakness, life after being near death. But then there is also the essence of renewal, the core, the epitome of renewal itself. It is the month of *Nissan*, the birth month of the Jewish nation.

How appropriate it is, that we honor *Nissan*, which is the *essence of renewal*, by giving new coins, *machatzis hashekel*, the half-shekels, the center and essence of Jewish generosity and giving.

It is written, "God spoke to Moses and said: When you number (*Ki Sisa*) the children of Israel for the purpose of registration, each man shall give a ransom for his life to God. . . . he shall give half a shekel . . ." (Exodus 30:11–13).

The words *ki sisa* also mean to lift up. The heads of the Jewish people will be uplifted when they give the half-shekel.

The spiritual world works with balances. When evil increases, goodness increases to balance it. And similarly, when good is increased, evil rises up against it. When God wants to raise the heads of the Jewish people, there is great opposition from the evil in the world. How then can it be done?

We can compare this to a king who was speaking to his court. His son, advisors, elders, and sorcerers were all there. The prince gave brilliant and practical pieces of advice several times during the meeting. As the king praised his son for his brilliance, the others seethed with jealousy. Their faces turned red as they grumbled about the king's unfairness. The king called to his son, "Son, I was just about to give all my advisors a bonus for their loyalty. Please fetch the box of newly minted coins and give each one his due." As the prince doled out the coins, they noticed that the prince had no air of conceit or unfriendliness. They calmed down and accepted him.

When God raises the Jewish people, they humble themselves. They immediately awaken their compassion for the lowly, for the poor and downtrodden. They use their generosity to help the poor by giving their money. They are high and low at the same time. They balance the scale. The opposition loses its strength, and the Jewish people are saved from suffering.

It is written, "The rich man shall give no more than a half-shekel and the poor man shall give no less . . ." (Exodus 30:15).

Would it not be fairer to tax the rich man more than the poor man? Why is it that both the rich and the poor give equally? This practice teaches us an important lesson. Although the rich man possesses more gold and silver, his "generosity" is no greater than that of the poor man. This generosity is at the core of the giving; it is the kernel of kindness that God planted into every Jewish heart. So then why is it that one person has more than another? The truth is that part of the rich man's share is not his at all. God gives the share of the poor man to the rich man for safekeeping. It is God's will that the share of the poor man should come through an *intermediary*. When the rich man gives, he is merely returning the poor man's money. He is no more charitable or generous than the poor man. They are both equally generous at the core.

A king wanted to reward his servants. He appointed a few of them to distribute the payments and said, "When you are finished distributing the money, please take an equal share as the others, and an extra share for your work."

It is written, "And you shall love God your Lord with all your heart, with all your soul, and all your possessions" (Deuteronomy 6:5).

Many have asked, How is it possible to be commanded to love God? You might be commanded to obey Him, but to love is an emotion, an attitude, a state of mind. Can you be forced into it? The answer is that even before *love*, one must first have awe and fear of God. We must remember that God is the All Powerful Lord of the universe Who created us and everything that exists. He is the one who controls the destiny of every creature, and our very life and death depends on Him. He is all knowing, and nothing is hidden from Him. And when we realize all of this, we are filled with awe and fear and totally humbled before Him. Therefore, awe depends on the level of our understanding and perception. The "closer" we are to God, the more we are in awe of Him.

But the love of God is entirely a gift received from God Himself. As it is written, ". . . they should give gold and silver (*kesef*) . . ." to the building of the Tabernacle (Exodus 25:1). *Kesef* also means to yearn, to hope, and to pine with love of God. This yearning and love are planted in the hearts of the Jewish people. They form the core of generosity, which is given as a gift.

Let us show our appreciation for God's gift of love by using it with pride—by opening our hearts to the plight of the poor and taking care of their needs. We will be met in return with God's love for us.

It is written, "The rich man shall not give more, the poor man shall not give less. . . ." This can also be referring to spiritual matters. Those who are rich spiritually should remember the others less fortunate than they and share with them. Those who are rich in understanding should share with the others who are not.

THE COIN OF FIRE

The Midrash relates that when God commanded Moses concerning the shekels for the census, he was puzzled. He didn't clearly understand what type of coin was required. God showed him a coin of fire that was the size and shape of the required shekel. Then Moses knew exactly what it was. As it is written, "This they shall give . . ." (Exodus 30:13). The word *this* signifies that Moses saw the coin that was required, and it was a divine coin of fire.

It is important for each one of us to reach within and contact our inner core of generosity. But how does a person contact the depths of his heart? Some reach it through wisdom, whereas others reach it through awe and fear of God. No matter how we reach it, we

know that the inner generosity of each Jew is the same, as it is written, "The rich man shall not give more, and the poor man shall not give less." The amount is always the same—a half-shekel, no more no less.

A king assembled his servants to reward each for his loyalty. Some servants worked for the king in the palace, whereas others traveled in dangerous places. The king gave each one a diamond-studded gold medallion. The servants all admired their gifts, but began to wonder out loud why they all received the same identical thing. The king noticed and said, "You are probably wondering why each of you received identical gifts. Each one of you has absolute loyalty to me, your king. Some of your jobs are in the palace, while others travel far and through danger. Yet the dedication in your hearts is identical."

Similarly, in the case of charity, although some may have more to give than others, the inner generosity in the deepest depths of each of our hearts is identical.

The world must maintain a balance between good and evil. When destructive forces become more powerful, then the good must increase. If a balance is not maintained, the world can be destroyed altogether, as it nearly was by a flood in the days of Noah.

This is also true of the universe as a whole; there must be harmony. And it is the job of the Jewish people to maintain that harmony. The question is, How can the physical Jewish nation bring about the spiritual harmony that is needed? It is because the Jewish nation is a "coin of fire"; they are the energy that gives life to the universe. The coin of fire has a face engraved on it, the face of Jacob our forefather, whose face is also engraved on God's Throne of Honor.

What is the Throne of Honor? It is God's plan of dealing with the world. And which people symbolize God's plan? It is Jacob and his children, the nation of Israel.

An engineer lived with his son in a village, which was miles from the nearest market. The son often asked his father, "Father, how will we get to the market, so far away?" Finally, the father built a machine that would transport them. When the locomotive was ready, he and his son admired it. Others criticized him saying, "This engine of yours is evil. It will kill people by crashing and exploding." The engineer invited his critics to examine the locomotive. He showed them each of its parts and how it worked. He also introduced them to the conductor, his own son, who helped build the engine. "I built this engine to help people get from place to place, and really hope that it is never used to hurt or kill anyone. And to guarantee this, my own son will drive it, and . . . look here," the engineer added, pointing to a metal name plate on its side, "see the etching of my son's image. That will remind everyone that this locomotive was built with love."

Similarly, God's plan for dealing with the world, His Throne of Honor, is one of love. And we know this plainly because Jacob's "face," the face of his beloved nation of Israel, is engraved on it. And this same face is engraved on the coin of fire, the enthusiastic desire of the Jewish people to do good and overwhelm the forces of evil.

Every person has a *yetzer tov*, an inclination to do good, and a *yetzer hara*, an inclination to do evil. They are two angels appointed by God to accompany man wherever he goes. One is on the right and the other on the left, as it is written, "The heart of the wise man faces right, but the heart of the fool faces left" (Ecclesiastes 10:2). They are like the two plates at the sides of a scale. If a person does a good deed, he tips the scale toward good. If he does an evil deed, he tips the scale toward the side of evil. Man's soul, however, is the balancing arm. It must remain very still, being sure not to lean in either direction. Thus, it radiates the strongest spiritual energy, and is called, *machatzis hashekel*, the half-shekel. *Machatzis* also means in the middle, that it must remain balanced in the absolute middle. And in that spot it is truth, which is in the absolute center and core of the universe.

Similarly, a tightrope walker in the circus starts to walk on the tope with great care. There are people watching and cheering him on the right and the left. If he looks to the right and is distracted by what he sees, he then leans to the right. And if the noise of the crowd on the left attracts his attention, then he leans to the left. In either case, he can fall and break his bones. He must lean neither to the right nor to the left. He must stay very calmly and quietly in the absolute center. That is the path of truth and of safety for him; all other paths are lies and dangerous.

The same can be said of us. We must stay poised in the middle and allow the truth to lead us through life. We thus give the half, the center position of the shekel, the balancing arm, and consecrate our life to God.

The word *shekel* also means to weigh. This teaches us to weigh each deed that we do and compare it to the coin of fire within us, the inner holiness that God has placed inside each Jewish person.

It is written, "So God created man in His own image; in the image of God He created him" (Genesis 1:27).

The core of every Jew is from the highest spiritual realm. Yet his body is of the earth, material and unholy. How can he raise himself to spiritual heights? He can, if he yearns to be a vessel for spirituality, if he longs to be pure and just, if he wants to follow the teachings of the Torah of justice and charity. These yearnings caused the Jewish people to say, ". . . we will do and we will listen . . ." (Exodus 24:7). Their hearts were always yearning and prepared to listen and follow.

And because they are always prepared to do what is right, God too responds to them in a similar manner. He gave them 613 commandments, one for each part of the body. Each one of these commandments purifies and prepares a part of the body to be a vessel for the spirit of God. This happens because the Torah is ". . . from His right hand a fire of law . . ." (Deuteronomy 33:2) It is a fire, like the coin of fire; which cleanses from the inside.

"Moses wondered what sort of coin the shekel might be, and God showed him a coin of fire" (*Exodus Rabbah* 25).

Moses knew that every Jew has a physical body and a spiritual soul. But he wondered, how will the outside half become as pure as the inside half? With fire, the fire of the law, the Torah that is formed with the twenty-two letters of the Hebrew alphabet. And these twenty-two letters influence the physical body to be like the inside soul.

A student asked his teacher what a table was made of. The teacher explained that each material object is made of molecules. "And what are those made of?," asked the student. "They are made of atoms, and they in turn are made of smaller particles still," said the teacher. The student looked puzzled and persisted, "And what are those made of, I wonder?" "They are mostly space," answered the teacher. "You mean that the table is made of space? " said the student. "Yes," said the teacher, "if only you would know what space is really about."

Similarly, the universe was created with the twenty-two Hebrew letters, the letters of the Torah. Therefore, although the body is physical, it is nevertheless made of Hebrew letters. It therefore can become as pure as the spirit within. The outside *can* match the inside. The physical world was created with two letters, and the World to Come was created with two letters to teach us that they are the opposite sides of the same coin. They are as the *machatzis hashekel*, which seems to be merely a physical coin, but actually it is of fire; it is spiritual.

The activities of the Jewish people are only half of what happens. The truth is, however, that whatever we do on the physical plane is accomplished on the spiritual plane too. It has an effect on the world of the spirit. And this is symbolized by the half-shekel, that all that happens on this plane is but half of the whole story.

———————

"The greatness of God is that every human face is different, yet their mold is the same" (*Numbers Rabbah* 16:22).

Moses wondered about the commandment that the poor man should not give less than the rich man (they both give half a shekel). How could it be required of every poor man to give the identical amount, unless the generosity in each of their hearts was identical. Therefore, it must be that the soul of the Jewish people possesses a coin of fire, a core of generosity of such spiritual purity that it is identical inside each of them. And where does this core of generosity reside? It lives in the congregation of Jacob; the face of Jacob that is engraved on the Throne of Honor. This face of Jacob is the collective heart of the Jewish people. And in this collective heart there is great generosity. Thus each Jew has to participate in the giving in order to be part of the *collective heart*. Therefore, if you want your heart to be part of the coin of fire, you too must give the half-shekel. The "half" comes to show that no one's giving is complete without the other. If you think that you are complete on your own, then, on your own, you are not complete. But if you are merely part of the whole, then your giving is whole and complete.

———————

There are righteous people, and there are sinners. When the righteous do good deeds, they gain merit and spiritual standing. But what happens to the good deeds of the sinners? The merit of those deeds go directly to the righteous and raise them even higher.

When the Jewish people stood by Mount Sinai to receive the Ten Commandments, they were rewarded with two crowns: one for saying "we will do," and another for saying "we will listen." Soon afterward they made and worshiped an idol, the Golden Calf. This act caused the two crowns to be removed from

them and to be transferred to Moses in the form of rays shining from his face when he descended from the mountain. But then the Jewish people repented, Moses gladly gave back the crowns to them in the form of the twin commandments of *Shabbos*—"Keep the *Shabbos* holy", and "Remember the *Shabbos* to make it holy." Thus the Jewish people regained the crowns because of their reverence for the Sabbath. And Moses was very happy, as we recite in the prayers, "Moses rejoiced in the gift of his portion." This can mean that Moses was happy when he returned the portion, the crowns, that he had received from the Jewish people.

Similarly, the lesson of the half-shekel is that each of us has a share in the fortunes of the other—the rich with the poor and the poor with the rich. And in the event that we are "rich" because of another's sins, then we should rejoice in eventually returning what is theirs.

———————

"O Master, raise the light of your face upon us, and let me raise a shekel in the firm and exalted Temple" (*Yotzer* Prayer for *Parshas Shekalim*).

Why does it say "shekel" if only a half-shekel was given? It is because the shekel that we give becomes raised and complete together with the other, heavenly half-shekel. Just as we give here on earth, so too God *gives* from the heavens above.

———————

The shekel coin is the material, and the fire is its form, the spiritual essence of it. The physical coin is on the outside, and the spiritual essence is its inner being. Similarly all our deeds that we do with our outside can be focused with the inner spirit, the essence of the deeds. And thus by giving the half-shekel, or reading about it, we connect ourselves with the inner essence of generosity and raise the Jewish people to heights from where they can defeat their enemies.

REPENTANCE AND MERIT

After the Jewish people worshiped the Golden Calf and then repented, God commanded them to give shekels for the *Mishkan*, the Tabernacle, so that they be pardoned and forgiven completely. It is therefore written, "It will thus be a remembrance for the Israelites before God to atone for your lives" (Exodus 30:15).

———————

It is written, "How beautiful are your sandled feet, O prince's daughter" (Song of Songs 7:2), and also,

"My sister my bride is a garden close-locked, a fountain sealed" (Song of Songs 4:12).

When a person sins, he falls down to a very low spiritual level. How can he ever recover? This is done through the generosity in the heart of the Jewish people. When he connects with the generosity in his heart, he is made a vessel for complete repentance. Where do these wonderful feelings come from? From the innermost and hidden part of a person's heart, a place where it could never get ruined by sin. It is like "sandaled" feet and as a garden "close-locked."

The Jewish people made a Golden Calf and sinned miserably. How were they able to return to God? They were told to give the half-shekel to the Temple. This generosity awakened the protected and unblemished part of their heart.

We can compare this to a fire that destroyed most of a house. A builder was asked to assess what could be done and how the house could be rebuilt. The builder said, "The burned material will have to be removed. We will remove everything untill we reach the part that was not damaged by the fire. Then we'll start building anew."

When you sin, your spiritual health is destroyed. Where then can any healthy spirit be found in you? It is found hidden in the depths of your heart. You can be made completely new with it. And the month for this renewal is the month of the Exodus, the month of *Nissan*. As it is written, "This month shall be for you the head of the months" (Exodus 12:2). Therefore, immediately before that, we give the shekel, which is begotten by generosity, "the completely new," locked within our hearts.

God is always good and giving, but human beings are not always ready to receive. What can we do? We can clear the way for Providence to descend from heaven to the earth.

A king announced that he will distribute the finest oil to all who are his loyal servants. The date was set for two weeks. Thousands upon thousands of his subjects received this news with great enthusiasm. Most of them were only counting the days. But some of them thought seriously. How will they receive the oil, and how will they take it home? They checked their vessels for cracks and holes. After repairing them, they were ready to receive the pure oil from the king.

The physical world is finite and incomplete. But even the spiritual world, which seems infinite and whole, is incomplete to some extent. When the spiritual world makes no contact with the physical world, it lacks in perfection too. How can the world reach a state of wholeness? How can the physical and spiritual world be whole? Through the Torah and commandments. The purpose of all the commandments is to bring Providence from heaven. When we observe the commandments of the Torah, our body becomes a vessel to receive the gifts of God. And when God gives, that gift connects us with the spiritual world. There is union between the heaven and earth, and all is infinitely wholesome.

Similarly, this happens to us on *Shabbos*. The union between the heaven and the earth is very strong on that day. On *Shabbos*, the spirit in us is of the highest quality, and is called the *neshama yeseirah*, the extra soul. How is it extra? Because it is infinite and our finite vessels cannot contain its exuberant holiness. Therefore, we must prepare vessels to receive such high levels of spirit.

When we repent from sin, our vessels need major repairs. We can speed this repair by opening our hearts in generosity, which is a spiritual trait. We thus unite with the spiritual world and are wholesome once more.

It is written, "Happy is the man of Your choice, whom You bring near to dwell in Your courts; let us enjoy the blessing of Your house, Your Holy Temple" (Psalms 65:4).

"The man of Your *choice*" refers to the Jewish people who were chosen to be the nation of God and brought forth from Egypt. The phrase, "whom You bring near," refers to the time they sinned and went astray in the desert, but found their way back with repentance. All this happened so that future generations could follow the same path.

There is a physical as well as a spiritual nature to the world. Each material thing in the world has a spiritual portion, a Divine, holy spark. And when a person sins, he scatters these sparks, and the world is in disarray. Finally, when a person repents, he gathers the holy sparks and makes the world whole again. ". . . let us enjoy the blessing of Your house. . . ." As the years pass, more and more of the sparks are gathered together until the final redemption occurs.

The verse "Happy is the man of Your choice, whom You bring near to dwell in Your courts; let us enjoy the blessing of Your house, Your Holy Temple" (Psalms 65:4) has another meaning as well.

The Jewish people had two leaders, Moses and his brother Aaron. Moses was the righteous one. From the moment of his birth until his death, he was unblemished by sin. When he was born the room "filled with light," and when he died, he was called the "man of God." He was the "man of Your choice" and remained without sin from the moment he was chosen. He therefore merits to dwell in the house of God, as it is written, ". . . in My entire house he is trustworthy" (Numbers 2:17). On the other hand, Aaron helped make the Golden Calf, an idol that the Jews worshiped near Mount Sinai. Aaron is "whom You bring near"; he had to be brought near after he repented. But by being brought near, by God, he is elevated to a level even higher than Moses. He therefore merits being in the Holy Temple.

The Jewish people also went through these two phases. At first they were chosen and delivered from Egypt by Moses the righteous one. Later they sinned and worshiped the Golden Calf, repented, and built the *Mishkan*, the Tabernacle, where Aaron the repentant reigned.

It is written, "Happy is the man whose strength is in You; in whose heart are Your ways. As they pass through the valley of Beka they make it a well; the rain covers it with blessings" (Psalms 84:6–7).

The *valley* is the part of our life where danger lurks and we stumble and sin. God sets even the righteous in such places, who sin and repent, so that others will learn from them.

A king and his men were once going to one of his provinces through the fields. They came to a rough piece of land where boulders and thorns covered the terrain. His men were reluctant to advance because of the danger. He called to his best soldiers and said to them, "You men go forth and blaze the trail for me!" The brave soldiers went. As the others waited and watched, they saw the brave ones get torn by thorns, fall into crevices, and slip on the rocks. They finally got through to the safer fields. When the king saw this, he said, "All right men, we can go now. Our trailblazers have shown us the way. We know which pitfalls to avoid." The valleys and pitfalls, the lowest points of our lives, can become the highest ones. Those low points taught us how to find the higher planes of spiritual life.

Similarly, when the Jews were in Egypt, they were in the severest of all the exiles. It was said that no slave had escaped from Egypt. It was a time of murderous oppression and enslavement. The redemption, too, arrived with storm and fury. Egypt, instead of a symbol of oppression, became the symbol for complete subservience to God. Thus it is mentioned in our first and most important encounter with God at Mount Sinai, in the first words of the Ten Com-

mandments, "I am God your Lord who has delivered you from Egypt from the house of slaves" (Exodus 20:2). We are also admonished to ". . . remember the day that you left Egypt all the days of your life." (Deuteronomy 16:3) Those words obligate every Jew to mention the event of the Exodus every morning and every evening. Never are we to forget that great event.

Our ancestors were trailblazers and showed us paths of Jewish survival. Even if we sin, we must not give up, but rather continue and seek the path of truth.

It is written, "Happy is the man whose strength is in You; in whose heart are Your ways. As they pass through the valley of Beka they make it a well; the rain covers it with blessings" (Psalms 84:6–7).

Every Jewish heart is healthy and alive to the call of God. It is sensitive to its obligations and is open with great generosity. When a person sins he deadens his heart. His heart hardens, cell by spiritual cell, until the whole thing turns to stone. It becomes hard as rock, insensitive and unresponsive. If he mends his ways, his heart is repaired, and he starts serving God with new enthusiasm. Those ". . . in whose heart are your ways . . ." can now serve God with ". . . all their hearts . . ." every part of them.

The word *bocho* (Beka), also means crying. There are those who go into the valley, stumble into sin, but afterward regret their deeds. They cry over their lost past and their years wasted and return to God with all their hearts. Those repentants cool the fires of *Gehenom* (hell) with their tears (Eruvin 19a).

It is written, "Many are there who say of my soul, 'There is no help for him in God, Selah.' But You God, are a shield for me: my glory and lift my head high" (Psalms 3:3).

When you listen to the commandments and follow the Godly path, everyone has praise for you. But if you slip and sin, then you can expect scorn and abuse. Who has a good word to say about the sinner? No one. And even if you repent and cleanse your heart, most people still regard you with doubt. They still insist that there is no hope for you. But they are very mistaken. Because the repentant is lifted up higher even than the level of the righteous. "In the place where the repentant sinners stand, even the wholly righteous cannot stand" (Berakhos 34b). And why is that? It is because a sinner defiles and ruins the spiritual levels of his soul. And when he repents he must start from a place that has not yet been defiled. Therefore God lifts him far above the ruins.

He is raised high up, higher than a person normally reaches. And he is exalted beyond the levels reached by those who have never sinned.

Therefore when the Jewish people made the Golden Calf and fell into sin, they repented and were lifted high up. As it is written, "When You will lift up the heads of the Jewish people...." God Himself lifted them up when they repented.

It is written, "It is a continual whole offering, which was made at Mount Sinai for a sweet savor, a sacrifice made by fire unto God" (Numbers 28:6).

When the Jewish people came to Mount Sinai they said, "We will do, and we will listen." To God they promised their desires and actions, their entire beings. Therefore they received a gift, the whole-offering sacrifice, which signified what they had done. God promised to bring them near to Him with the sacrifice, called *korban*, a thing that *brings near*. When they sinned and worshiped the Golden Calf, however, they were not whole any more. They had ruined their actions, but their desire was still pure. Therefore, directly after this idol worship they repented and were asked to be generous with their contributions to the Temple. It was their generosity, their desire, that was still intact and the one thing they still had in its original purity.

There are two realms, the physical and the spiritual. The spiritual realm sustains the physical realm and is therefore always giving. The physical realm is needy and is therefore always receiving. These two worlds are always moving toward each other, and there is a dynamic relationship between them.

Man has ten virtues (*midos*) and he focuses them toward and for the service of God. Similarly, there are ten *sfiros*, spiritual virtues that sustain the world. When man's ten virtues are focused on God, then God's ten virtues are focused on man. There is then harmony, and the world is in the finest state.

These are the two half-shekels; man gives one-half and God gives to man the other half. The shekel is equal to twenty *gerah*; each half equals ten *gerah*. These refer to the Ten *Midos* of man and the Ten *Sfiros* of God. When the ten move toward the other ten, then there is harmony and health.

There is always a dynamic, twin relationship between God and the Jewish people. It was first expressed at Mount Sinai when they said, "... we will do and we will listen...." We will do our share; those are our ten virtues. And we will listen, receiving the ten that come from heaven.

"The rich man shall not give more ..." (Exodus 30:15). This verse refers to the *tzaddikim*, "righteous ones," who have never sinned. And what happens to *tzaddikim* when the majority of the Jewish people are sinful? Can the righteous assume that because they have more merit they are above and beyond the others? Should they consider themselves innocent? No. Even the "rich" one does not have more to give. He too is part of the group and participates in their sinfulness, even if passively. Then how is he saved from punishment? Just as is the "poor" man, by opening his heart, being generous, and making contributions. By nullifying himself and his "riches" to the rest of the congregation of Israel, he too is uplifted with them.

A king's servants once rebelled and refused to do his bidding. The king was very upset and angry. He rounded up the rebels and threatened to banish them from the palace. The servants relented and wanted to apologize. Each one crawled to the throne and begged forgiveness. Suddenly the king noticed among them the most loyal of his advisors. "What are you doing among the rabble?," The king asked in astonishment. "Your servants have rebelled," their spokesman said," and we are your servants too. We too must apologize."

It is written, "Is not my word like a fire? said God; and like a hammer that breaks the rock in pieces?" (Jeremiah 23:29), and it is also written, "Many waters cannot quench love, no flood can sweep it away; if a man were to offer for love the whole wealth of his house, it would be utterly scorned" (Song of Songs 8:7).

The word of God is as a fire. The Talmud explains that the fire of a *mitzvah* can be extinguished by sin, whereas the fire of the Torah cannot. (*Sotah* 21a). Why can a sin extinguish one and not the other, although they are both the word of God? The answer can be found in another teaching of the sages. "Any love that depends on a specific cause, when that cause is gone, the love is gone; but if it does not depend on a specific cause, it will never cease" (*Ethics of Our Fathers* 5:19). A commandment is dependent on a physical object. The fire, which is God's love for us, is contained and dependent on the physical object and can therefore be extinguished. But the study and understanding of the Torah represent the fire itself. That can never be extinguished.

Similarly, God's love for an individual Jew may depend on his deeds. But God's love for that same Jew as a member of *Klal Yisrael*, the Congregation of Israel, is not dependent on any deeds. As it is written, "For God's portion is His people; Jacob is the lot of His inheritance" (Deuteronomy 32:9). It is also written, ". . . yet I loved Jacob, and I hated Esau . . ." (Malachi, 1:2–3). If God loved Jacob merely because of his deeds then why announce it? We know that God loves the good and hates the wicked! It must mean that although Jacob is undeserving, God still loves him because His love for Jacob is not dependent on a specific cause, and therefore will never cease.

Therefore, as a mirror, the Jewish people too love God back, "for no reason," and give charity with generosity.

It is written: "When you take the sum of the children of Israel after their number, then shall they give every man a ransom for his soul to God, when you count them. . . . And you should take the atonement money of the children of Israel, and shall appoint it for the service of the Communion Tent; that it may be a memorial for the children of Israel before God, to make an atonement for your souls" (Exodus 30:11–16).

At Mount Sinai, God spoke to the Jewish people face to face. That was the strongest spiritual experience that a human being could have and remain alive. But, soon afterward, they worshiped the Golden Calf and lost it all. Their "face" was now one of shame. As we recite in our morning prayers, "To You God is righteousness and charity, and to us is the disgraced face." How can we ever hope to fix our disgraced face? We can, with generosity and giving. By opening our hearts generously to our fellow man, we fix our disgraced face. God reciprocates, by coming to us face to face.

Accordingly, the word shekel has the same numerical value as *nefesh*, "soul." By giving the shekel, our soul is mended and we are again face to face with God.

When *Adar* Begins, Happiness Is Increased

"Rabbi Yehudah quoted in the name of Rav: Just as we have learned that when the month of *Av* begins we should minimize our merriment, similarly when the month of *Adar* begins we should increase our merriment. In addition to this, Rav Papa said, that if one has a judgment with a non-Jew, he should make himself scarce in the month of *Av*, because it has bad

mazal (ruling constellation), and he should let himself be found in the month of *Adar* because it has good *mazal*" (*Taanis* 29b).

When Moses asked the Jewish people to help build the Temple, they did so with great merriment and joy. That joy came from the depths of their hearts—the genuine generosity of the congregation of Israel. That joy was deeply ingrained in their hearts and passed down from generation to generation. As our rabbis have taught, "A commandment which the Jewish people received with joy is still done with joy" (*Shabbos* 130a).

A prince was the youngest child of the royal family. His brothers were always asked to help their father with errands and other royal chores. Finally one day, the king called for him and said, "You are now a big boy, and I need big help. The bridge over the garden brook is cracked, and I need you to fix it." The boy was ecstatic and jumped with joy. "I am ready, Father; when can we start?" He excitedly ran to the bridge and helped the workers. It was the happiest day of his life as he got to share in the life of the palace. Even when he was older, he did not forget the deep joy of that day. And whenever someone mentioned repairs of the palace he experienced the same excitement.

Whenever the Temple was being improved, the Jewish people got excited and happy. And therefore, as soon as they heard the call to give the half-shekels used for buying sacrifices in the Temple, they became ecstatic and filled with happiness.

"And you should love God your Lord with all your *heart*, and with all you *soul*, and with all your *might* (possessions)" (Deuteronomy 6:5).

These three phrases symbolize three major events. "With all your heart" symbolizes the Exodus, "with all your soul" symbolizes the experience at Mount Sinai, and "with all your might" (possessions) symbolizes the building of the *Mishkan*, the Tabernacle.

Heart: when the Jewish people left Egypt they did so with faith and trust in God. They ignored the dangers and followed God into the desert. Soul: when they stood at Mount Sinai to hear the word of God, they risked death; from fright their souls departed from their bodies. As it is written, "My soul departed when he spoke" (Song of Songs 5:6). Possessions: finally, when they built the *Mishkan*, they did so with utmost generosity.

Therefore, when *Adar* arrives, we feel a completion in our lives as we serve God with every part of our being and are filled with great happiness.

When man sins, he is spiritually dismal and empty. If he returns to observing the Torah, what has he to offer? Hence, God gives him money so that he can do a good deed with all his heart. When *Adar* arrives, we are overjoyed to contribute to the Temple. Although we have sinned, we still have something to offer.

A prince rebelled against his father and became a thief. He was so angry at his father that he destroyed anything that reminded him of the palace. He shaved his head, changed his clothing, and walked barefoot. Some months later he regretted his deeds and schemed his return. He found a secret entrance and stole onto the palace grounds. He was shocked to learn that it was his father's birthday and that guests had assembled to offer spectacular gifts. Reluctantly, he edged toward his father. Suddenly he stood before him. He reached into his pocket and pulled out the last vestige of the palace, a gold coin. He gazed at the coin with the royal inscription and thought, "I really have nothing to offer but this. Still, I am lucky to have it!" He sheepishly handed it to his father. The king smiled and forgave him saying, "Get this boy dressed, and make him look like a prince again."

Similarly, after we sin and give charity with generosity, God returns to us all the spiritual levels that we destroyed during our rebellion.

It is written, "Rejoice with Jerusalem, and be glad with her, all you who love her; rejoice for joy with her, all you who mourn over her" (Isaiah 66:10).

There are happy times and sad times. When we had the Holy Temple it was a very happy time. Later, it was destroyed in the month of *Av* and we missed it and yearned for it. We show sadness during the month of *Av* and minimize our rejoicing. But when *Adar* arrives, and we contribute the shekels to support the Temple, we feel as if the Temple was rebuilt. We rejoice.

Our yearning for the Temple is not in vain. Because God does not ignore any spiritual intention or yearning, He takes all our yearnings and connects them with the deeds of all the previous generations. Consequently our mourning over Jerusalem turns into a celebration for all those who love her. May we see this soon in our lifetime, with the coming of the *Mashiach* and the total redemption of the Jewish people.

He Uplifts the Jewish People

We are human and are part of a material world that exists in space and time. That means that we live always in a specific place and a specific time. A person cannot be in two places at once, nor can he exist in two different time periods in the same instant. That is true in our limited, finite world. But for God it is all different. There are no limitations or boundaries for Him. God is infinite; He is beyond the confines of space or time. Hence, He is in the past, the present, and the future at every instant. Thus, if we had spiritual yearnings but were unable to fulfill them, and others had done deeds but without proper intentions, God takes them all together. He gathers all the intentions, yearnings, and deeds from the past, present, and future into one. But how can the intentions of one person be put together with the actions of another? Because there is a *Klal Yisrael*, the congregation of Israel, and they are, as a group, infinite, and without limit.

Still, our deeds become part of this great collective body only if we participate with and nullify ourselves to the *klal*, the congregation. And if every single Jew nullifies his self to the *klal*, then they are all uplifted and stand tall.

It is written, "And the work of righteousness will be peace; and the effect of righteousness quietness and assurance forever" (Isaiah 32:17).

There is the work of charity; that is the actual giving. And there is also the effect of charity: the sincere intention. Even if we had only promised charity, it is already a righteous deed and will lead to peace and blessing. And immediately we are uplifted.

It is written, "Though the good man falls down seven times, he is soon up again, but the rascal is brought down by misfortune" (Proverbs 24:16). When the good man falls, this fall is only in the material and lower levels of his spirit. But in the purest spiritual sphere all is complete and whole still.

We can compare this to a rope hanging on a nail from the top of a building. When someone shakes the rope on the bottom, it shakes with a very wide swing. The closer the rope is to the nail, the smaller is the swing. All the way on top, where it is attached to the nail, there is no swing at all. The same is with our life. Sin shakes our lower levels with a frenzy, but the higher levels are not harmed at all. In fact, although the righteous fall, it is only to rise up again. And better still, the higher the spiritual level of the righteous, the more they want everyone to be uplifted. For Moses prayed, "If You forgive them, good, and if not, erase me from the book that You have written" (Exodus 32:32). If the Jewish people could not be uplifted, then Moses did not want to be uplifted either.

The wicked behave in the opposite manner. Even if they are high up, it is only to fall again. As it is written, "... though the wicked grow like grass and every evildoer prospers, they will be destroyed forever.... I lift my head high, like a wild ox tossing its horn..." (Psalms 92:7–9). Although the wicked seem high, do not be dismayed for they are surely falling spiritually. But you, in contrast, who opens your heart with generosity, lift your head high. Because God is lifting you up to the place where all is whole and spiritually healthy.

"When the wicked gather, it is bad for them and bad for the world. When they disperse, it is good for them and good for the world. When the righteous gather, it is good for them and good for the world" (*Sanhedrin* 71a).

The wicked, just like the righteous, have a source for their energy. When they are focused and receive their evil energy directly, they are the most dangerous. We have seen this throughout history, and most recently with the Germans, *yimach shmam*. They used their "high" culture, good education, and training to accomplish their evil plans. They reached for their roots and connected with their energy. And thus they carried out the most heinous crime ever in recorded history.

Similarly, Haman the Amalekite was wicked. When he focused his energy, he was able to do the most harm. He gave the king 10,000 shekels to kill the Jews. This made him the chief peddler of the Jewish people and the top Amalekite. He became the arch-criminal of the world, and he gloated in his fame. That was his undoing. As it is written, "Amalek was the first of the nations; but in the end he shall perish forever" (Numbers 24:20). When they are "first," at their height, they fall apart. The opposite is also true. When the righteous are connected with their source of energy, they too are at their best. Their goodness overflows and is good for the whole world.

Accordingly, the righteous among the nations, the Jewish people, quickly give the shekels; they do their deeds of goodness before the wicked are able to do their evil deeds. The wicked give money to enslave, whereas we give to redeem and rescue.

THE TORAH READING OF *SHEKALIM* ON *SHABBOS*

Shabbos is the witness that God created the world. By not working on *Shabbos* we show concretely that we rely on God to provide for us. We show also that we are free men and are slaves to no one. The weekdays,

in contrast, do not bear witness that God is the creator. Because *we* work and try to accomplish everything through our efforts, as if we are the masters of our destiny. We leave God out. Therefore, *Shabbos* should be the focus for all our energies and deeds. And when we focus on *Shabbos*, then everything we do is Godly and spiritual.

We can learn the same lesson from the first words of the Torah reading: *Ki Sisa*, literally, "when you lift up," (when you take the sum); *es rosh bnei Yisrael*, means the heads of the Jewish people (the numbers). This means that every Jew should lift his head and his whole being toward God. His only desire should be to serve Him and be close to Him. And when he lifts his head, the rest of the body is sure to follow.

We observe that when some animals walk they keep their heads bowed and look only at the grass they are eating. In contrast, a human being should keep his head lifted high and look toward heaven. He should be drawn toward the source of life and negate his being in search of it. Similarly, in each thought, word, and deed, the very first part must be devoted to God. That first portion is the "head," and wherever the head is the rest of the body follows. So that when we think, our first thought should be of God, and then the rest of our thoughts are sure to follow. When we speak, our first words should be to God, and then the rest of our talking will follow in the same direction. When we do a deed, we should begin with a deed for God, and then the rest of our deeds will follow.

An engine pulls a long line of railroad cars. The conductor comes to a juncture and chooses which track he will take. Once he chooses the track for the locomotive, the other cars just follow. Similarly, wherever the head goes, the body is sure to follow.

The Jewish people give the half-shekel in generosity and with an open heart. It does not really matter who is actually giving the half-shekel because the giving adds up in the collective heart and desire of the Jewish people. Everyone who participates is uplifted, as it is written, "When you lift up the heads of the Jewish people...." When we *participate* with the Jewish people, we are uplifted. As Hillel said, "When I am for myself who am I?" (*Ethics of Our Fathers* 1:14) When I separate my deeds from those of *Klal Yisrael*, the congregation of Israel, who am I? How could I possibly accomplish anything? I must nullify my being and join together with the Jewish nation. When

I am not for myself and I join the Jewish people, then I really am somebody.

———————

The Jewish nation was chosen by God as a role model for the other nations of the world. Their lives set an example for the others. Other nations, some living in spiritual ignorance, can look to them and say, "We like what we see. We appreciate your lifestyle and would like to learn more about your Torah." When the people of God behaves as if they cannot exist without Him and they nullify themselves to Him, then the whole creation does the same.

The strength of each Jew and of the nation as a whole comes from totally nullifying one's self to God. Otherwise, a Jew has no spiritual strength at all. Hence, if a Jew thinks he can get along without God, he is mistaken and off the right path.

The ones who steer the Jewish people off the right path are the Amalekites, who constantly plan their physical and spiritual annihilation. They attack them to weaken their faith and oppress them for believing in the One. Their goal is to lead the Jews astray.

In contrast, the commandment that keeps us on the right path is the observance of the Sabbath. The Sabbath balances the arrogant thoughts that we accumulate during the six days of work. It is a day of introspection, complete rest, and renewal of spiritual values. It instructs and reminds us that God created the world. He is the only cause of events, and we are servants to no one but Him. While the weekdays keep us busy with many material tasks, the Sabbath returns us to God. We gather all our deeds and nullify them to the Creator of the world.

The commandment of the Sabbath is one of the Ten Commandments. Unfortunately, soon after receiving the Ten Commandments the Jewish people made an idol, the Golden Calf, and worshiped it. This was because their faith had been weakened by the attack of Amalek. They were not strong enough to reject the many gods and choose the One God. But then, as the holy nation that they are, they repented and were about to build the *Mishkan*, the holy Tabernacle. Again, God commanded them to observe the *Shabbos* day and keep it holy. They had to be reminded to nullify their deeds to the one true God, the creator of the universe.

———————

When the Jewish nation left Egypt they believed that God was all powerful and that there is nothing better than to serve Him. Then the Amalekites attacked.

They weakened their faith in the Creator and cooled their pride in being His servants. Fortunately, Moses was there and, lifting his hands in prayer, reminded them that God is all powerful and the only one who can save them.

Similarly, in each generation, the *tzaddikim*, the righteous ones, keep us away from evil and protect us from sin. But to fight an adversary such as the evil Amalek, even a *tzaddik* might shy away. Hence the Torah says, "The rich man shall not give more, nor the poor man give less than the half-shekel" (Exodus 30:15). The person who is richer in spirituality should not separate himself from the rest of Israel. Rather, he must nullify his being to them. Doing so will strengthen the others who are poorer in spirit, and then they too will not give less than their share. They too will have the strength to withstand Amalek.

———————

When the Jewish nation said at Mount Sinai, "We will do and we will listen," six hundred thousand angels came to tie two crowns on the head of each Jew. When they worshiped the Golden Calf, these crowns were removed. After they repented and observed the sanctity of the Sabbath, Moses returned the crowns to them, and he does so every *Shabbos* (*Shabbos* 88a).

When the Jewish people worshiped the Golden Calf, they broke their promise "to do." Their actions were no longer pure. But they were able to heal their actions by observing the Sabbath. Because the Sabbath is observed mainly by not doing, it is a day of complete absence of work, a day of rest. Although it is desecrated by working, it remains spiritually intact. It really has no material content that can be defiled by bad actions. Hence, the Sabbath was never defiled by the actions of idol worship and is therefore a place of healing for anyone who wants to correct his actions. As our sages have taught, "Whoever observes the Sabbath, even if he worshiped idols as the generation of Enosh, still, he is forgiven" (*Shabbos* 118b).

Therefore, in the spiritual realm, the Holy Temple and the sacrifices still exist on the day of Sabbath. Their spiritual essence was not harmed by physical destruction. Accordingly, on the Sabbath, it is most appropriate to read about the half-shekel tax used in purchasing the sacrifices for the Temple service.

———————

When Moses asked the Jewish people if they would accept the Torah, they answered, "We will do and we will listen." It was very brave of them and a great risk to commit themselves. They had no idea what their new obligations would entail. They literally threw aside all selfish desires and nullified themselves to God's will.

A king once asked, "Whom can I send to an undisclosed country and carry out a secret mission?" Immediately the most devoted of his servants said, "I will go!" "Now I see that you are not only devoted but also brave," said the king. "You are the most fitting for this assignment!"

The rabbi of Parshis'che said that this is the meaning of the verse, "And these are the laws you should place before them . . ." A Jew should always place the laws of the Torah before himself, before any selfish desires. He should throw everything aside, as his ancestors did at Mount Sinai, and nullify himself to the will of God.

We nullify our desires to observe the Sabbath, and likewise, we set aside our selfishness and share generously by giving the half-shekel. We are then following in the tradition of our ancestors and their extraordinary devotion.

It is written, "When you will raise the head . . ." (Exodus 31:12); in Hebrew, "*Ki sisa es rosh. . . .*" If we raise up, we move up one level above the word *rosh*, which is spelled *reish, aleph, shin*. We get the following: one letter higher than the letter *reish* is the letter *shin*, one letter higher than the letter *aleph* is the letter *beis*, and one letter higher than the letter *shin* is the letter *saf*, which spells *shin-beis-saf*, Shabbos.

The spirit of the Sabbath is to unite with God. We should negate our thoughts and intentions, our "head," to the One above. And when all of *Klal Yisrael*, the congregation of Israel, do that and are of a similar mind, they are united as one and protected by God. But if their heads are filled with disparate intentions, they are then broken into pieces and in danger.

When the people have singularity of purpose, they are then at one with their spiritual nature, which is oneness and unity. But if they are separated and divided in their thought and actions, they are more like their physical nature. And being physical, the nature of the physical world dominates them, with its limitations and accidents.

A king was leading his troops into battle. When they arrived at the battleground, the king ordered them, "Men, stay close together and move as one!" The soldiers obeyed and followed close to the king. Suddenly, thousands of arrows flew in their direction. Most of the men stood their ground and in tight formation. But a number who were frightened scattered in all directions and were hit.

We need to lift our heads, above the physical realm, to unite ourselves with the One above and live with the spirit of the Sabbath.

Whenever the Jewish people are raised high, there is great jealousy among the nations of the world. They complain, "Why are the Jews more deserving than we?" And this question needs to be answered with truth and justice. Thus, if the Jews are not "deserving," then the nations will be right! Therefore, the Jewish people must demonstrate that they are deserving and quickly give the shekels to charity. This act helps raise them high and bring them close to the One.

A king called his servants and promoted one to a higher position. The others reacted with jealous grumbling. The servant sensed this and immediately said, "In honor of my new position I donate a chest of gold to the city's poor." The king said, "Now no one can deny that you are deserving of your new position!"

It is written, "And Moses took half of the blood, and put it in basins . . ." (Exodus 24:6).

The Torah teaches us that the Jewish people are "children" of God, and the "chosen" people. This does not refer to physical superiority. On the contrary, the more the Jewish people are uplifted and prosper, the more they share with and benefit others. That is one of the signs of a genuine Jew—that he generously shares his blessings with others. This is symbolized by the basins. Both are vessels for the blessings of God. We are ready to receive, not only for ourselves but also to give and share with others.

The Sanhedrin, the Jewish Supreme Court, possessed the same virtue and therefore sat in a semicircle when it judged matters of law; it sat in the shape of a vessel ready to receive blessing. And when members of the Sanhedrin received blessing and knowledge, it was not for themselves. They shared it with the rest of Israel and the world. As it is written, "From Zion shall go forth the Law and the word of God from Jerusalem" (Isaiah 2:3).

Let us closely examine our blessings received from God and, with true generosity, immediately share them with others.

SHEKALIM FOR THE TABERNACLE OF WITNESS

After the Jewish people repented from their brief idol worhsip of the Golden Calf, they built the *Mishkan*. Their contribution of coins helped buy the sacrifices used there for atonement. It was called a witness because it is a witness that although they sinned, God still dwells among them.

It is written, "God has made everything for His purpose . . ." (Proverbs 16:4). Further, it is written, "You are my witnesses, says God . . ." (Isaiah 43:10).

The entire creation is witness to God's creation of the world. There are three realms, however, and in each, a witnessing takes place. The three realms are soul, time, and space. The holiness residing in the soul of the Jewish people is a witness in the soul of the world. The holiness residing in the day of *Shabbos* is a witness in the realm of time. And the holiness residing in the Holy Temple is witness in the realm of space. Both the Sabbath and the Holy Temple are brought into the world by the Jewish people. Each of them, therefore, reflects on the other. The Sabbath bears witness that the Jewish people are ready to be witnesses. After all, they are the ones who observe the Sabbath and the ones who with love and devo-tion built the Holy Temple. In sum, it is the love, generosity, and devotion of the Jewish people that cause the entire universe to bear witness that God created the world.

This devotion is renewed each year. Similarly, during each holiday a new batch of coins is taken from the treasury to buy sacrifices. But the primary occasion for separating the shekels occurred in the month of *Nissan*, which is the head of the months. Since the Jewish people were chosen to be a nation of God in the month of *Nissan*, their desire to say witness is also renewed.

A king had an advisor whose devotion was unparalleled. Each opportunity he had, he would praise the king publicly and encourage allegiance to him. The king did not hide his admiration and fondness for him and rewarded him often. Once a year the king promoted his servants. The trustworthy advisor was also promoted. But, unlike the others, he used the occasion to renew his devotion to the king.

We too, when we receive from God, renew our devotion to Him, by being witnesses for His kingdom.

30

The Torah Reading of Zachor

"REMEMBER WHAT AMALEK DID"

 n the Sabbath preceding Purim, two Torah scrolls are removed from the Holy Ark during the synagogue service. In the first, the portion of the week is read. In the second, we read from Deuteronomy 25:17–19, as follows:

> Remember what Amalek did to you on your way out of Egypt. When they encountered you on the way and you were tired and exhausted, they cut off those lagging to your rear, and they did not fear God.
>
> Therefore, when God gives you peace from all your enemies around you in the land that God your Lord is giving you to occupy as a heritage, you must obliterate the memory of Amalek from under the heavens. You must not forget.

Our sages have taught in the Talmud, "One ought always to cause his *yetzer tov*, his desire to do good, to be in anger over his *yetzer hara*, his desire to do evil" (*Berakhos* 5a).

A prince was very fond of his father. When visitors came, he stood next to his father and received them. Of course, not every visitor was loyal to the king, nor did each show adequate respect. The prince became upset with those who showed little respect for the king. He could not understand how anyone could think badly of such a beloved person. One day the prince rebelled and ran away from the palace. He needed a place to stay, and went immediately to a subject who disliked the king. After a short stay he was comfortable. One night he dreamed that he was in his father's garden talking to him. His father took his hand and talked with him for a long time. He woke up with his heart pounding. "My father loves me so much," he thought. "How can I be here with his enemy?" It made him sick to think of it, and he quickly escaped and ran back to the palace.

When we become estranged from God and forget how much He loves us, then we become "comfortable" with His enemies. But as soon as our heart wakes up with renewed generosity, when our desire to do good becomes active by giving the shekels to the Temple, we then have contempt for God's enemies.

Therefore, when we cause the *yetzer tov* to be angry at the enemies of God, then we are about to be rid of all our enemies.

The enemies of God are obstacles to the redemption of the Jewish people. And certainly they will not be removed if the Jewish people are on good terms with them. This seems especially true in our time when there seems to be no end to our enemies. How, then, will their end come about?

Amalek is the opposite of respect for God's Name, and he must be removed. There are two ways that this can happen. One is by nullifying our own desires and thinking only of God's will. The other way is to awaken the love of God in our heart so that then we would suddenly shudder with contempt for those who hate God and His people and would be ready to remove Amalek.

God could remove Amalek easily, so that he would be easily destroyed. And if not He directly, then other nations could easily get rid of Amalek indirectly. But God wants the Jewish people to do it so that they can be a witness to His name and bring honor to Him. Truthfully, *only* the Jewish people can get rid of Amalek, because Amalek is in everything. Every deed, word, and thought contains some of Amalek's evil in it—his rebellion against God, his denial of His honor. Therefore, only the Jewish people, who are the children of God and are close to Him, have the true determination to rid the world of Amalek. They will look for him in every crevice and hunt for him until there is no trace of him left in the world.

——————

There are two types of memory. One is the "holy" memory of remembering God, of being aware of His presence without interruption. And there is the remembering of Amalek, the "unholy" memory of his evil deeds. Likewise, we can experience the world in two distinct ways. Either we experience the outside material portion or the inside spiritual portion. If we relate only to the material part of the world, then we relate to a limited part and in a limited way, by wanting to use, dominate, and control. We then forget the Master of the world and think instead that we are the masters.

Thus, by relating only to the superficial, material aspect of things we are in danger of forgetting God. And if we do, then we are getting closer to Amalek, and he may overpower us. The forgetfulness that Amalek causes is on the outside shell of everything. It is on the surface of thought, of speech, and of action. It is on the surface of everything that exists in the universe. Then how do we combat it? Only by remembering that beneath the shell there is a spiritual world, God, who causes everything to exist. When we remember that, then Amalek is about to be defeated.

When you open your heart by giving the shekels, you start to remember. And soon the memory that is dear to every Jewish heart is awakened in you, and it says, "Do not be misled by appearances. Remember God your Creator. He is the cause of all things and events in the world."

——————

The Jewish people say, "There is one God, and one nation was chosen to tell it to the world." The nations of the world say, "There are many gods, and any nation may be superior to any other." And the one who says this most forcefully, with anger, wrath, indignation, vengeance, and war, is Amalek. Amalek laughs at our belief in One God. We saw this during the Second World War, when the Germans spat in our faces as they said, "Where is your God now, Jew?" in one breath denying both God and His nation. Hence, as long as Amalek is in the world, he is an obstacle to declaring that God is the one and only. And when we say the verse, "Hear O Israel, God our Lord, God is One," we must first overcome the obstacle of Amalek.

A prince loved his father more than anything in the world. When visitors would come to see the king, the prince would welcome them with heroic tales about his father. Within the palace walls there was a magnificent garden, and, strangely, the gardener was very jealous and resentful of the king. The gardener missed no opportunity to secretly influence the prince. He made veiled but negative comments and planted seeds of doubt in the boy's mind.

One day, as the prince was about to praise his father to some nobles, the questions of the gardener echoed in his mind. He suddenly realized the evil of that man and became very angry. He said, "I wish I could get rid of that gardener right now, but I can't." Instead, and to the surprise of his guests, he prostrated himself to the ground and called out, "Long live his majesty the king, my father, in honor and glory!" Suddenly all the doubting thoughts left him, and he resumed greeting the guests as always.

We may not be able to get rid of Amalek right now, but we can still remove him as an obstacle to our special mission by totally nullifying our being before our Creator. If we affirm that we are as nothing before God's greatness, that we are in service for God's sake, then Amalek ceases to be an obstacle.

Let us open our hearts and feel the majesty of our Creator. Then we are no longer dominated by the forces of evil and are able to do what we ought.

——————

Our sages have taught, "When the Jewish people read the portion dealing with the giving of the shekels, then God lifts up their heads. Just as it is written in their war against Amalek, 'And it was when Moses lifted his hand that Israel prevailed, and when he let his hand down, Amalek prevailed'" (*Midrash, Tanchumah, Exodus* 17).

When the heads and hearts of the Jewish people are in the right place and are raised in prayer, they can annihilate the evil Amalek. This refers to the faith that each Jew carries in his *head* and the yearning and hope that he has in his *heart*. When these are lifted up and dedicated to God, we can be confident that Amalek will soon be cleared from the earth.

These were the two strengths that the Jewish people used in the days of Esther to vanquish Haman the Amelekite. Mordechai was a model of true faith in God when he refused to bow down to Haman, and Esther showed the people the power of prayer by fasting and praying for three days and nights.

It is written, "Therefore it shall be, when God your Lord has given you rest from all your enemies on every side, in the land which God your Lord gives you for an inheritance, you should blot out the memory of Amalek from under the heaven: you should not forget it" (Deuteronomy 25:19).

There is much work to be done before we can hope to blot out Amalek. We can compare this to a prince who was put in charge of the garden within the palace walls. He took a stroll to see its condition. He noticed that a wild vine was thriving and strangling many of the trees. The brook that fed water to the plants was about to dry out. And to his great dismay, a fungus was clinging to some of the leaves and was about to spread and destroy all the trees. The prince decided that first he would remove the killer vine. He worked hard hacking and cutting until all of it was cut away. He then spent time removing the obstacles from the brook and renewing its flow of water. Once completed, he was ready to deal with the most dangerous problem of them all: the fungus.

Before we deal with the worst evil, Amalek, we must first remove other obstacles that prevent us from serving God. One is the outer covering that surrounds each thing in the world. It makes it hard for us to have contact with the spirit inherent in material things. The other obstacle is the *yetzer hara*, the urge to do evil. If we prevail over those two, then we are ready to deal with the most difficult obstacle of them all, Amalek.

Our life has some good and some evil. We are constantly struggling to rid our life of evil. We are commanded to choose the good life, obey the commandments, and fear and love God. Then God helps us and gives us the strength to overcome the evil. He helps us by giving us the three major holidays of the year: Passover, Shavuos, and Sukkos. Each one of them helps us get rid of another degree of evil and uncleanliness. So that by the year's end, the month of *Adar*, we could have most of the evil under control. We are then ready to tackle Amalek. Hence we read the portion dealing with Amalek during the month of *Adar*.

As we listen to the commandment to blot out Amalek, let us be thankful for the other small battles we have won against evil during the year. And then we pray, "Just as You have helped us with our small enemies, You should help us also with the ultimate enemy of the Jewish people."

The commandment to blot out Amalek is preceded by the commandment to appoint a king. Once the king is appointed, his first order of business is to deal with Amalek.

The appointment of a king refers to what is required of us in order to overpower Amalek. How would we behave in the presence of a king? What would we think when he asked us to do something? That should also be how we relate to God. What we need to do is ignore our selfish desires and focus on His commandments. When we are totally humbled to God, no obstacle can stop us from listening to Him. We are merely servants of our Master the King, and if He wants something we immediately do it. We do not stop to think if it is convenient or difficult, but we do it right away without hesitation.

Every Jew should fear God. We can compare this to those who come to the king's palace. The visitors look around and are astounded by its splendor and riches. They are astonished and awed by the abundance and grandeur. They realize that the king is powerful and can mete out punishment for those who do not conform to his will. When they leave, the splendor remains in the palace. The only thing left with them is the fear of the king's power. But the king's servants and advisors who remain with the splendor never cease to be awed by it.

Some are unfamiliar with the teachings of the Torah, and are not close to God. Yet, they fear God, remembering that their very lives are in His hand. Such thoughts only come occasionally and do not last very long. There are others, however, who are "in" the king's palace, who walk among the splendor and are awed by it. They are permanently engaged, anchored, and focused in the fear of God, regardless of what is happening around them. Although the world turns round and everything is changing, they remain steadfast in the fear of God. It is the permanent condition in their life compared to the other things that are only transient. As it is written, "And you should love God your Lord with all your heart . . . and these words . . . should be . . . *on your heart* . . . when you *sit* in your house and when you *walk* on the path" (Deuteronomy 6:4–10). This teaches us that even when you are on the move, when all is in flux and changing, your heart and mind should have a quiet, settled, permanent faith in awe of God.

After the Jewish people left Egypt, they were occupied with their journeys and travels. Their faith in God was not in its full strength. And therefore Amalek was able to have a partial victory. But when the Jewish nation is in her full strength and has the power of faith, then Amalek's power is useless against her.

It is written, "And it happened, when Moses held up his hand that the Israelites prevailed: and when he let down his hand, Amalek prevailed" (Exodus 17:11). Was it because of the hands of Moses that Israel won or lost the war? But the reason is that when Moses lifted his hands, the people looked toward heaven and focused their minds on God, and then they prevailed. In contrast, when they no longer thought of God, then they were defeated (*Mishnah, Rosh Hashanah* 29a).

The Jewish people exist in two realms. On the one hand they are God's chosen people with a special place in the spiritual realm. On the other hand they are human beings who live in the physical world and subject themselves to its laws. Therefore, when their heart is in the spiritual realm, Amalek has no power over them. But if their heart and mind are focused on the material world, then Amalek can overpower them, if only on a material level. He cannot touch the spiritual levels of the Jewish people.

Amalek and the Jewish people are exact opposites; they are like two sides of a scale. When one side of the scale rises then the other descends, and when one descends the other rises. That means that the way the Jewish people escape from the clutches of Amalek is to rise upward toward God. Therefore, when the hearts of the Jewish people warm up to God by giving the shekels, they rise upward to the spiritual realm and out of the reach of Amalek.

We must always "remember and never forget" what Amalek did to the Jewish people. We must despise him at the core of our being. And if you ask, why we should despise him, it is because of our love of God, the Jewish people, and the Torah; that is why we loathe him. Because he is the antithesis of all that is good and pure in the world. Hence, to the extent that we love the good, in that measure we despise the evil.

The prophet Samuel told the first king of Israel, Saul, to annihilate the Amalekites. Saul made an error. He allowed his soldiers to keep the fat sheep and some of the enemy alive. Obviously, Saul's soldiers did not have a great love of God or of Israel and therefore did not despise Amalek with vigor. And Saul too was insecure about his own attitude. He was worried that he did not despise Amalek enough. And even if he did, how would he convince his soldiers that his attitude was the right one? Therefore, Samuel rebuked him, "Even if you are small in your eyes, still, you are the head of the tribes of Israel" (1 Samuel 15:17). He should have assumed his role as leader and been the model for them. Still, Saul himself loved the Jewish people dearly and despised their enemies.

The same is true in our case. When our hearts open with the generosity of giving the shekels, it fills with love toward our people. And at the same time a passion is awakened against those who attack and oppose the Jewish people; namely, Amalek.

It is written, "With the merciful You will show Yourself as merciful; with an upright man You will show yourself as upright. With the pure You will show Yourself as pure; with the perverse You will show Yourself as perverse" (Psalms 18:26–27).

The "merciful" refers to Abraham whose entire life was dedicated to loving-kindness. The "upright" refers to Isaac who was complete in his uprightness. And finally, the "perverse" refers to Esau, whose perverse conduct dominated his life and the life of his descendants, and to Amalek, the arch-enemy of the Jewish people.

We can also say that by being merciful and upright we can be worthy of ridding the world of the perverse Amalek. And this is the reason for the order of the Torah readings before the month of *Nissan*. We start with the reading about the shekels, before the month of *Adar*. This *parshas* refers to the loving-kindness of Abraham. When we give the shekels, the kindness in our hearts is awakened. Then we remember God's kindness with us and vow to serve Him with new zeal. We are even ready to sacrifice our life for Him, like Abraham who was prepared to sacrifice his son Isaac on the altar. Although he did not actually do it, the sacrifice was considered done on a spiritual level. As a result *spiritual* ashes lay in a heap on the altar. These ashes are a constant reminder that the Jewish nation is prepared to give up everything for God's sake. That is the essence of the portion of *Zachor*, "*remember* what Amalek did."

The following reading is the portion about the Red Cow, which is *burned* and its ashes sprinkled on those who need to be purified. This is similar to Jacob, about whom it is written, "And the house of Jacob shall be a *fire*, and the house of Esau shall be as straw" (Obadiah 1:18). The fire of Jacob burns away all chaff.

We too, if we awaken the loving-kindness in our hearts, we then fill with memories of our people. We remember our primary goal to spread God's honor throughout the world, and we pray for the cleansing of the world of all evil.

THE POWER OF AMALEK

Amalek is called "first among the nation" (Numbers 24:20). Amalek was the grandson of Jacob's brother, Esau, who lived by the sword. The aggressive and murderous tribe became the arch-enemy of the Jewish people.

In general, our activities can be divided into two categories. One category contains reflexive and automatic actions such as the heartbeat or breathing. These actions are done without thinking and immediately, without a time lapse. They are vital and essential to our life. The second category contains cerebral actions that we think about before we do. These are done with some hesitation, the time it takes for us to decide whether to do them or not. The hesitation is harmless, because those actions are not critical for our survival.

To do something without hesitation is a sign that it is essential for our very life. To hesitate, think, and wait is a sign that it is not as essential. This is why the Jewish people answered *without hesitation* at Mount Sinai, "We will do and we will listen." They were aware that the Torah, the guidance of God, was essential to their life. They reacted reflexively and immediately.

When the Jewish people left Egypt, they were charged with a great energy and eagerness to follow God wherever He would lead them. Suddenly Amalek attacked. He attempted to take this quality of enthusiasm and spontaneity from them. He wanted to rob them of their hunger for the Torah. He wanted them to hesitate, to think, and procrastinate. Amalek nearly succeeded. Fortunately, the Jewish people humbled themselves and reaffirmed their total dependence on God. They were then able to defeat Amalek.

When we are totally humbled and feel our dependence, we are filled with joy. And how do we become humbled? When we think how undeserving we are and how far we are from God, our Creator. This is symbolized by the word *zar*, "stranger," or, one who is far removed. This word can also be read as *zer*, "a crown," one who is deserving of honor. Therefore, if we think of ourselves as strangers, *zar*, to God, because we are undeserving, then we are deserving of the *zer*, a crown of honor around our head.

The word *zar*, when read backward is *raz*, "secret." The word *raz* also appears in the verse "*Or zaruah la'tzaddik*—light is sown for the righteous" (Psalms 97:11). The last letter of the first word and the first letter of the second word spell *raz*, "secret." This tells us that if we conduct our life secretly, if we do our good deeds secretly and with great humility, then God sows light for us, and our reward is great. Similarly, it is written, "O how great is Your goodness that You have hidden for them that fear You . . ." (Psalms 31:20). If our deeds are hidden, if we do not parade around with them, then God too hides a great reward for us.

Humility is best expressed when we do our good deeds promptly and without hesitation, when we do not make major public preparations to slowly and flamboyantly do our good deeds. And it was this wonderful quality in us that Amalek wanted to destroy. And were it not for God's mercy, the enemy may have succeeded. Still, they did succeed partially and cooled our enthusiasm. Therefore, we must always be reminded that it was Amalek who weakened us and we need to be strong and serve God with true humility again.

It is written, "God has called your name, a green olive tree, fair, and of goodly fruit" (Jeremiah 16:16).

Olives were used in the service of the Holy Temple. The first and purest drop was used for the Menorah. The Menorah was lit by applying a flame and waiting till the "flame rises on its own" (*Numbers Rabbah* 16:22). The rest of the oil, with some sediment remaining in it, was used for offerings on the altar. This shows that if we lift up the pure drop of oil and allow it to shine forth, then we will find pure oil even within the mixture.

The first drop of oil symbolizes the kernel of divine spirit that is in each thing. This is a gift from God. We must acknowledge this gift and return it to Him. And if we do, then we will find the divine kernel in everything, even in places where it is obscure and full of sediment.

The physical oil in the Menorah is drawn upward by the divine oil, the spiritual essence of it. Similarly, it is the yearning of the Jewish people to be close to God that helps them find the Divine kernels in the world. And it is this yearning that Amalek wants to deaden in us. He wants us to forget; therefore we must always remember.

In our bedtime prayers we recite, "Tremble and sin not. Reflect in your hearts while on your beds, and be utterly silent. Selah." (*Prayer Book*, bedtime prayers)

If we tremble and are shaken up from the memory of what Amalek did to us, then we will not sin. But if we forget, and sin, then the wrath of God will deal with Amalek anyway, for his evil deeds.

There is a parable about a prince who was befriended by his wicked cousin. The prince began to imitate his cousin's behavior. The king was told of this and immediately banished the wicked cousin from the palace. The prince was embarrassed about his mistakes and promised to behave. Whenever he remembered what his cousin caused him to do, he was filled with indignation and promised himself to be good. But on occasion when he forgot the incident, he slipped into mischief again.

Similarly, we must always remember that Amalek caused us great harm by cooling off our faith in God and our yearning for the truth. And when we remember, we can then be sure that we will not sin, but walk on the path of righteousness.

It is written, ". . . you should erase (*timcheh*) the memory of Amalek . . ." (Deuteronomy 25:17). The word *timcheh* has two meanings: you *should* erase, and you *will* erase. Not only are you obligated to get rid of Amalek but it is also a promise that you will be able to get rid of him.

It is written, "For he said, 'God has lifted His hand to His throne and sworn that God will have war with Amalek from generation to generation'" (Exodus 17:16).

Why is there an endless war with Amalek? Because Amalek is the antithesis of the Jewish people. Just as the Jewish people risk their lives for holiness and closeness with God, the people of Amalek risk their lives for sinfulness. And because they are ready to lose everything for evil, their punishment fits the crime. In the end they will lose everything. And when the end of the exile comes, with the advent of the *Mashiach*, Amalek will have no part in the redemption.

During the exile, the Jewish people are hampered in their special mission to teach that God is the Master of the universe. Therefore, God's Name is neither whole nor revealed now, but is concealed. When the *Mashiach* comes, God's Name will be one and whole again. All the earth's inhabitants will know that God is the origin of the universe. They will plainly see that God is the Master, and there is no place empty of his presence. Everyone, that is, except Amalek. That will be his due punishment, because he fought against faith in God.

Therefore, God will not allow Amalek to live in the days when "God is One." So He waits until Amalek has been erased totally before He will reveal the unity of His name.

We can compare this to a popular general who became rebellious and ran away from the palace. He joined a band of thieves and soon became their leader. He and his band attacked the messengers of the king when they traveled through the province. They especially enjoyed annoying the prince and hindering him in performing his work for his father.

The general's treachery was a bad influence on the citizens of the kingdom. They became especially disillusioned when they heard about his attacks on the prince. Finally the king had enough! He gathered an army, surprised the band of rebels, and with little effort had them dragged off to the dungeon. When the people heard of the king's success they all rejoiced and were inspired. "Now that we are rid of the trouble makers, we can celebrate the unity of my kingdom," the king announced. "And the punishment of the rebels will be their absence from the celebrations."

The Jewish people have a special mission in the world. It started as far back as Abraham, who broke with the tradition of his culture and his father to proclaim the belief in one God. Ever since then, Abraham's defendants, the Jewish people, have been teaching the same truth. And therefore, when the time will come, speedily in our days, for the honor of God to be fully revealed in the world, the Jewish people will have a great share in it. They will have a great understanding of God and His kingdom. And even other nations who shared in this belief will share in the understanding. Thus the whole world will be filled with the knowledge of God. Everyone, that is, except Amalek. He will be cut off completely from sharing in this great knowledge. As it is written, "... Amalek was the first of the nations; but his latter end shall be that he shall perish forever" (Numbers 24:20).

As the earth turns toward the sun, morning comes. Little by little the eastern sky loses its deep blue darkness. The color lightens; the sky fills with spectacular hues and morning slowly takes hold. Darkness is banished, and it is day.

The same is true of the exile. It is dominated by Amalek and his ilk. But as the exile nears its end, the redemption comes closer and with it the end of Amalek. The more the honor of God is revealed, the more Amalek is erased. And whoever hopes for one is also hoping for the other.

Let us pray that the power of Amalek be broken soon in our days. This will release the great energy of all beings to understand the unity of God, and all will be redeemed.

The Jewish people left Egypt in the month of *Nissan*. It was during the Exodus that they became a nation of God. It was their birth month, and they were lifted to the highest spiritual levels. It was, in a word, their finest moment in history, so significant that it must always be remembered. As it is written, "... that you may remember the day that you came forth from the land of Egypt all the days of your life" (Deuteronomy 16:3).

The spiritual realm is always striving for balance. When the holy becomes strong, the unholy becomes weak. And because he is weakened he tries deliberately to hurt his opponent. This was true of the angel of Esau. When Jacob was at his greatest strength, the angel tried to weaken him by dislocating his thigh. The same is true of Amalek, Esau's grandson. When the Jewish people are at their peak, then Amalek attacks, trying to weaken the Jewish people.

The strength of the Jewish people is their voice in prayer and Torah study. Amalek tries to weaken their strong and determined voice by weakening their faith. Consequently, the Jewish people cannot rejoice. For surely, one whose voice is stilled cannot rejoice in full measure. But when the end of Amalek is imminent, with the coming of the *Mashiach* we will be filled with joy. As it is written, "... then our mouths shall fill with joy..." (Psalms 126:2). Because the power of our "voice" will be restored, Jacob will prevail and Esau will be vanquished.

Therefore, during the month before *Nissan*, in *Adar*, we already feel close to the point of our highest elevation, and we rejoice. And with the rejoicing

comes the strength to destroy Amalek and his descendant Haman.

It is written, "God has called your name, a green olive tree, fair, and of goodly fruit..." (Jeremiah 16:16). The Midrash comments, "The Jewish people are as olives; to get oil from them we lay heavy stones on them until the oil drips out. So too the Jewish people. God puts them through heavy exiles so that they give forth their best teachings and good deeds" (*Exodus Rabbah* 20).

And just as the olive, although it contains oil mixed with sediment, yet can give forth pure oil, so too the Jewish people. Out of every situation, no matter how murky a mixture it is of good and evil, the Jewish people are able to extract the good. And just as the oil of the olive can be mixed with any liquid, yet stays separated from it, so too the Jewish people. They can live in any culture and environment, yet maintain their distinct identity. And by maintaining their identity and being true to their special task, they are able to lift up the nations of the world.

When the Jewish nation left Egypt they were ready to bring salvation to the world. They were full of enthusiasm. Then Amalek attacked and made them weak and discouraged. And this weakness left them open to other spiritual mistakes. Not long afterward they worshiped an idol, the Golden Calf, complained about their food, refused to enter the promised land, and rebelled against their fatherly leader Moses.

Therefore, as powerful as Amalek is, so too will his downfall be complete and total. And then the Jewish people will give forth their best "oil." And all the nations will realize the great benefit they had from the Jewish people. They will be uplifted and redeemed.

It is written, "So Joshua did as Moses had said to him, and fought with Amalek: and Moses, Aaron, and Hur went up to the top of the hill. And it came to pass, when Moses held up his hand, that Israel prevailed: and when he let down his hand, Amalek prevailed. But Moses' hands were heavy; and they took a stone, and put it under him, and he sat on it; and Aaron and Hur held his hands up, the one on the one side, and the other on the other side; and his hands were steady until the going down of the sun" (Exodus 17:10–12).

Each one of us has a soul that is spiritually close to God. It is a kernel of spiritual essence. We also have a body that has a material nature. Thus we are connected to both the physical and the spiritual world. We are able to be close to God, yet at the same time relate to people in the physical world. And when we are with people, we can draw them closer to God by means of our soul.

Similarly, on a much higher plane, this was true of Moses, about whom it is written, ". . . Moses, the man of God . . ." (Deuteronomy 33:1). He was half-man, and half-Godly; he was able to relate to God in the realm of the spirit and to men as a man.

The Jewish nation, too, is close to God on the spiritual level, yet can easily relate to the other nations. And by relating to them, the Jewish nation elevates them from their purely materialistic striving and helps them live a life of spiritual value.

Accordingly, Moses lowered his hands; he used his lower level, "the man," and tried to lift up Amalek spiritually, but was unable to do so. He then resumed his spiritual level and lifted up his hands in prayer.

Amalek refused to be uplifted and, without a share in the spiritual world, is consequently punished.

It is written, "So Joshua did as Moses had said to him, and fought with Amalek: and Moshe, Aaron, and Hur went up to the top of the hill. And it came to pass, when Moses held up his hand, that Israel prevailed: and when he let down his hand, Amalek prevailed" (Exodus 17:10–12).

"But could the hands of Moses wage a battle or lose a battle? This is rather to teach you that whenever Israel looked on high and subjugated their hearts to their Father in Heaven, they prevailed, but if not, *they fell*" (*Mishnah, Rosh Hashanah* 3:8).

There are two problems with this mishnah. First, why can't the hands of Moses wage war? Weren't the hands of Moses the ones that performed all the miracles in Egypt? Why is war so much more difficult? Second, why does it say "they fell"? In the Torah verse quoted above it says, "Amalek prevailed," but it does not mention that Israel fell.

The answer is that the prayers of Moses depended on the behavior of the Jewish people. If their faith was strong then the prayers had a strong effect and the Jewish people won. But if their faith weakened, then Moses could not even lift his hands in prayer. "They"—his hands—literally fell down, and he was totally helpless.

If we want our spiritual leaders to pray for us we have to be strong in our own faith. We will then have the strength to erase Amalek and never need to remember him again.

In the spiritual realm there is a balance between good and evil, between the spiritual and the physical, be-

tween the holy and the profane. Human beings are at the center. They move from one extreme, far from God, to the other extreme, being close to Him. And thus there is a constant back-and-forth movement between the spiritual and the physical world. As it is written, "And the living creatures ran and returned as the appearance of a flash of lightning" (Ezekiel 1:14).

We can compare this to someone who spent many hours in the freezing cold. He then entered a warm house and sat near the roaring fireplace, not realizing how hot it was until he thawed out. Then slowly he began to feel the warmth, until he became too warm. He moved bit by bit away from the fire and then a bit more. Later, he felt cooler and returned to be near the fire again (Baal Shem Tov *Al Hatorah*).

Some nations are materialistic, whereas others are outright evil. Yet, they move a little toward spirituality. Some small part of them is good and redeemable. And they will be uplifted when the *Mashiach* comes. But Amalek is the furthest extreme of evil and profanity. He wants no share in the good nor of anything spiritual. Therefore in the end, even as others move toward the warm fire, he will be left out in the cold. And because he has totally alienated himself from God, he will therefore perish and be totally forgotten.

It is written, "Then came Amalek and fought with Israel in *Rephidim*" (Exodus 17:8).

The word *Rephidim* also means *rafa*, "weak": their good deeds became weak there, and therefore Amalek fought at that place. This is like a prince who lusted for his father's riches. One dark night the prince dug through the wall of the treasure house and stole a large amount of gold. As he was making his getaway, the guard dog pounced on him and mauled him severely. The boy started to cry and scream for help. The palace guards quickly pulled him to safety and treated his wounds. The king was awakened and came to see his son. "How did this happen that you were attacked by our trained dog?" the king asked. The prince cried as he admitted his evil deed. "Let that be a lesson to you, my son. Whenever you remember the pain of the dog's bites, also remember that you had wronged your father" (*Exodus Rabbah* 17).

Amalek is the tribe who serves as a "whip" when the Jewish people show weakness. If the Jews would obey God and live according to the precepts of the Torah, there would be no need for Amalek. Therefore, God promised that the day will come when he will be erased from the earth.

If we want to see Amalek erased, we must resolve to be better than we are now. But aren't we good enough already? No, that couldn't be true. Because if we were good enough, then why would Amalek still be in the world? Hence, we must improve and follow God's Torah, cleanse our hearts of all idol worship, and exercise our faith. Then we will finally see the end of Amalek, speedily in our days.

Isaac had two sons, Jacob and Esau. To each he gave an inheritance according to his nature. To Jacob he gave the "voice," as it is written, "the voice is the voice of Jacob," and to Esau he gave the hands, as it is written, "the hands are the hands of Esau" (Genesis 27:22). Jacob's inheritance is faithful prayer and scholarly study of the Torah. Esau's inheritance is the sword, war, and the ability to amass wealth by might. When the descendants of Jacob are in trouble they revert to their inheritance. They quickly drop everything else and pray to God, as it is written, ". . . the children of Israel lifted their eyes, and, behold, the Egyptians marched after them; and they were afraid: and the children of Israel *cried out* unto God" (Exodus 14:10). But when the descendants of Esau are approached, they respond with their inheritance. As it is written, "And Edom said unto him, you should not pass by me, lest I come out against you *with the sword*" (Numbers 20:18).

Although their inheritance is the opposite, they are both equally proud of it. Esau puts his whole life into the power of the sword and is confident that he will win his wars. "There is no successful war that does not have some of the descendants of Esau" (*Gittin* 57b). And when the Jewish people put their whole life into their inheritance and have no doubt about God's help, then they are saved from Esau's sword. If they totally nullify their strength and rely only on divine salvation, they are helped immediately.

We too, in our lives, should depend solely on the power and help of God. We should not take credit for our success as a sign of *our* strength. Rather, we should always say, "Whatever we accomplished, we could not have done it without the help of God." And if we live our life as the true inheritors of Jacob, then Amalek's sword will be broken and made harmless.

Amalek is opposed to the Torah and to faith in God. And as long as he is in the world, the name of God cannot be complete.

The name of God is composed of two parts: *yud* and *heh*, and *vov* and *heh*. And it is written, "And God

said further, 'You must tell the Israelites this, that the God of their forefathers, the God of Abraham, the God of Isaac, the God of Jacob, who has sent you to them. This is my name (*shemi*) for ever; this is my title (*zichri*) in every generation'" (Exodus 3:15). If we take the first part of God's name, *yud heh*, and add *shemi*, it has the numerical equivalent of 365: the number of days of the year, the amount of sinews in our body, and the number of forbidden commandments. And if we take the second part of God's name, *vov heh*, and add *zichri*, it has the numerical equivalent of 248, equal to the number of limbs of the body and the number of positive commandments. Therefore, the complete name of God contains all the commandments of the Torah. And as long as Amalek, who is opposed to the Torah, is in the world, God's name cannot be complete.

By observing the *mitzvos* of the Torah, we can help banish Amalek. We can help break his power and bring wholeness to our own being, completeness to the name of God, and peace to the world.

Isaac blessed his son Esau and said, ". . . and by your sword you shall live . . ." (Genesis 27:40).

The sword is the tool of Esau for domination and wealth. He idolizes it. Yet, *he* rules over his idol, as do all the wicked, who use their gods as tools for their selfish interests.

In contrast, the Jewish people allow God to stand over them. They subjugate themselves to His will. And even if they use a sword to protect themselves from enemies, it is God's sword that they use. As it is written, ". . . the Blessed One is your glorious sword . . ." (Deuteronomy 33:19). They know that, although they hold a sword, it is being held also by God. He is the one who actually protects them. They therefore consider themselves helpless without the help of God. They constantly pray that they be worthy of His help. As it is written, "The lofty praises of God are in their throats, and a double-edged sword is in their hand—to execute vengeance among the nations, rebuke among their governments" (Psalms 149:5). They pray that, when they lift their swords against their enemies, one edge should belong to them and the other to their Master. Even in the final battle with the chief villain, Amalek, they want God's strength to be there with them. As it is written, "God will have war with Amalek from generation to generation" (Exodus 17:16).

Let us pray that God holds our hand and makes war against Amalek. We do not have the strength to overpower him, nor to defeat him. But with the help of God we will.

Just as the soul is a light to the body, the Jewish people were created to be a light for the world. The darkness is the evil of Amalek, and to get rid of him you must prepare an inner light. As it is written, "And Moses said to Joshua, Choose us men and go out and fight with Amalek: tomorrow . . ." (Exodus 17:9). You must prepare an inner light today in order to fight Amalek tomorrow and to light up the darkness.

Similarly, the Sabbath is the light of the six work days. During the workdays the light of creation is hidden; it is concealed in nature. Come the Sabbath and you see the light clearly and declare that God created the world. But it is not enough that the Sabbath is spiritual. You must also bring the light of the Sabbath into the darkness of the weekdays. And when you are prepared to receive the holiness of the Sabbath in its full strength, the evil Amalek has no place and disappears entirely.

Amalek waits for an opportunity when we are weak and then attacks. And it was for this reason that Amalek could not tolerate the Jewish people at the Exodus. Egypt was devastated with the Ten Plagues; the Sea of Reeds split for the Israelites. Clouds protected them, and heavenly bread and water fed them. They had such marvelous strength and were united so completely, and miracles surrounded them.

We can compare this to a bath of boiling water. Not even the bravest of men attempted to bathe in it. Then someone brazen ran and jumped into the hot bath. When the others saw this, although they were still hesitant, they were no longer scared to jump in themselves (*Exodus Rabbah* 17). Amalek cooled the Jewish people from their enthusiasm; he weakened them, so that he could attack them again later.

Amalek can only attack us when we are separated and apart. As it is written, "Remember what Amalek did to you on the way as *you* [plural] left Egypt" (Deuteronomy 25:17). Because you were plural, were not united, therefore Amalek was able to attack you. But if we are united and shine as one light, then we can erase him, as it is written, "*You* [singular] shall erase the memory of Amalek." When we are as one, then we can break his power.

It is written, ". . . you shall erase the memory of Amalek . . ." (Deuteronomy 25:19). You shall make the memory of Amalek dust of the earth. And if you do not, you will be returned to Egypt to make bricks from the dust of the earth. And just as Amalek waited for you as you left Egypt and attacked you at a weak moment, you too will wait for the proper time to rid the world of all evil.

It is written, "Go and cry in the ears of Jerusalem, saying, Thus said God; I remember for you the kindness of your youth, the love of your bridal days, when you followed me into the wilderness, through a land unsown" (Jeremiah 2:2).

The Israelites left Egypt and entered an unfertile land; God had not yet given them the Torah. They did not have the merit of the Torah to protect them. What then was the great merit that protected them? It was their complete devotion to God and to following Him into the desert. They knew not where their next drink of water would come from nor how they would fight off warring tribes. This made Amalek's attack even worse. The attack cooled their devotion and planted seeds of doubt into their minds.

The day will come when we will attempt to get rid of Amalek. Then all the beautiful memories of our devotion to God will again come to our aid, and we will erase Amalek completely from the face of the earth.

It is written, "Man and beast will be helped by God" (Psalms 36:7). This passage refers to people who are intelligent like humans but make themselves like animals (*Chullin* 5b).

The Jewish people are intelligent, yet they humble themselves completely as if they were animals. They act as if they lost their intelligence and are no smarter than animals. Just as animals, they follow their Master as He leads them into the desert. They do not think, plan, or question. And when they act that way, *then* they are considered human. Because it takes a human being to understand fully that God is the Master, that we are but clay in the hands of the potter. As it is written, ". . . and you are my sheep, the sheep that I shepherd, you are human . . ." (Ezekiel 34:31). When you are like sheep, then you are truly human.

On the other hand, some people appear to be human, but they are not. They are less than human, are "dumb" as an animal, if they are not intelligent enough to know the Master of the world. This is Esau, who was born mature in body, as are some animals, but refused to know the Master of the world. His maturity was only skin deep. He was as a mature fruit, ripe and quick to rot.

This was also the mistake of the Amalekites. When they met the Jewish people at the Exodus, they mistook them for a bunch of dumb animals, and they attacked them. But their Master Whom they had followed into the desert protected the Jewish people. And they prayed and fought intelligently like the humans that they really were.

The same is true about each one of us. If we humble ourselves and consider ourselves animals, then we truly know our Master. And when the evil urge comes to attack us and tries to distract us from our good deeds, we ward him off. We are then worthy of the title of "human" being. And then we have the strength to overpower Amalek and tear the evil urge out by the roots.

It is written, "For the Lord your God goes around in your camp, to keep you safe and to hand over your enemies as you advance, and your camp must be kept holy for fear that he should see something indecent and go with you no further" (Deuteronomy 24:15).

Wherever a Jew goes, his job is to reveal the kingdom of God. The covenant for this job is symbolized in circumcision, which reveals that which is covered. The name of God is hidden in the world, and we reveal it. And where is the name hidden? In the words for man and woman, *ish* and *ishto*; *ish* has a silent *yud*, and *isho* has a silent *heh*. *Yud* and *heh* spell God's name. When a man and a woman marry and have a child, God's name is hidden until the circumcision. The ceremony consists of two acts: cutting off the foreskin, *milah*, and pulling the skin downward until the "crown" is revealed, *p'riah*. Both of these words have the name of God, *yud* and *heh*, silently hidden in them. Hence by performing the commandment of circumcision properly, we reveal the name of God.

As we prepare to fight Amalek, we want to remove the evil that covers, that does not allow God's name to be revealed in the world. And when we remove him, God's name will be revealed.

Amalek against the Covenant

God chose the Jewish people with a covenant, as it is written, "Now if you obey Me and keep my covenant, you shall be My special treasure among all the nations, even though all the world is mine" (Exodus 19:3–5).

". . . You are my witnesses . . ." (Isaiah 43:10).

The Jewish people are the witnesses that God cre-

ated the world. By their actions, their very being, they bear this important witness.

In the book of the Zohar, Rabbi Shimon bar Yochai states that the ten words with which God created the world correspond to the Ten Commandments, matched up one to one. Hence, the commandment, "Thou shalt not bear false witness," corresponds to the words, "Let us make man in our image." If a person's image is true to the nature that God intended for it, then it does not bear false witness. On the contrary, he bears true witness that God created the world.

Abraham was the first witness after the flood. He proclaimed to one and all that God is the creator. But what would happen when Abraham had children? Would his children be witnesses too? This question was answered by God's covenant with Abraham. Abraham was circumcised, a sign on his body and on those of his descendants, that they are witnesses for God. With his circumcision Abraham promised that all his descendants would belong to God. They would live an exemplary life.

This promise was sealed with Joseph, who lived and ruled in a land foreign to his heritage, yet maintained his image as a true witness. He was a pioneer for the Jewish people in the time of exile. He showed them how to live in an idol-worshiping culture, yet bear witness about the one and only God. He showed how to be true keepers of the covenant. And when the Jewish people left Egypt they were ready to continue their dedication. They would keep the covenant and make God's name known throughout the world.

Then Amalek came. Amalek opposed the covenant. He didn't want witnesses that God is the master. He wanted to be master. He was the true heir of his grandfather Esau who said, "By my sword, by my might, I shall defeat, subjugate and rule. My might cannot be challenged."

We must be strong in our resolve to keep the covenant and continue to be witnesses for God.

Great Strength to Do the Will of God

When we are about to do one of God's commandments, a *mitzvah*, we ought to look up to the angels and see how they do the will of God. This is especially important with a difficult *mitzvah* such as the obliteration of Amalek.

It is written, "Bless God, you, His angels, that excel in strength, that do His commandments, listen to the voice of His word" (Psalms 103:20). An angel is created to do the will of God. He is nothing but a messenger of God; there is no other will or intention in his being. Hence, he completes his mission with great strength and zeal with no ulterior motive or distraction.

Similarly, each of us was sent to earth with a mission. And in order to be true, we must feel it through and through. Even the deepest, most hidden part of us must be true to the mission. Then we are able to complete it, because every part of us "remembered" the mission that we set out to do.

Amalek wants us to forget. He doesn't want us to be true to our mission, to teach that God is the master of the world and not he. He wants to weaken us, to make us dishonest on the inside.

Therefore, we are admonished to remember, never to forget. Not to allow Amalek to weaken us in our zeal to spread the truth.

It is written, ". . . and I will give you places to walk among these that stand by" (Zechariah 3:7).

Angels "stand" in their spiritual level, whereas man keeps moving. An angel has only one desire; his intentions and actions are one and the same. They are identical. We cannot even say that the angel's intention ended and his actions began. It all happens in the speed of light. It is impossible to perceive when one ends and the other starts. It is as if they are standing still.

Man, on the other hand, has countless thoughts, intentions, desires, and plans that pull him in various directions. We hope he will carry out his plans, but we will never know until the end when he finally acts whether he will do so. He is constantly being pulled away, being distracted from his intentions. He must always struggle and be constantly on the move. He rises and falls and rises and falls, each time gaining strength. The more his strength increases, the less he struggles, the less effort he needs to put into his actions. He becomes more and more like an angel.

This strength made the Jewish people able to say, ". . . we will do and we will listen." They did not have to listen first to the commandments. Their deeds were as good as done. They were on the level of angels.

But Amalek had already corrupted their deeds before they came to Mount Sinai. Therefore, they fell into the trap of idol worship and made the Golden Calf.

We must never forget the spiritual place we could have attained if not for the attack of Amalek. This will strengthen us to struggle until we fix our actions. And then we will again be able to say, "We will do and we will listen."

It is written, "The voice is the voice of Jacob, but the hands are the hands of Esau" (Genesis 27:22).

Jacob was a man pure of heart, as it is written, "Esau was a cunning hunter, a man of the field; and Jacob was a plain man, dwelling in tents" (Genesis 25:28). Jacob's strength was his good intentions to voice his prayer and speak the words of the Torah. His power came from the faith in his heart and the awe of God in his mind. On the other hand, Esau's strength was physical, in the power of his hands.

When we have faith and pray or study, then the blessings of Jacob are in it. And when we act physically, then some of the Esau's energy is in it. How then do we deal with the defilement of Esau on our hands? The Jewish nation at Mount Sinai rose to the challenge and said, ". . . we will do and we will listen." They gave their action away to God. "Doing doesn't even belong to us, it belongs completely to God," they said. Well, if a person's hands belong to God, could he do anything wrong? No. We can cleanse our hands from the defilement of Esau even more by purifying the intentions of our deeds. By lifting our hands to the level of Jacob's intentions, they become united with our heart and mind. They become the voice of Jacob.

Thus, Moses lifted his hands during the war with Amalek. As it is written, "And it came to pass, when Moses held up his hand, that Israel prevailed: and when he let down his hand, Amalek prevailed" (Exodus 17:10–12).

This is the reason for lifting the hands during prayer, the blessing of the *kohanim*, and washing the hands before eating bread.

Let us lift our hands to the holy levels and the "voice" of Jacob, and live a life of Torah deeds.

It is reasonable that a person should first want to hear what he is supposed to do before he does it. It is also sensible that he should understand clearly what is required of him. But the Jewish people did the unreasonable and the insensible thing. Before listening, they jumped in and said, "We will do and we will listen." They put their doing, their hands, above their understanding. They lifted their hands "above their heads."

A prince had the bad habit of tearing flowers from his father's garden. This so infuriated the king that he was about to punish him for it. The prince realized this in time. The next time he passed the garden he kept his hands above his head. We too in our daily life must lift our hands above our heads. We must always guard them so they do not degenerate to the level of "the hands of Esau," whose hands are always below where he can make trouble. And Amalek, who attacks every weakness in us, we will defeat by lifting our hands above our heads.

It is written, "Bless God, you, His angels, that excel in strength, that do His commandments, listen to the voice of His word" (Psalms 103:20).

At first, before the Jewish people sinned, they were on the level of "that *do* His commandments." They were as the angels of heaven, whose whole being is one of total readiness, poised to carry out the will of God. Hence, even if they did not yet do anything, it was as if they did. There was no separation between their desire to do and the deeds they finally did.

After they sinned and made the Golden Calf, all that changed. Although they may have had good intentions, no one could be sure if they would act on them in the end. Their deeds were tainted.

When God presented them with the second set of stone tablets inscribed with the Ten Commandments, they learned how to fix their deeds. They knew they had to listen first, understand well, and then do. That sort of listening was a cure for their deeds.

A servant was given two crystal vases by the king. The servant was careless and broke one of them. The king summoned him and said, "You were careless and broke one of the vases. Be careful that you don't break the other one." (*Exodus Rabbah* 32).

We no longer have the strength of action and must listen carefully. Our intentions must be pure, so pure that it purifies even our deeds.

It is written, "Bless God, you, His angels, that excel in strength, that do His commandments, listen to the *voice* of His word" (Psalms 103:20).

God created the physical world with Ten Commands, and each particle of the world contains one of them. For example, light comes from the sun. Nevertheless, there is within it the command of God, "Let there be light" (Genesis 1:3). So there are two aspects to each thing: the physical part and the word of God within it, which is completely spiritual. This is the "*voice* of His word."

Similarly, there are the *hands* of Esau, and there is the *voice* of Jacob. When we do anything physical we are using the hands of Esau. Can we ever do a good deed with purity and holiness? Only if we ignore the physical and focus on the word of God within. The more we strive to reflect the word of God, the more it becomes the voice of Jacob and the farther it moves from the hands of Esau.

When the Jewish people left Egypt they were ready to do everything on the highest level. They were the voice of Jacob, and Amalek was the prime model for the hands of Esau. Amalek attacked the Jewish people and weakened them. Ever since then, the Jewish people must do their deeds with great strength if they want them to be pure and holy.

When the Jewish people were in the desert they were surrounded and covered by a blanket of clouds. They had a domain of holiness wherever they went and spent their day. After the attack of Amalek, they were commanded to build the *Mishkan*, the holy Tabernacle. The presence of God resided there. Whoever needed to have communion with the word of God came to the *Mishkan*. It was the voice of Jacob protected in a small place, from the hands of Esau.

A prince lived in the palace. He dressed royally, strolled, and conversed with his father. One day his father sent him on an errand through enemy territory. Soon the king's enemies were trailing the prince and finally attacked him. With the help of the palace guards, he was able to repel the attack and barely escaped. The prince then disguised himself as a peasant. "It is best that I hide my identity for now," the prince said. "I don't want my enemies to know of my relationship with the king."

When we are attacked by evildoers, or evil thoughts, it is time to hide. We must guard our relationship with God lest it fall into the hands of Esau. We struggle to protect our heritage from defilement and our deeds from blemish. Then our deeds stay pure, and our people live as the nation of God.

It is written, "Bless God, you, His angels, that excel in strength, that do His commandments, listen to the voice of His word" (Psalms 103:20).

The Midrash comments, "His angels," some of His angels, but not all His angels. Real angels, messengers of God, complete their assignments to their conclusion. But the sons of man, who are also messengers of God, cannot always carry out their assignments to their conclusion (*Numbers Rabbah* 13).

Every action begins with a thought. And from the thought it moves through the nerves and muscles until it concludes with a physical act. There are thousands of obstacles between the thought and the act on a microscopic level, as the thought travels through the nerves, and we are amazed that the act is done at all. A real angel, on the other hand, has but one single nature: to do the will of God. And whatever the assignment is, he does it immediately, without hesitation.

At the Exodus, the Jewish people were ready to complete their task of teaching the faith in one God. Amalek came, interfered, and did not let them conclude their task. We had just become a nation and were highly enthusiastic, and it all came to naught. The enthusiasm of the Jewish people was cooled off, and they became discouraged. They doubted if they would ever finish anything they started out to do. Their faith in *action* was damaged.

For this reason, whenever we are ready to do anything, we need great strength to overcome the obstacle of Amalek. We are always with a prayer on our lips, that God should help us finish what we started. As it is written, "God will accomplish His purpose for me. Your love, O God, endures forever; leave not your work unfinished" (Psalms 138:8).

Thought ends in two types of action. The first, which seems to be the easiest, is speech. And what sort of speech is especially appropriate for the Jewish people? They need to speak words that proclaim God's name and make it known in the world. That is their covenant of the tongue.

Abraham also started his actions with his tongue; he traveled to proclaim God as the master of the world. That was the beginning.

The next type of action seems to be the hardest, and it is procreation. To have a child is like the last of our actions; we are ready to leave the world in the hands of our offspring. This act is protected with the covenant of circumcision. The covenant is a promise that our children, just as we had, will proclaim the kingdom of God.

When we left Egypt, we were finally free to complete our task, to speak freely and proclaim that God is one. Amalek realized that the Jewish people would continue doing this task for generations to come, so he attacked quickly. He wanted to break the power of our generations, the covenant of circumcision, the end of all our actions. Therefore, God declared war with Amalek for all generations, until the "end of days."

We must have the strength to conclude that which we started out to do. We must guarantee that we will raise children in the image of Jews, true to their mission to the end of days, until the *Mashiach* comes. Thus, Amalek will disappear and our own story, long as history itself, will come to a happy conclusion.

Nissan is the first of the months and represents the beginning of action, the act of speaking, the covenant to declare the singularity of God. *Adar* is the last month and represents the end of all actions, the act of procreating, the covenant of circumcision, our children who will continue our mission.

Therefore, in *Nissan* we speak; at the Passover Seder we tell the story of the Exodus. And in *Adar* we take care of children; we erase Amalek, his memory, his descendants. We rescue our children from the clutches of the enemy, even if the work proves to be very difficult. Because as long as the descendants of Amalek are in the world, we have no guarantee that our children will be true Jews. The only insurance is our rededication to the two covenants: speech, and circumcision. Speech: to communicate to them in the strongest way that God is the master of the world. And circumcision: to promise that our children will be witnesses to God's oneness on earth.

REMEMBERING AMALEK ON *SHABBOS*

On the *Shabbos* preceding Purim two Torah scrolls are removed from the Holy Ark during the synagogue service. In the first, the portion of the week is read. In the second, we read from Deuteronomy 25:17–19, "Remember what Amalek did to you on your way out of Egypt."

We must remember; but how? If our essence, our thoughts, and our actions are one, through and through, then we do not forget who we are. We do remember.

We can compare this to someone who bought a gold-plated watch. He showed it to his friends as if it was made of real gold. Some time later he himself forgot what it was made of. One day, to his astonishment, he noticed that the gold was worn off, and underneath it was plain nickel.

If we remember that we have no life without God, then we cannot forget. We are constantly before God and in awe of him. Whatever we do is with our entire being; no part of us is left out. Each part of us wants to be where we are and to do what we are doing. This also brings us quietude and peace.

Amalek is the opposite of all this. He does not want us to be true to God nor to act with this quality of tranquility. He wants us to be in turmoil and weakness. He does not want us to have peace; instead he makes war.

But when the Sabbath comes, everyone becomes one, united, with the One. All creatures become unified as they feel their essence become one with God. Hence, Amalek is *erased* on *Shabbos*; he is totally powerless against God Who dwells in each of us on the day of *Shabbos*.

It is written, "Remember the Sabbath day to keep it holy" (Exodus 20:8).

God is the vitality and life of the world. This vitality is in the depths of our heart, in the place where our very life resides. But how do we receive this vitality? Through the Torah. The words of the Torah are the very essence and life that He grants to all His creatures. That is why the Torah was given on Sabbath, because the Sabbath and the Torah are identical. Sabbath is the secret, the inner truth, and the essence of all. It is the singularity, the unity of all things, the soul and core of everything.

A bird makes her nest in the spring. Later in the year, we watch the bird fly to a warmer climate for the winter and then return again in the spring. Again she builds her nest. "How does she *remember* the way to build it?" we ask. It is because the nest is part of her; it is intrinsic to her nature. She will not forget it.

Similarly, that which is part of us and is our essence, we do not forget. The inner core, the deepest most secret part of our being is the word of God, His *name*. And therefore, the word *zachor*, "remember," is composed of these Hebrew letters: *reish* and *zayin* spell *raz*, "secret," and *chof* and *vov* are numerically equal to 26. The name of God, *yud* and *heh* and *vov* and *heh*, also equals 26. This comes to teach us that the word *remember* is a "secret" with *God's name* in it. The reason we remember it is because it is part of the deepest secret in us.

Therefore, on the Sabbath, Amalek is erased. He has no room in the place where there is only God's name and His presence.

When the Jewish people came to Mount Sinai they declared, "We will do and we will listen" (Exodus 24:7). They were as the angels who have no other desire except to do the will of God. Unfortunately, they did not remain on that high level; they sinned and worshiped a Golden Calf. Ever since then we have had to struggle constantly between good and evil. It is not easy for us to live a righteous life.

Despite everything, one day of the week was untouched by our sin and remained on the highest spiritual level. This is the day of the Sabbath. On the Sabbath we are still on the level of Mount Sinai when we said, "We will do and we will listen." On the Sabbath, our spiritual being has no other desire, but to do the will of God. Therefore it is a day of complete rest. Nothing has to be done; it is already done. We are at rest in the essence of our being. It is our home, the place where we belong. When our entire being is at home with the will of God, Amalek has no power. The essence of the Sabbath invalidates his existence.

God created the world in six days and "rested" on the Sabbath, the seventh day. The six days represent the natural, created world. The Sabbath represents the spiritual world. It comes from the world of rest, a place where nothing has to be done.

The nations of the world represent the natural world. They live and die within its rules and laws. But the Jewish people represent the spiritual world. Their life and death do not necessarily conform to the laws of nature. Because according to the laws of nature, the law of averages, we should have long been extinct. Our mere existence is no small miracle.

The day of the Sabbath is called *m'ayin*; it is similar to the World to Come, is a taste of the other world, the miraculous and perfect one. Therefore, the day of the Sabbath and the Jewish people are from the same "world"—not from the "natural" one. Amalek cannot come near the day of Sabbath. He has power only in the natural world, but not in the spiritual world of the Sabbath.

God's kingdom is concealed in this "natural" world. We can look around and think, "Everything seems to be working merely with the laws of nature. Where is God?" However, if we just scratch away the surface we find the Master of the world. We realize that God is the one who created and makes everything happen.

We await the day when God's kingdom is revealed to one and all. As we recite in our daily prayers,

> And therefore we put our hope in You, our God, that we may soon see Your mighty splendor, to remove detestable idolatry from the earth, and false gods will be utterly cut off, to perfect the universe through the Almighty's sovereignty. Then all humanity will call upon Your name, to turn all the earth's wicked toward You. All the inhabitants will recognize and know that to You every knee should bend, every tongue should swear.

Even before that day arrives, God's kingdom is revealed one day each week. As it is written, "Between me and the children of Israel it is a sign forever that in six days God made heaven and earth, and on the seventh day He rested and was refreshed" (Exodus 31:17). On the Sabbath we have a taste of the revelation of God's kingdom, but in private. Still, Amalek has no place in the kingdom of God, even if it is only revealed privately. And therefore he is nowhere to be found on Sabbath.

A prince's cousin came to stay at the palace. The cousin was very mischievous, pestered and hurt the prince as long as no one was looking. The prince was very upset, but did not know what he could do. So each day he accompanied his father for a stroll through the garden. When he was near his father, the pest was out of sight and would not dare come near him.

On the Sabbath we have the opportunity to be rid of Amalek. Let us spend the time being close to the King. And while we are, the evil Amalek would not dare come near us.

God created the world in six days and rested on the Sabbath. Then the Sabbath complained, "Each day has a pair, but I don't?" And God answered, "You too will have a partner: the Jewish people" (*Genesis Rabbah* 11:9).

The six days of the week belong to the world of nature; they are made of parts and counted with numbers. The seventh day, the Sabbath, belongs to the spiritual world; it is without parts and without numbers. Hence, even if the Jewish people are in parts, are separated during the six days of the week, they are united on the Sabbath. They are one, and the Sabbath is their partner.

Amalek can only attack those who belong to the world of nature, those who are divided and separated and can be made weak. He only attacks stragglers, as it is written, ". . . and he attacked those stragglers among you. . . ." But he cannot attack those who are from the spiritual world, who are without fault or weakness and are united as one.

It is written, "What profit has a man of all his labor that he labors under the sun?" (Ecclesiastes 1:3). The Midrash comments, "Under the sun he has no profit. But above the sun, he does have profit" (*Numbers Rabbah* 28:1).

The world under the sun refers to the world of nature. Do we have any profit from it? But the world above the sun—that is, the spiritual world—we definitely profit from it. Amalek only has power to attack those who are under the sun, in the world of nature, but he has no power over those who live a life above the sun. That place is the World to Come, *Olam Habah*, where evil does not exist and Amalek's memory is totally erased.

The Jewish people received the *manna*, "bread" from heaven, while traveling through the desert. It was in the form of seeds and was found each morning in the Israelite camp. All the families gathered the amount they needed. On the sixth day of each week they were told to gather two portions so that they had enough for two days, for Friday and the Sabbath. On the Sabbath day they were not permitted to gather the *manna*.

However, "And it came to pass, that there went out some of the people on the seventh day to gather, and they found none" (Exodus 17:27). They desecrated the Sabbath, and, soon after, Amalek came and attacked them. Our sages comment: "If the Jewish people would have kept the first Sabbath, Amalek would never have been able to attack them" (*Shabbos* 118b).

The first Sabbath refers to the essence of the Sabbath, the "Sabbath of the Sabbath." The place and root of the Sabbath is in the heavens above, in the spiritual realm. That place is the root of all holiness and the root of all life and vitality in the world. It is the word of God Himself, and it is the home and resting place of all created beings. So that if the Jewish people would have rested *in* the Sabbath, they would have found their home in the essence of the Sabbath and then Amalek could not have touched them.

We recite in the Sabbath prayers, "He who spreads the shelter of peace upon us, upon all his people Israel."

True and everlasting peace will not come until the *Mashiach* comes. Then all the nations will live in peace and harmony with each other, as it is written:

> Then the wolf shall live with the lamb, and the leopard lie down with the kid; the calf and the young lion and the fatling together; and a little child shall lead them. The cow and the bear shall be friends, and their young shall lie down together. The lion will eat straw like cattle; the infant shall play over the hole of a cobra, and the young child shall dance over the viper's nest. They shall not hurt or destroy in all my holy mountain; for as the waters fill the sea, so shall the land be filled with the knowledge of God. (Isaiah 11:6)

The Hebrew word for "He who spreads" is *haporeis*, which also means, He breaks off a piece. There is a piece, a part of the week, the day of Sabbath, which has a taste of everlasting peace. We can experience Sabbath as if the *Mashiach* came already, and Amalek has no place there. In fact he is completely forgotten, so that no one can even remember his name.

When the Israelites left Egypt they were united in purpose and full of enthusiasm to carry out their special mission in the world. They went forth with a mighty hand to declare the kingdom of the one and only God. Soon after, Amalek attacked them. Amalek is the tribe that shatters, splinters, crumbles into fragments, and disintegrates the unity of the Jewish people.

The Sabbath is the opposite of all that. The Sabbath brings unity, wholeness, and integration. Therefore, on the Sabbath Amalek has no place; he has nothing to do and leaves immediately.

We recite in our Sabbath prayers, "For He is our God and we can be the sheep in His charge—even today, if we but heed His call. Do not harden your heart as at Merivah, as on the day of Massah in the wilderness; when your ancestors tried Me; they tested Me; though they had seen My deed" (Psalms 95:5–7).

God is the Master of the world. When we realize it, we humble ourselves to Him. Then we are true servants of God, and He does not allow anyone to use us as servants. But if we are arrogant and think that we are the masters of the world, then we fall into the hands of "masters," of Amalek, the chief villain among the nations. Hence, "Do not harden your heart. . . ." Do not be arrogant lest you fall into the hands of Amalek.

On the other hand, the Sabbath helps us recognize the Master of the world. Just as we bear witness that God created the world, we also declare that we are His servants. And therefore we stand in rapt attention when God speaks, "even today, if we but heed His call." And when we do, Amalek no longer has power over us.

The Sabbath is the completion of all that we did during the six work days. Similarly, there were Jacob and Joseph. Whatever Jacob worked on, Joseph completed. He was the seal of all of Jacob's striving. Therefore, Joseph got to ride in the king's coach, which was called "the chariot of the ruler." In Hebrew, it is *mirkeves hamishneh*, literally, the *double* chariot. That means that whoever completes the work gets a double portion.

Similarly, the Sabbath also has two portions. "Remember, (*zachor*) the Sabbath to keep it holy," and "Observe (*shamor*) the Sabbath day as holy." In addition, we take two breads for each of the Sabbath meals. One bread represents bread of the earth, and the other represents bread from the heaven.

And finally when the *Mashiach* comes, the name of Amalek will be erased. That will complete the work to repair the world and restore God's kingdom. Therefore, the war against Amalek is also waged with double language: ". . . I will utterly blot out the remembrance of Amalek . . ." (Exodus 17:14). In Hebrew, the words are *mo'choh em'cheh*, a double emphasis.

Likewise, when the Jewish people got rid of Amalek's grandson, Haman, he was first killed and then hung. He was, so to speak, killed twice. The *Megillah* has to be read on the night of Purim and "*repeated*" in the daytime—*twice*. Esther tells King Achashverosh, "Enjoy the party today, and tomorrow I shall do the king's desire"—twice (Esther 5:8). When David fought with Amalek, it is written, "And David smote them from the evening to the morning . . . .*twice*" (2 Samuel 30:17). And lastly, when Moses fought Amalek, it is written, ". . . tomorrow I will stand on the top of the hill . . ." (Exodus 17:9); again, today and tomorrow—*twice*.

And when Amalek is finally erased, the two will fuse into one. Then "God will be the king over all the earth. That day God will be one and His name will be *one*" (Zechariah 14:9).

It is written, "Then shall the house of Jacob be fire, the house of Joseph flame, and the house of Esau shall be chaff, they shall blaze through it and consume it" (Obadiah 1:18).

When the wheat plant grows, it has a stalk and seeds. After the seeds are removed, the stalks falls to the ground, dry up, and are straw. The seed itself has a cover, a shell that is removed as chaff, and then the peeled fruit can be eaten. Hence, although the chaff protects the fruit, it also keeps it in "prison." All fruit is in prison until the cover is removed.

Similarly, Amalek is the chaff who keeps the good deeds, the fruit, of the Jewish people in prison. Finally, he will be removed. But how? By the fire of holiness.

Therefore, on the Sabbath, when we feel the warmth of the holiness, we can be rid of Amalek. And he is consumed and disappears forever.

It is written, "*Remember* the Sabbath day to keep it holy . . ." (Exodus 20:8), and "*Remember* what Amalek did to you . . ." (Deuteronomy 25:17). Are these two memories identical? Can the memory of the most holy and the most despised be the same?

We can compare this to a landlord who sat and ate by his table. While the table was full of delicious food, he talked about his friends. When he finished eating and the table was empty, he spoke of his enemies (_Midrash, Tanchumah, Deuteronomy_ 25).

Each of us is composed of two major parts. The first, the spiritual and eternal part of us, is our _neshama_, the "soul." The second, the physical and impermanent part, is our body. We need both in order to do the will of God. The soul by itself would not have free choice, nor would it need to struggle to attain higher spiritual levels. The body on its own would merely fall into purely physical pursuits. But because the soul is in the body, it must strive for purity, holiness, and more spirituality.

We can compare this to a pitcher with a handle. We reach for the pitcher, take hold of the handle, and pour a delicious drink into our glass. It seems to us that the most important part of the pitcher is the handle. But what is a handle without the contents of the pitcher? Likewise, what is the action of the body without the _neshama_, the soul? The body is only a means, a handle to relate to the world.

Amalek has power in his hands, as it is written, ". . . and the hands are the hands of Esau . . ." (Genesis 27:22). He is very capable of grabbing things such as handles and destroying them. He can attack the physical part of us, but he cannot harm our soul, the spiritual part.

During the week we may favor our body because we are active and involved with the physical world. But when the Sabbath comes, our "table is full," and holiness, peace, and tranquility take hold of us. We soar to new heights and climb to view new vistas. Our body unites with our soul to be one and act as one integral whole. It is no longer a handle, but takes on the quality of the spiritual world. Then Amalek has no handle to grab and destroy.

It is written, "As the whirlwind passes, so is the wicked no more: but the righteous is an everlasting foundation" (Proverbs 10:25).

We can compare this to a house that stood on cement piles. A hurricane came and totally demolished and carried away every last splinter of it. Not a trace of it remained, and it was quickly forgotten and never remembered. On the other hand, if our house had a foundation and the wind ravaged it, the foundation would not be destroyed. It is not forgotten; it is still there to be remembered.

Similarly the wicked have no foundation. Their character is superficial, and when problems come they wither and are blown away. Their memory is fleeting, and they are soon forgotten. But the righteous, their life comes from their roots and essence. Their strength is genuine and deep. Therefore no wind or adversity can harm them. They are not forgotten.

Just as the righteous one is a foundation of the world so is the Sabbath. The Sabbath is the essence and inner being of everything that was created. It is the permanent memory of everything, and because of it nothing is forgotten.

Amalek can attack those who have no foundation, no memory. But when he approaches the day of the Sabbath, he is stopped in his tracks. He feels the power of remembrance, the foundation of the world. He knows that he cannot harm that and is totally bewildered. He runs away and is heard from no more.

It is written, ". . . the voice is the voice of Jacob . . ." (Genesis 27:22).

The voice of Jacob is heard from one end of the universe to the other. What is his voice? It is identical to the voice of God calling to all of creation to remember Him as the creator. And who remembers Him? The Jewish people: they use their voice to proclaim that God created the world. Hence Jacob is the soul, the inner truth and voice, for the physical world.

Amalek has power only over the physical world, which dominates the six work days. On the Sabbath, however, each of us gets a _neshama yeseirah_, "a reinforced soul." We become much more spiritual, and even our physical body is uplifted. We attain a much higher level of spirit, and suddenly we are no longer within the grasp of Amalek.

When the Jewish people left Egypt they were attacked by Amalek, as it is written, ". . . how he met you by _the way_" (Exodus 25:17).

On the regular everyday path, in the natural normal world, you can meet Amalek. And if you meet him you are in big trouble, especially if you belong to a nation that is controlled by the laws of nature. But if you are of the Jewish nation, you may survive his attack because then you are not controlled by natural laws. As it is written, ". . . God led them not through _the way_ of the land . . ." (Exodus 16:17). He did not lead them through the regular path, the way of natural laws, but through a different path—the path of the miraculous. The Jewish people are not controlled by the laws of nature, but survive because of miracles.

The physical world was placed in the control of Esau, whose hands and sword rule. Amalek is the inheritor of the hands of Esau; with the power of the sword, he is the boss in this world. He cannot be defeated by any nation naturally. The Jewish people can only defeat him super-naturally: if we are on *the way, the path* of miracles. That special way is ours through the Torah, the word of God, the creator of miracles every moment.

The Sabbath is the essence of the word of God and the Torah. We find rest and peace in the words of God. And therefore on the Sabbath, where the word of God dominates, Amalek has no grasp and is gone in an instant.

"When God was about to create the world and mankind, Truth said to God, 'No, it should not be created because it will be full of lies.' Peace said, 'God, don't create it! It will be full of quarrelling and war'" (*Genesis Rabbah* 1).

This is true of other nations. But the Jewish people were blessed with truth and peace; they do not belong to the world of lies and wars. They belong to the World to Come, to *Olam Habah*, to the perfect world filled with God's blessings. This was already the case with our ancestor Jacob, who attained the virtue of truth, as we recite in our Sabbath prayers, "Give truth to Jacob . . ." And similarly with Joseph who attained the virtue of peace by overcoming the rift between him and his brothers and marrying the daughter of the same master who threw him in prison.

Amalek, on the other hand, embodies all the reasons for not creating the world. He is full of lies, deceit, dispute, and war. He is the warlord of the physical world.

This whole discussion applies only to the six weekdays, the days of work, the physical world. But when the Sabbath arrives all this changes. The Sabbath fulfills what the six days are lacking—peace and truth—and it is a taste of the World to Come. Therefore Amalek has no place at all in Sabbath, and we cannot even find him when Sabbath arrives.

"When God created the world, there was a great debate if man should be created or not. Kindness argued, 'Create him! He will do acts of loving-kindness.' Righteousness said, "Create him! He will do acts of charity'" (*Genesis Rabbah* 1).

If you do not give to the unfortunate or share your gifts, you may remain false. Your character and your hidden self would never be put to the test. But if you constantly share, you must attain the truth because you keep reaching inside yourself and sharing with others. After a time your inside will match your outside. You become more and more genuine to others as well as to yourself. And then you are worthy of peace too, as it is written, "Righteousness and peace have kissed each other" (Psalms 85:11).

Therefore, Jacob, who is "truth," causes his descendants to have another virtue, as it is written, "Righteousness will uplift a people" (Proverbs 14:34). Because the righteousness of Jacob, the Jewish people, comes from the deepest depths of their being, therefore they are uplifted and their physical life is also elevated by their deeds. But Esau, representing the nations of the world, even if he does kindness, ". . . the kindness of the nations is sinful" (Proverbs 14:34). (Another, non-literal translation reads, "To do wrong is a disgrace to any nation.") Because it does not come from their true nature, his kindness is only superficial, pretentious, and false.

The Sabbath is unique in this regard. It is a day filled with truth and peace. The Sabbath is truth, a witness of the Divine creation of the world. The Sabbath is peace, the resting place of the world. And therefore Amalek, the exemplar of all that is evil in the world, cannot tolerate the Sabbath. And soon he is gone and never comes again.

It is written, "And God blessed the seventh day and made it holy" (Genesis 2:3).

In the Zohar there is a question: Something was created each day of the week and therefore needed a blessing. On the Sabbath nothing was created, so why did it need a blessing? The answer is that the Sabbath is higher than the physical world and therefore nothing was created in it. "And God blessed . . .": it is so highly spiritual that God made it the root of all blessing.

The Sabbath is the witness that God created the world, and the Jewish people are also witnesses. They are a pair: the Sabbath depends on the Jewish people, and the Jewish people depend on the Sabbath. Similarly, Sabbath is empty of anything physical and so is *Olam Habah*, the World to Come, which is everlasting. In fact, the Sabbath is called "*may-ayn Olam Habah*"; it is similar to the World to Come.

The Jewish people did not inherit the physical world. Their inheritance is the World to Come, the "full table," the everlasting table. Amalek, on the other hand, was given the entire physical world, and therefore his future world is empty. Amalek has an "empty table."

Sabbath is the "full table"; with no physical content, it is full of spirit just as is the World to Come. Therefore Amalek has no place in the Sabbath and departs without a trace.

———————

God created the world in six days and rested on the seventh. In a larger time frame, we are commanded to work our fields six years and to let them rest during the seventh year. Then we count seven times seven years, and we have the *yovel*, "the Jubilee," in which we rest our fields and set all servants free. Similarly, the physical world has a life span of six thousand years, followed by one thousand years of desolation (*Rosh Hashanah* 31a). On a micro-scale of one week and the macro-scale of thousands of years, there is the Sabbath, the rest period at the end.

Amalek does not let us rest. He disturbs us from doing our job of making God's name known. And neither does God have "rest" from him, because His kingdom and Name cannot be complete if Amalek is still in the world. Hence we can say that ever since the first Sabbath of creation God did not have rest because of Amalek. And finally, when Amalek is defeated God will have complete rest. The universe will be tranquil, and all creatures will know that God is the one and only King and no other.

———————

"Sabbath is the name of God" (Zohar, Exodus 88).

God created the world with ten commands. And although each of the commands is different, they have something in common. They are all the words of God, and the word of God sustains each creature. Deep in the inner core and concealed, the word of God is like the soul in our body.

The entire Torah is actually names of God. What is a name? It is the word that identifies and defines. And God's name is the divine nature of all things. Because below the physical surface, it is God's vitality that keeps things alive. And this same vitality from God is the essence of the Sabbath. The Sabbath is the inner core of every created thing and is therefore the name of God.

Amalek does not allow the kingdom or the name of God to be complete and therefore cannot survive with the Sabbath.

The Jewish people, however, are just the opposite. Our name and God's name are bound together. When the Jewish people are at their best, then God's name is magnified. And similarly, when God's name

becomes known, then the Jewish people are also blessed. The peace and harmony that result from all this will have the sweet taste of the Sabbath. And it will be everlasting.

———————

It is written, "In the beginning God created the heaven and the earth" (Genesis 1:1). The Hebrew word for beginning is *bereishis*, *with* the beginning. To whom does this *bereishis* refer? The Jewish people, because of whom the world was created (*Genesis Rabbah* 1).

Every part of the physical world has a beginning, but it is only temporary, and does not last until the end. This is true also of the chief villain of the nations, Amalek. As it is written, "Amalek was the first of the nations, but his end shall be that he shall perish for ever" (Numbers 24:20). How did Amalek become the "first" of the nations? The Amalekites banded together for their physical survival, for hunting for food and fighting their enemies, thus becoming a powerful tribe. But this togetherness is merely physical and thus has no permanence. It does not last, but soon disintegrates, falls apart, and then is no more. And how many nations had this very fate since Amalek! As even in our own lifetime we saw it happen in the Soviet Union. Who would have believed that such a powerful amalgamation would ever fall apart! But their whole union was for falsehood and evil. It was totally of the physical world, and therefore the impermanence affected it sooner or later. They started with great tumult, but ended in the dust of history.

The Jewish people, on the other hand, *seem* to be separated, and scattered. As it is written, "And Haman said to King Achashverosh, There is a single people scattered and dispersed throughout your kingdom . . ." (Esther 3:8). On the outside they seem to be scattered and dispersed, but in truth, in the deepest depths of their heart, they are absolutely single and one. Their souls are joined with the one and only God. They are united on the spiritual level, in the world everlasting and without end. Therefore, the Jewish people are the beginning and will similarly be the "end."

———————

If the Jewish people would have kept the first Sabbath, then no nation in the world would have been able to attack them. This means that had they been genuine, they would have been the first of the nations and not Amalek. As it is written, "And it shall come to pass, if you *listen diligently* to the voice of God, to observe and do all his commandments which I command you this day, that God will set you *high above all the nations of the earth*" (Deuteronomy 28:1). Amalek would have not only had no end but also no beginning.

How then do we repair that first Sabbath? By observing the last Sabbath in the most perfect way. And when is the last Sabbath? It is the Sabbath right before the *Mashiach* comes. If we do that, then Amalek will be erased.

All this will happen right before the Jewish people begin. And they "begin" in the month of *Nissan*, the time of the Exodus. So that in the month of *Adar*, the month in which Amalek meets his end, we must keep the Sabbath in the most perfect way. And when we do, we will see miracles not seen since our Exodus from the land of Egypt.

It is written, "Death and life are in the hands of the tongue" (Proverbs 18:21). We can compare this to a coal that was cool on the outside, but was still glowing with fire on the inside. If you blow on it, it lights up again. But if you spit on it, it becomes extinguished (*Leviticus Rabbah* 33).

The world is full of falsehood and lies. The Torah is truth and lies deeply embedded in the false world. The Jewish people can awaken the vitality of the Torah. But even then, it would not be revealed completely, because the world is false. It would be as a glowing fire of truth inside a false exterior.

And what is the inner fire of the Torah? It is like the total commitment that Joseph had for the covenant of God. As it is written, "And the house of Jacob will be a fire, and the house of Joseph a flame" (Obadiah 1:18). Jacob is like the coal and its warmth, and Joseph is the flame deep inside it. He is the essence of the glow that comes from the coal.

Thus, when we awaken the flame, when we conduct our life with enthusiasm for the Torah, then we have life. But if we ignore the flame of the Torah and we spit on the coal, then the Torah in our lives is extinguished. We should rather spit on the unimportant part, the physical matter, and then the Sabbath is revealed. The holiness inside the world becomes revealed, and then Amalek, the falsehood, disappears.

It is written, "In the beginning God created the heavens and the earth" (Genesis 1:1). The Hebrew word for beginning is *bereishis*, *with the beginning*, and it refers to the Torah that existed before the world was created. The Torah was God's blueprint for the creation of the world, and "He looked in it" and created the world (*Genesis Rabbah* 1).

Everything in the world is connected to the Torah, the beginning and root of all. And the Jewish people were given the ability to connect everything with the Torah, as it is written, ". . . the voice is the voice of Jacob. . . ." Their voice, their connection to the Torah is in the depths of their heart. Their verbal declaration has a powerful effect. And therefore, when they declare with all their heart that God created the heavens and earth in six days and rested on the Sabbath, the holiness of the Sabbath immediately descends to the world. With it comes peace and rest.

Every nation has a small part of the "beginning" from the time of the creation. Therefore, at the end, when the *Mashiach* comes, they will survive because they are connected to that beginning. But Amalek will perish, since he is entirely evil. He is severed from the Torah, the beginning of all things. He is a self-appointed "first" among the nations. In truth, he neither has a beginning nor a lasting end. And when he is erased, we will return to the spiritual level of the very first Sabbath when peace and tranquility reigned and God's name ruled.

It is written, "Remember the Sabbath . . ." (Exodus 20:8). The Sabbath represents the permanent good and holiness in the world. There are other pursuits that bring temporary good, and still others that are merely distractions. Amalek tries to make us forget the Torah, so that we indulge in unimportant, useless, and wasteful activities. Therefore, the Sabbath is his opposite. The Sabbath helps us remember, and when we do, Amalek fades and disappears.

31

Purim

THE SIGNIFICANCE OF PURIM

n entire tractate of Mishnah deals with the *mitzvos* and traditions of the holiday of Purim. The tractate deals principally with the dates, places, rules, and the correct reading of the *Megillah* on Purim and the laws of how it is to be written. The Talmud, which devotes 32 pages to explaining the four chapters in this tractate, also goes into the details of other aspects of Purim: the *mitzvos* of sending *monos*, a "gift of food," to a friend, of giving gifts of charity to two or more poor people, of celebrating the Purim feast, and of rejoicing by drinking wine. There is also a fascinating discussion of the story of Purim.

The holiday of Purim falls on two days: the fourteenth and fifteenth days of *Adar*. People who live in cities without walls read the *Megillah* on the fourteenth of *Adar*, whereas those from walled cities read it on the fifteenth.

It is written,

In the twelfth year of King Achashverosh, in the first month, *Nissan*, they cast lots, *Pur* as they were called, in the presence of Haman, taking day by day and month by month, and the lot fell on the thirteenth day of the twelfth month, the month of *Adar*. . . . Therefore these days are named Purim after the word *Pur*. Accordingly, because of all that was written in this letter, because of all they had seen and experienced in this affair, the Jews resolved and undertook, on behalf of themselves and their descendants, and all who should join them, that they would without fail keep these days as a yearly festival in the prescribed manner and at the appointed time; that these days should be remembered and kept, generation after generation, in every family, province, and city, that the days of Purim should always be observed among the Jews, and the memory of them should never cease among their descendants. (Esther 3:7 and 9:26–28)

Purim is the singular, and *Purim is the plural*. But was it not merely Haman who cast lots? That was a total of only one set, or *Pur*. Who else cast lots so that we call it Purim? The answer is that the nations had their luck, and so did the Jewish people have theirs. Haman cast his lot to signal the right day to annihilate the Jews, an impossible hope. The Jewish people cannot be annihilated. They are a miraculous people and indestructible. Therefore, the day that signaled for Haman what he should do, that very same day signaled for the Jewish people that it cannot be done. It was as if two lots were drawn—one as a signal for Haman, and one as the signal of the Jewish people.

A handsome and wise prince was beloved by his father. One of the generals was jealous of him and plotted against him. The general planned to embarrass the prince on the king's birthday in front of all the visitors. The king found out and called his son. "My son," he said, "there is a plan to harm you, but do not worry, I am still your father." On the king's birthday the king had his son sit next to his throne as the guests paid homage. And to the chagrin of the general, the king criticized him before all the assembled, for his poor planning during a recent battle. The very day that the general chose as the prince's downfall, the king chose to bring honor to him and his kingdom.

Similarly, the very day that Haman chose for the destruction of the Jewish people, God chose to elevate and exalt them before the eyes of the entire world.

When Haman cast lots, they were random. Any month and any date could have been chosen. It was all in the realm of probability. The date that *was* chosen is the date that had the most chance, the most probable one to be chosen. It was like a natural law, the nature of the physical world. But the Jewish people are not controlled by the laws of nature. If natural laws would control them, they would long ago have disappeared. They live with the miracles that God is constantly doing for them. And thus they survive natural calamities that befell other nations.

The Midrash relates that Haman, at first, cast lots on the days of the week, but he was not successful. Later when he cast lots for the days of the month, he was successful (*Esther Rabbah* 3).

If he had trouble with the days of the week, why then had he no trouble with the days of the month? For whatever date is chosen will still be on some day of the week.

The Sabbath is a day made holy by God; it is His day of rest and belongs totally to the heavenly realm. It is not physical at all and does not follow the laws of nature. Rosh Chodesh, the New Moon, is made holy by the Jewish people. Their court decides when the New Moon should be declared. And when it is declared then, the stagnating world, dominated by "unchangeable" laws of nature, is renewed.

Similarly, the name *tzaddik*, "of he who makes righteous," signifies that he draws holiness into the everyday world. Just like Rosh Chodesh, he brings life and vitality to the world of nature. And the name *rasha* signifies being cut off from the roots of life.

This was the complaint of Haman: "There is a particular people who are spread out and dispersed throughout your kingdom." They bring unity even within the "dispersed." They revitalize that which seems dead.

Haman could only bring harm to the days of the month; they are made by man. But he could not bring harm to the days of the week, because they are connected to the Sabbath. And the Sabbath is entirely in the spiritual realm; it cannot be touched by Amalek.

It is written, "The Jews gathered themselves together in their cities throughout all the provinces of the King Achashverosh, to lay hand on all who sought to harm them: and no man could stand in their way; for the fear of them fell upon all people" (Esther 9:2). Simi-

larly, when they stood at Mount Sinai, God told Moses, ". . . gather to Me all the people, and I will make them hear My words . . ." (Deuteronomy 4:10).

Each of us has a multitude of energies, thoughts, and feelings. We must gather them together and unify them for one purpose. We must be ready to give all of them away to God—the only One worth living for. Everything else is impermanent and perishes. Compared to eternity, all is worthless.

A king's advisor saved the kingdom from imminent attack. The king honored him by inviting his many allies to come to the palace for a grand celebration. The event passed with pomp and ceremony. The advisor was introduced to many important persons and spoke with them. An elaborate meal was consumed, and spectacular entertainment followed. Finally, the festivities were over, and everyone left. The advisor was finally alone with the king. "I sincerely appreciate the honor that you prepared for me today," the advisor said. "But all the guests who were just here have now left and are gone. Now it is only you and I. To be with the king is best of all."

We unify our energies and stay with the King. Then no one can harm us, not even the evil Amalek.

It is written, "The Jews gathered themselves together in their cities . . ." (Esther 9:2). It is most important to gather together, to be together as one, to be unified. And it is also written, "With seventy souls, your forefathers went down to Egypt" (Deuteronomy 10:22). The Hebrew word for the plural noun of "souls" is *nefesh*, which is singular. How do the seventy people become one soul? All those who worship One God and are united are called one soul. That unity revitalizes the collective soul of the Jewish people, who become all the more powerful.

But who could unite the Jewish people so powerfully? Only the *tzaddik*, the righteous one of the generation. He supervises and watches over the unity of their souls, and the masses look up to him and subjugate themselves to him. And because the *tzaddik's* entire being is focused on God, whoever is with him unifies his being and focuses on God too.

We must become unified in our own inner life, and then with the rest of the Jewish nation. And if we do, we will soon see the redemption and the disappearance of Amalek.

It is written, "The Jews gathered themselves together in their cities throughout all the provinces of King Achashverosh to lay hand on those who sought to hurt them: and no man could withstand them; for fear of them fell upon all people" (Esther 9:2). And it is also written, "But the other Jews that were in the king's provinces gathered themselves together, and [amod—singular] stood for their lives . . ." (Esther 9:16).

When the Jewish people gather together, they unite as one, and then they are referred to by the singular noun because they are singular and undivided. Similarly, when Jacob and his children immigrated to Egypt, ". . . all [nefesh—singular] the souls of the house of Jacob, which came into Egypt, were seventy" (Genesis 46:27). All those who worship the one God are called "one soul," are united. When we unite with our friends and other acquaintances, we revitalize the collective soul of the entire nation of Israel. This is all the more powerful.

Who has the energy to unite the nation so powerfully? The tzaddik, the righteous one of the generation. It is he who has worked on the unity of his own being and has been concerned with the unity of the souls of all of Israel. And by nullifying ourselves to the tzaddik, we too become united with each other.

Purim is calling to us to become whole again, to abandon all nonsensical reasoning, and rather to love our fellow Jews, to unite with them, and to make all of Israel one soul.

Amalek has a hold only on the physical part of the Jewish people. The more spiritual the Jew, the less that Amalek has control of him. And where is the part of every Jew that is the closest to spirituality? It is the part that is connected to the source of life. That is a part Amalek cannot touch. Therefore, with the power of the source of life, Amalek can be defeated.

There is thought and there is action. First we merely think of doing something. How does thought change to action? It becomes more and more like action, until we finally do it.

At first a thought is abstract. But when it is a deep conviction and devotion in your heart, it is then only a heartbeat away from action. That is as close as thought can come to action. It is nearly done, but it is not yet done. There is only a hair between them.

For example, you can know that some food is dangerous to your health. If you have high blood pressure and your doctor tells you, "If you eat another drop of salt, you will die," you know that his warning is true, but still only on the level of knowledge. But if your desire to live is strong you believe that life is good, and you do not want to die, then it is more than knowl-

edge. You don't have to think about it. You remember not to eat salt. It is inseparable from your life; you are the memory, and the memory is you.

If you know something, then it can be forgotten. But if it is part of your very being, through and through, then just as you don't forget yourself, neither do you forget that memory. As it is written, "And these days should be remembered and kept . . ." (Esther 9:28). The Talmud comments, "First remembered, then kept . . . and not first kept, then remembered" (Megilla 2b). This means, that if you remember in the strongest way, then surely you will also keep it. It will move from thought to action. But if it is not that strong and is merely a weak memory, then there is no guarantee that you will keep it.

Let us then remember the days of Purim in a way that it is part of our very being. And then when we remember who we are, Amalek will surely be forgotten.

The miracle of Purim happened after the destruction of the First Temple of Jerusalem. Destruction and desolation followed. Most of the population had been carted off as slaves, but some were less fortunate and died by the sword. As the prophet Jeremiah said, "How does the city sit solitary, that was full of people! how is she become as a widow! She that was great among the nations, and princess among the provinces, how is she become tribute!" (Lamentations 1:1). The exile was to last seventy years, and then God would allow the Jewish People to return to their land.

How could a nation so battered and tortured, feeling weak and forlorn, return and rebuild their homeland? They needed to have an invigorating experience, a miracle, to bolster their spirits. And that was the miracle of Purim. Haman's plot was foiled, and their enemies were defeated. The Jewish people realized that they are still the children of God; they are not forsaken. They can pray for help and be answered, can study Torah and live an inspired life, are not helpless, and can defend themselves if need be.

Now too, in this present exile, which is long and never ending, when so many have already given up the hope of ever returning en mass to the land of our fathers, surely God will again make a great miracle that will jolt us out of our apathy and prepare our hearts for the final redemption coming soon in our lifetime.

It is written, "When these days were over, the king gave a banquet for all the people found in the city of

Shushan, the capital city, both high and low; it was held in the garden court of the royal pavilion and lasted seven days" (Esther 1:5).

We find the same expression used to describe the destruction of Sodom, "And when the morning arose, then the angels hastened Lot, saying, Arise, take your wife, and your two daughters, which are *found* here; lest you be consumed in the iniquity of the city" (Genesis 19:15).

We can compare this to a king who heard strange noises coming from the treasure house. Suspecting that a thief was stealing his gold, the king sent his guards to grab the thief. They entered with empty sacks and after a brief struggle came out with two writhing sacks. They dumped the two sacks before the king. How surprised and amused the king was when he saw his two children before his throne, who were very embarrassed and indignant. "So, this is what you have *found* in my treasure house!," the king laughed.

The Jews who participated in the feast of the King Achashverosh committed a grave sin. It was not their place to celebrate according to the customs of the idol worshipers. There were days and nights of drunken revelry, a mockery of civility and defilement of the stolen vessels from the Holy Temple. Yet their presence there was eventually part of a divine plan. They were *found* there.

Later, after Haman's decree was known to all, Esther said to Mordechai, "Go and assemble all the Jews to be *found* in Shushan and fast for me; take neither food nor drink for three days, night and day, and I and my maids will fast as you do. After that I will go to the king, although *against the law*; and if I perish, I perish" (Esther 4:16).

The Jews of Shushan fasted to repent for the sin of participating in the decadent feast of the king. Their repentance was so complete that their sin was repaired completely, so that on a divine level where there is no past and future, their presence at the feast of the king was free of sin. They went there to sin, but when God *found* them, (in the future's past), they were free of sin. They were merely his children whom He loved and protected.

The feast was returned to them through repentance. Thus Esther said, "I will go to the king, although *against the law*." I am going to the King of the universe, with the merit of that which was *against the law*; the Jews of Shushan at the feast of the king. Now that they repented, I can bring their "sin" as merit.

From the sin of feasting with the king sprouted the redemption; it caused the demise of the queen Vashti at that very feast.

On Purim, we too can experience the great love that God has for us. We too should seize the opportunity to repent for our sins and bring great miracles.

It is written, "*Day by day* Mordechai passed along by the forecourt of the women's quarters to learn how Esther was faring and what was happening to her" (Esther 2:11).

From the time that Esther was taken until Haman was defeated, several years passed; yet, Mordechai continued to walk to the palace *each and every day* to check on the welfare of his niece, the orphan girl. And what a great merit this was for him! The outpouring of his generosity allowed him to receive divine kindness. Therefore, when he needed mercy and help he received it immediately. As it is written:

> And all the king's servants that were at court bowed down to Haman and did obeisance. But Mordechai did not bow nor do obeisance. Then the attendants at the court said to Mordechai, 'Why do you flout his majesty's command?' *Day by day* they challenged him, but he refused to listen to them, so they informed Haman, to see if Mordechai's refusal would be tolerated, for he had told them that he was a Jew. When Haman saw that Mordechai was not bowing down to him or doing obeisance, he was infuriated. On learning who Mordechai's people were, he scorned to lay hands on him alone, and looked for a way to destroy all the Jews throughout the whole kingdom of Achashverosh and all his people. (Esther 3:6)

Because he did kindness day by day, he too received kindness day by day. He was able to outmaneuver and overpower Haman and save his people from imminent death. He gave life as a gift, by caring for his niece; therefore, life was also given to him as gift.

It is written, "Now there in Shushan the capital city was a Jew named Mordechai son of Yair, son of Shimi, son of Kish, of the tribe of Benjamin" (Esther 2:5). Mordechai was also a descendant of Saul the son of Kish, the first king of Israel, so why was not Saul's name mentioned? It is because Saul was commanded to destroy the Amalekites, but did not. Mordechai, on the other hand, was successful in destroying Haman the Amalekite. Therefore, Mordechai stood in the place of Saul, repaired his mistake, and is himself called the son of Kish.

"Therefore these days are named Purim after the word *Pur*" (Esther 9:26). The holiday of Purim grew out of the lots that were cast by Haman. His evil plan and his downfall were all contained in the casting of the lots.

Why is it that the evil plan of that beast became the name of the holiday? And why is his downfall foretold just when he seems to be at the height of his power?

We find the answer later in the *Megillah*. "The king rose from the banquet in a rage and went to the garden of the pavilion, while Haman remained where he was, to plead for his life with Queen Esther; for he saw that there was evil determined against him (*at its very end*) by the king" (Esther 7:7). The career of Haman the Amalekite as a killer of Jews was coming to an end. Amalek had reached his peak and now was about to fall. Although his descendants would continue to live by the sword of their grandfather, Esau, still, they would no longer be invincible like Amalek was.

Let us pray that the final end comes to Amalek and we be free to follow the Torah undaunted.

It is written, ". . . while Haman remained where he was, to plead for his life . . ." (Esther 7:7).

This is a repeat of the events that happened with Saul, the first king of Israel, when he fought to destroy the Amalekites. "But Saul and the people took pity on Agag, and the best of the sheep, and the oxen, and the fatlings, and the lambs, and all that was good, and did not utterly destroy them: but everything that was vile and repulsive, that they destroyed utterly" (1 Samuel 15:9).

Amalek survives because he is mistaken for an ordinary criminal. But he is not; he is evil through and through. And when he begs for mercy, it is but a trick. We have experienced this with the captured Germans after their defeat in World War Two. They cried for mercy, distracted their guards, and killed them.

When Amalek says, "I am going to kill you," we should not doubt him for a moment, even if he says he is sorry and claims a change of mind.

The *Megillah* mentions the following words three times: ". . . but on the spoil they laid not their hand" (Esther 9:10, 15, 17).

The Jews fought against Haman, his sons the Amalekites, and the other enemies of the Jewish people. They had permission, by the king's decree, to take all the spoils. Yet they did not in order to repair the sin of Saul and his men who also fought Amalek but took all the spoils. They followed the commandment of the Torah to leave no trace of Amalek. Because if there is, someone will see it and say, "See, that thing is from Amalek." And then he will again be remembered. Amalek must never be remembered; but, forgotten entirely.

All this extreme wrath arises because Amalek blocked the path of the Jewish people as they streamed forth with great enthusiasm from Egypt. They were on their way to reveal God's name, and Amalek cooled them down, discouraged them, and weakened their faith.

We should not have the memory of Amalek before us in any shape or form. Rather, we ought to rededicate ourselves to the Torah and the Godly way of life.

It is written, "And Mordechai told him of all that had happened unto him, and of the sum of the money that Haman had promised to pay to the king's treasuries for the Jews, to destroy them" (Esther 6:7).

Mordechai was very downcast by the generosity of Haman. He knew that generosity was the hallmark of the Jewish people. It was one of the signs that indicates that a person is a Jew. So how is it, Mordechai wondered, that an Amalekite is so generous? It must be because the Jewish people are on a very low spiritual level, and therefore the energy of giving is transferred to the nations. It reflects the spiritual balance in the world: when one rises, the other falls.

In the end Haman never gave over the money, so that his generosity was for naught. Instead, the kindness of Mordechai and his people prevailed. Haman was hung; yet, the Jews took none of his money.

"A person is obligated to drink wine on Purim till he doesn't know the difference between 'cursed is Haman' and 'blessed is Mordechai'" (*Megillah* 7b).

What is the difference between one who is cursed and one who is blessed? The difference is one of the forty-nine levels. There are forty-nine levels of defilement and forty-nine levels of holiness. We can descend deeper and deeper into the abyss, the evil of degeneration. Or we can climb higher and higher to infinite goodness and growth. Amalek is on each of the steps descending to unholiness.

The forty-nine steps in either direction are the Tree of Knowledge. On the fiftieth step, however, there is only purity, unity, and singularity. On that level there is neither good nor evil. It is the source of all and is one. That step is the Tree of Life. It is the source of all knowledge of God; it is the Torah. When we reach the fiftieth step, in either direction, which is humanly impossible, suddenly it is the Torah.

To defeat Amalek we must reach out for the fiftieth step, just as Moses did when he fought against Amalek. He lifted his hand, and the Israelites were victorious. In the opposite direction, in the realm of the defiled, Haman made a tree fifty cubits high to hang Mordechai. He too was reaching out for the fiftieth level of defilement. But it is unattainable.

Therefore, when we reach the level of Purim, we reach beyond the forty-ninth level to the fiftieth level, the Tree of Life, the Torah. On that level there is neither curse nor blessing. There is but the One and Only God whom we can only experience, but say not one descriptive word. We cannot describe our experience as blessed nor as cursed. It just is, and it is all one.

———————

"A person is obligated to (*livsumi*) drink wine on Purim till he doesn't know the difference between 'cursed is Haman' and 'blessed is Mordechai'" (*Megilla* 7b). The word *livsumi* also means to be filled with fragrance.

When the Jewish people listened to the Ten Commandments at Mount Sinai, it was their ultimate encounter with God. After each word that was heard, the entire planet filled with a spicy fragrance, *besomim*. Similarly, each God-fearing person who teaches Torah has the fragrance of spices and causes his student to smell of spices too.

This was true of Mordechai. He helped his generation of assimilated Jews repent and rededicate themselves to the Torah. He was a powerful source of fragrance, as it is written, "Take you three principal spices, of pure myrrh" (Exodus 30:23). This is translated in the *Targum*, the Aramaic, as *mori dach'ya*, which can be pronounced as Mor–de–chai.

Let us therefore fill ourselves with the fragrance of Purim, which comes from Mount Sinai. And then we can, starting immediately, imbue others with the delicious fragrance of the Torah.

———————

It is written, "After these things, the King Achashverosh appointed Haman the son of Hammedasa the Agagite, and advanced him and set his seat above all the princes that were with him" (Esther 3:1).

Why was Haman elevated? To attract attention and publicize his catastrophic demise. Does God bestow honor on the wicked so that they should later fall? Is that a good enough reason for a wicked man to receive all that honor?

The reason for Haman's elevation was to punish him, measure for measure. For Haman, it was beneath his dignity to kill Mordechai alone. As it is written, "On learning who Mordechai's people were, he scorned to lay hands on him alone, and looked for a way to destroy all of the Jews throughout the whole kingdom of Achashverosh, Mordechai and all his race" (Esther 3:6). Therefore it was beneath the Divine dignity to destroy Haman the way he first was. Hence, he was elevated to the highest position, and then he was destroyed.

———————

Haman said to the King Achashverosh, "There is a singular people scattered abroad and dispersed among the people in all the provinces of your kingdom; and *their* laws are diverse from those of every people" (Esther 3:8).

Amalek opposes the Torah and anything that contains Torah. He opposes not only the Written Law, the Torah written by Moses and received by all of Israel but also the Oral Law, the Torah originated by them—*their* Torah. Amalek makes weak our enthusiasm for Torah regardless of its form.

Therefore, whenever Amalek is dealt a blow, our enthusiasm for the Torah increases. When Haman and his sons were hung, the Jews celebrated the victory by their rededication to the Torah.

We too must open our hearts to God's call, as He calls from Mount Sinai, "Rid your lives of all evil, come to Me, and together we will prepare every heart for the Torah."

———————

It is written, "Remember what Amalek did. . . ." Remember the misery you suffered lest you sin and Amalek will come again.

A shepherd neglected his sheep; the wolf came and ate several of them. The next day, some of the owner's workers got drunk and destroyed the shepherd's shed. He grieved for the sheep and the shed for a while, but later regained his composure. Some weeks later, the owner noticed that the shepherd was again careless. He came to him and said, "Remember the wolf that ravished the flock. Don't ever forget it!" The shepherd turned to him and said, "And you, my lord, please don't forget what your workers did to the shed."

The entire *Megillah* is a reminder of Amalek's attack on us and of our weak spiritual state. It reminds us to observe God's commandments. And just as God reminds us of our obligations, we ask God, "Remember O God the children of Edom, in the day of Jerusalem; who said raze it, raze it to its very foundation" (Psalms 137:7). Remember the nations who pester us constantly and don't allow us to make Your name known in the world. Remember, O God, that Your name and Your throne will never be whole until Amalek is totally destroyed. Your name is the Torah, which is made up entirely of the names of God. And Your throne is Jerusalem, the seat of all holiness for the Jewish people.

It is written: Then were the king's scribes called at that time in the third month, that is, in the *month of Sivan*, on the twenty-third day; and it was written according to all that Mordechai commanded to the Jews, and the lieutenants, and the governors, and rulers of the provinces, which are from India to Ethiopia, one hundred twenty-seven provinces, unto every province according to their writing, and to every people according to their writing, and according to their language (Esther 8:9).

When the Jews received the letters in the month of *Sivan*, they saw the light of redemption and rejoiced. But why didn't they rejoice when Haman was hung? Because when Amalek perishes the Torah is revealed. And not long after Haman was hung came the holiday of Shavuos in the month of *Sivan*, and the Jewish people felt a special inspiration and light during that holiday. They realized that the end of Amalek is near; they will be able to defeat him altogether. Then and only then did they rejoice. Not only was Amalek destroyed and the nation of Israel rescued, but it also ultimately led to the building of the second Holy Temple in Jerusalem.

"The Jews *had* light, and gladness, and joy, and honor" (Esther 8:16).

The Jewish people always *had* light, but the light was covered up by the misdeeds of the wicked. Similarly, the light of the Jewish people cannot be revealed while Amalek is in the world. But when Amalek is destroyed, the joy and splendor of the Jewish people are revealed. And therefore after Haman was hung, Mordechai walked out of the palace with royal garments. "And Mordechai left the king's presence in robes of violet and white, wearing a great golden crown and a cloak of fine linen and purple, and all the city of Shushan shouted for joy" (Esther 8:15).

It is written, "But the (*sheor*) other Jews that were in the king's provinces gathered themselves together, and stood for their lives . . ." (Esther 9:16). The word *sheor* means the leftovers. When we think *we* are important, and totally independent, we do not need anyone, not even God. We are then separated from God and the people of Israel. The result of that thinking is that we are not important, but are actually weak and alone. On the other hand, if we consider ourselves as leftovers to the *tzaddik*, the righteous one of the generation, then we are united as one and ready to receive God's blessings.

The Jewish people completely humbled themselves to Mordechai, the *tzaddik* of his generation. They considered themselves as mere leftovers to him, and that helped them to be humble before God too. Therefore they were able to destroy Haman and his followers.

It is written, "When Mordechai learned all that had been done, he rent his clothes, put on sackcloth and ashes, and went through the city crying loudly and bitterly" (Esther 4:1).

Did Mordechai think that Haman's plan would succeed and that all the Jews of the 127 provinces would be annihilated? Didn't he believe in the word of the prophets who declared that the exile will return to Jerusalem at the end of seventy years? Yes, he certainly did! But he thought, "What if all the Jews are killed, but God plans to save me and Esther to produce a new nation of Israel?"

A king made a picnic for the prince and his friends. He treated them to climb up a steep hill to his private residence. The boys hardly were able to climb up and complained the whole time. When they got to the top, there were long tables set with an exquisite feast. When the feast was over the king said, "Everyone is invited to come up here again on your next holiday." The boys looked at each other and laughed. "You expect us to make that hard climb again?" they said. But the prince and his closest friend spoke up, "We want to come, even if no one else does."

Mordechai and Esther were united as one, and therefore Haman could not harm them, as it is written, "There is a single people . . . scattered abroad and dispersed among the peoples . . ." (Esther 3:8). "There is a single people"—those were Mordechai and

Esther; "scattered"—those were the Jewish people. Haman may be able to kill them because they are spread apart, and there is no unity among them.

When Purim comes, let us abandon our differences and unify as one people. And when we do, Amalek cannot harm us at all.

———————

It is written, "And that these days should be remembered and kept throughout every generation, every family, every province, and every city; and that these days of Purim should not fail from among the Jews, nor the memory of them perish from their descendants" (Esther 9:28).

God gave many gifts to the Jewish people, and He does so still. One was the Torah, a Divine guide for our life. Another gift was the Holy Temple in Jerusalem, a place of worship and prayer. Although gifts are wonderful, it is embarrassing to receive them if you did not earn them.

Later, the Holy Temple was destroyed, and Torah study became weak among the people. Then, in the era of Esther and Mordechai, the Jewish people repented and rededicated themselves to the Torah. They again received the Torah and the Holy Temple, as a gift, but they had earned it.

A prince's father treated him with great compassion. He constantly showered him with affection and gifts. Although the prince behaved fairly well, he realized that he was undeserving of the many gifts. His cousins were not receiving as much; yet they were as good as he was. One day, the prince spoke rudely and insulted his father. The king ignored him for several days and of course gave him nothing. Finally, the prince approached his father and begged forgiveness. "I will always respect and honor you, Father; just please forgive me," the prince said. The king hugged his son and said, "Of course you are forgiven. After all, you are my son. And I will give you a gift; you earned it."

It is Purim. We look around and see all the gifts that God has given us. Let us at least be worthy of one of them.

———————

It is written, "... Amalek was the first of the nations; but his latter end shall be that he perish forever" (Numbers 24:20).

For Amalek, his beginning and end are destruction. He attacks every beginning, any good thing that is about to happen for the first time, such as the new nation of Israel emerging from Egypt. He cannot tolerate someone being first. And we are the "first," as

it is written, "This month shall be unto you the beginning of months: it shall be the first month of the year for you" (Exodus 12:2). And just as the Jewish people have their strongest energy in *Nissan*, so does Amalek. Haman uses the first month, *Nissan*, for evil; "... in the first month, *Nissan*, they cast lots, *Pur* as it is called, in the presence of Haman ..." (Esther 3:7)

Since *Nissan* is the first month of the year, it is also the beginning of Amalek, the height of his power. His end is in *Adar*, the last month of the year. In that month he will experience the dissolution of his strength because that month has the strength to destroy Amalek, as we learned, "Whoever has a judgement with a non-Jew, should avoid him till *Adar*, because that month has a strong fortune" (*Megilla* 14a).

Therefore, when Haman cast lots, no matter how they fell they kept skipping to *Adar*. He was actually choosing a month for his own downfall because *Adar* is the end of Amalek. So shall it be in our own lifetime.

———————

Esther is like the morning star, which is the meaning of her name. Why? Because the morning star is the last visible star before the morning. It is nearly light, but still dark enough to see one last star. With a bit more light even that star would not be seen. Esther also was the last miracle before the final redemption. It is a preparation for the *Mashiach*, when Amalek will fall and never rise again.

———————

It is written, "And these days should be remembered and kept throughout every generation, every family, every province" (Esther 10:28). We also recite in our prayers on Purim, "You have been their eternal salvation, and their hope throughout generations."

Why is Purim remembered in every generation? It is because Haman wanted to get rid of all the Jews and their generations forever; he wanted total annihilation. Therefore, his punishment is that his downfall will be remembered by all generations. Could you imagine the punishment of someone who wants to annihilate the entire nation of Israel?

Each generation that makes God's Name become known, each of us who makes God's Name holy brings more punishment on Haman's head and similarly brings blessing on the head of Mordechai.

———————

It is written, "And these days should be remembered and kept throughout every generation, every family, every province" (Esther 10:28). The manner that you remember the holiday of Purim, that is how you will keep it.

Amalek has power over every aspect of the physical world: space, time, and the soul. On Purim he was destroyed on all three fronts. Hence we celebrate a total victory over Amalek. We got back all the things he took from us. "In every generation" refers to the aspect of *time*. "Every family" refers to the aspect of *life*. "Every city and province" refers to the aspect of *space*: the world.

Amalek is always fighting with us, and trying to dominate the world. He does not want to leave any part for us. How will we ever be free of him? The prophet answers, "It is a time of travail for Jacob, and (*mimena*) from her he will be helped" (Jeremiah 30:7) The word *mimena* has the same letters as *mehaman*, "from Haman." Although Haman-Amalek gives us much trouble, still we will be helped. Where does the help come from? "*Mimena*," from her, the trouble itself. As it is written, "God is our refuge and strength, a very present help in trouble" (Psalms 46:1). The help is found in the trouble itself. Similarly, the Hebrew word *bitzur* means prayer, to pray for help, and *b'tzara* means in trouble. The prayer and strength are found in the suffering itself.

When the king elevated Haman, the wicked Amalekite, the Jews thought they would never see the end of their troubles. But it was precisely because he was elevated that the help came. Mordechai refused to bow to Haman, causing him to plot the murder of the Jews, which led to his downfall.

When we are in trouble, let us pray and we will find salvation sprout from the affliction itself.

It is written, "And I will (*haster aster*) surely hide my face in that day for all the evils which they have done, that they turned to other gods" (Deuteronomy 31:18). The Hebrew word for "I will hide" is *aster*, which is very similar to the name Esther. There was hiddenness in her time, she was forbidden to reveal her Jewish background, the Jews felt completely abandoned, and their fate was in the hands of murderers.

The Torah too is both hidden and revealed. Sometimes we see the light coming from the hidden part and sometimes from the revealed part. As the Zohar teaches, Purim is like Yom Yippur. Purim is hidden in Yom Kippur, and some day the holiday of fasting and pain will change to feasting and pleasure. Also, another similarity, is that the one day a year that the *Kohen Gadol* may enter the Holy of Holies in the Temple of Jerusalem was Yom Kippur. It was the most hidden part of service. And although he does enter, the Torah says, "And God said to Moses, Speak to Aaron your brother, that he *should not come* at all times to the holy place within the vail before the mercy seat, which is upon the ark. . . . Thus *shall he come* into the holy place . . ." (Leviticus 16:2–3). His entering the holy place is hidden in the words "he should not come." He enters a place that *he should not*.

Similarly, Esther was not permitted to come to King Achashverosh. And yet she did. The help of God, the light, came to the Jews from the hidden place, a place where one ought not tread. This was brought about by the destruction of Haman. When Amalek is destroyed, all the gates open, and the world is flooded with light and help.

If we do not experience our help from the obvious sources, we ought not give up. With prayer, all obstacles will be removed. Then our help will come even from the most obscure and hidden place.

"And Esther set Mordechai over the house of Haman" (Esther, 8:2).

Whatever happens in the physical world happens also in the spiritual world. Now that Haman was hung and Amalek destroyed, the impure gave way to the pure. As it is written, "Instead of the thorn shall come up the fir tree, and instead of the briar shall come up the myrtle tree: and it shall be to God for a name, for an everlasting sign that shall not be cut off" (Isaiah 55:13). Where there was idol worship was now holiness; wherever Amalek's name was erased, was now revealed the name of God. The house of Haman, all the honor he represented in the world, was now in the hands of Mordechai. As it is written, "He may prepare it, but the just shall put it on, and the innocent shall divide the silver" (Job 27:17). The honor for Haman that people had turned into the honor for God's name. This is symbolized also by the large crown that Mordechai wore after the fall of Haman. It represents the two large letters in the reading of the *Shma*; "Hear O Israel, God our Lord, God is one." The two large letters are *ayin* and *dalet*, which spell *eid*, "witness." Every Jew is a witness that God is one. But Amalek does not allow us to bear witness. So when he is defeated, our role as witnesses becomes magnified. And thus Mordechai wears a large crown on his head, where everyone can see it. The Jewish people were again able to advertise, to announce to the nations of the world that God is one.

Neither will we be lazy. It is Purim. We have defeated Amalek. Let us quickly resume our task and spread our message: God is one.

"King Achashverosh took off his ring and gave it over to Haman. And with that, he sealed the fate of all the Jews in Haman's hands. This did more to pressure the Jews to repent, more than the words of forty-eight prophets" (*Megilla* 14a).

The relationship of God to the Jewish people is one of essence. They are connected with Him on the highest spiritual level. Nothing can break this bond between them—no nation nor even their own sins, although if they do sin, they are given over to the hands of the nations. And when they sinned in the time of Mordechai, they were given over into the hands of Haman. The nations could only dominate them on the physical level. But on the spiritual plane, they were still as close as ever, with God. As it is written, ". . . God's share is His own people" (Deuteronomy 32:9).

This is another similarity between Purim and Yom Kippur. When we sin during the year, we feel severed from God. We no longer have a connection with Him. Then Yom Kippur comes. We suddenly realize, in the strongest way, that we have never left the presence of God. He is as close as ever to us. As it is written, "Though your sins be (*shani*) as scarlet, they shall be as white as snow . . ." (Isaiah 1:18). The Talmud explains: If your sins be as *shani*, or, *shanim*, as the years which progress regularly one after the other from creation; still, they will be white as snow. (*Shabbos* 89b).

Although it appears that our sins will stay red forever, it is normal and natural, expected and probable. Still, if we repent, we will be forgiven, completely and unconditionally.

Similarly, Esther said, "I will go to the king, although *against the law*. . . ." A Jew stands before God, the King, regardless of what the laws of nature say. Regardless of how logical it may seem to think that we are no longer the nation of God, still we are.

It is Purim. What are we waiting for? Let us immediately resume our work as the nation of God. There is really nothing in our way.

Referring to Mordechai, the king asked Haman, "What shall be done to a man whom the king delights to honor?" (Esther 6:7).

Why does the king delight to honor him? No reason is given; he just does. Similarly, with the nation of Israel, God delights to honor them, but for no reason. They are His people, and that is reason enough.

A prince walked into the throne room just as the king was receiving dignitaries. The king said, "Come my son, and sit at my side." The guests exchanged puzzled glances. The king responded, "I see you are wondering why this boy is getting honored. You see, he is my son!"

Therefore on Purim we drink wine, more than usual, until, ". . . he doesn't differentiate . . ." Just as God Himself does not make a difference between when we are good or when we are bad, we are always His people. We too on Purim reach for the level when we don't know, the level beyond reason and understanding. Even those whom we have no reason to honor, even those whom we have no reason to love, still we should honor and love them for no reason.

When we are in danger of sinking through the fiftieth gate of uncleanliness, God wrests and pulls us up to the fiftieth gate of holiness. The first time this happened was before the Exodus from Egypt. The Jewish nation was worshiping idols and were about to abandon all hope of ever being redeemed. Therefore, God quickly led them out of Egypt and into the desert. There, they counted forty-nine days and stood before Mount Sinai to receive the Torah. When God spoke to them, they reached the highest spiritual level attainable. Thus, they jumped from the lowest point in the deepest pit to the highest point on the tallest plateau.

Similarly and strangely, Haman, who was on the highest social level, was respected by the king and queen, ended his career hanging from a tree fifty cubits high. He falls by being raised high in the air, for all to see.

Neither should we despair if we are low and downcast. God cares even for the lowly, and he will surely lift us up. And then we will be raised to a level that we would never have attained on our own.

It is written, "Go, gather together all the Jews that are present in Shushan, and fast for me . . ." (Esther 4:16). And also, ". . . they gathered themselves together, and stood for their lives . . ." (Esther 9:16).

When the Jewish people gather together, then Amalek has no power against them. Their true state is unity. The truth about Amalek, on the other hand, is that he is fragmented and apart. His banding together is a deception. The Amalekites stand together only while they attack and make war with other nations. They are a false nation, and their leader is falsely honored as a leader.

When God created the month of *Adar*, he used the

letter *kuf*, which in Hebrew means monkey. A monkey mimics man and his actions, but it is not man. It is rather the false man. In *Adar*, which is the last part of the year, we find the false man, Haman. The year is coming to an end; it is almost gone and is no more. That is when the people "who are no more" appear.

How do we combat the evil of Amalek? By uniting as one by sharing our food with others and acting charitably with the poor, by gathering our families together to feast and enjoy, we abolish falsehood.

During the first Purim, we loved our neighbors, even for no reason, and were united as one people. Amalek was destroyed, and the Second Temple was rebuilt. Many years later, unfortunately, that Temple too was destroyed. Why? Because Jews hated each other for no reason. This brought disunity and destruction.

Let us therefore gather our families and our neighbors and unite with all of the nation of Israel. Thus we will be one and will help rebuild the Third Temple speedily in our days.

It is written, ". . . in the day that the enemies of the Jews hoped to have power over them, though it was *turned to the contrary*, that the Jews had rule over them" (Esther 9:1). And, ". . . the month which was *turned over* for them from sorrow to joy, and from mourning into a good day . . ." (Esther 9:22). And finally, "For then I will *turn* to the people a pure language, that they may all call upon the name of God, to serve Him with one will" (Zephaniah 3:9).

Adar is the month and Purim is the day that turn over. They do not "change" from sorrow to joy; they turn over. What is the difference? Haman had to lead Mordechai around the city and honor him, the king's ring was given over to Mordechai, the fifty-cubit tree was used to hang Haman instead of Mordechai, and the house of Haman, the headquarters for all his wickedness, was given to Mordechai. In sum, whatever Haman did to gain power led to his downfall. And whatever might have harmed the Jewish people turned over and became their salvation. An even more shocking turn of events took place. The very people who were plotting to harm the Jews became Jews themselves. As it is written, "And many of the people of the land became Jews . . ." (Esther 8:17).

This is in a small measure of what will happen in *Mashiach's* time. All the evil and oppression that the nations perpetrated against the Jewish people will become a great salvation. Therefore, do not be overly concerned with the signs of hard times and misery for the Jewish people. With one turn, the afflictions themselves can become their salvation.

Haman had the character of severe and strict judgment. He was a true Amalekite who lived by his sword. Esther wanted to blunt his sharp blade, so she invited him to her banquet to soften him. Amalek is not really high; he just appears high; but stands on nothing, because there is no foundation under him. Therefore, Amalek has the numerical equivalent of *Ram*, meaning high (240). Then, when Amalek is hit he falls all the way down. The Jewish people, on the other hand, are low, but grow with the power of the Torah. They are really high. So when they are hit, they fall down one step at a time.

Let us soften the harshness of the nations by being strong in our traits, the virtues of Jacob, who sat in the tent of Torah and perfected himself more and more.

Rabbi Masya ben Charash said . . . be a tail to lions rather than a head to foxes (*Ethics of Our Fathers* 4:20).

Amalek is the head of the nations, the head of foxes. He attained this position with his tongue of deceit, lies, and falsehood. As it is written, "Who have said, With our tongues we will prevail; our lips are our own: who is lord over us" (Psalms 12:5). He thinks he is the most high and that he will prevail, and no one can lower him from his spot. However, in truth he is only the head of foxes, and his power will soon end, as it is written, ". . . but a lying tongue is but for a moment" (Proverbs 12:19).

On the other hand, the Jewish people are the descendants of Jacob, the younger brother of Esau, the smaller and weaker one. Yet, Jacob is the man of truth whose voice does not lie. It always sounds like his real self, as his father said, ". . . the voice is the voice of Jacob. . . ." It cannot be mistaken. It is him. His words are true, as it is written, "You will show the truth of Jacob . . ." (Micah 7:20). He is the tail to the lion, to God who is a God of truth. He is an appendage to the truth that is always true. And therefore he endures, as it is written, "The lips of truth shall be established forever" (Proverbs 12:19).

It is said of Haman, "No one had a more wicked tongue than Haman" (*Megilla* 13b). Therefore his end was assured, and it quickly came.

We, the people of the Book, the people of truth, justice, and mercy, let us use our inheritance to the utmost. And thus we will break the false power of Amalek, and relegate him once more to be the tail of foxes.

Moses blessed the Jewish people before his death, saying, ". . . and you shall (*tidroch*) tread upon their high places" (Deuteronomy *33:29*).

When Haman was ordered by the king to lead Mordechai on the king's horse, Mordechai was reluctant to get on.

"Why don't you get on?" Haman asked.

"I am too weak from fasting," said Mordechai.

"So what will you do?" asked Haman.

"You bend over, and I will step on you, and get on the horse that way," said Mordechai.

And Haman did just that (*Esther Rabbah* 6). Similarly, the Jewish people will literally tread upon their enemies.

Tidroch also means to tread on a new path, to blaze a new trail. Until the story of Purim, the Written Law prevailed. But after the defeat of Haman-Aamlek, a new Torah path was started. The miracle of Purim was the last miracle to be written as part of the Torah. After that, everything was transmitted orally.

Therefore, the *Megillah* has both the qualities of the Written and Oral Law. It must be written precisely as a Torah, but, it is called a letter, a letter written by Mordechai and Esther to the Jews of all the provinces.

Purim is the big step for the Jewish people. We hold on to the strength of the written Torah, while at the same time we gain strength from the Oral Torah.

In the *Megillah*, the Jews are called *Yehudim*, "of Judah," not by their regular name of *Bnei Yisrael*, the Children of Israel.

The root of the name Yehudah is *modeh*, "to acknowledge a favor, to be thankful and grateful." He who admits that there is one God and denies idols is called a Yehudi, a Jew (*Kiddushin 40*). That is really the barest minimum that a Jew must do. It is the lowest level. This teaches that the *Megillah* and Purim are significant even for the lowly generations, those called *Yehudim*, ordinary Jews. Because no matter how lowly we are, we still have circumcision, *tefillin*, and the holidays. As it is written, "The *Yehudim* (Jews) had light, joy and honor" (Esther 8:16).

The root name of Yehudah is also the four letters of God's name, *yud* and *heh* and *vov* and *heh* (YHVH) plus the letter *dalet*, which means poor. As in the verse, "I will leave in the midst of you an afflicted and poor people, and they shall trust in the name of God" (Zephaniah 3:12). Even if you will be spiritually poor, (*dalet*), still, you will trust in the name of God.

We too, no matter how spiritually poor we are, still

are Yehudim, Jews. And as such, we are worthy of all the miracles of the Purim of old. May it happen in our days.

REDEDICATION TO THE TORAH

"Rabbi Avdimi said, 'When the Jewish people received the Torah at Mount Sinai, God arched the mountain over their heads as a tub, and said, 'If you accept the Torah, then all is well. But if you don't, then you will be buried, here and now.' Later, however, in the days of Achashverosh, they accepted it with all their hearts" (*Shabbos* 88a).

It is written, "The Jews observed and took upon themselves, and their children . . ." (Esther 10:27).

Why did they rededicate themselves to the Torah? It was because the miracle of Purim evoked a feeling of love for God and the Torah in their hearts.

A second interpretation of the same verse is, that in heaven they observed that which the Jewish people accepted on the earth.

There are two realms: the realm of action, which belongs in the physical world, and the realm of speaking and being commanded, which belongs to the spiritual world. When we do the will of God, it cannot become more nor less than our action. It already took its place in the finite world. But the *desire* to do, that is without limit; it has not yet been done and is therefore still infinite. It is connected to a higher plane than is materially possible. And out of the desire grows a commandment, which is the voice of the action. Thus, when the Jews had a strong desire to celebrate Purim, it connected to the voice, to that which was higher than the material world and was infinite. They observed in heaven that which the Jews accepted and desired on earth. They made Purim happen on the earth at the highest spiritual level.

Before the Jewish nation received the Torah, God sent Moses to ask them if they wished to accept it. They answered, "We will do and we will listen!" Then they stood at the foot of Mount Sinai to receive the Torah. God lifted the mountain over their heads and said, "If you accept it, then all will be well. But if you don't, you will be buried right here!" Later when Moses ascended the mountain to receive the Ten Commandments, the Jews worshiped a golden calf. Thus they broke one part of their promise, "We will do . . ."

Now they were left only with the other part of their promise, ". . . and we will listen."

In the days of King Achashverosh they rededicated themselves and accepted the Torah with all their hearts (*Shabbos* 88a). Why did they need to rededicate themselves to "accept" the Torah, when they had never broken the promise to "listen."

Why did God lift the mountain over their heads? And what, allegorically, is a mountain? It symbolizes obstacles that prevent one from observing the Torah. Those obstacles loom before you like a huge mountain that you cannot get through. And God says, "If you agree to live your life guided by the Torah, with all your heart and without reservation, then, even mountains in your way will be lifted."

On Purim, Amalek has been destroyed. He is no longer here to weaken our resolve and dedication. Watch as God lifts the mountains of obstacles from our lives so that we can live a life of Torah.

The Jewish people said, "We will do and we will listen." Then they stood at Mount Sinai, and God lifted the mountain over their heads and said, "Accept the Torah, or you die right here!" Later they worshiped an idol and broke their promise.

Why did they need to be forced to accept the Torah? If they were forced, then they would possess it against their will and not because of a promise. Therefore, when they worshiped an idol, thereby violating one of the commandments, it was as if they did not break their promises. After all, the Torah was not given to them because of their promises, but was forced upon them.

How can lifting the mountain, which happened later, repair their damaged promises? It is because, on the divine level, with God Himself, there is no separate past and future. A thing that happens in the future can repair that which happened in the past. It is possible, for example, to recover from illness because of the future merit of grandchildren who are yet to be born. The future can affect the past, and the past can affect the future.

Of course, if Amalek had not attacked the Jews when they left Egypt, their dedication would have been flawless. They would never have worshiped the Golden Calf, nor would their promises have been broken. There would have been no need to lift the mountain over them, to force them to accept the Torah. Then their promises would have stayed intact, strong, and powerful as their pure hearts.

On Purim, when the Jews destroyed Haman-Amalek, they again experienced their "promises" in their undamaged form. They felt close to the Torah and promised never to leave it again.

It is written, "Therefore the Jews of the villages, that lived in the unwalled towns, made the fourteenth day of the month of *Adar* a day of *gladness and feasting*, and a good day, and of sending portions of food to another" (Esther 9:19). Then later it says again, ". . . that they should make them days of *feasting* and joy . . ." (Esther 9:21).

On Purim we celebrate with feasting and on Yom Kippur with fasting. The forgiveness of Yom Kippur comes after much preparation. Starting with the month of *Elul* and until Yom Kippur, we observe forty days of prayers and repentance. And even on Yom Kippur, the day of forgiveness, we still fast. Then when Yom Kippur is over, we are finally mended.

Purim, on the other hand, requires little preparation. After just a one-day fast on the eve of Purim, we then go right to feasting. Yet everything is mended on Purim day. How? It is mended because we get reconnected to the promises that we made at Mount Sinai. We regain the spiritual level that we had *before* we worshiped the Golden Calf. On Yom Kippur, however, we connect to the forgiveness of the original Yom Kippur. And that was the day that God forgave the Jews *after* they made the Golden Calf.

In some way we can reach a higher spiritual level on Purim than on Yom Kippur, and instead of fasting, we are feasting.

If we are forced into a legally binding action, we can legally protest it in court. And if the Torah was given to us by force, the mountain was held over our heads, why can we not protest? (*Shabbos* 88a).

Had we marched from Egypt straight to Mount Sinai, we would have accepted the Torah with enthusiasm. But Amalek came between us and the Torah, and he weakened our faith. We still wanted the Torah, but had doubts because of Amalek. And therefore we had to be compelled to accept it.

The year that Haman was killed, the holiday of Shavuos followed soon after. The Jewish people felt a great enthusiasm for the Torah. They thought, "Why are we suddenly so excited about the Torah? It must be because Amalek will soon be destroyed, and he will no longer be an obstacle." Therefore they were confident to confront those who hated them. They immediately wrote letters to all the Jewish communities saying that they have the king's permission to fight back.

In the spiritual realm, during Purim each year some of the power of Amalek is erased. We can easily regain our closeness to the Torah, if we desire it with all our hearts.

The most powerful part of the miracle of Purim happened on the night of Passover, as it is written, "On that night the sleep of the king was disturbed . . ." (Esther 6:1). The night of Passover, the anniversary of the Exodus, the "sleep" of the King of the universe was disturbed. How possibly can the King "sleep" if His children are in trouble? And He really never sleeps, but guards Israel. And immediately the miracle started when the servants read that Mordechai saved the king's life.

The spiritual light of the miracle descends on Purim day. We also can experience the levels of spirituality that the Jews attained during that very first Purim, especially their rededication to the Torah. The Torah, after all, is the inheritance of every Jew, to which we can all connect and be part of.

It is written, "So He drove out man; and He placed at the east of the Garden of Eden the cherubim, and a flaming sword which turned round and around, every way, to protect the way of the Tree of Life" (Genesis 3:24).

The sword prevents man from reaching the Tree of Life. The Tree of Life is also the Torah, which gives life to all those who hold it dear. And this sword was also given into the hands of Esau, when his father blessed him with the words, "And by your sword you shall live . . ." (Genesis 27:40). And his grandson, Amalek, attacked the Jewish people on their way to Mount Sinai with his sword. The Amalekites acted in the tradition of their grandfather, who sought always to sever the ties of the Jewish people with God and the Torah. To counter the awesome power of Amalek's sword, God gave the Jews a sword too. As it is written, ". . . with (*lefi*) the *edge* of the sword . . ." (Joshua 11:11). Literally, *lefi* means with the mouth. The Jews have a sword that has a mouth. And also, "Let the high praises of God be in their mouth, and a two-edged (*pipiyos*) sword in their hand" (Psalms 149:6). Literally, *pipiyos* means with two mouths. The power of the Jewish people lies in their two mouths, reciting Torah and prayers to God. The voice of Jacob is the only thing that can counteract the hands of Esau. Only a sword with a "mouth" can destroy the sword of Esau.

The "turning sword" also refers to the sword that cuts around the foreskin that covers the covenant. Amalek blocks the path of those who want to stand at Mount Sinai to receive the Torah. And he also opposes the covenant of circumcision because he does not want the Jew to identify with God. And therefore his sword is also called, "And I will bring a sword upon you, that shall avenge the quarrel of my covenant" (Leviticus 26:25).

On Purim we defeated the sword of Amalek with rededication to the Torah and endless prayers. Let us do the same again now.

"The Jews observed and they took upon themselves." They reaccepted the Torah; and it was as if they had a new Torah just for Purim, the *Megillah*. And what is the special Torah of Purim? It is a story that says decisively that God will never forsake the Jewish people nor allow their total annihilation. As it is written, "And yet for all that, when they be in the land of their enemies, I will not cast them away, neither will I abhor them, to destroy them utterly, and to break my covenant with them: for I am the Lord their God" (Leviticus 26:44).

If the Jewish people are worthy then the misfortune does not happen. But even if they are not worthy and the misfortune does come, still, it can turn into salvation. As it is written, "And it shall come to pass, that as the Lord rejoiced over you to do you good, and to multiply you; so the Lord will rejoice over you to destroy you, and to bring you to nought" (Deuteronomy 28:63). That means, that if you are bad and it is decreed to destroy you, still He will rejoice, because from that decree itself will sprout your redemption. As it happened with Haman.

It is also written, "His anger endures but a moment. Life results from His favor" (Psalms 30:6). The Hebrew word for moment is *rega*, and it is an acrostic that spells *reishis goyim Amalek*: Amalek is the head of the nations. The reign of Amalek is but for a second, because what God really desires is life. Therefore, "So they hanged Haman on the gallows that he had prepared for Mordechai. Then the king's wrath abated" (Esther 7:10). The reason why the King's wrath abated is because that was what he really wanted: to destroy Haman and Amalek.

Let us therefore connect to the new Torah of Purim, that God desires us and He will not abandon us.

Whatever is not eternal and infinite is a lie, deceit, and falsehood. Why? Because sooner or later, eventually the lie will end, and it will be no more. Consequently, the thing that is eternal and infinite is true. As it is written, ". . . and you shall be like a watered garden, whose waters do not become false" (Isaiah 58:13). A spring never dries up, it is forever, and therefore it does not lie. It is true.

Amalek is constantly trying to cut us from the Torah, the eternal word of God. He tries to make the Torah seem like it has an end, that it has a limit. He wants us to think that the Torah is a lie, that it is not eternal. But when Amalek is defeated, the Jewish people discover that the Torah is infinite and will always be part of them. They rededicate themselves and continue what they started. They make the Torah live longer in their own lives; they make it true.

The Torah is written with black ink on parchment using letters to form words, sentences, and paragraphs. This is the first phase of writing. There is also writing on a higher level. As it is written, "And God said to Moses, Write this for a memorial in a book, and rehearse it in the ears of Joshua: for I will utterly blot out the remembrance of Amalek from under the heaven" (Exodus 18:14). It is a writing that is etched into the human heart in the place where there is no forgetting. That is the final form of writing, after which there is no writing.

A prince was taught calligraphy by the royal scribe. When he knew how, he wrote letters to his father in beautiful script. Then one day the king called him and asked him to bring his paper and pen. "Now stand next to me," said the king, "while I dictate my new edict."

To communicate the desire of the king, that is the final form of writing. Similarly, when the words of the Torah are inscribed in us and communicate to us the desire of the King, that is the final form of writing.

God wants the Jewish people to be in the world always, and this desire is etched into our body with the commandment of circumcision. Amalek wants to destroy the Jewish people and at the same time erase the writing, the Torah, from our body. Therefore, on Purim when we got rid of Amalek, it is as if the Torah was renewed.

It is written, "And (Anochi) I will surely hide my face in that day for all the evils which they have done . . ." (Deuteronomy 31:18). The very word Anochi is used in the Ten commandments: "I am (Anochi) God your Lord who took you out of Egypt" (Exodus 20:2).

When God gave the Torah on Mount Sinai, it was with a spectacular display of light and sound. The entire world stood silent as God spoke to His nation, Israel. But then the Jews worshiped the Golden Calf and abandoned the teachings of the Torah. For a while. Then they repented, and God again gave them the tablets with the Ten Commandments. This time it was given quietly, without the public ceremony of the first tablets.

The Torah is sometimes hidden and sometimes revealed. The "open" tablets did not last, but the "hidden" tablets did. The Torah starts with the creation; the whole universe was in upheaval as God created the world. At the end of the Torah, Moses blessed the Jewish people. His last words are ". . . and you will tread on their high places" (Deuteronomy 33:29). That is at the end, when Amalek is defeated; Mordechai steps on Haman's back to mount the king's horse and be honored.

When Amalek is defeated, the Torah again becomes revealed and gives us light to the end of days.

"The Jews observed and they took upon themselves. . . ." They observed in heaven that which was accepted down below (Megilla 7a).

The spiritual order was turned upside down. Usually it starts in heaven and ends up on the earth. This time, it all started down below: Esther fasted, Mordechai pleaded, the Jews prayed, and the children studied Torah. Similarly the name Haman was turned upside down and it spelled Mordechai, the left hand became the right, and the beginning became the end.

On a normal day, we have to erase things in order; on Purim the order does not matter. It can be done backward, forward, or upside down. And it is all possible because it is Purim.

Thus we can be rid of Amalek, in thought, in speech, and in deed—if only we want it with all our hearts.

Torah Is Light

Haman the Amalekite wanted to extinguish the light of the Torah by annihilating the Jewish nation. What did Mordechai do? He gathered the young children of Shunan and studied the Torah with them (Esther Rabbah 3).

It is written, "The Jews had light, gladness, joy and honor" (Esther 8:16). "Light" is the Torah (Megilla 16b).

If the word light means Torah, why isn't the word Torah used in that passage? It was because of their repentance that they experienced the Torah as light. They were uplifted to the highest level of faith, just as when they stood at Mount Sinai. Then, God darkened the sky with the darkest clouds, but they saw the light.

A student went to study at a yeshivah. When he returned, his father asked him, "Well, what did you learn, my son?" The boy answered, "I believe in God, and I believe in the Torah." The father replied, "You still need more study. Go back for another year." The next year when the son returned, his father again asked him about his progress. The boy said, "There really is a God; and we can't live without the Torah." The father smiled; he was pleased with his son's achievement.

Amalek prevents the Jewish people from experiencing strong faith. When the Amalekites are wiped away and are no longer a threat, the light of faith will shine into the Jewish hearts again, as it did at Mount Sinai. And suddenly the heavens will open, and the light of both the Written and the Oral Law will light up the sky. As it is written, "Write this for a memorial in a book, and rehearse it in the ears of Joshua: for I will utterly blot out the remembrance of Amalek from under the heaven." When Amalek is wiped out, then the writing in the Book and the rehearsing of the ear will both be returned. The complete light of the Torah will be revealed.

It is written, "God talked with you face to face in the mountain in the midst of the fire" (Exodus 5:4). There exists also, the face of shame, as it is written, "O God, righteousness belongs to you, but to us belongs the shame of the face . . ." (Daniel 9:7). On the deepest level, this verse reads as follows. While we are busy doing shameful acts, still God is busy doing acts of kindness. While the Jews were worshiping and dancing around the Golden Calf, God was busy carving the Ten Commandments on the stone tablets.

A prince's father loved to have him nearby. The king enjoyed looking at his son and admired him constantly. One day the prince was disobedient. He sat down at his father's desk and played with the ink; it spilled and soiled several important documents. While the prince was busy, the king was on his throne thinking of a favorite toy he should fashion for him. The king had it made quickly and looked for the prince to give it to him. The prince was also on his way to his father, but to apologize for spilling the ink. As they turned a corner, they suddenly came face to face, eye to eye.

How different that sudden meeting was than the other ones. The king was excited with the new toy that he had made for his son, while the prince was red with shame for destroying his father's documents.

Both the Jewish people and God want to be face to face. But Amalek always gets in the way, weakens our faith, and we have instead the face of shame.

Purim is the day when Amalek has no power over us. We can renew our faith and dedication to the Torah. Let us encounter God on this day, face-to-face.

"The commandment is a lamp; and the Torah law is (or) light" (Proverbs 8:23). In the *Megillah* we read, "The Jews had (orah) light, gladness, joy and honor" (Esther 8:16).

When the Jews had "light" (orah instead of or) after the downfall of Haman, it was of a special nature. Just as its spelling, the light was longer and more powerful than usual and spread into every part of their body. It filtered into their deepest depths, the most secret and hidden places. It made their whole body, the 248 limbs and 365 tendons, a vessel for the Torah and its commandments.

The entire Torah is composed of the names of God. All its teachings help reveal God's name. Amalek attacks the Jewish people and prevents them from observing the Torah. He weakens their faith and their enthusiasm and makes the light of the Torah dim.

Therefore, when Amalek is defeated, when Haman and his cohorts are destroyed, then the light of the Torah shines brightly once more. Consequently, Purim is a holiday that is full of Torah light. Let us not be lazy to collect every particle of it.

"The Jews had light, gladness, joy, and honor" (Esther 8:16).

It is not enough to accept the Torah; rather, we must cleave to the Torah and hang on to it for dear life. We must take hold of it, must take possession of it so that it does not just slip out of our hands. And to take possession of it we must use every one of the forty-eight qualities taught by our sages: study, attentive listening, articulate speech, intuitive understanding, discernment, awe, reverence, modesty, joy, purity, ministering to the sages, closeness with colleagues, sharp discussion with students, deliberation, knowing the written Torah, the Mishnah, limited business activity, limited sexual activity, limited pleasure, limited sleep, limited conversation, limited laughter, delayed anger, a good heart, faith in the sages, acceptance of suffering, knowing one's place, being happy with one's lot, making a hedge around one's utterances, claiming no credit for one's self, being beloved, loving God, loving other people, loving charitable acts, loving justice, loving reproof, keeping far from honor, not being arrogant with his learning, not enjoying halachic decision making, sharing his fellow's yoke, judging him favorably, setting him on the truthful course, thinking deliberately in his study, asking and answering, listening and contributing to the discussion, learning in order to teach, learning in order to do, making his teacher wiser, pondering over what he has learned, and repeating a saying in the name of the one who said it. For you have learned that whoever repeats a thing in the name of the one who said it brings redemption to the world, as it is written, "And Esther said to the king in the name of Mordechai" (*Ethics of Our Fathers* 6:6). And if Torah is that precious to us, then it gives us a spectacular light.

Not only did God give us the Torah, which is a treasure house of goodness, but He also planted it into our hearts.

A king once gave his son an ivory chess set. Then he said to him, "Come, sit down, and we'll play with your new chess set." The king played with his son and continued to admire the pieces, telling him what a pleasure it was playing with him. When they finished playing, the boy said, "I never realized what a wonderful game chess is. And all the more so that it is made of ivory. And best of all, to play it with you, father!"

God gave us the Torah; that is the Written Law. And he planted the Torah firmly in our hearts; that is the Oral Law. On Purim, not only did God perform miracles as the Written Law, which descended from heaven, but He also made us good. He planted a love for it into our hearts, and we accepted it.

Isaac blessed his son Jacob with, ". . . the voice is the voice of Jacob." Jacob has the voice for prayer and words of Torah wisdom. If only he could pray and study properly! What would his prayers consist of then? He would express the love that he has for God and how much he needs Him. But Amalek is always there on the threshold. Just when Jacob is about to pray or to receive Torah wisdom, Amalek attacks and stops him.

Thus when Amalek is destroyed, the love that the Jewish people want to express overflows. There is a great outpouring of gratitude and Torah study. We are free to do what we do best. And for this reason,

before every prayer we first mention that God redeemed us and since He did, therefore we can pray. Prayer and redemption then are two sides of the same coin. On one side of the coin is the destruction of Haman, "Cursed is Haman!" And on the other side, is the formulation of prayer, "Blessed is Mordechai!" And as the sages of the Talmud commented, on Purim one really doesn't know which one should cause celebration.

"The Jews had (*orah*) light."

When light comes from its source, it is *or*, as in, "And there was (*or*) light" (Genesis 1:3). But when light is being received, then it is *orah*. The Jewish people *received* the light of the Torah. They were vessels for it, as the flame is to the wick. And as long as there is a wick, there is also a flame. Torah is constantly being given without end and without limit. As it is written, ". . . a great voice that did not end. . ." (Deuteronomy 5:19). But Amalek is also always there to prevent the flame from burning the wick. And when he is destroyed, an infinite light will be seen that will shine from one end of the world to the other.

It is written, "And God said, Let there be light, and there was light" (Genesis, 1:3).

Our sages taught us that wherever it says, "and there was," it is a sad occasion. What was sad about the light that God created? It was, it passed, and it was no more. That light was so powerful that one was able to see from one end of the universe to the other. But God hid it for the use of the righteous in a future time. The light that remained was incomplete, and therefore there was sadness when God created it. It was only in the world for a very short time. Therefore, light always follows darkness, as it is written, "And it was evening, and it was morning . . ." (Genesis 1). It is incomplete.

There is a light, however, that is still whole. This is the light coming from God by way of the Torah, as it is written, "In the light of the king's countenance is life, his favor is like a rain cloud in the spring" (Proverbs 16:15). When we experience that light, we are happy, and thus "The Jews had light, and joy. . . ."

A SINGULAR NATION

"And Haman said to the king Achashverosh, There is a singular people scattered abroad and dispersed among the peoples" (Esther 3:8). The words "there is" are one word in Hebrew: *yesh-no*.

When the light of God fills the world, it is called *yesh*; there is *substance*. As it is written, "That I may cause those that love me to inherit *substance*; and I will fill their treasures" (Proverbs 8:21).

The name *Yisrael*, Israel, is composed of two halves: *yud* and *shin* and *reish-aleph-lamed*. The letters *reish-aleph-lamed* are numerically equal to 241. The substance of the Jewish people is that they follow the 241 paths to wisdom. Those paths are usually hidden, but on Purim they become revealed through the *Megillah*. The word *Megillah* itself means, it reveals that which is hidden.

Let us therefore become people of substance on this happy holiday of Purim. And while you are joyous, make your treasures ones of substance.

The Talmud asks, Why don't we say *Hallel*, the festival prayer of praise, on Purim as we do on the other holidays? Because we only say *Hallel* for miracles associated with the land of Israel. It is said on Passover and on the other major holidays because the Jewish people were on their way to the land of Israel. But Purim happened in Persia and its provinces, and therefore we do not say *Hallel*. Another answer is that the reading of the *Megillah* is like *Hallel*; it is a prayer of praise in story form (*Megillah*).

When the Jewish people are in desperate need of help, God may save them with a miracle. He changes the rules of nature, and He makes the improbable, the astonishing, and impossible happen.

A king was riding through the countryside with his entourage and a group of soldiers. They came upon a coach and its horses mired in the mud. A whole family was working feverishly to push it out of the mud, but it did not budge. As the king passed, he felt pity for the family and called out, "Stop!" Everyone came to a sudden halt. The king called to the family, "All right, move out of the way, and I will get you out of the mud!" The soldiers immediately dismounted, fastened their group of horses to the coach, and with one command, the coach was out of the mud. The family cheered and came to thank the king.

To do a miracle, God tells you to step aside also, and He takes over. On Purim, God did not tell us to step aside. But rather, everything happened through the work of people: Mordechai and Esther, and the Jews of all the provinces. The miracle did not break the rules of nature. Nothing impossible or supernatural occurred. And therefore we do not say *Hallel*.

"A person has to drink wine on Purim till he does not know between 'Cursed is Haman' and 'Blessed is Mordechai'" (*Megilla* 7b).

There are two ways that God saves the Jewish people. In a worthy generation, God uplifts the *tzaddik* spiritually and saves the generation by his merit. But if the people are unworthy, and do not have enough merit, then God saves them in another way. He sends Amalek or his cohorts to attack the Jews. And because Amalek is so vile and wicked, God destroys them, and consequently the Jews are saved. As it is written, "Were it not that I feared the wrath of the enemy..." (Deuteronomy 32:27). This means that sometimes when Jews are punished, they are put into the hands of a fearful enemy so that later they can be saved.

Therefore, we wonder what saved us on Purim: was it the merit of Mordechai, so that we should say "Blessed is Mordechai" or was it rather the wickedness of Haman the Amalekite that brought his downfall, so we should say, "Cursed is Haman"?

And that is the true spirit of Purim. On the one hand, we are proud of the activities of the righteous among us, such as Mordecai. But, at the same time, we must be humble enough to think that it was the wickedness of Haman that brought about his downfall, rather than our own merit.

"And Haman said to the King Achashverosh, There is (*yesh-no*) a singular people scattered abroad and dispersed among the peoples..." (Esther 3:8).

The Hebrew word *yesh-no* also means, *yashen*, "he is sleeping." Haman argued that the God of the Jewish people is sleeping, and as proof he offered the fact that numerous tragedies had befallen them and He did not help them. Therefore, Haman argued, now is the best time to attack and annihilate them. Haman was not far from the truth. It seemed as if God was "hiding" in that period of history. The First Holy Temple was destroyed in that era, the Jews were exiled from their land, and many were even sold as slaves. What was hidden?

We know God on two levels. One is the *yesh*, "there is," the aspect of God that we experience. Everything we see, feel, or imagine, everything tangible that has substance, is defined by *yesh*. Then there is the highest level, which we cannot experience in any manner whatsoever. That is the aspect of God known as *ayin*, "not"; there is nothing to say about it. It is of such high spirituality that it is utterly beyond our realm. We cannot speak of it because speaking involves words, and words are *yesh*; they have substance.

The *yesh*, the divine presence of God, seemed to be sleeping, because the Jews were "scattered abroad, and dispersed."

Still, there was one Jew among them who was a model of true faith. He was not bothered by the fact that God was "sleeping." He knew that an aspect of God's greatness and strength was to be silent even when the nations have the upper hand. This man was Mordechai, and he was able to rekindle the faith of the Jewish people.

MORDECHAI THE JEW

It is written, "Now in Shushan the capital city there was a man, *a Jew*, whose name was Mordechai, the son of Yair, the son of Shimei, the son of Kish, a Benjaminite" (Esther 2:5).

The words, "a Jew," in Hebrew are written *Yehudi*. The Talmud says not to read it *Yehudi* but rather as *yechidi*, singular (*Megilla* 15).

We are all made of a variety of experiences and opinions. If a unifying thread pulls everything together, then we are whole and singular. Otherwise we are torn apart. The Jewish people, too, are made of many thousands of individuals. Yet, they are one people when the Torah is the unifying thread in their lives. Otherwise they are a loose band of individuals.

The Jews of that time were spread out and dispersed, but Mordechai was one complete Jew. He was whole, unbroken, wholly undivided. When a Jew is in such spiritual condition, Amalek cannot touch him. When can Amalek harm us? When we are separated, the way we were when Amalek first attacked us on the way from Egypt. He came to fight the Jews in *Rephidim*, a word similar to *mefuradim*, "spread out." When the Jews are not united, then Amalek has power over them.

Mordechai, who was totally whole himself, helped unite the Jewish people and thus bring the redemption. The words of Esther to him were "Go and gather together . . ." and later, when they fought their enemies, ". . . gather themselves together and stand for their lives. . . ."

Accordingly, after the victory, in honor of Mordechai the Yehudi, the singular one, we celebrate Purim with symbols of togetherness. We read the *Megillah* in the congregation; we celebrate Purim as a family holiday, as it is written, "every family," and we send presents and treat the poor with extra kindness. And we honor Mordechai by singing about him on Purim: "The rose of Jacob was cheerful and glad, when *they joined together* and saw the royal blue robes of Mordechai" (*Prayer Book*).

Let us therefore without hesitation unite within and without and bring the redemption that we are all waiting for.

It is written, "Then said his wise men and Zeresh his wife unto him, If Mordechai be of the *seed* of the Jews, before whom you have started to fall, you will not prevail against him, but you will surely fall before him" (Esther 6:13). It is also written, ". . . is then not a man's life like a tree in the field? . . ." (Deuteronomy 20:19). And it is also written, "Light is planted for the righteous . . ." (Psalms 97:11).

Some trees grow fruit and others do not. Similarly, there are Jews who are good in many ways but only for themselves; they are called *yishrei lev*, "who are straight in their heart." But the *tzaddik*, the righteous one, makes more good Jews by planting the seeds of righteousness in others and thus grows fruit.

To fight Amalek one needs to be a *tzaddik*, righteous beyond himself. Therefore, Mordechai is called "the *seed* of the Jews"; he plants seeds in the Jewish people and makes more Jews. He was like the first Jew, Abraham, who dedicated his whole life to planting the seeds of faith in the hearts of other men. Even the Amalekite Zeresh and the co-conspirators of Haman, recognized the power of such a man. They knew that all Jewish enemies will fall before him.

We too should be like Mordechai and plant seeds of the Jewish faith wherever we go, thereby helping protect our people from all harm.

Another interpretation is that God plants light into the *tzaddik*, the righteous one, so that he can light the way for the generation. In each *tzaddik* He plants the measure that the generation needs. The masses who want to receive light and guidance from the *tzaddik* must connect with him, and thereby become "straight of heart."

The spiritual world is dynamic and always balancing itself. When impurity increases, so does purity. When evil is on the increase, righteousness is not far behind. And thus, when the Amalekite, the wicked, corrupt, vile, malicious, and hateful Haman, was on the rise, God brought Mordechai the Jew, who was his opposite. He was good, honest, just, moral, pure, and generous. And in the *Megillah*, Mordechai is mentioned first and then Haman, because God always prepares the cure before He brings the blow. Mordechai was the cure for the blow that the Jewish people were about to receive through the evil designs of Haman.

Mordechai is called *Yehudi*, "a Jew," in the *Megillah*. The truth is though that anyone who rejects idol worship, is called a *Yehudi*, a Jew (*Megilla* 13a). So why was Mordechai singled out with that title?

The rejection of idol worship has to be done with every fiber of one's being. Unfortunately, the Jews of that generation were not strong enough to do that; they could not challenge the wicked Haman, who made everyone bow to him like to an idol. Then along came Mordechai, who was a real "Jew" in every fiber of his being, and he challenged Haman.

It is written, "There was a *man*, a Jew, whose name was Mordechai . . ." (Esther 2:5). And it is written, "If it were not for God who was on our side when a *man* rose up against us" (Psalms 124:2).

The Talmud comments, "A *man*, but not a king" (*Megilla* 11a). This means, that because Haman was only a man, and not a king, his challenger was also only "a man, a Jew." But if the wicked enemy would have been a king, then the challenger also would have had to be a king, as was the case in Egypt. Since the wicked enslaver was the Pharaoh, he was challenged by Joseph and Moses, both of whom were members of the royal household. Joseph was sold to an officer of the Pharaoh and later elevated to be second in rank to king, whereas Moses grew up in the palace of the Pharaoh, as the adopted son of the princess Basyah.

Similarly, when the *Mashiach* comes, the wicked oppressor of the Jews will be a king, and the redeemer of the Jewish people will have to be a king, as well.

Although the Jewish people were in exile, God prepared a *tzaddik*, a righteous one, who was himself not in exile. This was Mordechai who refused to bow to Haman. So that in the mind and consciousness of Mordechai, Haman was just an ordinary human being, not one to fear or to be intimidated by.

We too, on Purim, renew our spiritual strength and reject our exile, our fear and trembling before the earthly rulers. We re-establish in our minds the singularity of God, and humble ourselves completely before Him.

AND MORDECHAI WILL NOT BOW DOWN

"And all the king's servants that were in the king's gate, bowed, and did reverence to Haman: for the king had so commanded concerning him. But Mordechai will not bow down nor do him reverence" (Esther 3:2).

In every generation there is a *tzaddik*, a righteous one who is the exemplar of the Jewish faith in its strongest and purest form. In his generation, it was Mordechai. Therefore, it is not written of him, that *he did not* bow down, but, he *will not* bow down. He never had any doubt, not for a moment, whether he should bow down or not. As soon as Haman was elevated and all the people bowed down to him, Mordechai knew immediately that he would never bow down to him. When other Jews saw Mordechai they saw his utter conviction, without the smallest doubt. This helped them be stronger in their faith and rely on God for their salvation.

We should not hesitate when challenged by the evil in the world. We should rather go forward with the power of our faith, and we will see our enemies falling by the wayside.

It is written, "On learning who Mordechai's people were, he scorned to lay hands on him alone, and looked for a way to destroy all the Jews throughout the whole kingdom of Achashverosh, Mordechai and all his race" (Esther 3:6).

Haman looked at the Jews in Shushan and noticed that many of them were assimilated. He met them at the banquets of the king and drank and reveled in their company. But he also knew that Mordechai, the Jew who did not bow to him, was representative of what a Jew was supposed to look like. He knew that he was a *tzaddik*, that he followed the Jewish tradition with complete righteousness. And therefore, when Mordechai did not bow to him, Haman felt as if the entire Jewish nation was refusing to bow to him, and he decided to kill all of them.

The decision of Haman to kill all the Jews, in the spiritual realm, turned out to be their best defense. Because, if in the mind of the arch-enemy of the Jews, all the Jews are equal to Mordechai, than how much more so in the "mind" of Him who loves the Jews?! Therefore, not only was it decreed that Mordechai be saved but all of the Jews must be saved too.

DAYS OF FEASTING

It is written, "As the days wherein the Jews rested from their enemies, and the month which turned for them from sorrow to joy, and from mourning into a good day: that they should make them *days of feasting* and joy, and sending portions one to the other, and gifts to the poor" (Esther 9:22).

How do we make them, transform them, into days of feasting? By remembering. And what is remembering? Reaching into our heart where there is no forgetfulness. And where is that? It is the place where we stand before the Creator with complete humility. In that place Amalek has no dominion.

What are ordinary days? They are days when we forget who we are and are disconnected from the inner core of faith of our heart. Then our days follow the laws of nature, the regular and ordinary happenings of life. But if we are connected with God, then we have the miraculous, the new, and the ever exciting and joyous.

Let us then remember, and transform our ordinary days into days of feasting and joy.

It is written, "The voice is the voice of Jacob" (Genesis 27:22). There are two uses for the voice of Jacob. One is prayer and reciting words of Torah; the other is to be silent. They both come from two facets of wisdom. The lower level of wisdom gives us silence, which protects our soul, whereas the higher level of wisdom gives us the voice in Torah and prayer.

Jacob met two sisters, his cousins, Leah and Rachel. Leah used her voice, and Rachel used her silence. When Jacob was about to marry Rachel, he realized that her father would trick him. He gave Rachel a secret word that she could whisper to him during the marriage ceremony. Rachel also knew that her father was going to trick Jacob and told the secret word to her sister Leah. Then she remained silent. Her silence saved her sister from embarrassment and possibly worse. Later, when her son Joseph was sold to Egypt, her other son Benjamin was silent about his whereabouts. And even later, Esther, a descendant from the tribe of Benjamin, was also silent: ". . . Esther had not disclosed her people nor her family, because Mordechai had forbidden her to do so" (Esther 2:10).

Leah was constantly praying and her eyes were worn from tears. Each child who was born to her was named for one of her prayers, and especially her fourth one, whom she named Yehudah, saying, "Now I will praise God . . ." (Genesis 29:35).

There are two types of fruit that have a very strong effect on our senses, mind, and body. They are spices with strong fragrance and grapes made into wine. As our sages have taught, "Rabbi Nathan says; When one would grind the incense, the other would say, 'Grind thoroughly, thoroughly grind,' because the sound is beneficial for the spices" (Kerisos 6a). Talk-

ing makes the fragrance of spices even better, but wine is better when it is pressed in silence.

Silence protects the body lest it became too physical and overpower the soul, as does wine. We need to be silent to keep the power of wine within bounds. But the fragrance of spices is on the level of the soul itself and is like prayer and Torah study.

Mordechai had both qualities. He was called Yehudi because he had the quality of Yehudah, the son of Leah, the one who prays and studies Torah. And he also had the quality of Benjamin; he was a Benjaminite and was able to be silent when necessary.

We have days of feasting and joy: we feast with wine that must be protected with silence, and we have joy, with fragrant spices, to voice our happiness with words of Torah and prayer.

The Talmud says, "The meal of Purim which is eaten *at night* is not considered complying with the requirements of the law" (*Megilla* 7b). This means that the meal and celebration of Purim were not given so people could walk or sit around in the darkness but rather to make Purim a day of happiness and joy.

Wait not for next year, but right now celebrate this wondrous holiday with happiness.

It is written, "This people I have formed for me, and they shall proclaim my praises" (Isaiah 43:21).

The Jewish people's mission in this world is to witness that God created the world. Their well-being and their very existence are bound inseparably to the Kingdom of God. Without God they do not exist; and on the human level, without the Jewish people, God's kingdom is not known in the world. Thus, when the Jews heard the king's decree that they were about to be annihilated, they were deeply saddened. They were in great pain knowing that no one would be left to witness for God. This pained them more than their own death.

This is true even for a Jew on the lower level. His life is crowded with material concerns, and he has little time for spiritual matters. Yet, when the moment arrives, near death, he gathers all his strength, and prepares to hand over his soul to his Maker. Haman's purpose in killing the Jews was to make God's name forgotten; may it never happen! And when Haman was destroyed, there was great rejoicing in heaven, just as for the people on earth.

Who made Purim into a feast day? It started with a celebration in heaven. The Jews survived! All the angels rejoiced, knowing that just as they call to each other, "Holy, holy, holy, is God the Lord of hosts, the whole world is full of His glory!" (Isaiah 6:3), the Jewish people on earth will continue to do the same.

SENDING GIFTS

Then Mordechai set these things on record and sent letters to all the Jews in all the provinces of King Achashverosh, far and near, binding them to keep the fourteenth and fifteenth day of the month of *Adar*, year by year, as the days on which the Jews got relief from their enemies and as the month which was changed for them from sorrow into joy, from a time of mourning to a holiday. They were to keep them as days of feasting and joy, days for sending presents of food to one another and gifts for the poor. (Esther 9:20–22)

Why is Purim the only holiday when we send gifts to one another? The answer is that unity is the weapon against Amalek. Jacob and the twelve tribes, already at the infancy of the Jewish nation, used this weapon against Esau, the grandfather of Amalek. Jacob and his children banded together to defeat his evil plans.

The Jewish people make God's name known in the world, and they are God's name, so to speak. And if one letter, or even part of a letter, is missing then it is not the name any longer. Thus by loving each other, the Jewish people connect and together form the letters of God's name. As a result they make God's name known in the world. But how can we unite when Amalek keeps stopping us? We can, if we erase Amalek, but how? Only by uniting!

Therefore, on Purim, both happened simultaneously. Mordechai gathered together the Jews, Haman attended Esther's banquet, the Jews gathered and united even more, Haman was found guilty of plotting the death of the Jews and was executed, and the Jews united even more to the extent that they were ready to challenge all their enemies. The Jews were saved, Amalek was defeated, and Purim was established as a holiday.

The essence of Purim then is to unite all the Jews. We can safely say that everything that we do on Purim should reflect this unity. Let us not wait until next year to do this, but do it right now in the proper time.

It is written, "Now in Shushan the capital city, there was a singular Jew, whose name was Mordechai . . ." (Esther 2:5).

The word Jew in Hebrew is *Yehudi*, and the Midrash comments, "Don't read it *Yehudi* but *yechidi*, singular" (*Midrash, Esther* 6:4).

Mordechai united the Jewish people and made them one and singular. How did he do this? What quality did he possess that he could bring people together as friends? He loved every single Jew and planted the seeds of love in their hearts.

We are commanded in the Torah, "You should love your friend like yourself. I am God" (Leviticus 19:18). "Your friend" also refers to God. You should love your friend and God like yourself. Because to love one and not the other is incomplete. And therefore, the word *Yehudi* itself is *yechidi*, "to unite"; to be a real Jew we must be uniting and helping unite the Jewish people.

How do we make one people from such a variety of people? Only if we connect with the spark of vitality that is in all of us. After all, in essence, we are one. If we could only ignore that which separates us and look only at that which unites us, then we would always be a singular people.

On Purim we have no reason to favor one Jew over the other, rich or poor, slave or freeman. We shower them all with love, gifts, and good will.

There is the Written Law, the Torah, and there is the Oral Law, the explanation and commentary to the Torah. During the First Temple period, the Written Law was supreme, and the Oral Law was only secondary. The spiritual energy of the Temple came then from the Written Law. And because it is written, it gave a very strong energy to the Temple. When the Jews sinned, it was not destroyed until they committed the three cardinal sins of idol worship, murder, and incest.

During the Second Temple, on the other hand, the Oral Law was supreme, with a renewed vigor and interest in all its details. The spiritual energy of the Second Temple came from the Oral Law, which is taught with words and is weaker as a means of communication than writing. Therefore, when the Jews sinned during the Second Temple, as soon as they merely disliked one another, it was destroyed because the Oral Law itself depends on one person liking another person. Otherwise why would a person orally teach another the Torah? So if there was hatred, the Oral Law ceased to exist.

The Written Law is the Torah that we receive from God; the Oral Law is the Torah that we live. And if we do not live it, then calamity befalls us.

The *Megillah* has both qualities; it has to be written like a Torah scroll, with precision, yet it is called a letter (Esther 9:26,29), and the laws of its writing are much more lenient than those of a Torah scroll. It is therefore the link between the First and Second Temple; its miracle helped the Second Temple be rebuilt.

If we remember to love one another, to give to one another, to share whatever we have with the other, then the threads of the Oral Law will be strong. We would be worthy to uncover the place of the Second Temple, which is an oral tradition, and ultimately rebuild the Third Temple soon in our days.

The Torah is the light of all souls; it unites all those who have a share in it. When the Jews throw off the yoke of the Torah, they throw away the unity too. And similarly, when the Jewish people do not love one another, then the Torah too becomes weak among them.

Let us therefore break the stone shell around our hearts and replace it with a heart of flesh. Starting with this Purim day, we will strive to love our friends and help bring unity to the Jewish nation. With that we will strengthen the Torah among us, which will instruct us to the end of days.

THE TRANQUILITY OF PURIM

It is written, "On the thirteenth day of the month of *Adar*, and on the fourteenth day of the same, they rested, and made it a day of feasting and gladness. But the Jews that were in Shushan assembled together on the thirteenth day thereof and on the fourteenth day thereof, and rested on the fifteenth day, and made it a day of feasting and gladness" (Esther 9:17–18).

After all the struggles of this world, a person comes to a resting place, literally and spiritually. He lived the good and just life, repaired whatever was amiss, and all is finally in its proper place. Gone is the tumult and turmoil, the struggle and conflict, the challenge, strain and effort. All is still.

Amalek's war against the Jews is to prevent them from ever reaching this level of rest, peace, and tranquility. Because Amalek knows that we can only destroy him if we are at rest, the place of our greatest strength, as it is written, "Therefore it shall be, when God your Lord gives you rest and peace from your enemies from every side, in the land which He is giving you to occupy as your patrimony, you shall blot out the memory of the Amalekites from under the heaven" (Deuteronomy 25:19).

Amalek himself is full of tumult and chaos, as it is written, "But the wicked are like the troubled sea,

when it cannot rest, whose waters cast up mire and dirt" (Isaiah 57:20). Quiet is their antithesis; and with quiet, they disappear.

When the time came, the Jews destroyed their enemies by fighting them. But they destroyed more of them with quietude. As it is written, "But the other Jews who were in the king's provinces gathered themselves together, and stood for their lives, and had rest from their enemies, and slew off their foes seventy-five thousand; but they did not touch the plunder" (Esther 9:16). When the Jews were finally at rest, they got rid of more of the enemy than they did with the war.

Therefore the holiday was established on the day of rest, after the victory. That day they had total victory over Amalek, because they were finally at rest.

We, too, should enjoy the tranquility of Purim. It is the highest spiritual level that one can attain in one's lifetime. It is a taste of the World to Come, the infinitely peaceful and serene place where the souls of the righteous enjoy the light of the Divine presence.

Amalek prevents the Jewish people from giving honor to God's name. He oppresses, persecutes, and subjugates them. And while persecuted, the Jews don't realize what they are missing. Rather, they are too busy tending to their miserable daily needs. But when Amalek is destroyed, we rejoice. We are again able to witness to the world about God, the creator of heaven and earth. And suddenly we realize all that we missed; what we could have been and done all the years of our oppression. Therefore it is written, ". . . when God your Lord has given you rest from all your enemies . . ." (Deuteronomy 25:19). When you finally rest, you realize the evil that Amalek has committed against you, and you hate him even more. Similarly, after Haman and the other murderers were crushed, and the Jews rested, they finally realized the misery they endured and they hated him even more.

On Purim, our day of tranquility, let us realize all that the enemy has prevented us from doing. Now, we are free. We can finally do our utmost in Torah and good deeds. When do we begin?!

THE HAPPINESS OF PURIM

It is written, "On the thirteenth day of the month of *Adar*; and on the fourteenth day of the same, they rested, and made it a day of *feasting and gladness*. But the Jews that were in Shushan assembled together on the thirteenth day thereof and on the fourteenth day thereof; and rested on the fifteenth day, and made it a day of *feasting and gladness*" (Esther 9:17–18).

The Midrash says, "The joy of Purim is as beloved to God as the joy of Sabbath. As it is written, '. . . that they should make them days of feasting and joy . . .' (Esther 9:22). And of Sabbath it is written, 'These are the words which God has commanded, that you should do them'" (Exodus 35:1). In Hebrew the word in both places is *la'asos*, "to do."

Ever since Esau and then Amalek came into the world, God battled with them endlessly. It is almost as if the world has lost its day of rest. But when Amalek is finally defeated, the wars end; tranquility returns. The world gets Sabbath back. Sabbath is the joy of each of the weekdays. With the defeat of Amalek and the return of Sabbath, we also get back joy.

Let us treat the joy of Purim with great respect. It is, after all, the joy of Sabbath itself that we experience.

———————

It is written, "Stone is a burden and sand is a dead weight, but to be angered by a fool is more burdensome than either" (Proverbs 27:3).

Who makes God tired? Doesn't He have a day of rest, the day of Sabbath? The truth is, that although God gets to rest from all the ordinary burdens of the world, He gets no rest from the anger of the fool. And when the fool is defeated, rest, and joy return to the world. When the wicked Amalek was finally defeated, the joy was boundless. We can all feel the heavy burdens that have been lifted from us. We will rejoice knowing that God rejoices with us, too.

———————

". . . to be vexed by a fool is more burdensome than both of them." The anger of the wicked is very strong. As we find, "I said I would scatter them into corners, I would make the remembrance of them to cease from *among men*. Were it not that I feared the wrath of the enemy, lest their adversaries should behave strangely, and lest they should say, Our hand is high, and God had not done all this. For they are a nation void of counsel, *neither is there any understanding in them*" (Deuteronomy 27–28). The last three letters of the last three words spell Haman. The fact that God placed the Jewish people in the hands of Haman was a great favor for them. It was the remedy before the blow, to place them in the hands of "men." Had they been in the hands of a king, the redemption would have been more difficult. Because the king would realize that he is a messenger of God, and wouldn't have rested until he completed his mission. But in the hands of a man there was hope of saving them.

"The wrath of the enemy," thinking that they have infinite power over the Jews; and that they are "men" rather than a king, that saved the Jewish people from annihilation.

Finally, on Purim, the wrath of the enemy is quiet and so is their oppression. Our burden has been lifted and we are saved. Now we can be truly happy.

———————

The Talmud says, "When *Adar* arrives we increase our happiness" (*Mishnah, Taanis* 26b).

Adar is the time for happiness and laughter. Happiness comes from the covenant that God made with us, and laughter is from the covenant that we made with God. The covenant that God made with us is the one He made with Abraham concerning circumcision. God pledged to Abraham that he, his children, and all his descendants shall be witnesses to Him. They will be the chosen ones to proclaim God's kingdom. And He placed a mark on his body, as a symbol of an irreversible pledge.

The covenant that we made with God is the words that we uttered as we stood at Mount Sinai, ". . . we will do, and we will listen." Those words came from the inner soul of the Jewish people, from the blessing that Jacob received, ". . . the voice is the voice of Jacob. . . ." We pledge that every time we open our mouths it will be in thanks, prayer, and study of the eternal truths.

These two covenants, circumcision and the voice of Jacob, are linked one to the other. If we and our descendants are witnesses to God through circumcision, then it follows that we sanctify our mouths to tell others of God's kingdom. As it is written, "A man has joy by the answer of his mouth: and a word spoken in due season, how good it is!" (Proverbs 15:23)

The greatest joy for God and the Jewish people is the covenant of circumcision. It is this powerful link with the Almighty that brings true joy to our hearts. Similarly, the joining together of a man and wife is pure joy. It is merely lust that covers this joy and makes one sad and depressed. Lust is the "shell" of Amalek, which covers the connection that the Jewish people have with God. As it is written, "You have changed for me my lament into dancing; You undid my sackcloth and girdled me with gladness. So that my soul may make music to You and not be stilled . . ." (Psalms 30:12–13) The word sackcloth is *sa'ki* in Hebrew. The sack covers up the last letter i, or *yud*, which is the letter and symbol for circumcision. When the foreskin is removed, the connection between God and Jewish people is revealed, and the result is great joy.

Similarly, Haman the Amalekite covers up the light and joy of the circumcision. He doesn't allow the Jews to serve God. Instead he wants everyone to bow to him. This is the deeper meaning of the conversation between Esther and Mordechai. "When Mordechai learnt all that had been done, he rent his clothes, put on sackcloth and ashes, and went through the city crying loudly and bitterly. He came within sight of the palace gate, because no one clothed with sackcloth was allowed to pass through the gate." And then Esther sent garments to Mordechai so that he could change. But Mordechai refused (Esther 4:1–4).

Mordechai put on sackcloth to symbolize the wickedness of Haman; his sack, his evil, covers the light of the covenant. He prevents Jews from doing their task. Esther hinted to Mordechai that he should remove the sack; it was within his power to continue to reveal God's kingdom, and ignore Amalek. But Mordechai disagreed. He refused to take off the sack, so that Esther should understand that first Amalek had to be removed, for his sack to be removed.

If we ever find darkness, we can be certain that it hides light. The more darkness that covers, the more light is hidden beneath it. We must have faith and patience to uncover it, because if we do, we will have great joy.

Purim is replete with disguises and masks, to teach us this great truth. We cover our faces with masks; we read the *Megillah*, which is part of the Torah, camouflaged as a letter; and perform our deeds of kindness hidden within laughter and merriment.

May it be the will of the All Mighty, that the sack of Amalek will soon be removed, and a great new light shine over us, and Jerusalem, and our mouths shall fill with laughter, to rejoice with God in peace and tranquility forever, as it is written, "Then our mouths will be filled with laughter and our tongues with glad song" (Psalms 126:2).

32

Abbreviated Background and History of the First Purim

Year 441 B.C.E. (3319) The fourth year in the rein of Yehoiakim, king of Judea, the Land of Israel. Nebuchadnezzar, heir to the throne of Babylonia, routed the Egyptian army at Carchamish on the banks of the Euphrates. After father's death, the same year, Nebuchadnezzar was crowned king of Babylonia. The policy he adopted was intended to ensure his domination over Syria and Palestine, preparatory to a final conflict with Egypt.

That same year, Ashkelon refused to open its gates to Nebuchadnezzar; he laid siege to the city, captured it, and laid it waste. A great fast was proclaimed in Jerusalem in response to the events in neighboring Ashkelon. Yehoiachim became a vassal of Babylonia, fought a battle against Egypt, but was defeated. Following that, he rebelled against the king of Babylon, who was too busy on other campaigns. Quarreling in Jerusalem—some sided with Egypt, and others, (including the prophet Jeremiah), demanded surrender to Babylonia. Yehoiakim suppressed his opponents with a strong hand, killing them mercilessly.

Year 444 B.C.E. (3323) In the seventh year of his reign, Nebuchadnezzar laid siege to Jerusalem. King Yehoiachim died in the fourth year of the siege, the eleventh year of his reign. His eighteen-year-old son, Yehoiachim, was crowned king. After three months and ten days, the young king opened the gates of Jerusalem and surrendered.

Year 440 B.C.E. (3327) The king of Babylonia crowned Zedkiahu, an uncle of the deposed Yehoiachim, as king. This was not accepted by the people. The prophet Jeremiah warned the Jewish people.

Zedkiahu asked Egypt for military aid, and with the help of other armies, rebelled against Babylonia.

Year 421 B.C.E. (3340) In the ninth year of Zedkiahu's reign, the forces of Nebuchadnezzar arrived to crush the rebellion. The siege was renewed on the tenth of *Teves*. On the ninth of *Av*, after Jerusalem had withstood one and a half years of siege, the foreign armies pillaged the city, destroyed the king's palace, as well as the Holy Temple. The Babylonian "exile," dating from the time they dominated the region, was in its twelfth year.

Year 423–370 B.C.E. (3342–3389) Nebuchadnezzar was succeeded by E'vil Merodach twenty-four years after the destruction of the Temple. He was assassinated after only two years and replaced by his brother-in-law, Nergal-Sharezzer, who reigned for nine months. He was displaced by Nabonidus, who campaigned in Arabia for ten years while his son Belshazzar wielded power in Babylonia. Cyrus, king of Persia, attacked at this opportune moment. Belshazzar was killed by his own men, and with the coming of the Persians, the political power of Babylonia was at an end. Cyrus consolidated his kingdom and ruled over Media, Persia, Babylon and the "countries." In the first year of his reign, he granted the Jews permission to rebuild the Holy Temple.

Year 368 B.C.E. (3387) Achashverosh became king of the Persian empire. In the second year of his reign he went off to Egypt and forced it into submission and when he returned, he made a great banquet, in the year 365 B.C.E. Flushed with wine he commanded that Queen Vashti be brought before the guests. The queen refused to come and was therefore severely punished. She was deposed, and her crown was to be given to "one who was better than she." In order to choose a successor to Vashti, beautiful maidens were gathered in Shushan from all the provinces of the empire. One of these maidens was Esther, whom Mordechai the Jew had adopted after the death of her parents, to whom he was related. After undergoing beautifying treatments in the harem, Esther found favor in the king's eyes, and he chose her as his queen in place of Vashti (361 B.C.E.—3394). At this time Mordechai discovered a plot against the king, and his deed was recorded in the royal chronicles.

A man named Haman then rose to power. The king made him the highest of all the ministers and ordered all his ministers to do obeisance to him. Only Mordechai disobeyed the royal command and refused to bow down to Haman. Infuriated, Haman tried to destroy Mordechai's people, the Jews, and obtained the king's consent to this act.

Mordechai told Queen Esther to go to the royal presence and plead for her people. Esther asked him to proclaim a three-day fast, at the end of which she would come before the king, even though she had not been called to him and was thereby endangering her own life. No one dared appear unsummoned in the king's presence, and unless the sovereign held out his golden scepter to the intruder, he would be put to death, as prescribed by law and court etiquette.

After three days of fasting, Esther came before the king, who held out his scepter to her. When the king asked what her request was, she invited him to come to a banquet the same evening, and another banquet on the next. Haman, hearing this, felt himself favored and left the king's presence in high spirits. He had a gallows fifty cubits high erected, on which to hang Mordechai once the king's authorization was received.

That night, the king could not sleep, and had his attendants read to him the section of the royal chronicle relating Mordechai's act in saving his life. The king discovered that Mordechai had not yet been rewarded. In the morning, when Haman came to request the king's permission to hang Mordechai, the king asked him what should be done to the man that the king wished to honor. Haman, thinking that he himself was to be honored, replied that the man should be clothed in royal attire, and led through the streets of the city on the king's own horse. The king ordered Haman to do to Mordechai as he had advised. Haman carried out the king's order, but returned home "mourning and with his head covered."

At the second banquet given by Esther for the king and Haman, she revealed Haman's dastardly designs to the king, who thereupon commanded that Haman be hanged on the gallows that he had prepared for Mordechai (356 B.C.E.—3400). On the same day, Mordechai was appointed to Haman's high office, and the king gave orders that Haman's decree regarding the Jews be revoked and that the Jews should be permitted to defend themselves.

On the thirteenth of *Adar*, the Jews destroyed their enemies in the provinces, and on the thirteenth and fourteenth of *Adar* they destroyed their enemies in Shushan, the capital, and the cities, and killed Haman's ten sons. They therefore made the fourteenth and fifteenth days of *Adar* a festival in commemoration of their deliverance for themselves and future generations. The two days of feasting are called Purim because of the lot, *pur*, which Haman cast for the destruction of the Jews.

(The famous Greek thinkers, Hippocrates, Euclid, and Plato, lived in the time of Mordechai and Esther.)

Darius, the son of Achashverosh and Esther, also known as Artachashastah, in the second year of his reign, permitted the Temple to be rebuilt. In the year 347 B.C.E. (3409) the Second Temple was completed and dedicated. The next year, Ezra came from Babylonia to the Holy Land.*

---

*I would be remiss in my responsibility to my readers if I ignored to mention this note on Jewish chronology. It was brought to my attention by my dear cousin, Mordechai Friedman, a true scholar and historian of holy books.

In 1961, Rabbi Shimon Schwab wrote an article, recently reprinted in a book of his writings, entitled, "Comparative Jewish Chronology." In his article, Rabbi Schwab deals with the issue of Jewish chronology compared with the chronology according to secular sources. After careful analysis, Rabbi Schwab concludes that there are 165 years "missing" from the Jewish calendar.

That means, that while in Seder Hadoros, the destruction of the First Temple is calculated to have occurred in the year 3338 or 441 B.C.E., (the date quoted in this book, following traditional sources); according to others, it took place about the year 3173, or 586 B.C.E. That date is agreed upon by all the known secular historians as the date for the destruction of the First Temple, and it predates the "traditional" date by 165 years. If this dating system is correct, then we are today in the year 5917 since the Creation, and very close indeed to the year 6000. That is the year traditionally believed to be set for the ingathering of the exiles.

Whatever the case may be, we should all be worthy to see the coming of the *Mashiach* (Messiah) and the rebuilding of the Third Holy Temple, soon, in our lifetime.

33

Laws and Customs of Purim

he laws and customs of Purim are discussed in a separate talmudic tractate called *Megilla*; also in the Rambam in the portion of *Zemanim*, in *Hilchos Megillah;* and in the *Shulchan Aruch*, sections 686 to 696.

1. The Sabbath before the first day of *Adar* we read the portion of *Shekalim*. We take two Torah scrolls from the Holy Ark. In the first we read the portion of the week, and in the second we read Exodus 30: 11–16, starting with the words "*Ki Sisa.*" It is a reminder to us that the month of *Adar* is at hand, and we need to contribute to the holy work.

2. On the Sabbath preceding Purim, we read the portion of *Zachor*. We take two Torah scrolls from the Holy Ark. In the first we read the portion of the week, and in the second we read Deuteronomy 25: 17–19, starting with the word *Zachor*. It is a *mitzvah*, a commandment, enjoining us at least once a year to hear the reading of *Zachor*.

We must never forget what Amalek did to us, and our obligation to destroy him completely.

3. The thirteenth day of *Adar*, the day before Purim, is a fast day, called *Taanis Esther*, the "Fast of Esther." It is so named because of her central role in the rescue of the Jewish nation. Although all of Israel has accepted to fast on this day, it is not as mandatory as the four fast days that are commanded in the scriptures. Therefore, there are allowances for pregnant and nursing women, or those suffering even slightly from some ailment.

4. Before Purim, it is customary to give half of a standard coin that is currently in that place and time. This is called *machatzis hashekel*, half a shekel. The money is customarily distributed to the poor.

5. On Purim, each time we recite the silent prayer, the *Shemonah Esrei*, we add the prayer *Al Hanisim*.

6. Purim is on the fourteenth of *Adar*. We honor the *Megillah* reading by dressing in Sabbath garments.

7. All men, women, and children should attend the *Megillah* reading in the synagogue. At night it is read after the stars have already appeared, and it is definitely night.

8. The *Megillah* is spread like a letter and then the reader says three blessings. After the reading, the *Megillah* is rolled completely together, and then the blessing is said.

9. It is a custom for the congregation to make loud noises when Haman's name is mentioned. However, the reader should be sure that they hear each and every word.

10. In the morning, the Torah (Exodus 17:8–16) is read. These verses describe Amalek's attack. The *Megillah* is then read.

11. In a city with a wall from the days of Joshua the son of Nun, the *Megillah* is read on the sixteenth of *Adar*.

SENDING PORTIONS OF FOOD AND GIFTS FOR THE NEEDY AND THE PURIM FEAST

1. Each person, man and woman, is obliged to send two portions of food to at least one person. The food should be such that can be eaten without preparation.

2. Each person, man and woman, even one who accepts charity, is obliged to give two gifts to at least two poor people. We should not be particular about who receives the money; to anyone "who stretches forth" his hand to take charity, money is given.

270

3. Each person has to eat, drink, and be especially merry on Purim. On the night of the fourteenth one should rejoice and make somewhat of a feast. The main feast is held on the day of the fifteenth; at least the greater part of it should be held while it is still day.

4. "One is obliged to cheer himself up with wine on Purim, till he doesn't know the difference between 'Accursed is Haman' and 'Blessed is Mordechai'" (*Megilla* 7b). Still, everything that a Jew does should be according to the teachings of the Torah and the accepted traditions.

5. No work should be done on Purim, but it is permissible to attend to business, or to write even a letter of friendship. Of course, for the require-ments of Purim it is permitted to perform regular labors.

6. Shushan Purim is on the sixteenth day of *Adar*. It is customary to make somewhat of a feast then and to rejoice.

7. In a year with two months of *Adar*, Purim is cel-ebrated in the second one, the one followed by the month of *Nissan*.

However, even on the fifteenth day of the first *Adar*, somewhat of a feast is made.

Let us hope and pray that the joy of Purim will extend and spread throughout the entire year, with the arrival of the *Mashiach* soon in our days, *ba'agalah u'vizman kariv*!

34

Prayers and Blessings

The Kabbalists have authored the following prayer:

For the sake of the unification of the Blessed Holy One and His Divine Presence, with awesome reverence and love, to unify the name Yud Heh and Vov Heh in perfect union, by the power of He Who is hidden and concealed, in the name of all of Israel. I am prepared and ready now to perform the positive and negative commandment pertaining to the reading of the Megillah. May it be the will of the Master of the world that this reading shall be considered as if I have meditated on all the conjugation and combinations of the Holy Names therein, which are derived from the first letters and last letters of all the words, and as if I have all the sublime intentions of the Men of the Great Assembly.

The *Megillah* is opened as "a letter," and the reader recites the following three blessings.

Blessed are You, God, our Lord, King of the universe, Who has sanctified us with His commandments and has commanded us regarding the reading of the Megillah.
   Blessed are You, God, our Lord, King of the universe, Who has wrought miracles for our forefathers, in those days at this season.
   Blessed are You, God, our Lord, King of the universe, Who has kept us alive, sustained us, and brought us to this season.

After the *Megillah* is read, each member of the congregation recites the following blessing:

Blessed are You, God, our Lord, King of the universe, (the God) Who takes up our grievance, judges our claim, avenges our wrong; exacts vengeance for us from our foes, and Who brings just retribution upon all enemies of our soul. Blessed are You, God, Who exacts vengeance for

His people Israel from all their foes, the God Who brings salvation.

The following is recited in the evening. After the morning reading, only the last paragraph is said:

Who refused the counsel of the nations,
   and annulled the plans of the cunning,
When a man stood up against us,
   a wantonly evil branch of Amalek's offspring.
Conceited with his wealth he dug himself a grave,
   and his very greatness snared him in a trap.
Dreaming to trap, he became entrapped;
   attempting to destroy, he was fully destroyed.
Haman showed his forefathers' malice,
   and aroused the brotherly hate of Esau on the children.
He would not remember Saul's compassion, that
   through his pity on Agag the foe was born.
The wicked one schemed to cut away the righteous,
   but the impure one was trapped in the pure one's hands.
Kindness overcame the father's error, and the wicked one piled sin on sins.
In his heart he hid his cunning thoughts and devoted himself to doing evil.
He stretched his hand against God's holy ones;
   he spent his silver to destroy their memory.
When Mordechai saw the wrath commence,
   and Haman's decrees were issued in Shushan,
He put sackcloth and bound himself in mourning,
   decreed a fast, and sat on ashes.
"Who would arise to atone for error, to gain forgiveness for our ancestors' sins?"
A blossom bloomed from a branch;
   Hadassah stood up to arouse the sleeping.

*Her servants hastened Haman, to serve him wine
with serpent's poison.*

*He stood tall through his wealth and toppled
through his evil. He built the gallows on which
he was hung.*

*The earth's inhabitants all opened their mouth, for
Haman's lot became our Purim.*

*The righteous man was saved from the wicked's
hand; the foe was substituted for him.*

*They undertook to establish Purim, to rejoice in
every single year.*

*You noted the prayer of Mordechai and Esther;
Haman and his sons were hung on the gallows.*

*The rose of Jacob was cheerful and glad, when they
jointly saw Mordechai robed in royal blue. You
have been their eternal salvation, and their hope
through the generations. To make known that all
who hope in You will not be ashamed; they will
not be humiliated, those who take refuge in You.
Accursed is Haman who sought to destroy me,
blessed be Mordechai the Yehudi. Accursed be
Zeresh the wife of my terrorizer, blessed be Esther,
who did for my sake. And Charvonah, too, be
remembered for good.*

In the silent prayer, *Shemonah Esrei*, and in the Grace
after Meals, the following prayer (*Al Hanisim*) is
added.

*And for the miracles, and for the salvation, and for the
mighty deeds, and for the victories, and for the wonders,
and for the consolations, and for the battles which You
performed for our forefathers in those days, at this time.*

*In the days of Mordechai and Esther, in Shushan, the
capital, when Haman, the wicked, rose up against them
and sought to destroy, to slay, and to exterminate all the
Jews, young and old, infants and women, on the same day,
on the thirteenth of the twelfth month which is the month
of Adar, and to plunder their possessions. But You in
Your abundant mercy, nullified his counsel and frustrated his intentions and caused his designs to be return
upon his own head and they hanged him and his sons on
the gallows.*

May we all be worthy to rejoice and make
others happy.

And in the merit of our love and caring for one
another,

God with His infinite mercy will redeem us from
this last exile, speedily in our days.

35

Torah of Purim

Purim is a day of merriment. Therefore, excerpts from the book *The Handbook of Kabbalah and Astrology,* by Shlomo Pasmanter, are included here for your enjoyment.

The numerical value, *gimatreyah*, of the word *Purim* is 336, which is 7 x 48, the same as the word *kochav*, "star." The Persians used the astrology of the seven stars, or planets. The number 48 is equivalent to *mo'ach*, "mind"; their mind was influenced by the use of the seven stars. And thus Purim came to be.

Esther in Persian is *Ishtar*, which is the planet Venus, or *Nogah*, which also means radiance. Mordechai in Persian is *Marduk*, which is the planet Jupiter, or *Tzedek*, which also means righteousness. The ruling planet of *Adar* is *Tzedek*. Both these planets are *benevolent* planets. For example, whoever is born under the influence of *Tzedek* will tend to goodness, happiness, abundance, wealth, charity, philanthropy, and religion. These are all the qualities that we find in Mordechai and in the holiday of Purim.

There are Ten *s'firos*, "spheres." In the *s'firah* of *netzach*, "eternity," which belongs to Moshe, the exalted planet is Venus, or *Nogah*, meaning radiance. Moses gave us eternal teachings, and therefore his face radiated. Also, if we transpose the letters of *Nogah*, we can get *ha'gan*, "the Garden of Eden." The eternal teachings of Moses lead us into the garden of Eden for eternal bliss.

Moses was born in *Adar* and died in *Adar*. The word *Adar* has the numerical equivalent of 205; when we add the 3 letters of the word, it equals 208. *Or*, "light," equals 207, and with the word itself is 208. So that when Moses was born in the month of *Adar*, the room filled with light. Also, the *mazal*, the astrological sign, of *Adar*, is *dagim*, "fish." *Dagim*, is equal to 57; plus the word, equals 58, which is equivalent to *Nogah*, meaning radiance, equals 58. That means that Moses, whose face exuded radiance, was born in the month of fish.

Moses was born on the seventh of *Adar*. (My father, may his memory be a blessing, was also born on the seventh of *Adar*). Mount Sinai, *Har Sinai*, equals 336 with the word, and Purim too equals 336. This alludes to the rededication that the Jews undertook on Purim in regard to the Torah, which was given on Har Sinai.

Moses was born on the seventh of *Adar*, so that his *bris*, his circumcision, was held on the fourteenth of *Adar*, when Purim is celebrated. Therefore, we can say that Purim is a celebration of the *bris* of Moses. Amalek opposed the bris, the covenant that God has exclusively with the Jewish people. Therefore, the energy of the *bris* of Moses on Purim day gave the

Jewish people the strength to defeat Haman, the Amalekite.

Our tradition says that Moses was born already circumcised. The word *bris* equals 612, one less than the number of commandments in the Torah, because Moses was missing the *mitzvah* of the *bris*. Six hundred and twelve plus the *bris* equals 613, the entire Torah.

The Jewish people protect the sanctity of the *bris*, and therefore Mordechai is called *ish Yehudi*, the man the Yehudi, the one who protects the *bris* from Amalek. The first one who is called by the name of the nation was Jacob, who was called Israel. Jacob separated himself from his brother Esau, the progenitor of Amalek, at the brook of Yaabok, which, when multiplied three times, has the equivalent of 336, the same as Purim, which was the undoing of Esau's descendant Haman. And when Haman is defeated, then the name of God becomes revealed. And thus the two names of God, *Elokim* and *Yud* and *Heh* and *Vov* and *Heh*, equal 336 as well.

The Fast of Esther is on the thirteenth of the month of *Adar*. Esther equals 661, which can be added thus; 6 + 6 + 1 = 13.

Haman is equal to 95, and so is *Maadim*, Mars, the planet of "bloodshed." Daniel also equals 95, and according to some traditions, it was Haman who ordered the death of that prophet.

The planet of the month of *Adar* is *Tzedek*, Jupiter, which is also the ruling planet of *Kislev*, the month in which we celebrate the holiday of Chanukah.

We celebrate Purim with wine, which is equal to 70 and which is also the numerical value of *sod*, "secret." As it is said, "When wine goes in, the secret comes out." There are exactly seventy days between Chanukah and Purim. The secret of Purim becomes revealed after 70 days.

May it be the will of God to add up the years of our exile and see that we need to return to our land, with the coming of the *Mashiach* speedily in our days.

V

THE FREEDOM
OF PESACH

Introduction

Each holiday helps us commemorate and relive a principal event in the history of our nation. Passover, however, is different. Without it there are no holidays, and in fact, without Passover there is no Jewish people. It was the event of the Exodus, the liberation of the Israelites from the Egyptian exile, that produced the eternal people. Until that moment in history no enslaved people ever went free, nor did a slave nation ever live to establish the greatest civilization known to mankind. The seeds of a faith first sown by the patriarch Abraham germinated in the fertile soil of Egypt, the crucible and furnace that burned away all impurity. The seeds finally sprouted forth as the virile tree of faith, bringing to the world a civilization of justice and mercy, writing and measurement, study and action, theory and practice. It has changed the face of humanity from the mindless hoards controlled by their leaders to thinking individuals who are responsible for every choice and decision.

Without the liberation of the Jewish people, the chosen witnesses of God's kingdom, the world would have sunk into an abysmal routine of atheism and materialism. As the sages tell us in the Haggadah, "If God would not have liberated us from Egypt, then we and all our descendants would have remained enslaved to Pharaoh in Egypt." We would still have been in the quicksand of endless work that accomplished nothing. It was only because of the Exodus that we were able to move ahead and to change the world as we moved along.

True, God could have made a people that never tasted the pain of slavery. But this particular people, destined to lead the world from the darkness of idolatrous and oppressive beliefs, had to be first enslaved and then liberated. It had to be so, because their principal teaching would be negation of slavery in any of its forms. Therefore, the Exodus is the pivotal and most prominent event in our history, as it defines us as a people. No longer would we allow ourselves to be enslaved by our circumstances and oppressors. Rather, we would maintain our free will and volition and adhere to the high standards that God had set for us through Moses His servant.

The Exodus is also the ultimate act of separation. We were separated from our oppressors, their culture, and beliefs in a powerful and decisive way—by fleeing the Egyptians and seeing them perish in the Red Sea, "never to be seen again." This quality of being separated is also an integral part of who we are. We are a people apart, and all through the longest of exiles, now nearing 2,000 years, we have retained our integrity. This alone has made us unique; many other peoples have ceased, while we persist.

The Exodus has also established the unique relationship we have with the Creator. It established us as the miraculous people, the people for whom nothing is impossible, who survive even impossible circumstances. When we have true and unfailing faith, the miraculous becomes just as common as the irrevocable laws of nature.

Our liberation also established us as servants of God. We braved the harsh desert to gain his teachings and risked the security of our past for an unknown future. Propelled by an unquenchable yearning for freedom and knowledge of the ultimate truths, we did not hesitate, but rushed forth with great enthusiasm. That remained a hallmark of our being; we were ready always to risk everything for the sake of the ultimate knowledge.

And as we settle down to the Seder ready to perform all the commandments of the Passover night, we have the opportunity to identify, empathize, and connect with the lives of our ancestors of the Egyptian exile and be liberated, once again, with them. We can literally experience the slavery and subsequent freedom. We can literally experience the flood of emotion and spiritual elevation, the excitement and enthusiasm to do the ultimate of all human acts: to ignore the logical and rely on the improbable and impossible, to follow the unknowable God into a parched land.

But how can we ever hope to be spiritually uplifted by this most glorious of holidays when we are mostly engaged in mundane obligations? By discovering the deeper significance of the holiday through learning.

The chasidic masters have taught that each time one does a *mitzvah* it should be done as if it is the very first time. How can we accomplish this? By learning and relearning the significance of this joyful holiday. Thus, when one is ready to learn, one chooses the very best teachers. In my opinion, these are the chasidic masters who have revealed, illuminated, and clarified the deep secrets and symbolism of the Torah.

From this book, I pray you will learn to appreciate chasidic teachings and catch a glimpse of the Kabbalah. I pray also that you will acquire a taste of the deeper significance of Passover while learning to be free from all oppression and find peace as a servant of God.

By fully participating in Passover, you will be granted true and lasting liberty. You will find the roots of your soul as you bask in God's protection. You will unite with your people and live with their collective strength.

I pray that these teachings will sustain you not only during Passover but year-round.

36

The Order of the Four Portions

he *Shabbos* before Rosh Chodesh, the first of *Adar* (the month before *Nissan* in a leap year), is called *Shabbos Parshas Shekalim*. Two Scrolls of the Law are removed from the Holy Ark. In the first, the weekly portion is read, followed by the portion of *Shekalim*, which is read for the *Maftir* (Exodus 30:11–16). If Rosh Chodesh occurs on *Shabbos*, then the reading of the portion of *Shekalim* is done on that day. The reading deals with the giving of the half-shekel tax for the counting of the census.

The *Shabbos* before Purim is called *Shabbos Parshas Zachor*, when the portion of *Zachor* is read (Deuteronomy 25:17–19). It commands the Jewish people to remember the evil of the Amalekites and to never forget their deeds.

The *Shabbos* before we read *parshas Ha'chodesh*, which is read on the *Shabbos* before *Nissan*, is called *Shabbos Parshas Parah*, the portion of the Red Cow (Numbers 19:1–22). It tells of the ritual purification required of someone who became impure through touching a corpse. As a result of the ritual the person would be pure and allowed to bring the Passover-sacrifice.

The *Shabbos* before *Nissan* is called *Shabbos Parshas Ha'chodesh*, and the portion of the month is read (Exodus 12:1–20). It tells of the commandments of the Passover-sacrifice and the preparations for the Exodus from Egypt.

What is the spiritual significance of these four portions, and what can we learn from their particular order?

The first is *Shekalim*, the commandment to give coins to the Temple. Giving charity is the work of the heart. The Jewish heart is full of benevolence and gives freely; we always want to give and are always giving. It is our very essence. It is the part of our heart where there is no forgetting. We remember who we are and are aware of what we are doing.

Why do we remember? Because we are connected with the memory in the depth of our hearts of benevolence, which causes us to remember. As Jews, our true nature stands before God, and we remember and never forget. We do not forget the nation that is set to destroy our essence, nor do we forget Amalek who wanted to usurp our special relationship with God. And that is the portion of *Zachor*—to remember what Amalek did to us.

As we stand before God, we realize our insignificance and humble ourselves before Him. We are helped to achieve this humility by the ashes of the Red Cow, which are put into water and sprinkled upon those defiled by death. Then we remember that we are not more than ashes compared to the infinite glory of God.

How could anyone who remembers be anything but humble, as he stands before God? Thus, as we are humbled and dependent on Him, He suffuses us with life. The new life rushes into us, and we are renewed. This renewal is the theme of the reading of the portion of the New Month, *parshas Ha'chodesh*. It is about the renewal of the Jewish people during the Exodus from Egypt.

If we combine these four portions together, what is their lesson to us? If we want our life to be new, we must be close to God. And in the depths of our heart is a clear remembrance of who we are as we stand before God. And there a great benevolence for another human being is found. Feeling God's presence we humble ourselves and accept the blessings that He gives freely and in abundance. Suddenly, we are renewed.

Why is *parshas Zachor* read before *parshas Parah*?

Zachor reminds us that the evil Amalek attacked the Jewish people when they left Egypt. Amalek is the antithesis of the Jewish people, first mocking our chosenness and then saying that his people are the chosen ones instead. The Amalekites also mock our special relationship to God. They deny it, and they have nothing to fear. As a result they attack and make war against us. They weaken our faith in God and plant in us the seeds of doubt about our special mission. Then we cannot reach the level of purity that God had intended for us.

We conclude, therefore, that in order to reach a high level of purity, we must first get rid of the evil Amalek. We read in the *parshas Zachor* of Amalek's deeds and the commandment to be rid of him, and then we read the portion of cleansing with the *Parah Adumah*, the Red Cow. This teaches us that, once the obstacle is removed, we can move on to our place of chosenness and purity.

Similarly, in our own life, we should not allow obstacles in our spiritual path to remain and linger. We must remove them immediately and continue to grow and improve.

It is written, "Create a pure heart in me, O God, and a steadfast spirit renew in me" (Psalms 51:12).

Sometimes we feel a spiritual awakening in our heart, but unfortunately, it is only temporary and incomplete. What can we do to make it more permanent? We must immediately humble ourselves and return to God. We then remove the impurities from our heart and make room for the spiritual awakening.

The first awakening is in *parshas Shekalim*, which is done with the benevolence of the Jewish heart. We are suddenly overcome with a desire to give, but the desire is not as yet developed or complete. It needs to be purified. We cleanse it by remembering Amalek and the need to get rid of the evil completely and unconditionally. We remember God, and He remembers us by giving us life and vitality.

Our original desire was strong and pure, and now we made room for it and our heart fills with it. As a result we obtain even more strength from heaven.

A peasant stood in line to pay homage to the king. When the king passed he noticed the peasant's tattered clothing and emaciated body and took pity on him. He stopped and decreed that the peasant be granted a small cottage to live in and that his needs be met. The peasant was overcome with emotion. He wanted to thank the king and show his appreciation with a gift, but all he found was an old tarnished lamp, which was far from appropriate. He sat down to polish it. The cleaning was difficult and time consuming. Soon the original feelings of appreciation left him; all he thought about was the lamp. Later, as he finished polishing the lamp and admired his hard work, he suddenly felt the appreciation for the king even more than before. He realized that the king must love him as much as he loves the king.

When the love of God awakens in us with the portion of *Shekalim*, we cherish those feelings by helping them grow in our heart. We must immediately banish evil, purify our heart, and thus become renewed.

There is a controversy in the Talmud over which time of the year the world was created. Rabbi Eliezer said the world was created in the month of *Tishrei*, in the fall; Rabbi Yehoshua said the world was created in the month of *Nissan* in the spring. How can we reconcile these two opinions?

We can say that there was a creation and a re-creation. The world was created in *Nissan* with the Ten Utterances (*Asarah Maamoros*), and is re-created in *Tishrei* with the Ten Commandments (*Aseres Hadibros*). The *Asarah Maamoros* are hidden within the natural world. The *Aseres Hadibros*, the Ten Commandments, comprise the Torah, a guide that helps us reveal the word of God.

It is not always easy to recognize the words of God within the creation. There are evil forces that obstruct the spirit that God wants to give us. What can we do? We must first get rid of evil, purify our desires, and then receive the vitality that God has put into the world. This also corresponds with the order of the *parshiyos*, the four portions. Before we arrive at the creative power of *Nissan*, we struggle with the evil of Amalek by reading *parshas Zachor*. Then we purify ourselves to the ultimate with the *parshas Parah*, the Red Cow, and we are ready for the renewal of creation as we read the *parshas Ha'chodesh* concerning the new month of *Nissan* that renews us as a nation and brings new life into each one of us.

After Elijah the Prophet proved the sovereignty of God to the worshipers of the Baal, he ran for his life and hid in a cave. There, God wanted to reveal His great strength and power. Suddenly, Elijah heard a great howling wind that uprooted trees and moved mountains. "No," God said, "it is not with the wind that I come." Then a great and terrible earthquake came. "No," said God, "neither is it with the earthquake that I come." And after the earthquake there was a fire, but it was not with that either that God came. Finally a still, small voice was heard. When Elijah heard this quietest of sounds, he wrapped his face in his robes, went out and stood at the entrance of the cave. He knew that this was the voice of God (1 Kings 19:11–14).

The "wind" is the spirit of benevolence that is in the hearts of the Jewish people. This corresponds to the portion of *Shekalim*, when every Jew gave a coin to charity. The "earthquake" is the noise of the quake of the war with the Amalekites. It corresponds to the portion of *Zachor*, when we remember what Amalek did to us when we left Egypt. The "fire" signifies the fire that was used to burn the *Parah Adumah*, the Red Cow, which purifies the unclean, as described in the portion of *Parah*. After this we arrive at the softest, quietest voice. We have reached the very essence of life and stand before God in complete humility. We become totally renewed, as God suffuses us with His Divine life. This is a true renewal and corresponds to the portion of *Ha'chodesh* commanding the Israelites to observe the new moon of the month of *Nissan*, the month of redemption and renewal.

When our heart is awakened and we fight off the evil mingled in our feelings, purifying it with fire, we finally stand before God and are ready to receive a life of renewal.

It is written, "Thus spoke God, let not the wise man boast of his wisdom, nor the valiant of his valor, let not the rich man boast of his riches; but if any man would boast, let him boast of this, that he understands and knows Me, for that is what I desire, For I am God" (Jeremiah 9:23).

The Midrash comments: God gives three gifts to mankind: wisdom, strength, and riches. If a man thinks that the gifts belong to him, then he loses them. But if he recognizes them as coming from God, then he will possess them in full measure. (*Numbers Rabbah* 22:6).

These three gifts are alluded to in the four Torah portions that we read before Passover. The portion of *Shekalim* speaks about giving coins for the holy work in the Tabernacle. It is as if we are giving the coins back to God. This act of charity makes us realize that riches are not ours, but rather are a gift from

God. We then read the portion of *Zachor*, of how we fought with Amalek. It reminds us that our strength in war is not ours either, but rather comes from God. Then when we read the portion of the *Parah Adumah*, the Red Cow, we learn of a decree that we cannot understand. We realize that our wisdom is also not ours, but is from God. When we realize that whatever we possess is from God, we are ready for real life and renewal.

Therefore, after the three portions mentioned above we read the fourth, *parshas Ha'chodesh*. This tells us that the new moon of *Nissan* is about to appear and our redemption is at hand.

We too, in our lives, must first give everything "back" to God. Then in return we will receive the thing that we want most of all: new life and vitality.

We first read *parshas Parah* about the Red Cow and then read *parshas Ha'chodesh* concerning the new moon of *Nissan*. This comes to teach us that before we receive renewal we must first purify ourselves. As it is written, "Create in me a pure heart, O God, and a steadfast spirit renew in me" (Psalms 51:12). Before God renews one's spirit, his heart must first be purified. Therefore, before reading about the new moon of *Nissan*, we read of the purification of the Red Cow.

Ever since the Exodus, it had been the tradition to purify one's self during the month of *Nissan* as a preparation for the Passover sacrifice. We need to continue this tradition even now that the Temple is destroyed. First we must purify our heart and prepare for renewal.

Abraham chose to serve one God instead of worshiping idols like his father. In turn God chose him and instructed him to leave his father and homeland. Abraham chose to be close to God, and God brought Abraham close to Him. This is a twofold movement of choosing and being chosen, of drawing near and being drawn near. It is a movement that has been repeated throughout the history of the Jewish people, as well as in the lives of each individual Jew.

A subject of the king was uncompromising in his loyalty, but this loyalty was known to no one but himself. One day an unruly dispute escalated into an uprising. A mob rioted and wanted to march on the palace and harm the king. The subject was jolted into action. He risked his life and stood up in the midst of the crowd. He raised his arms and shouted, "In the name of the king, stop this mindless assault!"

The mob calmed down and eventually disbanded. When the king heard of his subject's bravery, he invited him to the palace. On the way, the man thought, "Who am I to be worthy of the king's company? What an honor to be chosen to come to the palace!" Reaching the palace, he immediately bowed. The king declared, "Come here to my throne. Is there anyone more worthy to be near me than you?" The man quickly stood up and took his place near the king.

Similarly, the Jewish people were chosen in the month of *Nissan*. And as the month of *Nissan* approaches, they humble themselves before God. They know they are not worthy of such honor. They prepare themselves with the purification of the *Parah Adumah*, the Red Cow. Then they feel worthy for the renewal of the month of *Nissan*.

In own lives, we must prepare for our being chosen and get ready for the invitation to the king's palace.

37

Parshas Parah—*Reading the Portion of the Red Cow*

PURITY FROM THE IMPURE

he *Shabbos* before *parshas Ha'chodesh* is read is called *Shabbos Parshas Parah*, when we read the portion of the Red Cow (Numbers 19:1–22). It tells of the ritual purification required of someone who became impure through touching a corpse. As a result of the ritual, the person was purified and allowed to bring the Passover sacrifice.

God spoke to Moses and Aaron, telling them that the following is declared to be the decree as commanded by God:

Speak to the Israelites and have them bring you a completely red cow, which has no blemish, and which has never had a yoke on it. Give it to Elazar the *kohen,* and he shall have it brought outside the camp. It shall then be slaughtered in his presence.

Elazar the *kohen* shall take the blood with his finger and sprinkle it toward the Communion Tent seven times. The cow shall then be burned in Elazar's presence. Its skin, flesh, and blood and entrails must be burned. The priest shall take a piece of cedar wood, some hyssop, and some crimson wool, and throw it into the burning cow.

He must then immerse his vestments and his body in a *mikvah*, and remain unclean until evening, after which he may come into the camp. The one who burns the cow must also immerse his clothing and body in a *mikvah*, and then remain unclean until evening.

A ritually clean person shall gather up the cow's ashes, and place them outside the camp in a clean place. They shall be a keepsake for the Israelite community to be used for the sprinkling water, as a means of purification. The one who gathers up the

cow's ashes must immerse his body and clothing, and remain unclean until evening.

All this shall be an eternal law for the Israelites and for any proselyte who joins them:

If one has contact with any dead human being, he shall become ritually unclean for seven days. In order to become clean, he must have himself sprinkled with the purification water on the third day and the seventh day. If he does not have himself sprinkled on the third day and the seventh day, he cannot become clean.

Any person who touches the corpse of a human being who has died, and does not have himself sprinkled, shall be cut off spiritually from Israel if he defiles God's Tabernacle by entering it. Since the purification water was not sprinkled on him, he remains unclean and is pervaded by his defilement.

When a man dies in a tent, this is the law: everything that comes into the tent or was originally in the tent shall be unclean for seven days. Every open vessel that does not have an airtight seal shall be unclean.

Similarly, anyone who touches a victim of the sword, corpse, a human bone, or a grave in the open field shall be unclean for seven days.

Some of the dust from the burnt purification offering shall be taken for such an unclean person. It shall be placed into a vessel that has been filled with water directly from a running spring.

A ritually clean person shall take some hyssop and dip it into the water. He shall sprinkle the water on the tent, on all the vessels and persons who were in it, and on anyone who touched the bone, a murder victim, or any other corpse, or a grave. The ritually clean person shall sprinkle the water on the unclean person on the third and on the seventh day. The purification process is completed on the seventh day, when the person undergoing purification must immerse his clothing and body in a *mikvah*, and then become ritually clean in the evening. If a person is unclean and does not purify himself, and then defiles God's sanctuary by entering it, that person shall be cut off spiritually from the community. As long as the purification water has not been sprinkled on him, he shall remain unclean.

This shall be to you a law for all times.

One who sprinkles the purification water must immerse both his body and his clothing. However, if he merely touches the purification water, he must only immerse his body and then be unclean until the evening.

Anything that a person who is unclean by contact with the dead touches shall become unclean. Moreover any person touching him shall be unclean until the evening.

There is much controversy among doctors and discussions in halachah over at what point a person is considered dead. Is it when the heart has come to a complete stop or when there is no longer any perceptible brain activity? Whatever the answer, that is all in the physical realm. But in the spiritual realm, death occurs when one no longer has the vitality of God in his body. And thus being "separated" from God, the body is unclean and transmits this uncleanliness to anyone who may touch it or be with it under the same roof. And how is this uncleanliness removed? It is removed by sprinkling water with ashes of the *Parah Adumah*, the Red Cow, on the unclean person. This symbolizes that when a person humbles himself as ashes, he can again receive the Godly life. This humbling not only returns the "old" life but also renews the life.

This is an everyday lesson for us. If we feel stagnant, without vitality, and lifeless, as if our life is going nowhere but heading toward death, we must humble ourselves before God. We will then regain our strength and vitality. A new life will surge inside us, and we will be renewed totally.

It is written, "Who can bring purity out of the impure? Not one" (Job 14:4).

Our sages read the last two words as follows: "Is it not the One and only?" Meaning that the only one who can make pure out of the impure is the One and only God.

Every Jew believes that God is, "One and only, and there is no singularity like Him anywhere in the universe" (Maimonides, *Thirteen Principles of Faith*). God is the absolute singularity; He is not composed of parts, and His being one is perfect and complete.

There is no exception to this whatsoever. Therefore, if we see something that is more than one, we know that it is no longer God, because two cannot be God. Therefore, in the desert, when the Jews made an idol, the Golden Calf, they declared, "These are your gods . . ." (Exodus 32:4). When there are more than one, it is obviously idol worship.

Similarly, the One is pure; more than one is not as pure. Purity is found in the one and only God. Impurity is found outside God. Thus if you want purity you must be connected to God. But how? Only by humbling ourselves before the one and only God can we be connected to Him and have true purity.

A king visited his subjects in a foreign land, asked to see some of their homes, and toured them. But as soon as he saw them adorned with the possessions of the owner, he gave a mere glance and left immediately. Finally he entered a house that was empty of all furnishings. The surprised king asked, "Tell me, my good servant, why is your house totally empty?" The servant answered, "I knew that the Your Majesty will visit our homes, and I had nothing that was good enough for my master's honor." "In that case," the king said, calling to his men, "bring into this house my finest furniture, dishes, and utensils and prepare a royal feast for me and my men."

The same is true in our daily life. When we fill our life with lowly desires and aspirations, we leave no room for God. But when we humble ourselves to the very earth, as the ashes of the Red Cow, then we make room for the purity of God to enter our "dwelling."

Before we are born God puts a clean and pure soul into our body. Left on its own, the soul would pursue wisdom and good deeds throughout our lifetime. But God has given us freedom to choose between good and evil. Thus we sometimes stray off the good path and end up in unclean places.

Similarly, there are righteous people who never sin. They always follow the prescribed path and never err. And there are, on the other hand, those who do sin. But even they can repent and mend their ways. They can find their way back to the path of charity and mercy, justice and righteousness. These are the *baalei teshuvah*, the repentants.

A king had two sons. One's conduct was perfect and flawless. The other was always in some mischief or another and was an embarrassment to his majestic surroundings. Years passed. The errant son, on his own, decided that he wanted to enjoy the pleasure of being close to his father. The king noticed his great effort and reciprocated by drawing him close. He invited his son for private walks and chats, things that he rarely did with the perfect son. This made the repentant son wish that he would never have been bad.

Our sages have taught, "In the place where the *baalei teshuvah* stand, even the righteous cannot stand" (*Berakhos* 34b). The love and closeness shown to a *baal teshuvah* are even greater than that shown to the righteous.

This lesson can also be learned from the events at Mount Sinai. Moses stayed on Mount Sinai for forty days and forty nights without food or drink. He studied the Ten Commandments and then received them carved on stone tablets. He was about to give them to the Jewish people, who were then pure and free of sin. But they did not remain so and made an idol, the Golden Calf, and said, ". . . These are your gods." Moses broke those tablets and then pleaded for God's forgiveness for forty days and nights atop Mount Sinai. Finally God forgave them and gave Moses another set of tablets. They received those as repentants, *baalei teshuvah*, with greater love than the first ones.

Turning from sin to repentance is like turning from death to life. We return to a level of purity just as before we were born. But how? By lowering ourselves to dust and ashes, we are vessels to receive new life from God, just as the ashes of the *Parah Adumah*, the Red Cow. It too first becomes ashes and then gives life and purity to those who need it.

————————

It is written, "And Abraham said . . . I am dust and ashes" (Genesis 18:27). In the merit that Abraham considered himself as dust and ashes, his descendants had the merit to receive the commandment of the *Parah Adumah*, the Red Cow (*Genesis Rabbah* 18).

Why are the Jewish people able to be completely humble before God? Because of Abraham, the father of them all. He taught them the spiritual feat of *mesiras nefesh*, of selfless devotion. To put aside one's will, and instead, do the will of God. Thus, in the presence of God, Abraham considered himself as dust and ashes, as nothing and nobody; he was completely humbled before God's will. We, the Jewish people can also humble ourselves completely because of him. But we lack the moral strength of Abraham and need help to attain humility. And this help comes to us through the ashes of the *Parah Adumah*, the Red Cow.

When we encounter death, we may feel devastated and helpless. We are then aware of our physical being, of our mortality and death. Our ego feels weak and without strength. Yet those feelings are not humility; they are merely depression. Therefore, along come the waters of the *Parah Adumah*. They contain the ashes of the cedar and the lowly hyssop bush. They teach us to lower our cedar-tall ego to the level of the lowly hyssop. And when we listen to its lesson, we realize that in death as in life, we are prostrated before God. That just as we are dust and ashes in death, we are dust and ashes before Him in life too. Suddenly we feel a great strength surge through us, and our weakness is transformed into true humility.

————————

There are forty-nine levels of purity and forty-nine levels of uncleanliness. We can purify ourselves more and more, and with each level come closer and closer to God. In contrast, we can become more and more unclean and move farther and farther from God. But to where do we move? Can there be a place that is so far from God as to be without God? We know that the opposite is true, that there is no place without God. Therefore we must conclude that in the lowest level of uncleanliness the pure and impure merge into one singularity. We have reached the roots.

The roots of all things are in God, and in Him there are no opposites, no divisions or fragments, no good and evil, no sizes, times, or places. Everything is one and the same in complete unity. And therefore if we take the unclean back to its roots, we realize that He is also the roots of impurity. As it is written, "Who can bring a clean thing out of an unclean? Not one" (Job 14:4). Is it not the One? Only in the One God can the unclean become clean. But if we believe that the uncleanliness has a power of its own, like death, then we remain in its hold.

Therefore, when we encounter death and are about to be caught in its clutches of impurity and depression, we must humble ourselves to the very earth, as dust and ashes, and completely surrender to God's power. We then return the uncleanliness to its roots, and it is stripped of its power. We are free of its domination.

————————

It is written, "Who can bring a clean thing out of an unclean? Not one" (Job 14:4).

The Midrash teaches: that this verse alludes to Abraham, who was pure, but came from his father Terach, who was an unclean idol worshiper. Similarly, the Jewish people are pure and were separated from among the unclean nations. The same is true of the World to Come, which is pure but which follows the unclean material world (*Numbers Rabbah* 19).

The world has both purity and impurity in it. If

we want to have purity we have to work very hard for it. For example, despite the fact that Terach was an idol worshiper, Abraham, his son, worked very hard to overcome the impurities of his upbringing. He inquired, questioned, analyzed, and studied the power of the idols and wondered which one of them was the master of the world. He finally concluded that the true God cannot be seen and is not an object or idol. The Jewish people, despite their impure surroundings, can attain purity with hard work. Mankind has a similar fate. Out of the "unclean" present, through their diligent effort, they will bring about the purity of tomorrow, the advent of the perfect world, the World to Come.

Do not think, though, that the purity you attain is a "result" of your hard work. It is merely a gift from heaven.

A king sent a group of his trusted servants to a faraway land. They went to induct monarchs to the king's service. They had many obstacles to overcome and worked very hard. After many months, they accomplished their mission and returned to the palace. The king rewarded them with a handsome salary and a sizable bonus. Then he called all of them to his private chambers where the royal heirloom coin collection was kept. He carefully took coins with the king's image engraved on them, and gave some to each of them. They realized that this was a special gift beyond their earnings. It was a personal gift from the king's heart.

This is true with us too. When we work hard to overcome impurity we ought to be rewarded. After all, we chose it with our own free will. Still, purity is not a result of our work. We can only clean ourselves from impurity. But the purity that follows is a gift from God Who is its exclusive source. It is from the treasure house of the "royal palace"; it is divine and a thing from heaven.

It is written, "Lift up your eyes to the heaven and see Who created these" (Isaiah 40:26).

We can interpret this verse as follows. When you lift your eyes to the heavens, you can see "Who created," . . . that there is one and only Creator. But if you do not focus, and your gaze wanders, then you see "these," a plurality, more than one. Anything more than one has impurities. And suddenly, while gazing at the same heavens, your mind can become filled with the impurity of the many and think perhaps that there is more than one god? What is the remedy for this? You must look again and see that even the many stars and galaxies obtain their energy from the one and only Creator of the world. Then you

declare, "who," the Creator, "created 'these,'" even "these" the many, were all created by the one and only.

What can we do that will help us see the one again? An act of total humility, of humbling ourselves to the very earth like dust and ashes. Then we see clearly, without interference of our ego. And it is then clear to us that there is one and only Creator.

It is written, "Who can bring a clean thing out of an unclean? Not one" (Job 14:4).

The Midrash compares this to a son of a maid who soiled the palace floor. The king said, "Let the mother come and clean up the mess." The same is true of the Golden Calf, the idol that the Israelites worshiped at Mount Sinai. God says, "Let the *Parah Adumah*, the adult cow, come to cleanse the sin of the baby, the Golden Calf."

When we do good deeds we realize that it was God who had provided us with the energy to do them. But when we sin, is it God who gives us life and energy to do evil? Yes, because even from evil something good can come. If we repent, do *teshuvah*, then the sin "changes" to merit. Therefore, even an evil act gets energy so that it can later "change" to merit. The impure changes to the pure.

Who feeds and sustains a child so that he could soil the palace floor? The mother. Does she keep him fit so that he should soil the floor? No, but each time that he does, she cleans and shines it to the utmost. It is as if the child's soiling is part of the reason why the palace floors are so shiny. It all becomes part of the service for the king.

So too the life-giving waters of the *Parah Adumah*, the Red Cow. Although the Jewish people made the Golden Calf, it became part of the service for the king when they later repented. The humbling ashes of the mother cow wipe up the mess of the calf. The purity that is produced is out of the impurity itself.

It is written, "Who can bring a clean thing out of an unclean? Not one" (Job 14:4).

There are two words in the Jewish tradition signifying closeness to God: *kedushah* and *taharah*, "holiness" and "purity." What is the difference between them? *Kedushah* is the level of closeness to God before we sin. This is the spiritual heights attained by our soul before we are born; of Moses our teacher whose prophetic vision was clear as the clearest glass; of the Jewish people as they stood by the foot of Mount Sinai and received the Ten Commandments; of the

Written Law, which is precise, clear, and unambiguous; and of *Shabbos*, the holy day in which the good is clear and right before us.

Taharah, purity, on the other hand, comes after we have sinned and are trying to get close to God again. We must then purify our actions, strive to do good, and separate the good from the evil in our life. This is the very level of the soul after we are born; of the Jewish people after they worshiped the Golden Calf; of the other prophets who saw through an obscured glass; of the Oral Law, which needs careful study until the purity of its logic is revealed; and of the six weekdays when we engage in activities of good and evil and we must constantly be on guard to do the right thing.

A prince grew up in the palace, with strict regulations for every activity. How the prince ought to dress, eat, play, study, greet royalty, and relate to his own parents, the king and queen—all was carefully taught as royal etiquette. The rules were clear and concise.

When the prince was older he was sent to a distant country. Suddenly everything changed. He was now in the company of men who were independent; some even contradicted the king's plans. He heard opinions contrary to those of his father and observed behavior that was not acceptable in the palace. The prince no longer had the pure mind that had been nurtured in him. He then had to think carefully before he gave an opinion or an order. He had to choose between good and evil, between loyalty and treachery.

We too, before we are born, are in the king's palace. There everything is clear, like the Written Law, "the rules of the palace." But after being born into a world with a mixture of good and evil, the rules are not so clear any more. In this place we must work hard to separate the good from the evil. We are no longer on the level of *kedushah*, but it is hoped that we can be on the level of *taharah*.

In what way does the sprinkling of the waters of the *Parah Adumah*, the Red Cow, produce purity? Rashi comments, "If one has been arrogant and sinned, (and is therefore impure) he should humble himself" (*Rashi, Commentary*, Numbers 19).

How does humility cause a sin to be forgiven? On the simplest level, a sin is committed when God commands us to do something and we do the opposite. But how could we? Don't we realize that our very life depends on God every instant? How dare we ignore His teachings? It must be that while we sin, we don't believe this truth with complete faith. At the instant of our sin we think that we own the world and our life and that no one can tell us what to do. These are the impure thoughts that lead to sin and impurity. Later, when we repent, we humble ourselves like ashes and realize our great mistake. We again profess our faith in God with strength and are made pure.

A mother was holding her baby in her arms. The mother must feed, clothe, cleanse, and care for each of the baby's needs. She tried to feed the baby, but the baby pushed the spoon away and refused to allow the mother to feed him. The mother wondered out loud, "Hey, big boy, what are you doing? So you want to be on your own? Let's see what you can do for yourself, you little big shot!" Of course the mother is right. Her baby could not survive without her for too long. Pushing his mother away is a mistake that he is simply too young to understand.

When we push God away and say, "We are on our own!" we also are very mistaken. Finally, when we are humbled, we are again ready to listen to God and His teachings. We are then off the path of sin and back on the path of purity.

THE DECREE OF THE TORAH

The commandments of the Torah are divided into two categories. Some are called *chukim*, "decrees," whereas others are *mishpatim*, "laws." *Mishpatim* are logical and sensible, whereas *chukim* are not. One of the more difficult *chukim* is the commandment of the *Parah Adumah*, the Red Cow. Even King Solomon, who was the wisest of men, said, ". . . I said I will be wise, but it is far from me" (Ecclesiastes 7:23).

It is written, "God spoke to Moses and Aaron, telling them that the following is declared to be the Torah's decree as commanded by God. Speak to the Israelites and have them bring you a completely red cow, which has no blemish, and which has never had a yoke on it" (Numbers 19:1–2). And it is also written, "This is the Torah, the law that Moses presented before the children of Israel" (Deuteronomy 4:44).

There are two aspects of the Torah, the laws of God. On the one hand it is the wisdom of God and therefore is beyond human understanding. It is placed before the children of Israel; it is there before them but they cannot reach it. On the other hand, the Torah is our way of life; it is practical and real. Similarly, the word *chukas* has two meanings. It means decree, a command that we do without understanding. It also means engraved—the Torah becomes marked and engraved into our heart and is concrete and real.

The Torah that is beyond our understanding, so to speak, is the Written Law, the law given directly from God to the children of Israel. The Torah that is engraved in our hearts is the Oral Law, which we live and is part of us. And this Torah is not only engraved in us but it is also engraved in each and every particle of creation because the Torah was the blueprint with which God created the world. And when we seek, study, and search for it we find it everywhere and in everything. And when we find it, it leaves a mark on us, too. This is the true *chukas*—mark of the Torah.

Thus we learned, "The righteous men of old made their Torah study their permanent activity, and their occupation their temporary activity" (*Berakhos* 32b). This can mean as follows. These righteous men learned "Torah" from everything they did. Even when they worked at their occupation they were searching for the word of God engraved in it. The Torah therefore became their permanent activity, and their actual physical work became merely temporary, of lesser importance in their life. And thus they succeeded at both; they gained the Torah that they were seeking and the work they were doing.

It is written, "This is the decree of the Torah . . ." and it is also written, "Praise Him, sun and the moon: praise Him, all the stars of light. Praise Him, heavens of the heavens, and the waters above the heavens. Let them praise the name of God: for He commanded and they were created. He has also established them for ever and ever: He drew a (*chok*) line, it shall not pass" (Psalms 148:6). The word *chok* also means decree.

God created the world with Ten Utterances. He said, for example, "Let there be light, and there was light" (Genesis 1:3). This command was not only active at the instant of creation but it also constantly makes light to exist. In every instant since the creation, light exists because of God's will. It is as if God is saying every instant, "Let there be light," and the creation responds. The same is true with each and every item of creation.

What is the decree of the Torah? It is God's command in each thing, a line that He drew to set its boundaries. Why is the sun in the sky? Why do the birds fly? Why does the heart keeps beating? Because God is drawing the line. He is the one that wills all of these things to be, every instant.

This is like a king who had a treasury containing many precious objects. He commanded the royal treasurer to secretly engrave the royal seal on each and every object. Only the loyal subjects knew the

shape of the seal. Some time later, clever thieves came to the palace and stole many of the royal treasures. The king ordered his soldiers to set up roadblocks and to catch the thieves and retrieve the treasure. He appointed his loyal subjects to stay with the soldiers and help identify the stolen goods. Each merchant was stopped and made to unload his wares. It was the loyal subjects who were able to find the king's seal on the items. Each item was carefully examined until the king's seal was found.

When we look for the *chukas hatorah*, the decree of God in each item of creation, we find it. And when we do, we realize that nothing in the world is without an owner. God owns each and every item. We then realize that they all bear the royal seal and they are all from the king's palace.

It is written, "This is the decree of the Torah . . ." (Numbers 19:2). Rashi writes in his commentary, "Since the nations of the world pester the Jewish people and taunt them saying, `What possible reason could there be for this red cow?,' therefore the Torah uses the word *chukas*, 'decree,' telling us to accept it as a decree, and not to think at all about the reasons."

The obvious question is, How does the word *chukas*, decree, answer the taunts of the nations, when they really asked, Why are we doing something that has no logical reason?

This is a lesson not only about the Red Cow but also about every commandment. We must accept every commandment as a decree. When we observe the *mitzvos* we are obeying the King. Perhaps we don't understand it, but since it is the Creator's will it must be done. And if we do it as a decree, we will suddenly find the deepest reasons for the commandment.

A king called his royal court together to discuss a vital problem. He ordered them to immediately saddle their horses and ride to the bridge precisely at midnight. Some of the servants questioned the wisdom of the plan. Others were lazy and grumbled at the inconvenience. The king's sons, however, were enthusiastic. They knew their father and trusted that if he ordered this plan, it must be with excellent reasons.

At midnight, the king rode to the bridge. He met his men and looked carefully into their faces. He saw their reluctance, doubts, and apprehension. This nearly upset him. But then he saw the eagerness, confidence, and trust on the faces of his sons, and he was immediately encouraged. He whispered to them, "To you I will reveal the secret plan."

Similarly, when we trust God, accept His commandments as decrees, and perform them with confidence and trust, then God reveals His secrets to us. Then we understand the deep meanings of the Torah.

It is written, "This is the decree of the Torah. . . ."

The decree, the mark of the Torah, is in each and every item of creation. Furthermore, each Jew has a portion of the Torah that corresponds specifically to his life. Some commentators say that each person has one specific letter in the Torah that belongs to him. Some say it is one word, and others say it is a sentence. Still, everyone agrees that the Torah and our lives are intertwined. We are part of the Torah, and the Torah is part of us. But this interconnection is not obvious. If we want to find our connection to the Torah, we have to seek it as one who seeks gold and precious jewels. Then it will be revealed.

This is like a set of crystal glasses and chimes. Each chime makes a different sound, and each sound makes another crystal glass resonate.

The same is true of us too. We each have a portion of the Torah that is exclusively ours, and when we find it and tap into its source, our soul resonates to its message and we spring to life. We are suddenly awake and full of energy. How did this happen? Because we have found the *chukas haTorah*, the mark of the Torah. We have discovered the specific mark that is written in the Torah and engraved in our souls too. And when these two marks find each other, they cause each other to become alive with divine life.

"This is the decree of the Torah" (Numbers 19:2). The Midrash comments, "To you, Moses, I am revealing the reason for this commandment, but for all the others it is a decree, without logic or reason" (*Numbers Rabbah* 19).

The commandments of the Torah deal with the day-to-day life of man. The Torah guides us in relating to ourselves, our fellow men, and our Creator. It guides us from our birth and to the moment of our death, throughout our entire sojourn in the physical world. This is true of all the commandments of the Torah, except one. One commandment in particular speaks about another world. It tells how death can be removed from a living man and is about a world where there is no death. This commandment is the decree to take a Red Cow and to use its ashes to remove the defilement of death from a living person. This commandment is beyond the realm of nature and is not of this world. Therefore, we, who are of

this world, cannot understand it. Only someone like Moshe, who was at home both in the physical and the spiritual world, who spoke to the Jewish people as well as to God, who stayed on Mount Sinai for forty days and nights without food or drink, he alone can understand a commandment whose roots lie outside of the natural world.

A married couple gave birth to a perfectly normal baby. Later, when the child started to talk, the parents were shocked. He spoke in detail about his life before his birth to the amazement and chagrin of his parents. Soon the rumor spread that the *wunderkind* was relating his prebirth experience. Many came to listen and learn. Unfortunately, when they listened, they only heard words. They had no idea what the child was saying. It was totally out of their realm of experience.

The same can be said of Moses, the greatest of the Jewish prophets. He was on such a high spiritual level that he was still in touch with the "before birth" world: the world where there is no death. That is the same spiritual realm from where the commandment of the Red Cow, the *Parah Adumah*, originates. And thus, although to others it sounded merely as so many words, to Moshe, its message was understood clearly.

"This is the decree of the Torah. . . ."

One of the chief motivators in the physical world is pleasure. If we derive pleasure or anticipate pleasure from an activity, we will most likely do it. But once we have done it, the pleasure may have quickly ended, or worse, it may turn into pain. Our relationship to the Torah is very different. We do not follow its precepts because they give us physical pleasure. We follow them because they are the words of our Creator Who knows what is best for us. When we have already done the *mitzvah*, the commandment, then we suddenly taste the pleasure, the logic, the reason and sense in it.

A king called his servants to a feast. The king had a reputation for being a connoisseur of delicious food, and his chef was an expert in satisfying his exotic appetite. Still, although everything looked and smelled delicious, some of the guests were reluctant to try the more exotic items. They were reassured by the more experienced guests that the king has never disappointed his visitors. Finally, the guests started to eat. When they took the first bite they only thought of their insecurities; then they started to experience the delicious flavor of the food.

We too, when we obey the *mitzvos*, the commandments of the Torah, at first we are only aware of the decree of the King. Later when we have done the *mitzvah*, we suddenly taste the wonderful and delicious flavors that are in it.

"This is the decree of the Torah . . ." and it is also written, "And this is the Torah that Moses placed before the children of Israel" (Deuteronomy 4:44).

The natural world is ruled by laws that seem to be immutable. They are repeated so often and with such regularity that we can reliably predict their occurrence. Thus we call them laws. Do we, for example, doubt that the sun will rise tomorrow? Can we predict with accuracy where the moon will be ten years from now in the April sky? We can with certainty! It is as if the laws of nature were independent and had a life of their own. And this really seems the case. But when we delve a little deeper, we discover that the laws of nature are really the will of God. It is His will that makes everything happen.

How can we know anything about God's will? We know it mainly through the Torah. The Torah expresses the will of God and guides us to the type of life He wants us to live. Thus, the laws of nature, which are also the will of God, have their origin in the Torah. Still, it takes someone on the level of Moses, the greatest teacher, to understand the natural laws on the level of the Torah. So that the words "And this is the Torah that Moses placed . . ." mean that Moses saw everything through the Torah. For Moshe, everything is Torah. But for us, who are merely plain and ordinary human beings, it is hidden, unclear, and without understanding. For us it is *chukas haTorah*, the decree of the Torah, which we do not understand.

"This is the decree of the Torah . . . ," and later it is written, "This is the Torah that Moses placed before the children of Israel" (Deuteronomy 4:45).

If the universe is like a gigantic machine, the sum of which are the commands of God, then each part is a command, law, or teaching of the Torah. Unfortunately, this deep and spiritual truth is hidden from us ordinary people. To us, the world is merely *chukas haTorah*, a decree of the Torah that we do not understand.

The Torah is hidden from us because we are not pure. But when we stood at Mount Sinai ready to receive the Torah, we were on the highest level of purity. We were then like our teacher Moses and had the same understanding of the world as he had. And that understanding left a deep impression in our hearts. But we then sinned and worshiped a Golden Calf. We lost our purity and understanding. Still, we yearn for

it and seek it within our hearts. And thus is reawakened the understanding that we had at Mount Sinai, the ability to see Torah wisdom in all things.

A prince was rebellious, ran away from the palace, and joined a band of thieves. At first he felt uncomfortable in the company of cruel, drunken, and mistrusting men, but soon he became accustomed to their ways and rules. He slowly forgot the fine and cultured ways of his father's court and looked at everything with the eyes of a thief. Yet at times he yearned to be back with his father at the palace. It was during those moments of yearning that his father's point of view became very clear to him.

We too, are not pure, and cannot see the world from the perspective of the Torah. To us it is merely *chukas haTorah*, the decree of the Torah. Still, we yearn to be in the King's palace and to be close to His teachings. And then, for an instant, we catch a glimpse of the world in light of the Torah. The secret decree changes and becomes, "And this is the Torah"; it becomes revealed as Torah.

"This is the decree of the Torah . . ." The Midrash asks, "Why is the word *decree* used? Because the nations of the world taunt the Jewish people saying, 'What is the reason or logic for this commandment?' And we answer them saying, 'It is God's decree'" (*Numbers Rabbah* 19).

The *mitzvah* of *Parah Adumah*, the Red Cow, is outside the realm of the natural world. It can only be understood by a man such as Moses who was spiritually elevated above the material world. But there will come a time when even we will understand it. As it is written, "And it will come to pass that day will not be a brilliant light, nor will it be a dim light" (Zechariah 14:6). The Midrash comments, "God will bring forth a light and everyone will see what they had done in their lifetime" (*P'siktah Rabathi* 48). It means that God will bring forth all the *mitzvos* that we did without understanding and He will reveal their deepest reasons. As it is written, "And I will lead the blind on a path that they do not know and on trails that they do not know, and the darkness before them I will transform to light, and straighten their twisted roads. These things I have done and have not forsaken them" (Isaiah 42:16).

The Jewish people are like blind men when they do God's commandments. Although they understand nothing, they obey His command. Similarly, they responded at Mount Sinai, "We will do and we will listen." The Jewish people were prepared to do without understanding anything.

This is like a ship sailing across the ocean. There is a wealth of knowledge that the captain of such a ship needs in order to bring her to port. He needs to know about the effect of the elements on the ship, the provisions, navigation by stars and wind, surviving storms and calm, and managing the crew. The captain took his young son along for the first time. The boy had no idea of all the skills needed for crossing the ocean. His father, with great patience, kept teaching and repeating his instructions. The son did not understand why all of those things had to be done in such a precise way. Yet he trusted his father. He knew that his life and the survival of the ship depended on it.

We too are crossing the great unknown ocean of life, for the "first" time. Our Creator has taught us all we need to know. He gave us the Torah. Although we do not understand the reason for each of the required *mitzvos*, still we must trust in God. Some day it will all be clear, and we will understand all of the teachings. Then our eyes will be opened like a blind man who is able to see for the first time.

"This is the decree of the Torah. . . ."

Some people make a mistake. They think that each commandment of the Torah opposes another pursuit, desire, or activity of the human being. Actually the opposite is true. The Torah is so perfectly synchronized to the life of the person that each commandment corresponds to another part of the human body. There are commandments that relate to the head, others to the feet, and still others to each and every part of us.

We know the function of most of our organs. But there are a few that still mystify us, and we still do not know what function they serve. Similarly there are commandments that we do not understand. These are the *chukim*, the decrees, the *mitzvos* based on reasons we simply do not understand. They are beyond reason and logic and must be from the highest spiritual realms. They are from a place that is very close to God, a place where, just like He, things do not change but remain the same. They are therefore decrees that do not change. Thus, only someone who has not changed since his birth can hope to understand them. Such a person was Moses whom God called, "Moshe, Moshe" (Exodus 3:4), meaning that he was the same, he did not change since his birth.

But even we, when we reach out for the time of our birth, in an act of repentance, we catch a glimpse of this commandment that defies logic. With repentance, we are newborn babes, and thus it is as if we have never changed. We are then in that special place near God where there are no changes and no death; it is the source of the commandment of the Red Cow, which negates death.

"This is the decree of the Torah. . . ." King Solomon commented, "I said I would be wise, but it is far from me" (Ecclesiastes 7:23). Although King Solomon was the wisest of men, he could not fathom the meaning of the commandment of the Red Cow. Why not?

Wise men like King Solomon contemplate the universe. They recognize the miracles that are inherent in the deep and complex nature of the world. They see the infinite and unfathomable wherever they look. And suddenly they are awe-struck by the greatness of the One Who created it all. And they declare, "O God, how great are your works, all of them you have made with wisdom!" (Psalms 104:24). But are these this wise men full of the deepest knowledge of God? No, they are not. Because their knowledge of God grew from their own human, limited thinking and is therefore also limited. It still has some confusion and doubt. Only with the infinite divine knowledge of the Torah can we hope to have true knowledge of God.

The lesson that the *Parah Adumah* teaches is also on the level of divine knowledge. It teaches the negation of death, that we are always alive with God, and with Him there is no death. This knowledge is divine, and we can not possibly understand it with our limited minds. Even King Solomon attempted to understand this, but he failed.

"This is the decree of the Torah . . ." (Numbers 19:2).

Purity comes to us through the Torah, the Tree of Life; it is always pure and cannot be defiled. It is from the same source as our ever-pure souls. In contrast, the Tree of Knowledge is full of confusion, doubt, and death. Therefore, when Adam and Eve ate from the Tree of Knowledge, they were immediately confused, and this sin resulted in their death.

If you stay on the level of the Tree of Knowledge and attempt to reach purity through your own understanding, you will not succeed. On the contrary you must use Divine knowledge, the knowledge in the Torah, to reach everlasting purity. As our sages have taught, "Every letter in the Torah has the power to bring the dead back to life."

Thus we yearn to find the letter, the exact place, that will teach us the way of purity.

"This is the decree of the Torah . . ." And it is also written, "The words of God are pure, silver refined in a crucible, gold seven times purified" (Psalms 12:7).

The Torah is nothing but purity, and if you want to reach it, if you ever want to fathom its depths, then you must purify yourself and not just superficially, but rather seven times seven, the ultimate level of purity. If you do, then not only will your actions, speech, and thoughts be purified, but your desires will also be pure. You will then be ready to receive the teachings of the Torah. And as soon as you receive some of the Torah, the Torah will purify you further, and thus you will become worthy of even more Torah.

A commoner once wanted to marry the princess. He came to the palace and presented himself to the king and his court. He tried to impress the king with his possessions and wisdom. The king was amused. He laughed and mentioned his own enormous wealth and dismissed him with a wave of his hand. But the man was persistent and refused to give up. He thought of a new tactic. He said, "Your majesty, a lowly man as your servant, will never be worthy of being accepted into your company." "Aha!" said the king, "Humble yourself, will you? You will need to humble yourself a lot more before I will speak to you about anything."

We too, if we want to come close to the King, must humble and cleanse ourselves completely from the minutest arrogance. And when we do, we will have the purity that we seek.

"This is the decree of the Torah. . . ." The commandment of the Red Cow is so difficult to understand that even the wisest of men, King Solomon, could not understand it.

Each of us possesses a physical body and a spiritual soul. It might seem that the soul is of a divine nature and the body is merely of a physical nature. This is not exactly true, because even the body, which is physical, is sustained by the command of God as is every created thing. Thus even the body is divine. This view, however, is not shared by the "body." Our physical self wants to understand the world with physical tools, with logic, and with human understanding. By limiting itself to the physical, it is likely to err and stray off the path of the Torah.

If we insist on reasons that are tangible to the body, then we risk straying into paths of doubt and confusion. But if we follow the teachings of the Torah and we accept her teachings as decrees, then we are sure to walk on the path of life. Therefore, if we are ever to reach the purity that we long for, we must reach for it through the power of the Torah.

There are various types of *mitzvos* in the Torah. Some are understood logically, whereas others are decrees and cannot be understood. One might think that the logical ones are the stronger of the two. But the opposite is true.

A king had many servants. Those who were not of the inner circle did whatever the king desired as long as it had a reason. There were others who belonged to the inner circle and were very loyal to the king. They trusted his judgment, his fairness, and his charitable nature. They did whatever the king asked them to, even if it was not "logical." And the king, in turn, only asked his most trusted servants to do his will when he could not reveal the reason for his actions.

The pride of the Jewish people is that they do God's will even when it is against logic. Therefore, we are considered the most trusted of God's servants. It is the Jewish people that God addresses when He would not reveal the reason for one of His commandments.

What is the difference between doing something because of a reason or doing it without a reason? If you do it because of a reason, then it cannot be everlasting. Either the person changes, or the reason is no longer valid. But if you do it without a reason, then it is beyond logic and is everlasting. It is not affected by changes in the person or changes in the reason.

This is similar to our everyday life. Before we do something we examine the reasons carefully. We try to act in the most logical manner possible. We think and think. That is because the decision is not critical to our lives. But if there were a fire around us and the decision was critical to our survival, we would not care whether the act was logical or not. We must be saved! Therefore, if the commandment is vital to our lives, then we do it, regardless of its logic. This is why the *chukas hatorah*, the decree of the Torah, is higher than all the other commandments.

BECOMING HUMBLE

It is written, "The cow shall then be burned in Elazar's presence. Its skin, flesh, and blood and entrails must be burned. The priest shall take a piece of cedar wood, some hyssop, and some crimson wool, and throw it into the burning cow."

"Why is the cedar, the tallest of trees, and the hyssop, the shortest of bushes, both thrown into the fire with the Red Cow? This comes to teach you that if one is as haughty as a cedar, he should lower himself like a lowly bush" (*Numbers Rabbah* 19).

If the Torah wants to teach humility, then why throw in the cedar, so proud and tall? Would it not be better to throw in only the lowly bush as a symbol of humility?

The answer is very instructive about true humility. To be humble is merely to know that everything that we have is from God. Even if we are arrogant, we must remember that God gives us life so that we can be arrogant. Thus we transform our very arrogance into humility. Therefore, the tall cedar is thrown into the fire together with the lowly hyssop. Because, once we realize that without God we cannot even be arrogant, then we will immediately humble ourselves before God.

Why do we burn the cedar together with the lowly hyssop bush? This teaches us another thing about humility. An arrogant person may one day realize how small he is before the Creator. Then he may wonder about his own stupidity: "How could I have been so arrogant?" He takes his arrogance and uses it as part of the healing process. With it, he humbles himself before God. Thus the tall cedar and the lowly hyssop bush are burned together, and both have an equal share in the service of God.

"And they should take for the defiled person from the ashes of the burnt offering and place water from a (*mayim chaim*) brook into a vessel" (Numbers 19:17).

The words, *mayim chaim*, "waters of life," refer to the Torah, which gives life to everyone. If you want to be worthy of the waters of life then you must be as lowly as the hyssop bush, completely humbled to the ground. But the truth is that even humility is not enough. It is not enough to be the dust of the earth. As long as you are part of the natural world, you grow older and older and closer and closer to death and deterioration. There is only one way to renew your life—by becoming connected to the waters of life, the Torah. The Torah comes from a higher place

than the material world and brings us life and renewal.

"And God formed man from the dust of the earth and breathes into him a spirit of life" (Genesis 2:7).

The body is of the earth and dies, but the soul is from heaven and is eternal. The soul of man is pure and from the loftiest heights. But the body is easily defiled by improper actions. What is man to do?

We can humble our body and make it a vessel for our soul. Our body then receives the vitality from our soul as well. Thus it is written, ". . . and he should put the waters of life into a vessel . . ." (Numbers 19:17). If we make the body a vessel for the waters of life, then it too receives life from the waters.

The Reading of *Parshas Parah* on *Shabbos*

There were two trees in the Garden of Eden, the Tree of Life and the Tree of Knowledge. The Tree of Life was of the highest perfection, it contained no evil, and whoever ate from it lived forever. The Tree of Knowledge, on the other hand, was good and evil. Whoever ate from it was confused and eventually died.

Before we are born our soul is connected to the Tree of Life; it is pure and without blemish. This is on the level of holiness, a closeness to God and a being apart from the material world. When we are born, we are thrust into the world of the Tree of Knowledge, with its mixture of good and evil and eventually death. In such a world we are on the level of purity, because we must purify each of our actions so that they are not tainted with evil.

Similarly, we have *Shabbos* and the six work days. *Shabbos* is on the level of the Tree of Life. It is and has always been holy from the days of creation. It shares the everlasting quality of the World To Come. The six work days, however, are on the level of the Tree of Knowledge. They contain a mixture of good and evil, confusion and doubt. They are not holy, but are more on the level of purity; we must work hard to get them to the level of purity.

The commandment of the *Parah Adumah*, the Red Cow, is a path that leads us from the Tree of Knowledge to the Tree of Life. When the waters of the *Parah Adumah* are sprinkled on us, we are cleansed from the defilement of death. We suddenly realize that there is no death for our soul, our spirit, and it is alive as it ever was. We nearly jump out of the level of purity up to the level of holiness. We realize that when we die we are in the same spiritual place we were before we were born. The work of purity, of working our way out of confusion, ends with holiness.

A prince was raised and educated in the palace. As a teenager he rebelled and ran off with some ruffians. The royal family and those loyal to the king insisted that the prince be caught and punished severely. He eluded the soldiers and stayed away several years. After some very bad times in which he suffered privation, the prince decided to return. Yet, he could not return openly to the palace for fear of capture and possible death. So he came one dark night and got on his hands and knees near the palace wall and started to dig.

In his chambers, the king heard the odd noises of scratching and looked out. He saw the dark shape of a young lad and suspected that it might be his son. He too took a shovel and pick, and started to dig from the inside. After many hours the boy's hand met the king's shovel. The king reached for his son with great emotion and love. His son had finally come home.

The Red Cow is the secret tunnel in the deep of the night. It brings us back from the realm of this world of confusion, the Tree of Knowledge, to the palace of the king, the Tree of Life. It catapults us from the six work days to the completely holy day of *Shabbos*.

Similarly, the *Parah Adumah* allows us to experience the world on the level of the Tree of Life, before the sin of Adam and Eve, when the world was perfect without blemish.

A prince's father proudly taught him how to administer his kingdom. The prince was a bright and willing student and was soon well versed in all laws, regulations, and decrees. How surprised his father was when he saw him breaking the most fundamental of the rules a few days later. He reprimanded the boy by removing the royal insignia from his small crown. The prince was saddened and humbly asked for his father's forgiveness. His father forgave him, but did not honor him with the insignia. The prince really yearned for it and begged to wear it. His father finally acquiesced and allowed him to wear it during royal visits. When the prince wore it, he felt the same pride as he did before his offense.

The same is true of us on the day of *Shabbos*. We can experience and taste the first tablets before we sinned with idolatry and can wear our two celestial crowns. And when we do, we can be in the realm of a world without sin, sickness, and death—the world of the *Parah Adumah*, the Red Cow.

When God offered the Torah to the Jewish people they proclaimed, "All that God has spoken we will do and we will listen" (Exodus 24:7). And because of their brave answer they received two crowns, one for saying "we will do" and the other for saying "we will listen."

How could a thinking person commit himself to do without first hearing what needs to be done? Why didn't the Jewish people first listen? Because they were then on the highest level of faith in God and did not have to think. This level is called the Tree of Life; there is no doubt or confusion. Therefore, the stone tablets they received were engraved by God with the Ten Commandments. It was without confusion or sin.

Unfortunately, soon after Mount Sinai, they worshiped the Golden Calf. Moses broke the first tablets, and God took back the two crowns from the people. With great effort Moses helped them repent for their idolatry, and he engraved a new set of tablets with the Ten Commandments. And what happened to their crowns? Moses returns these crowns at the arrival of the Sabbath, because they keep the commandments, "Remember the *Shabbos* to keep it holy" and "Keep the *Shabbos*." And therefore, when a Jew observes the Sabbath, he not only tastes the sweetness of the day, but also the taste of the first tablets and the gift of crowns that came with it.

The soul, has three strengths, and the body has three weaknesses. The *neshama* is pure, it is united, and it is aware that its wondrous nature is a gift of God. The body, on the other hand, is impure and confused. It is made of many parts and thinks in terms of pluralities; it thinks that all accomplishments are the work of its own hands.

The soul is connected to the Tree of Life. When the soul observes more than one thing, it sees them as one, but the body, on the other hand, is connected to the Tree of Knowledge. When it observes even one thing, it perceives it as two. Therefore, when the Jewish people worshiped the Golden Calf, they proclaimed, ". . . these are your gods . . ." (Exodus 32:4); they saw everything in terms of pluralities. Later, when they repented, they became united as one, and they again believed in the one and only God.

Shabbos similarly is a day connected to the Tree of Life. And like the Tree of Life, it is united, and in it everything finds its unity. The Jewish people are more united than ever, as one, on the day of *Shabbos*, but this unity is not a result of our work. Rather, God gives us this unity as a gift. It is not achieved because of our understanding, but is beyond understanding and beyond the Tree of Knowledge. And when we are in the realm beyond understanding, the limitations of our body no longer hinder us.

A prince was once sent on an important mission. He had to cross a raging river over a narrow bridge that was thousands of feet above sea level. "You'll have to be very careful," the king warned his son. "The air is very thin at such heights, and you might start to hallucinate. You may forget where you are and where you are heading. If that happens, do not despair; there is a remedy. Whenever you feel doubt, dizziness, and confusion setting in, quickly look back toward the palace. As soon as you see the palace, even if from a distance, you will remember every-thing, even if only for an instant. Even that will be enough to bring you back to life."

We too are on a narrow bridge, where we often are confused. What can we do? What is the remedy for this confusion? *Shabbos*! From the day of *Shabbos* we can look back and see the palace of the King, the world in its perfection, the Garden of Eden, and the Tree of Life. We can see a world that is the source of the commandment of the *Parah Adumah*, the Red Cow, where there is no death.

And when we fix our gaze in the direction of the palace, we are reminded of who we are, where we are, and our destiny.

38

Parshas Ha'chodesh—
The New Moon of Nissan

THIS MONTH IS FOR YOU

 n the *Shabbos* before the Rosh Chodesh of *Nissan* we take two Torah Scrolls from the Holy Ark. In the first we read the regular weekly portion. In the second *parshas Ha'chodesh* is read, from Exodus 12:1–20 as follows:

God said to Moses and Aaron in Egypt: This month shall be the head month for you. It shall be the first month of the year.

Speak to the entire community of Israel, saying: On the tenth of this month, everyone must take a lamb for each extended family, a lamb for each household. If the household is too small for a lamb, then he and a close neighbor can obtain a lamb together, as long as it is for specifically designated individuals. Individuals shall be designated for a lamb according to how much each will eat.

You must have a flawless young animal, a one-year-old male. You can take it from the sheep or from the goats. Hold it in safekeeping until the fourteenth of this month.

The entire community of Israel shall then slaughter their sacrifices in the afternoon. They must take the blood and place it on the two doorposts and on the beam above the door of the houses in which they will eat the sacrifice.

Eat the sacrificial meat during the night, roasted over the fire. Eat it with *matzah* and bitter herbs.

Do not eat it raw or cooked in water, but only roasted over fire, including its head, its legs, and internal organs.

Do not leave any meat left over until morning. Anything that is left over until morning must be burned in a fire.

You must eat it with your waist belted, your shoes on your feet, and your staff in your hand, and you must eat it in haste. It is the Passover offering to God.

I will pass through Egypt on that night, and I will kill every firstborn in Egypt, man and beast. I will perform acts of judgment against all the gods of Egypt. I alone am God.

The blood will be a sign for you on the houses where you are staying. I will see the blood and pass you by. There will not be any plague among you when I strike Egypt.

This day must be one that you will remember. You must keep it as a festival to God for all generations. It is a law for all time that you must celebrate it.

Eat *matzos* for seven days. By the first day you must have your homes cleared of all leaven. Whoever eats leaven from the first day till the seventh day will have his soul cut off from Israel.

The first day shall be a sacred holiday, and the seventh day shall also be a sacred holiday. No work may be done on these days. The only work that you may do is that which is needed so that everyone is able to eat.

Be careful regarding the *matzos*, for on this very day I will have brought your masses out of Egypt. You must carefully keep this day for all generations; it is a law for all times. From the fourteenth day of the first month in the evening, until the night of the twenty-first day of the month, you must eat only *matzos*. During these seven days, no leaven may be found in your homes. If someone eats anything leavened his soul shall be cut off from the community of

Israel. This is true whether he is a proselyte or a person born into the nation. You must not eat anything leavened. In all the areas where you live, eat *matzos.*

While the soul is still in the spiritual world, before it is sent down into a body, it is aware that God is the Master. It is also aware of constant renewal, of experiencing a new world every instant. But after the soul enters a body, it is in the physical world of rules and laws. The material world seems always to remain the same within the laws of nature.

Why does the physical body think that the world never changes? Because it has forgotten its lessons of the spiritual world! In the world of the body, there is nothing new. The same thing happens over and over, as nature seems to be a series of constants.

A young man went sailing on a ship. He noticed that the captain supervised every aspect of the ship's and passengers' safety. As he watched the captain check his ship and the safety of the crew and passengers, he was overwhelmed at the enormous responsibility that rested on the captain's shoulders.

Finally, the ship began to sail. After several days, the young man forgot the captain and his hard work. He took the uneventful journey for granted and enjoyed the sun and ocean breeze.

After we are born, we take the world for granted and forget the "captain," the Master of the world. Once we knew that He is the Creator and Re-creator of the world, but now we have forgotten. We need *parshas Ha'chodesh* to set us straight. *Ha'chodesh*, "this renewal"; *hazeh*, "this very one," this real and ever-present one; *lochem*, "is for you." God gave *Nissan* to the Jewish people to reconnect with renewal. It is the month that instructs them how to live. It says to them, "Do not stay on the fringes of the world of laws and stale days and nights. Get on the world of renewal, the month of renewal. And when you do you will experience the new, the heavenly, and divine."

"This month shall be a head month for you . . ." (Exodus 12:2). The Midrash comments, "There is nothing more new than this . . ."(*Exodus Rabbah* 12).

After the creation of the heaven and earth and the entire universe, Adam and Eve were in the Garden of Eden. There, among plentitude they saw that God was the Master of the world. They saw Him and heard His voice on the breeze. The next generation, however, knew less of Him, as they were farther away from the days of creation and from the Creator. As generations passed, this knowledge was less

and less clear. Some of the people began to worship the sun, moon, and stars. They forgot the Creator and the words with which He created the world.

Then God brought plagues upon the Egyptians, and Moses led the people out of bondage. Suddenly everyone realized an old and forgotten piece of history: God is the creator of the world. The newness of the world was again clear and obvious to all.

Therefore the month of *Nissan* is so new and is the first of all the months. It is the month that reminds us that the world is constantly new and that God is the ever-present Creator.

The Midrash comments on the first commandment in the Torah: "This month shall be the head month for you. It shall be the first month of the year" (Exodus 12:2). It asks why the Torah starts with the story of creation. "Because God wanted to tell His people about His great deeds."

There are two beginnings: the beginning of the world and the beginning of the Jewish people. The beginning of the world is told in the story of the creation, "*Bereishis barah Elokim*—In the beginning God created" (Genesis 1:1). And the beginning of the Jewish people is told with the words, "*Ha'chodesh hazeh lochem*—This month shall be the head month for you" (Exodus 12:2).

The beginning of the world was made with the words of God. Those words are the ones with which He created the world and are revealed only in the Torah. Thus, nothing has a beginning without the Torah. Only with the words of God that are in the Torah can anyone hope to have a beginning.

How can we get a hold of the Torah? How can we connect with it so that we have a beginning? By looking for the words of the Torah hidden in the ordinary and natural world. And when we look for them in the natural world, they are revealed to us in the Torah. Therefore before we receive the first piece of Torah, the first commandment, we must first find the Torah in the story of creation. Thus we first fix the concealment, the words of God that are hidden in creation, and then we receive the commandments of the Torah.

We too in our own life must first correct our everyday, natural life in order to reveal God's word. And when our regular, everyday life becomes Godly, then we will be worthy to learn the Divine knowledge of the Torah.

The oppression of the Jewish people in Egypt was total. They were robbed of their freedom, culture, traditions, and children. It was said that no slave ever left Egypt, and no one expected the Jewish people to ever leave either. Yet God showed that He was the Master of the world and the Jewish people did leave. Everyone realized that these people did not belong to anyone in the natural world. They must therefore belong to someone higher—the Creator and Master of the World.

After the Exodus, when the Israelites came to the Red Sea and could not cross it, no one expected them to be saved. But the unexpected happened, and the sea split. The people crossed on dry land. It was again clear to everyone that God was the Master of the world.

It is therefore written, "This month shall be a head month for you . . ." The fact that *Nissan* is the first of the months bears witness about you, that you belong to no one except God. Because in this month you left Egypt, a place that no slave has ever left. You are different, not an ordinary people; you belong to the Creator and Master of the world.

———————

The Jewish people were oppressed as slaves and subjected to misery and suffering. They were downtrodden and treated as the dust of the earth. Their spirit was like broken reeds, hopelessly despairing. Then God sent Moses and Aaron, the many plagues, and miracles all around them. They were impressed, and their spirits were uplifted. Then God did even more. He led them from Egypt and took them as His people.

When miracles happened all around them, that was an external renewal. But the Exodus happened internally, inside their very souls. They became renewed as a nation. This was the greatest miracle of all. And therefore it is written, "This month shall be the head month for you." This is your special month. This month is more important to you than all the months when the plagues happened. Those were only occurring around you, but in this month you became renewed on the inside. You became completely new through and through.

The Head of the Months

Rosh Hashanah, New Year's Day, falls in the month of *Tishrei*, but the first month of the year is *Nissan*, which is six months later. How can that be? The answer is that there is a beginning for the natural year, in *Tishrei*, and there is a beginning to the miraculous year, and that is in *Nissan*. The New Year of *Tishrei* is for all mankind, as the Mishnah says, "All the inhabitants of the earth pass before God in judg-

ment . . ."(*Mishnah, Rosh Hashanah* 1:2). That is the natural New Year. But the new month of *Nissan* is only for the Jewish people, as it is written, "This month shall be the head month for you. . . ." It is for you, and no one else.

A prince came to ask his father for a favor. As he waited his turn, he overheard the king refusing the very request that he was about to make. "I am sorry," said the king, "I simply cannot do it!" The prince was sure that he too would be refused. But when he asked the king for the favor, it was granted immediately. "Why did you agree to my request and refuse that of your subject," the prince asked. "Because," the king replied, "with my subjects I have rules, but with my own son, I have my own way."

The rules for the natural world start with Rosh Hashanah, the New Year's Day of *Tishrei*. And the miraculous, the path of above and beyond the rules, starts for the Jewish people in the month of *Nissan*.

We too can reconnect our life to the path of the miraculous when we find our place in the month of *Nissan* and realize that the miracles are meant for us. Even if we find all the doors of the natural world closed, still we have the doors of miracles. Thus we shall never again say that we cannot do because "there is no way." Because for the people of miracles there is always the possibility of a miracle.

———————

It is written, "Who is that who looks out like the dawn, beautiful as the moon, bright as the sun, majestic as the starry heavens?" (Song of Songs 6:10).

The Jewish people are unique in that they infuse light wherever there is darkness. The special blessing of God for the Jewish people is that wherever they go, even the darkest place in the world, they can light it up. They are bright as the sun and a sky full of stars.

The life of people who live by habit, by the laws of nature, can become stagnant and old. But the Jewish people, the people of the Torah, are always renewing themselves and thereby spreading light into the world. This is the power of the month of *Nissan*, the month of renewal. Every slave of darkness is able to become free, and every creature is born anew.

———————

"This month shall be the head month for you. . . . They must take the blood and place it on the two doorposts and on the beam above the door of the houses in which they will eat the sacrifice" (Exodus 12:1–22). The Midrash comments, "The 'beam over the doorpost' symbolizes our forefathers, Abraham, Isaac, and Jacob."

The strength of the Jewish people is our fore-fathers. Our origins in those great and righteous men and women give us strength. They help us always to find new life when we think that all is lost. They help us pull ourselves out of despair and exile. But if we are severed from them, we sink to the lowest of levels. Therefore, we always have to reach out and touch the "beam" over the doorpost. We must always find a connection to the path of our forefathers and emulate their way of life.

A king had a very dear friend. The kingdom was in a state of collapse. Widespread anarchy and law-lessness spread throughout the land. The king's friend saw the desperate situation and immediately traveled throughout the kingdom, gathering sup-porters for the king. He spoke about the king's great-ness, his mercy and justice, and the good life that would result if only they obeyed him. Slowly his words took effect. The new "loyalists" continued to spread the word until the kingdom was back under the control of the king once more.

The king's friend died and left a son. The king treated the son with great respect, especially when the son showed the same degree of loyalty as his father. But when the son neglected his duties and for-got about the king, the the king was saddened and remarked, "Oh, how I miss my dear friend."

Abraham was the friend of God and made His kingdom known throughout the world. We are the children of God's friend and emulate his ways. When we do, then God draws us close to Him, to His power of renewal and the realm of freedom.

"And this month shall be the head month for you" (Exodus 12:2). The Midrash comments, "The Torah should have started with the first commandment, about the New Moon and the Passover sacrifice. Why does it start with the story of creation? Because God wanted His people to Know of His strength, so He can give them the inheritance of the nations" (*Genesis Rabbah* 1).

When Abraham first began teaching about God, he was still part of an idol-worshiping nation. So God said to Him, "If you chose to do this, you may as well be my emissary and spread my name throughout the world. Go forth then, from your land and family, to the land that I will show you." To separate him from the nations of the world, God commanded him to be circumcised. Thus he was elevated to a new position.

The same is true with the Jewish nation. At first they were merely part of the other nations; they were in exile and enslaved. Then they were chosen by God to be a unique and singular nation. They were com-manded to be emissaries for the word of God. The Torah, too, is organized in this manner. First, it tells the story of the creation of the universe. Every-thing is included in the story. Not one detail seems to stand out over another. Then, gradually, first with Abraham, Isaac, and Jacob and later with the Jewish people, a separation takes place. The special messen-gers and witnesses are chosen to proclaim God's Name throughout the world.

"This month shall be the head month for you" (Exo-dus 12:2). The Midrash comments, "'Behold the voice of my beloved, behold, he comes leaping upon the mountains, skipping upon the hills' (Song of Songs 2:8). When Moses came and told the Jewish people of their imminent redemption, they argued, 'The time has not yet come! We are decreed to remain here in Egypt 400 years. How can you tell us that we are leaving already?' And Moses answered, 'Because God wants to redeem you, He ignores the exact cal-culation'" (*Exodus Rabbah* 1).

The Jewish people were in slavery and exile under Pharaoh, a powerful king, and in Egypt, a powerful country. The Egyptians enslaved many peoples, which was typical behavior in those times. In addi-tion, God had decreed that the descendants of Abraham should fall into the Egyptian hands for four hundred years. This was merely a physical enslave-ment. But on the spiritual level, they were always exclusively the servants of God. They could not be slaves or enslaved under any circumstances. They were truly free of any human bondage.

A prince rebelled against his father, the king, and joined a band of criminals. The king, disguised, roamed the countryside along paths frequented by thieves. He rode singing songs of royal vintage. The prince was hiding in a tree when he heard his father's voice. Sud-denly, the attractions of the criminals dissolved. His "chains" opened as he jumped from the tree and pros-trated himself before his father. "Father, please forgive me, and I will come with you right now! My vows to these rogues mean nothing now that I hear your voice." "And my banishment of you for seven years is likewise revoked! " said the king. "You were always precious to me, and shall always remain so."

So it is with the Jewish people. They turned away from God and became enslaved to the nations of the world. There was a decree; they gave their word that they would not leave before the appointed time. They were in chains and were powerless before their enslaver. But when they heard the "voice" of their "beloved," then all restraints fell away, and they were ready to leave the exile.

"This month shall be the head month for you. It shall be the first month of the year" (Exodus 24:7–8). The law concerning the New Moon is given in the hands of the Jewish courts (*Rosh Hashanah* 22a).

Why is the commandment concerning the New Moon joined with the commandment of the Passover sacrifice?

We are born, mature, decline, and die. Yet, in our hands are two ways to reverse the inevitable decline. By having children and by speaking the right words, we can renew our life and the lives of those around us. Is it then a wonder that we have been taught, "Whoever teaches Torah to another is as if he gave birth to him" (*Sanhedrin* 19b).

The Jewish people are blessed with two covenants. The first is a blessing for their children; they are ". . . all the seed blessed by God." The second is His blessing of their teachings, the Torah, the most Divine knowledge. These are the two factors that guarantee the immortality of the Jewish people.

In the month of *Nissan*, when we were freed from bondage and became the nation of God, we derived strength from both our blessings. Our children were spared during the plague of the firstborn, and we regained our freedom of speech that was robbed from us during our slavery. We therefore teach our children the story of the Exodus. Our way of combining the renewal of the world through our children and through our speech is to impart the Torah to the next generation. Therefore, the time of the Passover holiday is the best time to learn about the Jewish court declaring the New Moon. By declaring the new month they attest to the fact that through speech the world can be renewed. This teaching is hidden in the word "Passover," which can be separated into two words, *PE–SACH*, "the mouth is talking."

It is a daily observation that the natural world falls apart. Old buildings crumble, the beach is washed away by the sea, stars lose energy, and we too become frail with age. The wise men have said that the whole universe is composed of elements, and slowly it is falling apart. Like a big clock that has been wound with a spring, slowly the spring is unwinding. This rule is true for all things in the world of nature. They are composed of parts and of elements.

But there is also a world higher than the world of nature—the spiritual world. There, this rule of a constant state of deterioration does not apply.

God chose the Jewish people for a spiritual life, to be free from the rules of the natural world. Still, we are flesh and blood, and we deal with the world of nature on a daily basis. So how can we be saved from the decaying world in which we live? Through the commandment of the New Moon. Each month we are reminded about our constant state of renewal. We are the opposite of the crumbling world of nature. We, the Jewish people, do not age. On the contrary, we are getting younger all the time. As it is written, "And they that wait upon the Lord shall renew their strength; they shall mount up with wings as eagles; they shall run, and not be weary; and they shall walk, and not faint" (Isaiah 40:31). Therefore, it is written, "This month shall be the head month for you. It shall be the first month of the year" (Exodus 12:2). The New Moon will teach that you will always be rejuvenated and never grow old.

"This month should be for you. . . ." The Jewish people count the months with the moon, whereas the nations of the world count with the sun (*Exodus Rabbah*).

There is yesterday, today, and tomorrow. There is the past, the present, and the future. That is time. Time marches forward. It keeps passing and moving on. It separates our present moment from the one that just passed. It seems to march on and on without end.

This is the kind of time given to the nations of the world. They are dominated by the sun. The sun seems always to be there. Days come and go, on and on, without end. One day, one hour, one moment, and one second are separated from the next and are thus fragmented. The time of the nations is static. It does not change, but rather remains the same.

The Jewish people are different. They count their months with the moon. The moon varies in size throughout the month until it disappears altogether. Then it is born anew. A new month has begun. Time for the Jewish people is dynamic. It is always changing and being renewed.

The Jewish people are equally connected to the present, the past, and the future. Their time is constantly being renewed, so that they can just as easily be in their past or their future as in their present. Therefore they are the eternal people.

In which month was the world created? Rabbi Elazar said, in the month of *Tishrei*, and Rabbi Yehoshua said, in the month of *Nissan* (*Rosh Hashanah* 10b). *Tishrei* is also the New Year for counting the years of the non-Jewish kings, whereas *Nissan* is the New

Year for Jewish kings. *Tishrei* is the month of judgment and is dominated by the fear of God, whereas *Nissan* is the month of mercy and is dominated by the love of God.

While the Jewish people were enslaved, they were in the realm of fear and judgment. But when Moses came and announced the redemption, they realized God's love for them. Therefore, their year shifted to *Nissan*. "This month shall be for you the beginning of the month of the year."

———

All renewal comes through the Torah. But while the Jewish people were enslaved, they were not connected to the Torah. Their life became dull and dreary, full of work and drudgery. They grew sick and old, without hope or purpose to their lives.

Then Moses came and renewed their connection to God's ways. Suddenly, their life was infused with renewal, and they heard the words, "This month shall be for you the first of all months." They realized that they were starting anew. Life would begin again, and they would endure. Their hope was reawakened, and they yearned for freedom.

A prince was marooned on a desert island. He had not heard from his father or seen any searching vessels for a long time. Months later, he had already given up hope and despaired of rescue. But one day he found some papers in the lining of his clothing. They were his father's instructions to him in case he ever got lost. Suddenly he felt his father's caring and closeness reaching out to him. His heart filled with hope. He realized that his father would be desperately searching for him. His heart quickened with hope for his father's arrival.

Likewise, in their exile the Jewish people were sad and felt forsaken. They thought that they were abandoned in Egypt forever. But then they heard the words of the Torah, from the mouth of Moses, "*Pokod pokadeti*—I have remembered." They immediately became alive. They realized that God loved them and would eventually free them.

———

"The voice of my beloved, behold, he comes leaping upon the mountains, skipping upon the hills. . . . behold he stands behind our wall, he looks from the windows, and peers through the lattice" (Song of Songs 2:8–9).

"The voice of my beloved" is the voice of the Torah, the word of God; it leaps over the mountains. There are no mountains in the world too high for the voice of God to scale. There are no hills too steep for the voice of God to skip over. There are no walls too strong for the voice of God to break through, and there is no crack too small for the voice of God to penetrate.

The voice of God is the Torah and the Commandments. And therefore Moses came to the Jewish people to redeem them with the words, "This month shall be for you the first of all the months." It was the first commandment to the Jewish people and the first words of Torah that they heard. And in face of these powerful words, no chains, however strong, could enslave the Jewish people. Chains are broken, windows burst open, walls fall down, and whole mountains are skipped over with the power of God's voice.

How can we comprehend the power of this voice?

A king took a liking to his servant girl and later married her. The longer he knew her, the more he liked her. Finally, he never wanted to be without her. One day the king had to leave for battle and was much distressed to leave his beloved. While he was gone, his beloved was captured, taken, and jailed in a high tower. The young queen tried every trick to escape, but to no avail. Finally the king himself went to find her. He found the tower, but the walls were too high to climb. He took his axe and banged on the door, but it was too thick to break. Finally, he started to sing his favorite royal tunes.

When the young queen heard the voice of her beloved, she was filled with strength and courage. She tore her chains and broke through the walls and the doors. Every obstacle melted before the great love that she and the king shared.

Likewise, when the Jewish people hear the word of God, there is no obstacle that can stand in their way.

THE MIRACULOUS MONTH

The nations of the world are ruled by the sun, which symbolizes the world of nature with its seemingly constant and unchanging light. And the Jewish people are ruled by the moon, symbolizing the world of renewal with its waning and waxing phases.

A clock tower was in the middle of the palace property. All servants, workers, advisors, and noblemen were ruled by that clock. Every appointment was kept according to its time.

One day the king called his son and said, "My son, I am giving you the keys to the clock tower. From now on you will be the one to set the time."

God gave the Jewish people the power to declare the New Moon. They are the ones who set the time. They have power over time. The nations of the world follow the time and are under its power.

While the Jewish people were slaves to Egypt, they

thought that they must follow the clock. They were slaves to the world of nature and thought they would never be redeemed. But then Moses said to them, "This month shall be for you the first of all the months," they suddenly realized that they were the ones who have the power over time. They rule time, and time does not rule them. They then knew that their redemption was at hand and they would soon be freed.

"This month shall be for you the first of all the months" (Exodus 12:2). There shall be nothing more new to you than this month (*Exodus Rabbah* 12).

Isn't the greatest news that God created the world?

A king fought many wars and conquered many lands. He finally found a very fertile stretch of land on which to build his kingdom. His servants tilled the soil, cleared thousands of acres of unwanted stones and brush, and landscaped it to look like a heavenly garden. When the work was completed, he rejoiced at the sight of his beautiful kingdom.

Then tragedy befell the king and his servants. They were attacked by a hostile and jealous tyrant who ravished the countryside and made them all his prisoners and slaves.

Years passed. After many years of suffering and servitude, the king and his loyal servants were able to overthrow the tyrants and banish them from the land. The king and his men stood on a hilltop and looked down at their beautiful land. They remembered how they had toiled the first time, making it a beautiful place to live in. Yet now it seemed to sparkle with an amazing freshness as if they had just received it.

The Jewish people knew that God created the world. But that idea became forgotten during their enslavement. Then they saw the plagues of God upon the Egyptians. They were thrilled that God was taking them out of slavery and exile. The whole world seemed new, as if it was just created. Suddenly nothing mattered to them, but that they were free and were servants to God once more.

"This month should be for you the first of all the months."

"Moses had difficulty understanding about the new moon. Then God showed him, `This month,' this is what you will see when you declare the new moon" (*Exodus Rabbah*).

God created the world in six days and rested on the seventh day. And ever since then the world has been in existence. Does that mean that God no longer has anything to do with the world? On the contrary. We believe that God wills the universe into existence every instant. And if there was a moment when He would not will it, then the world would cease to exist. Then why does it seem as if the world is going on by itself, as if it does not need God's will? Because God hid His will in the cloak of nature's disguise. God's will is revealed in the Torah, and those who are connected to the Torah are aware of it.

Those who look only at the world of nature will see an ordered world, a world that seems to run by itself. They will see a world that is old and has been in existence for a long, long time. But the Jewish people who are connected to the Torah are able to perceive the will of God that wills the world to exist. They see a new world, a miraculous world that has just been willed into existence.

A king once sent his servant to a distant city. The servant organized the city's government according to the orders of the king. After some time the city was running smoothly as part of the kingdom. The citizens no longer noticed that the king was running the city. Some months later the king received reports of crime and corruption in the city government. He visited the city with a group of brave soldiers. He expelled the corrupt officials and re-established law and order. Suddenly the citizens realized that their smooth running city was always run by the laws of the king.

The Jewish people, too, had great difficulty seeing the newness of the world. Then God brought great plagues upon Egypt, and they realized that the world, although weary with its old ways, is run by God's laws, which are always new. They looked up at the moon and saw that, although it is very old, it is constantly new.

"This month should be for you the first of all the months." As it is written, "In me the kings reign, and the princes decree judgement" (Proverbs 8:15; *Exodus Rabbah*).

It is during the month of *Nissan* when we realize that God is the Master of the world. It is the month that God took the Jewish people out of Egypt with great and powerful miracles. There can be no doubt of His greatness. We see it all in the open, and it is not hidden from us. The month of *Tishrei*, in contrast, although it is also very important to us and is our New Year, is not revealed clearly. Just as the moon is as yet barely visible on the day of the New Year, it is as if the kingdom of God is hidden too. Therefore, the month of *Nissan* is the New Year for the Jewish kings. That is the month that God's kingdom is revealed in the world. The month of *Tishrei* is the New Year for the non-Jewish kings for in that month the kingdom is really hidden.

"In the first of *Nissan* is the new Year for kings and also for the holidays of the year" (*Mishnah, Rosh Hashanah* 1:1).

What is the connection between kings and holidays?

The world of nature works with great regularity. Fire is very hot and burns our skin. We would not expect to put our hand into fire and to remove it without physical damage. This is a law of nature: the fire will burn the skin. We cannot breathe under water, and we would not expect a human being to stay under water for an extended period of time and survive. It too is a law of nature. It is also a "law" that a slave cannot be free, especially if he is enslaved to a ruler as mighty as Pharaoh. That is the decree of nature, which includes the stars and the power of astrology. So how did the Jewish people ever leave Egypt? Because they were raised above the natural world. The natural world came crashing down on the heads of the Egyptians with ten terrible plagues. The Jewish people were then separated from them, remaining unharmed. Each time the Egyptians were punished, the Jewish people were blessed and rewarded. They were elevated above and beyond the world of nature, of stars and astrological powers. They were removed from the slavery of Pharaoh and became the royal subjects of God. They were now part of the miraculous kingdom and were no longer subject to the laws of nature. They received their own miraculous calendar beginning with the month of *Nissan*.

A prince was taken captive by a band of thieves. Their personal schedule was suited to their thievery. They slept in the day and were awake at night. Their weeks and months were likewise organized around their thievery. The prince lived this way for many years until he had all but forgotten the royal calendar and routine. Luckily, the king was able to rescue him and return him to the palace. He no longer was a slave to the thieving band and resumed his royal schedule.

"It is the first of the months of the year" (Exodus 12:2). The word *year* is the name for the unit of time that the earth revolves around the sun. In Hebrew the word for year is *shanah*, which also means to sleep. What is the connection between sleep and year? A year is a unit of natural time, of the laws of nature. The laws of nature are limiting. They set limits as to what may happen and what may not happen.

God is without limit; He is boundless and infinite. Yet the world He created is defined by limitations. God is miraculous, but the world of nature follows strict laws. Compared to the infinite nature of God the world of nature is asleep. Sleep is in the head, and although the year has a "head," still, it is asleep because the year, the world of nature, is asleep.

The moon is the symbol of renewal and of the world of the miraculous. The word for moon is *levana*, also meaning *lev*, "heart." And although the head is asleep, the heart beats on. It is awake, as it is written, "I sleep, but my heart is awake" (Song of Songs 5:12). That means that deep within the world of nature, in its heart of hearts, is a spectacular world of renewal, the miraculous.

A king built a most spectacular kingdom. After some time he noticed that the people were really not worthy of enjoying all his hard work. He enclosed all the beautiful gardens, orchards, pools, and buildings within the palace walls. Within those walls only the royal family was permitted to stroll. Outside, to the public, he left only a few plain buildings and gardens.

One day a wise man visited from a distant land. When he saw the kingdom, he suspected that there had to be more to it than what he saw. He knew that the king had his real palace somewhere and that it must be hidden from sight. He requested permission to see the real palace. When he saw the magnificent interior he realized the greatness of the king.

The same is true if we look at the world of nature, the finite world. We get the impression that God's world is asleep. But then we look up at the moon; we look deeper into the work of God and realize that God's world is full of miracles and renewal.

This month should be for the first of all the months. Because the Jewish people left Egypt during this month, therefore it is the first, the most prominent.

The nations of the world appreciate that God created the world. They are thankful to God for the opportunity to live in this world and enjoy its pleasures. They are happiest when things remain in their status quo. They are connected with the static condition of the world. The Jewish people, in contrast, were freed from slavery. They broke the chains of oppression and limitations. They transformed their enslavement into freedom. They changed their limitation to opportunity. They are connected with the dynamic condition of the world. Therefore their first month is *Nissan*, the month of their redemption and Exodus.

The work of the nations of the world is to be thankful of their own existence, whereas the work of the Jewish people is to release themselves from the limitations of the natural world and to serve God.

The Light of the Moon

The nations of the world count their months with the sun, whereas the Jewish people count with the moon. What is the difference between the light of the sun and the moon? The light of the sun is much brighter and generates heat. It seems to be a more powerful light. Yet, the light of the moon, although it is much dimmer and is only a reflection of the sun's light, still shines and gives light in the darkness.

Such is the difference between the nations of the world and the Jewish people. The nations of the world might be stronger, richer, and more numerous, but the Jewish people are the ones who make light within the darkness. They are like the moon shining a quiet and steady light, which can light up the entire world.

Just as there are two lights in the heavens, the sun and the moon, there are also two lights in a person. One is the mind, in the head, and the other is the emotions, in the heart. The sun is a ball of burning gases that can bring great benefit, but can also harm by its burns. The moon has a cool, soft light.

The heart is composed of two chambers, the desire to do good and the desire to do evil. It is as if the heart is torn in two, each part fighting the other. What a person needs to do is to bring unity to the two parts and make his heart one. Then his heart will be pure and shine with a soft, quiet light. And when he does, it will influence his mind to be pure and quiet too.

The sun represents the consistency of nature. It is constantly shining in the sky. The moon is different. It waxes and wanes and even disappears. It reappears again as a new moon in a most delicate thin, soft light. The moon therefore represents renewal and the world of the miraculous.

The Maharal of Prague answers a question of the "philosophers." They ask, "How is it possible for miracles to happen in a natural and orderly world?" Isn't the order of the natural world the will of God? He answers that the world is truly orderly and is dominated by the laws of nature. Its orderliness never leaves. However, there is another sort of order, and that is the miraculous. This order is reserved for the Jewish people.

We can explain this conception on an even deeper level. The true nature of the universe is that it is the constant, ongoing, ever-present will of God. God has to will it into existence every instant. This concept fits more into the idea of "chaos" and quantum mechanics, in which you may calmly expect the unexpected. The world that we see and know is but a tiny moment, a tiny bubble in the greater scheme of things. Nature and its laws are a tiny but revealed portion of an immense miraculous universe.

This is also the difference between the Ten Commands with which God created the world and the Ten Commandments of the Torah and the guide of the Jewish people. The creation of the world took place with orderly laws and is "nature." The Torah, on the other hand, is the key for every Jew to enter the miraculous world.

The same is true with the two months of *Tishrei* and *Nissan*. *Tishrei* is the Jewish New Year and represents the world of nature. *Nissan* is the "first of all the months" and represents the miraculous world. It is during this month of *Nissan* that the Jewish people experience the true nature of the world. They read about the Ten Plagues, the Exodus, the splitting of the Red Sea, and the Ten Commandments. They realize that the life of our people is one that is full of miracles.

39

Shabbos Hagodol—
The Great Sabbath

he Sabbath before the holiday of Passover is called *Shabbos Hagodol,* the Great Sabbath. Why is this Sabbath greater than any other?

"Six days a week you should labor and do all your work. And on the seventh day it is *Shabbos* to your God, you should refrain from all work" (Exodus 20:9). During the six work days we think that everything that happens is a result of our actions. We are part of the natural world, a world that works according to laws that never change. But then when *Shabbos* comes we realize that whatever happens in the world is not our doing at all. It all must be done by God in order for it to happen. Then the greatness of God is revealed, that He is the Master of the world and the Lord of all that happens.

Abraham taught this very idea, that God is the Master of the world and that nothing happens outside His will. This made people realize that God is great because His power is in the human realm, the world of nature, and everything that is experienced. Therefore God promised Abraham, "And I will make you a great nation" (Genesis 12:2), because Abraham taught the greatness of God.

Before the Jewish people left Egypt, they were commanded to take a lamb and sacrifice it four days later. This was a great risk, since the lamb was the Egyptian idol. The Israelites knew that if caught they would be killed instantly. But they trusted that God's greatness lies in His direct intervention in their life. And they did all this on *Shabbos,* the very day that is a witness to God's greatness.

Therefore, the *Shabbos* before Passover is called the Great *Shabbos.*

The Midrash tells us that while Moses lived in the palace of Pharaoh, he begged the king to allow his Hebrew slaves to have a day of rest. Pharaoh agreed. Thus the Sabbath was established as a day of rest even during their years of slavery (*Exodus Rabbah*). After the Exodus they stood at Mount Sinai and God commanded them to keep the *Shabbos* holy. What was the difference between the original *Shabbos* that they kept in Egypt and the one they kept after Mount Sinai?

There is a physical *Shabbos* and a *spiritual Shabbos.* When the Jews worked as slaves, as some of us work even today, they rested from their physical work on *Shabbos.* They would rest and lie exhausted in the fields while their wives brought water to wash them and cooked fish to feed them. Still, this was merely an absence of work; it was the negative aspect of *Shabbos,* as it is written, "Observe the *Shabbos* to keep it holy . . ." (Deuteronomy 5:12). Do not do types of work forbidden on *Shabbos* and thus you will keep it holy. And, although physical, it is nevertheless *Shabbos* and is holy.

Then there is the spiritual *Shabbos,* the higher positive aspect of the day. As it is written, "Remember the *Shabbos* to keep it holy" (Exodus 20:8). We must remember and suffuse the mind, fill our every thought with *Shabbos* and that there is no one but the Creator Who is the Master of the world.

A king's subject administered one of the provinces. Each month he was allowed one day off, which he spent at a mountain retreat. One day he received an invitation from the king: on his next day off he was to be at the palace and spend the day in the king's company.

The *Shabbos* before they left Egypt, the Jewish people were told to "(*Mishchu*) Gather the people and get yourselves sheep . . ." (Exodus 12:21). *Mishchu* also means to draw; you can be drawn closer to your roots by taking the sheep, the idol of Egypt, and abandoning idol worship. Run from the uncleanliness of Egypt and turn to be a holy nation to God. Do not merely rest in the countryside, but come and stay with the King in His palace. Thus, the *Shabbos* before the Exodus was the first Sabbath that the Israelites experienced on the spiritual level. And it is therefore called *Shabbos Hagadol*, the Great *Shabbos*.

"If the Jewish nation would keep two days of *Shabbos*, they would immediately be redeemed" (*Shabbos* 118b). One *Shabbos* that they kept was the regular weekly one. And the second one was the *Shabbos* before the Exodus, when their yearning for God was at its peak. And into this *Shabbos* there assembled the spiritual essence of the fifty *Shabbos* days of the entire year. And it thus became a very big *Shabbos, Shabbos Hagodol*.

What made that *Shabbos* so special? It was because the Israelites had to take a sheep on that day, inspect it, and keep it until the fourteenth day of *Nissan* for the Passover sacrifice. By pulling the sheep, God said, "Pull your hand away from idol worship and take a sheep to do a *mitzvah*." You must first pull away from idol worship in order to do a *mitzvah*, to serve God, because as long as you are enslaved to anyone else you cannot be a true servant of God. *Shabbos* is a statement that a Jew is totally free from domination, that he is a slave to no one. A Jew who keeps *Shabbos* does not become a slave to anyone, even during the weekdays. Therefore, if you keep the first *Shabbos* properly and throw off the yoke of slavery from your back, then you will work for six days as a "free man," and then will keep the second *Shabbos* as a free man and on a higher level.

Thus the two phrases concerning *Shabbos*: "Observe the *Shabbos* to keep it holy . . ." (Deuteronomy 5:12), and "Remember the *Shabbos* to keep it holy" (Exodus 20:8). To observe means not to accept foreign domination. To remember means to remember God and accept His sovereignty. And on the last

Shabbos before the Exodus, both the "observe" and the "remember" came together. They pulled the sheep, the Egyptian idol, and tied it to their bed. They created a distance between themselves and idol worship. And furthermore, they prepared to do the *mitzvah*, the Passover sacrifice as commanded by God. They accepted His word as their command. Therefore it is called the Great *Shabbos*.

God created the world with Ten Commands. As each of the commands was uttered, it was hidden within the creation. The command, "Let there be light," was hidden within the light itself, so that when we look at light today, we are unable to see the command of God within it. It lies concealed. When were these commands revealed? When the Israelites stood at Mount Sinai and heard the Ten Commandments, at that instant they "saw" clearly that God's words are at the root of each created thing. The Ten Commands were then revealed.

A king wrote edicts and laws to improve the lives of his countrymen. The edicts were posted in each of the town squares for all to see. Some of the rebellious subjects rode around and tore down every one of the posters. Visitors who came from other kingdoms wondered, "Does this king ever tell his subjects what to do?" Because they did not see any of the king's commands, they thought that he never communicated with his subjects.

Similarly, when the commands of God are concealed, we think that God is speechless. And this is the misery of the exile and especially of Egypt. Speech itself was in exile, as if God did not "say" anything to His world. We therefore have different blessings. When we hear good news, we say, "Praised are You Who is good and does good" and when we hear bad news we say, "praised is the true judge." Why are there two different blessings? Because the bad is not recognized as good; it is hidden. But when the redemption comes, we will use only one blessing for all occasions, and we will say, "Praised are You Who is good and does good." Then the commands of God will be revealed, that His word is in control of all events. Therefore, now in the exile, we only have "*razah d'Shabbos*—the secret of *Shabbos*." *Shabbos* reveals that which is concealed in the weekdays and during the exile: that God created the heavens and earth, that He is one always and everywhere. But when the Exodus was at hand it became abundantly clear that He and no one else orchestrated all events. On that last *Shabbos* the commands of God were free from the exile and were crystal clear for one and all to see. Thus it is the Great *Shabbos*, *Shabbos Hagodol*.

During the six work days we sometimes are arrogant and feel that we have limitless power. Such arrogance can lead to idol worship. When you think that you are independent of God, you remove the yoke of heaven. But when *Shabbos* comes, we realize that God is the source of everything, He made and does everything, and our arrogance melts away. Thus the *Shabbos* before the Exodus, the Israelites realized that the only one who helped them was the One and Only. It was the most powerful realization anyone could have had. And therefore it was called the Great *Shabbos*.

There is physical enslavement and spiritual enslavement. When our physical activities are dominated by another and we cannot act independently, we are then slaves. We were slaves in Egypt. Similarly, we can be spiritual slaves, too, when we are totally dominated in our spiritual decisions. As an antidote to these two forms of enslavement come the two aspects of *Shabbos*. *Shabbos* is a day of physical rest, it releases our body from slavery. And there is also the spiritual freedom of *Shabbos* that frees our soul to serve God. And when we accept God as our King and refuse to be slaves to anyone else, then we are free the entire week, although we may appear to be enslaved. When *Shabbos* comes we are elevated to new heights, as we experience a spiritual liberation. And thus, the last *Shabbos* before the Exodus, we experienced both a physical and a spiritual liberation. And thus it was the Great *Shabbos*, *Shabbos Hagodol*.

It is written, "You must remember that you were slaves in Egypt, when God your Lord brought you out with a strong hand and an outstretched arm. It is for this reason that God your Lord commanded you to keep the *Shabbos*" (Exodus 5:15).

There are fifty Sabbaths during the year, and in each one we mention the Exodus during the *Kiddush* service. Corresponding to this, there are fifty times that the Exodus is mentioned in the Torah. Similarly, there are fifty gates of wisdom, and each one has an obstacle that must be overcome in order to enter it. And not only are there gates for deeper understanding but even for the smallest understanding there are

fifty gates. When the obstacle is removed, it is like at the Exodus, when the door was wide open. And when all the gates are open, it is a sign that all the obstacles were removed, as at the moment of exodus. Then it is the Great *Shabbos*.

The Great *Shabbos* before Passover is similar to the *Shabbos* of Repentance before Yom Kippur, the Day of Atonement. Before Yom Kippur, we are frightened of what God will decree. We repent out of fear. A mind that is afraid is in a diminutive state; it is small and depressed. But the moment before the Exodus, the hearts of the Jewish people were filled with thankfulness for the Divine miracles and wonders, and they repented with great yearning and love. Their minds and hearts then were open and receptive, grand and spacious. Thus the *Shabbos* of the Exodus is called the Great *Shabbos*.

It is written, "Speak to the entire community of Israel, saying: On the tenth of this month, each of them must take a lamb for each extended family, a lamb for each household" (Exodus 12:3).

The tenth day of *Nissan* of that year fell on *Shabbos*, and therefore the Sabbath before Passover is celebrated as a special day. The question is: why do we not celebrate the tenth day of each *Nissan* instead of the Sabbath?

There are two phases in performing a *mitzvah*: (1) the thought in the mind and the feeling and emotion in the heart and (2) the physical performance of the deed. The Israelites obligated themselves to serve God, to prepare the sheep by pulling it into their homes, before they actually sacrificed it. This obligation was far more valuable to God than the deed itself, because the yearning to do a *mitzvah* is much more pure and perfect than doing the *mitzvah*. After all, how perfect are our deeds? There is none without fault.

The day of *Shabbos*, too, is a day without physical activity, a day of pure will and desire. It is a day when you need not do a thing in order to produce the *Shabbos*. It is holy from the time of creation, regardless of what a person does or does not do. Therefore it is like the World to Come when everything will revert to the original intention, the perfect state that God intended for it. Thus, the pure intention of the Jewish people meshed with the pure intention of *Shabbos*, and the two created the Great *Shabbos*, *Shabbos Hagodol*.

Similarly, in our everyday life, we must know that every deed that we do with the purest intentions, although completed with shortcomings, will one day blossom into its fullness and completeness.

The spiritual world is in balance. Just as there are forty-nine levels or faces of impurity, there are also forty-nine levels of purity. Where are these forty-nine faces of impurity? They dwell as an obstacle at each of the forty-nine gates of wisdom that we approach during the six work days. And by removing each of the obstacles, we are able to enter a gate of wisdom on the day of *Shabbos*. The first *Shabbos* and the first gate that we enter are called, "the beginning of wisdom," because we do not yet have wisdom. However, with the proper fear and awe of God we enter the gate of wisdom. And the last *Shabbos*, the very last fiftieth gate, is called "the world of total liberation." We enter this gate when we have no attachments to the material world. And that gate takes us into a realm where purity and impurity dissolve into a singularity. There are no opposites there—only unity, wholesomeness, and peace. It is the Great *Shabbos*, the level that the Israelites reached on that last *Shabbos* before their liberation.

In the Torah there are two reasons for the existence of the Sabbath. The first is given in the Ten Commandments, "It was during the six weekdays that God made the heaven, the earth, the sea, and all that was in them, but He rested on the seventh day" (Exodus 20:11). Then later, it is written, "You must remember that you were slaves in Egypt, when God your Lord brought you out with a strong hand and an outstretched arm. It is for this reason that God your Lord has commanded you to keep the *Shabbos*" (Deuteronomy 5:15). Therefore, until the Exodus, the Sabbath had only one reason for its existence. On the *Shabbos* before they left Egypt, when the redemption was imminent, the second reason was added to it. It was the first *Shabbos* with two reasons and was therefore twice as powerful than all the Sabbaths that preceded it. It was therefore called the Great *Shabbos*, *Shabbos Hagodol*.

The Zohar says, On the one hand there are the impure forces and political enslavement, and on the other hand there is complete servitude to God. In other words, either we are servants of God or slaves of

tyrants. But even if we are servants of God and we serve Him with awe and reverence, it is not the highest level or best relationship. This is accomplished on *Shabbos*, when we "rest" even from being servants of God. On that day we are children of God, we are spiritual kin to the Creator, and we are created in His image.

During the six work days this relationship is hidden, for two reasons: the material nature of the physical world hides the world of the spirit; and the holiness of the spiritual world is so awesome that we could hardly hope to come near it. This is why we praise God, *min haolam ad haolam*—literally, from one world to the other world. *Olam* also means *helom*, "hidden"; we praise God from one hiddenness to the other. During the six work days we relate to the physical world. We work, organize, and make changes in the material world. And if we are able to overcome the material nature of the weekdays and strive to uncover the spiritual that is hidden below the surface, then we receive a gift on *Shabbos*. We merit being free of physical enslavement; we do not have to work. This is the lower level of *Shabbos*, the "small" *Shabbos* that is defined by the words, ". . . and there is no other ruler . . ." (Zohar, *Parshas Tetzaveh*). The higher level of the *Shabbos* is when we are not only free of physical enslavement but are also elevated even above being servants of God to the level of His children.

In Egypt, the Israelites went through two stages. In the first they were freed from the work of slavery on *Shabbos*. They did not have to work and therefore had the "small" *Shabbos*. Later, in the second stage, just before the Exodus, they were elevated even higher to be the children of God. That *Shabbos* was the Great *Shabbos*, the highest and most spiritual one and is therefore called *Shabbos Hagodol*.

The Midrash says, "*Shabbos* complained to God, 'All the weekdays have a pair; day one with day two, day three and day four, and so on. Why haven't I a pair?!' God answered, 'The Jewish people will be your pair,'" (*Genesis Rabbah* 1).

When God gives a gift, there must be a vessel to receive it. Each day of the week is like a vessel to receive a particular blessing from God. *Shabbos*, however, is above and beyond the physical realm. What can it possibly receive? Hence its complaint. But when the Jewish people were about to leave their exile, on the *Shabbos* before the Exodus, they were elevated to the realm above the physical world. Thus *Shabbos* became a vessel for the Jewish people, and the Jewish people became a vessel for *Shabbos*. They had gone through the highest form of spiritual education with the ten plagues. Their level was awesome, but not at all a result of their effort. *Shabbos* too, just before they left, was on the most awesome spiritual level. At that instant they had the purest and most free choice: to worship idols or sacrifice the sheep to God. And because its pair, the Jewish people, was on such an awesome level, it is therefore called the Great *Shabbos*, *Shabbos Hagodol*.

The Zohar (Leviticus 101) says, the Israelites could not perform the *mitzvah* of the Passover sacrifice properly because whoever is a slave to another cannot be a servant of God. Therefore, right before the Exodus, they were free of Egyptian domination and were able to complete the *mitzvah* in its fullness. And since they performed the *mitzvah*, it was a merit for their redemption. That last *Shabbos* became the greatest of all Sabbaths and is therefore called *Shabbos Hagodol*.

The *Shabbos* itself was yearning for the redemption of the Israelites from Egypt, because it did not have a pair until the Israelites became a people. And truly, no part of the creation was a proper vessel to receive the *Shabbos*. Thus when the Exodus came, *Shabbos* finally had a place in the world. Therefore it is called the Great *Shabbos*.

It is written, "Remember the *Shabbos* to (make) keep it holy" (Exodus 20:8). *Shabbos* is holy since the creation of the world and is a gift from God. How is it possible for anyone to "add" to its holiness? Only the Jewish people whose souls receive extra power on the Sabbath, who are the "pair" for the *Shabbos*, are able to add to the holiness of the Shabbos. Thus, at the time of the redemption, when the Israelites became a nation, the *Shabbos* itself became bigger and greater and is therefore called *Shabbos Hagodol*.

Shabbos is the ultimate peace and tranquility, a state that cannot be attained in the physical world. Yet, the day will come when the world will be transformed, and we will have "a day that is totally *Shabbos* forever." Therefore, in miniature, the *Shabbos* is a sample of the World to Come. On the Sabbath before the Exodus, as the Israelites were about to leave the slavery of Egypt, they experienced the sweet joy of total

freedom and peace. Similarly, we too are reminded each *Shabbos* to keep hoping for wholeness and tranquility such as the *Shabbos* is. We hope for a day when our present exile will end and God will be the recognized King over all the nations of the earth.

The Israelites were commanded to take each a sheep on the tenth day of *Nissan*, on the *Shabbos*, and to inspect and hold it till the fourteenth, when they would sacrifice and eat it. Why was it necessary for them to have the sheep four days before they would sacrifice it? God wanted them to yearn and hope for the redemption and especially on *Shabbos*, which is a day of yearning and hope. On *Shabbos* we yearn and hope for the day when the entire world will change to a state of *Shabbos*, with peace and tranquility forever. And this hope itself created their merit for a spectacular redemption.

Similarly, we too yearn and hope for the final redemption, and that creates the merit for it. Thus we are instructed by our sages to begin asking and expounding about the laws of Passover thirty days before the holiday. Therefore we start yearning for the redemption of Passover right after Purim. And that yearning creates the merit for the final redemption. May it come quickly in our lifetime.

The creation has four major categories: inanimate objects, such as stone, water, air; vegetation, such as trees, plants, grasses; animate, such as animals of every description on land, sea, and air; and man, the communicator. Each was created with its own potential, and before it becomes actual it remains in *katnus*, in a minor aspect of its being. But when a potential is realized, then it is in *gadlus*, the major aspect of its being.

We find this to be true even concerning *Shabbos*. When God rested on the seventh day it is written, "Because He rested in it" (Genesis 2:1). It is passive, in potential, in the *katnus*, the minor aspect of the *Shabbos*. Later it is written, "And the Israelites should keep the *Shabbos* to make the *Shabbos*." When the Jewish people are keeping the *Shabbos*, it is the *gadlus*, the major aspect of the *Shabbos*. When the *Shabbos* is in potential, we are merely witnesses to it, as a servant of a king who observes what the king does but does not grasp the full impact of it. So too, when we witness and say, "God created the world in six days and rested on the seventh day," it is as an observer to the work of the king. But when we make the *Shabbos*, we are like the king's child who delves into all of the secrets of his father and understands what he is doing. This then is the *gadlus* of *Shabbos*, and hence *Shabbos Hagodol*.

Although there was *Shabbos* before, it was only in potential, until the Jewish people brought it out into the actual world.

When witnesses come to the Jewish court, the judges put them through a corroboration process with seven types of cross-examinations until their testimony is crystal clear and truthful. Similarly, the Jewish people are witness that God created the world, and they too went through a process in which their integrity was tested: the exile with its pain and suffering. And thus, on the *Shabbos* before the Exodus, their qualification as witnesses was already established. That particular *Shabbos* had bona fide witnesses that God created the world, and it was therefore the first Great *Shabbos*, *Shabbos Hagodol*.

It is written, "A stone is heavy and sand is weighty, but a fool's wrath is heavier than them both" (Proverbs 27:3).

The anger of the fools who block the Name of God from being revealed is the heaviest of all burdens. It causes the Divine Presence to be in exile and instead be concealed in the world of nature, as if God is carrying a load that keeps Him in exile. Thus God rested from the six days of creation, but He rested so much more when the stubborn Pharaoh was forced to release the Israelites. So that on the *Shabbos* before the Exodus the "heavy stone" was already lifted, and the Name of God was already revealed. Therefore that *Shabbos* was a Great *Shabbos*, *Shabbos Hagodol*.

It is written, ". . . the Lord has said to me, You are my son; I have begotten you" (Psalms 2:8).

The Zohar says that when a child reaches the age of responsibility and is obligated to do *mitzvos*, a boy at the age of thirteen years and a girl at twelve, it is as if he was just born. It is the day that he is called a *godol*, "mature." Similarly, when the Israelites were about to leave Egypt they were commanded to do the *mitzvah* of the Passover sacrifice. It was the first commandment to the brand-new nation, and with that they reached a new level of maturity. Hence that *Shabbos* was called *Shabbos Hagodol*, the mature, grown-up *Shabbos* when we were born as a nation of God.

The entire world is ordered on many levels. Some animals dominate over others, some mountains are bigger than others, and the same is with trees and even with human beings. Some nations dominate over others, and some are enslaved to others. All things, all creatures and all people, except the Jewish people, stand in relation to one another. However, the Jewish people have been removed from the natural cycle of domination and subjugation. Therefore, they are called a great nation, because they are elevated over every nation. No nation can legitimately call them their slaves. On the *Shabbos* preceding the Exodus, the Israelites became a nation of God and therefore a great nation. We therefore call it the Great *Shabbos*, *Shabbos Hagodol*.

We too should rise to the occasion, lift our heads high, and be the great nation that we are.

When a Jew observes *Shabbos*, he is a witness that God created the world in six days and rested on the seventh. He proclaims that the natural world has a Master and Creator. But what about the ability of God to perform miracles, to change nature, and ignore its laws? When does one say witness about that? This happened on the *Shabbos* before the Exodus. After the Israelites witnessed the Ten Plagues and other great miracles in Egypt, they were ready to leave. On that last *Shabbos* they realized that God is the Master not only of nature and its laws but also that He is the Creator of the laws of nature. It is His Will that makes the laws function, and His Will also makes them not function. He makes nature, and He makes miracles. They are both totally in His hands. As it is written, "You must remember that you were slaves in Egypt, when God your Lord brought you out with a strong hand and an outstretched arm. It is for this reason that God your Lord has commanded you to keep the *Shabbos*" (Deuteronomy 5:15).

Therefore, that *Shabbos* before the Exodus was so much greater than any other. It was the Sabbath that bore witness to God as the Master of the natural, as well as the miraculous, world. It is therefore called the Great *Shabbos*, *Shabbos Hagodol*.

It is written, "I sleep, but my heart is awake: the voice of my beloved is knocking, and says, Open to me, my sister, my love, my dove . . ." (Song of Songs 5:2). The Midrash comments, "Open for me an opening of repentance the size of a needle's eye, and I will open for you doorways that ox-drawn carts can fit through" (*Song of Songs Rabbah* 8:2). When it was the time of the redemption, the Israelites were without merit or good deeds. Therefore God commanded them to do two *mitzvos*: circumcision and the Passover sacrifice. Both are covenants of blood, as it is written, "The blood will be a sign for you on the houses where you are staying. I will see the blood and pass over you. There will not be any deadly plague among you when I strike Egypt" (Exodus 12:13). God "saw" the blood and had mercy on them and skipped over their doors. The doors symbolized those tiny openings that they opened in their hearts for repentance. God had compassion on those small openings, embraced them, and made them infinitely large. And upon that opening God built the entire redemption and all that followed. Therefore, the *Shabbos* in which all this happened is called the Great *Shabbos*, because God made the doorways of the Jewish hearts infinite.

This is a lesson to every one who wants to repent. Let him have the strongest resolve and determination. Then even if he merely opens his heart a tiny crack, as the hole of a needle, God will do the rest and will use that opening to penetrate to the deepest depth of his heart and soul.

It is written, ". . . The gate of the inner court that faces east shall be shut the six working days; but on the *Shabbos* it shall be opened, and in the day of the new moon it shall be opened" (Ezekiel 46:1).

During the six work days the spiritual gates are closed; they are concealed. But on the *Shabbos*, the gates are open, and it is clear to all that God created the world. And just as the natural world yields its secrets on the *Shabbos*, so too do the hearts of the Jewish people. Their hearts open to receive the Divine spirit. And when all of them open, as gates, then the time of the redemption has arrived. Therefore, on the *Shabbos* before the Exodus, all the gates were wide open, and it was a Great *Shabbos*, *Shabbos Hagodol*.

Although the Israelites rested on the *Shabbos* even before the Exodus, still, up to that time, they had not made a total commitment to be a nation of God. But on the last *Shabbos* they left idol worship completely by taking the idol of Egypt, the sheep, as the Passover sacrifice. Therefore the redemption already started on that *Shabbos* and made it the most significant day in Jewish history.

Shabbos is holy and is with us since the creation of the world; it is the first of the holy days. Passover, too, is the first of the three major holidays of the Jewish nation. Therefore, the *Shabbos* before the Exodus was an introduction to the holiday of Passover. And as holy as it usually is, it became so much more holy and special. Therefore it is the Great *Shabbos*, *Shabbos Hagodol*.

It is written concerning the ultimate redemption of the Jewish people, ". . . I the Lord will hasten it in its time" (Isaiah 60:22). The Talmud asks: If it will come in haste, then it is before the appointed time; and if it is in its appointed time, then is it not in haste? The Talmud answers: if the Jewish nation is worthy, then God will hasten the redemption. And if they are not worthy, they will ultimately be redeemed, but at the appointed time (*Sanhedrin* 98a).

It is written, "To everything there is a season, and a time to every purpose under the heaven" (Ecclesiastes 3:1). Anything that is under the heaven, in the natural world, has an appointed time. But the Torah is higher than the heaven and is above nature and time. In fact, time is a vessel for the Torah, and without it the Torah would not be able to be in the natural world. But The Torah itself is higher than time and the world of nature. It is high up there, transcendentally hovering over the material world. It waits for an opportunity to land in a vessel. Therefore, when the Jewish people are connected with the Torah, with its teachings, with its hope, and they yearn for it as they did in Egypt, then they too rise above the confines of time. Then the redemption comes hastily, before its time. As it is written, "It is time to act for God, for they have made void Your Law" (Psalms 119:126). When it is time for God's work, for His redemption, then the fixed time is void, and it arrives in haste before its time.

This is also the contrast between the six work days and the *Shabbos*. During the six work days, the Days of Creation, time is uplifted and repaired by our good deeds. Our deeds are physical and affect the physical world. Therefore, the physicality of time is repaired and uplifted. But on the *Shabbos*, time itself is uplifted to the level beyond time, to the level of the Torah. It is the seventh day of the week, but it is beyond the days of the week and beyond time. It is above the natural realm and is on the level of the Torah, which is itself beyond time. As it is written, "Today, if you will hear His voice" (Psalms 95:7). "His voice" means the Torah. And "today" is the *Shabbos*. What is *Shabbos* about? It is about the Torah, which is beyond time and the natural world.

Thus, the *Shabbos* before the redemption was already beyond time; the redemption was rushing at the Jewish people and they were rushing to leave. And it was therefore higher than anything the Israelites had ever experienced and is the Great *Shabbos*, *Shabbos Hagodol*.

The Midrash (Exodus 4) relates the following conversation between Moses and the Israelites: Said Moses, "The month of your redemption has arrived." The people answered, "But we are supposed to be here four hundred years; why are we leaving so early?" Moses answered, "Since God wants to redeem you, He skips over the years and takes you earlier, as it is written, 'He skips over the mountains . . .'" (Song of Songs 2:8).

The question is: if God wanted to redeem them before the time, then why was it "decreed" that they remain in exile four hundred years? A similar scenario took place when God created the world. The Midrash relates that the *mazikim*, "demons," were created right before sunset on the sixth day and they would have had a physical body, but it got dark and became *Shabbos*, and so they did not get a body. Again, the question is: if they were created so late, in an instant before *Shabbos*, how would they have had a body?

The answer to both questions is the same. God created the demons, spiritual creatures, in an instant before *Shabbos* to teach us that regardless of what you are in the middle of doing, even if it be the holiest of things, such as creating spiritual creatures, you must stop immediately when the *Shabbos* arrives. Nothing should delay the arrival of the *Shabbos*.

Similarly, the Exodus of the Israelites could not be delayed even for a second, because they would have sunk to the lowest levels of depravity. They had to leave without delay to teach us that if we have merit then nothing will delay our redemption. They were decreed four hundred years of exile, but could merit an earlier redemption on their own. Thus, if the four hundred years had passed, they would leave "naturally," but since they were worthy, they left "miraculously."

With the Exodus and the miraculous haste with which the redemption came, we realize the great love that God has for us always and in all circumstances. And we realize this the most on the *Shabbos* before Passover, and it is therefore the Great *Shabbos*, *Shabbos Hagodol*.

It is written, "Then you shall delight yourself with God; and I will cause you to ride upon the high places of the earth, and feed you with the heritage of Jacob your father: for the mouth of God has spoken" (Isaiah 58:14).

This verse describes three types of pleasure that we experience when we observe the *Shabbos*: to delight, to ride high, and to be fed the heritage. These three pleasures correspond to the three awesome Sabbaths: the *Shabbos* of Creation, the *Shabbos* of the Exodus, and the *Shabbos* of the Ten Commandments. The greatest of these events was the Exodus, which established the Israelites as the people and witnesses of God. Why did the *Shabbos* of the Exodus precede the commandment to keep *Shabbos*? The answer is that the Exodus is the fruition of the words of the Torah. If we listen to the Torah, then we are the free people of God that no one can enslave. It is the embodiment of the ideal, of the world in its perfect state. And because the Israelites followed the path of God even before they knew where it led, they were rewarded with the World to Come even before they received the Torah. The Exodus was the *yom shekuloh Shabbos*, a day that is totally *Shabbos*, is liberation and freedom from all obstacles. The Jewish people rushed out of Egypt, they did not hesitate, and their reward was the Torah that enables man to be totally free.

Thus the Exodus is the highest of the three awesome Sabbaths, and is therefore called the Great *Shabbos*, *Shabbos Hagodol*.

The Midrash (Genesis 1) says that when God created the world it was expanding without limit until God said, "*Dai!*—Enough!" and it stopped expanding. How did the world expand? God created it with laws, and when set in motion it continued without end, or so it seemed, until God said "Enough!" It appeared as if it was on its own, independent, and did not need the Creator to keep it going. But all this was merely an appearance. The truth was that the universe could not exist without a Creator even for an instant. And as witness to this, we have the day of *Shabbos*, when we proclaim God as the Master of the universe. And if a regular *Shabbos* is witness to this truth, how much more so it is true of the *Shabbos* of the Exodus, when God flipped over the laws of nature and produced countless miracles. And, therefore, the *Shabbos* of the Exodus is the greatest *Shabbos* of them all.

There are three types of Sabbaths. There is the *Shabbos* of Creation, the *Shabbos* of the Exodus, and the *Shabbos* of the World to Come, the everlasting and eternal one. Each one is awesome in its own right, but each has a special quality that is exclusive. The first *Shabbos*, that of the Creation, is special because it is the very day in which God rested. It is the resting day of God and of the entire universe. The *Shabbos* preceding the Exodus had an even higher quality in that the nature of the world was changed and was filled with miracles. And finally, the *Shabbos* of the World to Come will be the greatest of them all, because it will be eternal and everlasting. As it is written, ". . . and God alone will be exalted in that day" (Isaiah 3:17), meaning that on that *Shabbos*, God will reign supreme and all will know that only He is the ruler and Creator. This aspect of *Shabbos* was given to the Israelites before the Exodus. Why? Because the essence of the *Shabbos* is a secret between God and the Jewish people, as it is written, ". . . it is a sign between me and the children of Israel forever . . ." (Exodus 31:17). The "forever" aspect of the Sabbath is a sign that only I and the Jewish people understand.

A king confided in his advisors. But each night he would go to the prince's room and speak with him privately. Those intimate conversations he shared with no one. Those secrets belonged to the two of them, whose royal bloodline extended twenty generations into the past and to the infinite future. Similarly, the eternal portion of the *Shabbos*, which we will experience in the World to Come, is a secret shared between God and the Jewish people. And it was on the *Shabbos* of the Exodus when the Israelites became a people of God and the secret was shared with them. And therefore it is called the Great *Shabbos*, *Shabbos Hagodol*.

As soon as Abraham discovered God, he started to teach others about Him. He went from place to place, gathered people, and taught them his newly found faith. He set up his tent, too, with a door on each of the four sides, to reach out to wayfarers, to befriend and plant the seeds of faith in their hearts. But his deepest yearning was to have children, to establish a tribe whose faith would be of such strength that no power on earth would be able to weaken it. And because of this, he was called "a great man among the *Anakim* (giants)" (Joshua 14:15). Thus, on the *Shabbos* before the Exodus, his yearning and hope were finally realized. So it is named after him, the great man—the Great *Shabbos*, *Shabbos Hagodol*.

The Zohar quotes two verses that seem to contradict each other. "For who is a great nation like you . . ."

(Deuteronomy 4:7), and "But you are the smallest among the nations . . ." (Deuteronomy 7:7). Are they small, or are they great? The verses can be reconciled as follows. The Jewish nation is physically the smallest in number among the nations, but spiritually they are the greatest. They are a unique people apart from the nations, with a special mission to establish the kingdom of God. And God, too, lifts them above the natural world and relates to them with miracles.

We see this in the life of Abraham, the progenitor of the Jewish people. He did not have a son to call his own and worried lest he die before he establish a faithful tribe. Then God lifted him above the stars and said to him, "Look down upon the stars. As one cannot count the stars, so too, your offspring will be counted" (Genesis 15:5). God showed him that he was not under the astrological influence of the stars, but was above them. Therefore, although Abraham was nearly a hundred years old, he gave birth to a child. And therefore Abraham is called "a great man among the *Anakim*" (giants) (Joshua 14:15). The word *anakim* means that he wore the sun as a necklace around his neck. It means that he was above the influence of the sun and the forces of nature. He was raised to the level of the miraculous and is therefore called a great man.

Thus, although the Jewish people are the smallest, they are "among the nations," and therefore the nations benefit from them. It is because of their miraculous ways that the nations are able to survive their own ordeals. But when the Jewish people leave, as they did from Egypt, the country is left empty and bare, open to attack by natural events. In truth, then, the Jewish people are great, and became great at the Exodus from Egypt. Therefore the *Shabbos* of the Exodus is called the Great *Shabbos*, *Shabbos Hagodol*.

It is written, "To Him who punished the Egyptians with their firstborn" (Psalms 136:10). The Midrash (Exodus 11) relates that on the *Shabbos* before the redemption, the firstborn of Egypt, knowing that they were doomed to die in a plague because of the king's intransigence, incited a rebellion against the Pharaoh. There was a civil war, and many Egyptians died in the fighting so that the Egyptians were punished "with their firstborn." But why did that happen? It was because the redemption already had started in the spiritual realm, and in that world, when one rises the other falls. So that as soon as the Israelites were being raised up high, their enemies had to fall. And they did. Thus the *Shabbos* before the Exodus was transformed to a Great *Shabbos*, *Shabbos Hagodol*.

There are the six work days and the *Shabbos*. We do physical work during the six work days, but it is incomplete without the blessing of God. God blesses the work of our hands, and these blessings come to us through angels. The blessings for the *Shabbos*, however, come directly from God. *Shabbos* is in a realm where there is not even a hint of the natural world. It is in a place where only God reigns supreme.

Similarly, when the Jewish people are in trouble, their help sometimes comes by human intervention, such as with the victories of Purim and Chanukah, which were brought about by brave Jews. At other times God sends an angel to help them, as it is written, "And it came to pass that night, that the angel of God went out, and killed in the camp of the Assyrians one hundred eighty-five thousand: and when they arose early in the morning, behold, they were all dead corpses" (2 Kings 19:34). But the Exodus from Egypt was even more divine, since it was done by God Himself, as we read in the Haggadah, "And I will pass through the land of Egypt. . . . 'I' and not an angel, 'I' and not a fiery angel, 'I' and not a messenger, 'I' and no one else." God could have redeemed the Israelites naturally without miracles. Yet He redeemed them with great miracles, because he wanted them to have an order and law of their own, different from the laws of nature.

If the Exodus would have happened naturally, we would soon have forgotten it. But since it was miraculous, it is not bound within the space and time of nature and is infinite. And therefore, "So that you should remember the day that you came out of the land of Egypt all the days of your life" (Deuteronomy 16:3). There is no time that you can forget the Exodus, because it did not happen within time. It happened in the miraculous, the infinite, in its own order and law. And that infinite place is identical to the *Shabbos*; they are one and the same.

Therefore the *Shabbos* of the Exodus is called the Great *Shabbos*, because it is identical with the glorious redemption. It is therefore *Shabbos Hagodol*.

It is written, "Great are the doings of the Lord; all men study them for their delight" (Psalms 111:2).

The natural world is awesome, and the more you study it the more wondrous you discover it to be. But its wonder is hidden, is well concealed in the habit of natural laws. But the Exodus, full of great wonders and miracles, caused people to pause suddenly and contemplate, to wonder about the ordinary world.

This is the same with the *Shabbos*, which is also a day to pause, reflect, and contemplate the wonders of God's creation. As it is written, "A song for the day of *Shabbos*. It is a good thing to give thanks to the Lord, and to sing praises to your name, O most high. . . . O Lord how great are Your works! and your thoughts are very deep" (Psalms 92:1, 2, 6). The day of *Shabbos*, when the entire creation was complete and God rested, is a perfect day to relax, let go of all attachments, sit back, and delve into the deep thoughts, plans, and works of the creation. This is true of even an ordinary *Shabbos* and how much more true it is of the *Shabbos* in which miracles happened, the *Shabbos* of the Exodus. When the Israelites rested on that *Shabbos*, contemplated the wonders of God's work, and suddenly saw miracles unfolding all around them, it changed the *Shabbos* from an ordinary one to an awesome one. And thus it became a Great *Shabbos*, *Shabbos Hagodol*.

Two reasons are given for the *Shabbos*; one is that God rested on that day, as it is written, "For in six days God made the heaven and the earth, the sea, and all that is in them, and rested on the seventh day: therefore God blessed the *Shabbos* day and made it holy" (Exodus 20:10). The other reason is that we were slaves and it was God who redeemed us, as it is written, "And remember that you were a slave in the land of Egypt, and that God brought you out with a mighty hand and by an outstretched arm: therefore God commanded you to keep the *Shabbos* day" (Deuteronomy 5:15).

Similarly, there are two aspects of *Shabbos*. There is the *Shabbos* that God gives to the Jewish people, and then there is the *Shabbos* that the Jewish people make themselves. As it is written, "And the Israelites shall keep the *Shabbos*, to make (observe) the *Shabbos*" (Exodus 31:16). The question is: what can anyone do to increase the holiness of the *Shabbos*? Is it not already as holy as it can be from the time of the creation? It is true that the *Shabbos* is a gift from God, but still we must prepare ourselves for its holiness in order to receive it in full measure. When we cleanse our thoughts, speech, and actions to be worthy of holiness, then we connect the Jewish people with God and the earth with heaven.

Thus, until the Exodus the entire *Shabbos* was given by God, but there were no vessels to receive it. With the birth of the Jewish people on the *Shabbos* before the Exodus, the vessels for the Sabbath were also born. There was now a giver and a receiver, a pair, and together they made the *Shabbos* great, *Shabbos Hagodol.*

The Exodus took place in three stages. On the New Moon, the first day of the month of *Nissan*, the Israelites were commanded to take a sheep, inspect it, and have it ready for the Passover sacrifice. On the tenth of the month of *Nissan* they actually took it and tied it to their bedposts, much to the chagrin of the Egyptians. On the fourteenth of the month they slaughtered it. Similarly, on the New Moon, God warned that the plague of the firstborn of all the Egyptians is imminent; on the tenth day, *Shabbos*, the Israelites took the sheep and tied it to their bedposts and by this act resolved to completely abandon idol worship; and on the fourteenth, God freed them completely, utterly, and unconditionally.

Similarly, their hope was released from bondage on the New Moon when Moses told them that the redemption is at hand; their soul was released from bondage on the tenth of *Nissan* when they abandoned the idols of Egypt; and on the fourteenth their bodies were finally freed from bondage and slavery. Thus, the high point of the Exodus was that they abandoned the idols of Egypt and their souls were free to worship the one and only God. And since this happened on the *Shabbos*, therefore it became elevated and of prime importance. It became the Great *Shabbos*, *Shabbos Hagodol.*

"The one who is commanded to do a *mitzvah* and does it is greater than the one who is not commanded to do it but does it" (*Kiddushin* 31a).

The *Shabbos* preceding the Exodus was kept holy by the Israelites because of the command of God, and therefore, it is called great. It was the first one that they kept because they were commanded to do so. They were greater that *Shabbos* than on any other. The question is: our sages have taught that our forefathers kept the Torah even before it was given, so what more was gained when they were commanded to keep it?

When our forefathers kept the Torah, it was as a child who keeps the Torah. He is trained to do the commandments so he can be in the habit of observing them and they should not be strange to him. Similarly, the Sabbaths that the Israelites kept before the Ten Commandments were kept as a child who was being trained. But then came the *Shabbos* on the tenth day of *Nissan* when they tied the sheep to their beds and abandoned idol worship forever. That *Shabbos*

was kept with the same dedication and maturity as if they were already commanded. And therefore it is greater than any other *Shabbos*.

We can understand this concept even deeper. We can do a commandment because it is logical. It makes sense to us, and we do it. Thus, it is limited within that logic. Our observance is bound to and limited by the logic that made us do it. Even if it is the logic of the wisest of men, as King Solomon, it still bears the limitation of his mind. On the other hand, if we observe the commandment because God told us, because we were commanded and not because we understand it, then it is infinite as God Himself.

This same lesson can be gleaned from the fate of the two sons of Aaron the *kohen*, Nadav and Avihu, who brought a sacrifice based on their understanding and were rejected by God. Obviously, their logic was limited.

Therefore, when we observe a *mitzvah* because of God's command, it is on the highest level. And so was the *Shabbos* of the Exodus, which was observed because of God's command. And it is therefore the highest and is called *Shabbos Hagodol.*

In the Sabbath *Kiddush* service we recite, "It is the first among the holy days."

All the holidays are called *Shabbos*, as it is written, ". . . on the first day shall be a *Shabbos*, and on the eighth day shall be a *Shabbos*" (Leviticus 23:39). Still, the original *Shabbos* of Creation is higher than all of them. Each holiday gives us merely one aspect of holiness, but *Shabbos* is the total negation of the self to God. It is totally Divine, as it is written, "Thus spoke the Lord, Let not the wise man boast of his wisdom, neither let the mighty man boast of his might, let not the rich man boast of his riches. But if any man would boast, let him boast of this, that he understand and knows me. For I am the Lord. . ." (Jeremiah 9:22). The "wise man" is one with the wisdom of the Torah, corresponding to the holiday of Shavuos, the day we received the Torah. The "mighty man" is a man with the might of escaping slavery, corresponding to Passover and the Exodus from Egypt. The "rich man" is a man with an abundance of produce and crops, which corresponds to the holiday of Sukkos, the ingathering of the harvest. Now all these holidays boast, but the boast is incomplete. The true boast should come from the man who "understands and knows Me," which corresponds to the day of *Shabbos*, when we are totally negated to God, the One and Only.

Therefore, on that *Shabbos* before the Exodus, we understood that God is the Creator and not any idol;

it was therefore greater than all of the other holidays. Therefore it is *Shabbos Hagodol*, the Great *Shabbos*.

There is both greatness and insignificance in the world. As the renowned Kabbalist, Rabbi Isaac Luria, explained, before the world was created there was only God. Then God created a void, a place for the creation. He created the world and it was expanding infinitely until God said, "Enough!," and it ceased expanding. The boundaries of the material world are the laws of nature, the command "Enough!" that resounds throughout the universe. Those laws are the limitations of the world, from which stem its insignificance. But every once in a while the Divine and Godly nature of the world peeks through. When that happens there is the infinite, miraculous, boundless greatness of God. It is the Name of God spelled *yod* and *heh*, *vov* and *heh*, and meaning became, becoming, and will become. It is the happening of everything that there is, with quantum leaps and chaos.

The creation of the six days was complete; nothing new comes from them. Any new creation must come by means of the *Shabbos*, which is the root and place of all. It is the place where the command of "Enough!" is not heard. It is still infinite and parallels the World to Come. Therefore, when the redemption was at hand, the miracles revealed the world's infinite nature, its greatness beyond its limitations. Thus the *Shabbos* of the redemption is called the Great *Shabbos, Shabbos Hagodol*.

40

S'firas Ho'Omer—
Counting of the Omer

God spoke to Moshe, telling him to speak to the Israelites and say to them:

When you come to the land that I am going to give you, and you reap its harvest, you must bring an *omer* of your first reaping to the *kohen*. He shall wave it in the motions prescribed for a wave offering to God, so that it will be acceptable for you. The priest shall make this wave offering on the day after the first day of the Passover holiday.

On the day you make the wave offering of the *omer*, you shall prepare an unblemished yearling sheep as a burnt offering to God. Its meal offering shall be two-tenths of an ephah of wheat meal, mixed with oil, a fire offering to God. Its libation offering shall be one-fourth hin of wine.

Until the day that you bring this sacrifice to your God, you may not eat bread, roasted grain, or fresh grain. This shall be an eternal law for all generations, no matter where you live.

You shall then count seven complete weeks after the day following the Passover holiday when you brought the *omer* as a wave offering, until the day after the seventh week, when there will be a total of fifty days. On that fiftieth day you may present new grain as a meal offering to God.

From the land upon which you live, you shall bring two loaves of bread as a wave offering. They shall be made of two-tenths of an ephah of wheat meal, and shall be baked as leavened bread. They are the first-harvest offerings to God.

Together with this bread, you shall sacrifice seven unblemished yearling sheep, one young bull, and two rams. These, along with their meal offerings and libations, shall be a burnt offering to God, a fire offering as an appeasing fragrance to God.

You shall also prepare one goat as a sin offering, and two yearling sheep as peace sacrifices. The *kohen* shall make the motions prescribed for a wave offer-

ing before God with the bread for the first-harvest offering and the two sheep. They belong to the priest as something sacred to God.

This very day shall be celebrated as a sacred holiday when no service work may be done. This is an eternal law for all generations, no matter where you may live.

Furthermore, when you reap the land's harvest, do not completely harvest the ends of your fields. Also do not pick up individual stalks that may have fallen. You must leave all these for the poor and the stranger. I am God your Lord. (Leviticus 23:9–22).

---

he Talmud comments, "God said to the Jewish people, 'Bring to me the Omer offering so that the grain in your fields should be blessed" (*Rosh Hashanah* 16a).

After Adam and Eve sinned the earth was cursed, as God said to them, "The ground will therefore be cursed because of you. You will derive food from it with anguish all the days of your life. It will bring thorns and thistles for you, and you will eat the grass of the field" (Genesis 3:17–18). The ground was no longer pure and grew a confusion of edible and nonedible plants. It needed to be liberated by people who were themselves liberated, who were first cursed slaves in Egypt and became a blessed nation of God. Thus when the *omer* is brought as an offering, it repairs the confusion of the land. And whenever the Jewish people are uplifted, the land is uplifted with them. So that at each holiday some aspect of the land, of the earth and its ability to sustain edible vegetation is repaired. During Passover the grain receives blessing and is uplifted; in Shavuos, the holiday of weeks, the fruit of the trees is uplifted; and during Sukkos, the holiday of booths, the water is blessed.

We can learn from this how precious our deeds are. We can bring about the repair of the land that was cursed from the beginning of time by the first sin of man on earth. Imagine how much more we can repair and improve our environment by doing good deeds and living a blessed life.

The Talmud comments, "God said to the Jewish people, 'Bring to me the Omer offering so that your grain in your fields should be blessed" (*Rosh Hashanah* 16a).

It is with judgment that each creature receives its sustenance. How much he receives is determined by the spiritual laws set down by God. But the law is not a sentence, and it can be mitigated: the judgment can be changed to mercy and loving-kindness by humbling one's self and returning to the path of the Torah. One can again become a vessel to receive the blessings of God.

Similarly, there is a difference of opinion about what was the main feature of the Exodus. The Zohar says it was the utter judgment and punishment of the Egyptians. Rashi says that, on the contrary, it was the rescue of the Israelites. Both these opinions can be reconciled. There truly was sheer judgment for the Egyptians, but the Israelites turned that very judgment into mercy and kindness, with their good deeds. The same judgment that was destroying the firstborn of the Egyptians was simultaneously rescuing the Israelites.

We find similar examples in the history of our people. Abraham lived totally by the virtue of loving-kindness. His son Isaac, born on Passover, was different, living by the virtue of strict judgment. This indicates that the judgment of Passover, the nature of Isaac, can be changed to mercy through Abraham.

This is also true of the world as a whole. The universe was created from nothing with strict judgment, which underlies the laws of nature. From nothing God made something, and it must follow Divine rules. How can those rules be broken, how can the laws of nature be altered to accommodate the needs of man? When we take the something, the grain, the *omer*, and make from it nothing, when we offer it and return it to God, then the laws no longer have power over it. It is then nothing, is Divine, and is not subject to judgment and laws. Thus mercy prevails and the creatures are sustained and live.

Let us lift our sustenance up to God. On each day of the Omer let us lift another aspect of it and change judgment to mercy and live to walk in the Divine path.

The Zohar states: The seven weeks of the Omer are the central focus of the entire year, and whoever can mend all those days will not be in need of judgment during the Days of Judgement of Rosh Hashanah and Yom Kippur. Why is this so?

It is written, "You shall then count seven "complete" weeks after the day following the Passover holiday..." and also, "The Torah of God is complete" (Leviticus 23:15). Everything in the world was created with the energy of the Torah. When the Jewish people relate to the world with the energy of the Torah and realize that their existence depends on the Torah, they receive sustenance with kindness. The same is true of the Omer. By returning it to God, and negating all the energy that we put into its growth, we cause great blessings to come our way.

"When you come to the land that I am going to give you, and you reap its harvest, you must bring an Omer of your first (*reishis*) reaping to the (*kohen*) priest" (Leviticus 23:10).

"In the beginning (*bereishis*) of the creation of the world...." The world was created for those who are called *reishis*, "first," the Jewish people the first of His grain. The Torah, too, is first, for with it God created the world.

The instant something begins, it is in its purest form; for example, the first step that a baby takes, the first time in our life that we see something, the first time a complete nation believes in God. Later it can become mixed with impurities. Who can untangle the good from the evil, the pure from the defiled? It is only the Jewish people who, with the power of the Torah, the very plan of the universe, can find and elevate the very first particle of energy in each thing. And thus, by lifting the *omer*, the first cutting of the grain, to God, they elevate the very essence of their produce and give it back to God.

With our liberation from Egypt we learned that nature itself is caused by He Who makes miracles, the One Who brought the plagues upon the Egyptians. We realized that all that happens, from the most spiritual to the most mundane, is caused by God.

The same idea can be found in the blessing of Jacob to his grandchildren: ". . . the God who has been my shepherd from the day that I remember until this day, sending an angel to deliver me from all evil" (Genesis 48:16).

"My shepherd" means the one who sustained me; "deliver me" means to liberate me from exile. To have food to eat and to be liberated from exile are both on the same level. We must realize that it takes God to liberate us from exile; it can hardly be done by human intervention. But even food, which we think is acquired naturally, even that only God can get for us. Just as redemption comes directly from God, so does sustenance. And the converse is also true; just as sustenance is given by God, each and every day, so is redemption. And we bring the *omer* offering during Passover to witness that just as the redemption of Passover was caused by the one and only God, so too is the sustenance that comes from the grain.

May we merit the understanding to see how God takes care of us all the time in every way. And then, we will experience our redemption through our sustenance and our sustenance through our redemption.

41

The Haggadah *Service*

e are commanded in the Torah to "remember the day that you have left Egypt all the days of your life" (Deuteronomy 16:30). This obligates us to mention the Exodus twice a day—once in the morning and once in the evening, every single day of the year, including the holiday of Passover. There is, however, a special commandment for the night of Passover that is above and beyond merely mentioning the Exodus. "On that day you should tell your son, 'This commemorates what God did for me when I came out of Egypt'" (Exodus 13:8). We must not just mention, but also tell and in a fashion that is clearly understood and instructive. Therefore, we have a special service on the night of Passover in which, through symbolism, unusual customs, and a special order of events, we evoke the curiosity of children and motivate their learning and absorption of teachings about the Exodus. It is called the Seder, order, and includes all of the commandments we observe on the night of Passover: relating the story of the Exodus to our children, eating *matzah* and *moror*, and drinking the four cups of wine.

THE SEDER

The natural world has laws. The sun rises and sets, and similarly thousands of events can be predicted because they follow a set pattern. On the other hand, miracles occur that do not follow those set laws of nature. They are not ordinary and are out of order.

The Maharal of Prague gives a deeper interpretation of miracles. There is an order of the physical world, which follows cause and effect. And there is another order that is chaotic and spiritual. We never know what to expect. We never know what will happen. This is the order of the miraculous world. When Moses threw down his stick, it should have fallen on the ground. Instead, it turned into a snake. When the Israelites walk into the Red Sea, they should get wet. Instead, the sea parted and they walked through on dry land. This is the law for the Jewish people who are above the world of cause and effect. They are ruled by miraculous laws, the will of God Who does whatever pleases Him in the heavens and the earth.

Therefore, the events of the night of Passover are called Seder, order, although they are replete with chaos and disorder. The firstborn dying, slaves escaping from an escape-proof kingdom, kings pleading, enslavers giving gifts to their captives, dogs silent, and a night as bright as day. This is order? Yes, it is the order of the miraculous world, where there is nothing but the pure will of God. But the Israelites did not merit this kind of order; therefore, they had to rush out of Egypt.

A prince brought a beggar to the royal chef and asked for something to eat. The chef gave the beggar some food, and said, "Okay, hurry, hurry along now; you can't stay here too long." The beggar left and the prince continued to stay in the kitchen. "Why can I stay in the kitchen but not that beggar?," the prince asked. "The beggar is lucky that I didn't hit him with this ladle and throw him out. You, on the other hand, are the king's son and may go wherever you please."

Similarly, when the Israelites left Egypt with the order of miracles, they had to rush. They were not as yet on the spiritual level required to stay in the king's palace. It was not yet their place. But when the *Mashiach* comes, it is written, "But you shall not come out in urgent haste, nor leave like fugitives . . ." (Isaiah 52:12). The Jewish people then will assume their role as the children of God and will not need to rush through miraculous events. Therefore, on all the nights of the year we merely mention the Exodus; we are in exile and have little connection with those great miracles. But on the night of Passover, the night of our liberation, we elaborate the events of the Exodus, and talk about them endlessly. We bring the miraculous story into the realm of normal time, preparing ourselves for the ultimate redemption, soon in our days.

THE FOUR CUPS OF WINE: THE FOUR EXPRESSIONS OF REDEMPTION

There are four expressions of redemption, as it is written, "I am God. I will take you away from your forced labor in Egypt and free you from their slavery. I will liberate you with a demonstration of many powers, and with great acts of judgment. I will take you to Myself as a nation . . ." (Exodus 6:6).

The four expressions of redemption represent the four exiles, meaning that just as the Israelites were redeemed from Egypt, so too they will be redeemed from all of the exiles. It is only because God himself had liberated the Israelites that they became free, and only God made other redemptions possible. It is therefore written, "I am God. I will take you away. . . ." Once the big knot of exile was untied, it can never again be tied. The Jewish people are and will always remain free. And all the 430 dimensions of space and time in a man's spirit that needed redemption were redeemed, once and for all. Thus, *nefesh*, "soul," has the numerical equivalent of 430 and so does Raamses, the place of the Egyptian exile. And from the pit of oppression we moved to the refuge of God, as it is written, "And they moved from Raamses to Sukkos" (Exodus 12:37).

The four *mitzvos* of the night of Passover are to eat the Passover sacrifice, to eat *matzah*, to eat *moror*, and to relate the story of the events of the Exodus. These four correspond to the four exiles, from which we will be redeemed as well. They correspond also to the four cardinal sins, which are the private exile of each person. The four sins are idol worship, cohabitation with forbidden women, murder, and speaking evil about another.

The *mitzvah* of the Passover sacrifice, the idol of the Egyptians, mends the sin of idol worship. The eating of the bitter herbs repairs the sin of the bitterest suffering, which is death. The *mitzvah* of *matzah* repairs the sin of relations with forbidden women, of love going sour, just as we guard the drop of dough from becoming sour. And finally, the retelling of the story of the Exodus repairs the tale of evil told about another, which is the cause of the present and last exile.

I will take you out from under the burden of Egypt—that alludes to their idol worship. I will redeem you—from the sin of relations with forbidden women. I will save you—from murder. And I will take you—and unite you into one nation, and you will no longer speak evil one against the other.

We too, sitting at the Seder and waiting for the final redemption, can be redeemed from the four carnal sins immediately by observing the *mitzvos* of Passover. And when we do, we will be ready for the long-awaited redemption.

The four cups of wine correspond to the four portions of writing from the Scriptures that are placed inside the *tefillin*. The first portion is, "Make holy . . . ," which is followed by, "And it will be when God will bring you. . . ." The third is the *Shma*, "Hear O Israel, God is One," and the fourth is, "And it will be if you listen to the commandments. . . ."

One of the most astounding things that God did is to make the Jewish people holy even before He redeemed them. Before He liberated the Israelites from Egypt, He had already made them holy. This is like hiring someone for work even before he is released from jail. Therefore, we pour the first cup of wine and recite the *Kiddush* service, which expresses the holiness of God, the Jewish people, and Passover. Then we pour the second cup of wine and recite, "We were slaves to Pharaoh in Egypt" and the entire story of the redemption. Again, we mention the holiness of the Jewish people before we speak of the redemption. We pour the third cup of wine and recite Grace after the Meal, as the *Shma*, declaring that there is One God and He is the Tree of Life. We pour the fourth cup and say, "Pour Your wrath on the nations . . . ," as we pray and hope for the final redemption when we will leave the exile for the Promised Land. This corresponds to the portion, "And it will be when you listen to the commandments," as God promises to keep us safely in the land of Israel. And we sing, "God is Mighty! May He soon rebuild His Temple."

The four cups of wine correspond to the four *leshonos*, expressions of redemption that God mentioned to Moses. The word *leshonos* literally means tongues. There are four tongues that need to be redeemed. There is a river, the root of which is connected to the root of all, the One and Only; it has four tributaries that need to be uplifted and freed from exile. They are the four rivers coming from Eden and also the Four Kingdoms. And how are they uplifted? With wine, because it is wine that causes the secret, the exile, to come into the open. Wine opens the inside, the core and depth, and thereby brings about the redemption. And thus *Pah'ro*, which means bad mouth, becomes *Pe-sach*, the mouth that talks. From the exiled speech comes the liberated mouth.

The four cups of wine correspond to the four faculties of sight, hearing, remembering, and knowing. These are the four ways that God paid attention to our suffering in Egypt: "And God heard their cries"; "And God saw the Israelites"; "And God knew"; "And God remembered His promise to Abraham."

There are similarly four senses: hearing, seeing, tasting and smelling. To liberate those four senses, which are in the head, so that they do not enslave us with attachments to the physical world, we harness them for the service of God by tying the *tefillin* on our head. God ties all our senses and physical abilities together toward the left. God turns all our strengths and liberates them, so we then can serve God with those self-same strengths. As it is written, "And God turned the people" (Exodus 13:18). And it is also written, "His left hand is under my head . . ." (Song of Songs 2:6). He turns my right hand, which I consider my strength, and makes it a left hand, which is considered weak, yet is strong in the service of God.

The four cups of wine correspond to the four expressions of redemption that God promised Moses. As it is written, "I am God. I will take you away from your forced labor in Egypt and free you from their slavery. I will liberate you with a demonstration of my power, and with great acts of judgment. I will take you to Myself as a nation . . ." (Exodus 6:6). But when Moses came to the Israelites and told them about the imminent redemption, they did not listen to him, because they were exhausted and drained of energy. Soon they had to leave in great haste, because they just could not attain the level of meriting the redemption.

A parent took her child on vacation, but had no time to explain the details of the trip. Once they were settled on the bus, they both had time and patience to share the details of the trip in a calm way.

When the Israelites were in Egypt, they were too tired, too ignorant, and too weak to listen to the details of the four expressions of redemption. But they heard them often enough, and they stuck in their memory. After the Exodus, and being protected by the clouds of glory and fed the *manna* from heaven, they slowly came to understand the details. And

therefore the four expressions became part of the Torah and the Seder service for all generations.

The Seder, then, is a detailed description of the four types of redemption. It is like a king who taught his son a secret code. Later the prince was kidnapped by bandits and taken to the mountains. The king managed to send a secret message to his son. When the prince was freed and resting in his own room, his father came to see him. Together they told and retold the story of the boy's capture and rescue. They especially spent time talking about the secret code and the meaning of the message that the king sent, why he used those exact words and not others, and how he fulfilled his promise in a daring raid that freed the prince.

We too, especially at the Seder, feel the love of God for us and spend a lot of time with the secret code, the four-faceted message of redemption. We tell and retell the story of God's promises and how He fulfilled each of them. The more we talk about it, the happier and the more loved it makes us feel.

START WITH SHORTCOMINGS AND END WITH PRAISE

Our sages have said, "He should start with the shortcomings and end with the praise" (*Pesachim* 116a). He should relate how at first we were enslaved and then later were redeemed. He should relate how our forefathers were idol worshipers at first and later came to know the Lord and to worship Him. Therefore, the Haggadah starts with the words, "*Ho lachmo anya*—this is the bread of affliction . . . that our forefathers ate in Egypt.

All those who are hungry—let them come and eat. All those who are needy—let them come and celebrate the Passover with us. Now we are here; next year may we be in the land of Israel. Now we are slaves; next year may we be free."

Why is *matzah* called poor man's bread? A poor man does not have all the things he needs. Similarly, *matzah* reminds us that when the Israelites left Egypt, they also did not have what they needed; they did not have the understanding of what would happen to them. Thus, they were led by God into the desert. They had no idea where they were going or how they would get there. There was no logic. The Exodus was before logic and beyond logic.

This was because Egypt was the land of enslavement, the place of limitations and boundaries. Egypt is called *Mitzrayim*, which can be read as *metzarim*, "limitations." And the Israelites took these limitations and transformed them into a quality of faith. Even if they did not understand the Exodus, even if it was not logical, still they would follow God into the desert.

And to where were the Israelites headed? To *Eretz Yisrael*, the Land of Israel, which is the opposite of Egypt. It is a place that does not breed poverty, stinginess, or miserliness. As it is written, "It is a land where you will not eat your bread with poverty, nor want for anything. . . . You will have plenty to eat and will bless the God your God for the rich land that He has given you" (Deuteronomy 8:9, 10). In the new land the Jewish people were full of understanding and were rich in logic. That they were worthy later to understand everything was their reward for following God at first without understanding.

We were taught by our sages, "Whoever observes the Torah while he is poor, will be worthy to keep it when he will be rich; and he who doesn't observe it when rich, will not be able to keep it when he will be poor" (*Ethics of Our Fathers* 4:9). Thus, the Israelites who observed the commandment of God when they were poor in understanding, at the Exodus, later merited to observe the Torah in the Land of Israel with all her abundance and riches. And unfortunately, the opposite was also true. When the Jewish people did not observe the commandments in the prosperous land of Israel, they were sent in exile.

Whoever among you who is hungry now, physically or spiritually, and still observes the commandments of the Passover holiday can be sure that next year he will be keeping it in prosperous circumstances.

It is written, "The voice is the voice of Jacob . . ." (Genesis 27:22). Jacob and the Jewish people were blessed with the voice; it is part of them, their essence, always true and recognizable. It is the voice of prayer and study of the Torah, the way of God. But it is not always revealed. It is sometimes concealed under the rubbish heaps of exile and domination by foreign powers. Then the voice of Jacob is stilled and heard no more.

This happened when the Israelites were oppressed by the Egyptians. They suffered physical cruelty. But worst of all, their hosts attempted to destroy their spiritual essence by stilling their voice. They robbed them of their hope and their teachings. The voice of Jacob was still and was hardly heard in the land of Egypt. With the redemption, the Israelites were able to pray, sing, and dance for joy and to stand before Mount Sinai and hear the teachings of God. *Matzah*, the symbol of the Exodus, was the medicine for the voice of Jacob. The Exodus healed the voice of Jacob and redeemed it from exile.

"The voice is the voice of Jacob" in Hebrew is "*Hakol kol* Yaakov." The first *kol* is spelled *kuf lamed*; the second is spelled *kuf vov lamed*. The second *kol* has the numerical equivalent of *oni*, "affliction," teaching us that the affliction in Egypt was the enslavement and stilling of the voice of Jacob. And when the voice was released from prison, both aspects were released, the voice of prayer and the voice of Torah study. Therefore, *matzah*, which represents the redemption, also has two spellings. There is *matzah*, *mem tzadi heh*, which is a symbol of freedom of prayer, and *mitzvah*, *mem tzadi vov heh*, a symbol of freedom and Torah study. When the *kol* and the *kol* of Jacob are released from exile, the Jewish people immediately resume their prayers and their Torah study.

Let us therefore neither hesitate nor be lazy on this holiest of nights in exercising our freedom. Let us pray with all our heart for the final and complete redemption of the Jewish people, and let us also relate the story of the Exodus with all its beautiful details.

THE FOUR QUESTIONS

Why is this night different from all other nights?
    On all the nights we eat either leavened bread or unleavened *matzah*; on this night why only *matzah*?
    On all other nights we eat herbs of any kind; on this night why only bitter herbs?
    On all other nights we do not dip our herbs even once; on this night why do dip them twice?
    On all other nights we eat our meals in any manner; on this night why do we sit in a reclining position?

The four questions correspond to the four sons whom we need to instruct on the night of Passover. The first is the wise son who wants to know and understand all of the commandments, the *mitzvos*. He is represented by the *matzah*, which symbolizes our quick Exodus from Egypt and also represents all the commandments of the Passover holiday. The second is the wicked son, who does not want to exert himself or suffer in order to attain anything. But the truth is that the wicked contributed to the suffering by refusing to leave Egypt; the bitter memories, represented by the bitter herbs, are caused by him. The third is the simple son, who asks only when he sees a clear change in the ordinary, as when we sit in an reclining position at the Seder. These are the types of people who needed great changes and miracles to impress upon them the work of God. And the fourth is the son who cannot even ask and must see unusual things, such as the repeated dipping and eating of the vegetables, in order that he remember the unusual nature of the night.

Why is this night different? It is because the night of the Exodus was as bright as day. As it is written, "And you should tell your son that day . . ." (Exodus 13:8), and "The night will be as bright as day . . ." (Psalms 139:12). Similarly, we recite the psalms of *Hallel* on the Seder night, and we say, "From the east where the sun rises . . . ," and "This is the day that God has made . . ." (Psalms 113:3, 118:24). All these references emphasize that the night of Passover is like the day with its bright and broad daylight. Therefore the child asks: tell me about the events that led up to the Exodus so that I could understand the unusual nature of this night, which was as bright as day.

THE ANSWER

We read in the *Haggadah*,

> We were slaves of Pharaoh in Egypt, and God our God brought us forth from there with a strong hand and an outstretched arm. Now, if God had not brought out our forefathers from Egypt, then even we, even our children, and our children's children might still have been enslaved to Pharaoh in Egypt. Therefore, even if we were all wise, all men of understanding, and even if we were all old and learned in the Torah, it would still be our duty to tell the story of the departure from Egypt. And the more one tells of the departure from Egypt, the more he is to be praised.

Abraham was getting very old and was concerned that he still had no heir to continue his uncompromising belief in one God. Why was he concerned? Because he foretold, with his knowledge of astrology, that he would have no son. God lifted him above the heavens and stars and said, "You are not ruled by the stars. You are above the world of nature. The only one who is over you is I, God Himself. Similarly, the Jewish people who will come forth from you will not be dominated by the stars or natural forces."

Therefore, God said about Abraham, "And I have increased his seed, multiplied his children, and gave him Isaac." With one son He has multiplied his children? Yes. Although in the natural world one offspring is in danger of perishing and thus ending the

lineage, Abraham was above the laws of nature. His one offspring was like many children. And Isaac's chances of survival were so high that although his own father tried to kill him, he could not do so.

The children of Abraham are above the laws of nature and therefore have no place in the natural order of things. They wander in the lands of strangers, as strangers, and are enslaved by those who are rooted firmly in this world, as were the Egyptians, who worshiped the sheep, the chief among the astrological powers. But in truth, the offspring of Abraham belong to no one, and are just as suddenly extricated miraculously from slavery. They are sustained in an uninhabitable desert and brought to the Land of Israel, of which the nations say, "It naturally belongs to us." And it is true. It was given to the Jewish people miraculously, and it is a land that stretches miraculously as its population increases.

Therefore, before they leave Egypt, the Israelites slaughter the idol representing the astrological sign of Egypt. And they, who are above natural space and time, are able, through their actions, to make the time of the year holy and make it into a holiday forever.

Therefore we say, we were slaves to Pharaoh, and would still be had we been a people ruled by the laws of nature. Who could ever have left the powerful kingdom of Egypt? But God took us out with His miraculous power, because we are above those laws. And therefore, we were able to create a holy day forever for the purpose of witnessing the miraculous ways of God and our being chosen as His people.

The Zohar says, "Whoever is chained to another cannot serve God in truth" (Leviticus 101).

Before the Jewish people were taken from Egypt they could not be the servants of God. They were totally enslaved with no room in their heart for God. Then God released them from the exile and took them to Himself. After that event, no nation has been able to dominate or enslave them completely. They have tried, but to no avail. They may even have had the Jewish people in their clutches for a while, but then, sooner or later, they realized that they belong to the One and Only God. The Jewish people quickly leave their enslavers and their gods and return immediately to worship the God of the Exodus.

Even at the Exodus, there were those who were immediately able to abandon the slavery of Egypt and become the servants of God. But there were others for whom the miracles of the Exodus were not strong enough to cut off their enslavement to Egypt, and they said, "Let us alone, that we may serve the Egyptians. For it had been better for us to serve the

Egyptians than that we should die in the wilderness" (Exodus 14:12). They meant that they were not ready to serve God. They still felt obligated to Egypt, and therefore, how could Moses expect them to serve God? For their sake God split the sea. And that great miracle opened their eyes that God "needs" them too, as they sang after the Red Sea split, "May fear and terror befall them, at the greatness of Your arm may they be still as stone; until Your people passes through, God, until this people You have acquired passes through" (Exodus 15:16). There is no king without a people, and He acquired them with the great miracles on the Red Sea. By the time the Jewish people crossed the sea, every one of them was free of the attachments of Egypt; the core of each one's heart and soul was ready to worship God.

Thus, if God would not have taken us with His strong hand and outstretched arm, then we would still be chained, unable to serve God. How fortunate we are that we have no chains! So let us remove all of our chains. They can only hinder us from serving God because the true condition of the Jewish people is to be free of all earthly domination. And if we are under the rule or clutches of a foreign power, it will not last.

The question is asked. Then the answer begins with the words, "We were slaves to Pharaoh..." and continues "... and if God had not brought out our forefathers...." Why does the answer switch from "we" to "forefathers"?

When Abraham was told that he would have a son, on that very day he was also told of the slavery of Egypt. His son, Isaac, was born into the era of Egyptian slavery, and from that moment on, all the unborn souls of the Jewish people became enslaved to Egypt. Why was the Egyptian exile so important that every single Jew had to pass through it? As we read in the *Haggadah*, "Now, if God had not brought out our forefathers from Egypt, then even we, even our children, and our children's children might still have been enslaved to Pharaoh in Egypt." And the first commandment of the Ten Commandments is "I am the Lord your God, who has brought you out of the land of Egypt, out of the house of bondage" (Exodus 20:2). God communes with the Jewish people on the basis of their enslavement. Why?

The Jewish people had to be slaves to understand the concept of freedom and that their freedom comes from God. And this is true on the physical as well as the spiritual plane. And although the Israelites who were redeemed from Egypt were not worthy—after all, they worshiped Egyptian idols—still, the redemption had to be. Otherwise, who would ever have been wor-thy? Therefore, both the slavery and the redemption had to happen to them before they could serve God.

It thus matters little how wise and smart we are. If we would not have been slaves and redeemed from Egypt, we would not have understood the concept of total freedom nor the idea of being a total servant of God.

Let us then act with the full maturity of our knowledge. We are free of all human bondage. Let us cut the chains of illusion and act as the free men that we are.

It is written, "To Him who alone performs great wonders, for His kindness endures forever" (Psalms 136:4).

Whatever God Himself does, lasts forever. But if it is done through a messenger or an angel, then it is within the natural world and is therefore affected by the laws of nature of decay. It is limited and finally perishes. Therefore, God announced in the first of the Ten Commandments, "I am the Lord your God who has brought you out of the land of Egypt, out of the house of bondage" (Exodus 20:2). Because I am the one who brought you out, you will stay out forever. Had it been someone else who brought you out, the redemption would not have lasted. For then time and space and the laws of nature would have had power over it.

The New Year for Jewish kings is on the first day of the month of *Nissan*, the month of the redemption. The kingdom of Israel represents freedom from foreign domination, which is the Exodus, and it lasts forever. Our hopes are that the king will have a long reign, just as the Exodus in the month of *Nissan*.

But does it not say, "And He sent an angel and took us out of Egypt" (Numbers 20:16)? Yes, but no specific angel is mentioned. The redemption is not limited by boundaries, and therefore it is infinite and forever.

Therefore, we tell our child that we were slaves in Egypt, and if God himself would not have been the one to redeem us, then our freedom would not have lasted forever. Then we and our children would still be slaves there. But since God Himself redeemed us, therefore it is forever, and there is no time that we may slacken from relating the story of the Exodus.

Let us therefore connect to the eternal quality of the redemption and free ourselves and all the future generations from exile.

We were slaves to Pharaoh in Egypt. The Midrash comments, "The king was a tough one and so was the entire country" (*Exodus Rabbah* 16)

You can imagine how hard it was for slaves to leave Egypt. It was said that no slave had ever escaped from Egypt. Therefore, if God had not taken us out, we would still be there.

First God removed the Jewish people from the land of Egypt: that was the Exodus. Then God saved them from the king Pharaoh at the Red Sea. By splitting the sea and allowing the Israelites to cross and the Egyptians to drown, they were saved forever from the king of Egypt. Once He removed them from the clutches of evil, God was able to draw them to the good. He brought them to the land of Israel and built the Holy Temple, which symbolizes the kingdom of God.

God said to Moses, "Certainly I will be with you; and this is the sign, that I have sent you: When you bring the people out of Egypt, you will serve God on this mountain" (Exodus 3:12).

Another way of reading the words is that the way you bring them out of Egypt, that is how you will serve God on this mountain and receive the Ten Commandments. In the measure that you help the Israelites be released from bondage and leave the idol worship and abominations of Egypt, to that degree you will be able to come close to God, worship Him, and receive the Torah on Mount Sinai. Similarly, there is an Exodus for each individual Jew and for the Jewish people as a whole, each and every day. As it is written, "I am the Lord your God who brought you out of the land of Egypt, to be your God: I am the Lord your God" (Numbers 15:41). "I am" means that during each and every day, in every instant of your life, I am your God to the extent that "I brought you out of the land of Egypt." The farther you get from "Egypt," the closer you can get to your Creator so He can be your God.

A prince was kidnapped by thieves and taken far from the palace. At first he hated his new life, but little by little he got to like the thieving lifestyle. The king's men searched desperately for him and finally found him. At first he did not want to leave the thieves, but was finally convinced. Still, he left on the condition that he be allowed to send letters to his new friends and visit them from time to time. On the way to the palace, the prince's entourage was attacked by a band of thieves. The soldiers and the prince valiantly fought them off. It was then that the prince said, "I don't ever want to see those wretched people again!" "Finally," thought the king's men, "the prince is ready to return to the palace and be close with his father again."

We too were slaves to Pharaoh in Egypt. And it was because God extricated us from there in a most powerful way that we were able to leave the abominations of Egypt and stand before Mount Sinai.

At the Seder, let us resolve to get as far from Egypt and whatever she represents. Then we can come close to worship God with all our hearts.

"And even if we are old and well learned in the Torah. . . ."

We have learned, "Rabbi Chanina Ben Dosa says: Anyone whose fear of sin takes priority over his wisdom, his wisdom will endure; but anyone whose wisdom takes priority over his fear of sin, his wisdom will not endure. He used to say: anyone whose good deeds exceed his wisdom, his wisdom will endure; but anyone whose wisdom exceeds his good deeds, his wisdom will not endure" (*Ethics of Our Fathers* 3:11–12).

Each day we tie *tefillin*, "phylacteries," containing portions of the Torah to our hand and head. The one on the hand, says the Zohar, represents our physical, bodily strength and energy, that we must put under the yoke of God's service. We must train it as an ox that is trained to do the farmer's will. Because if the ox does not accept the yoke, then what else can be done? He must first wear the yoke, and then he can work. But if he refuses the yoke, no clever trick will get the work done. Similarly, if we first have fear of sin and subjugate our ox, our physical body, to the yoke of the kingdom of heaven, then we can serve God. Then we can move to the spiritual realm, the *tefillin* on our head, the Torah and wisdom of God.

The Exodus happened in the same order. First God removed us from the physical slavery of Egypt. He forcefully removed the yoke of Egypt from us. We were then ready to don the yoke of the kingdom of heaven and come closer to God. Therefore, because we were slaves and were released with great energy from bondage, no matter how wise we may be, we must still give prime importance to the physical redemption. We must tell and retell the story of the physical Exodus before we ever mention our wisdom, that we received the Torah.

Thus, we first have the holiday of Passover, which represents the physical redemption. It is followed by Shavuos, Pentecost, when we received the Torah at Mount Sinai. This is followed by Sukkos, the Holiday of Booths that combines both the physical and spiritual qualities of God's service. The *sukkah* surrounds us, just as a uniform of those who are the king's servants clothes them. The final step in the service of the king is when we don his uniform and continue to serve him.

We are fortunate that God has released us from Egyptian bondage. Let us not hesitate and incessantly tell of our great fortune and relate the story of our redemption.

"... it would still be our duty to tell the story of our departure from Egypt...."

We are obligated to tell the story of the Exodus. And by telling and retelling it, we uncover the miracles that happened. Our words give the miracle a physical place in the world. The miracle is a spiritual energy that visits us each Passover, but it has no place to exist. And when we speak the words and tell the story of the Exodus, the very words become the resting places for the spirit of the miracles, and suddenly they enter the physical realm. They then bring more and more redemption to the Jewish people. As we say, "... all the days of your life includes also the time of the *Mashiach*." This can be read to mean that if you tell and retell the story of the Exodus all the days of your life, you will help bring the *Mashiach*. The words of the story will prepare a place for a miraculous redemption.

Let us pray that with our own telling of the story we are hastening the final redemption, soon in our days.

"And the more one tells of the departure from Egypt, the more he is praised."

Normally we should refrain from saying too much praise about God. A leader of prayer in the company of Rabbi Chanina once said, "The great God, the powerful, the awesome, mighty, omnipotent, strong, feared, sure, and honorable." The rabbi waited until the man finished his prayers and then said, "Have you completed all of God's praise? Why did you elaborate so much? Our prayer only has three adjectives, 'the great, powerful, and awesome,' and we only include them because Moses said them, and the rabbis included them. Otherwise we would not even say them. Let me explain, we can compare this to a king who owned a million dinars of gold, and his subjects were praising him because of the silver that he also owned. Would that not be a great embarrassment? Similarly, God who is the all powerful, whatever you praise Him with, will be less than He deserves."

The question is: why do we praise God so much on the night of Passover? We can compare this to a king whose son was captured in battle and taken to a foreign land. The king did not rest and attempted

to rescue his son. But none of his subjects was successful in rescuing the prince. The king himself went, and in middle of the night, in a daring raid, he saved his son. On the way to the palace, the son praised his father for his bravery, cleverness, strength, and speed. He praised his father during the entire time that they rode in the royal coach. Finally, while still praising his father, the prince, tired from the ordeal and the journey, fell asleep.

One whom the king saves may praise him without limit. And we, who would still today be in Egyptian bondage were it not for the redemption, are obligated to praise Him without end.

"And the more one tells of the departure from Egypt, the more he is praised."

The Torah is eternal. Not only are its teachings eternal but also are the stories that occur in each of the generations. And just as the Israelites escaped from the land of Egypt, *Mitzrayim*, so too we escape from Egypt, the root of all evil and limitations, *metzarim*. By telling the story we give the redemption a physical place to take hold and spread in the world.

"And the more one tells of the departure from Egypt, the more he is praised."

It is written, "He does great things and unsearchable; marvelous things without number" (Job 5:9). The great things, the miracles of God, are unsearchable; they are infinite. But when put into the hands of the *tzaddikim*, the righteous ones, then they multiply and become more and more. This is like the Torah. Each of its teachings has infinite knowledge. But put into the hands of the *tzaddikim*, they multiply and find new meanings, relationships, and understanding.

Therefore, the more we talk of the miracles, the more and more they are praised: they multiply in the physical world.

"And even if we are old and well learned in the Torah, it would still be our duty to tell the story of our departure from Egypt."

Although you move up higher and higher in the spiritual realm with wisdom, and even if you reach the highest level, you are still connected to the beginning of your journey. The end is connected to the beginning, the beginning to the end. Similarly, in the end lies the beginning, and in the beginning lies the end. Therefore, you are never too far away from the original historical Exodus; it still operates in all your possibilities and the pinnacle of your spiritual life.

A mountain climber left his base camp at the foot of the mountain and started his climb. Finally, after two weeks of freezing weather, howling winds, sheer cliffs, and gaping chasms he finally reached the summit. He looked down and faintly saw the speck of dust that was his base camp. In his delirium he called out, "I am too high up to have started out at that lowly base camp!"

Can he say he is too high for starting at the base of the mountain? Ridiculous! His accomplishment is inextricably bound to his first step up the mountain. His standing on the summit cannot be separated from his first step at the base. His first step is connected to his final one and his final one to the first one, as a circle.

Similarly, we who may be wiser now, after two Holy Temples, four exiles, many tortures, and incessant oppression, the Holocaust, the Talmud and its commentaries, still we are never too wise, never too free to retell the story of our beginning. Those were our first steps, and without them we would not be here today.

Thus we recite in the *Haggadah*, "How much more do we have to be thankful for the manifold and manifold blessings of All Mighty." The word "manifold" means it folds on itself. The beginning of the redemption was the Exodus from Egypt, and it folds onto itself as a circle, the last of the redemptions, the coming of the *Mashiach*, soon in our days.

In the *Haggadah*, we read:

> Rabbi Elazar the son of Azariah said: Here I am a man of seventy years, yet I did not understand why the story of the Exodus should be told at night, until Ben Zoma explained it. The Torah commands us, saying: 'That you may remember the day that you left Egypt all the days of your life.' Ben Zoma explained: the days of your life might mean only the days, but all the days of your life includes the nights also. The other sages, however, explain it this way: the days of your life refer to this world only, but all the days of your life includes the time of the *Mashiach*.

It is written, "As the days when you came out of Egypt I will show him marvelous things" (Micah 7:15).

Why does it say, "As the days . . ."? It did not take days to leave Egypt. It only took one day, one hour, one instant, when they left all at once. It means, rather, the days since you left Egypt. Ever since you left Egypt there have been revelations of miracles and of the Divine presence. And we need all of those, each one of those revelations, to lift us up and bring the *Mashiach*. As it is written in the *Haggadah*, ". . . all the days of your life includes the time of the *Mashiach*. We need to transform each and every day of our life so that each adds up to bring about our redemption. How can we do this? If we remember the Exodus each day of our life, and we obtain an our spiritual sustenance from it to guide us and help us get through each day. If we remember that no matter how lowly a slave we may be, we are always redeemable, just as God pulled us out of the impossible slavery of Egypt. If we realize that no miracle is too big or too strange for God to bring about our redemption—then our redemption, too, will come quickly in our days.

The Four Sons

"Blessed is God, Who gave the Torah to His people Israel. Blessed is He. The Torah speaks about four sons: one who is wise and one who is wicked; one who is simple and one who does not even know how to ask questions."

God spoke to Moses and reassured him, ". . . and I will take you away from under the burdens of the Egyptians, and I will rescue you from their bondage, and I will redeem you with an outstretched arm and with great judgments: And I will take you to me for a people, and I will be to you a God . . ." (Exodus 6:6,7).

There are four expressions of redemption: I will take you away, I will rescue, I will redeem, and I will take you. These four types of redemption correspond to the four types of exiles, both in the physical and spiritual realm. There are spiritual exiles into which we can fall. They start in our mind when we make mental analyses and ponder the commandments of the Torah. There are basically four doubts that may creep into the our mind. The first doubt is similar to the question of the wise son, who asks: "What is the meaning of the rules, laws, and customs that God has commanded us?" This question is the first doubt: why does God not tell us the reason for all the commandments? The answer to the wise son is also the answer to the first doubt. And we answer: ". . . shall explain all the laws of the Passover sacrifice: including the fact that we may not eat dessert after eating the Passover sacrifice." The delicious taste we have when we do a commandment is sweeter than the best of reasons. We experience the commandments on a much higher level when we do not know the reasons for them.

The second doubt is also the question of the wicked son: "What is the meaning of this service to you?" What use is it to observe the Torah; what can the deeds of lowly creatures like us, made of flesh and blood, add or diminish from the Divine plan? And we answer the wicked son, "Because of this God did for me when I came forth from Egypt." Because of this itself, because we are flesh and blood and not angels, we need the commandments of the Torah to reach spiritual levels even higher than the angels.

The third doubt corresponds to the question of the simple son, who asks, "What is this?" And we too, when reaching a high spiritual level, can become arrogant and think, "What is this?" Why is this such a big accomplishment? The answer is the same one we give to the simple son, "With a mighty arm God took you out of Egypt." You did not deserve to be taken out of Egypt; God forced you to leave. Similarly, do not think that you deserve the spiritual heights! It is but the grace of God who grants it to you without merit.

The fourth doubt is perhaps the worst. It is the numbing oppression of the exile that makes us unable to even ask a question and that deadens our senses and intellect. And the answer is the same as we give to the son who does not even know how to ask, ". . . you must begin for him. . . ." You can become sensitive again and be educated about the Torah regardless of the pain and suffering of the exile. But you must begin.

The four sons symbolize the four attitudes that people have when they confront the Egyptian Exodus.

The wise son asks, "What is the meaning of the rules, laws, and customs which God has commanded us?" He is less interested in the physical benefit that we gained from the redemption. He realizes that the best part of being freed by God was our being able to serve Him and make His Name known throughout the world.

On the other hand, the wicked son wants no part of the spiritual gain and asks, "What is the meaning of this service to you?" What do you, on the earthly level, get out of it? And we say to him, "I do this for me and not for him," meaning that it is for God's sake and not for selfish reasons. But if you do it for God's sake, you too will benefit greatly. The simple son asks, "What is this?" He sees a wonderful new order of events. The path of miracles has been revealed. He

is fascinated and in awe. And the son who cannot even ask is the one who realizes that we cannot ask for a repetition of such miraculous times. The Exodus overwhelms him to such a degree that he cannot even begin to understand it. He stands there dumbfounded.

As we sit at the Seder, we too wonder about our relationship to the Exodus. How do we fit in with those great events? What did God accomplish when He took us from Egypt? What benefit do we have from it now? How do we connect to the path of miracles? We pray that by retelling the events of the Exodus we will have answers to our questions.

The four cups of wine that we drink in the Seder symbolize the four sons.

A king appointed his most trustworthy servant to go and proclaim his kingdom in one of his provinces. The servant went as commanded, reached the town square, assembled the citizens, and made the proclamation. The people who heard of the king's great wealth and powerful army realized that they would be of great benefit for their safety and prosperity. They looked around the marketplace, noticed some of the rebels, and gave them a good whipping.

With the first cup of wine we say the *Kiddush* service. We are consecrated for the task of making God's Name known throughout the world. This is the attitude of the wise son. With the second cup of wine we recite the *Haggadah*, the miraculous story of the Exodus and God's intervention in history. This is the attitude of the simple son, who is astonished and to whom you must relate the Exodus in the strongest of terms. With the third cup we recite Grace after the Meal. This is the attitude of the son who does not even know to ask. We open his eyes to see that God had been good to us and our obligation to thank Him. With the fourth cup we recite, "Pour out your wrath upon the nations who do not know You." This is for the attitude of the wicked son who will be punished for turning away from the Kingdom of God.

Let us therefore fulfill our obligations as servants of God and commit ourselves totally to the task of making God's Name known.

The wise son asks, "What is the meaning of the rules, laws, and customs which God has commanded us?" And you should explain to him the laws of Passover.

The history of the Jewish people is one of constant climbing to higher spiritual levels, starting with their witnessing the Ten Plagues, the Exodus, their standing at Mount Sinai and receiving the Ten commandments, having the *Mishkan*, entering the Promised Land, and building the Holy Temple in Jerusalem. The wise son wonders which of these events was the most prominent, the most important one. The answer is that although every one of the events brought the Jewish people closer to God, the most important one was the liberation of the Israelites from slavery in Egypt. As it is written, "You should therefore keep this decree in its season (*miyamim yamima*) from year to year. The words, *miyamim yamima*, can also be translated to mean the day of days. Passover is the day of days; it is on the highest level of spirituality. And if we experience it properly, then there is really nothing else to say. It is the highest! Therefore, if you "keep the decree," even if it is a mere decree to us and we do not fathom all its meaning, still it brings us to highest levels of spirituality. And even if we are wise, still the holiday is so much higher and deeper.

It is written, "As the days when you came out of Egypt I will show him marvelous things" (Micah 7:15). No matter what sort of miracles we anticipate with the final redemption, they will be "as" the ones visited upon us by the Exodus. They will always be compared to the original mother of all redemptions. No matter what delicious events happen to us, the taste of the Exodus miracles will never leave us. And therefore we say to the wise son, "Yes, there will be other redemptions, but they will never surpass this one. And all will be compared to the Exodus." Just as we do not eat dessert after the Passover sacrifice, so that the taste of the observance stays with us, so too the good taste of the Exodus shall never leave us.

It is written, "I remember the unfailing devotion of your youth, the love of your bridal days, when you followed me in to the wilderness, through a land unsown" (Jeremiah 2:2).

When we left Egypt to follow God to the desert, we were as youth, undeveloped and immature. We had no understanding of spiritual matters, of God, or the Torah. We had no idea where we were going nor what God wanted from us. Then why is that moment so exalted in the eyes of God that He can never forget it? It is precisely because we were raw, young, and immature, and yet we still followed God into a land unsown, uncharted, and unknown. We went with trust, cutting off our recent past, making a complete break and moving toward the God of Israel. Ah, the glory of that moment, replete with

faith and brimming with trust! Who can repeat it? Passover is therefore called the season of our liberation; it is the time that each one of us can become free of all attachments and entanglements. We can become totally liberated to serve God.

The wise son therefore asks, "What is the meaning of the rules, laws and customs. . . ." He is not satisfied and asks, "Why are you rejoicing over the mere fact of the liberation when there is so much more to the holiday?" To answer him, "You shall explain to him the laws of Passover . . ."—you explain to him that the mere fact of the Exodus is really the highest thing that there is. To follow God with a childish naivete and be drawn to Him through a parched desert, to be free totally and unconditionally, to choose God freely and trust in Him completely—there can never be anything higher than that.

Similarly, when we yearn for the final redemption, we hope for "As the days when you came out of Egypt I will show him marvelous things" (Micah 7:1). We do not want anything but the redemption and follow God wherever He may lead us. And, just as then, the redemption took the Jewish people into the desert, a new and unknown frontier, so when *Mashiach* comes, the Jews will enter a spiritual territory they have never experienced before. It will be a path of new revelations and experiences. All we yearn for is to get out of this exile.

Let us hope that by retelling the events of the Exodus we too can connect to the simple faith and trust of our forefathers in Egypt and be ready to go with God to the unknown, unexplored realms of spiritual attainment.

To the wise son we ". . . explain the laws of Passover, even to the last detail that after the Passover sacrifice no dessert is eaten."

To become a loyal servant of God is the foundation for everything; even if afterward you rise spiritually, you will never surpass that basic quality. Nothing can be higher than the simple, basic, unconditional subservience we have as a servant of God, without intellectualization. After the Passover sacrifice, the act of severance from Egyptian idol worship, nothing more is needed.

The wise son wants to know the meaning of the *chukim*, the decrees of Passover. Why does the wise son want to know the meaning of the decrees when decrees have no reason in the Torah? Yet, we find that decrees are understood, as it is written, "He relates His word to Jacob, His decrees and judgments to Israel" (Psalms 147:19). It seems that God gives both judgments and decrees to the His people. How is that?

The Jewish people do all the commandments of God, whether they understand them or not, whether they get pleasure from them or not. They do them because they accept the word of God as servants who do the bidding of the king. This is similar to eating *matzah*. *Matzah* itself has no seasonings; it is neither an exotic nor an especially tasty food. From where then does it get its taste? It gains its taste because by eating *matzah* we are refraining from eating the forbidden leaven, as servants who obey the decree of the king. That is the "taste" that we experience in the *matzah*. Similarly, although decrees have no taste, logic, or reason, by observing them because we are servants of the king we immediately taste a sweetness all its own.

We too, as wise as we may be, let us observe all of the laws of Passover with the same devotion as the true and trusting servants of the king.

The wicked son asks, "What is the meaning of this service to you?" Saying you, he excludes himself, and because he excludes himself, he denies a basic principle. You may therefore tell him plainly: "Because of what God did for me when I came forth from Egypt I do this. For me and not for him; had he been there, he would not have been redeemed."

What is the basic principle? It is to believe that the observance of the commandments are for God's sake and not for selfish interests. The wicked son cannot understand why he should do things that do not benefit him directly. But the wise son, who does everything for the sake of heaven, comes to understand everything. Now, when the wicked son sees the dedication of the wise son, he is impressed and realizes the error of his ways, repents, and also seeks enlightenment.

This explains a puzzling verse, "When you come to the land that God will give you, as He promised, you must also keep this service. Your children may then ask you, 'What is this service to you?' You must answer, It is the Passover service to God. He passed over the houses of the Israelites in Egypt when He struck the Egyptians, sparing our homes. The people bent their heads and prostrated themselves." They prostrated themselves to thank God for the promise of the land and the children.

The question is: The children mentioned are the wicked sons who ask "What is this service to you?"

So then why are the Israelites so thankful? The answer is that, after all the children ask their questions, they finally concur with the point of view of the wise son and become loyal servants of God. They too are finally worthy of redemption, and the fathers all rejoice.

We say to the wicked son, "Because of this God did for me...." Because of what? So that I should observe His commandments.

The Israelites did not deserve the redemption; they too were worshiping the idols of Egypt. And God wanted them to earn it with their own deeds so that it would become part of them. This is what God said to Moses when he asked him for His Name," ... I will be Who I will be." Although the Israelites are not yet ready, they do not have the deeds to warrant the awesome miracles I am about to do, still, in My future they will certainly add up enough merit for their redemption, "I will be." Thus, although the Exodus took place long ago, it takes place in every generation, at all times. And regardless of how little their merit was, the Israelites were redeemed through their own deeds.

The wicked son denies the good deeds of the Jewish people. He argues that it does not matter what a person does and that God will either favor him or he won't. He says, "What is the reason for this work?" Why do you waste your time observing the commandments when doing so doesn't make a difference? With this he is denying a basic principle. There *is* a Judge and reward and punishment. It does matter if one does good deeds or is wicked.

Let us add our deeds to the merit for the Exodus and perhaps become worthy for the final redemption, soon in our days.

The wicked son asks, "What is the meaning of this work for you?"

The purpose of the redemption was in order that the kingdom of God should be revealed to one and all, from the lowliest slave to the Pharaoh who sits on his throne. Each one of them should realize that God is the Lord over all the land and His kingdom endures forever in all places and all times. But the wicked son excludes himself and asks, "Why are you all participating in the Passover observance?" He exempts himself from the revelation. He is unimpressed and untouched by it. He thereby denies a basic principle—the purpose of the Exodus.

The wicked son has to either humble himself to the

wise son's position or say, "Although I am wicked and lowly in the spiritual world, still, the redemption was for everyone, even me." And by saying that and including himself, he is redeemed with all of Israel.

Thus we see that the Torah speaks to each one of the four sons in his language. We too should not be discouraged or frustrated in our own attitudes and logic. We should allow the Torah to speak to us. And if we listen carefully, we will hear the echo of the call of Moses to the Israelites in Egypt, and it will likewise be the call for us to hasten and leave the present exile.

HAGGADAH

In the *Haggadah*, we read:

> One might think that the Seder ceremony should be performed on the first day of *Nissan*. The Torah therefore tells us, "on that day"—on Passover. Saying "on that day," one might suppose that the Seder should be conducted during the daytime. But inasmuch as the Torah adds "because of all this," I learn from it that the ceremony does not begin until the time when *matzah* and *moror* are set before you—on Passover night.

When you sit at the Seder and relate the events of the Exodus to your child, with what spirit, with what energy should you do it? You should do it with the spirit of the day of Exodus, as we have recited, "on that day"—*bayom Hahu*, in that day, meaning in the spirit of the day. When the *matzah* and *moror* are before us and we are retelling the story of our redemption, then we will be filled with the spirit of that very day, the special day of the Exodus.

Similarly, it is written, "O God, we have heard for ourselves, our fathers have told us all the deeds which You did in their days, all the work of Your hand in days of old" (Psalms 40:2). The days of old, which ones are they? They are the primeval days of creation, when from nothing God created everything. More miraculous days than those we have never heard of. But our fathers, the generation of the Exodus, told us tales of the miracles that they experienced, and these tales sounded very much like those days of old. They have told us also of another day, the day they crossed the Red Sea, which was just as miraculous, as it is written, "And God saved Israel that day out of the hands of the Egyptians; and Israel saw the Egyptians dead on the sea shore" (Exodus 14:30). Which day is meant by "that day"? It refers to that special day, the all-miraculous day of the Creation.

We too, when we sit at the Seder and relate the story of the Egyptian Exodus, have an opportunity to connect with the miraculous nature of the day. And when we do, we can even sense the excitement of the days of creation, as God creates a new world from nothing.

It is written, "I have formed these people for myself, and they shall proclaim my praises" (Isaiah 43:21). We are the witnesses that God is the master of the universe. And it is our duty and obligation to proclaim this truth to one and all until the whole world will know. And therefore we must always mention, speak about, elaborate, discuss, articulate, announce, and declare the greatness of God and His miraculous redemption of our people from Egypt. Therefore we might think that from the first of the month we must already start retelling the story of the Exodus. We must have a special verse to excuse us from this obligation before the night of Passover.

During the exile, however, the truth of God's miraculous ways is concealed by the deeds of the wicked, who parade their wickedness and mock the Name of God. With the end of the exile, the end of the wicked kingdom, the revelation of God's Name will return. As we are taught in the *Sefer Yetzirah*, ". . . and He created the universe with three books (*sepharim*), with text (*sepher*), with number (*sephar*), and with communication (*sippur*)." The world, with its macroscopic and microscopic detail, is a *sepher*, an open book for all those who care to look into it. And the one who can decipher it, who delves into the secrets and intricacies of nature, is the *sephar*, the counter of the number of words and letters of the text of the book. And when he deciphers and understands it and is able to teach it and reveal it, then it all amounts to a *sippur*, a story. It is the story that communicates the ultimate truth about the world—that God is the Master and Creator and no one else.

Let us therefore not minimize the importance of relating the story of the Exodus. It is the loftiest and most important thing that we are doing on the night of Passover. Although we have other *mitzvos* to observe on the same night, the story of the Exodus is the book with which God created the world.

We read in the *Haggadah*:

> Long, long ago our forefathers were worshipers of idols. Now God has drawn us near and we worship

Him. As it is written, "And Joshua said to all the people: Thus said the God of Israel: In the days of old your forefathers lived beyond the river; that is Terach, the father of Abraham and Nachor. They worshiped other gods. Then I took Abraham, your father, from beyond the river. I led him through the whole land of Canaan. Then I increased his family by giving him a son, Isaac. And I gave Isaac two sons, Jacob and Esau. To Esau I gave Mount Seir as a possession, but Jacob and his sons went down to Egypt.

We have learned in the Mishnah, "According to the understanding of the child, so should his father teach him. He starts with the shortcomings and ends with the praise." The Talmud explains, "What is meant by shortcomings? Rav holds that he should start with the words, 'We were slaves unto Pharaoh in Egypt.' And Shmuel holds that he should start with the words, "Long, long ago our forefathers were worshipers of idols'" (*Pesachim* 116a).

Our teachers of ethics, discipline, and moral conduct say, "If you wish to criticize, then criticize yourself. But if you wish to praise, then praise the Lord." Beauty of character and virtuous deeds are gifts from God, Who possesses all the good. As it is written, "You have established justice and equity . . ." (Psalms 99:4). Whatever good is found in the world is from the root of all good: God. On the other hand, the crookedness and wickedness in the world come from the people themselves. As it is written, "This alone I have found, that God, when He made man, made him straightforward, but man invents endless subtleties of his own" (Ecclesiastes 7:29). When God first created man, he could have been totally good, but he went on the crooked path on his own.

Therefore, we start with our shortcomings and end with the praise of the Lord. We start with the fact of our forefathers' idol worship, which caused them to be sent to Egypt to be purified.

Not only do the sins of those days, long ago, have to be repaired but also the sins of the first humans, Adam and Eve, must also be repaired, although not completely until the *Mashiach* comes. And what was their sin? They ate from the Tree of Knowledge in the Garden of Eden. And what fruit did they eat? The Talmud says it was either a wheat tree or a grape tree. Both of these always need great protection lest they become corrupt. The wheat is flour, which needs protection on Passover so that it does not become leavened, *chometz*. And wine needs protection all the time so that it is not offered to an idol, making it unfit to drink. As it is written, "And wine that makes glad the (*levav*) heart of man, and oil to make his face shine, and bread which strengthens man's (*levav*)

heart" (Psalms 104:15). The word *levav* means two hearts. The heart has two parts: the inclination (*yetzer tov*) to do good and the inclination (*yetzer hara*) to do evil. They find their roots in the Tree of Knowledge, which brought confusion to the heart of man. He no longer knew the good from the evil. And if man wants to follow the straight path of God, he has to be very careful. He must watch his wine and bread from turning sour and uneatable.

Thus, on the Seder night, we acknowledge our shortcomings and realize that we had better watch the two parts of our heart. We eat the strictly supervised *matzah*, the unleavened bread, and wine, to get back on the path that God wants all His creatures to be on.

"Long, long ago our forefathers were worshipers of idols. Now God has drawn us near and we worship Him."

It is written, "Rid silver of its impurities, then it can go to the silversmith [who makes vessels] . . ." (Proverbs 25:4). When the dirt is removed, then the silver can be used to make a vessel. The dirt is our sins, our idol-worshiping past. But how is the dirt removed? In the melting pot, a name synonymous with Egypt, as is written, "For they are your people, Your inheritance, which You brought forth out of Egypt, from the midst of the furnace of iron" (1 Kings 8:51).

Why does dirt get into the silver? It mixes with the silver so that when it is melted and the dirt removed, it is richer in mineral content and atomic bonding material. The same was with our forefathers. They worshiped idols, dirt got into them, they were purified in the furnace of Egypt, and were stronger and better than ever before at the time of the Exodus. They had picked up the rich thought and culture of Egypt and adapted it to fortify their own faith in God. Thus, because we once worshiped idols and we were put through the fire of Egypt, we can now be drawn to God and worship Him in a deeper and more meaningful way than ever. This is what the Kabbalists call "lifting the holy sparks."

We too, let us take the errors of our past, transform them to spiritual strength with the fires of repentance, and worship the one God, Creator and Master of the world.

First we were idol worshipers; then God drew us near. First we were slaves to Pharaoh in Egypt; then

God redeemed us. The question is: why do we rejoice with the Exodus? Would it not have been better if we would never have been in exile?

The exile and the Exodus were both necessary to make the Jewish nation who they are and to establish their role in the world. First they needed to be part of the regular everyday world, mixed with others, and unrecognizable. Then they were separated, removed, and sent on their mission to proclaim the sovereignty of God and the singularity of His Name. As we have learned in the *Baraisa* of Rabbi Yishmael, "Anything that was included in the general statement, but was then singled out from the general statement in order to teach something, was not singled out to teach about itself, but to apply its teaching to the entire generality" (*Siddur*, Morning Prayers). Similarly, the Jewish people were first part of the whole and were then singled out, not only for their own sake but also to teach the entire generality, the whole world.

The Egyptian exile is the root of all the exiles. During their oppression in Egypt, the Israelites were exposed to the four cardinal sins of idol worship, cohabitation with forbidden women, murder, and speaking evil against another. These four originate from the four bad habits of jealousy, lust, honor, and hatred without cause. Each corresponds to the four sons mentioned in the *Haggadah*. If one is jealous of the gods of another nation, one becomes an idol worshiper and is the wicked son. If a person misuses his wisdom and regresses into lust, he cohabits with forbidden women and is the wicked son. If an individual is so concerned with his own honor that he cannot respect another, he becomes a murderer and is the plain son. And if a person is so corrupt that he hates without cause, then he is the lowest and is the son who cannot even speak; he is totally lost.

It would take four exiles to cleanse the Jewish people of these flaws. The Babylonian exile repaired the sin of idol worship. It was during that exile that Hanania, Mishael, and Azariah were thrown into the fire for refusing to bow to the idols of Babylon. The following exile of the Greeks repaired the sin of lust and forbidden cohabitation. It was then that the Maccabees made a stand against the abominations of the Greek rulers and the rebellion began. This was followed by the exile of Media, an exile that exposed the Jewish people to the murderous ways of that nation. It was during that exile that the Jewish people decided to have even more respect for each human life. And the last exile that we are presently in, Edom, is one of hatred for no reason. It is now that we must dedicate ourselves to the moral ways of the Torah and refrain from speaking evil against anyone. We must increase the love between one another and thereby bring about the end of the last chapter of the fourth exile with the coming of the *Mashiach*, soon in our days.

First we were idol worshipers; then God drew us near. First we were slaves to Pharaoh in Egypt; then God redeemed us. We suffered a great deal in Egypt, and from the pain we called out to God to save us. Our suffering, followed by our cries and prayers, brought about our redemption. It became as one process; the suffering and cries were as much a part of the redemption as were the signs and miracles. Therefore, at the Seder when we relate the story of the awesome redemption, we start with the shortcomings. Those were an integral part of the redemption as much as the Exodus itself.

We read in the *Haggadah*, "Come and learn what Laban the Syrian tried to do to our father Jacob. While Pharaoh decreed only against the males, Laban desired to uproot all. For so it is written: A Syrian sought to destroy my father; and he went down to Egypt and dwelled there, a handful, a few in number. There he became a nation, great, mighty and numerous."

Laban was evil, cunning, and conniving, and he really wanted to hurt Jacob and his children. He really wanted to uproot and destroy them. And his wickedness caused the exile of the Israelites and their descent into Egypt. But it was not only harm that was caused to them. The result was the most awesome redemption with miracles of a sort that the world had never seen. Laban was a tool in the hands of the smith to make the vessel.

The land of Egypt was also chosen for a good reason. The Egyptians were sunken into the lowest of evils and were ripe to be punished. Therefore God placed the Jewish people in Egypt so that the Egyptians would quickly be punished and the Israelites removed.

While Pharaoh decreed only against the males, Laban desired to uproot all. It was because Laban schemed to uproot the Jewish people to the very last one that God foiled his plans. Similarly, Haman, because he planned to kill every last Jew, as it is written, "... to destroy, to kill, and to cause to perish, all Jews, both young and old, little children and women, in one day ..." (Esther 4:13), therefore he was not successful. Even

Hitler, the ugliest and most monstrous of Jew killers, planned to kill all the Jews under his rule, and therefore, although he nearly succeeded, still, he failed.

The Exodus is active in every generation, and God protects us from the tyrants of today as He did then in the days of Pharaoh.

"He went down to Egypt." Why did he go down to Egypt? He was compelled by God's decree.

"He dwelled there" means that Jacob our father did not go down to Egypt to settle there but only to stay for a short while; for so it is written in the *Haggadah*, "And they said to Pharaoh, we have come for to dwell in the land because there is no pasture for the flocks of your servants, since the famine is very bad in the land of Canaan; and now let your servants dwell in the land of Goshen."

The Jews were originally "few in number," as it is said, "Your fathers went down into Egypt with seventy persons. Now God has made you as numerous as the stars in heaven."

"And there he became a nation." From this we learn that Israel became a distinct nation in Egypt.

"He went down (*vayered*) to Egypt." The word *vayered* can also be read *v'yerd*, as in the verse, "And He (*v'yerd*) ruled . . ." (Psalms 72:8). What can this mean? It means that he, the Israelites, went down to Egypt, and thereby, He, God, ruled. It is also written, ". . . and have dominion over the fish . . ." (Genesis 1:28). If man is worthy, he rules over the sea, and if he is not, the sea rules over him. God sent them to Egypt to be humbled; they would accept God as their King, He would become their ruler, so that afterward they would rule over the sea and walk through the parted sea.

"He went down to Egypt." Why did he go down to Egypt? He was compelled by God's decree (*dibur*).

Why do you say that Jacob was compelled? Didn't he want to go to see his son Joseph? Yes, he did. But we can interpret his going on a spiritual level. The mission of the Jewish people is to declare the kingdom of God. Ever since the creation, the Ten Utterances with which God created the world are hidden within nature. When the Jews are in exile, their voice, their *dibur*, is silenced, and thus the Commands of creation are hidden even more. How would they ever get revealed? With the Ten Plagues. Each plague was plain proof and witness that God is the Master of the world.

Jacob was thus forced to go down to Egypt, because the *dibur*, the speech, their voice that was in exile was

no longer able to witness for God. So he went to Egypt for the purpose of transforming the commands to plagues and releasing the *dibur* from exile.

We are, thank God, free. Let us therefore exercise this freedom and be loyal witnesses for the Master of the universe.

"And there he became a nation." From this we learn that Israel became a distinct nation in Egypt.

Jacob was afraid to go to Egypt. It was then a huge and expansive country with a distinct culture and idol worship, providing ample opportunity for a foreign group to assimilate and lose its distinct identity. God reassured him saying, ". . . I am God, the God of your father: fear not to go down into Egypt; for I will there to make you a great nation" (Genesis 46:3).

The truth is, though, that the children of Jacob never intended to assimilate, and therefore God guaranteed their separateness. He did this by allowing the Egyptians to inflict great pain and suffering on the Israelites. This is the meaning of the words *vayehi*—"and he became"; the word *vayehi* means pain. It was because of the pain that the Jews became a nation. The Israelites did not like their tormentors and kept their distance.

Let us learn at least that lesson from the Exodus. We are a people apart; let us stay apart without needing another exile.

". . . and the Egyptians did evil unto us and they made us suffer. They set upon us hard work."

The evil of the Egyptians was that they made the Israelites do work that was not needed. They only wanted to make them suffer. This is similar to what the Germans did to the Jews during the war. They forced the Jews to do work that they did not need at all. And even the work that they needed, they forced the Jews to do it in a way to made them suffer. But God did kindness with us, and ". . . (*v'ka'asher*) the more they afflicted them, the more they multiplied and grew" (Exodus 1:12). The word *v'ka'asher*, also means, and in the same measure. In the measure that the Egyptians oppressed the Jewish people, that is how much the Jews multiplied. And as much as they enslaved, humiliated, and debased them, that is how powerful was the Jews' liberation and freedom. They became so free with the Exodus that no nation could enslave them any longer. And the deeper they sank into the "house of slaves," the more they were privileged to go to God's house: the Land of Israel. And just as the Egyptians at first used soft words, seduction, and cunning to make them work and later worked them with great pressure, so too they heard from Moses the softest words to console them and strengthen their faith. And then again at Mount Sinai, they heard words of seduction from Moses in the name of God, how wonderful it will be for them to accept the Torah. And then God gave them the highest and full strength of spirituality, as much as their soul could bear. Thus, the spiritual world became balanced. *V'ka'asher*, just as the Egyptians made the Israelites work harshly, so too their enthusiasm for the Torah was so great that they will keep it in the hardest of times.

We read in the *Haggadah*, "And God brought us forth from Egypt, with a strong hand, and with an outstretched arm, and with great terror, and with signs and wonders."

"And God brought us forth from Egypt"—not by the action of an angel, not by a fiery angel, not by a messenger, but by Himself, in His glory, did the Holy One, blessed be He, as it is written, "And I will pass through the land of Egypt on that night, and I will smite all the firstborn in the land of Egypt from man to beast, and against all the gods of Egypt I will execute judgments. It is I, and none other" (Exodus 12:12).

An angel, although divine, is still a limited being and would have caused a finite redemption. But God is infinite, and His redemption is infinite and forever. Still, Moses asked of God, "Who am I (*mi Anochi*), that I should go unto Pharaoh, and that I should bring forth the children of Israel out of Egypt?" (Exodus 3:11). His question was based on a promise that God had made to Abraham, "And He said unto Abram, 'Know for sure that your descendants will be foreigners in a land that is not theirs for 400 years. They will be enslaved and oppressed. But I (*Anochi*) will finally bring judgment against the nation that enslaves them, and they will then leave with great wealth'" (Genesis 15:13,14). Moses asked, Why do You send me to liberate the Israelites? Didn't you promise to Abraham that You Yourself would do it, *Anochi*? This is a very deep and difficult question. And the answer is that since Moses was the most humble and said "Who am I (*mi Anochi*)?" he considered himself as nothing and nobody and was thereby totally nullified to God, it was as if God was doing it by Himself.

"And God brought us forth from Egypt"—not by the action of an angel, not by a fiery angel, not by a messenger. . . ."

Although God did send a messenger, Moshe, to redeem them, still it was as if He had not sent one. Why? Because the redemption was not natural, orderly, or rational the way a human being would have done it. Instead, it was miraculous, chaotic, and cataclysmic. How? As the Midrash says, in the verse "Come from Lebanon (*levonon*), my bride; come from Lebanon" (Song of Songs 4:8), *levonon* can also be read *leveinim*, the bricks that the Israelites made from the mud. "Come," God says, "come with me, come the way you are, from the very mud and straw with which you are now covered. Come, and be my bride, from your defiled and lowly condition. I'm taking you as my bride anyway—from the mud to the palace" (*Exodus Rabbah* 12). This is not normal, natural, or human. Therefore, it was surely only God Himself Who could have accomplished such a strange and astonishing feat.

We should realize the great love that God has for us regardless of our spiritual state. He is ready to take us the way we are. The question that remains is: are we ready to go to the palace?

We read in the *Haggadah*, "How thankful we must be to God, the All Mighty, for all the good (*ma'alos tovos*) He did for us."

The words *ma'alos tovos* also mean levels of spiritual attainment. All the good that God did for us was in order to raise us to higher and higher levels of spirituality.

Each month the moon is at first not visible, and then a thin crescent appears. The moon fills with more and more light until the fifteenth night of the month. There were also fifteen steps between the two courtyards in the Holy Temple. These correspond to the fifteen steps that one can climb in spiritual levels.

The Israelites in Egypt were sunken into the abominations of Egypt and after hearing the call of Moses yearned to correct their ways. Even one of the miracles of God would have been enough to draw the hearts of the Jewish people to seek spiritual enlightenment. Yet, God was so good to us by continuing to show us wonders and miracles beyond what we needed. He showed us altogether fifteen wonders, so that with each one we moved up one step.

We should accept the wonders of God and His kindness toward us. We should be aware of our open and receptive heart and should climb up the steps of the spiritual realm, all fifteen of them, until we reach the fullness and brightness of the moon.

In the *Haggadah*, we read, "Raban Gamliel said: Whoever does not explain the following three symbols at the Seder on Passover has not fulfilled his duty. The Passover offering, the *Matzah*, and the bitter herbs."

The Passover Offering

The Passover offering that our fathers ate in the Temple days, what was the reason for it? It was because the Holy One, blessed be He, passed over the houses of the forefathers in Egypt, as it is written, "And you shall say it is the Passover offering for God Who passed over the houses of the children of Israel in Egypt when He smote the Egyptians and spared our houses. And the people bowed their heads and prostrated themselves" (Exodus 12:28).

The *Matzah*

This *matzah* that we eat, what is the reason for it? It is because there was not time for the dough of our ancestors in Egypt to become leavened, before the Ruler of all, the Holy One, blessed be He, revealed Himself to them and redeemed them, as it is written, "And the dough which they had brought out from Egypt they baked into cakes of unleavened bread, for it had not leavened, because they were thrust out of Egypt and they could not tarry, nor had they prepared for themselves any provisions."

The Bitter Herbs

These bitter herbs that we eat, what is their meaning? They are eaten to recall that the Egyptians embittered the lives of our forefathers in Egypt, as it is written: "And they embittered their lives with hard labor: with mortar and bricks, with every kind of work in the fields; all the work which they made them do was rigorous" (Exodus 1:14).

It is written, "Hark! My beloved! Here he comes, bounding (*medaleg*) over the mountains, leaping over the hills" (Song of Songs 2:8)

The word should be *doleg*, "he is skipping," but instead it is written as *m'daleg*, "he makes skip." Not only does God skip over the houses of the Jewish people but He also makes their heart skip a beat. He makes them have the courage to skip ahead and reach for the spiritual levels of the forefathers, Abraham, Isaac, and Jacob. Step by step, they could

never have hoped to get there. As the Midrash relates: When the Jewish people were at the Red Sea and saw the Egyptians coming, they called out to God. Why? Because they seized the trade of their forefathers—praying and crying out in a time of trouble. But how did they have the nerve to try to do what men of such great stature did? Had they not been just released from slavery? Nevertheless, they seized, they skipped, they ignored their limitations (*Exodus Rabbah* 14).

We too, what we cannot do step by step we can do by skipping. Especially on this night when God skipped over the houses and nothing could stand between God, the beloved, and His beloved people.

In the *Haggadah*, we read, "The Passover offering which our fathers ate in the Temple days, what was the reason for it? It was because the Holy One, blessed be He, passed over the houses of the forefathers in Egypt. . . ."

God rules with judgment. But at times the judgment turns into loving-kindness. For example, blood is a symbol of judgment, yet in Egypt the Israelites smeared blood on their doorposts in order to ward off the judgment and to attract kindness. As it is written, ". . . and I will see the blood and skip over you . . ." (Exodus 12:13). I will see the blood, and although it is judgment, in this case it will cause me to skip over you. And it is also written, "Then I came by and saw you kicking helplessly in your own blood; I spoke to you, there in your blood, and bade you—live!" (Ezekiel 16:16). In the blood itself I tell you to live!

Similarly, God said to Moshe, "In the middle (*b'chatzos*) of the night, I will go out among the Egyptians . . ." (Exodus 11:4). The word *b'chatzos* can also mean, at the parting of the night. The night parted into two. On one side the Egyptians are dying; on the other part, the Israelites are being saved. The same happened at the parting of the Red Sea. In one part the Egyptians were drowning; in the other part the Israelites were being saved.

Similarly, God is a consuming fire, as it is written, "God is a consuming fire . . ." (Deuteronomy 4:24). Yet for the Jewish people, God is a source of life, as it is written, "And you who cleave to God are alive today . . ." (Deuteronomy 4:4). Although for you the closeness with God brings life, to others it is certain death.

All these contradictions puzzle the sons at the Seder. Why is this night called Passover, as if the night was filled totally with compassion, with skipping over the homes of the Israelites, when in fact there was pervading judgment resulting in the death of all the firstborn? But the truth is that the kindness and compassion are surrounded, hidden, and protected within judgment. What you see is the judgment, but scratch the surface and you find compassion at its core. What was seen on that awesome night was the death of all the firstborn, but within it, at the core, what was taking place, was the rescue of the Israelites. The *chometz*, the leavened, hides within it the *matzah*.

Whatever was in exile was redeemed with the Exodus. And there were three dimensions to the exile. One, was the Name, honor, and Divine presence of God, which was in Exile in Pharaoh's mouth, as he declared, ". . . Who is God that I should obey Him and let Israel go? I do not recognize God. Nor will I let Israel leave" (Exodus 5:2). And that had to be redeemed. This was the Passover sacrifice, with God skipping over the houses, as God Himself was released from exile. The second dimension of the exile was the soul of the Jewish people. It needed great protection lest it get sour like rising dough. And finally it was redeemed. The third dimension was the wicked who inflicted the pain and suffering of the exile. This is the *moror*, the bitter herbs.

MATZAH

There were two trees in the Garden of Eden, the Tree of Life and the Tree of Knowledge. With the Tree of Life one could discern good and evil clearly as opposites, as clearly as life and death. The Tree of Knowledge, in contrast, enabled one to experience the world in all its facets and required knowledge to separate the good from the evil. Once Adam and Eve ate from the Tree of Knowledge, they experienced the creation as a confusion of good and evil. It was their task to sort and find the good and evil in each thing. Such a task is called exile.

A prince lived with his father in the palace. As the son, he had the privilege of visiting his father any time and asking him anything he wanted. Sometimes, palace officials would tell him things in the name of the king. He would then go directly to his father and ask if the report was true.

One day the prince had to leave the palace and travel a great distance to one of the provinces. While there, he heard rumors and reports about edicts and other proclamations of the king. There was no way for him to check the truth of these reports, and he was very unsure of his decisions. He felt as if he was in exile.

With the Tree of Life, the King was approachable; one could know if his actions are leading to the King or in the opposite direction. But with the Tree of Knowledge one can never know.

Similarly the daytime is full of light, and with it one can discern objects and paths. But the night is dark, and one can hardly recognize anything and can easily get lost.

Chometz, too, is symbolic of confusion. It seems full and risen, although its weight does not change, it seems a good deal bigger and more substantial. It is like the Tree of Knowledge. *Matzah*, on the other hand, is what it appears to be. It is flat and has no more dough than what is seen. It is like the Tree of Life.

Therefore, the whole year in exile we eat *chometz* and *matzah*, leavened and unleavened bread, which are symbolic of the Tree of Knowledge. On the night of Passover, however, we eat only *matzah*, which is symbolic of the clarity of the Tree of Life. Although it is night, still "and for all the Israelites it was light in their dwellings." May we merit to experience this night of Passover.

Matzah is a dough that does not change; it stays flat and is no more than it appears to be. This is symbolic of the Jewish people who did not change in Egypt: they did not change their names, their language, or their distinct clothing. The way they entered Egypt was the way they left Egypt. And how was this possible? Was it not easier for them to assimilate and be like the Egyptians? We read in the *Haggadah*, ". . . because there was no time for the dough of our ancestors in Egypt to become leavened, before the Ruler of all, the Holy One, blessed be He, revealed Himself to them and redeemed them. . .," Because the Egyptians treated them miserably, the Israelites lost their appetite to become close to them and be accepted by them.

Therefore, the promise of God was fulfilled, "I will go down with you into Egypt; and I will surely bring you up, also to bring you up . . ." (Genesis 46:4). God promised, that for each and every step down that the Israelites took into the exile, He would bring them up a step out of the exile. And therefore, for each of the afflictions they suffered, God redeemed them. As it is written, "And He said unto Abram, Know for sure that your descendants will be foreigners in a land that is not theirs for 400 years. They will be enslaved and oppressed . . ." (Genesis 15:13). Because of the exile of being foreigners, they merited their own land. Because of the exile of being "enslaved," they merited becoming servants of God. And because of the exile of being "oppressed," they merited the Torah, as it is written, "Oh, how good it is for me to have had pain, to school me in Your statutes" (Psalms 119:71).

It is written, "The Lord will strike down Egypt, healing as He strikes . . ." (Isaiah 19:20).

Matzah is a medicinal food and at the same time is called the bread of affliction. It is medicine for the Jewish people and a plague upon the Egyptians. It separates the good from the evil, as the word *matzah* also implies conflict; there are still scores to settle and punishments to be meted out.

Similarly it is written, "And He said, If you will diligently listen to the voice of the Lord your God, and will do that which is right in His sight, and will give ear to His commandments, and keep His statutes, I will put none of the diseases upon you, which I have brought upon the Egyptians: for I am the Lord (*ani*) God that heals you" (Exodus 15:26). The question is: If God will not afflict you with disease, then why does He need to heal you? Normally, God would punish the wicked with sickness while He healed the Jewish people with miracles. But with the power of the Torah, I am God; the Torah is Me, My names, that have the power to heal you without inflicting pain on the wicked.

Similarly, "Six days you will eat *matzos*, and the seventh day is a day of solemn assembly . . ." (Deuteronomy 16:8). During the six days of Passover the *matzah* is sorting out the good from the evil; it heals and punishes. But on the seventh day, all the battles are over, and there is a solemn assembly between God and the Jewish people, and it is all healing.

Let us therefore connect with the healing power of the *matzah* and pray that we will no longer need punishments, but only healing.

We read in the *Haggadah*, "This *matzah* which we eat, what is the reason for it? It is because there was not time for the dough of our ancestors in Egypt to become leavened, before the Ruler of all, the Holy One, blessed be He, revealed Himself to them and redeemed them. . . ."

This sounds as if the Exodus started in the morning when the Jews were being expelled from Egypt. But did not their redemption start at night with the plague of the firstborn? At that time their dough was far from rising or leavening.

The answer is that there was both a physical re-

demption and a psychological redemption. The physical redemption started when Egyptians lost control over their Israelite slaves. That was at night. But the Jews were still enslaved to the Egyptians psychologically. They were still afraid of them. By the morning, when the clouds of glory surrounded them and they were in the refuge of God, then they felt completely redeemed. And this happened, as the *Targum Yonoson* says, immediately as soon as they moved from Raamses toward Sukkos.

Thus, the dough of the Israelites did not get a chance to rise in the morning before God suddenly revealed Himself with the clouds of Glory and redeemed them from their psychological exile.

We too have an opportunity to free our minds from the enslavement of the nations. When we eat the *matzah*, let us connect to its power of liberation. Then we can think as Jews and immediately know what to do as individuals and as a people.

We read in the *Haggadah*, ". . . there was not time for the dough of our ancestors in Egypt to become leavened, before the Ruler of all, the Holy One, blessed be He, revealed Himself to them and redeemed them. . . ."

It was the kindness of God that prevented the souls of the Israelites from becoming defiled in the forty-nine levels of abominations of Egypt. Because had that happened, they would never have been able to escape. They would have been lost forever, and we still would have been enslaved to Pharaoh. But God did not let our dough get sour. Instead, at the very last minute He liberated and saved us.

When we hold the *matzah*, let us remember that the liberation, although coming at the last minute, was the preeminent act that gave birth to the Jewish people. And in our personal exiles, we too would experience a redemption that would rival the Exodus if only we had the faith.

Matzah is called the bread of affliction, *lechem oni*. The great commentaries of Rashi and the Ramban say that *matzah* is the symbol, a reminder of our pain and suffering in the Egyptian exile. This is also the common understanding of the words, *lechem oni*, "poor bread," which imply poverty, and suffering in Egypt. The Maharal of Prague, on the other hand, says that *lechem oni*, *matzah*, is a symbol of the liberation and freedom of the Exodus. How? Because it is "poor" bread containing no other than the basic ingredients; it has no attachments, and it needs no leavening or seasoning to be called bread. Although bread is dependent on its ingredients, just as a rich man is dependent on his riches, a poor man is free, although merely a man. He can leave a country without any problem or regret. There is nothing tying him to the place where he is.

How do we reconcile these two contradictory views about *lechem oni*, the poor bread? Does it represent the poverty and slavery or the liberation?

The answer is that *matzah* is symbolic of both the exile and the redemption, because one depends on the other. We even praise God for the exile, when we recite in the *Haggadah*, "In the beginning our forefathers were idol worshipers." It seems that we need the exile in order to have the redemption.

When God wants to lift us to the very heights of spirituality, we must first be humbled. Otherwise, the arrogance that results from our lofty level would cancel the gain, and we would end with nothing. Thus, everyone who is about to be lifted up high is first humbled by God. And out of the sadness of the beginning comes the happy ending, as it is written, "...better the end of anything than its beginning..." (Ecclesiastes 7:8). Because we were slaves and utterly downtrodden, therefore we were able to become servants of the One and Only God with complete humility and obedience.

Matzah, then, is as much the symbol of poverty and suffering as it is a symbol of the prelude to the redemption. Although *matzah* is poor bread, with no leavening or seasoning, it is also liberated, independent, and free of all attachments.

The Talmud says, "Why is it called *lechem oni*? Because many things are said about it" (*Pesachim* 31a).

There is bread from heaven, and there is bread from the earth. The bread from the heaven was the *manna* that descended from the heaven without the work or merit of man. Regardless of who it was, there was *manna* outside his tent every morning. It was purely and entirely a gift from God. In contrast, bread from the earth requires much work—plowing, planting, and reaping—until it is ready to eat. It grows in the person's merit.

The Exodus was also without the merit of the Jewish people. It was a pure gift from God. But the Jewish people thought perhaps that they deserved it. After all, hadn't they risked their lives by taking the Egyptian idol, the sheep, on the tenth day of *Nissan* and tying it to their bedposts as a show of defiance? And hadn't they smeared blood on their doors, a direct confrontation with the authorities? But the truth was that compared to the miracles that hap-

pened and the awesome redemption, their merit was miniscule. And therefore we eat *matzah*, a food that, despite the work of mixing flour and water, was put into baskets and onto their shoulders. Although they worked, the dough baked "by itself" in the sun. It was poor bread, and not much work went into it. Still, the Israelites took credit for the results. Later they realized that their work was insignificant compared to the baking of the sun. First they thought it was "bread of the earth," but it was actually "bread from the heaven." Similarly, at first they thought they deserved the redemption, but they later realized that it was nothing less than a gift from God.

Therefore, the *matzah* needs many things to be said about it, until we realize that it is bread from heaven; it is not a result of our work, or our merit.

Although on the first two night of Passover one is obliged to eat *matzah*, on the rest of the days of the holiday eating it is not required. If a person wants to, he can eat *matzah*, and if not he can eat anything that is not leavened (*Pesachim* 120a).

Matzah is of such a pure nature. It is free of attachments and entanglements and is nearly in its original state, the way it grew. One can still taste its originality. We wonder then how could we, with all our entanglements, eat such a "pure" food. The answer is that we really would not be able to partake of the spiritual essence of *matzah* if not for the holiday of Passover. Although the holiday dwells on the miraculous, its freedom and liberation enter our earthly life. It is *zman cheiruseinu*, "the time of liberation." The miraculous liberation enters our earthly time. It lifts us to the level of no attachments. Thus we partake in the spiritual sustenance of the *matzah*. On the spiritual, the question arises: can we eat *matzah*, are we able to digest its spiritual nature? The answer is that yes, you are permitted to eat *matzah* whenever you please during the holiday of Passover.

When we eat *matzah* we must remember its high spiritual nature and, also, that without the Passover holiday we would not be able to experience it.

We read in the *Haggadah*, "This *matzah* which we eat, what is the reason for it? It is because there was not time for the dough of our ancestors in Egypt to become leavened, before the Ruler of all, the Holy One, blessed be He, revealed Himself to them and redeemed them. ..."

The ego of man rises and becomes inflated. But when it realizes that it is in the presence of God, it shrinks and dares not rise, just as dough, a second before it rises, is quickly baked into *matzah*, and remains flat as can be.

The Zohar explains that the difference between *chometz* [חמץ] and *matzah* [מצה] is the *heh*, which has a *yud* within the *dalet*. *Dalet* is the letter that means poor man. *Dalet* is a man who realizes that he is poor and has nothing without the *yud*, God, that is within him. How does he stay humble without inflating with arrogance? By realizing that it is God within him that makes him what he is. But if he inflates himself with arrogance, then the *yud* stretches and becomes a *vov*, the *heh* becomes a *cheth*, [ח] the *matzah* becomes *chometz*.

Thus, if we ever feel our ego expanding with arrogance, we must quickly allow God to appear before us. The dough is about to become leavened and must be baked quickly. And when we do that, we will merit to hasten the redemption, soon in our days.

The Passover sacrifice is to be eaten with *matzah* and *moror*, as it is written in the *Haggadah*, ". . . and eat it with *matzah* and bitter herbs (*al matzos um'rorim*)." When we celebrate the redemption, we are also thankful for the pain and suffering. Not only did God promise to go down (*eirid*) with the Israelites to Egypt, but also, just as He ruled (*rodeh*) after the redemption He also ruled during the exile.

It is written, "My beloved is for me a bunch (*tz'ror*) of myrrh . . ." (Song of Songs 1:13). The numerical value of *tzror* is 496, which is the same as *m'rorim*, "bitter herbs," and is equal to *malchus*, "kingdom." The kingdom of God, no matter where you are or what time it is, is there with you.

When we partake of the *matzah* and *moror*, let us realize that whether after the Exodus or during the exile, God is with us always. And no matter how long it lasts, He is with us during all our afflictions.

We recite in our daily prayers, "Who is like you, O Master of mighty deeds, and who is comparable to You, O King Who causes death and restores life and makes salvation sprout."

The exile and the redemption stem from the self-same will, just as do death and healing. Do not think then of the exile as the place and time empty of God and the redemption as finally having found Him. Instead, even during the exile, God is there just the same. And more than that, in order to obtain new life after the redemption one must first "die," put aside the life of the exile completely, be humbled to the very earth, and negate one's being entirely.

The Israelites in Egypt were in a twofold exile. They were in a physical exile of slavery and oppression. They experienced pain and suffered. At the same time they were also in a spiritual exile. Their soul was thirsting for direction and fulfillment. They had neither. And their biggest problem was that they no longer felt their spiritual exile. After they were liberated and climbed spiritual heights, they suddenly realized what they had been missing. Thus, when they remember their physical suffering, they realized that their spiritual suffering was just as bad. It was through the *matzah*, which is symbolic of the redemption, that they realized their *moror*, the bitterness of the spiritual exile.

We read in the *Haggadah*, "It is because there was not time for the dough of our ancestors in Egypt to become leavened, before the Ruler of all, the Holy One, blessed be He, revealed Himself to them and redeemed them. . . ."

The Israelites had almost sunk to the lowest of the forty-nine levels. Indeed, had they descended one more level, they would never have been able to recover. That is the fiftieth level and beyond redemption—the point of no return. God redeemed them from the forty-ninth level, but wanted to do even more for them. So He took them into the Red Sea. This symbolized the exile of the fiftieth level. And even from there God redeemed them, and they instead entered the fiftieth level of holiness.

We too, no matter how lowly we are and what troubles we may have, should never give up hoping for God's compassion to lift us from our miserable state and to catapult us to new heights of liberation and freedom.

The bitterness of the enslavement helped shorten the exile. The *moror* was part of the *matzah*, and as we eat it we realize that it was for our sake. The exile was as much part of the redemption as the Exodus itself.

REDEMPTION

We read in the *Haggadah*, "In every generation one must look upon himself as if he personally had come out from Egypt, as it is written, "And you should tell your son on that day, saying, it is because of that which God did to me when I went forth from Egypt." For it was not alone our forefathers whom the Holy One, blessed be He, redeemed; He redeemed us, too, with them, as it is said: "He brought us out from there that He might lead us to and give us the land which He pledged to our forefathers."

According to the Maharal of Prague, everyone understands that the Jewish people as a nation were redeemed. But how do we aspire to that redemption as individuals? It is by the faith that we are integrally part of the Jewish people. We experience the redemption as if each one of us was there and was redeemed: "and even if we are all wise." If our wisdom comes from the fact that we are part of the all, the collective soul of the Jewish people, that helps us tell about it. Thus, the *mitzvah* of telling the story of the Exodus is the obligation of each and every Jew.

This can teach us and help us be liberated from our own exile. When we join the collective soul of the Jewish people with faith, we can be sure that our redemption is soon to come.

It is written in the *Haggadah*, "One should visualize that he is leaving Egypt in each generation. As it is written, ". . . and He brought *us* out from there. . . ."

The question is: If we say, "He brought us out from there," that God actually took not only our ancestors, but even us out of Egypt, then why do we have to pretend and "visualize" as if we were brought out of Egypt? The answer is given in the morning prayers: "The Helper of our forefathers You alone are forever Shield and Savior for them and their children after them in every generation." The Exodus happened to the collective, the Jewish people. And each of us, too, the more we are part of the *Klal Yisrael*, the Jewish nation, the more we share in the reality of the redemption.

May we, and our children, until the *Mashiach* comes, merit to conduct the Seder with all of its revealed and hidden significance.

42

Shevi'ih Shel *Passover—*
The Last Day of Passover

THE SPLITTING OF THE RED SEA

After the Israelites left Egypt they went by the way of the wilderness toward the Red Sea. God guided them with a pillar of cloud in the day and a pillar of fire at night. They set out from Raamses and came to Sukkos and from there proceeded to Etham on the edge of the wilderness. By marching back toward Egypt, God made the Egyptians think that the Israelites were trapped. Pharaoh became stubborn, gathered his troops, mounted his chariot, and gave chase. It was not long before the Israelites saw the Egyptians coming and were terrified. This took place on the seventh day after the Exodus, and on our holiday calendar it is *Shevi'ih Shel* Passover, the seventh day of Passover. They called out to God, and He said, do not pray to Me at this time, but move forward into the sea. Moses lifted his staff, and God made an intense wind blow all night. The waters of the Red Sea were parted and made a wall for them on the right and left side. While the Israelites entered the sea, at the same time, the cloud moved between the two camps. It was light for the Israelites and dark for the Egyptians. In the morning, the sand became scorching hot for the Egyptian horses, and they galloped wildly toward the sea. They too entered the sea bed and pursued the Israelites with vigor. The Israelites had already all crossed and were out of the sea when the Egyptians rushed in. Moses held up his staff, and the waters returned and covered the Egyptian army. The entire Egyptian army was wiped out before the very eyes of the Israelites. They sang a song of praise to the Lord for this great miracle. Therefore, the seventh day of Passover is a day of rest as we celebrate the fullness of the Exodus, the parting of the Red Sea (Exodus 13:17–14:14).

It is written, "To Him Who divided the Red Sea into parts: for His mercy endures forever" (Psalms 136:13).

The Midrash says that the sea parted into twelve separate sections, one for each of the twelve tribes. Why was this so important? Would it not have been just as miraculous to have one path for all of Israel? That is precisely the reason. If there would have been only one path, then it would mean that the Israelites merited the miracle as a nation. Now that each tribe had a part, it was clear that each and every tribe had the merit for the sea to part. And not only an entire tribe, but each and every Jew had the merit that great miracles should happen just for him.

There is heaven, earth, and the sea. The Jewish people have dominion over each of them. Over the heaven, as Abraham, who was lifted above the stars in the heavens and astrological forces; as Jacob, who fought with the angel of Esau victoriously; as Moshe, who argued with the angels to allow the Torah to be given to the Jewish people; as Joshua, who made the sun and moon stop in their tracks; and as the prophet Elijah, who ascended to the heaven in a fiery chariot. They have dominion over the earth, as Isaac, who digs and finds water; as Jacob, who makes his sheep increase by using carved sticks; as Moses, who made a stick turn into a serpent, dust into lice, and ashes into boils; as the prophet Elisha, who put life back into a dead boy. And they have dominion over the sea, as Moses who parts the Red Sea.

Thus, every Israelite has dominion over the sky, earth, and sea and when the sea parted, it parted for each and every one of them. Similarly, when we sit at the Seder, we can feel our dominion over the world of nature. How can we still think that natural circumstances or inclinations can stop us from observing the Torah? We have been chosen to be above the world of nature and not to be dominated by it.

––––––––––––

It is written, "For since the beginning of the world men have not heard, nor perceived by the ear, neither has the eye seen, O God, beside You, what He has prepared for those who wait upon Him" (Isaiah 64:3). The Talmud comments, "All the prophets when they prophesied for the glorious future, it was about the days of the Messiah. But what awaits the righteous in the World to Come even they have never heard, or seen anything of it" (Berakhos 34b).

When the Israelites were crossing the Red Sea, they experienced awesome spiritual revelations. "What an ordinary maid saw while crossing the sea, no prophet had ever seen" (Exodus Rabbah 14). This is alluded to in the verse, "Have no fear," Moses answered, "stand firm and see the deliverance that the Lord will do for you this day . . ." (Exodus 14:12). The words "the Lord will do" refer to the World to Come, meaning that on this day you will see the ultimate of deliverance by getting a glimpse of Olam Habah, the World to Come.

Why were all the spiritual worlds revealed to the Jewish people during the crossing of the Red Sea? What was it about that experience that elevated them so? Why was that miracle so different from all the others?

When a miracle occurs, even if we witness it, it remains outside us. But the parting of the sea was different. The Israelites literally entered the realm of the miracle and were part of it. They walked on a "new earth" and under a "new sky," that of the World to Come. As they entered the sea, they stepped into a time warp and were suddenly in the future. Therefore, the song of praise for the parting of the sea was "Then Moses shall sing. . . ." "Then" means the future, in the World to Come. "Then Moses shall sing"? Didn't he already sing? Yes, he was singing, but also he will sing in the future, which was there within the sea.

––––––––––––

It is written, ". . . Your throne is firm from old (mai'az); from all eternity You are God" (Psalms 93:2). The Midrash comments, "Although your kingdom is

from days of yore, Your throne was not settled until the Israelites sang the song starting with the word az" (Exodus Rabbah 14).

The Jewish people must witness that God is the Master of the world, but cannot do this while they are slaves. Therefore, before they crossed the Red Sea, it says, ". . . and they believed . . ." (Exodus 14:31), not v'he-eminu, "they made others believe." They were thus stuck in their slave mentality and were unable to be witnesses for God's sake.

Liberating the Israelites from the slavery of Egypt, the Midrash says, was like a farmer who wants to help his cow give birth. He inserts his hand into the cow's womb to pull the calf out. He must pull gently but forcefully, with coaxing but with strength. Similarly, the Israelites were pulled with great force out of Egypt because they were not ready to leave. But once they passed through the Red Sea, they were totally liberated and removed from slavery. It was far behind them. Then they were ready to witness for God (Exodus Rabbah 13).

That is why, before we recite our silent prayer, we mention the parting of the sea. That miracle enabled us to pray to God.

The Talmud says that one ought to walk the distance of two doorways into the synagogue and then pray. These doorways are symbolic of the liberation; one is the Exodus, and the other is the parting of the Red Sea. When we are connected with those two doorways, we are removed from slavery and are able to pray.

––––––––––––

It is written, ". . . when the Israelites looked up they saw that (Mitzrayim) the Egyptians are close behind" (Exodus 14:10).

The Mitzrayim mentioned is the guardian angel of Egypt, just as, ". . . the Israelites saw the (Mitzrayim) Egyptians lying dead on the sea shore" (Exodus 14:30).

Our forefather Jacob fought with an angel and subdued him. God then changed his name to (Yisrael), Israel, which means, you have fought with an angel and have succeeded. This was a signal for Jacob that he and his descendants not only are above the world of nature but are also above the heavenly spheres. During the long and harsh exile in Egypt the Israelites forgot their great powers. And when they left and saw the Egyptians pursuing them, they were terrified of a war with the guardian angel of Egypt. "Have no fear," Moses answered, "stand firm and see the deliverance that the Lord will bring you this day; for as sure as you see the Egyptians now, you will never see them again. God will fight for you; so hold your peace" (Exodus 14:13).

The physical world and the spiritual world mirror each other. Whatever occurs in one happens in the other. During a war, just as there is a war on earth, there is also one in heaven. And Moses said, "You do what you have to, and God in heaven will do His work." First, the Israelites escaped from their physical slavery and bondage, and God subdued the guardian angel of Egypt before their very eyes. That completed the war in heaven. Just as there was an Exodus on earth, the physical exit from Egypt, there was simultaneously an Exodus in heaven, and that culminated in the parting of the Red Sea.

Thus, there are two names: Jacob and Israel. Jacob is he who acts physically on earth, and Israel is he who acts spiritually in heaven. When the Israelites left Egypt they took with them many physical gifts from their Egyptian neighbors. But even greater were the spiritual gifts that they received from defeating the guardian angel of Egypt. Its spiritual energy was given to them, and with that strength they sang a song of praise to God.

Whenever we remember the parting of the Red Sea, let it teach us that earth and heaven melt away before the man of complete faith. And we too, no matter the size of the obstacle that stands before us, can surmount it; if we do our share on earth, God does his share in heaven.

The Midrash says, "Then (*az*) Moses will sing . . ." (*Exodus Rabbah* 15) What is the meaning of the word "then" (*az*)? It is the same as in another verse, as it is written, "Then (*az*) you will go your way without a care, and your feet will not stumble" (Proverbs 3:23).

The Israelites had complete trust in God when they left Egypt. They became soldiers of God and warred with the kings of Canaan. They left a civilized country and entered a barren wilderness full of snakes, scorpions, and other poisonous creatures. To have the strength to endure, they needed to be bound to the Almighty with great strength. And it was during the parting of the Red Sea, followed by their song of praise, that their new faith was etched into their hearts. They were ready to risk all for Him and to follow His call in the most dangerous places.

This is similar to the time when our forefather Jacob went forth, "And Jacob went forth from B'er Sheva, and went to Choron" (Genesis 7:10). *B'er* means the brook, the root and origin, *sheva* means seven. What is the root of seven, the seven days of creation? It is the one, the *aleph*, the light of the seven days. This is identical to the word *az*, which is made up of the letters *aleph* and *zayin*, meaning the *aleph*, the root and origin of the *zayin*, the seven days of creation. *Zayin* also means weapon; the weapon of the Jewish people is the root of all: the *aleph*. When these two letters are together as in "Then (*az*) Moses will sing . . . ," it means that he sang with the strength he gained by realizing that every created thing is connected to the One, the Creator. And this knowledge gave the Israelites a surge of energy, and they too sang the song of faith to God.

Let us therefore refocus our attention to the *aleph*, the One and Only, the root of the world. And then we will follow God with confidence into the great unknown.

The Exodus had two parts. One was the physical escape from slavery, and the other was the spiritual freedom that they attained at the parting of the Red Sea. The symbol for the physical Exodus is the *matzah*, the bread of affliction and of poverty. How can a saved person ever thank his liberator enough? How does he show his gratitude? By completely humbling before his liberator, as we have learned, "Simon his son says: 'All my days I have been raised among the Sages and I found nothing better for the body [oneself] than silence . . ." (*Ethics of Our Fathers* 1:17). The body must be silent and humbled. The soul, on the other hand, can be proud and feel high because of its spiritual accomplishments, as it is written, " And his heart was lifted up in the ways of the Lord . . ." (2 Chronicles 17:6). Similarly, it is written, "From the straits did I call upon God; and He answered me with expansiveness" (Psalms 118:4). This verse alludes to the two aspects of the liberation. First, in the physical phase, we are in the straits and are humbled totally before God. Then God answers expansively, when our soul is liberated and we sing praises to Him.

This dichotomy of the body and soul is reflected in *tefillin*, which are put on the hand and the head. We are commanded to tie one *tefillin* on the hand, *yodecho*. It is tied on the weaker hand, which is usually the left one. And these words that God commands you should be "on your hearts," on both your hearts—the desire to do good and the desire to do evil. The heart itself is divided into two: the good and the bad. The other *tefillin* placed on the head represent *toe-toe-fos*, two parts of the head: the mind and the soul. The hand is the energy of Jacob, (*yaakov*), the letters of which can read *li-ekev*; *ekev* means heel as in I need to humble myself as low as my heel. And the head is the energy of *Yisrael*, the letters of which can be read, *li rosh*, I am raised up to my head with joy.

Thus, if we are totally humbled, we can experience

a physical redemption, which can be followed by the spiritual redemption that comes with a raised head.

When the Israelites came out of the Red Sea, they sang a song of praise to God (Exodus 15:1–21). This song contained several verses with repeated words and phrases: "I will sing to the God, for He has (*go-oh, go-oh*) risen up in triumph"; "Your right hand, God, is majestic in strength: Your right hand, God, shattered the enemy"; and "Who is like You, God, among the heavenly powers? Who is like You, majestic in holiness?" These repeated phrases allude to the spiritual balance that is in the world. There are opposing forces; up and down, far and near, that represent heaven and earth. There was also the physical Egypt, the Egyptian army that was pursuing the Israelites but was far from them, and the spiritual Egypt, the guardian angel of Egypt that was near them.

Each of these opposites is as a chord of music on its own, but a song makes them a symphony. It is a song of praise to the One and Only God, wherein we acknowledge the unity of all things, the common origin of all of them in God. The song pulls together all the strands and makes of them all one unity. Therefore, song is *shirah*, from the word *yashar*, "straight," as in the verse, "God, when he made man, made him straightforward (*yashar*), but man invents endless subtleties of his own" (Ecclesiastes 7:29). To most people the world is a collection of numerous things and many opposites. But the Jewish people are called *yeshurun*; "they make out of the many, one" (*E pluribus unum*); *yeshurun*, they sing, make a symphony, out of the many musical chords.

Shabbos also has a unifying quality, as the Zohar says, "*Shabbos* gets unified in the secret of the One." The upper world and the lower world move toward harmony. The higher aspect of the soul, the *neshama yeseirah*, descends to earth while the earth itself is uplifted. Peace reigns between heaven and earth.

Therefore, *Shabbos* is a very appropriate time to sing, as it is written, "A Psalm, a song for the *Shabbos* day. It is good to thank God and to sing praise to Your Name . . ." (Psalms 92:1).

On this night, when all opposites unite and become one, we have the opportunity to unify every facet of our personality. And when we do, the resulting song will be the sweetest music ever heard.

All the lands sang to God, but once the land of Israel was chosen, songs were only heard from there. All the nations sang, but when the Jewish people were singled out, then only they sang. This means that at first they were mixed with the voices of the other nations; their song was diluted with the voice of the others. After they were chosen, however, their song was heard loud and clear. It was the song of the Israelites when they emerged from the Red Sea. As it is written, "The song of all songs (*shir hashirim*)" (Song of Songs 1:1). And the Midrash says, "*shir hashirayim*" (*Song of Songs Rabbah* 1). It is the song to the One who made us *shirayim*, "singled out," leftovers in the world.

"Have no fear," Moses answered. . . ."

At first the fear of the Israelites was on the physical level. They were terrified. And there was a danger that the fear would turn into paranoia—into a fear totally physical that was devoid of any spirituality. After Moses spoke to them and gave them faith and hope, they raised their fear to a higher level—"And the people feared God" and they burst out in song. The fear of God lifts man's spirit, lightens his burden, and fills him with joy.

What is the test for the proper fear of God? If the fear causes you to sing out from a heart full of joy.

Let us therefore join the 600,000 Israelites who feared God and sang to Him with joy.

When the Jewish people left Egypt they became the armies of God, as it is written, ". . . for in this self-same day I have brought your armies out of the land of Egypt" (Exodus 12:17). At first they were the servants of Pharaoh; their bodies were enslaved to him. With the Exodus they became the servants of God Who brought them forth. The parting of the Red Sea raised them to new spiritual heights: they were then the children of God, as we recite in our prayers, "Who brought His children through the parts of the Red Sea" (*Siddur*, Evening Prayers).

Similarly, it is written, "Six days you shall eat unleavened bread (*matzah*), and on the seventh day shall be a retreat dedicated to God your Lord, when you may do no work" (Deuteronomy 16:8). This can mean as follows. Six days you will partake in *matzah*, as the word *mitzo*, "battle"; until the sixth day after the Exodus there was still a battle, and the Jews were as soldiers and servants of the king. They were on the level of Jacob (Yaakov), meaning cunning, in battle. By the seventh day, they had already gone through the Red Sea and were bound and dedicated to God, as children are to their father. They were then on the level of Israel (*Yisrael*), meaning straight, and also *shir kel*, "sing to God." Once you have finished with the battle, you are ready to sing to God.

It is written, ". . . in their terror they clamored to the Lord for help . . ." (Exodus 14:10). The Midrash comments, "They assumed the trade of the forefathers, of Abraham, Isaac, and Jacob, who all prayed whenever they were in trouble" (*Exodus Rabbah* 15).

Why did these downtrodden, humiliated, and oppressed slaves attempt to emulate the lofty traits of relatives of long ago? It was because those traits were indelibly etched into their hearts, although they were deeply concealed. As it is written, "I am dark but lovely, daughters of Jerusalem . . ." (Song of Songs 1:5). I appear dark because of my exile and oppression, but I am really lovely inside. And as soon as I am liberated, I can resume my lovely deeds and emulate the ways of my ancestors. Similarly, at the final redemption when the *Mashiach* will come, the hearts of the Jewish people that are covered by stone will be restored to flesh. And they will immediately resort to the ways of their forefathers, as it is written, "Look, I will send you the prophet Elijah before the great and terrible day of the Lord comes. He will reconcile the hearts of the fathers to the sons, and sons to their fathers" (Malachi 3:24). When the prophet Elijah comes to announce the final redemption, the hearts of the sons will immediately revert to the traits of the fathers.

And when the Jewish people are able to relate to God as their fathers did, then they become strong and full of energy and merit the full redemption. They no longer need to imitate; they can do it on their own. As it is written, "He is my God, and I will glorify Him; He is my father's God, and I will exalt Him" (Exodus 15:7). Not only could I relate to Him because He is my father's God, but now I can relate to him on my own—"He is my God." And we recite this in our prayers, too. "Our God, and the God of our fathers . . ." (*Siddur*, Silent Prayer). Not only can I pray to Him because I get strength from my fathers but I can also do it on my own, too.

Let us also look back to the deeds of our fathers and emulate their strong faith and trust in God. Then our hearts will be healed, and we will begin to feel the faith in the deepest depths of our heart on our own.

It is written, "While the king reclines on his couch, my spikenard gives forth its scent" (Song of Songs 1:13).

"While the King reclines on his couch" means, while the King of the universe, God, reclines, He has not yet given the Torah to the Jewish people. "My spikenard," my good deeds and my praise to Him after the parting of the sea, gives forth its scent; the song becomes part of the divine Perfume, the heavenly scent of the Torah. Although the Torah was not yet given, the song of the Jewish people is included in the Torah. And why did this happen? It is because the Jewish people are part of the Torah itself; their nature and the nature of the Torah are identical. The Torah is made of the Names of God, and so are the Jewish people.

A prince was captured by villains and taken to another kingdom. There he was made to serve a foreign king, until his father arrived with an army and fought for his release. The battle was fierce, resulting in many casualties. Finally the prince was saved, and the king greeted him with great love. As the armies marched back home, the prince, who rode on a royal steed, sang a song of praise to his father. He sang of the bravery and devotion, of the heroism and victory. Finally, the king and his troops arrived at the capital. The king was greeted with great jubilation and later with an official victory reception. How surprised the prince was to hear the words of his song being read as the official welcome to the king!

As the children of God, our very words can become part of the Torah scroll, the eternal praise of God, and the teaching for all generations. What an opportunity that was! How much more careful we have to be with what we say and, even more so, with what we say to our children. For our words will be the song sung by the next generation, and the next, until the *Mashiach* comes.

It is written, "The song of songs, which is Solomon's" (Song of Songs 1:1). The Midrash interprets the words as follows: *Shir*, "let us sing," *hashirim*, for He who made us leftovers, His chosen portion in the world (*Song of Songs Rabbah* 1). Another interpretation of this verse is, let us sing to Him who made us singers in the world. God made the Jewish people singers, as it is written, "This people I have formed for myself, they shall proclaim my praises" (Isaiah 43:21).

Betzalel was an excellent smith. His designs and workmanship were unparalleled. The vessels that he fashioned were of such high quality and perfection that people would remark, "Ah, look at this! A betzalel!" The vessel itself was synonymous with his name, and it would "sing" his praise. Similarly, when the creation is undamaged, it sings the praises of

God. And therefore, the Jewish people, who were created to be witnesses for God and fulfill their purpose, they too "sing" the praise of the Creator.

There is another and deeper meaning. There are the physical and the spiritual worlds. They are very different from each other, but are not separate. The physical world is incomplete without the spiritual world, as material is without form. Similarly, the spiritual world is like an idea without words. The Midrash compares this to a blind man who could walk but of course could not see, who carried on his shoulders a lame man who could see but of course could not walk. The body is the blind man, and the soul is the lame man. Neither the body nor the soul is complete without the other. But together they are a complete unit, and they sing praises to God. Therefore the Jewish people are called *Shulamis*, from the word *sholem*, "complete," because they are connected to the spiritual world.

Therefore, when we kiss the essence of the spiritual, when we are so close to God that we are suffused and enthused with His spirit, then our souls sing out the very song that our Creator put inside us. "*Shir*," we sing; "*hashirim*," the song, "*asher l'shlomo*," of God who is complete. "*Yishokeini m'neshikos pi'hu*—Let him kiss me with the kisses of His mouth." Because I am so close to God, as a kiss, therefore the song that comes out of me is the same one with which He kissed me.

It is written, "He brings out the prisoners (*b'choshoros*) into prosperity" (Psalms 68:7).

The Midrash interprets the word *b'choshoros* as *b'cho*, "crying," and *shoros*, "singing" (*Numbers Rabbah* 3). Literally, when God releases you from prison, you cry and laugh at the same time, as do people who are overcome with joy and relief. But there is a deeper meaning. When the Israelites were slaves in Egypt, both their crying and their singing were as in prison. When they cried they cried for the wrong reasons, and when they were thankful, it was also for the wrong reasons.

A prince was taken prisoner by a band of thieves. He was made to sleep on the rocky ground in their mountain hideout. The prince, who was terribly uncomfortable, cried himself to sleep each night. When they shared the stolen food with him, he thanked and praised their generosity. Finally, he was freed by his father and returned to the palace. Again, the prince cried to his father and praised him for his daring rescue.

Similarly, the Israelites, when freed from the bondage of Egypt, cried out to God at the waters of the Red Sea. They were already liberated from slavery; now they wanted complete freedom. And that they accomplished with the crossing of the Red Sea, and they sang a song of praise to God. Their praises were about their relationship to God, and not merely about their physical rescue. Their crying and their song were freed from prison.

We too, on this seventh day, have the opportunity to lift our voices and beg for the final redemption. And when we sing the song of the Red Sea, we can have a taste of what the final song will sound like.

In the song of praise after the parting of the Red Sea, the Israelites sang, "Who is like You, majestic in holiness, worthy of awe and praise, who works wonders?" (Exodus 15:11). The Midrash comments, "Not, who has done wonders, but who does wonders all the time" (*Exodus Rabbah* 15).

The Jewish people were chosen to be the witnesses for God's kingdom. They were blessed with special eyes to see the wonders of God and to tell the world about them. But when they are in exile, they are blinded by their oppression and can no longer see. And therefore, when they are finally liberated, they are once again able to see the perpetual wonders and declare, "Who is like God who does wonders all the time?" And what they see is the truth about the world. It is not merely governed by natural laws that are apparent to everyone. Rather, it is governed by God, Who, with His absolute free will, wills the world at every instant. There is no one and nothing in the world that compels God to continue the patters of the past. It is a wondrous universe that is renewed all the time. Still, its wonder is veiled behind its material nature, the laws of cause and effect, and it is not seen by the common folk. As it is written, "Take the veil from my eyes, that I may see the marvels that spring from Your law" (Psalms 119:18).

It is written, ". . . and behold the Egyptians were pursuing them, and the Israelites clamored to God . . ." (Exodus 14:10). The Midrash comments, "And how beloved is the sound of the prayer of the Israelites, as it is written in the Song of Songs, 'Let me hear your voice, for your voice is sweet' (Song of Songs 2:14)" (Exodus Rabbah 15).

The spiritual world is always balancing itself. When the Jewish people go forth to proclaim God as King, the powers of evil and perversity rise up against them. Then how do they ever manage to complete their mission? It is only by the power that God granted them at the Exodus, the power to be liberated from the severest oppression. Whenever they mention the event, they are uplifted by realizing that with God's help there is no power strong enough to enslave them. And God wanted this fact to be etched indelibly in their memory. Therefore, as soon as they left Egypt, He orchestrated a great problem for them. The Egyptians pursued them just so they could wonder how they would ever be rescued from them. They cried out to God and immediately the water parted, and they passed through unharmed. The mighty Egyptian army perished, and the Israelites emerged stronger and emboldened. Then they realized that with prayer they can have the redemption of the Exodus repeated; this is a lesson that they needed for all future troubles.

On the seventh day, nearing the end of the Passover holiday, let us call out to God, that He have mercy on us as in the days of old and redeem us one final time, quickly in our days.

It is written, "Moses took the bones of Joseph with him, because Joseph had exacted an oath from the Israelites: 'Some day,' he said, 'God will show His care for you, and then, as you go, you must take my bones with you'" (Exodus 13:19).

Joseph was the first one to live in the Egyptian Exile, and he prepared the land to receive the rest of his family and their descendants. His love for them was so strong, his empathy so real, that he already felt the pain of their future oppression. He therefore exacted an oath; his fate was tied with theirs. Whatever would happen to them would happen to him too. Therefore he merited the liberation of his bones from the Egyptian prison, and none other than Moses took his bones. As it is written, ". . . and to him who puts a way, I will show the salvation of God" (Psalms 50:23). Joseph is he who prepared the way, and he therefore receives the salvation.

Therefore, the exile starts with Joseph and ends with Joseph. It starts with Joseph, when the new king conveniently forgot all the benefit that Joseph brought to Egypt and was no longer favorably inclined to the Hebrew immigrants. And the exile ended with Joseph, when Moses took his bones and brought them out of Egypt.

What great merit we would have to bring about the final redemption by showing the way and making the way for others.

It is written, "We will make you plaited braids of gold set with beads of silver" (Song of Songs 1:11).

When God liberated the Israelites from Egyptian bondage, they were not yet worthy. They were removed with a strong arm, because of the great mercy of God; they were forced to leave against the Egyptians' will and the unworthiness of the Israelites. Although they were free, it was not complete salvation because it was dependent on the mercy of God. When they reached the Red Sea, however, they again needed to be saved. This time it was different. They trusted wholeheartedly in God and in Moses His servant, and that trust merited them complete freedom. Now their salvation was complete and made their "earnings," the spoils from the Red Sea, more numerous than that of the Exodus itself. And these are the "braids of gold," the golden salvation of the sea, in contrast to the silver, lesser salvation of the Exodus.

This is similar to another verse, "Show us Your mercy O God, and grant us Your salvation" (Psalms 85:8). First we need God's mercy because we are not worthy of His help; otherwise we would already have been helped. Then, because we realize that we cannot survive without Him, we merit His full salvation. Thus, in Egypt, we needed His mercy and were therefore forbidden to leave our premises or witness the event of the firstborn being smitten, lest we too perish in the plague. Were we then more worthy than the Egyptians? Later at the parting of the Red Sea, when the Israelites merited the salvation, they witnessed the destruction of the Egyptian army.

We too hope and pray that soon in our days, in the merit of our faith and trust in God's help, we will witness salvation of all that is good, and the redemption of our people from all the exiles.

It is written, "Then Moses and the Israelites sang this song to the Lord" (Exodus 15:1). The Midrash comments, "'Then,' but not before. Although God had been from all eternity, He did not settle into His throne until the Jewish nation sang praises to Him" (*Exodus Rabbah* 15).

Yes, God exists from the infinite past to the infinite future. But which of His creatures could possibly be worthy to receive Him as King? All is naught compared to His majesty, power, and awesome wisdom. Still, the truth is that He cares for each and every one of His creatures, as a parent would tend to the needs of his children.

We can compare this to birds who were in the care of an ornithologist, a professor who was the recognized world authority in his field. The birds wanted to communicate with their keeper, but were reluctant. After all, they thought, why would the professor, who is a thousand times smarter than they, want to have anything to do with them. An older bird admonished them, "This professor feeds you and studies you day and night. Of course he cares about you!"

Similarly, when the Israelites were in exile, they thought themselves too lowly to receive God as their King. Then when they were liberated, they realized that God cares for them all the time, and He freed them from bondage. They immediately broke out in song to proclaim God's kingdom.

We too, when we realize that God is the cause of all events down to their minutest detail and realize that we are in the care of the wisest and most powerful being, we are immediately filled with joy.

It is written, "Then Moses and the Israelites sang this song to the Lord" (Exodus 15:1). The Midrash comments, "'Then,' but not before. Although God had been from all eternity, He did not settle into His throne until the Jewish nation sang praises to Him" (*Exodus Rabbah* 15).

King Solomon said, "The glory of God is to keep things hidden, but the glory of kings is to fathom them" (Proverbs 25:2). Before God created the universe, He was the almighty, unfathomable God. After the creation, He became the manifest and knowable king. This is what separates the six week days from the *Shabbos*. The six weekdays are "the glory of God," whereas the *Shabbos* is "the glory of kings."

This is like a king who built his new palace on an island. The architects and builders worked year-round. No one was permitted to visit the site until the palace was completed. When it was finally completed, and thousands of visitors ferried back and forth to see the wonder, they spoke of its glory, marveled at its beauty, and praised the king for his majesty.

Similarly, before the universe was created, there was no one to praise God. But with the creation, there came also the kingdom: the manifestation of God's glory and omniscience. This was especially so after the creation of man, who, upon seeing the wonders of the universe, sang praises to the King. These songs of praise reached a peak with the Israelites, who, as the new subjects of the King, sang his praise at the Red Sea. Thus the fullness of God's sovereignty was not manifest until the Israelites said, "God will reign for ever and ever" (Exodus 15:18).

On this seventh day of Passover, let us fathom the glory of our King and see that His Kingdom is infi-nite. We will then quickly awaken from the slumber of the exile and sing the praises of God.

"The Lord said to Moses, 'What is the meaning of this clamor? Tell the Israelites to strike camp'" (Exodus 14:15).

The prophet declares, "And it will be, that before they call, I will answer; and while they are yet speaking, I will hear" (Isaiah 65:24). The answer of God, His salvation, needs only to become manifest; it is always really there. But being in exile we are blind to the divine plan. We do not see that the exile is leading to redemption. On the contrary, we feel that we will be stuck in the exile forever, as we unfortunately feel today. But as sure as the morning follows the night, so too our redemption will come. As it is written, "In the evening one lies down weeping, but with dawn—a cry of joy!" (Psalms 30:6).

This cycle of exile and redemption is alluded to in the blessing of Isaac to his son Jacob. He said, "The voice (*hakol*) is the voice (*kol*) of Jacob . . ." (Genesis 27:22). The first *kol* has no letter *vov*; it is not full. The second *kol* has a letter *vov* and is full. First there is the crying voice of Jacob in the midst of affliction, which is followed by the joy when the redemption comes. Fortunate is he who lives to see the outcome of God's plan in his lifetime, although often, we do not fathom it until we are in the realm of souls after our demise. Thus when the Israelites, after 210 years of slavery, saw the destruction of their oppressors in the waters of the Red Sea, the plan of God was manifest and they burst into song. The voice of Jacob was then full.

The Midrash says, ". . . the Israelites looked up and saw the Egyptians close behind. In their terror they clamored to the Lord . . ." (*Exodus Rabbah* 15). They assumed the trade of the forefathers, of Abraham, Isaac, and Jacob who all prayed whenever they were in trouble. But as soon as the dough soured, they said, "Were there no graves in Egypt that you brought us to die in the wilderness? See what you have done to us by bringing us out of Egypt!"

The first reaction of the Israelites to their plight was to call out to God. That is their true nature.

A prince was captured by villains and taken to a remote island. There, he was indoctrinated to serve the rogue chief. His captives asked him at every opportunity, "Who is your king?" And he had to answer, "Master Kahn, the king of the thieves." After months of brainwashing, the prince repeated the answer automatically. After a frantic search of some two years, the king's soldiers finally discovered the hideout of the kidnappers. Stealing into their camp in the dead of the night, the soldiers did not recognize the prince directly. They spotted a youth sleeping under blankets, held his mouth as they quickly roused him from his sleep, and asked him, "Who is the king?" The lad, shocked from his deep sleep, blurted out, "My father!," whereupon the soldiers seized him and whisked him away toward his home. But the villains woke and gave chase. When the prince saw Master Kahn, he yelled, "Oh, no, Master Kahn! Why are you taking me away from him? He is king of the thieves!"

Similarly, the Israelites were enslaved in Egypt against their will. When Moses heralded their imminent redemption, they left in great haste to be servants of God. And when the Egyptians pursued them, they reacted by calling out to God. Yet with time, their old habits took over.

This is like baking dough. When it is baked quickly, it is *matzah*; when let to stand, it is *chometz*, leavened bread, which is forbidden during Passover. Similarly, the Israelites had to leave quickly before they changed. They were unschooled to serve God; still, doing so was their nature, and they did so by reflex. When they received the Torah at Mount Sinai, however, they had the tools for proper conduct: faith and action. And therefore they were ready to serve God even after contemplating the commandments.

We too must quickly run to do the will of God and not hesitate, lest the influence of our environment get the better of us. When we are strong in our faith and steeped in the teachings of the Torah, we can afford to contemplate, investigate, and linger with the understanding of the commandments.

It is written, "Then Moses and the Israelites sang to the Lord. . . ." Then, but not before, although they had a lot to sing about after the Exodus, when they brought great riches out with them. But the spoils of the Red Sea were greater still. What was the nature of these spoils?

There were physical and spiritual spoils. The physical ones were the many utensils of gold and silver that the Israelites borrowed from their Egyptian overlords in lieu of payment for their slavery. And the spiritual spoils were the redeemable elements of Egyptian culture that the Israelites adapted to their way of life. These are called the holy sparks in exile. As it is written, "And that you may tell in the ears of your son, and your sons son, what things I have done in Egypt, and my signs (*o'so'sai*) which I

have done among them; that you may know that I am the Lord" (Exodus 10:2). The word *o'so'sai* also means letters. This refers to the letters of the Hebrew alphabet with which the Torah is written. Those letters were in exile among the Egyptians, and I liberated them, by liberating the Israelites from among them. They took those letters out with them. And from these letters were formed both aspects of the Torah: the written and the oral. The Written Torah is kept by mentioning the written verses pertaining to the Exodus daily. The Oral Torah that was formed was kept by the song that came forth from the hearts of the people at the Red Sea. The Written Law, associated with the Exodus, is ink on parchment. But the Oral Law that grew from the parting of the Red Sea is the very heart of the Jewish people, of they and their sons and of generations to come. Thus the spoils of the Red Sea were even greater.

Let us connect to the song of our people—a song sung to God for all generations past and future. And then we will hear the echoes of that very song from the hearts and mouths of our children.

It is written, "He brings out the prisoners (*b'choshoros*) into prosperity" (Psalms 68:7). The Midrash interprets the word *b'choshoros* as *b'cho*, "crying," and *shoros*, "singing." Literally, when God releases you from prison, you cry and laugh at the same time, as do people who are overcome with joy and relief.

Liberation sometimes comes because of crying and at other times because of singing. In the exile who can sing? It is then by crying that we prepare our hearts and humble ourselves to receive the help of God. But when help has already come, then we can achieve the same through joy and song. Thus at the inception of the Jewish nation these two paths were established. If we are not yet worthy, as was the state of the Israelites at the Exodus, then we achieve redemption by crying. And if we are worthy, then we can be redeemed with joy and singing, as by the parting of the Red Sea.

If we cleanse our hearts and have complete faith and trust in God, we too will be able to sing our way out of this present exile and merit the final and complete redemption. As it is written, "Then our mouths shall fill with laughter and our tongues with song. Then word will go round the nations, 'The Lord has done great things for them'" (Psalms 126:2).

The Israelites sang, "God is a warrior: God is His name" (Exodus 15:3). The Zohar comments, "Rabbi

Eliezer said, It is written, 'It is therefore told in the Book of God's Wars, Vahev and Suphah and the gorges of Arnon' (Numbers 21:14). Although it is God's war, still, it leads to love [*vahev* = *ahavah*] in the end [*suphah* = *b'sophah*]."

God's Name is Peace, (*shalom*), and He wars with His name. Therefore the outcome of the war is the establishment of peace by vanquishing tyrants and liberating the downtrodden and oppressed. And when peace comes at the end of a war, it is witness to its intention to establish God's kingdom and bring tranquility to the earth and its inhabitants. And even when the other nations want to war with us, we want peace, as King David said, "I am for peace, but when I speak, they want war" (Psalms 120:7). Thus if the Jewish nation is worthy, it establishes peace after a war with an aggressive nation.

All this is possible because of the Torah, whose paths lead to peace. And those who cleave to the Torah always strive and establish peace.

Peace is the final resting place where everything is supposed to be. And therefore we need to work during the six work days and rest on the *Shabbos*. During the work days our world is unsettled, is at "war," and needs fixing to find its place. We work. We help things, money, and people find their place. And when they do, they are at peace, and it is the *Shabbos*, the Divine day of rest.

Similarly, there were six days after the Exodus; on the seventh day the Red Sea parted, followed by the song of praise. For six days, the Israelites were at war with their own attraction to worship and the Egyptian culture that they had adopted. On the physical level, too, they were being pursued by their slave masters. Then, with a final battle, came peace at last; both the Israelites and the Egyptians found their place: the oppressors at the bottom of the Sea and the former slaves at the shore with a song of praise to God on their lips.

May we merit, soon in our days, the final and everlasting peace, for us and all of mankind.

"He brought them forth with silver (*kesef*) and gold (*zahav*) . . ."(Psalms 105:37). This is symbolic of the both the love and fear that were established in the hearts of the Jewish people with their liberation. The Exodus itself was done with the deepest love of God, as it is written, "I remember the unfailing devotion of your youth, the love of your bridal days, when you followed me in the wilderness, through a land unsown" (Jeremiah 2:2). Then, at the parting of the Red Sea, there came upon the Israelites an

awesome fear of God, as it is written, ". . . and the people feared God. . . ." The revelations at the Red Sea were far greater than at the Exodus, and they reached levels of prophesy. How is it that the fear of God raised them higher spiritually than the love of God?

Love and passion are emotional states that can be awakened in a person. They involve the physiology of the body—the quickening of the heartbeat, the secretion of chemicals of all kinds into the bloodstream, and the movement of cells. The person feels an actual tug; his heart starts to race and his feet start to dance, his voice breaks out in song, and his spirit soars. But unfortunately, as this surge of love rises, it also falls. The person can be left without any of the buoyancy and glow in his heart. And the love is gone. Awe, on the other hand, is a contemplative state of mind. The person establishes certain ideas in his mind about another that make him feel respect and reverence. This can remain with him forever, as it is written, "The fear of the Lord is pure, enduring forever" (Psalms 19:10).

A prince ran away from the palace and wandered through the provinces of the kingdom. One day as he thought about his parents, a passion welled in his heart, and he started out for the palace. After days of travel he was finally inside the palace walls. He was greeted with much emotion, given a bath and food, and was put to bed. Awakening the next morning, he was back to his brutish ways, as always. What happened to his passions? He lacked the awe, the respect and reverence for his parents.

Love is the movement toward; awe is being there. Love is the passion of courting; awe is the marriage based on mutual respect.

Let us also move to the level of awe of God, to have an everlasting bond for all time.

It is said of the Israelites at the Red Sea, ". . . and they believed in God. . . ." Why now? Didn't they already believe in God?

The Ramban, Rabbi Moses ben Nachman, writes in his commentary that the reason God lets us witness miracles is to establish that He is the Master of the Universe. That is because a miracle teaches us not to take the laws of nature for granted, as if they have an independent power. It is God who established and causes the laws to be effective. Therefore, when the Israelites saw the awesome miracles of the Red Sea, how all the natural laws were subverted, with water stiff as stone, yet viscous, while the seabed lay dry as a desert, they believed in the God of creation, and as if they had never believed before.

———————

The Israelites sang, "Who is like You O Lord among the powers, (*bo'eilim*) God? Who is like You majestic in holiness, awesome in praise, doing wonders" (Exodus 15:11). In the Midrash the word *eilim*, "powers," is read as *il'mim*, "mute ones": Who is like you, God, who tolerates the blasphemy of the wicked and is silent? Who is like You, God, who tolerates the desecration of Your own people, and is silent? (*Exodus Rabbah* 15).

There are times that the kingdom of God is concealed, as in the exile of His people. Then the laws of nature prevail. We look around and see nothing but immutable laws. God is silent. It is the historical moment of *il'mim*, "the mute." There are other times when God reveals His kingdom in all its glory, and His people enjoy liberation. It is then the time of "majestic in holiness, doing wonders." When the Israelites stood at the shore of the Red Sea and watched their salvation, they realized that both the mute and the majesty of miracles are one. It is the same God Who is silent in the time of exile and Who performs great miracles and liberates His people.

———————

The Egyptians made the Israelites work in the fields with mortar, stone, and bricks; they hauled, lifted, built, dug, and did numerous other tasks. For making the Israelites work, the Egyptians were punished with a multitude of plagues. At the Red Sea, the Egyptians chased them, united, and with singular purpose. Therefore they were punished in one single stroke and were drowned in the sea. Who could resist bursting into song at that instant?

Similarly there is the worship of God with the fulfillment of the 613 commandments and the multitude of laws and customs. And then there are acts, such as repentance, the love and awe of God, that allow you to stand before God in one stroke, in one instant.

May we merit that we return to God with one stroke, and cause the final redemption, which will also come in one stroke, which will unite the world and establish the kingdom of God forever.

43

An Abbreviated History of the Egyptian Exile and Redemption

Year 2018   Abraham was 70 years old, and on the fifteenth day of *Nissan*, God made a covenant with Abraham, saying, "Know for sure that your descendants will be foreigners in a land that is not theirs for 400 years. They will be enslaved and oppressed. But I will finally bring judgment against the nation who enslaves them, and they will then leave with great wealth." Five years later, when Abraham was 75, he left Haran.

Year 2023   Abraham leaves his land and his father's home.

Year 2034   Abraham was 86 years old, and Ishmael was born.

Year 2047   Abraham was 99 years old, and he was commanded to perform the covenant of circumcision.

Year 2048   Abraham was 100 years old and Isaac was born. Ishmael was 14 years older than Isaac.

Year 2085   Abraham was 137 years old and Isaac was 37 years old when God commanded Abraham to take his son as an offering. When Sarah, Isaac's mother, heard of this, she died at age 127, after giving birth at 90.

Year 2108   Isaac was 60 years old and Jacob was born.

Year 2123   Abraham died. Jacob was simmering a stew when Esau came home; he sold his birthright to Jacob.

Year 2171   Jacob was 63 years old. Esau went and married the daughter of Ishmael. Following this, Ishmael died.

Year 2185   Jacob was 77, and was in the house of Laban his uncle. In the year 2192 he married Leah and Rachel, who were both 21 years old. Rachel later died at age 36, and Leah was 44. Starting with the first year after his marriage, Reuven was born, the second year Shimeon, the third year, 2195, Levi was born (and died at age 137). Joseph was born in the year 2199, when Jacob was 91 years old, which was the fourteenth year that Jacob worked for his uncle. And he said to Laban, "Send me away and let me go to my land." In the year 2216 Joseph was sold into slavery and was taken to Egypt, and he was 17 years old. Isaac, Joseph's grandfather, lived another 12 years after Joseph was sold.

Year 2229   Joseph was 30 years old when he was brought before the Pharaoh to interpret his dream. (He spent one year in the house of Potifar, ten years in prison, plus 2 more, equalling 13 years.) Isaac died one year before Joseph stood before the Pharaoh.

Year 2238   Jacob was 120 years old, on the fifteenth day of *Nissan*, when he went down to Egypt.

Year 2332   The enslavement of the Israelites began. The "exile" lasted 400 years from the birth of Isaac; the "enslavement," from the death of Levi, when they had been in Egypt 94 years, lasted for 116 years; the "cruelest oppression" lasted 84 years, from the birth of Miriam in the year 2362 until the year 2448.

Year 2368   Moses was born to Amram the son of K'hos, the son of Levi, when his mother Yocheved was 130 years old, and was the twenty-sixth generation since the creation of the world. He was 80 years old when he stood before the Pharaoh and said,

"Thus spoke the Lord, Let my people go!" The following *Nissan* the Israelites were liberated from Egypt.

Year 2448 The Exodus. It was 400 years since the birth of Isaac. And the parting of the Red Sea occurred on the twenty-first day of *Nissan*, which is the seventh day since the Exodus. On the sixteenth of *Iyar* the *manna* fell from heaven, because for thirty days they ate from the *matzos* that they brought with them from Egypt. A few weeks later, on the sixth day of *Sivan*, the Israelites received the Ten Commandments at Mount Sinai.

44

Laws and Customs of Passover

he laws and customs of Passover are outlined in the Torah, and elaborated in a separate tractate of mishnah *Pesachim*, with talmudic commentary of some 156 pages. They are also derived from the Rambam (Rabbi Moses ben Maimon), in the *Laws of Leavened and Matzah*, and the *Shulchan Aruch, Orech Chaim*, chapters 429 through 493. They are far too numerous to mention fully, and the reader is referred to the traditional texts on the subject. However, several of the prominent ones are summarized below.

THE ORDER OF THE FOUR PORTIONS

The *Shabbos* before Rosh Chodesh, the 1st of *Adar*, the month before *Nissan* in a leap year, is called *Shabbos Parshas Shekalim*. Two Scrolls of the Law are removed from the Holy Ark. In the first the weekly portion is read, followed by the portion of *Shekalim*, which is read for the *Maftir* (Exodus 30:11–16). If Rosh Chodesh occurs on *Shabbos*, then the reading of the portion of *Shekalim* is done on that day. The reading deals with the giving of the half-shekel tax for the counting of the census.

The *Shabbos* before Purim is called *Shabbos Parshas Zachor*, and the portion of *Zachor* is read (Deuteronomy 25:17–19). It commands the Jewish people to remember the evil of the Amalekites and to never forget their deeds.

The *Shabbos* before *Parshas Ha'chodesh* is read is *Shabbos Parshas Parah*, the portion of the Red Cow (Numbers 19:1–22). It tells of the ritual purification required of someone who became impure by touching a corpse. As a result of the ritual the person would be pure and allowed to bring the Passover sacrifice.

The *Shabbos* before *Nissan* is called *Shabbos Parshas Ha'chodesh,"* when the portion of the month is read (Exodus 12:1–20). It tells of the commandments of the Passover sacrifice and the preparations for the Exodus from Egypt.

LAWS CONCERNING THE MONTH OF *NISSAN*

1. During the entire month of *Nissan, tachnun*, daily supplication prayers, are not said. Neither should one fast, except for the firstborn on the Eve of Passover, a bride and groom on the day of their wedding, and one who had an evil dream.

LAWS CONCERNING THE SEARCH FOR AND NULLIFYING OF *CHOMETZ*

1. On the night preceding the eve of Passover, immediately after dark, a search for *chometz* (leaven) should be made. A single wax candle is used.

2. Before the search, the premises should be carefully swept and cleaned. All rooms where *chometz* might have been brought, even wine cellars and sheds for wood, must be searched thoroughly. This includes rooms that are "sold" to a non-Jew with the leaven.

3. It is customary before beginning the search to place ten pieces of bread where the searcher may find them.

4. Before beginning to search, make this blessing: "Blessed are You God, our God, King of the universe, who has sanctified us with His commandments and commanded us to perform the removal of the *chometz*."

5. After the search, both the leaven found and the leaven left for eating must be put away in a safe place.

6. Directly after the search, he should nullify it by saying wholeheartedly, "Any *chometz*, or leaven, that is in my possession which I have not seen, have not removed and do not know about, should be annulled and become ownerless, like the dust of the earth."

7. The following morning, the *chometz* is burned, and again wholeheartedly nullified by saying, "Any *chometz*, or leaven, that is in my possession whether I have recognized it or not, whether I have seen it or not, should be annulled and become ownerless, like the dust of the earth."

8. If *chometz* is found during the *Chol Hamoed*, the intermediate days of Passover, it must be burned. If found on *Shabbos* or the Festival *Yom Tov*, it must be covered until the conclusion of the Festival or *Shabbos* and then it should be burned.

9. Anything that has a mixture of leaven in it, even if the leaven itself was already removed but the taste of the *chometz* is still present, it is forbidden to keep. But if it never had leaven in it and was merely cooked before Passover in a vessel used for *chometz*, it is permitted to keep it on Passover.

Laws and Customs Concerning Passover Eve

1. After one-third of the day has elapsed, it is forbidden to eat *chometz*, but it can be used for another hour as feed for animals or can be sold to a non-Jew. After that time it must be burned.

2. After mid-day one should refrain from any work that is not permitted on *Chol Hamoed*, the intermediate days of the Festival.

3. It is forbidden to eat *matzah* the entire day, but light foods may be eaten until the last quarter of the day. After that time, if necessary, one may eat fruit, meat, or fish in moderate amounts, so that he eats the *matzah* at night with great relish.

4. The firstborn should fast on Passover eve. If a feast is held concerning a *mitzvah*, such as the completion of a holy book, then he may join in the feast.

5. *Chometz* may be sold to a non-Jew before Passover, before the fifth hour of daytime on Passover eve. But the selling must be real and complete. After selling it, the non-Jew must remove it to his premises. Either the room where it is found must be let to him, or if the entire room cannot be let to him, then a partition should be made.

6. For vessels that were used to cook *chometz* that one wants to cook in on Passover, the following rules apply:

a) Earthen vessels cannot be purged of *chometz*.

b) Wood, metal and stone, can be purged, as follows: it must be thoroughly cleaned and all rust removed. No matter of any kind may be left in the vessel.

c) A vessel that has not been used for *chometz* for twenty-four hours is filled with water and boiled. The vessels that are being purged are immersed in fully boiling water and are then removed and washed with cold water. Then, they may be used on Passover.

d) A large vessel, which cannot fit into another, is filled with water and boiled. Also, a stone is heated on the fire and dropped into the boiling water so that it overflows.

e) If a vessel cannot be cleansed thoroughly, those spots may be heated until glowing hot and then it is purged as above.

f) The handles of vessels must also be purged, either by immersion, or pouring hot water that is boiling on them.

Laws and Customs of the Seder

1. The Seder table should be set up during the day and requires the following items: wine with a fine appearance; vegetables for the *karpas*; lettuce or horseradish for *moror*; a mixture of figs, nuts, dates, apples, pomegranates, almonds, cinnamon, and ginger for the *charoses*; salt mixed into water for the *mei melach*; three *matzos*; an egg for the *beitza*; the shank bone or neck of the chicken for the *zeroah*; cups for the four cups of wine; a cup for Elijah the prophet; the *Haggadah*; and a seat where one can lean to the left and eat comfortably.

2. The commandment to eat *matzah* and *moror* and to drink four cups of wine is to be performed especially at night. Therefore, the *Kiddush* service is not said until it is definitely night. Then the leader dons a *kittel*, a white robe, as a demonstration of freedom and starts the Seder immediately, so that the young children should not fall asleep before they hear the story of the Exodus.

3. It is important for the leader to explain the reason for each of the Seder elements, to each one according to his understanding.

4. After the *Kiddush* service, each one in the household should drink the greater part of the cup of wine while reclining on the left side. This too is a sign of freedom. Therefore, many women have the custom not to lean on their sides.

5. Then the leader washes his hands without a blessing, dips the *karpas* vegetable in salt water, and distributes it to each member of the household. Then the following blessing is said: "Blessed are You God, our God, King of the universe, who created the fruit of the earth."

6. Then the middle *matzah* is broken. The greater half is put aside for the *Afikomen*, and the smaller part stays in its place. The customs surrounding the *Afikomen* vary. Some hide it, and the children try to find it and give it back only for a price. Others only set it aside, and in some communities the *Afikomen* is grabbed by the children, one from the other. All of the customs have the purpose of keeping the children awake until the story of the Exodus is completed.

7. The dish with the *matzos* is lifted, and the *Ho Lachmo Anya* is recited.

8. The cups are filled again and the youngest child, or anyone else, asks the *Ma Nishtanoh*. The reading of the *Haggadah* follows, and it should be explained plainly, clearly, and dynamically.

9. When reciting the words *vehi sheomdo*, the cups are lifted, and afterward the leader uncovers the *matzah* and shows each item. When he reaches the words—*matzah zu*, this *matzah*, he shows it to his household; *moror ze*, he shows the *moror*; and so on, except with the Passover, he does not lift anything. This is followed by the blessing *Lefichach* and ends with *Go'al Yisrael*—"the One who redeems Israel." We drink the second cup of wine, leaning on the left side.

10. Everyone washes his or her hands and makes the blessing "Blessed are You God, our God, King of the universe, who has sanctified us with His commandments and commanded us regarding washing the hands." Then the leader says the following, "Blessed are You God, our God, King of the universe who brings forth bread from the earth," and "Blessed are You God, our God, King of the universe, who has sanctified us with his commandments and commanded us to eat *matzah*." Then *matzah* is eaten while reclining on the left side.

11. Then a measure as large as a *zayis*, an olive, of bitter herbs, *moror*, is taken, dipped into *charoses*, and the following blessing is made: "Blessed are You God, our God, King of the universe, who has sanctified us with his commandments and commanded us to eat *moror*." No reclining is required for the *moror*.

12. Again, *moror* is taken, placed between two pieces of *matzah*, and the following is said: "This is in memory of the Holy Temple, as Hillel would do; he wrapped the *matzah* and the *moror* and ate them together, as it is written, with *matzah* and *moror* it shall be eaten."

13. The Festival meal is then eaten, followed by the eating of the *Afikomen* and then Grace after the Meal. A blessing is said over the third cup of wine. Then the door is opened for Elijah the Prophet. After that the *Hallel* is recited over the fourth cup of wine. After the *Afikomen* no *matzah* or food should be eaten. One may drink water if very thirsty, but no wine should be drunk after the fourth cup. Then the Passover songs are sung, and we continue discussing the miracle of the Exodus until one falls asleep. It is customary on the first two nights of Passover to omit all the verses except the reading of the *Shma* before retiring for sleep.

LAWS OF THE COUNTING OF THE OMER

1. Starting with the second night of Passover and each night afterward, the *omer* is counted, day by day, until forty-nine days are counted. We stand and say the following blessing: "Blessed are You God, our God, who has sanctified us with his commandments, and commanded us concerning the *omer*." The first night we say, "Today, is the first day of the *omer*." And we continue this way until the seventh day, when we say, "Today is seven days, which is one week, in the *omer*" and so on until the forty-ninth day.

2. If one forgot to count the *omer* at night, he can count it in the daytime, but without a blessing.

3. Men and women should not do work during the days of the counting of the *omer* from sunset until after the counting of the *omer*.

4. In the days of the *omer* one should not marry nor have a haircut. However, some follow the custom of having a haircut or marrying on Rosh Chodesh, the first of the month and also on Lag B'omer, the thirty-third day of the *omer*, and the three days before to the holiday of Shavuos, Pentecost.

45

Prayers and Blessings

Eruv Tavshilin and Eruv Chatzeros

ne is permitted to prepare food to be eaten on the Festival. It is forbidden to prepare food on a Festival for use on another day. When a Festival falls on Friday, however, it is permitted to prepare food for the *Shabbos*. Even so, the rabbis attached a condition: to start cooking for the *Shabbos* on Thursday. This is called an *eruv tavshilin*. It consists of taking *matzah*, along with other cooked food, such as fish, meat, or an egg, and making the following blessing and declaration:

Blessed are You God, our God, King of the universe, Who has sanctified us with His commandments and has commanded us concerning the mitzvah of eruv.

Through this eruv may we be permitted to bake, cook, insulate, kindle flame, prepare, and do anything necessary on the Festival for the sake of the Shabbos, for ourselves and for all Jews who live in this city.

The rabbis also forbade carrying from a private domain of one person to that of another on the *Shabbos*. The sages provided that *matzah* be collected from the dwellings and placed in one of them, as if all those who contributed live in that one domain. This is known as *eruv chatzeros*. The following blessing and declaration are made:

Blessed are You God, our God, King of the universe, Who has sanctified us with His commandments and has commanded us concerning the mitzvah of eruv.

Through this eruv may we be permitted to carry out or to carry in from the houses to the courtyard, and from the courtyard to the houses, from house to house, from courtyard to courtyard, and from roof to roof, all that we require, for ourselves and for all Jews who live in this area, and for all who will move into this area, for all the Shabbos and Festivals of the year.

Kindling Shabbos and Festival Lights

Light the candles. Cover the eyes, and recite the blessing. Then uncover the eyes and look briefly at the candles.

Blessed are you, God, our God, King of the universe, Who has sanctified us with His commandments, and has commanded us to kindle the light of (the Shabbos and of) the Festival.

Blessed are you God, our God, King of the universe, Who has kept us alive, sustained us, and brought us to this season.

Kiddush Service for the Festival

If the *Kiddush* service is on on Friday night, add:

(whisper) And it was evening and it was morning; The sixth day! And heaven and earth were complete; then with the seventh day, God completed His work which he had made, and with the seventh day, He ceased from all His work which He had made. And God blessed the seventh day and made it holy, for with it He had ceased from all His work which He, God, brought into existence in order to continue the work of creation upon it.

Then continue with this prayer:

Welcome my teachers, rabbis, and all others!

Blessed be You, O God, our Lord, King of the universe, Creator of the fruit of the vine.

Blessed be You, O God, our Lord, King of the universe, Who has chosen us from among all peoples, exalted us above all tongues and has sanctified us by His commandments. And You have given us, O God, our Lord, in love, (Shabbos for rest) Festivals of assembly for rejoicing, feasts of rallying and seasons for delight, (this Shabbos day and) the day of this Festival of Passover, the season of our freedom (in love), a convocation to the Sanctuary, a remembrance of the Exodus from Egypt. For You have chosen us; You have sanctified us from among all peoples, (and the Shabbos) *and Your holy Festivals of assembly (in love and in favor) in joy and delight You have given us as an inheritance. Blessed be You, God, Who sanctifies (the* Shabbos) *Israel and the (festive) seasons.*

At the conclusion of *Shabbos,* we add the following:

Blessed be You, God our Lord, King of the universe, Creator of the flames of fire.

Blessed be You, God, our Lord, King of the universe, Who has made a distinction between holy and profane, between light and darkness, between Israel and the nations, between the Seventh Day and the six days of work. You have made the holiday, and You have sanctified the Seventh Day above the six working days; You have set apart Your people, Israel, and sanctified them by Your holiness. Blessed be You, O God, Who has made a distinction between holy and holy.

Blessed are You, O God, our Lord, King of the universe, Who has kept us alive, and has preserved us, and Who has brought us to this season.

This prayer authored by the Kabbalists was said before the counting of the *omer.*

For the sake of the unification of the Holy One, blessed be He, and His Divine Presence, with awe and love, to unify the Name Yud and Heh, and Vov and Heh in perfect unity, in the name of all of Israel. Behold I am prepared and ready to perform the commandment, of counting the omer, as it is written in the Torah: 'You shall then count seven complete weeks after the day following the Passover holiday when you brought the omer as a wave offering until the day after the seventh week, when there will be a total of fifty days. on that fiftieth day you may present new grain as a meal offering to God." May the pleasantness of my Lord, our God, be upon us—may He establish our handiwork for us; our handiwork, may He establish.

After the counting say:

The compassionate one! May He return for us the service of the Temple to its place, speedily in our days. Amen, Selah!

For the conductor, upon Neginos, a psalm, a song. May God favor us and bless us, may He illuminate His countenance with us, Selah. To make known Your way on earth, among all the nations Your salvation. The peoples will acknowledge You, O God, the peoples will acknowledge You, all of them. Nations will be glad and sing for joy, because You will judge the peoples fairly and guide the nations on earth, Selah. Then peoples will acknowledge You, O God, the peoples will acknowledge You, all of them. The earth has yielded its produce, may God, our own God, bless us. May God bless us and may all the ends of the earth fear Him.

We beg You! With the strength of Your right hand's greatness, unite the bundled sins. Accept the prayer of Your nation; strengthen us, purify us, O awesome One, Please, O strong One—those who foster Your oneness, guard them like the apple of an eye. Bless them, purify them, show them pity, may Your righteousness always recompense them. Powerful Holy One, with Your abundant goodness, guide Your congregation. One and only Exalted One, turn Your nation, which proclaims Your holiness. Accept our entreaty and hear our cry, O Knower of mysteries.

Blessed is the Name of His glorious Kingdom for all eternity.

Master of the universe, You commanded us through Moshe, Your servant, to count the omer count in order to cleanse us from our crust of evil and defilement, as You have written in Your Torah: "You shall then count seven complete weeks after the day following the Passover holiday when you brought the Omer as a wave offering until the day after the seventh week, when there will be a total of fifty days, so that the souls of Your people Israel be cleansed of their contamination." Therefore, may it be Your will, God, and the God of our forefathers, that in the merit of the Omer count that I have counted today, may there be corrected whatever blemish I have caused in the sefirah (insert the appropriate sefirah). May I be cleansed and sanctified with the holiness of Above, and through this may abundant bounty flow in all the worlds. And may it correct our lives, spirits, and souls from all sediment and blemish; may it cleanse us and sanctify us with Your exalted holiness. Amen, Selah!

A Prayer, *Yotzer,* for *Parshas Parah Adumah,* the Red Cow

It is impossible to fully express Your great wonders, nor to speak the depth of Your commandments, to understand the strength of Your deeds, to fathom the depth of Your marvels, nor to comprehend Your virtues, to unravel the secret of Your riddles, nor tell the fullness of Your praise, nor reveal the secret of Your commandments, the explicit is hidden, the revealed is unknown, the explained are sealed, the open ones are closed, the engraved ones are merely recorded, the incomplete ones are in surplus, the forbidden from understanding are open to knowledge, the obscure ones are clear, the revealed ones are concealed, the ones easy to interpret are difficult, the most elaborate is without understanding, the easy is difficult, He brings forth from most common the most lofty, from that which is forbidden He brings forth the permitted, and from the impure He brings forth purity. From the forbidden fat, He permits the fat on the heart; from the forbidden blood, He permits the blood of the spleen; from the forbidden meat cooked in milk, He permits the utters; from the forbidden admixture of wool and flax in clothing, He permits the same for the tzitzis; from the forbidden brother's wife whom we may not marry, He permits her when the brother dies without children; from the forbidden married woman, He permits her during battle; from the forbidden Niddah, He permits the virginal flow of the newlywed; from the permitted there is the forbidden, from the forbidden there is the permitted, from the unclean there is the clean, from the clean there is the unclean; a blemish on a part of the body is unclean, while if it spread over the entire body it is clean; if one dies in the house everything is still clean, but if the corpse leaves the house then all is made unclean; the scapegoat on the Day of Atonement forgives all sins, but whoever prepares it defiles his clothing; the Red Cow defiles all who prepare it, yet it removes the harshest of uncleanliness; while its ashes become a chief defiler, it removes the grossest defilement. Therefore, it is impossible to understand the secrets of the Torah, nor to clarify Your commandments, nor enlighten Your decrees. Likewise we must not exchange the explanations of our sages for the more "sensible" ones, nor to let our mind wander and argue against them. It is impossible to know, nor to make known; deeper than the Sheol, what can you know of it? "Her ways are unsteady, yet she doesn't know it" (Proverbs 5:6). Some laws were given with their logic, and others were decreed; some explained to the elders and others only to individuals; some were given to be asked about, and others to purse one's lips; some divinely secret and others are expounded; some spoken of and others to be silent about. And each of the laws where the word decree is found, we mustn't wonder and ask, "Why?" Because it was thus given, as a unit, and who can fathom all of it? But to one with understanding it is correct, and one with insight will comprehend, except of course the reason for the Parah Adumah, the Red Cow, which cannot be understood. And even those with wisdom will not understand it, not any of its details. She has five names as the Five Books of Moshe, [eigel, par, elef, shor, bakar], and unlike other purification offerings, it is a female, to gain atonement for the Golden Calf. They traded God's honor for a cow's offspring, and rebelled as a cow, let his mother come, the cow, and gain atonement for the people. They were insolent with red face, and defiled their pure bodies, let his mother come, the one with the red face, and may the white and ruddy one: God, and lift His face to us. They ground it to stand in the place of the faultless one: Moshe; let his mother who must be faultless, and with her the Faultless One will bring purity to the faultless people. They bowed to an idol full of defect, and were punished having become defective themselves; let the unblemished mother come, and wash off the blood of those who are without blemish. They planned to rebel with the Golden Calf, sacrificed to it and removed their yoke; let his mother who never had a yoke, come, and let her commandment be upon

them like a yoke. They gathered for the idol around the kohen, who became rejected and nearly put to death; let the mother come and be given to the kohen, and atone the sin of the kohen. And as the Golden Calf was burned, so too must the Red Cow be burned. And as it was ground to dust, so too must it be and made dust. And as the idol was thrown on the face of the water, so too must it be thrown on the water. And as the idol made three thousand fall, so too into it throw three kinds of objects [cedar wood, hyssop, crimson wool]. And just as the idol blemished the pure nation, so too, it will make unclean all those who are pure. And just as it made pure the nation that became defiled from it, so too the mother makes pure all those who are impure. And just as its sin was spread for all generations, so too it shall be guarded as an atonement sacrifice for all generations. To wash off the blood, to wash out as if unblemished, to make holy those who are holy, to make righteous those who are burdened; with the cedar branch, for those who branch out as a cedar; with the hyssop, for those who are oppressed and lowly; with the crimson wool, for those whose lips are as crimson; and of the worm, for those who but as worms should not fear. One should not be high as a cedar, because if he will not humble himself as a lowly bush and feel as a worm, he will not be purified with the cedar and the crimson thread; and if he will not allow his heart to flow as water, he will not become pure with the water. And how can a mere grass feel high, before God who is as a consuming fire; And how could a dry grass be haughty, before God who is on most high; the highest of the most high, higher than the cedars, lower than the hyssop, and formed five haughty ones, the ox among the animals, a lion among the beasts, an eagle among the birds, a cedar among the trees, and man from all of them, and a king over them all, who is clothed in majesty.

A Prayer, Yotzer, for Parshas Ha'chodesh, the New Month of Nissan

From the beginning the Lord established Nissan as the first, but he did not reveal its understanding in the book possessed by Adam—he first he revealed it only to You to expound. The calculation must reconcile the movements of the brilliant sun and the dark moon. This was hidden from every people and language and not given to Adam the first man. In this month Sarah regained her youth and was informed that she would give birth. The ripened Isaac who was born at year's end was bound to the altar with a rope; in this merit his offspring was promised redemption. This month that was not revealed to the ancients was reserved to contain new miracles and old ones; it was set as the first of the four New Years. It ushers in the Festivals for the people who camped around four flags; concerning it the Sanhedrin, the eyes of the people, assemble and dispatch witness to seek out the New Moon; it is counted as the New Year for kings and pilgrimage festivals. The *court inserts a month to maintain* Nissan *in its proper season: if crops and fruits are not ripe or the seasons will not be timely, for if only one of these occurs, it may be used in conjunction with another need. It was sanctified at its beginning, after a third, in its middle, and after its majority to observe: to sanctify the New Moon, to take a lamb for the Passover, to celebrate Passover, to cut barley for the* Omer, *and to complete the month in holiness. Its beginning is reserved in every generation for the coming of the pauper riding on a donkey (the Messiah). In observance of a third, Israel stood that day in the bed of Jordan, in the merit of the Passover flame of the middle of* Nissan *the army of Sancherib of Pul was destroyed, the salvation resulting from the cutting of the* Omer *stood by Mordechai the Benjaminite.*

A Prayer, Yotzer, for Shabbos Hagodol, the Great Shabbos

It came to pass at midnight!

Of old, most of the wonders You did perform at night. At the head of the watches is this very night. Full victory came to Abraham, when he divided his company at night.

It happened at midnight!

You judged the king of Gerar in a dream at night; You frightened Laban in the midst of the night; and Israel wrestled with God and prevailed at night.

It happened at midnight!

You struck down the first-born of Egypt at midnight;

and terrified Midian with a loaf of bread in a dream at night; the armies of Sisera You swept away by the stars of the night.

It happened at midnight!

The Assyrian armies that besieged Jerusalem were stricken at night; Bel and his pedestal were overthrown in the darkness of night; To Daniel you revealed Your mysteries at night.

It happened at night!

King Belshatzar of Babylon became drunk of holy vessels and was slain at night; Daniel, saved from the lions' den, interpreted the terrifying dreams of the night; Haman wrote his edicts of hate at night.

It happened at night!

May the day draw near that is neither day nor night. O God, make known that Yours is the day and also the night. Appoint guards over Your city all day and all night. Make bright like day the darkness of the night.

It happened at midnight!

Ended is the order of Passover, according to custom,   statute and law.

As we were worthy to celebrate it this year, so may   we perform it in future years.

O Pure One in heaven above,

Restore the congregation of Israel in Your love.

Speedily lead Your redeemed people

To Zion in joy.

NEXT YEAR IN JERUSALEM

VI

THE REVELATION OF SHAVUOS

Introduction

here were two separate instances of darkness related to the Egyptian Exodus. The first was the ninth plague, as it is written: "Hold out your arm toward the sky that there may be darkness upon the land of Egypt, a darkness that can be touched . . . and thick darkness descended upon the land of Egypt for three days. People could not see one another, and for three days no one could get up from where he was; but all the Israelites enjoyed light in their dwellings" (Exodus 10:21–24). The second instance of darkness happened as they crossed the Red Sea, as it is written: "The pillar of cloud moved from the front and took its place behind them and so came between the Egyptians and the Israelites. And the cloud brought on darkness and early nightfall, but lit up the night, so that one could not come near the other all through the night" (Exodus 14:20). Again, there was darkness for the enemy and light for the Israelites.

There is a stark contrast between these instances and the darkness at Sinai, where it is written, "I will come to you in a thick cloud, in order that the people may hear when I speak with you and so trust you ever after. . . . On the third day, as morning dawned, there was thunder, and lightning, and a dense cloud upon the mountain . . . " (Exodus 19:14). At Sinai the darkness was present not for the enemy, but for the Israelites themselves. It taught them that the world can be dark, without logic, or sense of purpose. Only the Torah can shed light on a man's life by providing the answer to three fundamental questions: where he came from, where he is, and where he is heading. It taught them that all powers and all beliefs are nothing but darkness by comparison.

Receiving the Torah from Sinai was the single most important event for the Jewish nation. It made them part of God's kingdom as His sons and daughters, with a code of conduct made in heaven. It was a demanding code for humans to follow, and they needed outstanding bravery to have accepted it. Who can be as perfect as the Torah demands? Yet, they took the courageous leap of faith. Logic was against them: Why Divine rules for humans? The other nations had already rejected it, and who can blame them? Each in turn had a legitimate excuse. "We are only human," they pleaded. "You can't expect us to keep these laws!"

Even the angels complained and said, "What is man that You have been mindful of him, mortal man that You have taken note of him." (Psalms 8:5). They implored, "Why are You giving the Torah to mankind; it is more fitting for the heavenly spheres." Moses answered the angels, "Although the ideals of the Torah are Divine, it was obviously meant for mankind." And to prove it, Moses challenged them with the following commandments—You should not kill, Honor your father and mother, Do not covet the wife of your neighbor, and so on—which were obviously not meant for angels, but rather for mankind. These commandments indicated that, although it would be difficult, with perseverance they can be observed. And with that, the angels agreed to have the Torah given to the Jewish people.

When the Jewish people heard the first words of God, they fainted lifelessly. With that they learned never to forget how vital the Torah is to their life and that without it there is no life.

And we have not forgotten. In our march through history, as a nation, we have never abandoned the Torah. On the contrary, young and old have tenaciously held firm to its teachings and studied it day and night. This closeness to the Torah not only influenced us but a major portion of humanity as well. They have learned the Torah from us, and several religions are based on its teachings. The entire world is influenced by the Torah's legal system, as it is the basis of the American constitution and the laws of many countries. Our responsibility as People of the Book is to hold the beacon of Divine light aloft for ourselves and the world and to judge ourselves and others with Torah standards, not with creeds of darkness, emptiness, and lies.

The essence of the Torah is wisdom, which lights the darkness of the world, its ignorance and falsehood. Torah teaches the truth about existence and bathes those who receive it with a brilliant light. The Talmud compares this to a man who walked in the dark and was constantly in danger of being injured by thorns, of falling into crevices, being attacked by wild animals, and losing his way. He did not see where he was going. When he lit a torch, however, he was no longer in danger of being injured by thorns, crevices, and wild animals and saw clearly the path for his destination. Similarly, without the Torah, one is totally lost and in great danger of spiritual injury. The Torah lights the path of man and saves him from all harm, setting him firmly on the path of life. As it is written, "Your word is a lamp to my feet, a light for my path" (Psalms 119:105).

The Torah is our most precious possession. Why then do some abandon it? Even if they have studied it once, it has grown stale over the years. It is time to have a new look and to learn some more.

The chasidic masters have taught: that each time one does a *mitzvah* it should be done as if it is the very first time. How can we accomplish this? By learning and relearning the significance of the *mitzvah*. Thus, when one is ready to learn, one chooses the very best teachers.

From this section, I pray you will acquire a taste of the deeper significance of Shavuos while learning the importance of Torah wisdom and the observance of its commandments.

By fully participating in Shavuos, you will be granted true wisdom. You will find the roots of your soul as you bask in God's light. You will unite as one with your people and live with their collective strength.

46

The Significance of Shavuos

he holiday of Shavuos is the anniversary of the giving of the Torah on Mount Sinai, as it is written:

In the third month when the Israelites left Egypt, on the first of the month, they came to the desert of Sinai. They had departed from Rephidim and had arrived in the Sinai desert, camping in the wilderness. Israel camped opposite the mountain.

Moses went up to God. Hashem called to him from the mountain and said, "This is what you must say to the family of Jacob and tell the Israelites: You saw what I did in Egypt, carrying you on eagles' wings and bringing you to Me. Now if you obey Me and keep My covenant you shall be My special treasure among all nations, even though all the world is Mine. You will be a kingdom of priests and a holy nation to Me. These are the words that you must relate to the Israelites."

Moses came back and summoned the elders of the people, conveying to them all that God had said. All the people answered as one and said, "All that God has spoken, we will do."

Moses brought the people's reply back to God. God said to Moses, "I will come to you in a thick cloud, so that the people will hear when I speak to you. They will then believe in you forever."

Moses told God the people's response. God said to Moses, "Go to the people, and sanctify them today and tomorrow. Let them immerse their clothing. They will then be ready for the third day, for on the third day, God will descend on Mount Sinai in sight of the people."

"Set a boundary for the people around the mountain, and tell them to be careful not to climb the mountain, or even to touch its edge. Anyone touching the mountain will be put to death. You will not have to lay a hand on him, for he will be stoned or cast down. Neither man nor beast will be allowed to live. But when the trumpet is sounded with a long blast, they will then be allowed to climb the mountain."

Moses went down from the mountain to the people. He sanctified them, and they immersed their clothing. Moses said to the people, "Keep yourselves in readiness for three days. Do not come near a woman."

The third day arrived. There was thunder and lightning in the morning, with a heavy cloud on the mountain, and an extremely loud blast of a ram's horn. The people in the camp trembled. Moses led the people out of the camp toward the Divine Presence. They stood transfixed at the foot of the mountain.

Mount Sinai was all in smoke because of the Presence that had come down on it. God was in the fire, and its smoke went up like the smoke of a lime kiln. The entire mountain trembled violently. There was the sound of a ram's horn, increasing in volume to a great degree. Moses spoke, and Hashem replied with a Voice.

God came down on Mount Sinai, to the peak of the mountain. He summoned Moses to the mountain peak, and Moses climbed up. God said to Moses, "Go back down and warn the people that they must not cross the boundary in order to see the Divine, because this will cause many to die. The priests who usually come near the Divine must also sanctify themselves, or else God will send destruction among them."

Moses replied to God, "The people cannot climb Mount Sinai. You have already warned them to set a boundary around the mountain and to declare it sacred."

God said to him, "Go down. You can come up along with Aaron. But the priests and the other people must not violate the boundary to go up to the Divine; if they do, He will send destruction among them."

Moses went down to the people and conveyed this to them.

God spoke all these words saying: "I am God your Lord, who brought you out of Egypt, from the place of slavery. Do not have any other Gods before Me. Do not represent such gods by any carved statues or picture of anything in the heaven above, on the earth below, or in the water below the land. Do not bow down to such gods or worship them. I am God your Lord, a God who demands exclusive worship. Where My enemies are concerned, I keep in mind the sin of the fathers for their descendants, to the third and fourth generation. But for those who love Me and keep My commandments, I show love for thousands of generations.

Do not take the name of God your Lord in vain. God will not allow the one who takes His name in vain to go unpunished.

Remember the Sabbath to keep it holy. You can work during the six weekdays and do all your tasks. But Saturday is the Sabbath to God your Lord. Do not do anything that constitutes work. This includes you, your son, your daughter, your slave, your maid, your animal, and the foreigner in your gates. It was the six weekdays that God made the heaven, the earth, the sea, and all that is in them, but He rested on Saturday. God therefore blessed the Sabbath day and made it holy.

Honor your father and mother. You will then live long on the land the God your Lord is giving you.

Do not commit murder.

Do not commit adultery.

Do not steal.

Do not testify as a false witness against your neighbor.

Do not be envious of your neighbor's house.

Do not be envious of your neighbor's wife, his slave, his maid, his ox, his donkey, or anything that is your neighbor's. (Exodus 19:1–20:14)

———————

The holiday of Shavuos commemorates the face-to-face communion that the Jewish people had with God at Mount Sinai. This communion had a double aspect. God descended on Mount Sinai and approached the Israelites, and similarly, the Israelites left their camp and came near the mountain, approaching God. Both these aspects are reflected in the names of the holiday. We call it "the day the Torah was given," which indicates how proud we are that God came to meet us, whereas the Torah calls it, ". . . the day of first fruit (*b'hakrivchem*), when you bring a new grain offering to God. . . ." The word *b'hakrivchem* means, you bring yourselves close. God is proud of us that we came close to Him.

A prince was in a foreign country for several years. When he was old enough to receive the royal signet ring, his father sent for him. He left for the palace the very next morning. How excited he was that in just three days he would meet his father. The king was equally excited and couldn't wait for his son's arrival. He too ordered a coach and started out toward his son. It was not long before father and son met. They embraced and lovingly told of their journeys. The prince told of his speedy preparations and adventurous travel. The king too told of his excitement and the details of his trip. Arriving at the palace, the king related the prince's adventures to the royal family while the prince told his brothers and sisters how his father came to meet him. Each was proud of the other's effort.

Let us therefore come forward and move toward God, and He will come toward us too.

———————

We recite in the daily prayers: "With His goodness He renews daily, perpetually the work of creation" (*Prayer Book*, Morning Prayers). Which ingredient in the creation is God's goodness? It is the Torah, as it is written, ". . . and God saw that it was good" (Genesis 1:13). It was the Torah with which God created the world, and it is the essence of the creation. This essence, however, was concealed until the Torah was given. Then, all the world knew the inner workings of the creation.

A king invited his subjects to a royal feast. When the guests arrived they were unprepared to behave according to royal etiquette. They tried their best to behave properly by imitating and watching the king's servants. The next morning, however, when the imperial rules were read in public, everything became clear.

Similarly, before the Torah was given, people did not understand how to relate to the world. When the Torah was finally given, all the laws were understood, and the inner truth of nature was revealed.

Let us therefore look for the Torah in each item of creation and each occurrence that happens. Then we will know the essence of the world and understand the language of all its creatures.

———————

It is written, "The words of God are pure words: silver refined in a crucible, gold seven times purified. You shall protect them, O God, protect them from this generation for ever" (Psalms 12:6–7).

The Midrash comments that King David's soldiers were not only good at warfare but were also scholars. They could give forty-nine reasons why something should be pure, just as well as they could give forty-nine reasons why it should be impure. And David worried about them and prayed for them. He wanted God to protect the Torah in their hearts from the evil of the generation (*Leviticus Rabbah* 21).

When there is both good and evil, then there are forty-nine levels of purity and forty-nine levels of impurity. But in the place where there is only good, on the level of God, then there is no impurity. It is all one unified singularity—the root and source of all purity and impurity. The root itself is neither pure nor impure.

How does God protect the words of the Torah among the Jewish people? By purifying their hearts and making them vessels to contain its words. Similarly, says the Zohar, God purifies the hearts of the Jewish people on the night of Shavuos and makes them vessels for the Torah. When the Torah enters one's heart, the heart itself becomes the source and no longer a place for good and evil, pure and impure. Thus at Mount Sinai the Israelites did not possess the *yetzer hara*, the desire to do evil; their hearts were focused and united as a singularity.

Therefore, it is the holiday of the first of the new fruit, which symbolizes the renewal that takes place in the world and in the hearts of the Jewish people. Aging is the reflection of the distance of a living being from the source of life. That distance is also the cause of impurity and evil. But if the living being is still connected to the source, it neither ages nor engages in evil.

On Shavuos we have the opportunity to reconnect to the roots of our life. Let us cleanse our hearts and make them vessels for the Torah, the root of our life.

It is written, "Create a pure heart in me, O God, and renew in me a steadfast spirit" (Psalms 51:10).

When God was ready to give the Torah to the Jewish people, He urged that they purify themselves, as it is written, "God said to Moses, 'Go to the people, and sanctify them today and tomorrow. Let them immerse their clothing. They will then be ready for the third day" (Exodus 19:14). Similarly, we purify ourselves during the forty-nine days of the *omer* before we receive the Torah. We ascend from level to level, until we reach the forty-ninth level and stand before God.

The Torah was given as "black fire on white fire" (*Midrash Tanchumah, Genesis* 1). This verse signifies that if a person wants the words of the Torah to make an impression on him, he must first purify his heart as the white fire.

A king's devoted servant worked in the village as a smith. Because, of his great loyalty he was the king's favorite. One evening, the king had just finished codifying the laws of the empire. As he would do nothing without his favorite servant, he had him sum-

moned at once. The servant had no time to change and entered the royal chambers in his soiled clothing. The king looked at him and smiled, "This document is too important to be read without preparation. Please bathe, dress, and then come to evaluate it."

The Torah is the most important document in our possession. We too must purify our hearts before we again receive it on Shavuos.

It is written, ". . . to Me every knee shall bend, and by Me every tongue shall swear" (Isaiah 45:23).

The Midrash comments that the phrase "every knee shall bend." is the day that man dies, and "every tongue shall swear" is the day that man is born (*Niddah* 30b). Before a child is born he is made to swear that he will be a *tzaddik*, righteous and not wicked. Similarly, when a man dies, he sees God, and the ultimate truth is revealed to him. His soul "swears" allegiance to God again. Thus, before man's birth and at his death, he is face to face with the Creator, and he negates himself completely. In that ultimate meeting, we are certain, man has no will or desire of his own. The only will is the will of God, and the only desire is God's desire. Does he need to swear that he will be a *tzaddik*? No, not at that instant, because the face-to-face communion with God is the oath itself.

An identical thing happened when the Israelites stood at Mount Sinai, as it is written, ". . . my soul left me when He spoke . . . " (Song of Songs 5:6). The souls of the Israelites left their bodies when God spoke to them face to face. It was just like an oath; they would do God's will exclusively. Thus, the expression, "He is under oath from Mount Sinai" (*Yoma* 73b). The Mount Sinai experience itself is an oath, a total negation of the self to God's will.

A villain, in chains, was brought before the king for judgment. The advisors demanded that he abandon his ways and swear allegiance to the king. The king motioned to one of the guards, who swung his sword and stopped it a hair's width from the villain's neck. "Will you obey me?," the king asked. "Yyyes, Yyyour Mmmajesty," stammered the villain. "That was an oath; you must all agree," said the king.

When we prepare to receive the Torah and stand face to face with the Creator, we swear our very being to Him. We have but one will, one desire, one focus. And that is to do the will of God.

It is written, "Bind them as a sign upon your arm, and let them be a phylactery between your eyes" Deuteronomy 6:8).

The verses that instruct us to have complete allegiance to God and the Torah, found in Deuteronomy 6:4–9, are written and placed in parchment boxes, the *tefillin*, which are bound to the hand and the head each day. The arm represents the physical body and its attributes. In order to connect the holiness of the Torah to the body, the Torah must be bound tightly to it. The head, however, represents the intellect and the soul. And since those are spiritual, the Torah needs but a lighter connection to them. Therefore, ". . . and let them be a phylactery . . . ," you need not bind them on your head, but it is sufficient if you merely let them be there.

We can glean the same lesson from the holidays of Passover and Shavuos. The Passover Exodus released the Jewish nation from their physical bondage. To accomplish this, God had to "bind" them with great force. He smote the Egyptians with ten terrible plagues and literally extricated the Israelites from their domination. Thus they were no longer the slaves of Pharaoh, but became instead the servants of God. Then on Shavuos, with the Torah, they were raised even higher so that even their intellect was released from bondage. But to achieve this, God needed to "bind" them lightly. He merely revealed himself and allowed the Israelites to learn.

A prince was captured by a band of thieves and kept in a mountain hideaway for many months. Finally the king found them and fought to free his son. The battle was fierce, but the king finally prevailed. He lifted his son unto his horse and galloped toward the palace at great speed. "Will I be able to relate to my son as before? Will he relate to me as a son?," the king wondered. Reaching the palace, the king dismounted and immediately took his son to his chambers. There, alone together, the prince broke down and cried about his separation. The king reassured him of his uninterrupted yearning and love for him. "Now that I see you face to face, father," said the prince, "there is nothing else I need to know."

It is written, "And God saw all that He had made and it was very good" (Genesis 1:31).

When the creation was still unified, the good it contained became manifest. As it is written, "And God saw the light and it was good" (Genesis 1:4). Light, which helped reveal the creation, was then very powerful. But God foresaw the deeds of the wicked who destroy the unity of creation and hid the light. Where then is it found? It is found in the inner part of every created thing. Thus, although on the outside, things appear to be separated, in their inner spiritual nature, they are united. And when God

reveals Himself, as He did on Mount Sinai, the physical differences disappear, and all that is left is the inner light, which is Divine and unified as one. It is the original light of creation that shines from one end of the universe to the other.

The outer nature separates and makes things different. As a result, there is a *yetzer hara*, an inclination to evil, to break apart and separate and destroy the inherent unity. This inclination, however, only has power when we deal with the outside, superficial nature of things. But when God revealed Himself, there was no place for the *yetzer hara*. Therefore, in describing the revelation at Mount Sinai, the word used is *vayidaber*, "and He spoke." However, its more precise meaning is, and He declared. God declared the nature of the entire creation, and every created thing listened. They were all made to face their inner essence. As the Midrash explains, "When God spoke on Mount Sinai the entire creation was silent" (*Exodus Rabbah* 20). It was the moment of truth, when the essence of every thing became revealed.

A king was about to hand over the control of his country to his beloved son. He needed also to reveal to him the names of his secret advisors and aides and describe the secret diplomacies and treaties with other monarchs and governments.

We too must be very still and attentive on the holiday of Shavuos so we can receive the secrets of the Kingdom, which lie right below the surface of nature.

"And Joseph could no longer contain himself, and he called out in a cry. . . . I am Joseph your brother whom you have sold to the Egyptians" (Genesis 45:2).

Joseph was sold as a slave and rose to be the second most important person in Egypt. In appearance he was the prime example of Egyptian culture, a wise, handsome, amiable, but all-powerful leader. He therefore had an enormous secret. He was a Hebrew, an *Ivri*, whose own brothers had sold as a slave. Yet, it was this identity, although concealed, that enabled him to interpret dreams, rule over Egypt, and save his father and brothers from starvation.

Similarly, Yocheved, the mother of Moses, hid him for three months after his birth to save him from Pharaoh's decree. And it is written, "And she could no longer conceal him, and she took a rush basket for him, made it watertight with clay and tar, laid him in it, and put it in the reeds by the bank of the Nile" (Exodus 2:3). The identity of Moses was hidden for months. But when the time was right, it became revealed. As it is written, "Pharaoh's daughter came down to bathe in the river, while her ladies-in-waiting walked along the bank. She noticed the basket among the reeds and sent her slave-girl for it. She took it from her and when she opened it, she saw a child. It was crying, and she was filled with pity for it. 'Why,' she said, 'it is a little Hebrew (*Ivri*) boy" (Exodus 2:5–6).

The inner nature of the world too, the divine light that is always new and renews, is concealed, but becomes revealed when the opportunity is right. And just as all created things have a concealed inner nature, mankind, as a whole, has one too. This inner nature is the Jewish people. But who would ever know? When God revealed himself on Mount Sinai, however, all the world was able to see that the Jews were chosen for a special mission—to reveal God's Kingdom that is hidden in the natural world.

It is written, ". . . because on it God ceased from all the work of creation that He had done" (Genesis 2:2).

The world was created long ago. It continues each day to be created by plant and animal life, as they give birth to their likeness. This is possible only by passing information from parent to offspring, from creator to created. We can observe this in the formation of a baby by watching the growth of cells. Each cell has an information center, the chromosomes made of genes, which instruct the cell about its shape, function, and activities. The offspring is formed when the codes of the DNA and RNA are replicated and instruct the cell to split in two. Then, those two cells again produce copies of themselves until many millions of cells are produced and take on a specific form. Hence it grows into a complete organism.

Similarly, when man creates, he uses information and passes it, imparting it to the object he is using. Thus, in a sense, there can be no offspring without information, without wisdom. And whereas the ultimate of this wisdom is the Torah, there can be no offspring without the Torah. The Torah is the highest form of information in the universe, and without it no offspring can be begotten. Therefore, when God gave the Torah on Mount Sinai, it is written, "And God spoke these words . . . (*leimor*) . . . to repeat them" (Exodus 20:1). God spoke these words, to create the world, and they can continue to beget offspring. The wisdom of the Torah is thus imparted to the entire creation and consequently causes the entire creation to be part of the Torah.

Not only the everyday world can be enlightened by the Torah but even the urge to do evil. Because when the light of the Torah fills some part of creation, it becomes totally nullified to its truth and thus is uplifted to the highest spheres. This is true of even the lowest levels of existence. When the knowledge of the Torah enters them, they are renewed by becoming an offspring of the Torah.

On the day of Shavuos, the whole world realizes that its existence has no meaning without the Torah and immediately nullifies itself to the Torah, the word of God.

The rabbis of talmudic times have debated how the holiday of Shavuos should be celebrated. Some said that it is best celebrated by devotion to spiritual matters. Others said that a physical celebration is more appropriate. Everyone agreed, however, that a physical celebration should be included (*Pesachim* 68b).

Our sages and the Kabbalists have taught that the physical realm and the spiritual realm are mirror images of each other. This is similar to the speculation of theoretical physicists about the existance of negative universes with an atomic structure opposite of ours, which have an influence one on the other. So too, man's world, the microcosm, and the universe, the macrocosm, are influenced by each other. Whatever man accomplishes in his little world is mirrored in the spiritual universe.

Although most of the spiritual universe depends on man's activities, portions of it are not dependent on it. Thus we had two groups of angels at Mount Sinai, one that depended on the actions of man and the other that did not. The angels that were independent of man said to God, "Do not give the Torah to the human race. Who is man that You should remember him? . . . " (Psalms 8:5). On the other hand, the angels who needed our good deeds in order to maintain their level of spirituality argued that the Torah should be given to the human race.

The Talmud relates that Moses argued with the angels, "The Torah teaches to respect one's father and mother . . . do you have parents? Why do you need the Torah's commandments? Also, one must not be envious of his neighbor's wife and possessions. Do you angels have jealousy among yourselves? Why would you need the Torah?! We humans need the Torah to curb our physical frailties and weaknesses. It is we who need the Torah, to buttress our weak constitution, while you angels are excluded from such matters all together" (*Exodus Rabbah* 20). Finally, the angels agreed that the Torah should be given to the humans.

Thus, the unanimous agreement of the angels came on account of our physical nature that needs the Torah. Therefore, all rabbis agreed, that the celebration of the holiday must also represent our physical nature. That is to teach us that the reason we have the Torah while the angels do not is that it guides us to the path of light and eternal life.

On the holiday of Shavuos the fruits of the trees are judged. We therefore bring an offering in the Temple of the first ripened fruit, the *Bikurim*, to pray for good crops and produce. What is the spiritual significance of this offering?

Our sages have taught, "Torah is great, it gives life for those who follow its precepts both in this world and the world to come" (*Ethics of Our Fathers* 6:7).

Torah gives life because it is the vessel for the spirit within nature. It was given so that humankind could raise the level of their activities and simultaneously raise the level of the material world too. And this task was given and accepted wholeheartedly by the Jewish people. They were therefore empowered to connect the material world with the Tree of Life, the Torah. And so, we raise the *Bikurim* to all the six directions of the universe, with the intention that the material world, no matter its location, be lifted up to a higher spiritual level.

However, the Torah is not only high but it is also the highest of spiritual entities. As it is written, "And it is hidden from the eyes of all living beings, and even from the birds of the heavens it is concealed" (Job 28:21). It is higher not only than the intelligence of humans but also that of the angels. Thus the Torah has two aspects: one that is more akin to the physical world and can be reached if we study it diligently and the other that is higher even than the realm of the angels and that we can never hope to reach. Nevertheless, by connecting with the outer portion, the fruit, we eventually reach the tree itself. And when we do, we have an experience like when we were first born, as the word *Bikurim*, from the word *bechor*, "firstborn," signifies. When we connect ourselves to the fruit of the Torah, we connect the world to its higher roots in the spiritual realm. Everything in our life, both material objects and people, is renewed. We experience them as being brand new, as if we had never before related to them nor knew them. Everything is renewed to its very roots and is transformed to new fruits.

Let us therefore not miss this opportunity to cleave to the Torah and renew our life from the lowest level to the highest.

It is written, "I was with Him as a confidant, a source of delight (*yom yom*) every day" (Proverbs 8:30).

The Hebrew *yom yom* means day by day. This verse refers to the two days in the Jewish calendar when the Torah is recognized as the confidant and source of delight. They are the days of Shavuos, when we celebrate the giving of the Torah, and Shemini Atzeres, when we rejoice for the fact of possessing the Torah. Both these holidays have similar names. In the Written *Torah Sh'b'ksav*, the eighth day of Sukkos is called Atzeres, a gathering. Similarly, in the oral tradition, *Torah Sh'bal peh*, Shavuos is called Atzeres.

The *Torah Sh'b'ksav* is the relationship that God has with us. The *Torah Sh'bal peh* is how we relate to God. As it is written

> *You have affirmed* this day that God is your God, that you will walk in His ways and you will observe His commandments and rules, and that you will obey Him. And *God has affirmed* this day that you are, as He promised you, His treasured people who shall observe all His commandments, and that He will set you, in fame and renown and glory, high above the nations that He has made; and that you shall be, as He promised, a holy people to God your God (Deuteronomy 6:19).

You chose Him as your God, and you made Him the One and Only through the Torah that you live, the *Torah Sh'bal peh*. And God chose you as His people, He made you the one and only with the Torah that He teaches, the *Torah Sh'b'ksav*.

We learn this also from the words, ". . . you shall be My (*segulah*), treasured possession, among all peoples . . ." (Exodus 19:5). The word *segulah* means a treasure that is customarily tied in a cloth so that it does not scatter nor get lost. The Jewish people have the power to unite the many into one. Just as they declare that God is one, so too they can unite the twelve tribes and even the entire human race to declare that God is the one and only. And just as they say witness that God is one in the heaven, so too God says witness about them that they are one on the earth.

Thus there is an ongoing action and reaction, a dialogue between God and the Jewish people. The day God spoke to us, the day the Torah was given, became the holiday of Shavuos. We respond to Him in the holiday of Shemini Atzeres as we rejoice with the Torah. The cloth in which this dialogue is wrapped is the Torah itself and is therefore our biggest treasure.

This is like a father and child who lived on a hill. For years the father taught his child the methods of survival with words of admonition and praise. Still he had no idea how well the boy had learned. One day the boy was playing in the field when suddenly he was caught in a terrible storm. He immediately ran to a nearby cave for shelter and was unharmed. When the storm subsided, father and son met. How happy the father was to hear that his son was able to save himself by following his teachings.

Let us therefore appreciate our great treasure, which helps save us from all danger, and remember it day by day.

It is written, "And *God saw* all that He had made, and found it very good. And there was evening and there was morning, the sixth day" (Genesis 1:30–31). After each day's creation the Torah has the words, "And God *saw* that it was good." What did God see?

The world was created with the commands of God, and these commands are the inner core of each created item in the universe. As the Midrash quotes, "There is not a blade of grass which has not an angel telling it to grow" (*Genesis Rabbah* 10). Although the blade of grass appears to grow from a seed nurtured by soil, water, and sun, it actually grows because of the spiritual essence that is at its core: the command of God. And all these commands in their totality comprise the Torah. So that what God saw, the good in the creation, was the Torah.

Therefore, the sixth day, which is symbolic also of the sixth day of *Sivan*, the day the Torah was given, is described with the words, "And found it very good." That sixth day contained all the good, all the commands, all the words of God without exception, the entire Torah. And where did God find the entire Torah? In "all that He had made"—a creature that is "all," a microcosm of the universe, with the ability to sway the creation toward good or toward evil. It is man. And the people who represent this to the fullest are the Jewish people. They, through example, influence the surrounding nations to worship the one and only God and discourage idol worship. They are the *all* of creation; it is entirely in their hands. They can bring the entire universe back to the moment of creation, its place of origin, They cause the words, "and it was good," to be found in the universe.

On this sixth day, when the Torah is given, let us immediately influence the world to recognize the word of God in everything that exists, and to cause all to be "very good."

It is written, "God spoke all these words (*leimor*), saying . . ." (Exodus 20:1). The word *leimor* means to relate, to tell. Thus, God spoke all these words so that they should be repeated and taught to everyone in the world.

The Zohar teaches that whenever the Jewish people are in exile, the *Shechinah*, the holy presence of God, is also in exile. Since the Jewish people are the ones who reveal God's kingdom, if they are oppressed, then God's name is concealed, and in exile also. In Egypt, because the Jewish people were in exile, Pharaoh was able to demand, "Who is God that I should heed Him and let the Israelites go?" (Exodus 5:2). And so do all the oppressive nations ask, "Where is their God?" (Psalms 79:10). The word of God and the fact that He is the master are also in exile.

Similarly, although the redemption of the world can come directly from God, it is nevertheless placed in the hands of the Jewish people. As the Midrash teaches, "When God said on Mount Sinai, "I am God your Lord . . ." the nations of the world thought that God is speaking to *them*, and *they* were chosen to reveal His kingdom. Then they heard, ". . . who brought you out of Egypt from the house of bondage. . . ." they realized that He was speaking exclusively to the Jewish people (*Exodus Rabbah* 20).

A king fondly called all his nephews "son."One day he had an expensive gift to give to the prince and called, "Son, come here, I want to give you a special gift!" All the royal family came running, thinking that he meant them. Glancing with a smile at all of them, the king explained, "My son the prince, please come here." They realized then whom the king had called.

Similarly, whenever God reveals His kingdom, the nations think that they are the ones being addressed. As it is written, "The sea saw them and fled, Jordan ran backward, mountains skipped like rams, hills like sheep" (Psalms 114:3). The nations think the message is directed to them, so we ask, "What alarms you, O sea, that you fled, Jordan, that you ran backward, mountains that you skipped like rams, hills, like sheep? Tremble, O earth, at the presence of God. . . ." You may still think that the message of God is to the entire earth, but no, the words mean "at the presence of the God of Jacob." The message is addressed to those who have the capacity and desire to reveal the kingdom of God, the children of Jacob, the Jewish people. The nations can see events, and they can even tremble, but to naught. It is only through the Jewish people that the other nations notice that the signs and trembling were from the God of Jacob, the creator of the world. Therefore, they are the ones chosen to perpetuate the revelation and experience of Mount Sinai and the giving of the Torah.

On Shavuos we offer two breads; one represents the Written Torah and the other the Oral Torah. As our sages have explained, It is written, "For this is not an (empty) trifling thing for you . . ." (Deuteronomy 32:47). "If it is empty," said they, 'if you find the Torah without meaning, then it is from you. It is due to your response to the Torah, rather than the Torah itself.' Just as God presents the Torah to you, you too must move toward Him and receive it. As it is written, "You have (heh'emarto) declared God to be your God, and God declared you as His people" (Deuteronomy Rabbah 26:18). God calls out to you, but you need to respond with your call to Him. By declaring God, finding God in the world, by revealing the spiritual treasures hidden in all things, the Jewish people become a vessel for His teachings. A mirror image is created: "You say that God is everywhere," says God. "Then I will allow you to experience My presence always."

The Ibn Ezra adds that the word heh'emarto can also mean, you made Him say. You, by your actions, have made God say the Ten Commandments. You, by declaring "We will do and listen," created the response from God. Your Oral Torah, the Torah that grows out of your own person, made Him give the Written Torah. The Jewish people create the vessels to receive the Torah. As it is written, "Truly Efraim is a dear son to me, a child that is dandled! Whenever I (midei dabri bo) have spoken about him, my thoughts would dwell on him still . . ." (Jeremiah 31:20). The Talmud teaches that the Hebrew words can be read as dai devori, meaning "My word that I have placed in him is sufficient" (Exodus Rabbah 20). God has given the Torah to the Jewish people to be part of them in their daily life. And if it would be part of their very life, they would need nothing else.

The tenth and final plague was the slaying of the Egyptian first-born. The Israelite first-born were spared and were therefore chosen to do the divine service in the Temple. Later, after they worshiped the Golden Calf, the firstborn were rejected and were replaced by the kohanim. The highest office in the avodah, the worship in the Holy Temple, was the Kohen Gadol. He was the leader and head of the kohanim, the select of the tribe of Levi. It was he who entered the Kodesh Hakedoshim, the Holy of Holies, in the Temple, only once a year. Nevertheless, the Torah is even more precious than the first born or the kohen, and even more than the Kohen Gadol. As it is written, "It is more precious than peninim" (Proverbs 3:15). The Torah is more precious than even the peninim, the Kohen Gadol who enters the peninim, the inner sanctum, the Kodesh Hakedoshim once a year. And it is also more precious than the first-born who are also called lifnim, "born before anyone else."

Shavuos also has holiness before it and after it. It is the middle holiday, with Passover before it, representing the first-born, and Sukkos after it, a holiday remembering the clouds of glory that surrounded the Israelites in the merit of Aaron, the Kohen Gadol. Thus Shavuos, being in the middle, is higher than both of them.

The Talmud teaches that when the Jewish nation received the Torah on Mount Sinai it was as if they swore to keep it: "Nishba v'omeid mei'har Sinai—he is sworn to keep the commandments from Sinai" (Yoma 73b). Similarly, when a person wants to rescue himself from the evil urge, he makes the yetzer hara swear in the name of God that it will not make him transgress against the Torah. That is what Boaz did on the night that he stayed with Ruth; he made his evil urge swear that it will not tempt him.

The Torah is composed of the names of God. If we cleave to it firmly, it is as if we swore to obey it and keep it. Then we do not stray and err from God's path. The Torah gives us strength, but only if we are as vessels to receive its strength and to be pure and virtuous. As it is written, "A fortress of strength is God's name, in it the righteous one is saved" (Proverbs 18:10). The name of God, the Torah, is the strength of the tzaddik, the righteous one. This was also the strength of Boaz—bo, "in him," and oz, "strength." The Torah was in him and gave him strength against his evil urge.

A prince was captured by thieves, forced to live with them, and learn their corrupt ways. He was tempted often to copy them. Still, when he saw the royal insignia on his clothing, reminding him of his father and the royal blood in his veins, he remembered his princely duty. He was thus able to thwart temptation.

The Israelites passed through three stages. In Egypt, they merely had the fear of God, then for forty-nine days they worked on their virtues, and finally on Shavuos at Mount Sinai they merited the ability to swear in God's name.

Similarly, we learned that before a soul is sent to the physical world, it is made to swear that it will be righteous and not wicked (Niddah 30b). Why is the soul made to swear even before it descends to earth? We can compare this to a prince who took to drinking and became an alcoholic. No amount of persuasion, not the severest oath, enabled the prince to stop his rebellious ways. Then a good physician got hold of him and slowly but firmly led him away from drink. The prince finally sobered up and was able to respond with a clear mind. He remembered that he was a prince and how he ought to behave. When he was lucid, the physician made him swear that he would never again drink in excess.

In order to swear one must be connected to one's true self. If a person is at a distance from his true self, then he is false and his oath is false too. When the prince was still drunk he was unable to swear in truth. Once he was removed from drinking and was back to his real self, he was able to swear in truth. The soul too is able to swear before it descends to this world. There, in the spiritual realm, it is in its true environment and is connected to its real and true self. There its oath is true.

It is written, "Did any flesh ever hear the voice of God and live?" (Deuteronomy 4:33).

To hear God's voice is the ultimate encounter with the Divine. And after a person hears that voice, can he remain in the physical realm? The soul, when experiencing so high a revelation, parts from the body. The body can no longer contain a thing so holy. How then did the Jewish people live through the encounter at Mount Sinai? They lost their life, but then received a new one from God, as we recite in our prayers, "He has planted in us an everlasting life" (Morning Prayers). After speaking to us, He had planted life into us again.

God is called *hatov*, "the good one," and *v'hameitiv*, "the one who makes good." He not only is good on His own but He makes others good as well. Those who connect themselves to the Torah, He plants the Torah truths into them.

The Torah has two aspects. One is the Written Law, which is outside the person; it is words written on parchment. There is also the Oral Law, the Torah lived in the real and actual world, which is inside the person. The Midrash comments on the word *Anochi*, meaning I am. "*Ano nafshi k'sovis yehovis*," I write and give Myself unto you; I place in you My essence that in turn makes you good. So much so, that the makeup of the physical body of the person corresponds to the commandments of the Torah. There are 248 limbs and 365 sinews for a total of 613, the amount of *mitzvos* in the Torah (*Exodus Rabbah* 20). This is to teach that the Torah belongs in the real life of the person, even in his physical body, a vessel ready to receive all the commandments. This interdependence of a person's life and the Torah may not be so apparent during the year, but on Shavuos it becomes perfectly clear.

Each of us in our lifetime goes through good times and hard times. We sometimes experience pain, illness, and other circumstances that make difficult the observance of the Torah and commandments. These may seem to us as obstacles, but at their source, in the spiritual realm, they are all good. They descend from heaven to earth to enrich our spiritual life. Thus when the *yetzer hara*, the evil urge, tempts us with traps that sway us from the path of Torah, we might think, "This is bad!" But actually, it is good. If we look further to the source, heavenward, we will see the good in it.

The root source of everything is the Torah, as it was the blueprint for the world's creation. Therefore on the day of Shavuos, the evil urge is nullified and does not exist. It has absolutely no power over us, because we see it in its heavenly form.

When the Jewish people received the Torah they became uplifted. Their power of communication became higher than that of other people. Thus their prayers, learning, and teaching became uplifted too. As it is written, ". . . from His mouth, wisdom and understanding" (Proverbs 2:6). The Jewish people receive from God directly. Just as when a mother chews food for her infant and gives it directly from her mouth, so too God gives understanding directly from His mouth. And it is written, "Who is like this great nation who has God so close to him, as our God whenever we call to Him; and who is like this great nation who has righteous laws and commandments as the Torah which God has given you" (Deuteronomy 4:8). This verse is a balanced scale: how one prays before God, as a creature before the Creator, that is how one receives the Torah. This works also in reverse; how one listens to God's Torah, the essence of one's life, that is how one prays. As it is written, "One who removes his ear from listening to the Torah, his prayers are also rejected" (Proverbs 28:9). If you are not connected to the source of your life, as a creature before its Creator, then how can you pray? Obviously your prayers are only words, not a plea, and therefore they are rejected. But when you listen to the Torah and learn who you are, your prayers are received in their proper place.

It is written, "The Torah of God is perfect, renewing life" (Psalms 19:8).

The physical body and the spiritual soul are at odds with each other, as a commoner who married a princess and whatever he offered her did not match the palatial delights that she was used to. How could he ever hope to satisfy her? Similarly, the soul is from the lofty spiritual realm; can physical *mitzvos* ever satisfy her? Yet, the Torah has a spiritual energy that satisfies the soul. It is a teaching of the most high, the Divine, and thus feeds the soul directly with its otherworldly teachings. If not for the Torah, the soul would be in a prison of the physical world. As we have learned, "No one is free except he who learns the Torah" (*Ethics of Our Fathers* 6:2). Even our fore-fathers, who lived before the Torah was received, were able to live loftily in the Torah's spirit. Because they were always ready to negate their lives for the sake of God, they received the light of the Torah even before it was given.

When the Jewish people left Egypt they were com-pletely united as one. Then Amalek came and dis-rupted their unity. They then needed forty-nine days to reconstruct their spiritual Gestalt, the form that they had at the Exodus. And finally, united as one, they were ready for the Torah, as it is written, ". . . and he camped at the foot of the mountain" (Exodus 19:2). This is also symbolized in the Omer, which is taken together and lifted. Finally, we were together. Our spiritual life was repaired, and we were able to receive the Torah.

The word *shavuos* also means to swear, to testify, to be a witness, as the Talmud teaches, "Being com-manded is identical to being sworn at Mount Sinai" (*Shevuos* 21b). And when is one obligated to testify? "When he had seen" and we too had seen the Torah being given at Mount Sinai. As my rebbe had taught: It is written, "And I will make witness with them (*bahem*), the heavens and the earth" (Deuteronomy 31:28). This can mean that *bahem*, with the Jewish people, I have a witness that I created the heaven and earth.

A prince was sent to a foreign country where the natives were not familiar with his father. When they watched ceremonies and customs of the prince, they became familiar with the king's ways too. Similarly, the nations of the world are not familiar with God's ways, and the Jewish people are sent as emissaries for this very purpose. By watching the conduct of the Jewish people, the nations become familiar with the Creator. They notice a people who conduct them-selves as if the King was watching, guiding, and pre-scribing their behavior. They are thereby a witness that God created the heaven and earth.

By receiving the Torah on Mount Sinai the Jewish people became witnesses that God is the Creator.

And on Shavuos we must assume the all-important task of being witnesses.

The Midrash comments: When God said the words, "I am God your Lord who . . . ," every part of nature trembled and called out, "I am the one whom God is addressing! It is to me that God is speaking!" (*Exodus Rabbah* 20). But then they heard the continuation of the words, "Who has brought you out of Egypt . . . ," they realized that God is not speaking to them but to the Jewish people. Why did nature change its mind and decide that God is, after all, not speaking to her but to the Jewish people?

Nature is the material world. It has the mistaken notion that God has abandoned her, that she is the master of her own destiny. She is never able to com-pletely believe that God is the Master of the world, a weakness that imprisons her. Only the Jewish people, because they were liberated from all prisons, from all slavery and enslavement, are free and able to accept the complete sovereignty of God. And because they accept the idea without reservation, they are able to impart it to the rest of nature and the world.

The Midrash says: We can compare this to some-one who walks into a perfume store. Although he does not buy any perfume, he walks out full of the fragrance. Similarly, the Jewish people received the fragrance of the Torah in full measure, and spread it throughout the natural world wherever they go. As the Midrash says: When God said the first word of the Ten Commandments, the entire world filled up with fragrance. This means, that by accepting the Torah, the entire world, even the material part, filled with the fragrance of the Torah.

It is written, "*Shma ami*—Hear, My people, and I will say witness with you" (Psalms 81:9). *Shma* also means to gather, as in "*Vayashma*—and Saul gathered the people" (1 Samuel 23:8). The meaning of the verse is thus, Gather together, my people, and be witness. By uniting, and being as one, they can also be witnesses to the singular One God. They are proper vessels to receive the Torah, which is but the name of God. As it is written, "God your Lord, I am" (Psalms 50:7).

Surely every creature can realize the existence of God in his own way and on his own level. But the Jewish people have the proper vessels. Because of their unity, they realize the true existence of God, as it is written, "*Anochi*—I am, God your Lord." "Your" in this verse is written in the singular, because the Jewish people are a singular unity; therefore, I am

God your Lord. As it is written, "Praised are the people (ha'am) who God is their Lord" (Psalms 145:15). The word ha'am means the united people. The people who are one people have God as their Lord. They receive the kingdom of God in full measure.

When the Jewish people receive revelations, comprehension, and understanding, the rest of the world shares in it too.

———————

The creation has two aspects: the static and the dynamic, the old and the new, natural laws and the world of renewal. Each thing that was created deteriorates and disintegrates. Nothing is permanent and everlasting; rather, everything is impermanent. The way things are is incomplete; wholeness and completeness are in renewal. Renewal comes from God Who is forever new. He does not change in any way, nor does He age or get old in any aspect of His being. Any instant that you encounter Him, He is totally fresh and new. Although you had already met Him yesterday and He is not a different one today, He is nevertheless not the same old God, but rather He is fresh and new. And the Torah, which is the revelation of God's name, is a means to connect to His renewal. Therefore we bring the Bikurim, "the first fruit." It teaches that just as a physical tree renews itself by producing new fruit each year, similarly, the Tree of Life, the Torah, renews those who cleave to it.

———————

Our sages have taught, "A gathering for the sake of Heaven will endure. But a gathering which is not for the sake of Heaven will not endure" (Ethics of Our Fathers 5:8).

This refers to the day the Torah was given on Mount Sinai. It was on that day that the Jewish people gathered together for the sake of Heaven, for God's sake, in order to receive the Torah. They begged for instructions for their spiritual life, and, therefore, that the Torah would be with them for ever. Similarly, the very definition of a Jew, his last words in face of death, is, "Hear O Israel, God our Lord, God is One!" (Deuteronomy 6:4). And because he is able to gather together his entire psyche for the sake of declaring God's name as one, he is able to receive the Torah.

———————

It is written, "God came from Seir, and shone forth from Paran . . ." (Deuteronomy 33:2).

The Midrash says: God presented the Torah to the nations of the world, and they refused it. Finally, the Jewish people accepted it. Similarly, on each Shavuos the identical activity is repeated on a spiritual level. God looks for His people, finds them, and again presents them with the Torah.

The gates of redemption and freedom open for all of humanity, as it is written, ". . . and He shone forth from Paran." From every part of the world the light of the Torah shone to bring freedom to its inhabitants. But although God shines His redemptive light to all the nations they do not have the vessels to contain it. The Jewish people, on the other hand, prepared for it and received the Law of freedom. They are permanently on that level. Yet they pray for the other nations, so they too may attain the capacity to receive freedom through the Torah. As it is written, "May you be praised by all the nations, may they rejoice . . ." (Psalms 47:4).

Even when the gates open, some are rejected, whereas others are welcome. We can compare this to a king who invited his subjects to the palace, and they all waited outside the main gate. The trumpets sounded, and the gates opened. Those who were loyal were thrilled at the opportunity to be near the king. But the villains shunned the palace; it was nothing but trouble and bother for them. Similarly, when God opened the gates and presented the Torah, Amalek was rejected, but Yisro (Jethro) was selected. Who selected him? He selected himself.

The very same occurs on Rosh Hashanah, the New Year. The gates of creation and renewal are opened for all of mankind. We offer sacrifices and prayers for all the nations that they be worthy to enter the gates. Finally, on the last day of Sukkos, on Shemini Atzeres, the only ones who are left to enter are the Jewish people, who stand united with God. So too, the gates of freedom open for all of mankind in the month of Nissan. We count seven weeks, during which time we attempt to repair the nation's vessels. Finally, on Shavuos, only the Jewish people are left, united and singular in their quest for the Torah. The Midrash sums this up by saying: Each word that God spoke divided into seventy languages, but in the end they all converged into one language, as it is written, "God speaks to the multitudes of armies."

———————

The purpose of giving the Torah was that the spiritual light descend to the material world. Similarly, the purpose of the soul is to spread its light in the body. The word neshama, "soul," is numerically equal to the word hashomayim, "the heavens." The soul is from the heavens and brings with it a heavenly light.

If a man pursues the longings of his body, he neglects his soul. If he is attentive to his soul, he may forget to care for his body. But if he allows his spiritual light to guide his body, then it too becomes enlightened. Therefore the Ten Commandments, the Torah from Sinai, start with the words: "I am (*Anochi*) God, the Lord your God who brought you out of the land of Egypt from the house of bondage" (Exodus 20:2). This verse can be interpreted to mean that the *anochi*, "the self," the persona of each individual, has to be suffused with God the Lord, and then his every fiber, muscle, and sinew, his total physical being will be consecrated to the service of God.

This is like a prince who was sent by his father to administer the kingdom. With unlimited funds at his disposal he attended lavish banquets and dined with the high and mighty. Soon his attention was diverted from his real goal as he moved from one party to the next. The king heard about his son's misdeeds and decided to visit him. The prince was surprised by his father's visit and begged his forgiveness. "No need to discuss this now," said the king. "We will review all the affairs of state tonight at the banquet." At the dinner, the prince asked, "You came to stop me from making elaborate banquets and you come and make one yourself?!" The king chuckled at his son's wisdom. "Your banquets were for yourself, my son, while this one is to establish my kingdom!"

Similarly, one can use the physical world, indulge in physical pursuits, and forget justice and mercy, or one can live a healthfully positive life, striving always to follow the Torah path and reveal God 's kingdom on the way.

The Midrash teaches that God used the Torah as His blueprint to create the world. The Torah is the pure will of God and is identical with Him. The Jewish people who live by this blueprint are spiritually tied to the Torah and are therefore one people, united and singular. As it is written, "The Torah of God is perfect, renewing life" (Psalms 19:8). All the souls are united in the purity and singularity of the Torah. Similarly, it is written, "The Torah was commanded to us by Moses, it is an inheritance to the congregation of Jacob." (Deuteronomy 33:4). The congregations become one Jacob, when they cling to the Torah's oneness and unity.

The Zohar says, "God's essence, the Torah and the Jewish people are all one." As we recite in the *Shabbos* afternoon prayers, "You are one, Your name is one, and who is like Your Jewish people, one nation on earth." But how could there be oneness in a world of fragments and plurality? The very nature of the

world seems to contradict unity. It is only because God is one that unity exists. Those who cleave to Him and His word, the Torah, also share in His unity.

The Talmud relates that a non-Jew came to the sage Hillel and said, "Teach me the Torah while I stand on one foot." And Hillel answered, "Do not do unto others, what you would not have others do to you" (*Shabbos* 31a). The words "one foot" refer to unity. The non-Jew wanted Hillel to teach him how to find unity within, and at the same time to feel unity with the rest of mankind. And Hillel instructed him that unity is only on one foot, as you cannot stand on one foot for too long neither can you be on the level of unity for too long. A person is a physical being affected by circumstances. Only God has the quality of never changing, as it is written, "I am God who does not change" (Malachi 3:6).

Although this is true of other human beings, it is different with the Jewish people. They are rooted in God and are one and indivisible. When a person negates his own being in order to be part of the nation of Israel, he becomes part of the oneness and unity that belong to them. Therefore, "do not do unto others"—if you have equal consideration for another Jew as for yourself, you negate your ego and unite with the *klal*, the nation, and then you are one, united and unchanging. As we say in the *Shabbos* prayers, "Who is like your nation Israel, one nation on earth."

On Shavuos, we receive the Torah and with it the opportunity to be part of the One by adhering to its oneness.

The word *Shavuos* also means to swear an oath. But the word *Shavuos* is plural and means two oaths. So who swears to whom? The Jewish people swore to God when they declared, "Whatsoever God has spoken we will do and listen" (Exodus 24:8). And God swore to the Jewish people too that He will eternally be their God. Just as God's oath is eternal, so is the oath of the Jewish people to keep the Torah eternally inscribed in their hearts.

There are two parts to a man's heart: a *yetzer tov*, a desire to do good, to strive for spiritual perfection, and a *yetzer hara*, a desire to do evil, to strive for physical desires for their own sake. How do these two parts of the heart ever unite? As it is written, "And these words (of Torah) shall be on your hearts (*levavecha*) . . ." (Deuteronomy 6:6); *levavecha* literally means two hearts. The Torah guides us to use both our spiritual and physical inclinations for divine purposes. Similarly, when the Jewish people received the Torah, God said, "May it be that the heart (*levavam*) remain with the fear of Me all the days" (Deuteronomy 5:26) *Levavam* is plural for heart; both of their inclinations shall be harnessed for the fear of Me. When we cleave to the Torah the inclination for evil is neglected, we are united, and the whole of us strives for the good.

Torah is wisdom and resides in the mind; desires and prayers for their fulfillment are in the heart. The Torah in the mind guides our desires and prayers. Those who are connected to its wisdom pray for spiritual enlightenment. Therefore, the reading of the Shma, the quintessence of Torah passages, "Hear O Israel, God our Lord, God is One," is said before a person prays for the fulfillment of his needs. Before we tend to the desires of our heart, we set our mind straight and connect to the singularity of the Torah. No longer do our mind and heart pull in two opposite directions. We are united as one, with one heart and mind.

It is written, "Gather together the people unto Me so I can let them hear my words" (Deuteronomy 4:10). Gather them for my sake, as a general who gathers his troops for the sake of the king. So too, when the Jewish people gather together for the sake of Heaven, they are able to bridge the gap between heaven and earth. As it is written, "Who built His chambers in heaven, and founded His *agudah*, "vault," on the earth" (Amos 9:6). The word *agudah* means bound together. When the Jewish people have unity on earth, they connect with heaven, as when they camped at the foot of Mount Sinai in unity and brought down the very heavens. Similarly on Shavuos, the day of ingathering, *atzeres*, when we unite as a people, we again have the opportunity to bring the Torah from heaven. This is like a king who, when in his palace, only knows the needs of his subjects. But on special occasions when they gather for his sake, he goes out to greet them and shares gifts and words of encouragement with them.

47

Torah Study on the Night of Shavuos

t is written, "And it will be if (*shamoah tishma*) you will listen . . ." (Exodus 16:26) The Hebrew word for listen is repeated. The Midrash comments: If you listen to the old, to that which you have previously been taught, then you will be able to listen to the new (*Berakhos* 40a). Therefore, on the night of Shavuos we study the Torah, to receive the Torah that we have already learned, and to prepare for the new.

It is written, "And I will sprinkle clean water upon you, and you will be purified . . ." (Ezekiel 36:25).

The Torah is a lofty spiritual teaching. How is it possible for it to enter a heart of flesh and blood, of physical feelings and emotions? The heart must first be made pure of all desires that contradict the Torah. Still, only the Torah can purify one's heart. So how can that purification take place? When we desire and long for the Torah, then the Torah enters to purify our heart and make it a vessel for the Torah.

This is like a king who traveled to a remote province of his kingdom. The people were poor, and not one of their homes was suitable to host the king. He stopped at one of the homes, with servants carrying all the royal comforts and amenities, entered it, and transformed a modest home into a palace fit for a king. Similarly, when the Torah enters our heart because of our longing for it, it transforms and prepares it as a spiritual vessel to contain its lofty teachings.

Therefore, by studying the Torah with diligence, on the night of Shavuos, by connecting it with the most private part of our heart's longing, we invite its

holiness and purity to purify our heart and make it a dwelling place for its teachings.

It is written concerning the angels, ". . . mighty creatures who do His bidding, to listen to the voice of His word" (Psalms 103:20). When the Jewish people follow the teachings of the Torah, they move the teachings from the potential to the actual. They make the words of God real by their actions.

This is like a king who wrote decrees and had them proclaimed in his provinces. He wondered if his laws are effective and ventured to observe his subjects. When he arrived at a remote province he was pleased to see the people observing his laws. This encouraged him to continue to promulgate laws for the benefit of his subjects.

Similarly, when the Jewish people study the Torah and adhere to it, they give, so to speak, strength to God to continue to imbue the hearts of the Jewish people with Torah. Therefore, by studying the Torah on the night of Shavuos we strengthen the very Torah that the Almighty planted into our hearts.

The Torah is of a high spiritual nature, and as humans we are at a great distance from it. How can we ever connect and be close to it? We were fortunate to have had a person who introduced us to the Torah, helped us fathom its depth, and taught us its proper respect. Without Moses our teacher, we could not have had any connection with the Torah. As it is written, "The Torah was commanded to us by Moses, it is an inheritance to the children of Jacob" (Deuteronomy 33:4). Moses' role as intermediary is itself an inheritance with the Torah, and we are therefore able to reach out and study it. Therefore, on the night of Shavuos, we study the Torah and receive with it Moses our teacher, without whom it is impossible to learn Torah.

There are two contradictory teachings from our sages: "Prepare to study the Torah for it is not an inheritance" (*Ethics of Our Father* 2:12) and "The Torah was commanded to us by Moses, it is an inheritance of the congregations of Jacob" (Deuteronomy 33:4).

The Torah is actually a lofty spiritual essence. It is the word of God, His name and kingdom in the world, His plan and goal for the entire creation.

This is like a king who sent his son to a distant province over steep mountains. Expert mountain climbers packed the prince's provisions and gave him written instructions in the use of every item, so he could survive the ordeals of the trip. Although he had all he would ever need in order to survive, the prince took special care to use each item as instructed and at the proper time. Although he received the entire package, he needed to apply himself to use it properly for his benefit.

Similarly, the Torah is our inheritance. We have it all, but we must apply ourselves if we are to live a full and spiritual life.

The universe is being created and re-created, as we recite in our prayers, "He renews each day the workings of the Genesis, as it is written, `He who makes the great luminaries, for His kindness endures for ever'" (*Prayer Book*, Morning Prayers). That means that constantly and always the universe is being renewed. This is contrary to appearances, in which everything seems to be old and familiar. Where is the newness in the world? It resides in its essence behind the facade of familiarity. It resides in the world of interacting subatomic particles and forces, which form the physical basis of reality. In the spiritual realm, it is God, the prime mover and Cause of all events commanding the universe to exist. And these commands are the Torah, the word of God, the origin of all renewal and creation. Thus, the renewal is there, and if we want to experience it we must prepare our hearts for it. And by studying the Torah on Shavuos night with great diligence, we connect to its core and can experience the vitality and newness of the words of the Torah and of the entire creation as well.

The Talmud teaches: "If this *yetzer hara*, the evil urge, meets you, pull him into the house of study, the *beis midrash*. Then if he is as a stone it will dissolve, and like metal it will shatter" (*Sukkah 52b*). Clearly the Torah is the antidote for the evil urges in our heart.

The Torah is the Tree of Life, the word of God, and it contains contradictory properties. It is water, as it is written, "Those who are thirsty go to water" (Isaiah 55:1), and it is simultaneously fire, as it is written, "Is not my word as fire, said God, and as a hammer that shatters stone" (Jeremiah 23:29). The *yetzer hara*, the evil inclination, challenges us to transgress both the *mitzvos aseh*, the positive commandments, and the *mitzvos lo saaseh*, the negative commandments. Refraining from *mitzvos aseh*, we cause vessels in our spiritual heart that carry spiritual vitality to become blocked with materialistic sediment, just as arteries in our physical heart become blocked by deposits of fat that hinder blood circulation.

Thus, by refraining from *mitzvos aseh*, our spiritual vessels sink to the level of the physical, they become heavy as stone. The waters of the Torah, however, dissolve the stone, and return our spirit back to health. Just as medicines dissolve blockages inside our veins, and return our blood circulation to normal, the Torah dissolves the hardness of our hearts and changes them into hearts of spiritual vitality.

By committing *mitzvos lo saaseh*, "prohibitions," our spiritual vessels become as metal. Just as an aberrant growth in a physical heart is best removed with laser surgery, which burns it away without damaging the healthy tissue, similarly the fire of the Torah burns away the metallic growths and heals the wounds of our spiritual heart, as it is written, "The teaching of God is perfect, renewing life" (Psalms 19:8). It renews it to its previous health.

But how? How can the burning away of growths possibly heal the heart? It is because the heart of the Jewish people constantly yearns for spiritual enlightenment and the Divine presence. Were it not for circumstances that challenge these yearnings, we would always seek to fulfill our spiritual yearnings. Once the impediments are removed, our essentially healthy heart is able to function again.

When we study the Torah diligently on the night of Shavuos, we invite both the water and fire of the Torah to repair our damaged heart and rejuvenate us to good health again.

Physical yearning and lust stem from a lack of stimulation. For example, the sensitive nerves in the mouth and throat crave for the stimulation of food tastes. When the nerves receive enough stimulation, the craving subsides. So too with the satisfaction of our other desires. The more often we satisfy our craving, the less impact and satisfaction it brings and the more intense our next indulgence has to be (*Sukkah* 52b).

In the spiritual realm it is just the opposite. Our soul has an infinite capacity; the more we connect with its nature, the higher we are able to reach. The Torah is the food for our infinite spirit and the more we study it, the more our capacity increases to understand, love, and be influenced by it.

We can compare this to fish swimming in the river. Although surrounded by water constantly, still, when it rains, they come to the surface and open their mouths as if they had never before tasted water. Each drop is precious to them. So too, the Jewish people, although they have studied the Torah, thirst for each new word, even one new letter of the Torah, as if they had never studied it in their life (*Genesis Rabbah* 97:5).

Thus when we study the Torah on the night of Shavuos we express our longing and love for it. That craving prepares our heart and makes it a vessel to receive the Torah with its infinite energy.

48

The Torah Was Given on the Sabbath

Our sages have taught: Everyone agrees that the Torah was given on the Sabbath. (*Shabbos* 72a)

n the physical world, coarse material placed in a vessel is affected little by the vessel that contains it. For example, sand placed in any of a variety of vessels is not affected by the type of vessel that contains it. Water, a liquid, is different in that it takes the shape of its container. Gas certainly is also changed by the nature of the vessel that contains it. In the spiritual realm, too, the energy from the spiritual essence depends on its vessel. *Shabbos* is a spiritual gift to the Jewish people and is the holiest of all the holidays. With their preparation the Jewish people create a vessel to receive the *Shabbos*. The better we are prepared to receive the *Shabbos*, the holier the *Shabbos* is in our domain. Therefore, the Torah was given on *Shabbos* to teach us that although it is the loftiest and holiest teaching in the universe, nevertheless, just as with *Shabbos*, the better vessels we prepare for it, the deeper and more powerful its teachings become.

What is the essence of the Jewish people? They are witnesses that God created the world. He is the Master Who with His free will chose us as His people. *Shabbos*, too, is witness that God created the world and He is the absolute Master without whom nothing can be accomplished. He is, in fact, the one who does everything in the universe. Thus, the Jewish people and *Shabbos* are two sides of the same coin. Just as the Jewish people are witness to the *Shabbos*, so is *Shabbos* a witness to the Jewish people.

We can compare this to a prince who was sent to a distant province to establish the king's legal system. He was accompanied by one of the king's advisors. Along the way they were surprised by a band of thieves who insisted that they were both impostors. The prince protested and called out, "In the name of the king, let him go!" And the advisor yelled, "I am the king's advisor and he is the prince. Let him go at once!"

Similarly, the Jewish people say witness that God created the world by resting on the day of *Shabbos*, and the *Shabbos*, too, says witness about the Jewish people. "Do you see who rests on *Shabbos*? They are therefore the witnesses chosen to testify that God created the world."

Similarly, the Jewish people are witnesses about the Torah. They proclaim that it is a heavenly teaching, and the Torah, in turn, with its heavenly laws, lofty morality, and way of life, is a witness for those who study it and perpetuate its teachings.

The Talmud states: Everyone agrees that the Torah was given on *Shabbos*. In the Ten Commandments we find the words "Remember the *Shabbos* to keep it holy"; and at the Exodus, "Remember this day that you have left Egypt" (Exodus 13:3). Just as the Exodus was in the very crux of the day, similarly, the Torah was also given on such a day—the day of *Shabbos*.

How is the Torah inextricably bound to the day of *Shabbos*?

When God created the world, it is written, "And God saw all that He created and it was very good, and it was evening and it was morning (*yom hashishi*), the sixth day." The other days of the week are listed plainly; *echad*, first; *sheini*, second; *shlishi*, third, and so on. Why is the sixth day called *hashishi* "the sixth day," as if it is very special? It is special because God declared: "These six days of creation are dependent on *the* sixth day of *Sivan*. If the Jewish people accept the Torah then I will allow the creation to continue to exist, but if they don't, then neither will these six days exist" (*Genesis Rabbah* 1).

When God saw all that He had created and it was very good, what did He see? He saw that there will be a Jewish people who will accept the Torah, and that is very good because the existence of the universe depends on it. God was satisfied with the creation; He was, so to speak, not in need or lacking. It was this divine satisfaction and contentment that became the peacefulness of *Shabbos*. Thus, the contentment and peacefulness of *Shabbos* are directly connected to the fact that the Jewish people accepted the Torah.

It is written, "And God completed His work on the seventh day and He rested in the seventh day" (Genesis 2:2). The Midrash asks this question. If God first completed His work on the seventh day, then did He not yet rest on the seventh day? The passage means, however, that God completed His work, but it was still missing the quality of rest. True, everything was already created, but still the final touch of rest was missing. As soon as it became *Shabbos*, rest came with it. Similarly, the creation was complete, yet it needed the Torah as a guide for life on earth, and it brought completeness with it. *Shabbos* became a complete and restful day only after the Torah was given. Therefore, it was given on *Shabbos*.

God created the world from nothing, ex nihilo, and it was manifest as material reality. It does not appear to be spiritual or divine. Yet, when we delve into it, we find it much more spiritual and divine than it appears. The deeper we go the closer we get to its roots, which are nothing.

The guide to help us reach the roots of the world is the Torah. It shows us the divine origin and root of everything so that we do not stray from the truth. This quality of the Torah is very similar to that of the *Shabbos*, as it is written, "Remember that you were a slave in the land of Egypt, and the Lord your God freed you from there with a mighty hand and outstretched arm; therefore the Lord your God has commanded you to observe the *Shabbos*" (Deuteronomy 5:15). You were once a slave; you were enslaved to the material world, the nations of the world who rule with their materialistic laws. They prevented you from having satisfaction and contentment. You could not find your place among them and were therefore far removed from your roots. Remember that God is the one who made you free and therefore observe the *Shabbos*. It is your day of freedom and contentment, the day you return to your roots, your resting place, your original and true nature. You were created free and return to that state of freedom.

Similarly, the Torah instructs and guides each one of us to find the root of our soul. It defines who we are and what our purpose is in the world. It helps us return to our roots and place of rest and contentment. Therefore, the Torah was given on *Shabbos* since both are the roots of our existence and the resting place of the Jewish people.

49

A New Offering

od created the world with Ten Commands. Each and every created thing is composed not only of its material part but also of the command of God that defines it. Where does the world really come from? From the word of God, from its moment of creation. Thus, every created being is as if it was created now with the command of God and is totally dependent upon it. Thus, each created thing is still at its roots and at its beginning.

In the natural world, the commands of God are hidden. It seems to us as if everything is independently alive. It is only through the Torah that the inner nature of the world is revealed and the commands of creation become manifest. The Ten Commandments become the Ten Commands. By heeding the commandments of the Torah, our eyes open to see below the surface of things to their inner core.

This is like a king who confers with his advisor in a hushed tone and tells him his desire. Later the advisor leaves the palace and tells the masses, loudly and clearly, the desire of the king. Similarly, the Ten Commands are called *maamoros*, words said in private conversation, whereas the Ten Commandments are called *dibros*, loudly spoken in public. The Torah reveals that which is within. Its public nature filled the entire world with fragrance from each of the Ten Commandments, and the words of the Torah were therefore translated into seventy languages.

We therefore offer a new *minchah* offering, as this holiday is identified by the newness and freshness of the universe, and we offer thanks to God for it.

Sinai experience revealed to the Jewish people all that which was hidden. It revealed the inner workings of reality and instructed humankind how to live on earth. And now that we know how to live, everything is fresh and new. As it is written, "He renews each day with His goodness the work of the creation" (Morning Prayers). The goodness refers to the Torah, because with it everything is made new.

We can compare this to a prince who begged his father to allow him to explore the woods around the castle. The boy left together with a soldier who looked after his safety. He entered the forest and went deep into the woods, stumbling along, discovering paths, brooks, and a variety of plants and animals. Later he told his father about his adventure. The king was pleased with his son's curiosity and perseverance. "Tomorrow," he said, "my expert scouts will take you into the woods."

The next day, two of the best scouts escorted the prince to the same forest. They showed him trees with edible berries, warned him of poisonous plants, and pointed to animal trails, bird nests, and underground tunnels. They taught him to find his way with the help of the sun and to build shelter in the trees. They taught him how to fish, lay traps, and make fire. As the prince looked at the forest with his new knowledge, he said, "This does not seem like the same forest I was in yesterday. Everything is fresh and new as if I was never here before."

Similarly, when we absorb the teachings of the Torah, the world becomes new to us. Therefore on Shavuos the offering is new, as everything in the world is really new.

"And God descended on Mount Sinai" (Exodus 19:20). The translation in the Targum of this verse is, God revealed Himself on Mount Sinai. The Mount

In offering the *minchah* in the Temple service we lift up two breads.

There is bread from the heaven, and there is bread

from the earth. The heavenly bread symbolizes the providence and kindness (*hashgocho*) we receive from God. Bread from the earth symbolizes what God gives us as a reward for our deeds. But even then, does God really owe us anything? Who are we, and what great accomplishments have we to our credit? Rather, the truth is that whatever we receive is from heaven and is the kindness of God.

We experienced this truth in its full impact on Mount Sinai as God spoke to the Jewish people and their souls departed, as it is written, "My soul left me as he spoke" (Song of Songs 5:6). Our sages call that experience "being sworn and remain sworn from Mount Sinai." Every Jew swore at Mount Sinai. The essence of swearing is that a person nullifies his being to the oath. He is ready to be nothing and not exist if he is not telling the truth. Similarly, at Mount Sinai, our very souls and lives were nullified and left our bodies lifeless, as we realized that life is from heaven and not from the earth at all.

The angels complained, "God, look, the souls of the Jewish people have departed! They are lifeless! Is it just for a king to marry off his daughter and kill his family?" And immediately, their souls were returned to them (*Exodus Rabbah* 19). As it is written, "The Torah of God is complete, it returns the soul" (Psalms 19:8). Even if a person's soul has gone astray and is lost in the materialism of the world, the Torah can bring him back. Even if his body is already lifeless without a spark of spiritual viability, the Torah reconnects him to his roots.

On Shavuos a new offering of the *minchah* is brought. It is a day of renewal. Even those who have gone astray, because the *yetzer hara*, the evil inclination, has misled them, even they are cleansed with the new energy of the Torah. The Talmud teaches "I have created the *yetzer hara*, the evil inclination, and I have created the Torah as an antidote for it" (*Kiddushin* 30b). The Maharal explains: If not that the Torah cures a life wrecked by the errors of the *yetzer hara*, there would not be a *yetzer hara*. Thus when one sees the *yetzer hara* pursuing him, he must not be frightened, nor surrender. Rather, he should say, "There is an antidote for this very inclination: the Torah." And he will surely find it; otherwise the urge would not exist at all.

This is like a king who had several sons. As soon as a prince would be old enough to venture out of the palace, the king would give him maps and information to survive in the forests around the palace. One of them contemplated the guide book and wondered aloud, "Why do I need all this information just to leave the palace?" The king answered, "It is because I know that boys your age are curious and adventurous and likely to get dangerously lost. Therefore, I offered you instructions to help you stay on safe paths, stay healthy, and reach your destination."

Similarly, it is because we are human and likely to fall into traps that God has given us the Torah. And even if we go astray, we are able to renew our life by following the instructions, returning to the path of life leading to the Tree of Life.

There are two types of humility. When a person is poor and lacking, he feels humble and lowly compared to others. The other type of humility is that of a person who is rich and prosperous but realizes nevertheless that his good fortune does not make him superior to others. We find these two types of humility in the story of the Exodus. When the Israelites left Egypt, it is written, ". . . and you were naked and bare . . ." (Ezekiel 6:8). They were poor, without merit, bare to the bones. Therefore, the offering on the morning after the Exodus is barley, a common food of animals who are humble because they lack the higher intelligence of human beings. Seven weeks later, after they sorted through their hearts and minds, they corrected their spiritual poverty, were rich in spirit, and were prepared to accept the Torah. Nevertheless, they realized that anything they have achieved and about to receive is a gift from God. They knew that they could never have gotten there on their own.

God and the spiritual world never grow old. On the other hand, the physical universe is forever disintegrating, growing old, and dying. Thus if we attribute our prosperity to our body and brains, then that prosperity has the same fate as the rest of the physical world. But if we attribute our prosperity to God, then it is from the world of renewal, being always new.

Thus the new offering of Shavuos is made of wheat, a grain common to humans, because we realize that our blessings are from Him. We realize, as humans, that all our prosperity comes from the realm of renewal and is forever new.

The Zohar tells us that bread is associated with faith. Bread symbolizes that which we receive from God. Whenever we receive, we must immediately activate and revitalize our faith in God, realizing that without God we have nothing and are naked and bare. And if we do that, then we are immediately in the realm of renewal. It is the world of human understanding as opposed to an animal's lack of understanding.

These two opposite sentiments can mesh together when a human being realizes that he really has no brains of any consequence and is as dumb as an animal. As it is written, "Man and beast will be helped by God" (Psalms 36:7). This verse refers to those who are intelligent as humans yet consider themselves animals. They consider themselves as ignorant as beasts before the all-knowing God, Creator of the universe.

Therefore, on Shavuos, we bring an offering of two breads: one representing the humility of ignorance and the other representing the humility that grows and grows. The wiser we are, the more we realize how little we know or understand. The wiser we are, the better and more effectively we are able to humble ourselves.

The Torah is the Tree of Life; it is the source of our life and the gifts with which God sustains us. When we are connected with the Torah, our life is renewed. We bring a "new offering"; we thank God for our new gifts.

All newness and renewal come from the Torah, the Tree of Life, as branches that grow from a tree. Just as the fruit of physical trees are judged on Shavuos, our spiritual fruit is being judged too. How well are our branches and fruit, our actions, connected to the Tree of Life? Although our attention is with the branches, we must constantly be aware of the Tree. And even if we stray, and forget the Tree, we can still return to it again and again. As it is written, "Now then, if you obey Me faithfully and keep My covenant, you shall be My treasured possession among all the peoples. Indeed, all the earth is Mine, but you shall be for Me a kingdom of *kohanim* and a holy nation. These are the words that you shall speak to the children of Israel" (Exodus 19:5–6). "Now then" is the virtual present, our real and actual situation. How do we fathom our real situation? By obeying God's covenant and being a holy nation. A person cannot be in touch with the truth of his being unless he studies the Torah and prays with all his might. Study and prayer are two aspects of our inheritance that return us to the very essence of our being, to who we are now, and bring us face to face with the Tree of Life, the essence of the Torah.

Our sages have taught that the daily prayers are in place of the daily sacrifices. And what is the origin of the daily sacrifices? It is written, ". . . a daily sacrifice which was made in Mount Sinai . . ." (Num-

bers 28:6). The sacrifices originate from Mount Sinai; their roots are in the Torah. Similarly, prayers also have their roots in the Torah, as it is written, "God is near to those who call Him, to all those who call Him in truth" (Psalms 145:18). Truth is the Torah, as it is the true word of God. Therefore, the roots of prayer are also in the Torah; prayer is the definition of our relationship with God, the God of truth. And it is because of the truth of our relationship with Him that we are able to pray at all. Prayer is but the reestablishing of the relationship between Creator and created. Thus, if God is called in truth, the truth of Sinai—the Torah that defines the relationship—then He is near, He is there directly for you.

On Shavuos both Torah and sacrifice, both Torah study and prayer, receive new strength and meaning.

The *hashgocho*, the Providence of God to His creatures, His constant uncoerced will to do kindness, is flowing from heaven to earth. In addition to that, there is also a providence, a divine granting of gifts as a response to the actions of people. Therefore sacrifices are described: ". . . the offerings of My bread, as offerings by fire of pleasing fragrance to Me" (Numbers 28:2). There is the bread from Me, from the heaven, which is called "My bread," and there is the bread of response, the "fragrance." As it is written, "Go (*lachmu be'lachmi*) eat My bread" (Proverbs 9:5). *Lachmu be'lachmi* symbolizes two breads, one from above and the other as a response to that which happens below.

The offering and response are symbolized by the twenty-six times that King David said ". . . and his kindness endures forever" (Psalms 106); they are the twenty-six generations from creation until the Torah was given. For twenty-six generations, God's kindness sustained the earth. It was not a response, but rather bread from heaven. After the Torah was given, there began the era of kindness as a response. Therefore, the Ten Commandments are introduced with the words, "And *Elokim*, the Lord, spoke these words saying. . . ." *Elokim* is the name of God that connotes judgment. Until Mount Sinai, the pure loving-kindness of God sustained the world. Now, at Mount Sinai, with the Torah and commandments, man had the opportunity to receive sustenance even with judgment, of *Elokim*, as a response to his actions.

This is like a baby who receives all his sustenance from his mother. She nurses, clothes, and shelters her baby. As the child grows in wisdom, she starts to deal with him in response to his actions.

Now that we have received the Torah, we can

merit God's sustenance by being faithful to its teachings and commandments.

The Torah is the relationship of God to the Jewish people and has two aspects. First there is the relationship to the individual, and there is the relationship to the person as part of the Jewish people as a whole. These two aspects are described in the two paragraphs of the *Shma*: in the first paragraph, speaking to the individual, ". . . which I command you today . . ." (Deuteronomy 6:6), and in the second, speaking to the people as a whole, ". . . which I command you today . . ." (Deuteronomy 11:13). There is *hashgocho*, "divine providence," that descends from heaven to the individual Jew and also to the entire Jewish people. How you are as an individual Jew determines how you are as a collective Jew. As Hillel said, "If I am not for myself who is? And if I am only for myself, what am I worth?" (*Ethics of Our Fathers* 1:14). Each person has to have worth on his own. And this worth is ultimately tied to the collective worth of the Jewish people as a whole.

The offering of the two breads also took place on the spiritual level. There is bread from the heaven and from the earth. There is bread that God grants you as a gift and bread that you receive as a response. As it is written, "Go and (*lachmu b'lachmi*) eat from My bread . . ." (Proverbs 9:5).

The Midrash tells us that the Jewish people responded to each of the Ten Commandments by saying "No!" to the negative commandments and "Yes!" to the positive commandments (*Exodus Rabbah* 20). Wasn't it strange that they interrupted God's words with their response? What did their response add? But the response was the essence of the Torah, the response of the created to the Creator.

Similarly, it is written, "This is the Torah law, if a man dies in a tent . . ." (Numbers 19:2). The Talmud comments: The Torah is found only with those who give their life for it as if they died in a tent (*Berakhos* 63b). Why is this so? Why is the Torah found only with those who give their whole life for it? Why does it need *mesiras nefesh*, a complete negation of the self? Because the Torah was given by God to the Jewish people without reservations. That was God 's relationship: bread from heaven. And the response of the Jewish people, the response of the created, also has to be without reservations. Thus the person becomes part of the Torah itself, made of the two halves, from the heaven and from the earth. The very definition

of teaching and instruction is the response. The student responds, mentally, verbally, or physically to the teacher's instruction. Therefore, our response makes the Torah complete. As it is written, "The Torah of God is perfect, it (*meshivas*) renews the soul" (Psalms 19:8). The word *meshivas* also means responds; the soul responds to it. And together with the response of the Torah it is complete; the two halves make it whole. It is also written, "My soul has left me when He spoke" (Song of Songs 5:6). The soul of the Jewish people left them when God spoke the Ten Commandments; that was their response: they cannot exist without the Torah.

Let us therefore respond to the Torah with all our soul and receive its teachings in full measure.

The two breads offered on Shavuos are the call of God to the creation and its response to God. As it is written, "And God spoke these words (*leimor*) to repeat them, to relate them" (Exodus 20:1). He spoke, and man is to relate those words—man needs to respond to God's words. Similarly, it is written, "He will kiss me with the kisses of (*fihu*) his mouth" (Song of Songs 1:2). The word *fihu* has two words: *fi*, meaning my mouth, and *hu*, Him. It is God's relationship and man's response. As it is written, ". . . your love is better than wine," the words of our sages, the Oral Law, *Torah Sh'bal peh*, is the love, the relationship of the Jewish people to God. It is even better than wine, better than the Torah *Sh'b'ksav*. The Oral Law, our response to the Torah, is even better than the Torah itself.

Our sages have taught: If one has more deeds than wisdom, he is as a tree whose roots are wide and deep (*Avos* 3). How can anyone have more deeds than his wisdom? How does he do without knowing? The answer is that if we act with *mesiras nefesh*, total resignation to God's will, our response connects us to the Torah. Our *Torah Sh'bal peh* response answers God's call; our soul literally jumps out to do good deeds, although we do not even possess the wisdom for it. As it is written, "Blessed is he who trusts in God, who trusts in God alone" (Jeremiah 17:7). The Talmud comments: One who worships idols becomes like the idol, as it is written, "Those who fashion them, those who trust in them, shall become like them (Psalms 115:8)" (*Rosh Hashanah* 24b). Surely the one who trusts in God will also be like Him.

Therefore, one who trusts and totally resigns his soul to God becomes "like" Him; he becomes the second half of God's call and completes it.

Let us respond to the Torah with complete commitment and resignation.

The offering of bread on Shavuos is called a new offering.

It is written, "There is nothing new under the sun" (Ecclesiastes 1:9). The Talmud infers: Under the sun there is nothing new, but over the sun there is something new (Leviticus Rabbah 28:1).

There is a world of nature, with its predictable laws: the sun rises and sets, flowers bloom in springtime, hydrogen and oxygen explode and form water. The world of nature also has dimensions; width, height, depth are three of them, and the fourth is time. There is the past, present, and future. As soon as the world is created, it is within time and can never get out of it. Therefore there is nothing new under the sun. Time grinds on and keeps getting older and older, with no way out. There is also the spiritual world, not bound by limitations nor by the laws of the material world. Whatever exists in a material form in the physical universe exists also in a spiritual form in the spiritual realm. Time, too, has a spiritual form, but there it is constantly being renewed, becoming new and being in the very present. This spiritual existence is the way of the Torah, the path that the Torah opens in the lives of those who follow its instructions. So that by connecting with the Torah we can rise above the natural "sun" and find the world of renewal. Therefore, it is uniquely available to the Jewish people who accepted the Torah with great enthusiasm.

Shavuos, then, is the day that the inner path beyond the world of nature, accessible to those who have the key, was given. It is therefore the holiday that enlivens all the other holidays.

Therefore, Pesach is composed of two holy days, the first and last, and Sukkos also has two days, but Shavuos has but one day. It is as a central beam that holds up the entire structure, just as the central beam that held together the entire *Mishkan*. As the Zohar comments, that the verse, "Days were created and He has one among them" (Psalms 139:16), refers to Shavuos. There are many days, many special days, but there is also one and only, the most special of days. It is the inner reality of the other holidays—the path of the Torah, the supernatural, the time of time. We can jump into each of the holidays and find the path of the Torah that is its renewal, the new time and reality that are in each thing.

As it is written, "They chose new gods, then the bread of the gates" (Judges 5:8). God can give you bread. He can also give you Torah, but it is heavenly and totally out of the reach of human beings and needs great preparation in order to receive it in its fullness.

The Zohar teaches: "Her husband is known in the gates" (Proverbs 31:23). How do the Jewish people understand God. By means of the gates that they open, as in, "Lift your heads, you gates" (Psalms 24:7). The amount of Torah one receives from God is dependent on the size of the gate one opens. The gates for the Jewish people at Mount Sinai were prepared by Moses and Aaron. The spiritual world is replete with blessings and wisdom waiting for people to prepare physical vessels to receive them.

There is a dual action and reaction. When a person yearns and pines for the wisdom of the Torah, then his brain becomes a vessel for it. And as the Torah enters, and because it is infinite, it transforms the physical vessel of a person's brain into a spiritually infinite vessel.

This is like a prince whose father appointed him to rule over the provinces. The prince wondered, "How can I ever do that? I am just an ordinary boy, although a prince by title." But as soon as he took charge, he immediately grasped the meaning of his office and was able to do his father's will. The very position uplifted him.

Similarly, when we were presented with the Torah, it seemed unfathomable, too deep for our tiny brains. But as soon as we started learning it, the Torah itself made room in our heads for its wisdom.

There are the outer gates and the inner gates.

This is like a poor woman who came to the king to appeal for help. She told her story to the guards at the gates and pleaded and begged to be let in. Finally they allowed her in. She thought that she could go directly to the king, but a guard corrected her, "Don't think you can speak to the king now. You still have to pass through the inner gates."

Similarly, there is the dichotomy, a two-aspected reality to everything—revealed and hidden. Even the revealed aspect has a gate that we must pass through before we can understand it fully. And when we pass through the gate, we again find a revealed and a concealed portion. We find outer gates and inner gates, one after the other, until our mind has no more capacity to understand further and we reach the fiftieth gate that we cannot open, but can only see, as was shown to Moses.

To reach God's palace we must first open the physical gates of slavery, which is accomplished with the Omer of Pesach. Next, we open the gate of the spirit, as we did at Mount Sinai. Those two gates are the two bread offerings of Shavuos.

Thus it is written, "Open to me the gates of righteousness" (Psalms 118:19)—those are the outside gates. "Open to me my sister my dearest" (Song of Songs 5:2)—these are the inner gates of a more intimate relationship with God.

The offering of the breads symbolizes Moses and his brother Aaron. Moses received the Written Law, the *Torah Sh'b'ksav*, for which the Jewish people promised, "We will listen." One must be attentive while the knowledge is being imparted. This knowledge took the form of stone tablets with the words of God etched into them. It was the bread that came directly from heaven. Then there was Aaron's part, whose role was the service in the *Mishkan*. Through deeds he eternalized the Torah in the minds and hearts of the Jewish people. His portion is *na'aseh*—we will do. We, the bread of the earth, prepare the ground and work the fields until the sustenance from above can be received. It is the *Torah Sh'bal peh*, the oral tradition that grows out of the actions of the Jewish people as they make holiness and serve God out of their daily lives.

There is bread that comes from the heaven as the *manna* that descended in the desert. There is also bread that is the result of man's deeds, such as plowing, planting, reaping, and threshing. These two breads are not exclusively separated. Even after the *manna* stopped falling and the Jewish people tilled the soil on their own land, the bread from heaven and of the earth would meet every seven years. The seventh year was *Shmitah*, when the earth must rest, as it is written, ". . . because the land is Mine" (Leviticus 25:23). The heaven and earth meet; although we work all the six years, we realize that the earth's produce originates from God. Our bread may look like bread from the earth, but it is in fact bread from heaven. Bread that we work for but is recognized as being from heaven is on a higher spiritual level than *manna* itself. Therefore, in the Temple service, the breads are lifted in every direction to symbolize that the bread from the earth reaches even higher.

This is like a prince who received a gift on each of his birthdays. On one of his birthdays his father gave him wooden boards and building materials to build a tree house in the garden. The prince was thrilled and set himself to the task. He spent many of his idle moments completing his house. After a month's time it was completed, and he begged his father to see it. The king was amazed at the elaborate structure and the fine workmanship. Then to the amazement of the king, the prince said, "Now, father, allow me to thank you for giving me the tree house as a gift." "Look at this wise son of mine," said the king. "Although I only gave him the raw material, he thanked me for the finished product."

We too, although we work very hard to understand the Torah, thank God for it as if He gave it to us as a gift.

50

The Earth Was Still

 t is written, "... the earth was afraid and was quiet" (Psalms 76:9). The Talmud asks, If the earth was afraid, what caused it to quiet down? And if it finally grew quiet, why was it afraid at first? The Talmud answers that God made the creation conditional: if the Jewish people accepted the Torah, He would allow the world to exist, but if they did not accept it, He would destroy the world. Therefore the world at first was afraid, not knowing whether the Jewish people would accept the Torah. Then when it saw that they accepted it, it calmed down and was quiet. But why was it necessary for God to give the Torah in such a manner that the earth should first be afraid and then calm down? That itself was a major teaching to the Jewish people. It showed them that no part of nature can oppose a Jew when he wants to do a *mitzvah*, a commandment of God, because all of nature would be destroyed if the Jewish people had not accepted the Torah.

Therefore, when difficult circumstances surround us and we think, "We are unable to observe the commandments of the Torah with these obstacles," we are very mistaken! Because the whole world, every stone and tree, every animal and person was waiting in suspense and hoping that the Jewish people accepted the Torah. So how could any part of the material world prevent one from studying, observing and perpetuating the Torah? That cannot be! It is only our weakness projected onto circumstances. And if we would desire it, we could simply ignore all these difficult circumstances and embrace the study of the Torah with all our hearts.

The earth was afraid and was quiet.

We can compare this to the subject of a king who came to beg for a favor. When his turn came to talk to the king, he became overwhelmed and in his confusion spoke without logic and made a fool of himself. The king was annoyed and sent him out empty-handed. The determined subject disciplined himself and said, "I am going back. And while I stand before the king I will only think of his great power and riches, and the awe that I have for him. That will help me control my feelings so I can speak with conviction."

When he returned, he was able to express his needs because of his awe and fear of the king. The awe and fear were a vessel for his words.

Similarly, we need the awe and fear of God in order to observe the commandments of the Torah. They focus our actions and make a vessel for them.

There are also two aspects to the *Shabbos*. There is *shamor*, "to observe and keep" the *Shabbos*, and there is *zachor*, "to remember" the *Shabbos*. What is the difference? *Shamor* is the negative aspect of not doing any work on *Shabbos*, of not participating in any weekday enslaving activity. *Shamor* means to watch one's actions that they not move from before God, that they not move into the realm of unholiness or ungodliness. We need to stand before God in reverence and truth, as a creature before the Creator in complete and true freedom. Then we can remember and feel the essence of our being as non-slaves before God always.

Let us therefore prepare ourselves and remain with awe before God to receive the Torah, a memory that is in each creature.

The earth was afraid and was still. Why was it afraid? Because the earth would revert to nothingness if the Jewish people did not accept the Torah. This seems to contradict another teaching of our sages. They have taught, "It is far better not to have been created;

but those who have already been created should examine their deeds and correct them" (*Berakhos* 5a). Now, if it is better not to have been created, then why was the earth afraid. For if it would merely become nothing, then it would be in an even better state.

The answer is that the earth reverting to nothingness and the "examination" of deeds are one and the same. What we have to think about is what our life would amount to if we did not follow the Torah. It would be desolation and nothingness. And this is precisely what we need to do more than anything else—to prepare our hearts to receive the truth, to be in tune with the truth. The Jewish people cannot exist without the Torah, and the Torah cannot exist without the Jewish people.

The material world is false; it is a world of appearances, illusion, and impermanence. We must be warned by God, "Don't think that because you exist you will amount to something. It is only because of the Torah that you can hope to attain the truth." Even when learning the Torah we cannot fathom its truth, because it goes through our material brain and becomes tainted with material interests and cravings. Only if we study it with fear and trembling before God can we hope to benefit from its message.

"In heaven You pronounced sentence, the earth was afraid and was quiet" (Psalms 76:9). At first the earth was filled with fear: what if the Jewish people do not accept the Torah and the whole world is destroyed. Later, when the Jewish people accepted the Torah, it quieted down. Yet, this verse is about the Jewish people at Mount Sinai when they stood waiting for the Ten Commandments. Why was the earth still afraid? Was it not already evident that the Jewish people were about to accept the Torah?

At the Exodus, too, it is written, "... Nations heard and trembled ..." (Exodus 15:14). Why did the nations, who were not anywhere near the Jewish people, tremble? Their trembling served a special purpose. It was the means that God used to prepare them to respect the Jewish people. After the Exodus the Jewish people became a role model for the rest of the world. Although only one nation received the Torah, the other nations learned from the Jews indirectly.

Similarly, the earth was afraid. It dared imagine a world without the Torah, which is an impossibility. There is nothing in the world that can exist without the Torah. And with its fear of the impossible, it made the natural world a vessel to contain the Torah. Therefore, there is nothing in nature that cannot be a vessel for the Torah.

There are two distinct periods in the spiritual history of the world. The first is from the creation until Mount Sinai, a period of twenty-six generations in which the world was sustained by God's Divine providence and mercy. After the Jewish people accepted the Torah on Mount Sinai, they were rewarded with providence for their good deeds. Therefore, the earth, in the hands of man, was fearful about its fate. As we recite in the prayers after meals, "Please God sustain us so that we never need the gifts of people." The earth, too, would rather receive sustenance from God than have people as an intermediary.

The earth was fearful and then quieted down and was still. Why was it frightened? Because it reasoned that if Adam, the first human being, was given one commandment and could not even observe it, then how would the Jewish people be able to observe 613 commandments. Later it quieted down. As our sages have taught: If a person's fear of God is more abundant than his wisdom, then his wisdom will endure (*Ethics of Our Fathers* 3). The question is, If fear of God is more important than wisdom, why does his wisdom, and not his fear of God, endure? The answer is that whatever you pursue with wisdom, you receive more of; in this case what is pursued is the fear of God. Thus, since the earth was fearful, it was able to receive Torah wisdom, and the fear stayed with it forever. What kind of fear did the earth experience? A fear that has wisdom in it, for we can always learn new ways to fear God from the trembling of the earth.

51

We Will Do and Listen

 nd the people answered: All that God has spoken we will do and listen" (Exodus 19:8). The Midrash relates: When the people answered with great devotion and dedication, 600,000 angels came to tie on each of them two crowns, one for saying *na'aseh*, "we will do," and one for saying *nishmah*, "we will listen" (*Exodus Rabbah* 19).

Each Jew has a spiritual light within, *Or Pnimi*, which illumines and gives him strength. There is another light, however, that is the root source of the soul. This light is outside the person, *Or Makif*, and surrounds him with a heavenly aura. How does the outer light connect with the inner light? If man sifts, chooses, and purifies his actions and obeys the commandments of the Torah, his material nature does not block the two lights from fusing together. And when they do, they produce a miraculous glow beyond the reach of humans.

The two lights correspond to the two promises made by the Jewish people. "We will do"—we will subjugate our material body to be a servant of the Torah and thereby allow the *Or Pnimi* to spread through us. "We will listen"—we will do even that which we have not yet heard and is therefore impossible to be done, thereby connecting us to the *Or Makif*, beyond the reach of man.

There are two spiritual forces in each of us; one is the *yetzer tov*, the inclination to do good, and the other is the *yetzer hara*, the inclination to do evil. The *yetzer hara* is mitigated by observing the commandments of the Torah. That fulfills our promise of "we will do." The *yetzer tov*, the craving to do good, to reach beyond limitations of the material world, is fed by the promise of "we will listen," although we cannot as yet do because it is beyond our reach.

Similarly there is also a dichotomy between *Olam Hazeh*, the world here and now, and *Olam Habah*, the World to Come. *Olam Hazeh*, the present material world, is sifted and purified by action guided by the Torah, by the *na'aseh*, "we will do." The *Olam Habah*, the World to Come, is reached by yearning for that which is beyond reach; *nishmah*, "we will listen," although we cannot do it now.

It is written, "Bless the Lord, O His angels, mighty creatures who do His bidding (*devoro*), ever obedient (*lishmoah*), to do His bidding; bless the Lord, all His hosts, His servants who do His will" (Psalms 103:20–21). *Devoro* also means His words, which literally are composed of letters and symbols. Just as the material world is composed of the tiniest common denominator—atoms, subatomic particles, forces, and energy exchanges—so too the spiritual world is composed of the names of God and ultimately of the letters of the Hebrew alphabet, which are the symbolic representation of the forces of the spiritual world.

When Bezalel, the great Jewish craftsman, formed the vessels of the *Mishkan*, the resting place of the Divine presence, he did so both on the physical and the spiritual levels. The Midrash teaches that he knew the combinations of the Hebrew letters and the name of God (Exodus Rabbah 28). Thus the physical vessels correspond to their counterparts in the spiritual realm. In this sense, when we observe the commandments, the word of God, we take the words, the letters, and ultimately the names of God, and combine them with the material world by translating them into action. This is just like $E=Mc^2$, which, when translated into the reality of this world, can release a great deal of energy, as in the atom bomb or nuclear-powered generators.

The Midrash asks: How are the Jewish people like a caterpillar? Just as a caterpillar produces silk from its mouth (orifice), so too the Jewish people produce Torah, spirituality from their mouth. They recombine the words and letters of the Torah to produce a new reality in the form of customs and laws called *Torah Sh'bal peh*. Those very people who know how to make letter combinations to say *na'aseh ve'nishmah* have the power in their mouths to create Torah (*Exodus Rabbah* 28).

The Jewish people said, "We will do and we will listen." Because they took a risk and reached far beyond their abilities, God also rewarded them with spiritual levels far beyond their reach. And because they understood this and were anxious lest they lose those levels, they begged Moses to receive the rest of the Torah for them. And the Torah that he received for them is an *Or Makif*, a surrounding light. They hoped that with adequate preparation they would attain the same level that Moses had received.

It is written, "As the apple tree among the trees of the forest" (Song of Songs 2:3). The Jewish people are like an apple tree that brings forth its fruit and then its leaves. So too, they offer their fruit to God by saying *na'aseh*, we will do, and then *nishmah*, we will listen (*Exodus Rabbah* 19). The Tosafos asks the obvious question. The verse about the apple tree is describing God—". . . so is my beloved. . . ." Yet the Midrash interprets this as if it describes the Jewish people.

The Baal Shem Tov taught that there is the means and the end. In order to build a table, we saw, cut, and nail. Cutting the wood is not the end of our plan; even nailing the boards together is not what we want. Our goal was to make a table, and until it is completed our plan is incomplete. All else that preceded it is merely a means leading to the end. This is our experience in the material world.

In the spiritual sphere, on the other hand, no activity should be regarded as a means. When we walk to give charity to a poor family, each step is a spiritual end, a good deed in itself. The same is true of every preparation to observe a commandment. It is a spiritual deed and needs the presence of mind that it deserves.

But why? If it is only a means, why regard it as an end? The reason is that in the world of Divine truth, God is in all, with all, and makes everything exist, regardless of limitations of time or space. In God's realm, the means are just as much the end as the end itself. The leaf is just as much the fruit as the fruit itself. The accomplishment of a tree in bringing forth a leaf, with all its intricate microscopic networks and processes, is just as miraculous and eventful as the fruit itself. Therefore, the Jewish people said *na'aseh*, "we will do"; whatever we do is not a means but an end. It is the goal of our activity, not a preparation, but is the actual observance of the commandment.

This is why they said *na'aseh* first. Had they said *nishmah* first, it would have meant, "let us listen so that we will know and then be able to do." Then *nishmah* would have been a means—because listening helps us do. But the truth is that listening is not a means to an end. Learning the Torah is an end, a connection to the infinite light.

It is true that God is the apple tree, the all in all, timeless and infinite, as an apple, the fruit of the tree, is here and now. And therefore the Jewish people who imitate God also relate to the world not as a means, but as an end, here and now.

The Midrash relates that when the Jewish people preceded to say *na'aseh*, "we will do," before *nishmah*, "we will listen," God declared, "Who is it who has revealed a celestial secret that only the angels of heaven know, as it is written, '. . . they do His commands to listen to His word.' First they do and then they listen" (*Exodus Rabbah* 19).

What is the great secret to do and then to listen?

It is written, "Eternal is Your word O Lord, planted firmly in heaven" (Psalms 119:89). This verse means that the spiritual root of all commandments is the word of God in the heavens, and when we take action and observe the commandments in the real world, the word of God, the root, is also awakened, and a ray of light descends from heaven into the activity. This is how angels take action; they anticipate the will of God—they have already done it and then hear the command of God as an echo of their deed.

This is like a prince who loved his father and always desired to please him by anticipating his needs. His father would call to him and say, "Could you please get my slippers?" and the prince would happily say, "It's done, my dear father." The king's words were merely an echo to that which his son had already done.

Similarly, the angels, as well as the Jewish people, say, "we will do," and as a result, we are ready to hear the echo. We will listen for the words that follow the action, and the heavenly light will descend and light up our deeds. They anticipated the will of their Father in Heaven, just as our forefathers observed the entire Torah even before it was given.

***

There is the word, *devar*, of God, and the voice, *kol*, of God. The word takes physical form, whereas the voice is still in the spiritual realm, the life and vitality in each created thing that give it the spirit to exist. Therefore, when the angels "do," they follow God's word and listen to His voice. They are in touch with the voice, the spirit within the action. Each and every created thing has God's voice within. And when man relates to a created thing properly, by observing the commandments, then the voice is heard from within. Therefore, they said, "We will do and we will listen," meaning if we do properly, we will surely listen and hear the voice of God from within.

On Shavuos we can tune in to the voice of God within our actions, to His voice within the natural world. When we act with the word of God, His commandments, we can hear the echo of His voice from within.

***

It is written, "If only now you will (*shemoah tishme'uh*) listen to My voice . . ." (Exodus 19:5).

The word of God is within the physical part of reality, limited in space and time, whereas the voice of God is infinite and gives vitality to the creation without end, always and everywhere. And that voice is the Torah, the inner voice of the entire creation.

Similarly, during the six days of the week, when we are active in the material world, we can hear the word of God. On *Shabbos* we can hear the voice of God, as in, ". . . *shomoah tishmah b'kol*, which is an acrostic of the word *Shabbos*. The manner in which we observe the word of God during the weekdays is how well we hear the voice of God on *Shabbos*. Similarly, *na'aseh*, "we will do"; if we do, we then can *nishmah*, "listen."

***

The Midrash teaches: A king gave two crystal glasses to his servant. After breaking one, the king said, "You have already broken one. Be careful not to break the other." Similarly, God said to the Jewish people, "You promised to do and listen, and have ruined your actions by worshiping the Golden Calf, now watch over your other promise to listen to the Torah. Just as Yisro, Moses's father-in-law, heard, and came to hear the words of the Torah, you too should always at least listen to the Torah" (*Exodus Rabbah* 20).

***

Why did the Jewish people first say "we will do," and then "we will listen"? Because the Jewish people are connected to the essence of the Torah, they need not think, but can do immediately. They are part of the Torah as the Torah is part of them. They need not hear anything. The ones who need to hear are those who are separated from the Torah in some way, such as Yisro, who was not as close to the Torah as the Jewish people. By saying *nishmah* the Jews were able to survive the sin of worshiping the Golden Calf; they still were connected to the Torah with listening, even if their action was defiled. Because they were still able to listen, that guaranteed that even those who cannot do can still listen. Their concern for their brethren on lower levels was rewarded. They were raised up high by God.

***

The Jewish people are called children of God, and as sons they risked all by proclaiming, ". . . we will do and we will listen. . . ." How could they have said such a thing? Is such a statement possible to fulfill? It is because when the Jewish people are united as one, they can collectively observe all the commandments of the Torah. Therefore, they proclaimed together, "And the whole people answered together saying, all that God had commanded we will do and listen" (Exodus 19). When they unite in this fashion they become as angels who do but one and only one thing: the will of God. Similarly, the entirety of the Jewish people will do that which God desires. And therefore God answered them in the singular as in "I am the Lord your God Who brought you out of Egypt." Our call as a people is as one, and God's response is also to the singular united soul of the Jewish people.

52

The Sinai Experience

 t is written, "God spoke to you face to face" (Deuteronomy 5:4). The Maharal explains this verse as follows. A master gives and the apprentice receives. The relationship of the master and the apprentice is one of total dependence. When the apprentice wants to receive, he needs to stand face to face; he needs to be prepared to receive and stand before his master. Similarly, God gives the Torah and at the same time supports you with life so that you can accept it. Moses was the one who prepared the hearts of the Jewish people to come face to face and accept the Torah.

The Midrash relates: Each word that God spoke, the entire world was filled with spicy fragrance. And all the fragrance was gathered and taken to the Garden of Eden (*Exodus Rabbah* 19).

The fragrance refers to the secret of residue; space–time itself, the material world, become infused with the fragrance of the Torah. One could breathe the air and actually experience that Torah had been there. Where is the place in which the very air, the very ground is infused with infinite spirituality? It is in the Garden of Eden, the ideal, wonderous, otherworldly place. Like the hallway that leads to the palace, so too, if we follow the fragrance of the Torah that is everywhere, we can reach the Garden of Eden.

What is this residue, this fragrance? The word of God is hidden inside each created thing and is the root of all existence. When the Torah was given, the word of God became revealed, not as the spice but as the fragrance. And if we follow this fragrance, we

are on the right track to discern the true nature of the universe.

With each word that God spoke, the world filled with fragrance. The Talmud asks: If the world filled with fragrance with the first word of God, how was there room for the second and third? The Talmud answers that a wind came, cleared the previous fragrance away, and then the second one followed (*Exodus Rabbah* 20). Similarly, when the Jewish people heard the first word, their souls flew out of them. How then did they hear the second word? God returned their souls for each of the words. As we say, "He brings death, He brings life" (*Prayer Book*). In order to attain the highest spiritual life, one must die and make room for a new one. Similarly, when one moves up to a higher spiritual level, one must also descend in order to rise again to an even higher level.

What is the secret behind these teachings? The Torah is the fulfillment and completion of the creation. If the creation is not lacking, then where is there room for the Torah? A person must realize his own imperfection in order to form a vessel for the perfection that the Torah brings. Therefore in order to bring the perfection that comes with the Torah, the wind blew away all the fragrance of the first word, and then the second word was able to come.

"God spoke with you face to face" (Deuteronomy 5:4). The Midrash comments: Sometimes a master-teacher wants to teach and the apprentice-student does not want to learn, and sometimes the apprentice wants to learn but the master does not want to teach. At Mount Sinai, however, both the master and the apprentice had the proper desire (*Deuteronomy Rabbah* 5). Surely this did not happen coincidentally, but was an act of Divine Providence. Both the Torah and the desire to learn it were gifts of God. As in the blessing before Torah study we recite, "He has given us a Torah of truth, and planted in us everlasting life." The desire to learn about and have the everlasting life was planted in us as a gift. Therefore, not only was the Torah a gift, but also standing before Mount Sinai was a gift. As we recite in the Haggadah, "If He would have only brought us before Mount Sinai, it would have been enough." We are grateful even for the desire to learn, which is a gift from God.

The Torah is made up of the combinations of the name of God and thus reveals the deepest secrets of the creation. Therefore, by learning the Torah, the Jewish people come to understand the place of each creature and its meaning in the universe. With Torah knowledge one can relate to each item of creation and place it in its proper place.

Man is a microcosm, a miniature universe, and each part of his body has a corresponding *mitzvah*. When man lives with the guidance of the Torah, when his yearnings and actions follow its prescriptions, he can then repair the whole world, because just like man, the entire universe corresponds to the words and letters of the Torah.

When we stood at the foot of Mount Sinai, we suddenly realized that the whole universe was waiting to be uplifted and restored to its original state. What an awesome encounter with the truth that must have been, although it lasted but a fraction of a second. Instantly, the souls of the Jewish people left them, as it is impossible to retain one's life during a revelation of such magnitude.

Let us allow ourselves a taste of that revelation and realize our awesome responsibility for the universe.

As the Jewish people stood before Mount Sinai, they realized that the great noise is the voice of God, as it is written, "The voice of God is with power" (Psalms 29:4). It does not say His power, but only power, meaning the power of each and every one of them who stood by Mount Sinai. God's voice varied in strength according to the strength of each and everyone. Realizing this, we know that whatever our intelligence or talents may be, whether a

lot or a little, we have a share in the Torah that was said just for us.

It is written, "God spoke to you face to face" (Deuteronomy 5:4). There were two events of clarity and concealment in the beginning. First, when God created light, it was supernal. With it humans would have understood everything, but it was concealed. Later, after the creation of man and before Adam and Eve ate from the Tree of Knowledge, the word of God was clearly experienced in each thing. After their sin, good and evil were in confusion. The good was concealed within an exterior that was not clearly good, thus concealing the word of God. At Mount Sinai, however, when God gave the Torah, for an instant the inner reality became revealed. For an instant the light of creation lit up the universe. Everything was clear again. Similarly, there is the Torah that comes from the outside, the Written Law, *Torah Sh'b'ksav*, and there is the Oral Law, the *Torah Sh'bal peh*, that comes from the inside. It is the pure good, hidden inside every Jew, that is never defiled nor mixed with evil.

On Shavuos we have the opportunity to reveal all the hidden, to see with the light from one end of the universe to the other, and to understand the meaning of the creation.

It is written, "God is my strength and my stronghold, who makes me strong" (Jeremiah 16:19).

God puts His strength inside me. Not only does a king supply a prince with soldiers to protect him but he also trains him to protect himself. It is written, "All the people saw how it thundered and the lightning flashed, and heard the trumpet sound and saw the mountain smoking, they trembled and stood at a distance" (Exodus 20:18). What did they see twice? First they saw the revelation itself—the fire, the sounds and quaking of the mountain. Then they suddenly realized that whatever they saw outside themselves was also happening inside them. Thus, face-to-face also means as one sees one's face in a mirror, ". . . as face answers face reflected in water" (Proverbs 27:19). When you look in a mirror you may think that you see someone else's face, as babies actually do. But with more wisdom you realize that it is your own face. This is just as when one discovers the light of the Torah and thinks that it is in the Torah, in its words and letters, but actually it is a reflection of the light that is in his own heart and soul. Therefore, when they stood at Mount Sinai and heard the first words of the Torah, the Jewish people also saw their own hearts, their very life, the root of their soul in the words, and immediately their souls could not be contained. They fainted dead away. It was awesome to realize that the words of the Torah are actually their very lives and the truth of their being.

Just as when a soul is sent into the physical body, they too realized that, although stuck inside a lowly body, their essence is in the highest realms and heavenly spheres. How could they possibly contain such awesome revelations? Then the Torah itself restored their souls, saying to them, "If you observe the commandments, you can remain intact while having deep revelations too."

Let us therefore look deeply into the waters of the Torah, and we will see how our souls are intertwined with the Torah.

It is written, "All the people (ro'im) saw how it thundered and the lightning flashed, and heard the trumpet sound and saw the mountain smoking, and the people saw and they trembled and stood at a distance" (Exodus 20:18). What is meant by ro'im, "they are seeing," and the repeat of the phrase, "and the people"? Not only did the people at Sinai see the sounds and become inspired but also did all the people of all times and generations, for all time to come. And when the Israelites realized that even the lowly generations can hear God 's voice from Sinai, it made them feel faint, and their souls left them, as it is written, ". . . my soul left when He spoke. . . ."

Those distant generations that the Israelites prophesied about are ours. Shouldn't we strive to deserve to hear the voice of God from Sinai so that the Israelites don't faint?

"(Vechol ha'am) All the people (ro'im) saw (es hakolos) how it thundered and the lightning flashed, and heard the trumpet sound and saw the mountain smoking, and the people saw and they trembled and stood at a distance" (Exodus 20:18). This can also be read to mean Vechol ha'am, and the whole of the people, every part of them, heard the sounds.

The Torah is a light that spreads from God and lands upon vessels that are ready to receive it. These are the 613 commandments, which represent every organ and sinew of the human body. Just as the flame on a torch can jump and land on a candle, so is a mitzvah a candle, as it is written, "A mitzvah is a lamp and the Torah is light" (Exodus Rabbah 20). Therefore the words es hakolos mean the sounds; why the additional word es? It means the spreading of the sounds; the light of the Torah spread and landed on the whole of the people. Kolos means voices. It was not merely one voice, but voices; the voice of God had an echo that bounced off the Jewish people and bounced back. It was the response that resounded from each Jewish person's body, and it was Torah Sh'bal peh.

"And all the people saw the sounds"—they were able to discern the voice of the Creator. This is just as it is said of Abraham, who as a three-year-old recognized the Creator, literally; he discerned the voice that he had heard as being that of the Creator.

Every soul recognizes the voice of the Creator before it is born inside a human baby. And that recognition is a powerful connection touching one's very being. Once in the body and through the filters of the physical world, the soul loses the sensitivity to hear God's voice. Yet, when the Israelites stood at Mount Sinai, there for an instant they regained the ability to recognize the voice of God. God's voice was so familiar to them then that their souls felt alien to the world. Therefore, their souls flew out of them, as it is written, "And my soul left me when He spoke. . . ."

This is like a prince who left the palace and joined a band of thieves. The king yearned and searched for him for many years. Finally, they came upon him on a hill. The thieves had escaped earlier when they spotted the king's soldiers while the prince lay fast asleep. The king saw his son from afar in the open field and called to him. Although asleep, the prince recognized his father's voice and responded. His father's voice touched the deepest part of his being where his love for his father was as strong as ever.

In the spiritual realm, too, there is a place in every Jewish heart where the love of God is never diminished. This love is represented by God's names that are (ainom nimchokim) not allowed to be erased. The words ainom nimchokim also mean, they are in fact never erased from our hearts. They are part of us and will never leave us. This can also be said about the words, "You shall have no other gods before me." You really cannot have any other gods, because the name of God is intrinsically part of you; it is engraved, never to be erased. Therefore, no god or no force or power can have power over you.

"And all the people saw the sounds. . . ." "All the people" means even the lowest level of the people, as when the Jewish people are in exile, still "I am with him," God says, "in his trouble" (Psalms 91:15). No matter where a Jew may be, even in the worst of situations, God's name is etched into his being. This was the significance of Ezekiel's prophesy on the River Kvor, outside the Holy Land. It teaches us that no matter where we are, even in exile, God has not forsaken us. In fact we are still prophets and the sons of prophets. Even if the Jewish people forget the Creator, He does not forget them, as it is written, "Can a woman forget her baby, or disown the child of her womb? Though she might forget, I never could forget you" (Isaiah 49:15).

This is similar to the laws concerning lost objects. We are obligated to return a lost object to an ignorant person only if he gives precise details about it. But a Torah scholar can identify it by merely looking at it because a scholar is trained to discern details, make comparisons, and recognize similarities. We too, because the image of God is engraved in our hearts, always recognize Him, even if idols became familiar to us. When put to the test, we know the true God immediately and call out, "God is One!"

A prince was gravely ill and in a state of delirium. Unfortunately, the king was out of the country and unable to be at his bedside. The wise men hired an actor to dress as the king to encourage the prince to recover, but to no avail. Finally, the next day, the king arrived, sat next to his ailing son, and whispered words of love and encouragement into his ear. Soon the prince responded and showed signs of improvement.

Similarly, although other cultures entice us, other gods beckon to us, we ultimately recognize our own Father in Heaven.

In the words of rebuke, it is written, "And I will turn to you . . ." (Leviticus 26:14). Our sages say: I will turn from all my chores and focus on you (*Leviticus Rabbah* 26). This focus, this turning away from all else, places the Jewish people directly before God—face-to-face. But can we say that God has distractions, and He needs to focus? Such is instead the weakness of material beings. Rather, this passage means that just as God's attention is always on the Jewish people, so should their attention be focused on Him. They should turn away from all distractions to study the Torah; they should turn away from all chores, leave their homes, and head for Jerusalem thrice a year and commune with God.

Similarly, at Mount Sinai, just as the Jewish people turned away from everything to listen to the words of God , so too God turned away from all else in order to be with His people.

53

Lest We Perish

t is written, "You speak to us," they said to Moses, "and we will obey; but let not God speak to us, lest we die" (Exodus 20:16). What were the Jewish people afraid of? They understood that the revelation of Sinai was so awesome that it was a miracle to have lived through it. They feared that because the spiritual heights they had attained were way beyond their reach, they would soon lose them. Therefore, they asked Moses to be an intermediary and to bring the Torah down to their level. Thus the Torah would be absorbed by them on their own level, and they would not lose it.

How could the Israelites be afraid of death? They knew that the Torah gives life, as it is written, ". . . and you shall live by them. . . ." (Leviticus 18:5). If they were sure to hold on to the Torah that they had just received, they would not have been afraid. But they could not hold onto it. Their souls left them when they listened to the first word of the Ten Commandments. They realized that they would never be able to survive the dose of spirituality that God was giving them. It was obviously the time for Moses on a human level to speak the words of the Torah.

Is it possible that the Israelites were afraid of dying? Hadn't they just risked their lives when they said, ". . . we will do and we will listen," without any idea what they were getting into? What indeed did they fear? They feared that, from the spiritual high that was totally out of their reach, they would fall so low and "die" spiritually, never to rise again—just as one who suddenly gains riches and then loses them all catastrophically and is left destitute. He can actually die, being so low, never to rise again. Similarly, after Adam and Eve ate from the Tree of Knowledge, God banished them from the Garden of Eden and kept them from the Tree of Life. If they had partaken also from that Tree, which was on a spiritual level unattainable by man, they would have fallen so low as never to rise again. Thus Moses admonished them saying, "Be not afraid," meaning, why has God done this for you? "in order that the fear of Him may be ever with you, so that you don't go astray" (Exodus 20:17). Aren't these two phrases contradictory? First Moses says, "Do not fear," and then he adds that God did this "in order that the fear of Him may be ever with you."

There are two types of fear. One is the fear of a dangerous situation, of God 's punitive power to do what He wills. The other type of fear is an awareness of God's being and presence. By humbling yourself before the Creator, an awe comes over you that is higher and out of reach of your emotions. It does not reach the emotions; you do not feel afraid, but are in a state of clear awareness and awe. Thus Moses meant, "Do not fear for your lives, but rather have the fear and awe of God with you always, and you will not sin."

Why were the Israelites frightened that they would die? At first they were not frightened of death, thinking that even if they would die, the Torah will survive. Then they realized that they were intrinsically tied to the Torah and that the Torah might not survive without them, with no one to study and perpetuate it. Then they were frightened.

Just as God is infinite, so is His love for the universe. And this love includes His guidance to help His creatures live in the world; it includes the details of their life story.

This is like a benevolent king who wished all his provinces to live in peace and harmony. With his wise men he devised a plan to help his villagers gain more tolerance and understanding, and he decreed laws to that effect. The villagers, being ignorant of the plan, thought that some of the laws were absurd. The king therefore sent his most trusted servant to explain its benefits to them.

The Torah, too, is the will of God, His love for the world. But its overall plan is hidden to human understanding, as it is written, "And it is hidden from the eyes of all beings . . ." (Job 28:21). There is no way we can fathom or understand it. But the details of the plan, the rules, the 613 commandments taught by the trustworthy servant Moses, those we can hope to understand.

This is like a prince who was sent to explore a distant island. The king had an experienced explorer instruct the prince about the exploration. He told him about the land and soil, trees and animals, the climate and weather. Then the older explorer gave him some practical advice. The prince really did not understand the advice until he lived through identical experiences.

At Mount Sinai the Israelites experienced the very roots of the Torah, which were impossible to endure. Moses, the experienced guide, was needed to teach and give them practical advice that they were able to digest and later understand.

It is written, "And they stood at the foot of the mountain" (Exodus 19:17). The Talmud explains that God lifted the mountain over their heads and said, "If you accept the Torah, all is well, but if you don't, then you will be buried" (*Shabbos* 88).

The life and vitality of God are in every particle of nature, and if people would see it they could not possibly sin. For how could they? If someone was about to use his arms or feet to commit a sin and would then clearly see God's vitality in the cells of his arms and legs, he would immediately give up his desire to sin. If he was about to use an object to commit a sin and would see God's vitality in it, he would immediately negate his desires. Why then do people sin? Because God's lifegiving and creative powers are not apparent, but are hidden in the creation. The only thing we experience are the laws of nature on the exterior of things. Few realize that the laws of nature are the word of God. When God appeared on Mount Sinai, however, He allowed the Israelites to experience His presence in every part of creation. It

was perfectly clear to everyone that sin is impossible. Therefore, if a person wants to defend himself from divine punishment, he can argue that he accepted the Torah at Sinai because it seemed so easy to keep. All of nature echoed its message. He could argue that he had no idea that the laws of nature would conceal the divine nature of the world. Still, although concealed, there is nothing in nature that negates the Torah. And whenever the Jewish people rediscover that truth, they rededicate themselves to the Torah, as they did in the days of Mordechai and Esther.

The Israelites gave over to Moses the power to listen to the word of God for them. Because to hear for yourself is one experience, but to listen for an entire people requires major intelligence and insight that only Moses our teacher possessed.

It is written: ". . . we have seen that man may live though God has spoken to him. Let us not die, then, for this fearsome fire will consume us; if we hear the voice of the Lord God any longer we shall die. For what mortal ever heard the voice of the living God speak out of the fire, as we did, and lived? You go closer and hear that the Lord our God says, and then you tell us everything that the Lord our God tells you, and we will willingly do it" (Exodus 5:22–24).

Because they negated their beings to God and thought they would die, therefore the Jewish people lived. And once they survived, they were concerned lest they perish.

The Talmud relates that the angels wanted the Torah, and it was also presented to all the nations. How could the selfsame document be presented to angels and the nations of the world? Wherein is the common thread in such dissimilar audiences?

The answer is that if the Torah would have been given to angels, it would have been read and interpreted on a very high spiritual level. On the other hand, if the nations would have received it, then it would have been read on a very materialistic level. In the end, the Israelites were the only ones to accept and receive it. Therefore, they received all the levels of the Torah—the spiritual ones of the angels and the materialistic ones of the nations.

This is like a prince at a royal banquet. He was served as a participant among a diverse group that included royalty as well as the common folk. He was therefore able to savor delicacies of both the upper crust and the lowly parts of society. Similarly, the message of the Torah is on every level, and the Israelites were able to get a taste of all of them.

It is written, ". . . and man became a living being" (Genesis 2:7). The Targum translates this as, ". . . and man was a talking being." The essence of man is his ability to communicate. And the ultimate use of this ability is to declare God's kingdom and say witness that God created the world.

The generations before Sinai forfeited their mission and gave up their gift of speech. They worshiped idols and all but banished the memory of God's power. The Israelites at Sinai accepted their mission wholeheartedly, and therefore, their souls jumped out of their bodies as God's presence was revealed. Just as the light of a candle is negated when in the presence of a torch, yet it is not extinguished but merely disappears. So too the souls of the Israelites in the presence of God faded before His great Divine light.

It is written, ". . . and the Israelites went up (vachamushim) armed out of the land of Egypt . . ." (Exodus 13:18). The Zohar comments that the word chamushim equals fifty, and the word Mitzrayim, Egypt, is mentioned fifty times in the Torah. This teaches us that although the Exodus was a liberation from slavery, it was not complete. It developed in levels as the steps of a ladder, and finally at the foot of Mount Sinai it was complete. Vachamushim—the Torah was as the contract given to the slaves declaring their freedom.

A prince was taken captive by a band of thieves seeking a ransom. The king organized a search and found his son on a remote island. Seeing his son he said, "Son, our fight for your freedom has just begun!" They braved rapids and climbed over boulders. After many days, they finally reached the palace walls. The gates opened, and as they entered, the king said, "Now you are free, my son. Bathe and get some needed rest."

Similarly, although the Israelites left Egypt, their complete freedom would wait until they stood at Mount Sinai. There they reached the palace of the King and were finally able to rest.

It is written, "(Vayitzer) The Lord God formed . . ." (Genesis 2:7). The word vayitzer is written in the Torah with two yuds, although one yud suffices.

God created man with two opposing desires, a desire for good and a desire for evil. Still, both of them must be harnessed to do the will of God, as it is written, "And you should love the Lord your God with all your heart . . . (Deuteronomy 6:5). A person must love God with both powers of his heart, the good and evil. But how can an evil desire be used to accomplish God's will? It can. Our ordinary physical life can be turned into Godliness and holiness. If the yetzer hara, the desire for evil, is like iron, the fire of the Torah will transform it. The Torah equalizes both the good and evil to be means of serving God.

Thus when the Israelites stood by Mount Sinai, they became as they were originally at creation, with both yods, both desires, in the employ of serving God.

"Do not fear," said Moses, "God is but testing you so that His fear should be on your face as not to sin." The Zohar comments that there are two levels of fearing God: a lower one, which fears punishment, and a higher one, which fears the greatness of God.

At Mount Sinai there was fire and smoke to prevent those who were unworthy from experiencing its essence. This is like a doctor who has just produced a miracle drug and is worried lest it fall into the hands of abusers, so he will not reveal its ingredients. So too, the Sinai experience was camouflaged with smoke and fire. But the Israelites, instead of being frightened, were emboldened by this camouflage, realizing that it must be a very precious intimacy needing much protection.

This is like the king's visit to a village. First the heavily armed cavalry marched into the village. The villagers assembled and were awed by the size and strength of the horses, the ceremonial uniforms of the soldiers, and their razor-sharp weapons. This sight inspired awe and fear of the great power of the king. The wise among them realized that the power of the king helps them live peaceful and orderly lives.

Similarly, there were two levels of reacting to the fire and smoke of Mount Sinai. The people of the lower levels feared the smoke and fire itself; they had a fear of death. The higher level saw in the smoke and fire the power of God Who desires true and everlasting life for all His creatures.

It is written, ". . . the Lord spoke in a great voice . . . (v'lo yosof) then said no more" (Deuteronomy 5:19). V'lo yosof literally means and it has no end. The sound of the thunder of Mount Sinai resounds throughout the universe, as it is written, ". . . which I (*Anochi*) command you today . . ." (Deuteronomy 6:6). The *Anochi*, the "I am the Lord," of the Ten Commandments can be heard still.

In the spiritual realm whenever the good increases, the evil increases, too, to balance it. And our sages have taught, the desire of man becomes stronger and stronger each and every day (*Sukkah* 52a). Each day man is in danger of falling into the exile of purely materialistic pursuits. But there is also the antidote, the Torah, which is given each and every day. With the Torah one can leave the exile, as it is written, "*Anochi*—I am God who brought you out of Egypt." With the *Anochi*, the giving of the Torah each day, one can be rescued from the ever-increasing strength of one's desires.

It is written, "Moses answered, `Do not be afraid. God has come only to test you, so the fear of Him may remain with you and keep you from sin'" (Exodus 20:20). He was testing them by lifting the mountain over their heads. But why did they need the test? Hadn't they just answered, "We will do and we will listen?" What other test did they need?

The Jewish people fearlessly risked everything and agreed to accept laws they had not even heard, yet were frightened of the fire and smoke on the mountain. Therefore, God lifted the mountain over them to teach them that, no matter what level one reaches, there are always other tests. They must hold to one spiritual level before they climb to the next one, like a mountain climber who reaches the top of a plateau and must acclimate himself to its height before attempting to continue. Similarly, in order to benefit from the Torah and to climb higher and higher in spirit, one must overcome the fright of being in a place so high. Once that is accomplished, one can go to the next level, but knowing that a similar experience awaits.

It is written, "Whenever Moses spoke, God answered him with thunder." The Midrash comments: God was speaking from the throat of Moses (*Exodus Rabbah* 20). How does the Midrash reach this conclusion?

Moses was asked to descend from the mountain so that the Israelites should not mistakingly think that God and Moses together wrote the Torah. How does his coming down from the mountain help correct that misconception? Even then they could say that Moses is the author of the Torah. Therefore, the Midrash concludes that it must be that when Moses spoke, it was not with his own voice, but with a Divine voice. Thus, God sent Moses off the mountain to speak with a Divine voice, and the people were certain of the Divine authorship of the Torah.

"They journeyed from Rephidim and entered the wilderness of Sinai" (Exodus 19:1). Rephidim is where the Amalekites made a surprise attack on the Israelites and dampened their spirit. What connection is there between that attack and their arrival at Mount Sinai?

It is written, "Many waters cannot quench love" (Song of Songs 8:7). Water and fire oppose each other. Yet, when drops of water fall on fire, they hiss, bubble, and cause a great tumult. So too, when the forces of evil block our path, keep us from reaching our goal, a great amount of energy is released, and we overcome. Thus, at Rephidim, where Amalek came to extinguish our fire of enthusiasm, the opposite happened. The fire became stronger, and we overcame them completely at Sinai.

This was the promise given to Isaac about his two sons soon to be born, "*U'leom m'leom ye'emotz*—one nation will overcome the other nation" (Genesis 25:23). There will be a struggle, but instead of being weakened by it, he will gain strength. Instead of breaking the Israelites entirely, the attack of Amalek helped strengthen them.

The Torah is compared to water, as it is written, "All who are thirsty go to water" (Isaiah 55:1). It is also compared to fire, "Is not my word as a fire?" (Jeremiah 23:29). Similarly, the body is made of the dust of the earth, whereas the soul is made of heavenly and spiritual stuff. As holy as the body becomes, even as of a *tzaddik*, it cannot escape its earthliness; it is buried in the ground, as even Moses, our greatest prophet, was buried. As it is written, ". . . for dust you are, and to dust you shall return" (Genesis 3:19). The water of the Torah descends from the high places to the lowest place, to the body that is the dust of the earth. If it is able to descend to the body, because of its humility, then it becomes as fire to raise man's soul to the highest heaven. And that is the proper way for things to be: the body should be as low as the dust of the earth, while the soul soars heavenward. The senses, being blind and unfocused, allow the body the pursuit of pleasures and prevent the soul from soaring. Those sensations then have nothing to do with the pursuit of spiritual goals.

A wise man from another country came to see the king. He prepared words of praise and a plea for help. At the throne he prostrated himself as the most worthless individual. Standing erect, he finally recited a most glorious praise of the king.

Similarly, when we lower ourselves to the very ground, when we negate our body, our souls are free to soar upward, as did Moses, our greatest teacher and prophet, who was "a man of God" (Deuteronomy 33:1). A man who was the most humble of human beings on the face of the earth, and his soul soared toward heaven with God.

After the Israelites saw the Ten Plagues and the splitting of the Red Sea, they were ready to be guided by the Torah. Then they would have received its teachings with perfect clarity, as glass without the slightest haziness. Then Amalek came and cast doubts in their hearts. Their enthusiasm weakened, and they were no longer ready to act. Forty-nine days passed. When they arrived at Mount Sinai and were again ready to receive the Torah, they had to energize themselves. They immediately said, "We will do and we will listen."

Since then, whenever Amalek is defeated we experience the enthusiasm of Mount Sinai, with the clarity of looking through a clear glass.

It is written, "As an apple tree among the trees of the forest, so is my beloved" (Song of Songs 2:3) Why are the Israelites compared to an apple tree? Just as with an apple tree, the fruit comes before the leaves, so too the Jewish people first are ready to bear fruit, to do good deeds and then to listen to instructions. Just as the apple tree has little shade, as God's protection is not apparent in this world, still the Jewish people want it and yearn for it (*Exodus Rabbah* 19). Yet, is this verse not about Jewish people but about God? It should say, rather, why God is compared to an apple tree.

The answer is that God relates to the Jewish people the same way that the Jewish people relate to Him. So if they visualize God as an apple tree, with protection that is not apparent, then they too are compared to an apple tree. Similarly, the Jewish people wanted to be like the angels who say we will do before they hear their orders: ". . . they went wherever the spirit impelled them to go . . ." (Ezekiel 1:12). They do without questioning, embodying the will of God. Therefore they become themselves like angels. And the Zohar adds: It is written, "*Noda ba'sheorim baaloh*—Her husband is known in the gates, of important places." The word *sheorim* also means to imagine or image. Whatever a person imagines or images about God, that is what God is to him.

54

The Ten Commandments

here is a spiritual essence that God gives to each of us, and there is the physical vessel that contains the essence. Our body is such a vessel for God's divine spark, which is our soul. And this vessel must be guarded and kept in condition to receive and contain the soul within. These two aspects correspond to the positive and negative commandments in the Torah. The *mitzvos aseh* are the positive commandments that fortify and give strength to our soul. The *mitzvos lo saaseh*, the prohibitions, protect the body so it can remain a proper vessel for the soul. And then it becomes subordinated to the soul and unites with it, so each invigorate each other. The purity of the soul shines through and enlightens its vessel.

The Ten Commandments are mentioned twice in the Torah. The first time is in the commandment of *Shabbos*, where we read "Remember, (*zachor*) the *Shabbos* . . ." (Exodus 20:8). The second time is in "Observe (*shamor*) the *Shabbos* . . ." (Deuteronomy 5:12) To remember is to do activities that remind one of the holiness of the day; for example, repeating the story of creation when reciting *Kiddush* over a cup of wine, lighting lamps in honor of the day, and bathing and dressing in its honor. On the other hand, there is the observance of the *Shabbos*—by refraining from doing any of the thirty-nine prohibited types of labor. When we observe the *Shabbos*, it becomes a vessel to receive that which is within the *Shabbos*, the holiness that we want to remember and never forget. Then the hidden and the revealed aspects of the *Shabbos* become one; a union and singularity are created.

The Midrash states that the words *zachor* and *shamor* both were said simultaneously, which no mouth can repeat and no ear can hear. This means that when we have both the *zachor* and *shamor* together, the vessel and the light within, then there

is unity, the vessel unifies with the spirit, and it no longer limits or hinders the inner light from shining forth. Therefore, no mouth could speak, no ear could hear—it is beyond the limitations of the physical body and essence.

The Torah has the power to unite the revealed and concealed. We can prepare vessels for the concealed by studying the Torah. Then the concealed part of the Torah becomes understood too.

"Do not utter God's name in vain." God's name is in each one of us from the time that He created the world. He said, ". . . and the Lord God said, Let us make man . . ." (Genesis 1:26). We must guard our life to keep the holy spark in us so that God will not have spoken in vain. That command is God's word in us, the holy spark of light, our soul, and it must be guarded carefully. As it is written, "Who may ascend the mountain of the Lord? Who may stand in His holy place? He who has clean hands and a pure heart, who has not taken a false oath by My life or sworn deceitfully" (Psalms 24:3–4). And who could be that pure? Only those who are helped by God. And if we exert all our energy to purify our deeds, then God assists us beyond human capabilities.

"I am the Lord your God. . . ." Why is it written as if speaking to Moses directly? In order to allow Moses to defend the Jewish people after their idolatry, when Moses said to God, "Forgive them. They err. You have commanded only me, not them, to worship You and no one else!"

On a spiritual level, the fact that God only spoke to Moses can be understood as follows. In every generation, there is one *tzaddik*, one righteous man to accept the commandments. It was Moses in his time; he, and not the Jewish people, accepted the yoke of the commandments. He could then legitimately defend them that they were not the ones commanded to worship one God, but only he.

———

We pray on *Shabbos* afternoon, "You are one, Your name is one, and who is like Your nation Israel, one in all the land." God, the Torah, and the Jewish people are one. What unifies them? The Torah is the word of God, and is the inner reality of all three. As it is written, "The Torah was commanded to us by Moses as the heritage of the congregation of Jacob" (Deuteronomy 33:4). Congregation is written in the singular. When do the Jewish people become one? Through the Torah, their inner reality. In addition, God said, "I am the Lord your God." God is one without number, without beginning or end. He is one as an absolute singularity, and so are the Jewish people, who mirror the ultimate reality. They were therefore removed from Egypt, *Mitzrayim*, which means limitations and boundaries. They left all limitations and were united as a singularity, just as is God Himself.

———

It is written, "And God spoke all these words saying, 'I am the Lord your God....'" All these words, the entire Torah is for one purpose: to know that I am the Lord your God. The Torah gives two gifts: the light of wisdom, the word *orah* in the word Torah, and awe, the word *yira* in the word Torah. Both wisdom and awe are contained in it.

There is fear and awe when we realize that the word of God is in each created thing. Fear must precede wisdom if it is to last. Fear is the feeling of one's inferiority, frailty, and impermanence. Awe grows from a feeling of fulfillment. Awe in realizing that God's Providence keeps everything alive is itself wisdom.

———

It is written, "*Anochi*—I am the Lord your God." The Midrash says that the word *Anochi* is a consolation for the Jewish people as it is written, "I (*Anochi, Anochi*) alone am He who consoles you" (Isaiah 51:12). Similarly in the Egyptian exile, God reassures Jacob as he is about to descend to Egypt, "I Myself (*Anochi*) will go down with you to Egypt, and I Myself (*Anochi*) will take you up..." (Genesis 46:4). The dialogue of *Anochi*, which God has with the Jewish people, is that which helps them survive (*Exodus Rabbah* 20).

The Torah gives strength before and after troubled times. It gave strength to the Jewish people in Egypt when they heard the words "When you have freed the people from Egypt, you shall worship God on this mountain" (Exodus 3:12). The promise to receive the Torah sustained them during their suffering and sustains them ever since.

———

It is written, "There's a people that dwells apart, not reckoned among the nations" (Numbers 23:9).

The Jewish people are insignificant among the nations; they are nothing and do not even count. Similarly, the Jewish people have no place in the world just as Abraham, a great astrologer, knew that according to the laws of nature, he would have no children. And God said to him, "True, within the laws of nature you cannot have children. But now you have joined my kingdom and follow My rules, the supernatural, the miraculous rules."

The Jewish people were slaves in Egypt, a country where no slave ever went free. In the natural order of things, no one ever escaped from there. But God said to them, "No one else can leave, but you have joined My kingdom, and function within the miraculous order." Therefore God said, "I am the Lord your God who brought you out of the land of Egypt, the house of bondage." This was a double removal: they were removed from Egypt and from the house of bondage. They were lifted higher than the natural world.

———

"And God spoke all these words, saying...." Whatever the prophets of any generation will say, it is already all from Sinai. All the souls of the Jewish people heard the words of God on Sinai. Not only their souls, but the Jewish people were on so high a level that even their physical ears heard. The other generations, only their souls heard it, and not their physical ears.

———

"I the Lord am your God who brought you out of the land of Egypt, the house of bondage." Why does this verse not read, "Who created you?" No, that would have been inappropriate for the Talmud already concluded that it is far better not to be created. However, once you are created you must check your deeds carefully and be sure they are pure. The Jewish people became purified and sifted thoroughly when they left Egypt. And although the love and awe of

God are of the highest virtue, still the Torah is the ultimate sifter as it is the word of God.

"I the Lord am your God." Those words are not only a command that every Jew must know that there is only one God but also indicate that God revealed Himself to the Jewish people and said, "Look, see, I am the one and only God. . . ." This revelation and encounter are inscribed in the hearts of the Jewish people, as it is written, "The Torah of God is perfect, renewing life" (Psalms 19:8). The Torah reunites the parts of the soul with each other, as it is written, "It is a tree of life to those who hold on to it" (*Mishlei* 3:18). Those who reconnect the parts of their body and soul by means of the Torah receive life.

It is written, "I the Lord am your God who brought you out of the land of Egypt, the house of bondage." The Midrash comments: Although I am the Lord over all of the natural world, nevertheless, with you I have a special relationship (*Exodus Rabbah* 20).

Nothing in the universe exists without God's free will. Nature is composed of elements, which are the smallest bits of any specific material. An element in nature could only survive within specific conditions. Limiting the power of God within the confines of nature is called "other gods," powers that come from God but manifest themselves in a very limited way. Those powers are inferior to God Who revealed Himself on Sinai as all powerful and infinite. The limiting power is called "the house of slaves," because anything that is not in its rightful place is in slavery. As it is written, "And He said to Abram, 'Know well that your offspring will be strangers in a land not theirs'" (Genesis 15:13). Therefore, "I the Lord am your God." Do not worship idols, because then you abandon the special relationship that I have with you. Yes, there are laws and forces of nature—but do not worship them. Do not accept them as the ultimate reality, but instead worship God Who orchestrates the forces and the universe as a whole.

The universe was created with Ten Commands, such as "Let there be light." And these commands are in the inner core of nature; they keep the natural world going. For example, how does light exist? The command of God, "Let there be light," is still active in light. The same is true with the other items of creation; the word of God within keeps them alive and makes them be. But the Jewish people heard the Ten Commandments from God Himself; therefore, their connection to nature is not to the material outer portion, but to its very core, to the word of God within. As it is written, "May he kiss me with the kisses of his mouth" (Song of Songs 1:1). We receive Torah straight from the mouth of God.

This is like a king who was giving portions to all his guests. When his baby crawled over to him, he picked him up and fed him from food that he himself had chewed. Similarly, while the other nations deal with nature even as a gift from God, the Jewish people relate to the word of God within, as it is written, "With the word of God the world was created and with the breath of his mouth all its hosts" (Psalms 33:6). Those who relate to the material portion of nature are in the house of slaves, but God removed the Jewish people from there to the realm of "I am the Lord." The Jews are no longer enslaved to nature, but go directly to the source, the word of God, the Torah, which is in everything.

55

The Story of Ruth

uth was a non-Jew who wanted to convert and join the Jewish nation. How is it possible to join a people who were set aside by God to declare His kingdom? It is because they are the ripened and mature source of truth in the world. They manifest what other nations may be in potential. Therefore, if a non-Jew desires to fulfill his potential, his earnest longing breaks through all obstacles, and he becomes a Jew.

The nations of the world are *nishmah v'naaseh*, people who demand first to hear about the nature of the commodity before they buy it. They need first to hear teachings to counter their resistance. But for those who are ready, God gave His people spiritual energy to help others join them in their brave enterprise of *na'aseh v'nishmah*, to first do and then listen.

When the *Mashiach* comes, all potential will be revealed, and the nations of the world will be speaking assuredly about God, as it is written, "For then I will make the people pure of speech, so that they all invoke the Lord by name, And serve Him with one accord" (Zephaniah 3:9). For now, the Gentile can hasten his progress to the era of *Mashiach* by converting to Judaism. Thus, King David was descended from Ruth, a birth that brought *Mashiach's* time full circle. *Mashiach* comes from a convert, and conversion hastens his coming.

———

Ruth decided to convert to Judaism because of the kindness she had experienced with Naomi and her family. It is the goal of the Jewish people to make others literally like themselves, as it is written, "And God said, `Let us make man in our image'" (Genesis 1:26) and also concerning Abraham, ". . . and the persons they had acquired in Haran . . ." (Genesis 12:5). It is an identical process with the individual. The more a person urges his physical being to be close to his soul, the more spiritual light shines into his body. Similarly, the more we allow the nations of the world to be close to us and the Torah, to enter our circle, the more light shines through us to reach them. But if the Jewish people are the inheritance of God, why should we reach out and share with others? Because doing so is part of being true and kind, and making others Jews is part of being a Jew. As it is written, "You will keep (*emes*) true with Jacob . . . (Micah 7:20). Because Jacob is true, it is his fundamental virtue, and kindness is his way, he must share his truths to maintain his integrity.

———

It is written, "*Anochi, Anochi*, I am He who consoles you . . ." (Isaiah 51:12). The word *Anochi* refers to the first word of the Ten Commandments, "*Anochi*, I am the Lord your God who brought you out of Egypt." Why is the word *Anochi* repeated? The first time it symbolizes the *Anochi* of Sinai, and the second time it symbolizes the *Anochi* of *Mashiach's* time, when God will console His people. The Egyptian exile cleansed the Israelites and prepared them for the redemption and Sinai. So too, this exile, which is longer and more intense, will lead to an absolute redemption and be followed by a Torah experience that will be more profound and powerful than Sinai. For the first *Anochi* at Sinai was restricted, "Beware of going up the mountain or touching the border of it" (Exodus 19:12), and the Jews were not permitted to have the full effect of the experience. But when the *Mashiach* comes, the second *Anochi*, the experience will be completed, as it is written, "When the ram's horn sounds a long blast, they may go up on the mountain" (Exodus 19:13).

Like Moses who ascended the mountain and received the Torah of the highest levels, so too when the *Mashiach* comes, the Jewish people will ascend to the mountaintop. They will attain the highest of all understanding. As it is written, "The end of a matter is better than the beginning of it" (Ecclesiastes 7:8), and "Behold, I will have redeemed you at the end as in the beginning" (*Kedushah* prayer of the *Musaf* service). The end will be even better than the beginning, as it is written, "For you will not depart in haste . . ." (Isaiah 52:12). You will not have to rush, as in Egypt, to reach the high spiritual levels. At that time you were unprepared for them, but in the *Mashiach's* time, you will be prepared to go to the very top. Similarly, the later years of Ruth were better than her early ones. She was consoled by joining the Jewish people. As a reflection of Ruth who abandoned her family's idolatry in favor of the Jewish people and the one God, so too the *Mashiach* will attract the nations to join the worship of one God.

It is written, "O Lord (*oozi*) my strength and my stronghold, my refuge (*me'oozi*) in a day of trouble, to You nations shall come from the ends of the earth . . . (Jeremiah 16:19). The word *oozi* refers to the Torah, as in "May the Lord grant (*oz*) strength to His people . . ." (Psalms 29:11).

There are two ways that the wisdom of the Torah reaches the world. One is by *oz*, "strength"—when the Jewish people are strong and exude Torah wisdom, thereby attracting other nations. Another way is by *me'oozi*, "my refuge in a day of trouble." God places the Jewish nation as a refuge among the nations where they can easily share their wisdom and culture with the nations of the world. This very thing happened with Ruth. Elimelech, the husband of Naomi, left *Eretz Yisrael*, the land of Israel, because of famine. He went, destined to attract the soul root of the *Mashiach*. After his death and Ruth's conversion, she met Boaz, whose name means, in him is strength. The Torah was shining through him, and that attracted Ruth, and together they became the progenitors of the *Mashiach*. Through them, both aspects of strength were realized—the strength of *oozi* and the strength of *me'oozi*. She was attracted by the Torah strength of Boaz, just as later the *Mashiach* will attract the nations of the world from all corners of the globe to do the will of God.

It is written, "Hope deferred sickens the heart" (Proverbs 13:12). But those who cling to the Tree of Life, their yearnings are fulfilled.

It is written, "I the Lord, will speed it in due time" (Isaiah 60:22). The Talmud explains: If the Jewish people are worthy I will speed their final redemption, and if they are not worthy, they will have to wait until they are sick of waiting. Nevertheless, there is still another way; they can bring the *Mashiach* with the energy of the Torah (*Sanhedrin* 98a). The Torah itself attracts *Mashiach* as Boaz attracted Ruth to beget the *Mashiach*. And not only our need for a redeemer can be attracted by the Torah, for whenever we pray for any of our needs, we should first recite a verse from the Torah to attract its fulfillment.

The spiritual world ultimately unites with the word of God, and then all exiles come to an end. "In due time," sometime, eventually, the redemption will come. But with the Torah, the Tree of Life, the word of God, "I will hasten it." The process is speeded up, and it happens quickly beyond time. It could even happen right now, this instant, without any waiting. This is exactly what happened with Ruth; her exile as a Gentile girl ended with a total immediate redemption, and she gave birth to the *Mashiach*, the redeemer of all time, who can come at any moment.

The Torah is the word of God in every item of creation, giving it its very life. It is the Tree of Life that gives life to lifeless creatures. It is impossible to bring life back to any creature unless it is connected to the Torah. As our sages have taught, Each letter of the Torah can quicken the dead, but unfortunately we do not know how (*Sanhedrin* 90b). Therefore, kindness done with the dead is called *chesed shel emes*, "kindness of truth"; the Torah is truth, and only with its energy can kindness be done. For otherwise how or why would anyone do kindness with the dead? Is there life in him any more? For whom are you doing kindness? However, with the Torah, God's word in every creature, there still is life in him.

Similarly, Boaz, a relative of Elimelech, the husband of Naomi and the husband of Ruth, offered to do kindness with the dead and to take over where Elimelech left off—to marry Ruth and bear children. Such kindness can only be done with the power of the Torah; *bo az*, "the Torah was in him."

The Israelites experienced the power of the Torah at Mount Sinai when their souls departed after hearing the first word. Then the words of the Torah itself quickened their lifeless bodies as their souls returned.

It is written, "Now then, if you obey Me faithfully, and keep My covenant, you shall be My treasured possession among all the peoples" (Exodus 19:5).

The Or Hachaim explains if you study the Torah, its energy will make you become the chosen of all the nations; you need not go into exile. Similarly, the words "*Anochi*, I am the Lord your God who brought you out of Egypt," mean that with the *Anochi*, the Torah, one is redeemed and removed from exile. Therefore, the story of Ruth is read on Shavuos to emphasize even more that if one receives the Torah fully and unconditionally, then one's redemption is imminent.

The Israelites proclaimed, "We will do and we will listen." They understood the importance of doing, just as they said, "If we continue to listen we will perish," meaning that if we continue only to listen, then we will perish. They knew that they must do, *hamaaseh hu haikar*, that action is of primary importance. Therefore, we read the book of Ruth on Shavuos to learn about the real flesh-and-blood lives of families with Torah values and deeds, as exemplified by Boaz—*bo az*, the Torah was part of him, was part of his real life.

The Midrash recounts that if Reuven would have known that the Torah would tell of him, that his deed would be recalled for posterity, he would have taken Joseph and carried him home on his shoulders. "But when Reuven heard it, he tried to save him from them. He said, `Let us not take his life.' And Reuven went on, `Shed no blood! Cast him into the pit out in the wilderness, but do not touch him yourselves,' intending to save him from them and restore him to his father" (Genesis 37:21). And if Boaz would have known that his deed of kindness would be recorded, that he gave Ruth some toasted wheat and vinegar, he would have roasted a calf for her. Yet, although neither did the ultimate action, the Torah still valued their acts as great deeds. We can assuredly say that neither Reuven nor Boaz thought their deeds great enough to be recorded, which is a witness to their righteousness; they did acts of kindness and thought nothing of them. They did not make a big deal of their good deeds unlike nowadays, says the *Sfas Emes*, when if a person does any one thing he thinks he deserves praise to the heavens.

The Jewish people were chosen by God to reveal His kingdom. They are like a prince who, wherever he goes, speaks of his father. They too are the children of God, as it is written, "You are the children of God . . ." (Deuteronomy 14:10). God also treats them with loving-kindness as His children, even when they are unworthy. It is no wonder that the nations of the world say, "They are just as unworthy as we, except that God has mercy on them." This is true now before the *Mashiach* comes. When he arrives, everyone will realize that it is not out of mercy and pity that the Jewish people survived all the terrible persecutions, but they deserved it, even with strict judgment. The nations will see that the Jewish people have served God in safety and in danger; ignoring comforts, they have observed the Torah and the commandments. Therefore, they deserve to survive even with the strictest of judgments.

The Jewish people receive gifts from God with loving-kindness because they are His children, but they are also His servants to whom He gives because they worked for it. The law is that if you work you get paid.

This is like the king who asked all the royal entourage to help set up a banquet. Servants, guests, and family members helped. Then the king gathered them and paid each one handsomely for his work. The prince too was among the helpers. The king smiled to him and gave him his due. The others saw the special regard the king had for his son, yet they realized that the prince deserved his reward. He had earned it with his hard work.

Moses said to God, "O Lord God, You Who let Your servant see the first works of Your greatness and Your mighty hand" (Deuteronomy 3:23). The Torah is the first works, the end is the coming of the *Mashiach*, and there too it is written, "My servant David shall be king over them; there shall be one shepherd for all of them" (Ezekiel 37:24). They both earned their reward as servants who work for the king.

Therefore, on Shavuos when we mention the Torah being given through Moses the servant of God, we must also mention David and the *Mashiach*, who is called a servant, too, as it is written, "My servant will be wise (*yaskil avdi*)" (Isaiah 52:13).

The souls of the Jewish people have their roots in the highest spiritual realms. There are other lofty souls, but for reasons unknown they are in exile among the nations of the world. What happens to those souls? They feel an attraction to the Jewish people and may convert to Judaism, just as Ruth did. Although the Jews are the ones chosen by God to serve Him, still they are commanded, "You too must befriend the stranger, for you were strangers in the land of Egypt" (Deuteronomy 10:19); he too belongs with you, a soul finally returned. As it is written, "God protects (*shomer*) the (*gerim*) converts (Psalms 126:9). The word *shomer* also means, He waits. God waits for the souls in exile among the nations to come home as *gerim*.

Our sages say: There are three things that were the most precious finds of God. One is the heart of Abraham, as it is written, "Finding his heart true to you" (Nehemiah 9:8). Two is the Jewish people, as it is written, "I found Israel as pleasing as grapes in the wilderness" (Hosea 9:10). And three is David, the progenitor of *Mashiach*, as it is written, "I have found David my servant anointed with sacred oil" (Psalms 89:21). Abraham was the first to find his way back to God after all the world went astray with idolatry and carnal sins. The *Mashiach* is the last to find his way; after he arrives, no new converts will be accepted, as all will have returned by then.

It is written, "When she opens her mouth, it is with wisdom, and *Toras*, a teaching of kindness is on her tongue" (Proverbs 31:26). The Talmud asks: is there a Torah with kindness and one without kindness? Torah with kindness is one who studied for the sake of the Torah itself, for God's sake. But one who studies for material gain, for his own glory so he can be called a scholar, such Torah is without kindness (*Sukkah* 49b). Because the Torah is very exacting and specific, *aish das*, it is the fire of the law and burns those who do not obey it. Then how can anyone hope to survive learning the Torah? Is it not fraught with danger? Because it is the word of God, it gives life to those who study and observe its commandments, but burns those who abuse it. Therefore, he who studies the Torah for its own sake, and not for fame and profit, the fire turns into honey, as it is written, "Like an apple tree among trees of the forest, so is my beloved among the youths. I delight to sit in his shade, And his fruit is sweet to my palate" (Song of Songs 2:3).

The nations of the world did not accept the Torah; they refused to sit in the shade of the apple tree. They shied away from its meager shade for fear of getting burned by the sun. They feared getting burned by the Torah law for it is fire. But the Israelites were brave and risked everything. They sat in its shade immediately and were rewarded; instead of the fire, they received sweet fruit. All those who come with complete resolve receive sweet fruit, whereas the others get burned with the fire of the law.

And because of this, the Jewish people are able to reverse the strict judgment of God to the sweetness of lovingkindness.

The custom of eating milk sweetened with honey on Shavuos is symbolic of the verse, ". . . honey and milk are under your tongue" (Song of Songs 4:11), and is a reminder that the Torah helps convert strict judgment to sweetness.

It is written, "And when you have freed the people from Egypt, you shall worship God at this mountain" (Exodus 3:10). To serve God refers to prayer, and Torah knowledge is also a service to God, as it is written, "Know the God of your father and serve Him" (*I Divrei Hayamim* 28:9).

To know and serve—one is in the mind, and the other is in the heart. Both our intelligence and sensations are harnessed in the service of God. Where one's mind is, one's heart is sure to follow. Consciousness and intelligence lead the rest of the person. The Torah is the mind of the Jewish people and leads the yearnings of their heart, their prayers, in the right direction. Therefore, we always precede prayers with words of Torah, which guide our hearts and prayers.

Moses initiated the Torah way, while David was "*ne'im zemiros Yisrael*—the favorite of the songs of Israel." His whole life was dedicated to prayer. The Torah of Moses shows the way for the prayers of David. Therefore by reading on Shavuos the story of Ruth, the progenitor of David, we connect the Torah, our mind, with our prayers, our heart. As it is written, "God is near to all who call Him, to all who call Him in truth" (Psalms 145:18). When one prays to God with the truth of the Torah, then one's prayers are accepted.

But even prayer has two aspects. We could be near, as in "God is near to all who call Him," and He could be far, as in "The people saw, had fear, and stood from afar" (Exodus 20:18). We can be far, being in need, and we then pray to God. At other times we are near, when we have what we need. In both cases we have to pray to connect our physical life to the spiritual realm. And always we pray with the guidance of the Torah, with the Torah in our mind guiding our heart.

It is written, "Man and beast You help, O God" (Psalms 36:7). At first we acted as a beast: we followed God into the parched desert without thinking, as does an animal that is not worthy of redemption. Then we prepared ourselves for seven weeks and stood before Mount Sinai to receive Torah wisdom and teachings of the highest caliber. We advanced from the level of a beast to the level of man, as it is written, "And you are my sheep, the sheep that I shepherd, you are men" (Ezekiel 35:31). At first you are sheep, are beasts; then you are men.

On a deeper level, however, relating to God as a beast that follows the master without thinking is a much higher level, as it is written, "... as a beast I was with you ..." (Psalms 73:22). King David said, "I have nothing from myself, but follow You, God, as an animal. I don't want a thing, I just want to pray and sing."

Reading Ruth on Shavuos teaches us the path of David, of following God as an animal, with complete faith and no questions.

Moses brought us the Written Law, and David was the root of the Oral Law. Yisro, Moses's father-in-law, was attracted to Sinai by the Written Law. He is also the one who attracted Moses and cared for him while he was a fugitive from Pharaoh. Ruth was brought to the Jewish nation through the Oral Law, when Boaz explained the words, "No Ammonite or Moavite shall be admitted into the congregation of God" (Deuteronomy 33:4). He said that Amon refers to men, so therefore females are excluded from the prohibition. She in turn brought David, who was the root of the Oral Law, into the world.

The story of Ruth teaches us that the primary and essential thing is action, not only study. The Torah is the guide to finding the right actions, as we say in our prayers, "... an everlasting life He planted in us." The Torah that He planted in us gives us everlasting life; it changes our temporary life into an eternal life by changing our actions to those that lead to an everlasting life.

Just as the Jewish people are witnesses that God created the universe, so too the Gentiles who are attracted to the Jewish people are witnesses to the holiness of Jewish people. And this is the sum of the story of Ruth—to tell us the greatness of the Jewish people who attract Ruth.

The Jewish nation received the Torah from God as a way of life. Reciprocally, when they follow its instructions, their life becomes part of that very Torah, as the story of Boaz and Ruth became a scroll, a *megillah*, and part of the Written Law. Thus the Oral became Written in the eternal mosaic; the impermanent life was transformed into the permanent teaching for all generations, until the coming of the *Mashiach*, who is a product of the story.

Thus, "If Boaz would have known that his deeds are being recorded ..." (*Ruth Rabbah*), if he would have realized the awesome value of a person's deeds that reach up to God's throne, becoming the Torah itself, "he would have behaved differently."

There is a twin symmetry. The Jewish people bring God's light and presence into the letters of the Torah, and reflectively, God engraves their deeds into the Torah scroll, and they become the actual Torah. The Midrash says, "Moses held onto the Tablets two *tefachim* (handbreadth) and God held on also two *tefachim*, and there were two *tefachim* in between them" (*Sukkah* 8a). This means that when the Jewish people hold onto the Torah, those actions become the very same Torah that God Himself holds onto. Thus the Oral Law and the Written Law are one and the same.

It is written, "Listen my people and I will speak" (Psalms 50:7).

The Jewish people listen. Only those who hear can be a witness, a vessel to receive the teachings of God. First there was no one to listen, as the nations turned a deaf ear and refused to accept the Torah. The Torah therefore had no place in the world. The Jewish people became the ears for the whole world. Therefore, Divine providence comes to the nations by means of the Jewish people. The nations realize this and want to be near them. They realize that the development of civilization is brought about by the Jewish people, as when their technology built the Pyramids in Egypt or when they introduced mathematics to Arabic tribes.

Similarly, Ruth was attracted by the Jewish people, and she came, as it is written, "Listen my daughter, and note, incline your ear: forget your people and your father's house ..." (Psalms 45:11). When our ears are open, we hear the greatness of the Jewish people and the Torah that they possess.

When Isaac was old and wanted to bless his son Esau, Jacob disguised himself as if he was the hairy son. His father touched him and said, "The voice is the voice of Jacob, but the hands are the hands of Esau"

(Genesis 27:22). On the physical level, it means that although Esau comes with the might of his hands, Jacob offers his voice, with Torah teachings and prayers. But there is a deeper meaning to the verse. The hands of Esau are his physical power and abilities. But from where does his power come? Where are its roots? All power comes from God, the root of all. He gives life to the lifeless and energy to the powerless. In truth, we possess nothing, but receive everything. Jacob was aware that he received and was therefore immersed in Torah study and prayer. Prayer is acknowledgment that one has nothing without God: we have nothing, but receive everything. On the other hand, Esau thought that he possessed power yet misused it. Therefore, just as the hands of Esau are active, the voice of Jacob is also active; it is the act of receiving from the roots, directly from God, as King David said, "... I am prayer" (Psalms 109:4). He had nothing but what he received from God.

At Sinai the Jewish people said, "We will do and we will listen." "We will listen" is to lend an ear to the Torah and study its teachings diligently, which is one-half of the voice of Jacob. "We will listen" is prayer, which goes to the roots of doing by realizing that we have nothing and do nothing, but only receive from God.

Both parts of the voice of Jacob are given prominence in the holiday of Shavuos. We rededicate our life to listening to the Torah as we read the story of Ruth, the progenitor of David, the pillar of prayer for all of Israel. Charity and prayer are the same acts. Who gives and who does not? A person who thinks that he possesses, that he owns his possessions, does not give or share with others. On the other hand, a person who acknowledges that all is received and he owns nothing and has nothing is quick to share. Therefore, charity and prayer go hand in hand. Just as we extend our hand to give to the poor, because our possessions are not ours, so too, we open our hand in prayer to receive from God, "Who opens His hand, and sustains all living beings with its heart's content" (Psalms 145:16).

It is written of the final redemption, "I the Lord, will speed it in due time" (Isaiah 60:22). The Talmud explains: If they are worthy I will speed it, but if not then I will bring it in due time (*Sanhedrin* 98a). How then will the Jewish people be worthy of redemption?

Only with the Torah. As it is written, "But take utmost care and watch yourselves scrupulously, so that you do not forget the things that you saw with your own eyes and so that they do not fade from your mind as long as you live. And make them known to your children and your children's children: The day you stood before the Lord your God at Horeb, when the Lord said to me, 'Gather the people to Me that I may let them hear My words...'" (Deuteronomy 4:9–10). It is a day that God remembers us; had not we, the collective soul of the Jewish people, stood before Him, even before the universe was created, and were chosen to stand before Him always because of the Torah that will be received from Sinai. It is a day that God remembers us, to redeem us, and therefore, the light of the *Mashiach* shines forth from this day, as in the story of Ruth.

There is the Written Law and the Oral Law hidden within it. When the Oral Law is revealed it is evident that it was the meaning of the Written Law all the time. As it is written, "And God spoke all these words (*leimor*) to be repeated" (Exodus 20:1). When we act according to that which is written, it is like truth and faith. If we have faith in the oral interpretation of the law and observe it, we reach the level of truth—the truth of the interpretation becomes obvious. It is like our physical life and the soul that is in each of us. If we have faith that a soul is in us, then the truth of it becomes obvious. By observing the Torah through faith, and struggling to reveal the hidden, we reach the level of truth. This truth is revealed through the words of the Torah, saying, "I am the Lord the God who brought you out of Egypt." With these words God is still speaking to us, and we hear Him and respond to Him. And they are still in our heart of hearts. And when we hear them we live that instant in truth, and the truth becomes revealed, as in the story of Ruth, when the truth of the Oral Law become revealed through the faith that Boaz had in the scholars of his generation.

Let us therefore be guided by our faith. Then all concealed sources of spiritual energy will be revealed to us. The hidden oath, which we swore at Mount Sinai, will once again guide us to fill the world with Torah. As it is written, "... and the earth will fill with knowledge of God as water covers the sea" (Isaiah 11:9).

56

Laws and Customs of Shavuos

1. On the fiftieth day of the counting of the Omer the holiday of Shavuos is celebrated.

2. It is customary in many congregations to decorate the synagogue with greenery and flowers to remember the landscape around Mount Sinai and the experience of receiving the Torah.

3. All the prayers of Shavuos are the same as for the holiday of Passover, except that we substitute the words, "This day of the Shavuos Festival, time of the giving of our Torah."

4. It is customary in many congregations to gather after the holiday meal in the evening and to recite the "*Tikkun* of the Night of Shavuos." These are verses and excerpts from all of the important texts of the Torah, both the written and the oral traditions. In some congregations the people stay up all night to study the Torah, and recite the *Shacharis* prayers at daybreak before they return home.

5. After the *Shacharis* morning services, the *Hallel* is said in its entirety.

6. Two Torah scrolls are removed from the Ark. The first person is called to the Torah, but before the Torah is read, the *Akdomos* poem is recited. The leader reads two lines, and the congregation responds with the next two lines. Then, in the first scroll, five congregants read from Exodus 19:1 to 20:23, relating the giving of the Torah on Mount Sinai. In the second scroll, the *Maftir* portion is from Numbers 28:26 to 28:31, which relates the sacrifices for the Shavuos holiday. Then the *Haftorah* from Ezekiel 1 is read, ending with an added verse from Ezekiel 3:13.

7. On the second day of Shavuos, before the Torah reading, the entire *Megillah* of Ruth is read. Then, two Torah scrolls are removed from the Ark. The Torah reading in the first scroll is from Deuteronomy 14:22 to 16:17. The *Maftir* is the same as on the previous day, and the *Haftorah* is Habakkuk 2:20 to 3:19.

8. It is customary to eat dairy foods during Shavuos. One reason is to remember the special sacrifice of the two breads. By eating a dairy and then a meat meal, two different breads will be required. (One must not eat bread that he had just eaten with a dairy meal and then eat it with meat). Another reason is that the Torah is compared to milk and honey, an ancient mixture for vigor and sweetness of the voice, both of which the Torah gives us.

9. On the second day of Shavuos, the *Yizkor* services are recited before the *Musaf* service.

57

Prayers and Blessings

Eruv Tavshilin and Eruv Chatzeros

One is permitted to prepare food to be eaten on the Festival. It is forbidden to prepare food on a Festival for use on another day. When a Festival falls on a Friday, however, it is permitted to prepare food for the *Shabbos*. Even so, the rabbis attached a condition, an *eruv tavshilin*, that enables one to start cooking for the *Shabbos* on Thursday. It consists of taking *matzah* along with other cooked food, such as fish, meat, or an egg, and saying the following blessing and declaration:

Blessed are You God, our God, King of the universe, Who has sanctified us with His commandments and has commanded us concerning the mitzvah *of eruv.*

Through this eruv may we be permitted to bake, cook, insulate, kindle flame, prepare, and do anything necessary on the Festival for the sake of the Shabbos, *for ourselves and for all Jews who live in this city.*

The rabbis also forbade carrying from a private domain of one person to that of another on the *Shabbos*. The sages provided that *matzah* be collected from the dwellings and placed in one of them, as if all those who contributed lived in that one domain, and this is known as *eruv chatzeros*. The following blessing and declaration is made:

Blessed are You God, our God, King of the universe, Who has sanctified us with His commandments and has commanded us concerning the mitzvah *of eruv.*

Through this eruv *may we be permitted to carry out or to carry in from the houses to the courtyard, and from the courtyard to the houses, from house to house, from courtyard to courtyard, and from roof to roof, all that we require, for ourselves and for all Jews who live in this area, and for all who will move into this area, for all the* Shabbos *and Festivals of the year.*

Kindling of the Lights

Before kindling the lights, the woman closes her eyes and says· these two blessings:

Blessed are You God, our God, King of the universe, Who has sanctified us with His commandments, and has commanded us to kindle the lights of (the Sabbath and) the Holiday.

Blessed are You, God, our Lord, King of the universe, Who has kept us alive, sustained us, and brought us to this season.

It is customary to say the following prayer after the lights have been kindled.

May it be Your will, God, my God and the God of my forefathers, that You show favor to me (my husband, my sons, my daughters, my father, my mother) and all my relatives; and that You give us and all of Israel a good long life; that You remember us in a good and blessed way; that You bless us with great blessings; that You make our households complete; that Your Presence dwell among us. Give me the privilege to raise children and grandchildren who are wise and understanding, who love God and fear Him, people of truth, holy offspring, attached to God, who illuminate the world with Torah and good deeds, and with every activity in the service of the Creator. Please hear my supplication at this time, in the merit of Sarah, Rebecca, Rachel, and Leah, our mothers, and illuminate our light so that it does not extinguish forever, and let Your Countenance shine so that we are· saved. Amen.

The Kiddush Service

While holding a cup of wine or grape juice, one should recite the *Kiddush*, beginning here when the holiday falls on a Friday night:

(Whisper: *And there was evening and there was morning. . . .*)

417

The sixth day. The heaven and the earth were finished, and all their array. On the seventh day God finished the work that He had been doing, and He ceased on the seventh day from all the work that He had done. And God blessed the seventh day and declared it holy, because on it God ceased from all the work of creation that He had done.

With your permission my masters and teachers:

Blessed are You, God, our God, King of the universe, Who has chosen us from all the nations, exalted us above all tongues, and sanctified us with His commandments. And You, God, our God, have lovingly given us (Sabbath for rest), appointed times for gladness, feasts and seasons of joy, (this Sabbath and) this Shavuos Festival, the season of the giving of our Torah (in love) a holy convocation in memorium of the Exodus from Egypt. For You have chosen and sanctified us above all peoples, (and the Sabbath) and your Holy Festivals (in love and favor) in gladness and joy You have granted us as a heritage. Blessed are You, God, Who sanctifies (the Sabbath) Israel, and the festival season.

On Saturday night, one should add the following two blessings. Two candles, with flames touching, should be held before the person reciting the service.

Blessed are You, God, our God, King of the universe, Who creates the illumination of fire.

While holding fingers up to the flame

Blessed are You God, our God, King of the universe, Who distinguishes between sacred and secular, between light and darkness, between Israel and the nations, between the seventh day and the six days of activity. You have distinguished between the holiness of the Sabbath and the holiness of a Festival, and have sanctified the seventh day above the six days of activity. You distinguish and sanctified Your nation, Israel, with Your holiness. Blessed are You, God, who distinguishes between holiness and holiness.

On all nights, we add this blessing:

Blessed are You, God, our God, King of the universe, Who has kept us alive, sustained us, and brought us to this season.

Akdomos is a famous liturgical poem, written by Rabbi Meir ben Yitzchok, in the eleventh century. It is recited before the Torah reading during the Shavuos morning service.

AKDOMOS

An introduction of words, and to start my speaking, I will ask authorization and permission.

In two or three sections, which I open with trembling, With permission of He Who created, and shields it till old age.

His strength is as the whole world, and cannot be described, Even if all the heavens were parchment.

If all the oceans were ink, as well as all the gathered waters, If all the earth's inhabitants were scribes, and writers of initials.

The glory of the Master of the heavens, and He Who rules on dry land, He alone established the world, and controlled its expansion.

And without fatigue He perfected it, and without constraint, And with a letter slight, and without substance.

He prepared all His work, in those six days, The splendor of His majesty ascended upon His fiery throne.

A host of thousand thousands, and tens of thousands to serve Him, New ones flow forth every morning, Your faithfulness is great,.

Even greater are the flaming Seraphim, each with six wings, Until permission is granted to them, they are still in total silence.

They receive permission from each other, in the same instant, without delay, The glory of Him who fills the universe, they chant with three times "Holy".

Like the sound from before the Almighty, like the sound of torrential water, Cherubim responding to Galgalim, they exalt with great shouts.

To the eye it seems as arrows shot from a bow, To every place that they are sent, they hasten anxiously.

They praise with "Blessed is His glory," in every spoken language, From the place of the dwelling of His presence, which needs no searching.

All the heavenly hosts express lovingly, and praise with great concern, "His kingdom does glow, from generation to generation, eternally."

The *Kedushah* service is scheduled among them, and when the appointed hour passes, It is forever ended, not repeated, even after seven years.

His precious inherited portion is better, for they, with regularity, Make Him their sole desire, at sunrise and sunset.

They are designated as His portion, to do His will, His wonders and praises, they recount at every hour.

He desired, longed, and coveted, that they toil in Torah study, And He therefore accepts their prayers, and their prayers are productive.

They are tied to the Eternally Living God, with an oath in a crown, It rests permanently beside His precious *tefillin*.

It is inscribed, with wisdom and with knowledge, The magnitude of Israel, reciters of the Shema.

The praise of the Master of the World is a pure statement, It behooves me to declare in the presence of kings.

The lost ones gather, appearing as waves, They wonder and inquire in the matter of proofs.

Whence and Who is our beloved, Nation of beautiful appearance, That for His sake you perish in the lion's den?

Precious and beautiful would you be, if you would blend in to our dominion, We would grant your wish in every place.

With wisdom she answers them, partially, to let them know, If only you wise men would know Him fully.

What value has your greatness compared to His Praise? Of the great things He will do for me when redemption arrives.

When He will bring me light, and cover you with darkness, When His glory will be revealed with power and with grandeur.

He will repay in kind, to the haters and the isles, But righteousness to the beloved people, with abundant merit.

When He brings total joy and pure vessels, To the city of Jerusalem as He gathers the exiles.

His honor He will set upon her, in day and night, His bridal canopy to build in her, with crowned praises.

The brilliance of clouds, to beautify the canopy, Each according to their toil, will the canopy be formed.

Upon armchairs of pure gold, and seven elevations, The righteous will be placed, before Him of many achievements.

Their appearance will be like one sated with joy, As the heaven in its splendor and the sparkling stars.

Beauty that cannot be detailed with lips, That was neither heard nor seen in prophetic vision.

Where no eye has reigned, in the Garden of Eden, There will dance in a circle, together with the Holy Presence.

To him they will point, "That is He!" but with trepidation, We hoped for Him in our captivity, with powerful faith.

He will lead us forever, we will be youthful, Because our predetermined portion, had been set aside and raised high.

The sport with the Leviathan and the ox of lofty mountains, When they will interlock with one another and engage in combat.

With his horns the Behemoth will gore with strength, The fish will leap to meet him with power.

His Creator will approach him with His mighty sword, A banquet for the righteous He will prepare, and a feast.

They will sit around tables, of precious stones and gems, Before them will be flowing rivers of Balsam.

They will delight and drink their fill from overflowing goblets, With sweet wine that from Creation, was safeguarded in pressing tanks.

Righteous ones, just as you heard the praises contained in this song, So may you be appointed among the company,

You should be privileged to sit in the foremost row, If you listen to His words that emanate in splendor.

Exalted is God, from the beginning to the end of time, He desired and selected us, and He gave us the Torah.

Glossary

Aaron Brother of Moshe, and first *Kohen Gadol*, High Priest, of the Jewish nation.

Abraham The first *Ivri*, "Hebrew," who taught the sovereignty of God.

Akiva One of the greatest rabbis and leaders during the Second Temple period and the all-time paradigm of the accessibility of the Torah. He first learned the Hebrew alphabet at the age of forty. After many years of study away from his wife and children, he returned with thousands of students, claiming, "All which I have learned and accomplished is to my wife's credit." He lived to suffer the deaths of large numbers of his students and was himself martyred by the Romans for defying the decree against teaching Torah.

Amalek A tribe that attacked the Jewish people as they left Egypt. With that attack the Jews lost their image of invincibility, became discouraged, and were easy prey to the other nations.

Angels *Malachim*, spiritual messengers of God. Angels are mentioned in the Five Books of Moses, as well as many times throughout the Prophets. They are described by the prophet Ezekiel as having wings, a body, and concealed faces. The Talmud, Midrash, and Zohar describe the work of the angels in more detail.

Aravah Branches of the willow of which two are tied to the *lulav* on the left side.

Astrology The influence of the spiritual aspects of the celestial universe, its order, and form. Although Abraham was a great astrologer, rabbinical authorities have wrestled with the question whether a con- flict exists between astrology and the omniscience of God.

Baal Shem Tov Literally, the Master of the Good Name, one who knows the power of the various names of God. A great sage and scholar, he revitalized Judaism in the latter half of the eighteenth century. He taught a fervent mystical way of observance that attracted giants of Torah scholarship, as well as many thousands of plain folk. Before World War II his approach dominated Orthodox Jewish life. After the slaughter of hundreds of thousands of chasidim during World War II by the Germans, the movement was brought back to life by a handful of surviving rebbes.

Baal Teshuvah A repentant who has completely left his former sinful ways to follow the Torah in every aspect of his life. Often, the *baal teshuvah* is lauded even more than the *tzaddik*, the righteous individual.

Chanukah The Festival of Lights, lasting eight days beginning on the 25th day of *Kislev* (November/December) and commemorating the Jewish victory over the Greek-Hellenist oppresstion in 164 B.C.E., and the miracle of a small jug of oil that burned for eight days.

Charity/tzedaka The Torah commands and admonishes time and time again to help those in need—the poor, the orphan, the widow, and convert—with money, food, and clothing.

Chosen People The Jewish nation chosen by God to carry out special responsibilities, such as learning and teaching the Torah and fulfilling His commandments.

Chukim/Mishpatim Decrees lacking reason.

Chuppah A canopy used in the traditional marriage ceremony, symbolizing the common home of the newlyweds.

David The second king of Israel, after Saul (1040–970 B.C.E.). His life is described in I and II Samuel and Kings. He fought many wars against the Philistines (who have no relationship whatsoever to the present-day Palestinians); established the Jewish kingdom; planned the construction of the Holy Temple in Jerusalem; and authored the Psalms, the most famous of all Jewish prayers. His son, Solomon, of legendary wisdom, continued his legacy by building the Temple and establishing *Eretz Yisrael*, the Land of Israel, as the hub of world commerce.

Days of Awe From the first day of *Elul*, the fifth month, until Yom Kippur, the tenth day of the sixth month, are forty days. They are traditionally set aside for meditation, fasting, and repentance. These correspond to the forty days that Moses spent on Mount Sinai, without food or drink, begging God's forgiveness for the sin of the Israelites worshiping the Golden Calf.

Divine Presence (Shechinah) The manner in which God is manifest in the world, in contrast to God's essence, which is unknown and unknowable.

Esrog The fruit of the citron, native to Middle Eastern countries, that is used on Sukkos as one of the four plant species.

Exile and redemption The Jewish people have gone through three exiles and redemptions. Now we are in the fourth exile and awaiting the final redemption.

Golden Calf An idol fashioned by the Israelites at Mount Sinai while Moses was studying the Divine Laws on the mountaintop. This caused Moses to break the first set of Tablets on which were engraved the Ten Commandments.

Greek Hellenists Hellenism was the form of Greek civilization that spread over the eastern Mediterranean and consequently the Middle East. It began with the conquest of the East by Alexander the Great in 134 B.C.E. and ended with the conquest of these territories by the Romans in the first century B.C.E.

Hallel Verses of praise in the Book of Psalms, traditionally from chapters 113 through 117.

Hebrew The Holy Tongue, or *Loshon Hakodesh*, the language of the Bible. It is an ancient language used in the creation of the universe, and at Mount Sinai. Linguistic scholars have traced tens of thousands of words from a variety of languages to their Hebrew roots.

Holiness A spiritual state accomplished by strictly observing all the positive commandments.

Holy Temple The building dedicated to the worship of God in eastern Jerusalem. (Since the Arab period dating from the seventh century, a mosque, the Dome of the Rock [Mosque of Omar], has stood on that site.) It was the religious and ritual center of all the Jews in *Eretz Yisrael* (Land of the Jewish nation) and the Diaspora, and pilgrims flocked to it from all countries.

Idol Worship (Avodah zarah) Worshiping anything in the universe beside God. It generally refers to the worship of a specific idol.

Isaac The son of Abraham whose virtue was stern judgment, in contrast to his father, whose virtue was loving-kindness.

Israel The collective name for the Jewish nation. In the biblical narrative, Jacob was so named because he had fought with an angel and prevailed.

Jacob The son of Isaac whose twelve sons became the progenitors of the tribes of Israel.

Joshua The prime and totally devoted pupil of Moses, who never left the presence of his teacher.

Kabbalah The mystical (esoteric) teachings imparted secretly from teacher to student. The Kabbalah deals with the nature of God, Creation, and the cosmos and the meaning of holidays, rituals, and Torah verses.

Kohen The priests (*kohanim*) were the specialists in worship and religion. The duties of the priests were: to serve God in a sanctuary (Numbers 8:26; Deuteronomy 10:8); to mediate between God and man by means of various acts, most notably making sacrifices (Leviticus 1:5–9) and burning incense (Exodus 30:7–9); to perform ceremonies of purification (Leviticus 16); to distinguish between harmless and dangerous forms of leprosy (Leviticus 13); to bless the people (Numbers 6:22–26); to make oracular pronouncements and interpret them (Deuteronomy 33:8); and to provide instruction in the Torah (religious obligations), essentially "instruction in the way of God" (Leviticus 10:10–11).

Kohen Gadol (High Priest)   The supreme administrator of the ritual of the Temple; his position dominated the life of the Jewish community. In Hellenistic times, he was the people's sole representative before the oppressive rulers.

Law, Written and Oral   Derived from the written part of the Torah (see Torah) by means of traditional methods of interpretation (exegesis). Moses learned both the methods and the laws thus derived from God, and he taught them orally. Later, when they were in danger of being forgotten, a compilation called the Mishnah (the Oral Law) was written.

Lulav   The leaves of a date palm used as the tallest and center of the four plant species.

Mashiach (Messiah)   A descendant from the family of David, King of Israel, who will redeem the Jewish nation finally and totally.

Mezuzah   A parchment inscribed on one side with the verses of Deuteronomy 6:4–9 and Deuteronomy 11:13–21 and on the other side with the Hebrew word *Shaddai* (a name applied to God) attached to each doorpost of the home.

Midrash   Part of the Oral Law, an interpretation clarifying or expounding points of law or developing or illustrating moral principles.

Mikvah   The Jewish ritual bath, consisting of 40 sah of water not previously contained in a vessel. The *mikvah* is used by women as purification after their menstrual period, and by men on Yom Kippur eve, at holiday time, and on Friday before the Sabbath. Some men use it every day before the morning services. It was used by the *Kohen Gadol* during the Yom Kippur service in the Holy Temple.

Mishnah   The first organized collection of the laws and traditions of the Torah.

Mitzvah   Any of the group of 613 commandments or precepts that are present in the Torah, or any good deed conforming to the spirit of a *mitzvah*.

Moses   Moshe Rebeinu, our teacher, the leader of the Exodus who received the Torah, the revelation of God, on Mount Sinai.

Prayer Book   The prescribed form of prayer, first written in the time of Patriarch Simeon Ben Gamliel. Other prayers were then composed and added, as those for the resumption of the ritual in a rebuilt Jerusalem and the malediction against *Minim* (heretics).

Prophet (Navi)   An individual who, through acts of purification, can attain a level of consciousness, so that he can discern the future and can admonish the masses to repentance. The Jewish people have a prophetic tradition.

Purim   The holiday celebrating the events recorded in the Book of Esther. It refers to the days fixed by Haman for the extermination of the Jews in the kingdom ruled by Achashverosh (Xerxes), the 13th and 14th of *Adar*. Specifically, it refers to the day of rest after the Jewish victory over their enemies, which occurred on the 14th of *Adar*; in the city of Shushan and all cities with walls in the days of Joshua; it is celebrated on the 15th of *Adar*.

Purity   A spiritual state of cleanliness accomplished by strict observance of all the negative commandments.

Rosh Chodesh   The New Moon, established by the Jewish court with witnesses testifying to having seen the new moon.

Rashi   The world-renowned scholar, Rav Shlomo ben Yizchok Yarchi (1040–1105).

Revelation   Revealing that which was hidden, usually by Divine inspiration.

Rosh Hashanah   The Jewish New Year, a day of remembrance and judgment for every member of the human race.

Sages   Traditionally the recognized Torah scholars of an era, usually referring to the rabbis of the talmudic period.

Shabbos   The seventh day of the week, a day of holy rest.

Shekel   The first fixed tax mentioned in the Torah. "Atonement money" of a half-shekel was imposed on every Israelite male aged 25 years and over. It was used to defray the ritual expenses of the Tabernacle and was equivalent to the weight of 320 grains of barley.

Shofar The horn of a sheep or ram used ceremonially to announce the New Year, to free all slaves on the Yom Kippur of every fiftieth or Jubilee year, to announce a fast, and to proclaim a call to arms. It originated with the substitution of a ram for the sacrifice of Isaac and will end with the sounding of the ram's horn for the advent of the Messiah.

Sukkah A temporary dwelling for the duration of the Sukkos holiday. The word specifically refers to the roofing.

Tallis A four-cornered shawl traditionally worn during prayer services. On the four corners are affixed, with knots and twists, the *tzitzis*, eight strings. One of those strings was dyed with *techeiles*, a bluish-purple dye extracted from the Hilozon, a cuttle-fish, or some other type of sea creature. During the long and painful exile, the art and knowledge of obtaining dye from the Hilozon was lost until Rabbi Gershon Henoch of Radzin (1839–1891), the Radziner rebbe, claimed to have found the Hilozon and proceded to dye his fringes with its blue-purple secretion. Many rabbis were opposed to this innovation, arguing that the long-hidden sea animal can await discovery with the advent of the Messiah.

Talmud The collection of Jewish law and tradition consisting of the Mishnah and the Gemara. One edition was produced in *Eretz Yisrael*, 400 c.e.; the larger, more important one was produced in Babylonia in 500 c.e.

Ten Commandments The major obligations between man and God and between man and man that were given through Moses on Mount Sinai, on the Sabbath forty-nine days after the Exodus.

Ten Commands The utterances of God with which the universe was created.

Ten Spheres In Kabbalah, the ten stages through which God's goodness and light descend to the material world.

Teshuvah Biblical repentance consisting of abandoning the evil path, remorse, and resolving to refrain from evil.

Thirteen Virtues of Kindness God's revelation to Moses of the Thirteen Virtues of Kindness, (Exodus 34:6) wherein it is taught that God is kind and benevolent in every and all circumstance.

Throne of Honor (Kisei Hakavod) Traditionally refers to the highest concept of God as the King of the Universe.

Torah Divine revelation from God which includes the entire body of Jewish law: the *Pentateuch* (or Torah), the Prophets (*Nevi'im*), Hagiography (*Kesuvim*), and the Talmud.

Tree of Knowledge/Tree of Life Two trees in the Garden of Eden; partaking in the fruit of the former gave one the capability to discern good and evil, whereas eating of the latter gave one eternal life.

Tzaddik The one who is constantly vigilant not to sin.

Tzimtzum The contraction, so to speak, of God's pervasiveness to permit the existence of corporeal reality. In the Kabbalah of Rabbi Isaac Luria, God contracted His being, so to speak, in order to allow for the creation of the universe. Thus, wherever there is matter, there is also a concealment of God's presence. The work of God's servant is to reveal that which seems hidden.

World to Come (Olam Habah) A future utopian existence promised as a reward for the righteous.

Yom Kippur The last of the Days of Awe, a day of atonement, fasting, and deprivation and the most sacred of all the holidays.

Zohar The Book of Splendor, traditionally accepted to have been written by Rabbi Shimon Bar Yochai while hiding in a cave to escape Roman persecution in the second century c.e. It is the prime sourcebook of the Kabbalah, Jewish mysticism.

Index

About the Author

Moshe A. Braun is director of Hope Educational Services, delivering educational initiatives to local communities, and also serves as a consultant with the Board of Education in New York City. He helped organize the Free Jewish University, a Torah outreach program for college-age youth. A Holocaust survivor, he has written and lectured on the subject at college campuses. He is also one of the pioneers in popularizing chasidic ideas and thought through lectures and published articles. The author of over ten books, including *The Talking B'somim Box* (1990), *Leap of Faith* (1992), and *The Magic Comb* (1993), he currently resides in New York State with his wife and children.